The Adams Papers

L. H. BUTTERFIELD, EDITOR IN CHIEF

SERIES II

Adams Family Correspondence

ORIGINALLY PUBLISHED BY
HARVARD UNIVERSITY PRESS

Adams Family Correspondence

L. H. BUTTERFIELD, *EDITOR*

WENDELL D. GARRETT, *ASSOCIATE EDITOR*

MARJORIE E. SPRAGUE, *ASSISTANT EDITOR*

———————————— ☆ ————————————

Volume 2 · June 1776–March 1778
Index

ATHENEUM

NEW YORK

1965

Published by Atheneum
Reprinted by arrangement with Harvard University Press

First Atheneum Edition

Funds for editing *The Adams Papers* have been provided by Time, Inc.,
on behalf of *Life,* to the Massachusetts Historical Society, under whose
supervision the editorial work is being done.

Contents

Descriptive List of Illustrations

William Trickett's trade card is pasted inside the front board of the second of a pair of letterbooks John Adams bought in Philadelphia at the end of May or beginning of June 1776. On 2 June he wrote his wife: "In all the Correspondencies I have maintained, during a Course of twenty Years at least that I have been a Writer of Letters, I never kept a single Copy." This "Negligence" had been a great inconvenience to him "on many Occasions," but he had come to a new resolution: "I have now purchased a Folio Book, in the first Page of which, excepting one blank Leaff, I am writing this Letter, and intend to write all my Letters to you in it from this Time forward" (p. 3–4, below). The bookbinder and stationer who supplied these letterbooks (which still survive in good condition) had announced himself "from London" as early as June 1774 in the Philadelphia newspapers; on 13 December 1775 his advertisement in the *Pennsylvania Journal* informed the public that he "Makes and sells all sorts of Merchants Account Books, bound in leather or vellum, with or without Russia bands, and ruled to any pattern." Located near the intersection of Front and Market streets "Facing *Black-horse* Alley," his shop was advantageously situated next door to the well-known Philadelphia printer William Bradford. From 1777 until 1780, when he died, Trickett occasionally supplied the Continental Congress and the Supreme Executive Council of Pennsylvania with stationery.

From an original in the Adams Papers.

Two cards of admission — one issued to ex-President John Adams in 1821 and the other to Secretary of State John Quincy Adams in 1824 — for the annual "COLLATION" at Faneuil Hall in observance of the Fourth of July. Both cards bear the same quotation from John Adams, perhaps the best-known words he ever wrote or uttered, but in a misdated and garbled form that became scriptural. The quotation consists of passages run together from two separate letters he wrote to Mrs. Adams from Philadelphia on 3 July 1776, the day after Congress actually voted independence. But well before 1800 the "Great Anniversary Festival" had been fixed in the public mind as the Fourth, the day on which the Declaration (rather than the *vote*) of Independence had been adopted. Adams' stirring letters, which had made their way into print in the 1790's, were therefore redated in subsequent printings to suit a popular preference. The texts of the letters as originally written are printed at p. 27–33, below, where there is also a fuller account of the early garbling and of unavailing efforts to correct it.

From originals in the Adams Papers.

The Billopp House or "Manor of Bentley" in Tottenville at the southern extremity of Staten Island on a slope overlooking Raritan Bay opposite Perth Amboy, N.J., was built about 1668 and was the site of the dramatic but fruitless conference between Admiral Lord Howe and a committee from Congress on 11 September 1776 intended (by Howe) to accommodate the dispute between Great Britain and America. Still standing in 1963 and known as the Conference House, it was owned during the Revolution by Col. Christopher Billopp, who had been a member of the New York Assembly and voted there against sending delegates to the first Continental Congress; later he was named in the New York Act of Attainder, had his property confiscated by the state, and was forced to flee to New Brunswick, where he died in 1827 (Harold D. Eberlein, *Manor Houses and Historic Homes of Long Island and Staten Island*, Philadelphia and London, 1928, p. 295–303). Benjamin Franklin, who was accompanied by John Adams and Edward Rutledge as the other members of the committee on the trip from Philadelphia to Staten Island, suggested to Lord Howe in a letter of 8 September that the meeting be held "either at the house on Staten Island opposite to Amboy, or at the governor's house in Amboy" (*Writings of Benjamin Franklin*, ed. Albert Henry Smyth, New York and London, 1905–1907, 6:463). The trip to and from Staten Island and the interview, lasting four hours, were graphically described by John Adams in his *Diary and Autobiography*, ed. L. H. Butterfield and others, Cambridge, 1961, 3:414–431, and in his letter of 14 September 1776 to Mrs. Adams, printed in the present volume, p. 124–125. This engraving of the Billopp House appeared in one of a series of articles on "Historic Houses of America" in *Appletons' Journal*, from the hand of the popular antiquarian and wood-engraver Benson J. Lossing ("The Bently or Billopp Manor-House, Staten Island," 11:161–163 [7 February 1874]).

Courtesy of the Boston Athenæum.

The Howe brothers, "Commissioners for restoring Peace to His MAJESTY's Colonies and Plantations in North-America," printed and distributed this broadside or "DECLARATION," dated 19 September 1776 (Charles Evans and others, comps., *American Bibliography*, Chicago and Worcester, 1903–1959, No. 14782), following the unsuccessful conference at Staten Island between Lord Howe and the committee from the Continental Congress. "Hen[ry] Strachey," whose name appears at the foot of the text, was the secretary to the British commission and wrote an account of it. For further information see John Adams' letter to Mrs. Adams, 14 September 1776, and the references given there, p. 124–125, below.

Courtesy of the Massachusetts Historical Society.

5. THE "CHOICE OF HERCULES," PROPOSED BY JOHN ADAMS FOR
   THE GREAT SEAL   102

John Adams was appointed to a committee on 4 July 1776 with Benjamin Franklin and Thomas Jefferson "to prepare Devices for a Great Seal for the confederated States"; he suggested an allegorical emblem which in the end he admitted "is too complicated a Group for a Seal or Medal, and it is not original" (letter to Abigail Adams, 14 August 1776, p. 96–98, below). This engraving by Simon Gribelin of the "Choice" or "Judgment of Hercules" appears on an internal titlepage in the third volume of the John Baskerville edition of Anthony Ashley Cooper, 3d Earl of Shaftesbury's *Characteristicks of Men, Manners, Opinions, Times*, 5th edition, Birmingham, 1773, a work owned by John Adams and still among his books in the Boston Public Library (*Catalogue of the John Adams Library in the Public Library of the City of Boston*, Boston 1917, p. 62). Shaftesbury published a short treatise on esthetics wholly based on the Judgment of Hercules theme in the first edition of the *Characteristicks* in 1714; for a titlepage decoration he commissioned Paulo de Matthaeis in 1712 to paint the "Judgment" and had it engraved by Gribelin the following year. The original fable is attributed to Xenophon in his *Memoirs of Socrates*, book II, chapter 1, to one Prodicus, a sophist and rhetorician of Ceos, who was admired by Xenophon and quoted by Socrates. Prodicus narrates a debate, or rather a succession of appeals to the young Hercules, by female impersonations of Virtue and Vice or Sensuality (or, to use Shaftesbury's terms, Virtue and Pleasure). Vice speaks first and points out the flowery path of self-indulgence; Virtue follows and adjures Hercules to ascend the rugged, uphill way of duty to others and honor to himself. The burden of Shaftesbury's treatise is that a successful treatment of such a theme, for either moral or esthetic purposes, must be natural, simple, and intelligible, and the artist must accordingly avoid the emblematic, cluttered, and exotic in both representation and style.

Gribelin's engraving, executed according to these principles, had a profound effect on Adams' attitude toward the fine arts, which to him typified luxury and therefore the threat of moral and social decadence. From Paris he wrote his wife in April 1780: "There is every Thing here that can inform the Understanding, or refine the Taste, and indeed one would think that could purify the Heart. Yet it must be remembered there is every thing here too, which can seduce, betray, deceive, deprave, corrupt and debauch it. Hercules marches here in full View of the Steeps of Virtue on one hand, and the flowery Paths of Pleasure on the other, and there are few who make the Choice of Hercules. That my Children may follow his Example, is my earnest Prayer: but I sometimes tremble, when I hear the syren songs of sloth, least they should be captivated with her bewitching Charms and her soft, insinuating Musick" (Adams Papers).

Courtesy of Mr. E. Harold Hugo, Meriden, Connecticut, and of the Boston Public Library.

6. JOHN ADAMS' PLAN FOR A MILITARY ESTABLISHMENT IN 1776 102

Broadside, without imprint, published in September 1776 (Evans 15167). While the Continental Army was being driven with heavy losses from Long Island and New York City, the Continental Board of War, over which John Adams had presided since its organization in June, was endeavoring to provide Washington with an ample and permanent body of troops. On 22 September Adams wrote his wife: "We have at last agreed upon a Plan, for forming a regular Army. We have offered 20 dollars, and 100 Acres of Land to every Man, who will inlist, during the War," by which he meant for the duration of the war (p. 131–132, below). The Board's report to Congress on 9 September, probably drafted by Adams and strongly advocated by him on the floor, was debated, amended, and adopted in stages during the following days, and on the 20th ordered to be published in the form here seen. Adams later cited this plan for "eighty-eight Battalions . . . to serve during the present War" as a standing refutation of Alexander Hamilton's politically inspired and damaging charge in the Presidential campaign of 1800 that Adams had always opposed a strong military establishment for the United States; see his *Diary and Autobiography*, 3:434–435.

Courtesy of the Massachusetts Historical Society.

7. ISAAC SMITH SR. IN 1769, BY JOHN SINGLETON COPLEY 103

Isaac Smith (1719–1787), younger brother of Rev. William Smith of Weymouth, carried on in Boston and Salem the mercantile vocation of the Smiths of Charlestown, Massachusetts, forebears of Abigail (Smith) Adams. Isaac Smith's extensive correspondence with John Adams, his nephew by marriage, most often deals with commercial matters and especially the difficulties of conducting trade during both the war and the disordered economic and political conditions that followed. Adams, who loved and greatly respected his uncle, once remarked that Smith "had been more largely concerned in the Cod Fishery than any Man excepting Mr. Hooper and Mr. Lee of Marblehead" (*Diary and Autobiography*, 4:5); and there can be no question that the interest of such friends and connections as Smith stiffened Adams' stand on American rights in the North Atlantic fisheries during the long and arduous negotiations for peace with Great Britain.

This portrait of a typical Boston whig merchant is unusually well-documented because many of the papers of Smith and his descendants are preserved in the Massachusetts Historical Society. In the collection known as the Smith-Carter Papers there is a bill in John Singleton Copley's hand for this painting and its companion piece of Mrs. Elizabeth (Storer) Smith which reads: "1769 Mr.

Isaac Smith to J. S. Copley Dr. / To painting his and his Ladys portrait in half Length at 14 Guineas—£39. .4. .0 / To two carved Gold frames for Do.—18. .0. .0 / [Total:] £57. .4. .0 / Recd. the contents in full per John Singleton Copley." The portrait of Smith, which measures 49 ¼" x 39 ½", was inherited by Isaac Smith Jr., then passed successively to a nephew of his, Thomas Carter Smith, to William Smith Carter, and to Theodore Parkman Carter. In 1843 Thomas Carter Smith paid George Howorth $50 "To restoring 2 portraits by Copley," which were identified on the receipt as "Grandfather & Grandmother Smith" (20 June 1843, Smith-Carter Papers). Both portraits were bequeathed to Yale University in 1943.

Courtesy of Yale University Art Gallery, Maitland F. Griggs Collection.

Cotton Tufts (1732–1815) of Weymouth, a Harvard graduate, a distinguished physician, and from time to time local manager of the Adamses' property and business interests, was an uncle of Abigail Adams on her maternal side and a first cousin on her paternal side. During John Adams' courtship of Abigail Smith, the lovers confidently committed the letters they exchanged to the hands of "Dr. Trusty." Thanks to the survival of later correspondence between Mrs. Adams and Dr. Tufts, we know a good deal not otherwise recorded about farming and building operations at the Adams homestead (the "Old House") in Quincy, which Tufts himself had negotiated the Adamses' purchase of in 1787 while they were still in London.

The present portrait was painted in 1804 by the youthful New England limner Benjamin Greenleaf (1786–1864), of Haverhill; his use of Chippendale furniture for props and the short curled wig, with everything painted in the flat style of the primitive painter, indicates not only a cultural lag on the part of the artist but perhaps also how basically 18th-century in outlook and habit was the subject, whose very name is a kind of essence of early New England. Tufts had been one of the founders of the Massachusetts Medical Society and served as its first president, 1787–1795, and so it was highly appropriate that the only known portrait of him should have been presented to the Boston Medical Library, still the headquarters of the Society, by Dr. William T. Brigham in 1878, on the occasion of the dedication of the Library's new building at 19 Boylston Place.

Courtesy of the Boston Medical Library.

James Lovell, a fellow Massachusetts delegate to the Continental Congress with John Adams, enclosed this manuscript copy of a map to Abigail Adams in his letter of 29 August 1777 from Philadelphia with the following explanation: "It is probable that Genl. Howe will waste the fall of this year between Chesapeak Bay and Delaware River. I send you a copied sketch of part of the country to which the Gazettes will frequently refer" (p. 333, below). Lovell's letter containing this thoughtful gift gave its recipient a terrible fright before she opened it; see her letters of 17 September to her husband and to Lovell (p. 343–344, below). Although Lovell's printed or manuscript source has not been identified, he perhaps made his copy from the "excellent Chart of the Schuylkill, Chester River, the Brandywine, and this whole Country, among the Pensilvania Files" that John Adams mentioned having seen on 15 September 1777 (*Diary and Autobiography*, 2:262). In any event Mrs. Adams must have found it useful, as the editors of *The Adams Papers* have, in tracing the movements of the opposing armies in the country lying between Philadelphia, Delaware Bay, Baltimore, York, and Lancaster.

From Lovell's manuscript copy in the Adams Papers.

10. "THE LOSS OF YOUR COMPANY ... I CONSIDER AS A LOSS OF SO MUCH SOLID HAPPINESS" 262

This page reproduced from a letter addressed on 8 July 1777 by John Adams in Congress at Philadelphia to his wife, then expecting her sixth child at Braintree, exhibits not only his hand but his inmost feelings. He had been away from home almost continuously for three years, and, because of the constant military crisis, he saw no hope of an early return. He thought himself entitled to sympathy, but he would ask for it from no one but his wife. For the full text of his letter see p. 276–277, below. For what was occurring in Braintree at almost the moment he wrote, see the following illustration.

From the original in the Adams Papers.

11. "I KEEP UP SOME SPIRITS YET, THO I WOULD HAVE YOU PREPAIRD FOR ANY EVENT THAT MAY HAPPEN" 262

In this hitherto unpublished note, dated 9 July 1777 but without salutation or signature, Abigail Adams reported to her husband the probable loss of a child she was carrying. Two days later she was delivered of a daughter, who according to the mother "appeard to be a very fine Babe" and whom the parents had agreed to name Elizabeth, but she was stillborn. For the texts of the letters reporting this event and its effect on John Adams, see p. 278–280, 282–283, 287–288, 292, and 298–299, below.

From the original in the Adams Papers.

12. SOME BOOKS THE ADAMSES READ DURING THE REVOLUTION 263

Mottin de La Balme's *Essais sur l'équitation*. "We shall have all the Sages and Heroes of France here before long," John Adams wryly observed to his wife at the beginning of a letter from Congress, 18 June 1777 (p. 267–268, below). Among other French soldiers of fortune whose arrival he reported was Capitaine Augustin Mottin

de La Balme, "a great Writer upon Horsemanship and Cavalry."
This officer had thoughtfully brought along with him a supply of
his own books, and he presented copies of two of them to Adams,
who La Balme knew was president of the Continental Board of
War and who was at this time, whether or not La Balme knew it,
an active collector of books on military science. The books presented
were *Essais sur l'équitation* . . . , Amsterdam and Paris, 1773, the
titlepage of which is reproduced here, and *Elémens de tactique pour
la cavalerie* . . . , Paris, 1776. Both remain among John Adams'
books in the Boston Public Library, along with other treatises attest-
ing their owner's eagerness to become a military expert even though
he never achieved his ambition to command troops in the field. La
Balme, as things turned out, proved merely troublesome to Washington, did not last long as inspector of Continental cavalry, and
wandered off to the Ohio country, where he was killed by Little
Turtle's Indians in 1780.

Smollett's *History of England.* History being so obviously in the
making all around them during the campaigns of the Revolution,
everyone in the Adams family read historical books with avidity.
On 2 June 1777 John Quincy Adams, then going on ten, wrote his
father: "I have Set myself a Stent, and determine to read the 3d
volume [of Tobias Smollett's *History of England*] Half out" by the
end of the week; on the 8th he reported he had "almost" done so by
spending several hours a day at his book instead of idling away
his time on "Trifles and play" (p. 254–255, 261, below).

Charles Rollin's *Method of Teaching and Studying the Belles Lettres.* Three days after Congress adopted the Declaration of Independence, John Adams sent his wife a long letter discussing the
education of their children and particularly the best means of their
acquiring a fluent and effective literary style. "There is a Book," he
wrote, "which I wish you owned, I mean Rollins Belles Letters, in
which the Variations of Style" — the epistolary, the oratorical, the
historical, &c. — "are explained" (7 July 1776, p. 39–41, below).
This three-volume work was procured (though precisely when is not
known) in a copy of the sixth edition, London, 1769, and joined
numerous other books by the very popular French writer Charles
Rollin (1661–1741), concerning whom see Mrs. Adams' letter to
her husband, 19 August 1774 (vol. 1:142–143).

Dodsley's *Preceptor.* In 1748 the London printer-publisher Robert
Dodsley issued *The Preceptor*, with a very long subtitle and a list
of the contents on the titlepage (here illustrated), aiming to fur-
nish in two stout volumes and numerous engraved plates "A General
Course of Education" embodying "THE FIRST PRINCIPLES OF
POLITE LEARNING" in all fields, from "READING, SPEAKING,
and WRITING LETTERS" through "ARITHMETIC," "GEOGRAPHY,"
"CHRONOLOGY and HISTORY," "DRAWING," "LOGIC," "NATURAL
HISTORY," "ETHICS," and "TRADE and COMMERCE," to "HUMAN
LIFE and MANNERS." Dr. Samuel Johnson wrote the preface, and
various sections were prepared by good authorities under Dodsley's

editorship. The volumes contain both expository essays and illustrative readings in the subjects dealt with, and the work as a whole forms a remarkable compendium of human knowledge at the time that deserved and obtained wide circulation and long use in schools and homes. The present edition, it will be noted, is the fifth, published in 1769. John Adams discovered *The Preceptor* when he was in college, and in a diary entry of 5 June 1771 he put down a reminder to himself: "I hope I shall not forget to purchase these Preceptors, and to make my Sons transcribe this Treatise on Logick entirely with their own Hands, in fair Characters, as soon as they can write, in order to imprint it on their Memories. Nor would it hurt my Daughter to do the same" (*Diary and Autobiography*, 2:24–25). In his letter to Mrs. Adams about their children's education, 7 July 1776, Adams recommended their reading particular letters of Pliny the Younger and John Gay, to be found in *The Preceptor*, as models of epistolary style, which should always be "simple, natural, easy, and familiar" (p. 39–41, below). In the set of *The Preceptor* now among the Adams books in the Boston Public Library, the first volume is a replacement copy, but on a flyleaf in the second volume appears the inscription "Abigail Adams 1772" in the round formal hand John Adams used for special occasions. This must indicate that he promptly carried out the intent of his diary entry in 1771 and then gave the books to his wife because she was the principal instructress of their young children.

Courtesy of the Boston Public Library.

Guide to Editorial Apparatus

1. TEXTUAL DEVICES

[These are listed only in the first volume of the *Adams Family Correspondence*, being applicable alike to all volumes in the series. See vol. 1:liv.]

2. ADAMS FAMILY CODE NAMES

[These are listed only in the first volume of the *Adams Family Correspondence*, being applicable alike to all volumes in the series. See vol. 1:liv–lv.]

3. DESCRIPTIVE SYMBOLS

[These are listed only in the first volume of the *Adams Family Correspondence*, being applicable alike to all volumes in the series. See vol. 1:lv–lvi.]

4. LOCATION SYMBOLS USED IN THIS VOLUME

For an explanation of editorial practice in citing locations of documents, see vol. 1:lvi.

CSmH	Henry E. Huntington Library and Art Gallery
DLC	Library of Congress
DNA	The National Archives
M-Ar	Massachusetts Archives
MB	Boston Public Library
MH	Harvard College Library
MHi	Massachusetts Historical Society
MQA	Adams National Historic Site, Quincy, Massachusetts
NN	New York Public Library
PHi	Historical Society of Pennsylvania
PPRF	The Rosenbach Foundation, Philadelphia

5. OTHER ABBREVIATIONS AND CONVENTIONAL TERMS USED IN THIS VOLUME

Adams Genealogy

A set of genealogical charts and a concise biographical register of the Adams family in the Presidential line and of closely connected families from the 17th through the 19th century. The Adams Genealogy is now (1963) in preparation and will shortly be issued in preliminary form to accompany the *Adams Family Correspondence*. An enlarged and corrected version of this editorial aid will, it is hoped, be published with, or as part of, the last volume of the present series.

Adams Papers

Manuscripts and other materials, 1639–1889, in the Adams Manuscript Trust collection given to the Massachusetts Historical Society in 1956 and enlarged by a few additions of family papers since then. Citations in the present edition are simply by date of the original document if the original is in the main chronological series of the Papers and therefore readily found in the microfilm edition of the Adams Papers (see below). The location of materials in the Letterbooks and the Miscellany is given more fully, and often, if the original would be hard to locate, by the microfilm reel number.

Adams Papers Editorial Files

Other materials in the Adams Papers editorial office, Massachusetts Historical Society. These include photoduplicated documents (normally cited by the location of the originals), photographs, correspondence, and bibliographical and other aids compiled and accumulated by the editorial staff.

Adams Papers, Fourth Generation

Adams manuscripts dating 1890 or later, now separated from the Trust collection and administered by the Massachusetts Historical Society on the same footing with its other manuscript collections.

Adams Papers, Microfilms

The corpus of the Adams Papers, 1639–1889, as published on microfilm by the Massachusetts Historical Society, 1954–1959, in 608 reels. Cited in the present work, when necessary, by reel number. Available in research libraries throughout the United States and in a few libraries in Europe.

The Adams Papers

The present edition in letterpress, published by The Belknap Press of Harvard University Press. References between volumes of any given unit will take this form: vol. 3:171. Since there will be no over-all volume numbering for the edition, references from one series, or unit of a series, to another will be by title, volume, and page; for example, JQA, *Papers*, 4:205. (For the same reason, references by scholars citing this edition should not be to *The Adams Papers* as a whole but to the particular series or subseries concerned; for example, John Adams, *Diary and Autobiography*, 3:145; *Adams Family Correspondence*, 6:167.)

PCC

Papers of the Continental Congress. Originals in the National Archives; microfilm edition, completed in 1961, in 204 reels. Usually cited in the present work from the microfilms, but according to the original series and volume numbering devised in the State Department in the early 19th century; for example, PCC, No. 93, III, i.e. the third volume of series 93.

Suffolk County Court House, Early Court Files, &c.

> Early Court Files and Miscellaneous Papers in the Office of the Clerk of the Massachusetts Supreme Judicial Court, Suffolk County, Suffolk County Court House, Boston.

Superior Court of Judicature, Minute Books, Records

> Massachusetts Superior Court of Judicature, Minute Books and Records in the Office of the Clerk of the Supreme Judicial Court, Suffolk County, Suffolk County Court House, Boston.

Thwing Catalogue, MHi

> Annie Haven Thwing, comp., Inhabitants and Estates of the Town of Boston, 1630–1800; typed card catalogue, with supplementary bound typescripts, in the Massachusetts Historical Society.

6. SHORT TITLES OF WORKS
FREQUENTLY CITED IN THIS VOLUME

AA2, *Jour. and Corr.*

> *Journal and Correspondence of Miss Adams, Daughter of John Adams,* ... *edited by Her Daughter* [Caroline Amelia (Smith) de Windt], New York and London, 1841–1842; 2 vols.

Amer. Antiq. Soc., *Procs.*

> American Antiquarian Society, *Proceedings.*

Austin, *Gerry*

> James T. Austin, *The Life of Elbridge Gerry. With Contemporary Letters,* Boston, 1828–1829; 2 vols. [Vol. 1:] *To the Close of the American Revolution*; [vol. 2:] *From the Close of the American Revolution.*

Biog. Dir. Cong.

> *Biographical Directory of the American Congress, 1774–1949,* Washington, 1950.

BM, *Catalogue*

> *The British Museum Catalogue of Printed Books, 1881–1900,* Ann Arbor, 1946; 58 vols. *Supplement, 1900–1905,* Ann Arbor, 1950; 10 vols.

Boston Record Commissioners, *Reports*

> City of Boston, Record Commissioners, *Reports,* Boston, 1876–1909; 39 vols.

Braintree Town Records

> Samuel A. Bates, ed., *Records of the Town of Braintree, 1640 to 1793,* Randolph, Mass., 1886.

Burnett, ed., *Letters of Members*

> Edmund C. Burnett, ed., *Letters of Members of the Continental Congress,* Washington, 1921–1936; 8 vols.

Cal. Franklin Papers, A.P.S.

> I. Minis Hays, comp., *Calendar of the Papers of Benjamin Franklin in the Library of the American Philosophical Society,* Philadelphia, 1908; 5 vols.

Catalogue of JA's Library
> Catalogue of the John Adams Library in the Public Library of the City of Boston, Boston, 1917.

Century Cyclo. of Names
> Benjamin E. Smith, ed., *The Century Cyclopedia of Names*, New York, 1894.

CFA2, *Three Episodes*
> Charles Francis Adams, *Three Episodes of Massachusetts History: The Settlement of Boston Bay; The Antinomian Controversy; A Study of Church and Town Government*, Boston and New York, 1892; 2 vols.

Chamberlain, *Beacon Hill*
> Allen Chamberlain, *Beacon Hill: Its Ancient Pastures and Early Mansions*, Boston and New York, 1925.

Col. Soc. Mass., *Pubns.*
> Colonial Society of Massachusetts, *Publications*.

DAB
> Allen Johnson and Dumas Malone, eds., *Dictionary of American Biography*, New York, 1928–1936; 20 vols. plus index and supplements.

DAH
> James Truslow Adams and R. V. Coleman, eds., *Dictionary of American History*, New York, 1940; 5 vols. and index.

Deane Papers
> Papers of Silas Deane, 1774–1790, in New-York Historical Society, *Collections, Publication Fund Series*, vols. 19–23, New York, 1887–1891; 5 vols.

Dict. Amer. Fighting Ships
> U.S. Navy Department, Office of the Chief of Naval Operations, Naval History Division, *Dictionary of American Naval Fighting Ships*, Washington, 1959– .

DNB
> Leslie Stephen and Sidney Lee, eds., *The Dictionary of National Biography*, New York and London, 1885–1900; 63 vols. plus supplements.

Evans
> Charles Evans and others, comps., *American Bibliography: A Chronological Dictionary of All Books, Pamphlets and Periodical Publications Printed in the United States of America* [1639–1800], Chicago and Worcester, 1903–1959; 14 vols.

Force, *Archives*
> [Peter Force, ed.,] *American Archives: Consisting of a Collection of Authentick Records, State Papers, Debates, and Letters and Other Notices of Publick Affairs*, Washington, 1837–1853; 9 vols.

Ford, ed., *Statesman and Friend*
> Worthington C. Ford, ed., *Statesman and Friend: Correspondence of John Adams with Benjamin Waterhouse, 1784–1822*, Boston, 1927.

Franklin, *Papers*, ed. Labaree
> *The Papers of Benjamin Franklin*, ed. Leonard W. Labaree and others, New Haven, 1959– .

Grandmother Tyler's Book
> Frederick Tupper and Helen Tyler Brown, eds., *Grandmother Tyler's Book: The Recollections of Mary Palmer Tyler (Mrs. Royall Tyler), 1775–1866*, New York and London, 1925.

Groce and Wallace, *Dict. Amer. Artists*
> George C. Groce and David H. Wallace, *The New-York Historical Society's Dictionary of American Artists, 1564–1860*, New Haven and London, 1957.

Heitman, *Register Continental Army*
> Francis B. Heitman, comp., *Historical Register of Officers of the Continental Army during the War of the Revolution*, new edn., Washington, 1914.

JA, *Corr. in the Boston Patriot*
> *Correspondence of the Late President Adams. Originally Published in the Boston Patriot. In a Series of Letters*, Boston, 1809[–1810]; 10 pts.

JA, *Diary and Autobiography*
> *Diary and Autobiography of John Adams*, ed. L. H. Butterfield and others, Cambridge, 1961; 4 vols.

JA, *Legal Papers*
> *Legal Papers of John Adams*, ed. L. Kinvin Wroth and Hiller B. Zobel (in preparation as a part of The Belknap Press edition of *The Adams Papers* under a grant from The William Nelson Cromwell Foundation to the Harvard Law School).

JA, *Letters*, ed. CFA
> *Letters of John Adams, Addressed to His Wife*, ed. Charles Francis Adams, Boston, 1841; 2 vols.

JA, *Works*
> *The Works of John Adams, Second President of the United States: with a Life of the Author*, ed. Charles Francis Adams, Boston, 1850–1856; 10 vols.

JA-AA, *Familiar Letters*
> *Familiar Letters of John Adams and His Wife Abigail Adams, during the Revolution. With a Memoir of Mrs. Adams*, ed. Charles Francis Adams, New York, 1876.

JCC
> Worthington C. Ford and others, eds., *Journals of the Continental Congress, 1774–1789*, Washington, 1904–1937; 34 vols.

Jefferson, *Papers*, ed. Boyd
> *The Papers of Thomas Jefferson*, ed. Julian P. Boyd and others, Princeton, 1950– .

Jones, *Loyalists of Mass.*
> E. Alfred Jones, *The Loyalists of Massachusetts: Their Memorials, Petitions and Claims*, London, 1930.

Lasseray, *Les français sous les treize étoiles*
> André Lasseray, *Les français sous les treize étoiles (1775–1783)*, Macon and Paris, 1935; 2 vols.

Mass., *House Jour.*
> *Journals of the House of Representatives of Massachusetts* [1715–   ], Boston, reprinted by the Massachusetts Historical Society, 1919– . (For the years for which reprints are not yet available, the original printings are cited, by year and session.)

Mass., *Province Laws*
  The Acts and Resolves, Public and Private, of the Province of the Massachusetts
  Bay, Boston, 1869–1922; 21 vols.

Mass. *Soldiers and Sailors*
  Massachusetts Soldiers and Sailors of the Revolutionary War, Boston, 1896–
  1908; 17 vols.

Mayo, *Winthrop Family*
  Lawrence Shaw Mayo, The Winthrop Family in America, Boston, 1948.

MHS, *Colls., Procs.*
  Massachusetts Historical Society, Collections and Proceedings.

NEHGR
  New England Historical and Genealogical Register.

Niles' *Register*
  Niles' Weekly Register, Baltimore, 1811–1849.

OED
  The Oxford English Dictionary, Oxford, 1933; 12 vols. and supplement.

Penna. *Archives*
  Pennsylvania Archives. Selected and Arranged from Original Documents in the
  Office of the Secretary of the Commonwealth, Philadelphia and Harrisburg,
  1852–1935; 119 vols. in 123.

PMHB
  Pennsylvania Magazine of History and Biography.

Quincy, *Reports*
  Josiah Quincy Jr., Reports of Cases Argued and Adjudged in the Superior Court
  of Judicature of the Province of Massachusetts Bay, between 1761 and 1772,
  ed. Samuel M. Quincy, Boston, 1865.

Rowe, *Letters and Diary*
  Letters and Diary of John Rowe, Boston Merchant, 1759–1762, 1764–1779,
  ed. Anne Rowe Cunningham, Boston, 1903.

Benjamin Rush, *Letters*
  Letters of Benjamin Rush, ed. L. H. Butterfield, Princeton, 1951; 2 vols.

Sabin
  Joseph Sabin and others, comps., A Dictionary of Books Relating to America,
  from Its Discovery to the Present Time, New York, 1868–1936; 29 vols.

Sabine, *Loyalists*
  Lorenzo Sabine, Biographical Sketches of Loyalists of the American Revolution,
  with an Historical Essay, Boston, 1864; 2 vols.

Shurtleff, *Description of Boston*
  Nathaniel B. Shurtleff, A Topographical and Historical Description of Boston,
  3d edn., Boston, 1890.

Sibley-Shipton, *Harvard Graduates*
  John Langdon Sibley and Clifford K. Shipton, Biographical Sketches of Grad-
  uates of Harvard University, in Cambridge, Massachusetts, Cambridge and
  Boston, 1873– .

Stiles, *Literary Diary*
> *The Literary Diary of Ezra Stiles, D.D., LL.D., President of Yale College,* ed.
> Franklin Bowditch Dexter, New York, 1901; 3 vols.

Stokes, *Iconography of Manhattan Island*
> I. N. Phelps Stokes, *The Iconography of Manhattan Island, 1498–1919,* New
> York, 1915–1928; 6 vols.

Warren-Adams Letters
> *Warren-Adams Letters: Being Chiefly a Correspondence among John Adams,
> Samuel Adams, and James Warren* (Massachusetts Historical Society, *Collec-
> tions,* vols. 72–73), Boston, 1917–1925; 2 vols.

Washington, *Writings,* ed. Fitzpatrick
> *The Writings of George Washington from the Original Manuscript Sources,
> 1745–1799,* ed. John C. Fitzpatrick, Washington, 1931–1944; 39 vols.

Webster, 2d edn.
> *Webster's New International Dictionary of the English Language, Second Edi-
> tion, Unabridged,* Springfield, Mass., 1958.

Weis, *Colonial Clergy of N.E.*
> Frederick Lewis Weis, comp., *The Colonial Clergy and the Colonial Churches
> of New England,* Lancaster, Mass., 1936.

Wharton, ed., *Dipl. Corr. Amer. Rev.*
> Francis Wharton, ed., *The Revolutionary Diplomatic Correspondence of the
> United States,* Washington, 1889; 6 vols.

WMQ
> *William and Mary Quarterly.*

VOLUME 2

Family Correspondence

1776–1778

Adams Family Correspondence

John Adams to Isaac Smith Sr.

Dear sir   Philadelphia June 1. 1776

Your favours of May 14. and 22d. are now before me. The first I shewed to Mr. Morris, as soon as I received it. The last contains Intelligence, from Hallifax of the Streights to which our Enemies are reduced, which I was very glad to learn.

I am very happy to learn from you and some other of my Friends that Boston is securely fortified; but still I cannot be fully satisfied untill I hear that every unfriendly Flagg is chased out of that Harbour.

Cape Ann, I am sensible is a most important Post, and if the Enemy should possess themselves of it, they might distress the Trade of the Colony to a great Degree. For which Reason I am determined to do every Thing in my Power to get it fortified at the Continental Expence. I cant be confident that I shall succeed but it shall not be my Fault if I dont.

I am very glad you gave me your Opinion of the Utility of that Harbour and of the Practicability of making it secure, because I was not enough acquainted with it before to speak with Precision about it.

Your Observations upon the oppressive severity of the old Regulations of Trade in subjecting Ships and Cargoes to Confiscation for the Indiscretion of a Master or Mariner, and upon the Artifice and Corruption which was introduced respecting Hospital Money, are very just: But if you consider the Resolution of Congress, and that of Virginia of the 15th. of May, the Resolutions of the two Carolinas and Georgia, each of which Colonies, are instituting new Governments, under the Authority of the People; if you consider what is doing at New York, New Jersey, Pensilvania, and even in Maryland, which are all gradually forming themselves into order to follow the Colonies to the Northward and Southward, together with the Treaties with Hesse, Brunswick and Waldeck and the Answer to the Mayor &c. of London; I believe you will be convinced that there is little Probability of our ever again coming under the Yoke of British Regulations of Trade. The Cords which connected the two Countries are cutt asunder, and it will not be easy to splice them again, together.

I agree with you, in sentiment, that there will be little Difficulty in Trading with France and Spain, a great deal in dealing with Portugal, and some with Holland. Yet by very good Intelligence I am convinced, that there are great Merchants in the United Provinces and even in Amsterdam, who will contract to supply you with any Thing you want, whether Merchandize or military Stores by the Way of Nieuport and Ostend, two Towns which are subject to the Empress of Austria, who has never taken any public Notice of the Dispute between Britain and Us, and has never prohibited her Subjects from supplying us with any Thing.

There is a Gentleman, now in this City, a Native of it, and a very worthy Man who has been lately in those Towns as well as Amsterdam, who informs me that he had many Conversations there, with Merchants of figure, and that they assured him they should be glad to contract to furnish us with any Supplies, even upon Credit, for an Interest of four Per Cent.[1]

Other Intelligence to the same Purpose, with Additions of more Importance, has been sent here. But the Particulars may not be mentioned.

Europe seems to be in a great Commotion; altho the Appearance of a perfect Calm is affected, I think this American Contest will light up a general War. What it will end in, God alone knows, to whose wise and righteous Providence I chearfully submit, and am with great Esteem and Respect for the Family, your Friend & servant.

LbC (Adams Papers). This is the first entry printed from JA's letterbooks in the present series of Adams Family Correspondence, though not quite the earliest entry in those letterbooks. It is the fourth entry in Lb/JA/1 (Adams Papers, Microfilms, Reel No. 89); the very first letterbook copy is dated 26 May 1776 and is a letter to James Sullivan (printed in JA, *Works*, 9:375–378). Concerning the Adams Letterbooks in general, see the Introduction to the Family Correspondence. For JA's purchase of his first two letterbooks, and his motives in doing so, see the letter immediately below (to AA, 2 June 1776). It should be noted here that the early entries in the JA letterbooks are actually drafts, which the writer corrected and then copied out fair for transmittal, and also that small variations in form and phrasing between letterbook and recipients' copies are not ordinarily recorded by the editors.

[1] Not clearly identifiable, but quite possibly William Bingham (1752–1804), College of Philadelphia 1768, who just at this time was appointed agent of the Continental Congress in Martinique, to serve under orders from the Committee of Secret Correspondence (of which he had been acting as secre-

tary). See *DAB; JCC,* 4:366; Force, *Archives,* 4th ser., 6:783; *Deane Papers,* 1:137; Burnett, ed., *Letters of Members,* 2:64, 96; Margaret L. Brown, "William Bingham, Agent of the Continental Congress in Martinique," *PMHB,* 61:54–87 (Jan. 1937), esp. p. 54–57.

John Adams to Abigail Adams

June 2. 1776[1]

Yesterday I dined with Captain Richards, the Gentleman who made me the present of the brass Pistolls. We had Cherries, Strawberries and Green Peas in Plenty. The Fruits are three Weeks earlier here than with you, indeed they are a fortnight earlier on the East, than on the West side of Delaware River. We have had green Peas, this Week past, but they were brought over the River from New Jersey to this Markett. There are none grown in the City, or on the West side of the River yet. The Reason is, the Soil of New Jersey is a warm Sand, that of Pensilvania, a cold Clay. So much for Peas and Berries.

Now for something of more Importance. In all the Correspondencies I have maintained, during a Course of twenty Years at least that I have been a Writer of Letters, I never kept a single Copy.[2] This Negligence and Inaccuracy, has been a great Misfortune to me, on many Occasions.—I have now purchased a Folio Book, in the first Page of which, excepting one blank Leaff, I am writing this Letter, and intend to write all my Letters to you in it from this Time forward. This will be an Advantage to me in several Respects. In the first Place, I shall write more deliberately. In the second Place, I shall be able at all times to review what I have written. 3. I shall know how often I write. 4. I shall discover by this Means, whether any of my Letters to you, miscarry.

If it were possible for me to find a Conveyance, I would send you such another blank Book, as a Present, that you might begin the Practice at the same Time, for I really think that your Letters are much better worth preserving than mine.[3] Your Daughter and Sons will very soon write so good Hands that they will copy the Letters for you from your Book, which will improve them at the same Time that it relieves you.

RC and LbC (Adams Papers). LbC is the first entry in Lb/JA/2 (Adams Papers, Microfilms, Reel No. 90), one of two folio volumes that JA had recently purchased from William Trickett, "STATIONER & BOOKBINDER from LONDON," in Front Street, Philadelphia. (Trickett's trade card is among the illustrations in the present volume.) In the first of these JA began entering letters relative to public affairs; the second he reserved for family letters, mainly to AA.

[1] In LbC the date is preceded by "Philadelphia," and this is the case in many of the letterbook copies that follow in 1776. Omission of the place in recipients' copies, like the omission of the writer's signature, was a device of concealment, springing from JA's experience with the famous intercepted letters of July 1775.

[2] Substantially but not literally true. A few retained drafts and copies of JA's letters prior to this date have been found among his papers, some of them in his Diary.

[3] AA kept a letterbook for only a brief period, 1779–1780, and then only fitfully; see Lb/JA/9 (Adams Papers, Microfilms, Reel No. 97).

Abigail Adams to John Adams

June 3. 1776

I received by Mr. Church a few lines from you; I wish to hear from you every opportunity tho you say no more than that you are well. I feel concernd least your cloaths should go to rags having nobody to take any care of you in your long absence, and then you have not with you a proper change for the Seasons. However you must do the best you can. I have a suit of homespun for you whenever you return. I cannot avoid sometimes repineing that the gifts of fortune were not bestowed upon us, that I might have injoyed the happiness of spending my days with my Partner. But as it is, I think it my duty to attend with frugality and oeconomy to our own private affairs, and if I cannot add to our Little Substance yet see that it is not diminished. I should enjoy but little comfort in a state of Idleness, and uselessness. Here I can serve my partner, my family and myself, and injoy the Satisfaction of your serving your Country.

I wish you would write me what I had best do with our House at Boston. I would advertise it if you think best. There are so many Houses torn to peices and so many others abused that I might stand a chance of Letting it perhaps as it is in so good repair.[1]

My Brother is desirous of Joining the Army again, but would chuse to be a field officer. I have mentiond him to some of the House and suppose he will be recommended to congress, for a commission. I hardly know where you will find Men to form the Regiments required. I begin to think population a very important Branch in the American Manufactorys.

I enclose a List of Counsel.[2] The House consists of more than 200 & 50 Members. Your former pupil A[ngie]r comes from Bridgwater, and 5 others. I hope they will proceed in Buisness with a little more Spirit than Heretofore. They are procuring two row Gallies, but when

4

they will be finished I know not. I thought they were near done, but find to day they are not yet contracted for. All our Gentery are gone from Nantasket road except the commodore and one or two small craft.

Every thing bears a very great price. The Merchant complains of the Farmer and the Farmer of the Merchant. Both are extravagant. Living is double what it was one year ago.

I find you have licenced Tea but I am determined not to be a purchaser unless I can have it at Congress price, and in that article the venders pay no regard to congress, asking 10. 8. and the lowest is 7.6 per pound. I should like a little Green, but they say there is none to be had here; I only wish it for a medicine, as a relief to a nervious pain in my Head to which I am sometimes subject. Were it as plenty as ever I would not practice the use of it.

Our Family are all well. It has been reported here that congress were going to remove 40 miles beyond Philadelphia. I gave no credit to the report, I heard no reason assignd for it. I had much rather they would come a hundred miles nearer here.

Adieu—Yours.

RC (Adams Papers); addressed in John Thaxter's hand: "To The Honble: John Adams Esqr. at Philadelphia To the Care of Coll. Warren"; docketed in one or more hands. For the enclosure see note 2.

[1] The state of the Adamses' Boston house after the British occupation is much less favorably described in AA's letter to JA of 20 Sept., below.

[2] Not found. AA probably sent the list of members of the new Council as printed in the *Boston Gazette* of this date.

John Adams to Abigail Adams

Philadelphia June 3. 1776

The last Evening, Mess. Adams, P[aine] and G[erry] and my self, by Agreement waited on the P[resident] at his House, in order to accompany him to the Generals, to request that Gates and Mifflin might be sent immediately, to take the Command at Boston. The P. we found very ill of a violent fitt of the Gout, unable to go abroad. At our Disire, he sent a Card to the G. requesting his Company, who soon afterwards came. This Conversation would make a Figure in History. It turned upon the general State of Affairs in the military Departments, and the Characters of the principal Officers in the Army.—I dont think it prudent to commit to Writing the Particulars.

But a few Reflections that occurred, may be safely written. One is this.

There is so much of Accident in the Appointment of Officers, even where they are chosen by the People or their Representatives, and their Characters are of such vast Importance, after they are appointed, and in Times like these when there are so many Jealousies, Envys, and Distrusts abroad from whence so many Calumnies arise, that it is absolutely necessary to support the Characters of Officers whenever you can, to be silent when you cannot, untill you are furnished with sufficient Evidence of their Faults and Guilt, and then censure, and punish.[1]

LbC (Adams Papers). This letter was almost certainly not sent; no RC has been found, and in JA's list of recent letters sent to AA (at the beginning of his letter of 26 June, below) he does not mention it. The text is probably incomplete.

[1] Following this entry in Lb/JA/2 there is another, shorter fragment of a letter presumably addressed to AA and never sent. It is dated at Philadelphia, 9 June 1776, and reads:
"The Intelligence from Canada, is very discouraging. Every Thing is in Confusion there.—Men discontented, dispirited, naked, starved. Officers chagrined. Canadians disappointed, and intimidated. Commissioners not very judicious, or penetrating—haughty not condescending. Rather Men of Dissipation than Business."

Zabdiel Adams to John Adams

Much Honored & dear Sir   Harvard June 9th 1776[1]

Having a very Convenient opportunity of Conveying a Line to you, by the Revd. Mr. Whitney (who being an invalid, sets out tomorrow on a journey to Philadelphia for his health,) I cannot but embrace it, just to let you know that though you are separated from me by a great distance of way, yet that *you*, and the respectable body to which you belong are often in my thoughts. I rejoice to find that the members of that illustrious house have been so generally united in the important measures of the present day, and that such immediate and ready obedience is yielded, by the respective Colonies, to your resolves and the significations of your Pleasure. It is truly surprizing that any body of men acting *above* and *without* the forms of the Constitution, and having no authority but what is founded in *reason, honor,* and *Love* of *Liberty*, should be able to manage the affairs of so great a Continent, and give harmonious motion to so many people, of different customs, educations, forms of Government and modes of religion! But strange as it is, we have found it realized in event. However, it appears to me that it is not safe long to depend on an authority held by such precarious tenure. Whilst in our present unsettled state with respect to Government we Lye exposed to a thousand dangers. Persons of enterprizing and disaffectd minds have too good an opportunity of forming parties, creating disunion and carrying into execution their evil designs. It is therefore, on this account, greatly to be wished that the Congress would declare us independant of Great Britain, and that one general form of Government might be soon instituted over the whole of the united Colonies. And if, as we hear, forreign assistance cannot be obtained till a declaration of independency is made, methinks this is another cogent reason why it should be made immediately. We have accounts of a very formidable armament coming against us, this summer. A vigorous and strenuous opposition must be made against them. But have we sufficiency of strength to make such an one among ourselves. I Doubt not. Why then is any time Lost in removing any obstacles in the way of our availing ourselves of forreign aid? With Pleasure I hear that most of the southern Colonies are now in favour of a Separation from Great Britain, and some have instructd their members to see that it is effected. We are very hearty in this measure in this part of the Continent, and are ardently wishing it may soon take place, as the most probable means of saving America from ruin. However, we confide in the well known abilities of the Congress, and patiently wait their determination on this most important Question.

Thus, with a familiarity becoming only the peculiar intimacy that formerly subsisted between us, have I communicatd to you my sentiments of independancy. I can assure you we hold the Congress in high estimation in this part of the world, and shall be very likely to submit with almost an implicit obedience to your resolves and directions; but as *Common Sense* teaches us that there can never be a cordial reconciliation between Great Britain and this Country, so we could ever wish to be heard as pleading for an immediate declaration of independence.

I have no material News to write you. The People this way do not appear intimidated by the reports of 55 Thousand men coming to attack and lay us waste. I hope our Courage will not fail us in the day of Battle. But we are not to trust in the number, valor, or regularity of well appointed and well disciplined Soldiers, but in the Lord of host[s] and God of armies; for as King Jehosophat said, we have no might against the great company that cometh against us, neither know we what to do, but our eyes should be up to God.

The People of Braintree I hear are in General well, and presume your family is so in particular. Mine is at present in comfortable circumstances. Sickness has much prevaild among the Children this way, and is not yet totally removed. The season is cold, dry in some places, and backward. Our Prospects with regard to the fruits of the earth are at present discouraging. The Lord be merciful to us.

I should be extremely glad to receive a Letter from you, telling me the news, and informing what are your views and expectations in the present perplexd state of our affairs. Watchman what of the Night? Whilst you in your exalted station, are concerting political measures for the Salvation of America, I in my meek and humble one, am pointing out the moral causes of our desorders, and calling upon the People to repent. In this, the way of Duty, we are hoping for better times, but if they never come to us in this world, I hope when we Leave it, we shall both go to a place of profound peace and tranquility, where, as there is no sin, so there is no sorrow; where Judah will not vex Ephraim, nor Ephraim envy Judah; where nation shall no more rise against nation, neither practise fighting any more.

I conclude by assuring you that my best wishes attend you and the other members of the Congress; that God would impart to you necessary wisdom, teach you the things that belong to our peace, guide your Counsels, continue your union, and make you the happy instruments of Establishing the Liberties of America on a perpetual basis.

I am your friend & humble Servant,   Zabdiel Adams

RC (Adams Papers).

[1] JA's "Cousin Zab," the settled minister of Lunenburg, was writing from nearby Harvard, Mass.

John Adams to Peter Boylston Adams

My dear Brother   Philadelphia June 15. 1776

I have an Account of the Politicks of the Town of Braintree; but it is an imperfect one. I wish you would write me, a clear, and distinct one....[1] I am told there was a Tie, between your Hon. Brigadier General and You, and that, in order to get a Decision in his Favour he was obliged to declare that he would leave the Board for the Sake of serving the Town.[2] I should be glad to learn a little of Motives and Politicks upon this Occasion.

How is it? You leave me in the dark: you dont tell me whether I have the Honour to be a select Man, or not, or who are select Men, nor any Thing about Town Affairs.... Do you think that, because I am half a thousand miles off, I never think about you and that I dont want to know this, and that and the other?—I do, indeed.—You may at any Time send a Letter to the Post Office in Boston, it will be brought to me free of Expence, to you, or me.... I am greatly at a Loss to account for the Conduct of your Hon. Councillor and gallant Brigadier, upon this Occasion. Pray explain it. Ask Mr. Norton[3]— what it means.

LbC (Adams Papers).

[1] Here and below, suspension points are in MS.
[2] Joseph Palmer is meant; see AA to JA, 27 May, above.
[3] Probably a slip of the pen for "Mr. Norton Quincy."

Mary Palmer to John Adams

Sir   Germantown June 15th 1776 Saturday

You will wonder at recieving a Letter from one who is very far from being Sufficiently qualified to write to a Member of the Grand Congress but I am under parental injunctions to do it, which every good Child ought to obey.—The Affair of fortifying the Harbour of Boston has long been in Agitation and tho' repeatedly urged by the Honourable Members of the Congress, and almost universally by the People of the Sea Coasts hereabouts, and by many others yet it has been delay'd by the Court from what Motives they best know who hinder'd its being done. Papa was one of those in its favour, and exerted himself as much as possible to get it done, the Council were for it but the House were afraid of Expences &c. There is now a New House of which he is a Member.—This House consented after some difficulties to let it be done immediately. I think this was last Saturday, and as the greatest Secressy was necessary in Order to prevent our Enemies having knowledge of our proceedings, (as there [was] too much reason to think they dayly reciev'd News of all our proceedings) the Time appointed for taking possession of the Heights was not known even to the House till the Day for its execution which was Thursday. 700 of the Continental Troops were Order'd to Long Island and Moon Island, 700 of Colony Troops and Militia to Nantasket, and 700 ditto to Pettucks Island and Spears Hill.—The Cannon, Military Stores, &c. were to be at their destinations at 9 OClock that Night, but as many of them, came by Water in Lighters which were becalmed, and some Missing their Way they did not bring the Cannon time enough to take possession of Pettucks or Nantasket that Night, which was a great Mortification to the Commanders at those places.—At this time there

were about 10 or 12 of the Enemies Vessels lying near Georges Island
some of considerable Force, and the Commodore a Sixty Gun Ship [1]
had moved nearer to Pettucks, and as they had within the Week
reciev'd recruits of Soldiers to the Amount of at least 700, it was fear'd
they wou'd take possession of that Hill or Nantasket that Night, which
our People cou'd not prevent for want of Cannon, their feelings may
be better immagin'd than express'd—they were dreadful.—The Night
was dark and so still that our People cou'd hear the Sound of the
Voices on Board the Ships in their common conversation.—Papa was
to command at Pettucks and Spears Hill, and went over to the former
with his Aid de Camps and 180 Men about 10 oClock and Staid till
two waiting for Recruits and Cannon to no purpose. Had the Enemy
known of their being there they say they cou'd have taken or kill'd
them all but providence order'd it otherwise. At two they returnd to
Spears Hill.—In the Mean Time the Fort at Long Island was carrying
on briskly so that before Seven in the Morning, they began to fire upon
the Ships.—Upon the first firing the little Vessels hoisted Sail, but the
Commodore and larger Ones stood it for about an Hour or more, 'tho
without returning the fire as it was to no purpose I suppose, the Advantage being so much greater on the high land than on the water.
Before 9 oClock the Commodore tho't proper to set sail with all his
Ships and Small Craft, after having stood a continued fire from Long
Island all that time, [...] [2] as it was calm they Sail'd but Slowly and
bro't to by the Light house, which they dismantled and blew up, taking
all their Soldiers from that place with the Cannon. This was about
one oClock Yesterday. Soon after they continued their Course out-
wards, tho not without some disagreable Salutes from Nantasket which
was then furnish'd with Cannon, and fired about 30 Balls at them
as they pass'd, some of which it is tho't struck the Commodore and
other Vessels.—About 5 or 6 OClock they were all out of Sight.—Some
of the Ships fir'd a few Guns as they past Nantaskett but without doing
any Damage.—There is little probability that any Lives were lost during
the whole of this Affair. Our Harbour is now entirely clear of the
Enemy, and it was entertaining to see the Privateers and little Lighters
parading it in the very places so long Usurp'd by the British Navy.—
The Day was clos'd by the discharging of Cannon and Small Arms,
in Token of Joy for their deliverance, by our People in Boston, and
the Forts. As this News will be agreable to you tho' told in a very
imperfect and faulty Manner, I the rather hope for your generous
Allowances in the behalf of the writer, whose Abilities are far from
being equal to the Subject. I shou'd not have presum'd so far, had

Mrs. Adams been at Home, but she set out for Plimouth, Thursday Morning, and so cou'd not have the Opportunity of writing so particularly as if she had been in Town at the Time of this Evacuation.— Papa is so taken up in Planing and executing the Plans of the Forts, in the Harbour especially Nantasket where he is now in person that he can't get a Moments Time to write, or even to Answer a Question, so that I can't tell certainly who the commanders were at the several places, and am at a Loss for other particulars.—My letter is too long already and I will not add to it by a Multitude of excuses. Your pardon for inaccuracies, Blots &c. I depend on and I believe you to possess too much good Nature, to expose the faults of an illiterate Girl.

I am Sir, Your most humble Servant,   Polly Palmer

Since I wrote the above, Papa has given me some Minutes, which I shall copy off just as they are—

> 500 Colonial Troops at Nantasket Hill
> 200 Militia from Lovels Regt. at Point Alderton
>   All these commanded by Colo. Lovel.

> 500 Continental and Colonial Troops at Pettucks Island
> 200 Militia from Bass's Regt. at Hoffs Neck
>   All these commanded by Palmer.

> 500 Continental Troops at Long Island
> 200 Militia from Gills Regt. at the Moon
>   All these Commanded by Wadsworth as I think—
>   with Cannon &c. to each place.

17th. Monday

Yesterday several of our Privateers fell in with and engag'd a large Ship of Force and a Brig. The two latter Maintain'd a kind of runing fight from Seven in the Morning till late at Night, still standing in for the Harbour which they were permited to enter followed by the Privateers. About 11 oClock at Night the Engagement was renew'd between the Vessels with great fury. I think I never saw such firing before. The flashes were almost without Intermission. At 12 they Yeilded to us having both run Aground during the fight. They had 200 Highlanders belonging to Frasiers Regt.

RC (Adams Papers); addressed: "The Honble. John Adams Esqr. Philadelphia"; endorsed: "Miss P. Palmer. an. June 5" (error for July 5); to this endorsement was later added the date "June 15. 1776" in the hand of William Gordon(?).

[1] That is, Capt. Francis Banks, R.N., in the *Renown*.
[2] MS worn and torn at bottom edge.

John Adams to Abigail Adams

June 16. 1776

Yesterday was to me a lucky Day, as it brought me two Letters from you, one dated May 27. and the other June 3d.

Dont be concerned, about me, if it happens now and then that you dont hear from me, for some Weeks together. If any Thing should injure my Health materially, you will soon hear of it. But I thank God I am in much better Health than I expected to be. But this cannot last long, under the Load that I carry. When it becomes too great for my Strength I shall ask leave to lay it down and come home. But I will hold it out a good while yet, if I can.

I am willing to take the Woodland Sister mentions, and the Watch and the sword. As to the Lighter, it cost more than five hundred Dollars in hard Cash.

I wish our Uncle [*Norton Quincy*] had as much Ambition, as he has Virtue and Ability. A Deficiency of Ambition is as criminal and injurious as an Excess of it.—Tell him I say so.—How shall We contrive to make so wise and good a Man ambitious? Is it not a sin to be so modest. Ask him how he can answer it? So! then it seems the Brigadier [*Joseph Palmer*] was obliged to step down Stairs in order to keep my Brother, out of the lower Room....[1] I am sorry for it.

Thanks for your Quotation from Sully. It is extreamly appropos.

I am very glad you are so well provided with Help. Give my Respects to Mr. Belcher, and his Family. Tell him, I am obliged to him for his Kind Care of the Farm. I wish I could go out with him, and see the Business go on, but I cant.

Thank your Father, and my Mother, for their kind Remembrance of me. Return my Duty to both.

Charles's young Heroism charms me. Kiss him. Poor Mugford. Yet glorious Mugford.—How beautifull and sublime it is to die for ones Country.—What a fragrant Memory remains!

The Rumour you heard of General Gates, will prove premature. I endeavoured both here and with the General, to have it so, and should have succeeded, if it had not been for the Loss of General Thomas.

Cruel small Pox! worse than the sword! But now I fear We must part with Gates for the sake of Canada.

Mrs. Montgomery is a Lady like all the Family, of refined Sentiments and elegant Accomplishments. Her Letter, as you quote it, is very pathetic.

Do you mean that our Plymouth Friends are in Trouble for a disordered son! If so, I am grieved to the Heart. God grant them Support under so severe an Affliction. But this World is a scene of Afflictions.

Rejoice to hear that the Enemy has not fortified. Hope they will not be suffered to attempt it.

Dont think about my Cloaths. I do well enough in that Respect. As to your House at Boston, do with it, as you please. Sell it, if you will, but not for a farthing less than it cost me. Let it, if you please, but take Care who your Tenant is—both of his Prudence to preserve the House, and his Ability to pay the Rent.

Your Brother, I hope will be promoted. He is fit for it, and has deserved it. If his Name comes recommended from the General Court, he will have a Commission for a Field Officer, and I will recommend him to the General for his Notice.

My Pupil, if he pleases, will do Honour to his Preceptor, and important service to his Country. I hope his Zeal and Fidelity will be found equal to his Abilities.[2]

I will endeavour to relieve your Head Ach if I can.

I send you all the News, in the Papers. Great Things are on the Tapis. These Throws will usher in the Birth of a fine Boy. We have no Thoughts of removing from hence—there is no occasion for it.

RC and LbC (Adams Papers).

[1] Suspension points in MS.
[2] See JA's fatherly letter of advice to Oakes Angier, 12 June 1776 (LbC, Adams Papers; JA, *Works*, 9:394–395).

Abigail Adams to John Adams

Plimouth June 17 [1776] a remarkable Day

I this day Received by the Hands of our Worthy Friend a large packet, which has refreshed and comforted me. Your own sensations have ever been similar to mine. I need [not][1] then tell you how gratified I am at the frequent tokens of remembrance with which you favour me, nor how they rouse every tender sensation of my Soul, which sometimes find vent at my Eyes nor dare I discribe how earnestly I long to fold to my fluttering Heart the dear object of my warmest affections. The Idea sooths me, I feast upon it with a pleasure known only to those whose Hearts and hopes are one.

The approbation you give to my conduct in the Management of our private affair[s] is very gratefull to me and sufficently compensates, for all my anxieties, and endeavours to discharge the many duties devolved upon me in consequence of the absence of my dearest Friend. Were they discharged eaquel to my wishes I should merrit the praises you bestow.

You see I date from Plimouth. Here I came upon a visit to our amiable Friends accompanied by My Sister Betsy a day or two ago, and is the first night I have been absent since you left me. Having determined upon this visit for some time, I put my Family in order and prepaird for it, thinking I might leave it with safety. Yet the day I set out I was under many apprehensions by the comeing in of ten Transports who were seen to have many Soldiers on board, and the determination of the people to go and fortify upon Long Island, Peticks Island, Nantasket and Great Hill. It was apprehended they would attempt to land some where, but the next morning I had the pleasure to hear they were all driven out, Commodore and all. Not a Transport, a Ship or a tender to be seen. This shews what might have been long ago done. Had this been done in season the ten Transports with many others in all probability would have fallen into our Hands, but the progress of wisdom is slow.

Since I arrived here, I have really had a scene quite novel to me. The Brig Defence from Connecticut put in here for Balist. The officers who are all from thence and who were intimately acquainted at Dr. Lorthropes,[2] invited his Lady to come on board and bring with her as many of her Friends as she could collect. She sent an invitation to our Friend Mrs. W[arre]n and to us. The brig lay about a mile and half from the Town, the officers sent their Barge and we went, every mark of Respect and attention which was in their power, they shewd us. She is a fine Brigg, Mounts 16 Guns, 12 Swivells and carries 100 & 20 men. 100 & seventeen were on board; and no private family ever appeard under better Regulation than the Crew. It was as still as tho there had been only half a dozen, not a prophane word among any of them. The Captain himself is an exemplary Man, Harden[3] his name, has been in nine Sea engagements, says if he gets a Man who swears and finds he cannot reform him he turns him on shoar, Yet is free to confess that it was the sin of his youth. He has one lieutenant a very

14

fine fellow, Smelden[4] by name. We spent a very agreable afternoon and drank tea on board, they shew'd us their Arms which were sent by Queen Ann, and every thing on board was a curiosity to me. They gave us a mock engagement with an Enemy, and the manner of taking a ship. The young folks went upon Quarter deck and danced. Some of their Jacks played very well upon the voilene and German flute. The Brig bears the continental Colours and was fitted out by the Colony of Connecticut. As we set of from the Brig they fired their Guns in honour to us, a ceremony I would have very readily dispenced with.

I pitty you and feel for you under all the difficulties you have to encounter. My daily petitions to Heaven for you, are, that you may have Health, Wisdom and fortitude sufficent to carry you thro the great, and arduous Buisness in which you are engaged; and that your endeavours may be crownd with success.—Canady seems a dangerous and ill fated place. It is reported here that General Thomas is no more, that he took the small pox and died with it. Every day some circumstance arises and shews me the importance of having that distemper in youth. Dr. Bulfinch has petitiond the General Court for leave to open a Hospital some where, and it will be granted him.[5] I shall with all the children be one of the first class you may depend upon it.

I have just this moment heard that the Brig on which I was on board a Saturday and which saild yesterday morning from this place fell in with two Transports having each of them a 100 & 50 Men on board and took them and has brought them into Nantasket road, under cover of the Guns which are mounted there. Will add further perticuliars as soon as I am informd.

I am now better informd and can give you the Truth. The Brig Defence, accompanied by a smaller privateer saild in concert a Sunday morning. About 12 o clock they discoverd two Transports, and made for them. Two privateers who were small had been in chase of them, but finding the enemy were of much larger force; had run under Cohasat Rocks.[6] The Defence gave a Signal Gun to bring them out. Capt. Burk[7] who accompanied the Defence being a prime Sailor came up first and pourd a Broad Side on board a 16 Gun Brig. The Defence soon attack'd her upon her Bows, an obstinate engagement ensued, their was a continual Blaze upon all sides for many Hours and it was near mid Night before they struck. In the engagement the Defence lost one Man and 5 wounded. On board Burk not one Man received any damage. On board the enemy 14 killd among whom was a Major and 60 wounded. They are part of the Hiland Soldiers. The other Transport mounted 6 Guns. When the Fleet saild out of this

Harbour last week they blew up the light House. They met 6 Transports comeing in which they carried of with them. Hope we shall soon be in such a posture of defence as to bid them defiance.

I feel no great anxiety at the large armyment designd against us. The remarkable interpositions of Heaven in our favour cannot be too gratefully acknowledged. He who fed the Isralites in the wilderness, who cloaths the lilies of the Field and feeds the young Ravens when they cry, will not forsake a people engaged in so righteous cause if we remember his Loving kindness.

We wanted powder, we have a Supply. We wanted guns, we have been favour'd in that respect. We wanted hard money, 22000 Dollors and an Eaquel value of plate are deliverd into our Hands.

You mention your peas, your cherries, your strawberries &c. Ours are but just in Blosome. We have had the coldest Spring I ever knew, thing[s] are 3 weeks back of what they generally used to be. The corn looks poor, the season now is rather dry.—Our Friend has Refused his appointment.[8] I am very sorry. I said every thing I could think to persuaid him, but his Lady was against it. I need say no more.—I believe I did not understand you when in a former Letter you say, "I want to resign my office for a thousand reasons." If you meant that of judge I know not what to say. I know it will be a dificult and arduous station but divesting my self of private intrest which would lead me to be against your holding that office, I know of no person who is so well calculated to discharge the Trust, or who I think would act a more consciencious part.

My paper is full. I have [only][9] room to thank you for it.

RC (Adams Papers); addressed in John Thaxter's hand: "To The Honble: John Adams Esqr. at Philadelphia To be left at the Post Office in Boston"; endorsed: "Portia. ans. July 3."

[1] Inadvertent omission by the writer.

[2] Nathaniel Lothrop (1737–1828), Harvard 1756, a physician of Plymouth (MHS, *Procs.*, 2d ser., 3 (1886–1887): 403, note).

[3] Seth Harding.

[4] Samuel Smedley.

[5] Thomas Bulfinch (1728–1802), Harvard 1746; M.D., Edinburgh 1757 (Sibley–Shipton, *Harvard Graduates*, vol. 12 [in press, 1962]). Bulfinch inoculated AA and the Adams children in the following month; see her letters to JA of 13–14 July *et seq.*, below.

[6] On "Cohasat Rocks" see JA's *Diary and Autobiography*, 4:7, and note there. The naval action described by AA, in which the transports *Annabella* and *George* were taken at the entrance to Boston Harbor by the *Defence* and four Continental armed schooners, is described in detail from the sources by William Bell Clark in *George Washington's Navy*, Baton Rouge, 1960, p. 160–165.

[7] Capt. William Burke of the Continental schooner *Warren*.

[8] James Warren had declined appointment as associate justice of the Superior Court.

[9] Word torn away by seal. (This sentence was added by AA in the inner margin of the MS.)

Cotton Tufts to John Adams

Dear Sr.   Weymouth June 17. 1776

Our vast Extent of Territory requires a great Land Forrce to defend it. The Spirit of Commerce and Privateering already operates to render the Difficulty of raising Soldiers great. If I am right in what is advanc'd, and as the grand Struggle will soon ensue and it is incumbent on us to make the best Defence that we are capable off, Might it not be of general Utility to prohibit any Vessells from going foreign Voyages and all others from Province to Province except such as can pass safely within Shores. No more Privateers to be fitted out—except such as are contracted for by the Colonies or Continent—I mean for a limited Time. The great Numbers of Provision Vessells taken from us by our Enemies, strengthens them in a most essential Point, and the Men taken in them are lost to us (perhaps for ever). I have thought, that it would have been for the Interest of the Colonies to have borne the immense Expence of Land Carriage for Provisions rather than to have risqued them by Sea. Connecticut might have supplied us and what Connecticut was drained off New York might have supplied and what New York, Pensylvania and so on—the one handing the other Provisions to be transported where most wanted. The non Exportation of Provisions to the West Indies, would probably oblige them to come to our Ports for them—in this Case we should be sure of running no Risque.

To encourage Soldiers to enlist might not the offer of 100 Acres of Land to every Soldier that would enlist during the War be a good expedient? Such offer to be made upon the Condition of his Fidelity and our finally succeeding in the Contest.

About 4th or 5th. Inst. a Jamaica Vessell taken by some of the Continental Cruisers arrived at Marblehead. About the same Time another of 700 Tons at Dartmouth richly laden with Jamaica Produce. On the 7th. the Yankey Hero of Newbury Port (Capt. Tracy Commander) was taken by the Lively Man of War after an obstinate Engagement of 1 & ¾ of an Hour. The Yankey had 4 Men killd and 11 or 12 Wounded, she was fitted for a Cruize to the West Indies and was coming to Boston to take on her Compliment of Hands, at the Time of the Engagement she had not above 35 or 36 Men as I have been informd.

On the 8th. the Continental Cruisers from Cape Ann took a Transport with upwards of 90 Highlanders and sent her into Marblehead. On the same Day a Vessell from Barbados arrived at Plimouth taken by a Privateer of Capt. Derby's—she was bound to Hallefax on the Kings Accountt loaded with Rum. The Vessell with Highlanders was from Scotland, being part of a Fleet of 30 Sail bound to Boston with which she parted some Days before, and was led into a Trapp by the Jamaica Prize who kept Company with her for some Time and undertook as she was a Stranger to pilot her into Boston; as the Scotchman was entering Marblehead he smelt a Rat and sheerd off—but too late to escape.

[On] the 9 and 10th 8 or 10 Transports supposed to be highlanders joind the Enemy in the Harbour.[1]

The highland Soldiers brot their Wives and Children being promisd 1 House and 100 Acres of Land on their Arrival and *no Doubt the Stock on our Farms*—the Women bro'tt their Milking Pails and plenty of Seeds to sow the Land. (Better late than never.)

It was determind to take Possession of the East End of Long Island, Petticks and Hull, all on the Evening of the 13th. The Artillery and Forces for Long Island reachd there in Season. By Reason of a Calm, the Plan with respect to Petticks faild and the Cannon for Hull did not get down there untill 9 the next Morning. On L. Island 1500 or 2000 Soldiers and Voluntiers, as many on Hull. On the Former a Breast Work was erected and a Battery formd by the next Morning mounting 2 or 3 Heavy Cannon and a Mortarr, on the Latter the Works were begun and an 18 Pounder carried over the Hill about 9. The 14th. at Day Break the Battery on L. Isld. opend on the 50 Gun Ship and other of the Enemy's Vessells then laying between Petticks and Georges Isld. They soon address'd themselves to Flight. This Battery was too far distant to do much Execution—had Works on Petticks and Nantasket been compleated according to a previous Plan, the 50 Gun Ship and a greater part of the Vessells must have fallen a Prey to us, for it was very calm. You could hardly Sea the Motion of the Ship. My Curiosity led me up Hunts Hill from whence I could see the Movements. It was 12 or 1, before she got to the middle of Hull. Here she was harrass'd with an 18 Pounder from Lorings Hill which obligd her to make all possible speed. The Boats were man'd to Tow her down and at length she made of with 16 other Topsail Vessells and 4 smaller. The Ships of War kept a perpetual Firing on Hull in their Way down, but no Life was lost on our Side nor One wounded.—Thus on the 14th of June 1776 the Harbour of Boston was cleared from every Ship of War and other Vessell belonging to Great Britain—it being just Two Years since it was blocked up (If I remember right). The Light House they blew up before they went off.

Last Night we were alarmd about 9 with the firing of Cannon

suppos'd to be at Nantasket and about 11 with a heavy cannonading and firing of Small Arms which lasted untill near 12. Yesterday a Ship and Brig were seen steering for the Harbour and 4 or 5 small Privateers in Chase of them maintaining a runing Fight. About Sun Set the ship and Brig were making their Way to the Light, about 9, they had got up to Nantasket and were saluted and orderd to come on Shore, the Brig catchd on Chamberlains Rocks, the Captain and 4 sailors came on Shore, the Ship continuing her Course up, the Tide rising cleard the Brig and she followed after the Ship notwithstanding she had struck to the Fort. The Privateers who had been galling them all day came up and a smart Engagement ensued between them [and] [2] the Ship and Brig (the Ship is said to have mounted 14. Guns) but at last they were oblig'd to submit and they were found to be Two Transports from Scotland, part of the aforementiond Fleet having on Board each 70 or 80 Highlanders with some Women and Children. One Major and 8 Sailors or Soldiers were killd in the Transports and [...] Wou[nded] [3] on our Side. The Captain of the Brig and Hands who came on Shore at Nantasket could not believe that Boston was in our Possession— they had not the least Idea of it. The Soldiers say that they had from 10 to 12 Guineas to enlist besides the Promise of 100 Acres &c. I am not without Hopes of our entertaining some more of these Gentrey. It appears from the Accounts of these and the former Vessell that the Fleet was parted in a Storm.— We have now a good Fort on Fort Hill, Noddles Island, Pulling Point, Castle Island, Dorchester Point, and new ones erecting on East End of Long Isld. and Nantasket, 2 Row Galleys building, and a Plan forming for immediately erecting a Foundery. I hope the present Court will act with more spirit than the Former. They see the Necessity of it and from the Complexion of Things there is no doubt they will.

I have many more Things to say, but finding a Tremor to affect my Nerves the Effect of much writing and fearing the Length of my Epistle will be tedious I must break off informing You that Yours the Braintree and Weymouth Families are well and that I am with much Affection, Yrs.

P.S. I have not received a Line from You, since my last to You.

RC (Adams Papers).

[1] This paragraph was added in the margin, evidently for insertion here.
[2] Editorially supplied for clarity.
[3] MS torn by seal.

John Adams to Zabdiel Adams

My dear Sir   Philadelphia June 21. 1776

Your Favour of the Ninth of this Month was delivered to me, Yesterday by Mr. Whitney, whose Health I hope will be fully restored by the Small Pox for which he was innoculated the day before. Your Letter, Sir, gave me great Pleasure and deserves my most hearty Thanks.

I am fully with you in Sentiment, that altho the Authority of the Congress founded as it has been, in Reason, Honour, and the Love of Liberty, has been sufficient to govern the Colonies, in a tolerable Manner, for their Defence and Protection: yet that it is not prudent, to continue very long in the same Way. That a permanent Constitution should be formed, and foreign Aid, obtained. In these Points and thus far the Colonies, and their Representatives the Congress are extremely well united.—But concerning a Declaration of Independency there is some Diversity of Sentiment. Two Arguments only, are urged with any Plausibility against such a Measure. One is that it will unite all the Inhabitants of G. Britain against Us. The other, that it will put us too much in the Power of foreign States. The first has little Weight in it, because the People of Great Britain, are already as much united against Us, as they ever are in any Thing, and the Probability is, that such a Declaration would excite still greater Divisions and Distractions among them.

The second has less Weight still, for foreign Powers already know that We are as obnoxious to the British Court as We can be. They know that Parliament have in effect declared Us independent, and that We have acted these thirteen Months, to all Intents and Purposes as if We were so.

The Reports of fifty five Thousand Men, coming against Us, are chiefly ministerial Gasconade. However We have reason to fear that they will send several very powerfull Armaments against Us, and therefore our most strenuous Exertions will be necessary, as well as our most fervent Prayers. America is yet in her Infancy, or at least but lately arrived to Man hood, and is inexperienced in the perplexing Misteries of Policy, as well as the dangerous Operations of War.

I assure you, sir, that your Employment, in investigating the Moral Causes of our Miseries, and in pointing out the Remedies, is devoutly to be wished. There is no station more respectable, nor any so pleasant and agreable. Those who tread the public Stage, in Characters the most extensively conspicuous, meet with so many Embarrassments, Perplexities, and Disappointments, that they have often reason to wish for the peacefull Retreats of the Clergy....[1] Who would not wish to exchange the angry Contentions of the Forum, for the peacefull Contemplations of the Closet. Where Contemplations prune their ruffled Wings and the free Soul looks down to pitty Kings? Who would not Exchange the discordant Scenes of Envy, Pride, Vanity, Malice, Revenge, for the sweet Consolations of Philosophy, the serene Composure of the Passions, the divine Enjoyments of Christian Charity, and Benevolence?

Statesmen my dear Sir, may plan and speculate for Liberty, but it is Religion and Morality alone, which can establish the Principles upon which Freedom can securely stand.... The only foundation of a free Constitution, is pure Virtue, and if this cannot be inspired into our People, in a greater Measure, than they have it now, They may change their Rulers, and the forms of Government, but they will not obtain a lasting Liberty.—They will only exchange Tyrants and Tyrannies.—You cannot therefore be more pleasantly, or usefully employed than in the Way of your Profession, pulling down the Strong Holds of Satan. This is not Cant, but the real sentiment of my Heart.— Remember me with much respect, to your worthy family, and to all Friends.

LbC (Adams Papers).

[1] Here and below, suspension points are in MS.

John Adams to Cotton Tufts

My dear Friend   Philadelphia June 23d. 1776

It is with Shame, and Confusion of Face, that I acknowledge that your agreable Favour of April the twenty sixth, came duely to my Hand and has laid by me unanswered to this Time. There has been as much Folly and Inattention to my own Pleasure, and Interest, in this Negligence as there is of Ingratitude to you, for in the sincerity of my Heart I declare, that none of the Letters of my numerous Correspondents, contain more important Information or more sensible Observations, than yours.

In a Letter I received last night from Boston, I have the Pleasure to learn that your Ideas of fortifying the Harbour have been adopted, and by the next Post or two I hope to be informed that every hostile ship is made to scamper.

The Danger, you apprehend, that our Armies will be thinned by the Freedom of Trade is real, but perhaps the Restraints laid upon it, by our Enemies may correct the Error, if it is one. The Voice of the People was so loud for it, that it was adopted altho some Persons thought it dangerous, and none expected any great Advantage from it before the next Winter.

You mention Independence and Confederation. These Things are now become Objects of direct Consideration. Days, and Times, without Number, have been spent upon these Subjects, and at last a Committee is appointed to prepare a Draught of Confederation, and a Declaration that these Colonies [are][1] free States, independent of all Kings, Kingdoms, Nations, People, or States in the World....[2]

There has been the greatest Scarcity of News for the last Fortnight, which has ever happened since the War commenced.... I make it a constant Practice to transmit to my Family, all the News Papers, where I presume you get a Sight of them. You will find by them, the Course of political Causes and Effects in this Colony. The Assembly [were] necessitated to rescind their Instructions, and [became] so obnoxious, and unpopular, among the Inhabitants their own Constituents for having ever passed them, as to be obliged to die away, without doing any Thing else, even without Adjourning, and give Place to a Conference of Committees and a Convention.[3] Every Part of the Colony is represented in this Conference which is now sitting, and is extremely unanimous, spirited, zealous, and determined. You will soon see Pensilvania, one of the most patriotic Colonies. New Jersey is in a similar Train. The Delaware Government the same.

Maryland is a little beside itself I think, but presently it will blaze out like a Fire ship or a Volcano. New York still acts in Character, like a People without Courage or sense, or Spirit, or in short any one Virtue or Ability. There is neither Spunk nor Gumption, in that Province as a Body. Individuals are very clever. But it is the weakest Province in point of Intellect, Valour, public Spirit, or any thing else that is great and good upon the Continent. It is incapable of doing Us much good, or much Hurt, but from its local situation. The low Cunning of Individuals, and their Prostitution plagues Us, the Virtues of a few Individuals is of some Service to Us. But as a Province it will be a dead Weight upon any side, ours or that of our Enemies.

LbC (Adams Papers).

[1] MS: "a."

[2] Here and below, suspension points are in MS. On 7 June Richard Henry Lee had moved "certain resolutions respecting independency," which he had composed but which were understood to

be submitted on behalf of the Virginia delegation in accordance with their instructions of 15 May by the Virginia Convention, directing the delegates "to propose [that Congress] declare the United Colonies free and independent states" (Jefferson, *Papers*, ed. Boyd, 1: 290–291, 298–299; JCC, 5:425–426). Although, as usual, the Journal does not record the name of either the mover or seconder of this motion, it has been generally accepted that JA seconded it; see his *Diary and Autobiography*, 3:392–393. Congress deferred considering the resolutions (one of which called for the preparation of a plan of confederation) until next day, a Saturday, when they were debated in a committee of the whole house; the debate was continued on Monday the 10th, but further debate on the first and crucial resolution was then deferred until 1 July; "and in the mean while, that no time be lost, in case the Congress agree thereto, that a committee be appointed to prepare a declaration to the effect of the said first resolution" (JCC, 5:427, 428–429). On the 11th it was *"Resolved,* That the com-

mittee, to prepare the declaration, consist of five members: The members chosen, Mr. Jefferson, Mr. J. Adams, Mr. Franklin, Mr. Sherman, and Mr. R. R. Livingston" (same, p. 431). For JA's principal accounts of the drafting of the Declaration of Independence in the weeks that followed (until the committee reported its draft to Congress on 28 June), see his *Diary and Autobiography*, 3:335–337, and references there. His arguments in the debate in the committee of the whole, 8–10 June, are summarized in Jefferson's Notes of Proceedings (Jefferson, *Papers,* ed. Boyd, 1:311–313).

[3] Two words (in brackets) have been editorially supplied in this sentence to clarify it. For the recent demise of the Pennsylvania Assembly, which had resisted moves toward separation from Great Britain, and its supersedure by a Provincial Conference, which first met on 18 June and was controlled by radicals, see J. Paul Selsam, *The Pennsylvania Constitution of 1776,* Phila., 1936, p. 129 ff.

John Adams to Abigail Adams

June 26. 1776

I have written so seldom to you, that I am really grieved at the Recollection. I wrote you, a few Lines, June 2. and a few more June 16. These are all that I have written to you, since this Month began. It has been the busyest Month, that ever I saw. I have found Time to inclose all the News papers, which I hope you will receive in due Time.

Our Misfortunes in Canada, are enough to melt an Heart of Stone. The Small Pox is ten times more terrible than Britons, Canadians and Indians together. This was the Cause of our precipitate Retreat from Quebec, this the Cause of our Disgraces at the Cedars.—I dont mean that this was all. There has been Want, approaching to Famine, as well as Pestilence. And these Discouragements seem to have so disheartened our Officers, that none of them seem to Act with Prudence and Firmness.

But these Reverses of Fortune dont discourage me. It was natural to expect them, and We ought to be prepared in our Minds for greater

Changes, and more melancholly Scenes still. It is an animating Cause, and brave Spirits are not subdued with Difficulties.

Amidst all our gloomy Prospects in Canada, We receive some Pleasure from Boston. I congratulate you on your Victory over your Enemies, in the Harbour. This has long lain near my Heart, and it gives me great Pleasure to think that what was so much wished, is accomplished.

I hope our People will now make the Lower Harbour, impregnable, and never again suffer the Flagg of a Tyrant to fly, within any Part of it.

The Congress have been pleased to give me more Business than I am qualified for, and more than I fear, I can go through, with safety to my Health. They have established a Board of War and Ordinance and made me President of it, an Honour to which I never aspired, a Trust to which I feel my self vastly unequal. But I am determined to do as well as I can and make Industry supply, in some degree the Place of Abilities and Experience. The Board sits, every Morning and every Evening.[1] This, with Constant Attendance in Congress, will so entirely engross my Time, that I fear, I shall not be able to write you, so often as I have. But I will steal Time to write to you.

The small Pox! The small Pox! What shall We do with it? I could almost wish that an innoculating Hospital was opened, in every Town in New England. It is some small Consolation, that the Scoundrell Savages have taken a large Dose of it. They plundered the Baggage, and stripped off the Cloaths of our Men, who had the Small Pox, out full upon them at the Cedars.

RC and LbC (Adams Papers).

[1] The Board of War and Ordnance, embryo of the U.S. War Department, was instituted on 12 June 1776; on the following day JA was named first among five members and hence became chairman or "President." He continued in this post until the close of his service in Congress late in 1777, or in other words throughout the entire period that the Board's work was directed exclusively by civilians. To that work, which soon imposed a crushing daily burden of correspondence and administrative detail, he was to give more time than to all the rest of his duties as a member of Congress put together. See JCC, 5:434-435, 438; JA, *Diary and Autobiography*, 2: 242; 3:342, 360, 394-395, and *passim*.

John Adams to Cotton Tufts

Dear Sir   Philadelphia June 30th. 1776

Your Favour of the 17th. I received by Yesterdays Post. Am much obliged, to you for your judicious Observations of the Spirit of Commerce and Privateering, and many other Subjects, which I have not Time to consider, at present. I mean to express my Sentiments of them in this Letter.[1]

You tell me a Plan is forming for immediately erecting a Foundery. I wish you would oblige me so much as to write me, who the Persons are who have laid this Plan: whether it is to be carried on by the Public or by private Persons—who are the Undertakers—where the Foundery is to be—whether it is a brass or an Iron Foundery or both? In short what the Plan is in all its Particulars. . . .[2] Are there any Artists sufficiently skilled with you? Have you Iron, or Ore, suitable to make Iron, proper for Cannon. Where shall you get Brass? Has Mr. Aaron Hobart of Abington done any Thing at casting Cannon. Has he an Air Furnace? Where does he get his Iron? And where, his Skill and Knowledge?

There are several other Subjects of Inquiry that occur to my Mind, which are of no small Importance.

Musquetts and Bayonnetts are excessively wanted in all the Colonies. Twelve Months ago We were distressed, to a Degree that Posterity will scarcely credit for Powder. This is now over. Now Arms are almost in as much Demand. The Convention of Virginia have taken as bold a Step to get Arms as the Massachusetts did to get Salt Petre. They have passed an ordinance for paying out of the public Treasury Twenty Dollars for every Musquet and Bayonnett which shall be made in the Colony for a year. Pensilvania makes very good Guns and in considerable Numbers. I fear the Massachusetts, in the Multiplicity of their Cares, have not done so much as they might in this Way. I am sure that Province upon a proper Exertion of its Ingenuity and Policy, as well as the Wit and Dexterity of her Tradesmen might make a vast Number of Arms annually. I want to be informed, what Number is now made Weekly or Monthly in the Province. How many are made by Mr. Orr; how many by Pratt, how many by Barrett of Concord, and how many by Pomroy of Northampton. . . . I sincerely wish that the Province would undertake in a public Capacity to encourage this Manufacture, and that they might do it with as much Wisdom and Spirit, and then I know they would have as much success, as they had in the Manufacture of Salt Petre.

There are several other Articles which deserve the public Attention.

Flints begin to be wanted, and I am convinced that those Colonies abound with the proper Flint Stone, and that nothing is wanting but a little Attention to find it, and a little skill, to brake it into the proper Sizes and Shapes. Orange County in New York abounds with it, and the People there use no other flints. I wish the general Court would set a Committee to search for it, or recommend it to the select Men of the Towns to look for it.

Sulphur is an Object which lies in your Way as a Philosopher and a Physician.... Is it to be found any where in the Province. Our Province has an Advantage of all others, in one Respect, the Division of it into Towns which are incorporated Bodies Politick and have public Officers and frequent public Meetings, gives the General Court Power, by ordering the select Men to call Town Meetings and to insert any subject in the Warrant, to diffuse and circulate any Information or Instruction and a Spirit of Inquiry into the whole Mass of the People at once. If some such Method was taken it is very likely that Sulphur Ore might be found in Plenty.

Lead is another Thing of great Importance, and there certainly is a great Quantity of the Ore in the Towns of Northampton and Southampton. It is a Pity that Something cannot be done to set the Manufacture agoing.

In one Word, my Friend, I cannot think that Country safe, which has not within itself every Material necessary for War, and the Art of making Use of those Materials. I never shall be easy, then, untill We shall have made Discoveries of Salt Petre, Sulphur, Flynts, Lead, Cannon, Mortars, Ball, Shells, Musquetts, and Powder, in sufficient Plenty, so that We may always be sure of having enough of each.

Another Thing my Heart is set upon is Salt. Pray inform me, what has been done with you towards the Manufacture.

The Intelligence you give me of your Success, in ferretting away, the Men of War, is some Consolation for the melancholly Accounts We have from Canada. It proves that Coll. Quincy was right when he wrote me, that with Powder and heavy Cannon, he would undertake to make Prisoners at Discretion of the Army in the Town and the fleet in the Harbour as he did last Summer.[3]

I am &c.

LbC (Adams Papers).

[1] JA clearly meant just the opposite: "I mean *not* to express," &c.

[2] Here and below, suspension points are in MS.

[3] See "An Old Friend" (i.e. Josiah Quincy) to JA, 11 July 1775 (Adams Papers).

John Adams to Abigail Adams

Philadelphia July 3. 1776

Your Favour of June 17. dated at Plymouth, was handed me, by Yesterdays Post. I was much pleased to find that you had taken a Journey to Plymouth, to see your Friends in the long Absence of one whom you may wish to see. The Excursion will be an Amusement, and will serve your Health. How happy would it have made me to have taken this Journey with you?

I was informed, a day or two before the Receipt of your Letter, that you was gone to Plymouth, by Mrs. Polly Palmer, who was obliging enough in your Absence, to inform me, of the Particulars of the Expedition to the lower Harbour against the Men of War. Her Narration is executed, with a Precision and Perspicuity, which would have become the Pen of an accomplished Historian.[1]

I am very glad you had so good an opportunity of seeing one of our little American Men of War. Many Ideas, new to you, must have presented themselves in such a Scene; and you will in future, better understand the Relations of Sea Engagements.

I rejoice extreamly at Dr. Bulfinches Petition to open an Hospital. But I hope, the Business will be done upon a larger Scale. I hope, that one Hospital will be licensed in every County, if not in every Town. I am happy to find you resolved, to be with the Children, in the first Class. Mr. Whitney and Mrs. Katy Quincy,[2] are cleverly through Innoculation, in this City.

I have one favour to ask, and that is, that in your future Letters, you would acknowledge the Receipt of all those you may receive from me, and mention their Dates. By this Means I shall know if any of mine miscarry.

The Information you give me of our Friends refusing his Appointment, has given me much Pain, Grief and Anxiety. I believe I shall be obliged to follow his Example. I have not Fortune enough to support my Family, and what is of more Importance, to support the Dignity of that exalted Station. It is too high and lifted up, for me; who delight in nothing so much as Retreat, Solitude, Silence, and Obscurity. In private Life, no one has a Right to censure me for following my own Inclinations, in Retirement, Simplicity, and Frugality: in public Life, every Man has a Right to remark as he pleases, at least he thinks so.

Yesterday the greatest Question was decided, which ever was debated in America, and a greater perhaps, never was or will be decided among Men. A Resolution was passed without one dissenting Colony "that these united Colonies, are, and of right ought to be free and independent States, and as such, they have, and of Right ought to have full Power to make War, conclude Peace, establish Commerce, and to do all the other Acts and Things, which other States may rightfully do." You will see in a few days a Declaration setting forth the Causes, which have impell'd Us to this mighty Revolution, and the Reasons which will justify it, in the Sight of God and Man.[3] A Plan of Confederation will be taken up in a few days.

When I look back to the Year 1761, and recollect the Argument concerning Writs of Assistance, in the Superiour Court, which I have hitherto considered as the Commencement of the Controversy, between Great Britain and America, and run through the whole Period from that Time to this, and recollect the series of political Events, the Chain of Causes and Effects, I am surprized at the Suddenness, as well as Greatness of this Revolution. Britain has been fill'd with Folly, and America with Wisdom, at least this is my Judgment.— Time must determine. It is the Will of Heaven, that the two Countries should be sundered forever. It may be the Will of Heaven that America shall suffer Calamities still more wasting and Distresses yet more dreadfull. If this is to be the Case, it will have this good Effect, at least: it will inspire Us with many Virtues, which We have not, and correct many Errors, Follies, and Vices, which threaten to disturb, dishonour, and destroy Us.—The Furnace of Affliction produces Refinement, in States as well as Individuals. And the new Governments we are assuming, in every Part, will require a Purification from our Vices, and an Augmentation of our Virtues or they will be no Blessings. The People will have unbounded Power. And the People are extreamly addicted to Corruption and Venality, as well as the Great. —I am not without Apprehensions from this Quarter.[4] But I must submit all my Hopes and Fears, to an overruling Providence, in which, unfashionable as the Faith may be, I firmly believe.

RC and LbC (Adams Papers). For the complicated story of early printings of this letter, in conjunction with JA's letter to AA written later on the same day, see note 9 on the letter that immediately follows.

[1] Mary Palmer to JA, 15–17 June, above. As frequently in JA's letters and Diary, "Mrs." (i.e. Mistress) stands for "Miss."

[2] Katharine Quincy (1733–1804), sister of Dorothy (Quincy) Hancock.

See Adams Genealogy.

[3] On 28 June "the committee appointed to prepare a declaration, &c. brought in a draught, which was read [and] *Ordered,* To lie on the table" until after the question of independence

itself (the first of the Lee or Virginia resolutions of 7 June) was dealt with (JCC, 5:491; see note 2 on JA's letter to Cotton Tufts, 23 June, above). That momentous question came up, as had been agreed, on Monday, 1 July, and Congress in a committee of the whole debated it and reported favorably on it; but "at the request of a colony" (South Carolina), the final determination was postponed until the 2d, when the delegates of twelve Colonies (those of New York, being bound by old instructions, abstaining) "*Resolved*, That these United Colonies are, and, of right, ought to be, Free and Independent States; that they are absolved from all allegiance to the British crown, and that all political connexion between them, and the state of Great Britain, is, and ought to be, totally dissolved"—the precise wording of the first of the Lee resolutions of 7 June (JCC, 5:504, 505, 506–507; Jefferson's Notes of Proceedings, in his *Papers*, ed. Boyd, 1:313–314; letters of JA and others, 1 and 2 July, in Burnett, ed., *Letters of Members,* 1:519–526).

It will be noted that JA's present version of the resolution of independence varies markedly from that in the Journal, but he was writing without a text to copy from. For his part in the debates of 1–2 July as he remembered them, see his *Diary and Autobiography*, 3:396–397, and references there. On 1 July the text of the Declaration as reported by the committee on 28 June was referred to a committee of the whole house, and

debate on it in committee of the whole began on the 2d, as soon as the vote of independence passed. This debate continued during the day on which the present letter was written and was resumed on the 4th, until the committee of the whole and the Congress were satisfied with the text to be given to the world, whereupon the text as revised and adopted was ordered "authenticated and printed" and distributed to the new states and the army (JCC, 5:504, 505–507, 509, 510–516; Jefferson's Notes of Proceedings, in his *Papers*, ed. Boyd., 1:314–319; various letters of 4 July in Burnett, ed., *Letters of Members,* 1:527–528). Thus, as scarcely needs to be pointed out any longer, though it once did, the present letter and the next one of the same date were written *between* the act of independence itself and the adoption of the statement designed to "justify it, in the Sight of God and Man."

⁴ The foregoing sentence is not in RC and has been supplied from LbC. Its omission from RC was unquestionably inadvertent, a result of mere haste in copying, because it is an essential and revealing element in the flow of JA's thought at this point. CFA printed this letter (or the critical portion of it) at least five times between 1841 and 1876, but since he used the RC exclusively and did not compare it with the text of the LbC, this sentence has been omitted in all subsequent printings and quotations of this famous letter.

John Adams to Abigail Adams

Philadelphia July 3d. 1776

Had a Declaration of Independency been made seven Months ago, it would have been attended with many great and glorious Effects....¹ We might before this Hour, have formed Alliances with foreign States.—We should have mastered Quebec and been in Possession of Canada.... You will perhaps wonder, how such a Declaration would have influenced our Affairs, in Canada, but if I could write with Freedom I could easily convince you, that it would, and explain to you the manner how.—Many Gentlemen in high Stations and of great Influence have been duped, by the ministerial Bubble of Commissioners to treat.... And in real, sincere Expectation of this Event, which they so fondly wished, they have been slow and languid, in promoting Measures for the Reduction of that Province. Others there are in the Colonies who really wished that our Enterprise in Canada would be defeated, that the Colonies might be brought into Danger and Distress between two Fires, and be thus induced to submit. Others really wished to defeat the Expedition to Canada, lest the Conquest of it, should elevate the Minds of the People too much to hearken to those Terms of Reconciliation which they believed would be offered Us. These jarring Views, Wishes and Designs, occasioned an opposition to many salutary Measures, which were proposed for the Support of that Expedition, and caused Obstructions, Embarrassments and studied Delays, which have finally, lost Us the Province.

All these Causes however in Conjunction would not have disappointed Us, if it had not been for a Misfortune, which could not be foreseen, and perhaps could not have been prevented, I mean the Prevalence of the small Pox among our Troops.... This fatal Pestilence compleated our Destruction.—It is a Frown of Providence upon Us, which We ought to lay to heart.

But on the other Hand, the Delay of this Declaration to this Time, has many great Advantages attending it.—The Hopes of Reconciliation, which were fondly entertained by Multitudes of honest and well meaning tho weak [2] and mistaken People, have been gradually and at last totally extinguished.—Time has been given for the whole People, maturely to consider the great Question of Independence and to ripen their Judgments, dissipate their Fears, and allure their Hopes, by discussing it in News Papers and Pamphletts, by debating it, in Assemblies, Conventions, Committees of Safety and Inspection, in Town and County Meetings, as well as in private Conversations, so that the whole People in every Colony of the 13,[3] have now adopted it, as their own Act.—This will cement the Union, and avoid those Heats and perhaps Convulsions which might have been occasioned, by such a Declaration Six Months ago.

But the Day is past. The Second Day of July 1776, will be the most memorable Epocha, in the History of America.—I am apt to believe that it will be celebrated, by succeeding Generations, as the great anniversary Festival. It ought to be commemorated, as the Day of Deliverance by solemn Acts of Devotion to God Almighty. It ought to be solemnized with Pomp and Parade, with [4] Shews, Games, Sports, Guns, Bells, Bonfires and Illuminations from one End of this Continent to the other from this Time forward forever more.[5]

You will think me transported with Enthusiasm but I am not.—I am well aware of the Toil and Blood and Treasure, that it will cost Us to maintain this Declaration, and support and defend these States.— Yet through all the Gloom I can see the Rays of ravishing [6] Light and Glory. I can see that the End is more than worth all the Means. And that Posterity will tryumph in that Days Transaction, even [7] altho We should rue [8] it, which I trust in God We shall not.[9]

RC and LbC (Adams Papers). Since this is a celebrated letter, several small but characteristic stylistic revisions made by JA when preparing his fair copy (the RC) from his draft (the LbC) have been recorded in the notes below. For the early celebrity and textual garbling of this letter, in conjunction with the preceding letter of this date, see note 9.

[1] Here and below, suspension points are in MS.

[2] LbC: "shortsighted."

[3] Preceding three words added in RC.

[4] Preceding three words added in RC.

[5] This word added in RC.

[6] This word added in RC.

[7] Preceding five words added in RC.

[8] LbC: "altho you and I may rue."

[9] This and the preceding letter, embodying JA's reflections in the course of the day after the United States became a nation, acquired early and deserved celebrity. But the history of their early publication and textual garbling offers a striking illustration of how difficult it is to overcome popular errors, or, to invert an idealistic saying, how error, crushed to earth, will rise again.

Only a summary of that history can be given here, and this summary is drawn largely from Charles Warren's article, "The Doctored Letters of John Adams," MHS, *Procs.*, 68 (1944–1947): 160–170, a learned and skillful piece of scholarly detective work. Warren points out that the two JA letters to his wife dated 3 July were apparently first printed (the first of them with an indicated omission at the beginning of the text) in the *Universal Asylum and Columbian Magazine* for May 1792 (8:313–315) as part of a series of JA's Revolutionary letters. No explanation of their provenance is given there, and the identity of the recipient is in both cases disguised by the salutation "Sir." (The texts as printed derive ultimately from JA's letterbook copies, are quite faithful, and were presumably supplied by some member of his actual or official family who had access to his letterbooks. JA himself, in a letter to JQA of 19 Sept. 1795 [Adams Papers], alluded to the printing of this "Letter," as he called it, and said he prized it "above a statue or a Monument —merely as Evidence of my Opinion at that time and of my Courage to avow it"; but he gave no hint of how publication occurred.) On 4 July 1792 the Philadelphia *Gazette of the United States* reprinted these texts, with a brief tribute to the Vice-President's powers as a prophet.

On 1 July 1795 the Federalist *Columbian Centinel* of Boston published a letter from "An American," who argued that his fellow Americans had all along been celebrating the wrong day (the Fourth of July) as the anniversary of independence; they ought, he said, to celebrate the Second. As evidence, he quoted "extracts of two letters, from Mr. JOHN ADAMS to a friend," consisting of the seventh paragraph of JA's first letter of 3 July ("Yesterday the greatest Question . . .") and the last two paragraphs of JA's second letter ("But the Day is past . . ."). "As a friend to propriety," he concluded, "I could wish to see the alteration take place."

Nine years later, in the same paper, 23 June 1804, "Seventy-Six" urged the same point, though in more sharply partisan terms. "Seventy-Six" cited the same passages from JA's "letters to a friend" of 3 July 1776 as proof that JA was the "efficient agent in this glorious work [of independence]," whereas Jefferson was an "adventitious" agent; merely "penning a bill, after the principles [had] been decided upon."

This argument having made little headway, a nameless Federalist writer took a different tack the next year. In the *Boston Gazette* for 4 July 1805 appeared a long, unsigned letter eulogizing the services of Washington and JA, and to this were appended the now familiar passages from JA's letters, run together and treated as if they constituted a single letter in and of themselves. The direction at the foot of the text reads: "To Mr. ———," which was by now canonical, but the date at the head of the letter as printed in 1805 reads "July 5, 1776," and in the passage on celebrating the national anniversary the second sentence is altered to read "The Fourth day of July 1776, will be *a memorable epocha*," &c., to square it with the doctored dateline.

This mode of reconciling the two national political parties' differing views on how (or rather *when*) the United States of America was born met with great and altogether undeserved success. Newspapers and holiday orators happily and frequently printed and quoted JA's "letter" on celebrating the "Fourth" of July. (In one case the hybrid document with its erroneous date appeared in the very same issue of a paper to which JA contributed autobiographical recollections on another subject; see the *Boston Patriot*, 4 July 1810.) Not until 1819 was there a clarification forthcoming, and it came directly from JA, who after AA's death late in 1818 had been rummaging among his old papers. On 16 Feb. 1819 JA wrote to Judge Thomas Dawes of Boston, a close friend and a connection by marriage, reminding him that "Once on a time, upon my Stony field Hill, you interrogated me concerning that extract [frequently printed in newspapers from JA's letter or letters of 3 July 1776] in so particular a manner that I thought you felt a tincture of pyrrhonism concerning its authenticity." To settle any such doubts, JA offered to show Dawes the originals in JA's own hand, but meanwhile he enclosed full texts of the two letters addressed to AA, "one in the morning, and the other in the evening of ... the day after the vote of Independence" (LbC in an unidentified hand,

Adams Papers). Dawes communicated both enclosures, together with JA's letter to him and a valuable introductory note of his own, to the *Columbian Centinel*, where all of them were printed on 3 July 1819.

Thus were made available, for the first time, complete and substantially faithful texts of JA's two famous and prophetic letters, with their correct dates and a correct identification of their recipient. (These texts were actually drawn from JA's letterbooks, without comparison with the recipient's copies.) They were given still wider circulation and made permanently available by being reprinted in Hezekiah Niles' *Principles and Acts of the Revolution in America* ..., Baltimore, 1822, p. 328–330. And yet just two days after they had appeared fully and correctly in the *Centinel*, another Boston paper, the *Independent Chronicle*, which held Republican views, printed an extract from one of them under the wrong date of 5 July 1776, "the day after the passage of the memorable Declaration of Independence"; and it did so again at the annual returns of the national anniversary in 1822, 1824, and 1826. Doubtless other papers did so too. What is more, the handsomely printed and decorated cards of admission to the Fourth of July feasts at Faneuil Hall in Boston now annually bore the old, telescoped, mangled, and misdated text of JA's "letter" from Philadelphia; two specimens of these—one directed to JA in 1821, and the other to JQA in 1824—are reproduced as illustrations in the present volume.

By this time even the Federalist *Centinel*, which had printed authentic texts and a full *éclaircissement* seven years earlier, was ready to cave in under dint of repetition. On 5 July 1826, the day after JA's death, it quoted him in support of celebrating "the Fourth of July" with "pomp, shows, games," and all the rest. Editor Niles caved in too. His obituary tribute to JA reprinted the garbled version of the letters that had been in circulation for decades (*Niles' Register*, 30:345 [15 July 1826]). That version remained standard through the first half of the century, even after correct (though normalized) texts from the recipient's copies had been printed in

JA's *Letters* (1841).

In printing these texts, CFA for some reason did not allude to the corrupt and popular version or versions of them until he issued the JA-AA *Familiar Letters* in 1876. There, at p. 193, he furnished an editorial note that almost apologizes for having upset a tradition by presenting accurate texts, and explains that the initial garbling was done by JA's nephew and sometime secretary, William Smith Shaw (1778–1826), later well known as "Athenæum" Shaw, on whom see the Adams Genealogy. Presumably the doctored text published in the *Boston Gazette* of 4 July 1805 was the one concocted by Shaw, but the present editors have not found the evidence on which CFA attributed it to him.

Mercy Otis Warren to Abigail Adams

Plimouth July 3d 1776

A Lame Hand still prevents me the free use of Either the Nedle or the pen. Yet I take up the Latter and Attempt a Line or two just to Let my Dear Friend know that both myself and Family are in better Health than when she was at Plimouth.

I Enclose a Number of papers which Came to hand yesterday from Philadelphia, with Directions to send them to the foot of Pens Hill when Read. I also send several Manuscripts Left in my hands for which am much Obliged.

When a Good opportunity presents should be glad you would Return two or three things which I wont say I Consented You should Cary away, but Confide in your Word that No one else should see them. Do with my Love to your amiable sister tell her I Cannot but Regret that I was prevailed upon by the importunity of Friendship to suffer Copies of Certain Letters to be taken and if you and she both Could make your selves willing Either to Return or to Destroy them it would Gratify one who loves them. I have Reasons sufficient for such a Request.

My paper and pen is too bad, my finger too sore, my time too limited and my Capacity too Circumscribed to Express the Ideas which ought to arise in Every Generous Breast on the Late Horrid Conspiracy.[1] Heaven will Frown the perpetrators of such Black Deeds into Distruction and shake to the Centre the Throne of Their Guilty Master.

I do not Expect to see you very soon. The accounts we have of the small pox at the Northward are such that I think it unsafe for any who have not had that Distemper to Venture beyond Braintree.

You will I hope soon write a Long Letter to your affectionate Friend,   M Warren

PS   Love to the Children.

RC (Adams Papers). Enclosures not found or identified.

[1] The so-called "Hickey plot," for which Thomas Hickey, a member of Washington's guard, was court-martialed and sentenced to death. Hickey had been suborned by New York City loyalists who were planning an uprising on the arrival of British forces there, but the rumors of a plot to assassinate Washington and his generals were exaggerated. See Washington, *Writings*, ed. Fitzpatrick, 5:161-162, 170, 179, 182 and note, 193-195.

John Adams to Mary Palmer

Miss Polly   Philadelphia July 5. 1776 [1]

Your Favour of June 15. 1776 was handed to me, by the last Post. ...[2] I hold myself much obliged to you for your Attention to me, at this Distance, from those Scenes, in which, altho I feel myself deeply interested, yet I can neither be an Actor nor Spectator.

You have given me (not withstanding all your modest Apologies) with a great deal of real Elegance and Perspicuity, a minute and circumstantial Narration of the whole Expedition to the lower Harbour, against the Men of War.—It is lawfull you know to flatter the Ladies a little, at least if Custom can make a Thing lawfull: but, without availing myself in the least degree of this Licence, I can safely say, that from your Letter and another from Miss Paine to her Brother, I was enabled to form a more Adequate Idea of that whole Transaction, than from all the other Accounts of it, both in News papers and private Letters which have come to my Hands.

In Times as turbulent as these, commend me to the Ladies for Historiographers. The Gentlemen are too much engaged in Action. The Ladies are cooler Spectators.... There is a Lady at the Foot of Pens Hill, who obliges me, from Time to Time with clearer and fuller Intelligence, than I can get from a whole Committee of Gentlemen.

I was a little mortified, at the unlucky Calm, which retarded the Militia from Braintree, Weymouth and Hingham. I wished that they might have had more than half the Glory of the Enterprize. However, it satisfies me to reflect, that it was not their Fault but the fault of the Wind that they had not.

I will inclose to you a Declaration, in which all America is remarkably united....[3] It compleats a Revolution, which will make as good a Figure in the History of Mankind, as any that has preceeded it—provided always, that the Ladies take Care to record the Circumstances of it, for by the Experience I have had of the other Sex, they are either too lazy, or too active, to commemorate them.

A Continuance of your Correspondence, Miss Polly, would much oblige me. My Compliments to Papa, and Mamma and the whole Family.... I hope they will see more serene Skies. I begin now to flatter my self, however, that you are situated in the safest Place upon the Continent.

Howes Army and Fleet are at Staten Island. But there is a very numerous Army, at New York and New Jersey, to oppose them. Like Noahs Dove, without its Innocence, they can find no Rest.

I am, with much Respect, Esteem and Gratitude, Your Friend and humble Servant, John Adams

RC (PHi:Dreer Coll.). LbC (Adams Papers). Enclosed "Declaratio⌐ not found; see note 3.

[1] There has been some confusion about the true date of this letter because an engraved facsimile of it was published a century ago with a dateline apparently reading "Philadelphia July 3: 1776" (William Brotherhead, *The Book of the Signers* . . . , Phila., 1861, p. 103–104; separates of the facsimile are also found in libraries). However, unlike the alteration in JA's letters to AA of 3 July, q.v., above, this change of date was probably an honest (though rather inexcusable) mistake, resulting from the engraver's misreading (or merely clumsy rendering) of the date as written by JA.

At the foot of the engraved facsimile appears the legend "In the possession of Mr. Teft Phila." This was Israel K. Tefft, one of the earliest and most zealous collectors of historical autographs in the United States. On 27 Nov. 1841, in answer to an appeal (not found) from Tefft, CFA sent him a letter in the hand of AA and a few miscellaneous autographs (CFA's letter is in NN:Ford Coll.). Tefft answered from Savannah, Georgia, 10 Dec. 1841, acknowledging the gifts, describing and quoting from JA's letter to Polly Palmer in his own possession, listing fourteen signers of the Declaration of Independence who were not adequately represented in his collection, and asking CFA if he would

supply "a letter, or note" by any or all of them from JA's papers (Adams Papers). There is no record of a reply.

[2] Here and below, suspension points are in MS.

[3] This must have been a copy of the broadside printed by John Dunlap—the first published text—of the Declaration of Independence, which was issued this day in accordance with Congress' vote of 4 July, and a copy of which is wafered to the "Rough Journal" of Congress as an official text. "You are still impatient for a Declaration of Independency," JA wrote Joseph Ward on this same day. "I hope your Appetite will now be satisfyed. Such a Declaration passed Congress Yesterday, and this Morning will be printed" (LbC, Adams Papers). (The Declaration was not printed in a newspaper until 6 July; see JA's 1st letter to AA of 7 July, below.) See Michael J. Walsh, "Contemporary Broadside Editions of the Declaration of Independence," *Harvard Libr. Bull.*, 3:31–43 (Winter 1949), which includes a facsimile of the Dunlap broadside and a census of the fourteen copies known to survive; also Julian P. Boyd, *The Declaration of Independence: The Evolution of the Text*, Washington, 1943, p. 8, 35, and pl. 10.

Cotton Tufts to John Adams

My Dear Sr.   Weymo. July 5. 1776

I wrote to You about the 17 or 18th. of last Month which suppose You have received.

Yesterday People in Boston were *openly* inoculated for the Small Pox. The Business had been carried on in private for some Time amongst the Soldiery and others; the Selectmen represented the Impossibility of preventing its Spread any longer and leave was given by the general Assembly for Inoculation in Boston.—It is probable that it will run thro' the Country. If so, no Care will hereafter be taken to keep it out. If there be any Inoculators of Eminence that you are particular acquainted with should take it kindly if You would enquire of Him his Method of Practice; as to Medicine, Diet, Air, Exercise— in short the whole Proccess. The Method of Practice is I suppose pretty generally known, that No one there would pretend to keep it as a Secret. Yet there may be some Improvements of late, that may be beneficial, the Knowledge of which might give much Satisfaction to an Inquisitive Mind, and any Gentleman of Benevolence and Literature would give in writing such a general Accountt of the Practice as might answer the Enquiry. If such You can obtain amongst your Acquaintance, be so kind as to forward it by the very first Conveyance.

We have my Friend Pestilence, We have the Sword, two thundering Messengers. May they bring us to our Senses, learn us to live as men ought to, despising Dress and Equipage and unbounded Wealth, Exercising Temperance and Frugality, Benevolence and Charity &c. &c. Oh my Dear Friend I am now entering into the Plan of public and private Happiness [and] [1] painting to myself a Scene delightful Indeed, which could I once behold Methinks I could [wil]lingly take my leave of Earth, satisfyed that the Day of American Redemption was [now?] at Hand.

Adieu. Yrs.

I have got leave to lodge this within Mrs. Adams Letter [2]—being wrote in Haste Youll excuse Errors.

RC (Adams Papers); addressed: "To Honbl. John Adams Esq Philadelphia"; added in AA's hand: "To be left at the post office"; postmarked: "BOSTON 11 IY" (i.e. July); endorsed: "Dr. Tufts," to which was later added, in the hand of William Gordon(?), the date of Tufts' letter.

[1] Here and below, MS is torn by seal.

[2] AA, however, merely forwarded Tufts' letter to the post office in Boston; see the descriptive note above; also JA to AA, 20 July (2d letter), and JA to Tufts, 20 July, both below.

Abigail Adams to John Thaxter

Sir   Braintree july 7. 1776

As you have always expressd a desire to have the small pox with my family I write to let you know that we go next thursday. If you chuse to enter as part of my family at 18 Shillings per week, paying your d[octo]r for innoculation which I hear is a Guiney you may send me word immediately. I will find a Bed and Bedstead, but should be glad if you could take 2 pair of sheets and a counterpain. All other necessaries will supply, Nursing &c. If we do well hope to return in 3 weeks. Mr. Cranch, wife and family and Sister Betsy go with us. The time allowed is short, so that we must go this week. Dr. Bulfinch is our Physician, says no occasion of any previous preparation. If you conclude to go, be at our House a wednesday Night.

My duty to your Pappa and Mamma. Love to your Sisters. Tell your Mamma we will take good care of you. If you was here I would shew you a coppy of some of Miss Grissys Letters intercepted.[1] If you have an opportunity of writing tomorrow Let me know your determination. I am most affectionately your Friend,   Abigail Adams

RC (MH:Autograph File); addressed: "To Mr. John Thaxter junr. Hingham"; endorsed: "Mrs. Adams 7 July 1776."

[1] This allusion remains obscure.

John Adams to Abigail Adams

Philadelphia July 7. 1776

I have this Moment folded up a Magazine, and an Evening Post[1] and sent it off, by an Express, who could not wait for me to write a single Line. It always goes to my Heart, to send off a Packett of Pamphletts and News Papers, without a Letter, but it sometimes unavoidably happens, and I suppose you had rather receive a Pamphlet or News Paper, than nothing.

The Disign of our Enemy, now seems to be a powerfull Invasion of New York and New Jersey. The Hallifax Fleet and Army, is arrived, and another Fleet and Army under Lord How, is expected to join them. We are making great Preparations to meet them, by marching the Militia of Maryland, Pensilvania, and New Jersey, down to the Scene of Action, and have made large Requisitions upon New England. I hope for the Honour of New England, and the Salvation of America, our People will not be backward in marching to New

York. We must maintain and defend that important Post, at all Events. If the Enemy get Possession there, it will cost N. England very dear. There is no danger of the Small Pox at New York. It is carefully kept out of the City and the Army. I hope that your Brother and mine too will go into the Service of their Country, at this critical Period of its Distress.

Our Army at Crown Point is an Object of Wretchedness, enough to fill a humane Mind, with Horror. Disgraced, defeated, discontented, dispirited, diseased, naked, undisciplined, eaten up with Vermin— no Cloaths, Beds, Blanketts, no Medicines, no Victuals, but Salt Pork and flour. A Chaplain from that Army, preached a Sermon here the other day, from "cursed is he, that doth the Work of the Lord, deceitfully."

I knew better than he did, who the Persons were, who deserved these Curses. But I could not help myself, nor my poor Country any more than he.

I hope that Measures will be taken to cleanse the Army at Crown Point from the small Pox, and that other Measures will be taken in New England, by tolerating and encouraging Inoculation, to render that Distemper less terrible.

I am solicitous to hear, what Figure, our new Superiour Court made in their Eastern Circuit. What Business they did? Whether the Grand Juries, and petit Juries, were sworn. Whether they tried any Criminals? or any civil Actions. How the People were affected at the Appearance of Courts again. How the Judges were treated, whether with Respect, or cold Neglect &c.

Every Colony, upon the Continent will soon be in the same Situation. They are erecting Governments, as fast as Children build Cobb Houses. But I conjecture they will hardly throw them down again, so soon.

The Practice We have hitherto been in, of ditching round about our Enemies, will not always do. We must learn to Use other Weapons than the Pick Axe and the Spade. Our Armies must be disciplined and learn to fight. I have the Satisfaction to reflect, that our Massachusetts People, when they have been left to themselves, have been constantly fighting and skirmishing, and always with success. I wish the same Valour, Prudence, and Spirit had been discovered every where.

RC and LbC (Adams Papers).

[1] The *Pennsylvania Evening Post* of 6 July contained the first printing of the text of the Declaration of Independence in a newspaper. See, further, AA to JA, 13–14 July, below.

John Adams to Abigail Adams

Philadelphia July 7. 1776

It is worth the while of a Person, obliged to write as much as I do, to consider the Varieties of Style....[1] The Epistolary, is essentially different from the oratorical, and the Historical Style.... Oratory abounds with Figures. History is simple, but grave, majestic and formal. Letters, like Conversation, should be free, easy, and familiar.

Simplicity and Familiarity,[2] are the Characteristicks of this Kind of Writing. Affectation is as disagreable, in a Letter, as in Conversation, and therefore, studied Language, premeditated Method, and sublime Sentiments are not expected in a Letter. Notwithstanding which, the Sublime, as well as the beautifull, and the Novel, may naturally enough, appear, in familiar Letters among Friends.—Among the ancients there are two illustrious Examples of the Epistolary Style, Cicero and Pliny, whose Letters present you with Modells of fine Writing, which has borne the Criticism of almost two thousand Years. In these, you see the Sublime, the beautifull, the Novell, and the Pathetick, conveyed in as much Simplicity, Ease, Freedom, and Familiarity, as Language is capable of.

Let me request you, to turn over the Leaves of the Præceptor, to a Letter of Pliny the Younger, in which he has transmitted, to these days, the History of his Uncles Philosophical Curiosity, his Heroic Courage and his melancholly Catastrophe.[3] Read it, and say, whether it is possible to write a Narrative of Facts, in a better Manner. It is copious and particular, in selecting the Circumstances, most natural, remarkable and affecting. There is not an incident omitted, which ought to have been remembered, nor one inserted that is not worth Remembrance.

It gives you, an Idea of the Scæne, as distinct and perfect, as if a Painter had drawn it to the Life, before your Eyes. It interests your Passions, as much as if you had been an Eye Witness of the whole Transaction. Yet there are no Figures, or Art used. All is as simple, natural, easy, and familiar, as if the Story had been told in Conversation, without a Moments Premeditation.

Pope and Swift have given the World a Collection of their Letters; but I think in general, they fall short, in the Epistolary Way, of their own Emminence in Poetry and other Branches of Literature. Very few of their Letters, have ever engaged much of my Attention. Gays Letter, concerning the Pair of Lovers kill'd by Lightning, is worth more than the whole Collection, in Point of Simplicity, and Elegance

39

of Composition, and as a genuine Model of the epistolary Style.[4]—
There is a Book, which I wish you owned, I mean Rollins Belles
Letters, in which the Variations of Style are explained.[5]

Early Youth is the Time, to learn the Arts and Sciences, and
especially to correct the Ear, and the Imagination, by forming a Style.
I wish you would think of forming the Taste, and Judgment of your
Children, now, before any unchaste Sounds have fastened on their
Ears, and before any Affectation, or Vanity, is settled on their Minds,
upon the pure Principles of Nature.... Musick is a great Advantage,
for Style depends in Part upon a delicate Ear.

The Faculty of Writing is attainable, by Art, Practice, and Habit
only. The sooner, therefore the Practice begins, the more likely it will
be to succeed. Have no Mercy upon an affected Phrase, any more
than an affected Air, Gate, Dress, or Manners.

Your Children have Capacities equal to any Thing. There is a
Vigour in the Understanding, and a Spirit and Fire in the Temper
of every one of them, which is capable of ascending the Heights of
Art, Science, Trade, War, or Politicks.

They should be set to compose Descriptions of Scænes and Objects,
and Narrations of Facts and Events, Declamations upon Topicks,
and other Exercises of various sorts, should be prescribed to them.

Set a Child to form a Description of a Battle, a Storm, a seige, a
Cloud, a Mountain, a Lake, a City, an Harbour, a Country seat, a
Meadow, a Forrest, or almost any Thing, that may occur to your
Thoughts.

Set him to compose a Narration of all the little Incidents and Events
of a Day, a Journey, a Ride, or a Walk. In this Way, a Taste will be
formed, and a Facility of Writing acquired.

For myself, as I never had a regular Tutor, I never studied any
Thing methodically, and consequently never was compleatly accomplished in any Thing. But as I am conscious of my own Deficiency,
in these Respects, I should be the less pardonable, if I neglected the
Education of my Children.

In Grammar, Rhetoric, Logic, my Education was imperfect, because unmethodical. Yet I have perhaps read more upon these Arts,
and considered them in a more extensive View than some[6] others.

RC and LbC (Adams Papers).

[1] Here and below, suspension points
are in MS.

[2] LbC adds "and Freedom," perhaps
unintentionally omitted from RC.

[3] Among JA's books in the Boston
Public Library is a copy of Robert Dodsley, *The Preceptor: Containing a General Course of Education,* 5th edn., 2

vols., London, 1769. The younger Pliny's letter that JA praises was addressed to Tacitus and is at 1:97–100. See also JA's *Diary and Autobiography*, 2:24–25.

⁴ JA could have encountered this letter, supposedly written by John Gay in 1718, either in Dodsley's *Preceptor* (see preceding note) or in one or another of the several editions of Alexander Pope's *Works* that he owned and that remain (though with numerous volumes missing) among his books in the Boston Public Library; see *Catalogue of JA's Library*. But the letter itself has a most curious and complex history. Judging from the texts and commentary in the latest and best edition of Pope's correspondence, it is still not possible to tell whether the letter was written by Gay, by Pope, by both of them in collaboration, or, since the story it tells is known in so many versions, perhaps by neither in its earliest form. The letter relates a sentimental tale, of a kind that soon became very popular, about two rustic and utterly virtuous lovers who were struck dead in each other's arms by lightning when they sought shelter in a haycock from a storm. Although Pope published Gay's version in 1737, *as by Gay*, Pope himself signed and sent versions of the tale in nearly identical language to sundry friends, including Lady Mary Wortley Montagu. Lady Mary did not admire the attitudes of the new school of sensibility and replied astringently:

"I must applaud your good nature in supposing that your pastoral lovers, (vulgarly called Haymakers) would have lived in everlasting joy and harmony, if the lightning had not interrupted their scheme of happiness. I see no reason to imagine that *John Hughes* and *Sarah Drew* were either wiser or more virtuous than their neighbours. That a well-set man of twenty-five should have a fancy to marry a brown woman of eighteen, is nothing marvellous; and I cannot help thinking that had they married, their lives would have passed in the common track with their fellow-parishioners. His endeavouring to shield her from a storm was a natural action, and what he would have certainly done for his horse, if he had been in the same situation. Neither am I of opinion that their sudden death was a reward of their mutual virtue" (Pope, *Correspondence*, ed. George Sherburn, Oxford, 1956, 1:523; see also p. 479–483, 494–496).

⁵ On Charles Rollin and his books, which were favorites in the Adams family, see AA to JA, 19 Aug. 1774, above, and note there. JA eventually acquired a copy (and it is now among his books in the Boston Public Library) of Rollin's *The Method of Teaching and Studying the Belles Lettres, or, an Introduction to Languages, Poetry, Rhetoric, History, Moral Philosophy, Physics, &c.*, 6th edn., 3 vols., London, 1769.

⁶ LbC: "most."

Isaac Smith Sr. to John Adams

Mr. Adams   Boston July 8th. 1776

You will hear by this Conveyance, itts probable that the small pox is likely to spread here chiefly by Innoculation As 4. or 500. I suppose are already received itt and people that have moved Out several times now tarry, Amongst which is Mrs. Edwards.—I am just agoing to set Out for Salem and am to meet Mr. Cranch and Mrs. Adams att Roxbury to settle About both families coming in and Cousin Betzey, and all of them to reside in Our house.

I have to inform you that Yesterday was sent into C[ape] Ann by Capt. Johnson of this port Two ships One Large One from Jamaica with 500 hhd. Sugar and rum and 39 bags Cotton &c.—A General and

Lady, passengers. The Other from Antigua on the Kings Account for Genl. How with 430 hhd. Rum all broad Air. They both made resistance both Vessells had more hands than the privatear.[1]

We wait to here from your way Anxiously and wish we may here something Agreeable.

I am Yr. &c.,   I.S.

RC (Adams Papers).

[1] The *Yankee* privateer, Capt. Henry Johnson, was shortly afterward captured by the prisoners aboard her from the two vessels she had sent into Cape Ann. See MHS, *Colls.*, 77 (1927):328.

John Adams to Abigail Adams

June [*i.e.* July] 10. 1776

You will see by the Newspapers, which I from time to time inclose, with what Rapidity, the Colonies proceed in their political Maneuvres. How many Calamities might have been avoided if these Measures had been taken twelve Months ago, or even no longer ago than last december?

The Colonies to the South, are pursuing the same Maxims, which have heretofore governed those to the North. In constituting their new Governments, their Plans are remarkably popular, more so than I could ever have imagined, even more popular than the "Thoughts on Government." And in the Choice of their Rulers, Capacity, Spirit and Zeal in the Cause, supply the Place of Fortune, Family, and every other Consideration, which used to have Weight with Mankind. My Friend Archibald Bullock Esq. is Governor of Georgia. John Rutledge Esq. is Governor of South Carolina. Patrick Henry Esq. is Governor of Virginia &c. Dr. Franklin will be Governor of Pensilvania. The new Members of this City,[1] are all in this Taste, chosen because of their inflexible Zeal for Independence. All the old Members left out, because they opposed Independence, or at least were lukewarm about it. Dickinson, Morris, Allen, all fallen, like Grass before the Scythe notwithstanding all their vast Advantages in Point of Fortune, Family and Abilities.

I am inclined to think however, and to wish that these Gentlemen may be restored, at a fresh Election, because, altho mistaken in some Points, they are good Characters, and their great Wealth and numerous Connections, will contribute to strengthen America, and cement her Union.

I wish I were at perfect Liberty, to pourtray before you, all those Characters, in their genuine Lights, and to explain to you the Course of political Changes in this Province. It would give you a great Idea of the Spirit and Resolution of the People, and shew you, in a striking Point of View, the deep Roots of American Independence in all the Colonies. But it is not prudent, to commit to Writing such free Speculations, in the present State of Things.

Time which takes away the Veil, may lay open the secret Springs of this surprizing Revolution....[2] But I find, altho the Colonies have differed in Religion, Laws, Customs, and Manners, yet in the great Essentials of Society and Government, they are all alike.

RC and LbC (Adams Papers).

[1] In the Pennsylvania Constitutional Convention, for which elections had just been held and which convened on 15 July. For its members and proceedings see Force, *Archives*, 5th ser., 2:1 ff.

[2] Suspension points in MS.

John Adams to Abigail Adams

Philadelphia July 11. 1776

You seem to be situated in the Place of greatest Tranquility and Security, of any upon the Continent....[1] I may be mistaken in this particular, and an Armament may have invaded your Neighbourhood before now. But We have no Intelligence of any such Design and all that We now know of the Motions, Plans, Operations, and Designs of the Enemy, indicates the Contrary.—It is but just that you should have a little Rest, and take a little Breath.

I wish I knew whether your Brother and mine have inlisted in the Army, and what Spirit is manifested by our Militia, for marching to New York and Crown Point.... The Militia of Maryland, New Jersey, Pensilvania, and the lower Counties, are marching with much Alacrity, and a laudable Zeal, to take Care of Howe and his Army at Staten Island. The Army in New York is in high Spirits, and seems determined to give the Enemy a serious Reception.

The unprincipled, and unfeeling, and unnatural Inhabitants of Staten Island, are cordially receiving the Enemy, and Deserters say have engaged to take Arms.—They are an ignorant, cowardly, Pack of Scoundrells. Their Numbers are small, and their Spirit less.

It is some Time, since I received any Letter from you; the Plymouth one was the last. You must write me, every Week by the Post. If it is but a few Lines, it gives me many Spirits. •

I design to write to the General Court, requesting a Dismission, or at least a Furlow. I think to propose that they choose four more Members or at least two more, that so We may attend here in Rotation. Two or three or four may be at home at a Time, and the Colony properly represented notwithstanding.—Indeed, while the Congress were employed in political Regulations, forming the Sentiments of the People of the Colonies into some consistent System, extinguishing the Remainders of Authority under the Crown, and gradually erecting and strengthening Governments, under the Authority of the People, turning their Thoughts upon the Principles of Polity and the Forms of Government, framing Constitutions for the Colonies seperately, and a limited and defined Confederacy, for the united Colonies, and in some other Measures, which I do not choose to mention particularly, but which are now determined, or near the Point of Determination,[2] I flattered myself that I might have been of some little Use here. But, now, these Matters will be soon compleated, and very little Business will be to be done here, but what will be either military or Commercial, Branches of Knowledge and Business, for which hundreds of others in our Province, are much better qualified than I am. I shall therefore request my Masters to relieve me.[3]

I am not a little concerned about my Health which seems to have been providentially preserved to me, much beyond my Expectations. But I begin to feel the disagreable Effects, of unremitting Attention to Business for so long a Time, and a Want of Exercise, and the bracing Quality of my Native Air: so that I have the Utmost Reason to fear an irreparable Injury to my Constitution, if I do not obtain a little Relaxation.

The Fatigues of War, are much less destructive to Health, than the painfull laborious Attention, to Debates, and to Writing, which drinks up the Spirits and consumes the Strength.—I am &c.

RC and LbC (Adams Papers).

[1] Here and below, suspension points are in MS.

[2] This undoubtedly alludes to the work of the committee, which had been appointed on 12 June and of which JA was a member, "to prepare a plan of treaties to be proposed to foreign powers," meaning (at this time) specifically France (JCC, 5:433). JA was himself the draftsman of the famous and influential "Plan" and instructions which resulted; see his *Diary and Autobiography*, 3:337–338, 393, 400, 412, 413, 414, 432–433, 435, with notes and references there. The committee submitted its report on 18 July, and debates on it followed intermittently for two months. JA considered the matter of such consequence that he would not ask for leave to visit his family even after hearing, on the 16th, that all of them were undergoing inoculation.

[3] JA's proposal to the General Court for "an Alteration in their Plan of Dele-

gation," urging that nine delegates be chosen annually so that part of them could always be on leave, is in a letter he apparently drafted on 17 July to John Avery, deputy secretary of state, but did not send until the 25th (M–Ar: vol. 195; printed in JA, *Works*, 9:426–427). See also the editorial note in JA's *Diary and Autobiography*, 2:251.

Abigail Adams to John Adams

Boston July 13 1776

I must begin with apoligising to you for not writing since the 17 of June. I have really had so many cares upon my Hands and Mind, with a bad inflamation in my Eyes that I have not been able to write. I now date from Boston where I yesterday arrived and was with all 4 of our Little ones innoculated for the small pox. My unkle and Aunt were so kind as to send me an invitation with my family. Mr. Cranch and wife and family, My Sister Betsy and her Little Neice,[1] Cotton Tufts[2] and Mr. Thaxter, a maid who has had the Distemper and my old Nurse compose our family. A Boy too I should have added. 17 in all.[3] My unkles maid with his Little daughter and a Negro Man are here. We had our Bedding &c. to bring. A Cow we have driven down from B[raintre]e and some Hay I have had put into the Stable, wood &c. and we have really commenced housekeepers here. The House was furnished with almost every article (except Beds) which we have free use of, and think ourselves much obliged by the fine accommodations and kind offer of our Friends. All our necessary Stores we purchase jointly. Our Little ones stood the opperation Manfully. Dr. Bulfinch is our Physician. Such a Spirit of innoculation never before took place; the Town and every House in it, are as full as they can hold. I believe there are not less than 30[4] persons from Braintree. Mrs. Quincy, Mrs. Lincoln, Miss Betsy and Nancy are our near Neighbours.[5] God Grant that we may all go comfortably thro the Distemper, the phisick part is bad enough I know. I knew your mind so perfectly upon the subject that I thought nothing, but our recovery would give you eaquel pleasure, and as to safety there was none. The Soldiers innoculated privately, so did many of the inhabitants and the paper curency spread it everywhere. I immediately determined to set myself about it, and get ready with my children. I wish it was so you could have been with us, but I submit.

I received some Letters from you last Saturday Night 26 of June.[6] You mention a Letter of the 16 which I have never received, and I suppose must relate something to private affairs which I wrote about in May and sent by Harry.

As to News we have taken several fine prizes since I wrote you as you will see by the news papers. The present Report is of Lord Hows comeing with unlimited powers. However suppose it is so, I believe he little thinks of treating with us as independant States. How can any person yet dreem of a settlement, accommodations &c. They have neither the spirit nor feeling of Men, yet I see some who never were call'd Tories, gratified with the Idea of Lord Hows being upon his passage with such powers.

Sunday july 14

By yesterdays post I received two Letters dated 3 and 4 of July[7] and tho your Letters never fail to give me pleasure, be the subject what it will, yet it was greatly heightned by the prospect of the future happiness and glory of our Country; nor am I a little Gratified when I reflect that a person so nearly connected with me has had the Honour of being a principal actor, in laying a foundation for its future Greatness. May the foundation of our new constitution, be justice, Truth and Righteousness. Like the wise Mans house may it be founded upon those Rocks and then neither storms or temptests will overthrow it.

I cannot but feel sorry that some of the most Manly Sentiments in the Declaration are Expunged from the printed coppy. Perhaps wise reasons induced it.[8]

Poor Canady I lament Canady but we ought to be in some measure sufferers for the past folly of our conduct. The fatal effects of the small pox there, has led almost every person to consent to Hospitals in every Town. In many Towns, already arround Boston the Selectmen have granted Liberty for innoculation. I hope the necessity is now fully seen.

I had many dissagreable Sensations at the Thoughts of comeing myself, but to see my children thro it I thought my duty, and all those feelings vanished as soon as I was innoculated and I trust a kind providence will carry me safely thro. Our Friends from Plymouth came into Town yesterday. We have enough upon our hands in the morning. The Little folks are very sick then and puke every morning but after that they are comfortable. I shall write you now very often. Pray inform me constantly of every important transaction. Every expression of tenderness is a cordial to my Heart. Unimportant as they are to the rest of the world, to me they are *every Thing*.

We have had during all the month of June a most severe Drougth which cut of all our promising hopes of english Grain and the first crop of Grass, but since july came in we have had a plenty of rain and now every thing looks well. There is one Misfortune in our family which I have never mentiond in hopes it would have been in my power to have remedied[9] it, but all hopes of that kind are at an end. It is the loss of your Grey Horse. About 2 months ago, I had occasion to send Jonathan of an errant to my unkle Quincys (the other Horse being a plowing). Upon his return a little below the church she trod upon a rolling stone and lamed herself to that degree that it was with great difficulty that she could be got home. I immediately sent for Tirrel and every thing was done for her by Baths, ointments, polticeing, Bleeding &c. that could be done. Still she continued extreem lame tho not so bad as at first. I then got her carried to Domet but he pronounces her incurable, as a callous is grown upon her footlock joint. You can hardly tell, not even by your own feelings how much I lament her. She was not with foal, as you immagined, but I hope she is now as care has been taken in that Respect.

I suppose you have heard of a fleet which came up pretty near the Light and kept us all with our mouths open ready to catch them, but after staying near a week and makeing what observations they could set sail and went of to our great mortification who were [prepared?][10] for them in every respect. If our Ship of 32 Guns which [was] Built at Portsmouth and waiting only for Guns and an other of [...] at Plimouth in the same state, had been in readiness we should in all probability been Masters of them. Where the blame lies in that respect I know not, tis laid upon Congress, and Congress is also blamed for not appointing us a General.—But Rome was not Built in a day.

I hope the Multiplicity of cares and avocations which invellope you will not be too powerfull for you. I have many anxietyes upon that account. Nabby and Johnny send duty and desire Mamma to say that an inflamation in their Eyes which has been as much of a distemper as the small pox, has prevented their writing, but they hope soon to be able to acquaint Pappa of their happy recovery from the Distemper.—Mr. C[ranch] and wife, Sister B[etsy] and all our Friend[s] desire to be rememberd to you and foremost in that Number stands your   Portia

PS   A little India herb would have been mighty agreable now.

RC (Adams Papers); addressed in John Thaxter's hand: "To The Honble: John Adams Esqr. at Philadelphia To be left at the Post Office"; postmarked: "BOSTON 15 IY"; endorsed: "Portia and. [i.e. answered (by JA)] July. 23d."

[1] Presumably Louisa Catherine (1773?–1857), daughter of AA's only brother, William Smith. Owing to her family's indigence and her father's early death, Louisa, who never married, lived for many years in the Adams household, served as amanuensis to JA in his old age, and was generously remembered by

both AA and JA in their wills. She is, of course, frequently mentioned in the family correspondence. See Adams Genealogy.

[2] Cotton Tufts Jr. (1757–1833), Harvard 1777; see Adams Genealogy.

[3] AA's listing and total are confusing at best. It is impossible to arrive at 17 as the total number of patients, whether or not the persons mentioned in the next sentence are included. (The "Little daughter" in the next sentence was Elizabeth [b. 1770], daughter of Isaac and Elizabeth [Storer] Smith; she later married John P. Hale. See Adams Genealogy.)

[4] First digit uncertain; possibly AA meant "50."

[5] "Miss Betsy and Nancy" were Elizabeth (later Mrs. Benjamin Guild) and Ann (later Mrs. Asa Packard), daughters of Col. Josiah Quincy by his 2d and 3d wives respectively. Mrs. Lincoln was doubtless Hannah, also a daughter of Col. Quincy but by his first wife; before her marriage to Dr. Bela Lincoln (1734–1773) in 1760, she had attracted JA's serious interest and is frequently mentioned in his early Diary; in 1777 she married Ebenezer Storer (1730–1807). "Mrs. Quincy" was probably the Colonel's 3d wife, the former Ann Marsh. All of these persons, though not close relations of the Adamses, are entered in the Adams Genealogy because of the numerous ties between the Quincy and Adams families.

[6] That is, a letter so dated; it is printed above, and so is JA's letter to AA of 16 June, evidently delayed in transit.

[7] No letter written by JA on 4 July 1776 is known to the editors. The possibility that he wrote a letter of that date to AA, enclosing in it the copy he had made of Jefferson's draft of the Declaration of Independence (see the following note), and commenting on the revisions made by Congress in the text of that paper—this possibility cannot be ruled out. But it seems to the editors an exceedingly doubtful one. If one supposes that such a letter was written and received, then one must at once explain why no entry for it can be found in JA's letterbooks, which he was keeping with great fidelity at this time, and how the recipient's copy of a letter of such mo-

ment could have disappeared without a trace from the family archives. This supposition, in short, raises more unanswerable questions than it resolves. Since AA mentions "two Letters" rather than three, she is almost certainly referring to the two separate letters JA wrote her during the morning and the evening of 3 July, both printed above; otherwise we must suppose that she failed to acknowledge one of *those* letters, which *are* extant.

[8] This remarkable paragraph raises questions to which only conjectural answers can be given. JA sent a copy of the Dunlap broadside of the Declaration of Independence to Mary Palmer on 5 July, the day it was printed (see his letter of that date, above), and he *may* have sent AA a copy in one of the packets of printed matter that he frequently forwarded from Philadelphia without covering letters. His earliest (surviving) reference to a text sent to her is in his first letter of 7 July (above), enclosing a *Pennsylvania Evening Post* of the 6th, which contained the first printing of the Declaration in a newspaper. AA had not received JA's letter of the 7th when she wrote the present letter. But printed copies of the Dunlap broadside had certainly reached Boston by 13 July from some source, and probably from several sources, for on that day Ezekiel Price visited his children, who were under inoculation in Boston, and wrote in his Diary: "The mail from New York brings the declaration of the Continental Congress for INDEPENDENCE" (MHS, *Procs.*, 1st ser., 7 [1863–1864]:260). The same mail probably brought JA's letter to Mary Palmer of 5 July and Elbridge Gerry's letter to James Warren of the same date, which enclosed two broadside copies of the Declaration, one for Warren and one for Joseph Hawley (Austin, *Gerry*, 1:202–203).

But what of AA's regret that "some of the most Manly Sentiments in the Declaration" as submitted by the drafting committee had been "Expunged" by Congress? How could she know, from the evidence in her hands, that any such thing had happened? Possibly JA had told her so in a letter now missing (see preceding note). Possibly letters (now lost) from other delegates in Philadelphia made observations to that effect, and the word spread rapidly in Boston. Neither of these explanations seems at all likely to the editors. The only other explanation is that AA received, most likely on the 13th, with JA's two letters of the 3d, his autograph copy of Jefferson's draft of the Declaration (see below) and made a quick but perceptive comparison of it with a text of Dunlap's broadside, either a copy sent to her or one sent to a friend with whom she was in touch in Boston. (Note that farther on in the present letter she mentions the Warrens' arrival in Boston from Plymouth on the 13th; and see Warren to JA, 17 July, in *Warren-Adams Letters*, 1:261.) Since, so far as we know, JA had said nothing to AA about the actual authorship of the Declaration, and since the copy of the draft that he had evidently sent on is *in his hand*, AA would very naturally have inferred that he was the author, and would, characteristically, have resented alterations by Congress in her husband's work. The Adamses' minister in Boston, Rev. Samuel Cooper, made the same inference and a similar comment in a letter he wrote JA on 14 Aug. (Adams Papers): "That Masterly Performance cannot fail of it's deserved Weight upon the Minds of the People. I could wish, however, that some great Strokes I saw in a Manuscript Draught had not been omitted." Cooper's letter makes clear beyond all question that JA had sent on his copy of Jefferson's "original Rough draught" during the summer of 1776, that it circulated in Boston, and that, since JA said nothing to the contrary (indeed apparently said nothing whatever about his handwritten copy when he sent it on), his friends in Boston assumed at this time that he was the author of the Declaration.

This is not the place to discuss the importance of the JA copy as a guide to the changes in the text of the Declaration while it was still in committee. It has remained ever since 1776 among the Adams Papers, except for a brief interval in 1943 when it was loaned to the Library of Congress for the purpose of making the first facsimile reproduction of it, which was published as plate 4 in Julian P. Boyd, *The Declaration of Independence: The Evolution of the Text*, Washington, 1943; see same, p. 6, 22–28; Jefferson, *Papers*, ed. Boyd, 1: 416; and John H. Hazelton, *The Declaration of Independence: Its History*, N.Y., 1906, p. 306 ff., 348–349.

⁹ MS: "remided."
¹⁰ Here and below, MS is torn by seal.

John Adams to Abigail Adams

Philadelphia July 15. 1776

My very deserving Friend, Mr. Gerry, setts off, tomorrow, for Boston, worn out of Health, by the Fatigues of this station. He is an excellent Man, and an active able statesman. I hope he will soon return hither. I am sure I should be glad to go with him, but I cannot. I must write to have the Guard relieved.

There is a most amiable, lawdable, and gallant Spirit prevailing, in these middle Colonies. The Militia turn out in great Numbers and in high Spirits, in New Jersey, Pensilvania, Maryland, and Delaware, so that We hope to resist Howe and his Mirimidons.

Independence is at last unanimously agreed to in the New York Convention. You will see by the Newspapers inclosed what is going forward in Virginia, and Maryland and New Jersey. Farewell! farewell, infatuated, besotted Stepdame. I have not Time to add, more than that I receive Letters from you but seldom of late. Tomorrows Post I hope will bring me some. So I hoped of last Saturdays and last Tuesdays.

Ever yours.

RC and LbC (Adams Papers). Enclosed newspapers not found.

John Adams to Abigail Adams, with Enclosure

Philadelphia July 16. 1776

In a Letter from your Uncle Smith, and in another from Mr. Mason which I received by this days Post[1] I am informed that you were about taking the Small Pox, with all the Children....[2] It is not possible for me to describe, nor for you to conceive my Feelings upon this Occasion. Nothing, but the critical State of our Affairs should prevent me from flying to Boston, to your Assistance.

I mentioned your Intention to Mrs. Yard at noon. This Evening our President was here. I was engaged abroad, the whole Evening till it was late. When I came home, I found the inclosed Card from the President. I have not yet had an Opportunity to thank Mr. Hancock for his Politeness, which in this Instance is very obliging, but I shall take the first opportunity of doing it, and of informing him, that your Uncles Kindness of which I shall ever entertain the most gratefull Sentiments, has rendered it unnecessary, as well as improper, for you to accept of his most generous Offer.

I can do no more than wish and pray for your Health, and that of the Children. Never—Never in my whole Life, had I so many Cares upon my Mind at once. I should have been happier, if I had received my Letters, before Mr. Gerry went away this Morning, because I should have written more by him.—I rely upon the tender Care of our Friends. Dr. Tufts and your Uncle Quincy, and my Brother will be able to visit you, and give you any Assistance. Our other Friends, I doubt not will give you every Advice, Consolation and Aid in their Power.—I am very anxious about supplying you with Money. Spare for nothing, if you can get Friends to lend it you. I will repay with Gratitude as well as Interest, any sum that you may borrow.—I shall feel like a Savage to be here, while my whole Family is sick at Boston. But it cannot be avoided. I cannot leave this Place, without more Injury to the public now, than I ever could at any other Time, being in the Midst of scænes of Business, which must not stop for a Thing.... Make Mr. Mason, Mr. any Body write to me, by eve

Post—dont miss one for any Cause whatever.—My dearest Love to
you all.

RC and LbC (Adams Papers). Enclosure: John Hancock to JA, 16 July,
printed herewith.

¹ Isaac Smith Sr. to JA, 8 July, above, and Jonathan Mason to JA, 9 July (Adams
Papers).

² Here and below, suspension points are in MS.

ENCLOSURE

John Hancock to John Adams

Sir   Philada. Tuesday Eveng. 16 July 1776

On a Visit to Mrs. Yard this Evening I was inform'd by her that
your Lady and Children propos'd to go into Boston, with an intention
of Taking the Small Pox by Inoculation, and as the Season is warm,
and the present process of Treating that Disorder, requires all the
Air that can possibly be had, and as my Scituation in Boston is as much
Bless'd with a free Air as most others, I make a Tender of my house
and Garden for their use if you Choose to improve it, and by a
Signification of your Consent I will write by this Express to that
purport. The fruit in the Garden shall be at their Controul, and a maid
Servant and the others in the House shall afford them every Con-
venience that appertains to the House.—It will give me pleasure to
be any way instrumental, however small, in adding to their Con-
venience.¹

I am Sir Your very hum sert.,   John Hancock

RC (Adams Papers); addressed: "To the Honl. John Adams Esqr. At Mrs.
Yard's." Enclosed in JA to AA of this date, preceding.

¹ The mansion of John Hancock, built
by his uncle Thomas Hancock in 1737,
stood on the southern slope of Beacon
Hill, overlooking the Common, on the
grounds of the present west wing of the
Massachusetts State House. Its gardens
and orchards were extensive, and the
house became a Boston landmark not
only because of its conspicuous site and
opulence but because it was visited by
so many eminent persons (including JA
and AA upon their return from Europe
in June 1788) and was described by
everyone who wrote about the city. Its
grounds were greatly reduced by the
building of Bulfinch's State House not
long after Hancock's death, and in the
1850's the house itself was threatened
with destruction to make way for more
modern dwellings. Attempts by the State
to acquire it as a governor's residence,
and by the City to remove and preserve
it as "an historical cabinet" or museum
of antiquities, failed. Though many
relics were preserved, the house was
demolished in 1863. The dwellings
which replaced it were razed when the
west wing of the State House was added
in the present century. See City of Boston, *Report of Committee on the Preservation of the Hancock House*, 1863;
Chamberlain, *Beacon Hill*, ch. 11, with

illustrations; and Walter Kendall Watkins, "The Hancock House and Its Builder," *Old-Time New England,* 17: 3–19 (July 1926), which is admirably illustrated.

John Adams to Isaac Smith Sr.

Sir   Philadelphia July 17. 1776

Your Letter of the Eighth contains Intelligence of an interesting Nature to the Public as well as to me, and my Family in particular.— The Small Pox is so terrible an Enemy that it is high Time to subdue it.—I am under the greatest Obligation to you, Sir, and Mrs. Smith for your kind Offer of the Accommodations of your House to Mrs. Adams and my Children. I shall be very, very anxious, untill I hear further, and if it was possible I would be in Boston as soon as an Horse could carry me. But this is the most unlucky Time, that ever happened. Such Business is now before Us, that I cannot in Honour and in duty to the public, stir from this Place, at present. After a very few Months, I shall return: But in the mean Time, I shall suffer inexpressible distress, on Account of my Family. My only Consolation is that they have no small Number of very kind Friends.

We are in hourly Expectation of some important Event at New York. We hope there will be a sufficient Number of Men there, to give the Enemy a proper Reception. But am sorry the Massachusetts have not sent along some of their Militia, as requested. My most affectionate Regards to Mrs. Smith and the family. I am yr.

LbC (Adams Papers).

John Adams to Abigail Adams

Philadelphia July 20. 1776

I cannot omit the Opportunity of writing you, a Line, by this Post. This Letter will I suppose, find you, in some degree or other, under the Influence of the Small Pox. The Air is of very great Importance. I dont know your Phisician, but I hope he wont deprive you of Air, more than is necessary.

We had Yesterday, an express from General Lee, in Charlestown South Carolina, with an Account of a brilliant little Action between the Armament under Clinton, and Cornwallis, and a Battery on Sullivans Island. Which terminated very fortunately for America. I will endeavour to inclose, with this a printed Account of it.[1] It has given Us good Spirits here and will have an happy Effect, upon our Armies at New York and Ticonderoga. Surely our northern Soldiers will not suffer themselves to be outdone by their Brethren so nearly under the Sun. I dont yet hear of any Massachusetts Men, at New York. Our People must not flinch, at this critical Moment, when their Country is in more danger, than it ever will be again perhaps. What will they say, if the Howes should prevail against our Forces, at so important a Post as New York for Want of a few Thousand Men from the Massachusetts?

I will likewise send you, by this Post, Lord Howes Letter and Proclamation, which has let the Cat out of the Bag.[2]—These Tricks deceive no longer. Gentlemen here, who either were or pretended to be deceived heretofore, now see or pretend to see, through such Artifices. I apprehend, his Lordship is afraid of being attacked upon Staten Island, and is throwing out his Barrells to amuse Leviathan, untill his Reinforcement shall arrive.

RC and LbC (Adams Papers). Enclosures, if actually sent, not found, but see notes below. Though not recorded in the *JCC* "Bibliographical Notes," there is a broadside printing, without imprint, of the Lee and Howe documents mentioned in JA's letter, in MHi:Broadsides, under date of 19 July 1776.

[1] Gen. Charles Lee's letter from Charleston, 2 July, was read in Congress on 19 July and an extract ordered printed (*JCC*, 5:593).

[2] Lord Howe's letter was a circular to the colonial governors, dated from his ship off Massachusetts on 20 June and enclosing a proclamation of the same date which announced his powers, jointly with his brother, to grant pardons to Americans who would return to their allegiance. These were read in Congress on 18 July and the next day were ordered printed (*JCC*, 5:574–575, 592–593). Texts will be found in Force, *Archives*, 4th ser., 6:1001–1002.

John Adams to Abigail Adams

Philadelphia July 20. 1776

This has been a dull day to me: I waited the Arrival of the Post with much Solicitude and Impatience, but his Arrival made me more solicitous still.—"To be left at the Post Office" in your Hand Writing, on the back of a few Lines from the Dr. were all that I could learn of you, and my little Folks.[1] If you was too busy to write, I hoped that some kind Hand would have been found to let me know something about you.

Do my Friends think that I have been a Politician so long as to have lost all feeling? Do they suppose I have forgotten my Wife and Children? Or are they so panic struck with the Loss of Canada, as to be afraid to correspond with me? Or have they forgotten that you have an Husband and your Children a Father? What have I done, or omitted to do, that I should be thus forgotten and neglected in the most tender and affecting scæne of my Life! Dont mistake me, I dont blame you. Your Time and Thoughts must have been wholly taken up, with your own and your Families situation and Necessities.—But twenty other Persons might have informed me.

I suspect, that you intended to have run slyly, through the small Pox with the family, without letting me know it, and then have sent me an Account that you were all well. This might be a kind Intention, and if the design had succeeded, would have made me very joyous. But the secret is out, and I am left to conjecture. But as the Faculty[2] have this distemper so much under Command I will flatter myself with the Hope and Expectation of soon hearing of your Recovery.

RC and LbC (Adams Papers).

[1] See Cotton Tufts to JA, 5 July, above, and notes there.
[2] The medical profession.

John Adams to Cotton Tufts

Dear Sir   Philadelphia July 20. 1776. Saturday

Yours of July 5th. never reached me, till this Morning. I greatly regret its delay. But that it might answer its End, without further Loss of Time, I waited on my Friend Dr. Rush, an eminent Phisician of this City, and a worthy Friend of mine, who with a Politeness and Benevolence, becoming his Character, promised to furnish me with his Sentiments, concerning Inocculation, so that I may forward them to you by the next Post, and I have obtained his Leave for you to publish them, in Print, if you please. He practices with great Success. Several of our Members, have been under his Hands and come out, almost without an Alteration of Countenance.[1]

You say you got leave to lodge yours in Mrs. Adams's Letter. But no Letter from her accompanied it, which has distressed me much, both because I was very impatient for a Letter from her, and because it creates a Jealousy of some unfair Practice in the Post Office....[2] I observe however upon the back of your Letter the Words "to be left at the Post office" in her Hand Writing, which makes it not improbable that she might send it without a Line from herself.

It is a long Time, since I heard from her or indeed any Thing concerning her only that she was determined to have the Distemper, with all my Children. How do you think I feel? supposing that my Wife and Children are all sick of the small Pox, myself unable to see them, or hear from them. And all this in Addition to several other Cares, public and private, which alone would be rather troublesome?

However, I will not be dejected. Hope springs eternal in my Breast, and keeps me up, above all Difficulties, hitherto.

I am, sincerely Yours.

LbC (Adams Papers).

[1] JA had first met Benjamin Rush (1746–1813), College of New Jersey 1760, M.D., Edinburgh 1768, in Aug. 1774, Rush being one of the party of Philadelphia gentlemen who rode out to Frankford to welcome the Massachusetts delegation to the first Continental Congress. JA characterized Rush in his Diary in 1775 as "an elegant, ingenious Body, [a] Sprightly, pretty fellow" and at first had some doubts about his substance. But they were soon warm friends. Rush served the Adamses as family physician in the 1790's, and despite their marked political differences the liking and respect of the two men for each other never diminished. During JA's years of political retirement they conducted an active and distinguished correspondence, their letters to each other being among the longest and best that either one of them ever wrote. It was Rush who, after long and pertinacious effort, brought about the reconciliation between ex-Presidents Adams and Jefferson in 1812, with remarkable results. See JA, *Diary and Autobiography*, 2: 115, 182; Benjamin Rush, *Letters*, 1:153–154 and *passim*; L. H. Butterfield, "The Dream of Benjamin Rush," *Yale Review*, 40:297–319 (Winter 1951).

Rush had learned the new or "Suttonian" method of inoculation in England during the 1760's and later published a tract on the subject that went through several editions (*Letters*, 1:66–67). See, further, AA to JA, 21–22 July, 1 Aug.; JA to AA, 23 July; Tufts to JA, 6 Aug.; all below.

[2] Suspension points in MS.

Abigail Adams to John Adams

July 21 1776 Boston

I have no doubt but that my dearest Friend is anxious to know how his Portia does, and his little flock of children under the opperation of a disease once so formidable.

I have the pleasure to tell him that they are all comfortable tho some of them complaining. Nabby has been very ill, but the Eruption begins to make its appearence upon her, and upon Johnny. Tommy is so well that the Dr. innoculated him again to day fearing it had not taken. Charlly has no complaints yet, tho his arm has been very soar.

I have been out to meeting this forenoon, but have so many dissagreable Sensations this afternoon that I thought it prudent to tarry at home. The Dr. says they are very good feelings. Mr. Cranch has passed thro the preparation and the Eruption is comeing out cleverly upon him without any Sickness at all. Mrs. Cranch is cleverly and so are all her children. Those who are broke out are pretty full for the new method as tis call'd, the Suttonian they profess to practice upon.[1] I hope to give you a good account when I write next, but our Eyes are very weak and the Dr. is not fond of either writing or reading for his patients. But I must transgress a little.

I received a Letter from you by wedensday Post 7 of July and tho I think it a choise one in the Litterary Way, containing many usefull hints and judicious observations which will greatly assist me in the future instruction of our Little ones, yet it Lacked some essential engrediants to make it compleat. Not one word respecting yourself, your Health or your present Situation. My anxiety for your welfare will never leave me but with my parting Breath, tis of more importance to me than all this World contains besides. The cruel Seperation to which I am necessatated cuts of half the enjoyments of life, the other half are comprised in the hope I have that what I do and what I suffer may be serviceable to you, to our Little ones and our Country; I must beseach you therefore for the future never to omit what is so essential to my happiness.

Last Thursday[2] after hearing a very Good Sermon I went with the Multitude into Kings Street to hear the proclamation for independance read and proclamed. Some Field peices with the Train were brought there, the troops appeard under Arms and all the inhabitants assembled there (the small pox prevented many thousand from the Country). When Col. Crafts read from the Belcona[3] of the State House the Proclamation, great attention was given to every word. As soon as he ended, the cry from the Belcona, was God Save our American States and then 3 cheers which rended the air, the Bells rang, the privateers fired, the forts and Batteries, the cannon were discharged, the platoons followed and every face appeard joyfull. Mr. Bowdoin then gave a Sentiment, Stability and perpetuity to American independance. After dinner the kings arms were taken down from the State House and every vestage of him from every place in which it appeard and burnt in King Street. Thus ends royall Authority in this State, and all the people shall say Amen.

I have been a little surprized that we collect no better accounts with regard to the horrid conspiricy at New York, and that so little mention has been made of it here. It made a talk for a few days but now seems all hushed in Silence. The Tories say that it was not a conspiricy but an association, and pretend that there was no plot to assasinate the General. Even their hardned Hearts ⟨*Blush*⟩ feel ——— the discovery. We have in Gorge a match for a Borgia and a Catiline, a Wretch Callous to every Humane feeling. Our worthy preacher told us that he believed one of our Great Sins for which a righteous God has come out in judgment against us, was our Biggoted attachment to so wicked a Man. May our repentance be sincere.

Monday morg. july 22

I omitted many things yesterday in order to be better informed. I have got Mr. Cranch to inquire and write you, concerning a French Schooner from Martineco which came in yesterday and a prize from Ireland. My own infirmities prevents my writing. A most Excruciating pain in my head and every Limb and joint I hope portends a speedy Eruption and prevents my saying more than that I am forever Yours.

The children are not yet broke out. Tis the Eleventh Day with us.

RC (Adams Papers); addressed in John Thaxter's hand: "To The Honble: John Adams Esqr. at Philadelphia"; endorsed: "Portia," to which was later added "July 21. 1776" in the hand of William Gordon(?). Evidently enclosed in Richard Cranch's letter to JA, 22 July, following.

[1] After Daniel Sutton (1735–1819), an irregular but highly successful practitioner of Ingatestone, Essex, and later of London (James Johnston Abraham, *Lettsom: His Life, Times, Friends and Descendants*, London, 1933, p. 189–194). His method required only a small puncture, rather than a gash, to infect the subject and made use of less virulent matter.

[2] The 18th.

[3] Balcony. A number of similar early spellings are recorded in *OED*.

Richard Cranch to John Adams

Dear Friend   Boston July 22d. 1776

Those that are dearest to you are here, under Inocolation. Charles was Inocolated with me on Thursday, the 11th. Instt. Our Symptoms are very promising; Mrs. A. and the other three Children underwent the operation the next Day. I suppose the enclos'd will be more particular.

The Declaration of Independency which took place here last Thursday, was an Event most ardently wish'd for by every consistant Lover of American Liberty, and was received accordingly by the loudest Acclamations of the People, who Shouted—God Save the united STATES of America!—We have various Stories current here of Vessels having spoken with Lord Howe, and that he inform'd them he had Powers to treat with Congress &c. *Beware of Punic Faith.*

Yesterday we had the Pleasure of seeing a Prize Ship with Provisions from Ireland, safely Anchor'd off Hancock's Wharfe. It seems by the Captain's account of things, that he was blown off to the W. Indies last Winter, was question'd by the Admiral at Jamaica, and roughly treated by him for coming so far to Leeward; he vindicated his Character; and after refitting, was sent off with a strict charge to go directly to Boston. He took a Pilot at Nantuckett, who foolishly told him that the Troops were gone from Boston, but happily the Captain would not believe him till our Fort at Nantaskett gave him full conviction. The chief of her Cargo is 1500 Barrells of Pork and Beef, with a Quantity of Butter. We have also just received the agreeable News, that an Arm'd Schooner, with Letter of Marque fitted out by the Derby's of Salem, has taken a large Jamaica Ship, with 394 Hhds. of Sugar, 143 Puncheons of Rum, 40 Pipes of Medaira Wine, and other West India Articles, and sent her into Sheepscutt. It is asserted that she has also 27 Pieces of Cannon in her Hold, from 4, to 9 Pounders. The above Schooner has also taken a Sloop from England with Dry Goods, bound to N: York, and carried her into Cape Ann. I hear you are President of a certain Board.—Cousin N:C. who has been in the Quarter-Master-General's Office from the very begining; and has been found, (what you k[new] him to be before,) a Person of the utmost Probity as well as good Abilities for Business; He, I say, has lost every thing that he had in the World, (amounting to several Hundred Pounds Sterg.,) because he quitted the Town without a Pass, after he had try'd Months in vain to get one.[1] The Neighbours say that the Provost came and carried off every Thing that he had, just after they found that he had made his Escape. He is now in the same office as a Clerk, at N: York. I mention the above to you, that if any Place shoud offer, in which he might serve his Country in a little higher Sphere, you would be so good as to think of him.

I am, with the greatest Esteem Yours &c.

RC (Adams Papers); addressed: "To The Honble: John Adams Esqr. at Philadelphia"; franked; "Free"; endorsed: "Mr. Cranch," with the date of the letter added in the hand of William Gordon(?). Enclosure was presumably AA's letter to JA, 21–22 July, preceding.

[1] Apparently Nathaniel Cranch (d. 1780), a nephew rather than a cousin of Richard Cranch. He was engaged to his cousin Elizabeth Palmer (who afterward married Nathaniel's brother Joseph) at the time of his death from a fall on the old fortifications at Boston Neck. See Richard Cranch to JA, 26 April 1780 (Adams Papers); *Grandmother Tyler's Book*, p. 55–56.

John Adams to Abigail Adams

July 23. 1776

This Mornings Post brought me yours of July 13 and 14 and has relieved me from an huge Load of Anxiety.—Am happy to hear that you are so comfortably situated, have so much agreable Company, and such fine Accommodations. I would very joyfully agree to have the small Pox, over again, for the Sake of the Company.

Since the Letters of July 3d. and 4th. which you say you have received,[1] I have written to you of the following dates. Two Letters July 7.—July 10. 11. 15. 16. Two Letters of July 20th.—This Morning I inclosed a Letter from Dr. Rush to me, containing Directions for managing Patients under Inocculation for the small Pox.[2] Rush has as much success as any without Exception.

You will find several dull Hours, and the Children will fatigue you. But if you had sent me a Present of an hundred Guineas,[3] it would not have pleased me so much as to hear that Nurse is there. You cant be low spirited, while she is there, and you cant possibly suffer for Want of Care. But I am somewhat afraid you have not Nurses and Servants enough in the House for so large an Hospital.

I dont know how I can better entertain you, than by giving you some Idea of the Character of this Dr. Rush.—He is a Native of this Place, a Gentleman of an ingenious Turn of Mind, and of elegant Accomplishments. He has travelled in England, where he was acquainted with Mrs. Maccaulay, with whom he corresponded while there, and since his Return. He wrote an elegant, flowing Letter to her, while he was in England, concerning a Plan of a Republic which she wrote and addressed to Pascal Paoli. He afterwards travelled in France, and contracted a Friendship there with M. Dubourg, with whom he has corresponded ever since. He has published several Things upon Philosophy, Medicine, and Politicks, in this City. He is a Lecturer in the Colledge here, in some Branch of Physick or surgery, and is a Member of the American Philosophical Society. He has been sometime a Member of the City Committee and was last Week appointed a Delegate in Congress for this Place, in the Room of one, who was left out.[4] He married last Winter, a young Lady, daughter of Mr. Stockton of New Jersey, one of the Judges of the Supream Court of that Government, and lately appointed a delegate in this Congress.[5] This Gentleman is said to be a staunch American, I suppose, truly.

Dr. Cooper has promised me, to visit you, and contribute all in his Power to amuse you and make your Stay agreable. I love him the more for this Kindness. I loved him much before.

Dont give yourself the least Pain about an incurable Lameness. Sell or give away the Creature, to a good Master; or keep her for the good she has done, and let her enjoy Life, in Ease for the future.—How shall I get home? I feel every generous Passion and every kind sentiment, rushing for Utterance, while I subscribe myself yours.

RC and LbC (Adams Papers).

[1] For reasons given above (AA to JA, 13–14 July, note 7), the editors believe that "the Letters of July 3d. and 4th." are actually JA's two letters of 3 July. JA is here simply parroting AA's phrasing.

[2] Rush's letter has not been found. It was doubtless handed on by AA to Dr. Tufts; see Tufts to JA, 6 Aug., below.

[3] Preceding four words supplied from LbC; their omission from RC must have been unintentional.

[4] Rush had been a member of the radical Provincial Conference and on 20 July was elected a delegate to the Continental Congress. He was thus able to sign the Declaration of Independence when the engrossed copy was ready for signing on 2 Aug., and he served until the end of Feb. 1777 (Burnett, ed., *Letters of Members*, 2:lxv).

[5] On 11 Jan. 1776, at Princeton, Rush had married Julia (1759–1848), daughter of Richard Stockton (1730–1781), who was to subscribe the Declaration of Independence with his son-in-law (Benjamin Rush, *Letters*, 1:97; *DAB*, under Stockton).

Abigail Adams to John Adams

[Boston, 24 July 1776] [1]

[First part of text missing.]

Respectfull Regards to Mr. Hancock with thanks for his very polite and generous offer and Let him know that I entertain a gratefull Sense of his kindness. My Regards to his Lady too who I hear is in thriveing circumstances. I wish they may be blessed with a fine Son. —Mr. Winth[r]ope deliverd me yours of july 7. Mr. Gerry is not yet arrived. We have not any news. My Eyes will suffer for this exertion. Adieu ever Ever Yours.

RC, fragment only (Adams Papers); addressed in Richard Cranch's hand: "To the Honble: John Adams Esqr. at Philadelphia"; postmarked: "BOSTON 25 IY"; endorsed: "Portia. ans. Aug. 3," to which was later added the date "July 24. 1776" in the hand of William Gordon(?). This is a detached leaf of folio size, the third and fourth pages only, of what was originally doubtless a large sheet folded to make four pages, with the text of AA's letter on the first through the third page and the address on the cover or fourth page. The first leaf was missing when this group of JA-AA letters was bound up in the 19th century; it may have been one of the specimens of AA's handwriting that JQA or CFA gave away to an autograph hunter.

¹ Date supplied from the docketing note (which must have been taken from the head of the letter) and confirmed by JA's acknowledgment in his reply of 3 Aug., below. That acknowledgment indicates that the missing portion of AA's letter had furnished a "particular and favourable Account ... of all the Family."

Cotton Tufts to John Adams

Dear Sr.   July 25. 1776

Yours of the 30th. of June came safe to Hand. A particular Answer to Your several Queries, for want of sufficient Information, must defer for the present. In general, Powder is made at two Colony Mills—Stotingham ¹ and Andover. Cannon is cast at Abington by Hobart, who has hitherto been unsucessful, not having cast above 8 or 10—he is still pursuing the Matter. Messrs. Nicho., Jos. and Jno. Brown of Providence equally unsuccesful at first, have now as I am informd, got into a good Run, casting in 24 Hours one 18. 12 and 9 Pounder. This I had from Mr. Will. Foster Mer[chan]t in Boston, but shall as Opportunity presents inform myself more fully.—Musquets and Bayonets may be manufactured in this Colony in prodigious Numbers. But to effect this Government should take into its Service a Lott² of Workmen—the Barrell Maker, Lock Maker, Stocker and Finisher, engage to take all the Arms manufactured by a certain Time, exempt them from all Military Duties, oblige them to Constancy and Fidelity under Penalties and to be under the Inspection of a Committee. Without some such Regulation No Assurance of a certain Number of Arms by a certain Time can be had. The same may be said with respect to many other Things of absolute Necessity.—The hard Hand of Necessity hath wrought Wonders. I have been surprizd to find Lock Makers spring out of Pail Makers, Boatmen and Farmers. I know some of each. A certain Micah Stockbridge of Abington, Pail Maker, has manufactured for Pratt a Number of fine Locks. Jno. Reed a Boatman and Farmer (formerly one of your Clients) has turned his Attention that Way and hath made a Number of substantial good Locks. These I suppose never ⟨wrought in Iron⟩ handled a Tool untill these Disputes came on. And Joshua Barrell of Bridgewater Lock Maker to Mr. Orr is suppos'd to make equal to any English Locks—will turn off one Lock dayly with his Apprentice.—Nil tam difficile &c.

A Vessell from Ireland with 1600 Blls. Pork, blown off last Fall to Jamaica, there refitted, bound to G[eneral] How and Troops at Boston, came into Nantasket Road last Sabbath and was invited by our Fort to stay with us, which she peaceably submitted to and was the same Day carried up to Boston. By this as well as former Instances we may see what Advantages might have resulted from an early fortifying this Place. I believe I gave You some Sketch of my Plan with respect to fortifying the Harbour. It was a Point my Heart was much upon, and which I digested into Form and laid before some Men of Influence. What Effect it had, cannot say but have the Pleasure to find that what I wished for, is in good Degree effected.

Jacta est Alea. Independency is declard. If we gain our Point, a System founded on the Principles of Virtue, productive of the best Interests of America and of universal Good to Mankind [I h]ope will be established. But if we fall the Words of Rochester on another Occasion I think may be applied—

> "By Jove 'twas bravely done
> first to attempt the Chariot of the Sun
> and then to fall like Phaeton."

Must not a Power be delegated by the People to the Congress, sufficient to hold all the several States in some kind of Subjection to it, such as will bind and oblige them wherein they of right ought to be bound, sufficient for regulating the general Interest of the whole, preventing one State from injuring another, for deciding all Controversies between them, for waging War, making Peace, for establishing a general Currency reducing all to one and bringing all Weights and Measures to one Standard, making general Regulations for Trade the same in all, establishing a Continental Revenue for discharging continental Debts, for supporting a Navy &c. &c.

The Small Pox prevailing in our Armies and Country has much retarded the raising Recruits. Inoculation has now ceased in Boston and will hereafter be carried on in Hospitals under the Direction of the Court of Sessions. One is orderd in Braintree. I have taken much Pains to get a Place but have met with many Obstructions and am as yet unsettled where We shall fix it. Shall probably engage with Dr. Phipps in it.

26th.

Am this day with my Friends at Boston. Mrs. Adams and your Children have all broke out, and have the Disorder light. Mr. Cranch and Family comfortable some with the Eruptions and others with the approaching Symptoms. My Son who is with them, has been inoculated 14 Days and no Complaints. The Disorder has hitherto provd very light.—I must break off with wishing You every Blessing and am Dear Sr., Yrs.

RC (Adams Papers).

[1] Now Sharon.
[2] Overwritten; perhaps "Sett."

John Adams to Abigail Adams

Philadelphia July 27. 1776

Disappointed again.—The Post brought me no Letter from you, which I dont wonder at much, nor any Intelligence concerning you, which surprizes me, a good deal....[1] I hang upon Tenterhooks. Fifteen days since, you were all inocculated, and I have not yet learned how you have fared. But I will suppose you all better and out of Danger. Why should I torture myself when I cant relieve you?

It makes me happy to hear that the Spirit of Inocculation prevails so generally. I could wish it, more universal. The small Pox has done Us more harm than British Armies, Canadians, Indians, Negroes, Hannoverians, Hessians, and all the rest. We must conquer this formidable Enemy without Hesitation or delay.

Sullivan is here, and in a Miff, at the Promotion of Gates, has asked Leave to resign his Commission.[2] I am sorry for this inconsiderate Step. It will hurt him more than the Cause. It is conjectured at New York, I am told, that he expects to be first Man in New Hampshire. If this is really his Motive, he ought to be ashamed of it, and I hope he will be dissappointed.—The Ladies have not half the Zeal for Precedence, that We find every day among the Gentlemen.

The Judge Advocate[3] came in this Evening, in fine Health and gay Spirits. The Army is the Place for Health—the Congress the Place of Sickness.—God bless you all.

Adieu.

RC and LbC (Adams Papers).

[1] Suspension points in MS.
[2] Brig. Gen. John Sullivan asked leave to resign on 26 July because he considered himself slighted by Gates' recent appointment as major general and commander of the northern army. A committee of which Jefferson was chairman drew a report intended to administer Sullivan "a proper rap of the knuckles" by accepting his resignation. But "on the advice of his friends" Sullivan withdrew his letter before this action was taken. See JCC, 5:612–613; Jefferson, *Papers*, ed. Boyd, 1:477–479, and notes and references there.
[3] William Tudor.

Nathan Rice to Abigail Adams

Mrs. Adams   Ticonderoga. July 27th. 1776

When I reflect on that Tranquil State, and agreable Scituation which I was in, while I had the Honour of being one of your Family, and compare it with my present, the Contrast appears so great and my Scituation so widely different, that the Reflection of past Pleasure, raises Desires, unbecomeing the Character of a Soldier; especially one fighting for every thing dear and valuable. Were I to attempt a Description, or Relation, of the Scituation and Sufferings of this Northern Army, Time as well as Words would fail me. Many I trust have been the Reflections which have been cast at us since the Retreat from Quebec, with how much Justice the World must Judge when they know the Circumstances which you in New England did not, if I may jud[g]e from the public Prints, which were filld with the most pompous Accounts of Victories gained by our Army. The Enemy might, and would, had they not been Paltroons, have forced our Army to have raised the Seige of Quebec any Day, the whole of the Winter. After the Defeat on the 31st of Decembr. we could never muster 700 Men fit for Duty: at the Time of the Retreat we could muster scarsely 400, not two Days Provisions in the Stores, nor twenty Rounds of Amunition for our Cannon, which did not exceed Nine Peices, among Inhabitants who were ready to cut our Throats when Opportunity might offer, without Money that would pass. Add to this, the small Pox raging and Destroying, and no Medicines for the Sick. In this Scituation I found our Army, when I came to Canada. Our Regiment (by an Order from Genl. Arnold) were inoculated as were a number of others, at Montreal. In the mean Time Genl. Tho[ma]s died with it. Genl. Sullivan arriving and taking the Command, proceeded to Sorel, 45 Miles from Montreal, with some Troops he brought with him, which joind with some of ours already there made him near four thousand strong; about 2 thousand of them Commanded by Genl. Thomson[1] went down to Three Rivers; to attack the Enemy, but by some bad Conduct proved unsuccessfull, himself being taken with some others by the Treachery of the Canadians. The Regulars soon proceeding up the River, and Genl. Sullivan knowing his weekness thought best to retreat, which he did at the Head of 6000 Men; 3000 and upwards of which were then unable to help themselves, and Nothing for Subsistance but Pork and Flower; very little of the latter. After distroying the Forts left behind; we retreated with all the publick stores, as far as Crown Point over Lake Champlain, 110 Miles: Upon a Council of Wars being holden after the Arrival of Genl. Gates, it was determined we should retreat to Ticonderoga, at the Head of the Lake; where we now are.—That we have been obliged to make this Retreat thro the Neglect of some Man; or Body of Men, is most certain. Whose it is, I shall not pretend to say. This I can say, that the Northern Army has been most scandalously neglected and abused. We have had an Army without Men, Commissarys without Provisions, Pay masters without Money, Conductors of Artilery and Quarter Masters without a Single Article in their Departments. Thus Madam the War in Canada has been carryed on: till we have lost 1400 Men or upwards. Indeed to say the truth such Conduct has made me sick of the Army. I hope however we shall be able to make a Stand where we now are. Our Army is upon the Recovery, trust we shall make a respectable Figure yet. Rejoice to hear of your peaceable State in the Massachusetts—hope you may enjoy it still. My Respects to Mr. Cranches Family, and Friends, Mr. Smiths in particular. Regards to the Gentlemen. Love to your little Folks.

Wishing you all the Happiness possible in the Absence of Mr. Adams, I subscribe myself, with the greatest Respect your very humble Servant, N Rice

RC (Adams Papers); addressed: "To Mrs. Abigail Adams in Braintree New England"; docketed in an unidentified hand.

[1] Brig. Gen. William Thompson of Pennsylvania (Heitman, *Register Continental Army*).

Abigail Adams to John Adams

Boston july 29 1776

I write you now, thanks be to Heaven, free from paine, in Good Spirits, but weak and feeble. All my Sufferings produced but one Eruption. I think I can have no reason to be doubtfull with regard to myself as the Symptoms run so high and my Arm opperated in the best manner. The small pox acts very odly this Season, there are Seven out of our Number that have not yet had it, 3 out of our 4 children have been twice innoculated, two of them Charles and Tommy have not had one Symptom. I have indulged them in rather freer living than before and hope they will not long remain doubtfull. Mrs. Cranch and Cotton Tufts have been in Town almost 3 weeks and have had the innoculation repeated 4 times and can not make it

take. So has Mrs. Lincoln. Lucy Cranch and Billy[1] are in the same
State. Becky Peck who has lived in the same Manner with us, has it
to such a degree as to be blind with one Eye, swell'd prodigiously, I
believe she has ten Thousand. She is really an object to look at; tho
she is not Dr. Bulfinches patient. Johnny has it exa[c]tly as one
would wish, enough to be well satisfied and yet not be troublesome.
We are ordered all the Air we can get, and when we cannot walk we
must ride, and if we can neither walk nor ride, we must be led. We
sleep with windows open all Night, and Lay upon the Carpet or Straw
Beds, Mattrass or any thing hard, abstain from Spirit, Salt and fats,
fruit we Eat, all we can get, and those who like vegetables unseasond
may Eat them, but that is not I.—This doubtfull Buisness is very
dissagreable as it will detain us much longer, but there are several
instances now of persons who thought they had had it, and were recoverd, and lived away freely, and now are plentifully dealt by. Mr.
Joseph Edwards wife for one, and queer work she makes of it you may
be sure. The Doctors say they cannot account for it, unless the free
presperation throws it of[f]. Every physician has a number of patients
in this doubtfull State. Where it does take and the patient lives any
thing free, they have a Doze of it. Cool weather is much fitter for
the small pox. I have not got rid of any terrors of the small pox but
that of not being liable to it again, which you will say is a very great
one; but what I mean is that I should dread it more now than before
I saw it, were I liable to it. If we consider the great numbers who have
it now, computed at seven thousand, 3 thousand of which are from
the Country, tis very favorable, tho not so certain as it was last winter
with many patients. Mr. Shaw who was innoculated at the same time
when I and 3 of my children were out of the same Box, and has lived
lower by his account than we have, has a full portion of it for all of
us. There is no accounting for it. We did not take so much phisick
as many others neither. If this last does not take I shall certainly try
them with some wine.

Dr. Sawyer of Newbury Port lost a child 9 years old last week with
the Distemper, and Coll. Robinson of Dorchester lies extreem bad
with a mortification in his kidneys. Some such instances we must expect among such a variety of persons and constitutions.

I rejoice Exceedingly at the Success which General Lee has met
with. I believe the Men will come along in a short time. They are
raising, but the Massachusets has been draind for Sea Service as well
as land. The Men were procured in this Town last week; we have
taken a vessel from Halifax bound to New York, which we should

call a prize but that it contain about 14 Tories among whom is that infamous Wretch of a Ben Davis the Ginger Bread Robber. How many little ones can say I was an Hungry and you gave me no Bread, but inhumanely took what little I had from me.[2] I wish the Sea or any other Element had them rather than we should be tormented with them. Friends and connexions are very bad things in such times as these. Interest will be made, and impartial Justice obstructed, we catch flies and let the wasps go.—Hark a General Huzza of the populace, these wretches are just committed to jail.

The Continental Troops are near all gone from this Town, all I believe who are in a Marching State. The small pox has been General amongst them and exceeding favourable.

I have requested of Judge Cushing to write you an account of his circut and he has promised to do it.[3] Both he and his Lady are under innoculation. When I came into Town I was in great hopes that if we did well we should be able to return in about 3 weeks, and we should have been able to have effected it, if it had opperated as formerly. Now I fear it will be 5 weeks before we shall all get through but I must not complain. When I cast my eye upon Becky whose Symptoms were not half so high as mine or some of the rest of us, and see what an object she is I am silenced, and adore the Goodness of God towards us.

Her Dr. says she is not dangerous. Col. Warren has sufferd as much pain as I did, but has more to shew for it, he is very cleverly spatterd. Mrs. Warren is now struling with it, to one of her constitution it opperates in faintings and langour. It did so upon Betsy Cranch, yet when it found it[s] way through, it opperated kindly.—I believe you will be tired of hearing of small pox, but you bid me write every post and suppose you are anxious to hear how we have it. The next post I hope to tell you that they all have it, who now remain uncertain.

I am at all times and in all States unfeignedly yours.

RC (Adams Papers); addressed in John Thaxter's hand: "To The Honble: John Adams Esqr. at Philadelphia To be left at the Post Office"; postmarked: "BOSTON 29 IY"; endorsed: "Portia."

[1] This is the first mention, individually, in these letters of William Cranch (1769–1855), Harvard 1787, a nephew of AA who will often be mentioned later and will have his own part in the Adams Family Correspondence. He was to enjoy a long and distinguished career as a federal judge in the District of Columbia and as a reporter of cases in his own court and the U.S. Supreme Court. See Adams Genealogy.

[2] Just what lay behind this remark by AA is not now known. Benjamin Davis Sr. (1729–1805) and his son Benjamin were captured at sea by the armed schooners *Hancock* and *Franklin*. Davis Sr. was a Bostonian, a Sandemanian, and a man of wealth, though in the

List of Addressers of Hutchinson in 1774 he is entered as a "Huckster" of Town Dock. During the siege of Boston he served in the Associated Loyalists. After his capture he remained imprisoned in Boston until June 1777, when he was exchanged and made his way to New York. Proscribed by the General Court in 1778, he settled after the war in Shelburne, N.S., but returned to Boston be-

fore his death. See *Boston Gazette*, 5 Aug. 1776; MHS, *Procs.*, 1st ser., 11 (1869–1870):392; Col. Soc. Mass., *Pubns.*, 5 (1902):269–270; 6 (1904): 126–127; Jones, *Loyalists of Mass.*

[3] Judge William Cushing did so in a letter of this date full of valuable information on the reopening of the Superior Court in Essex co. and the "eastern circuit" in Maine (Adams Papers).

John Adams to Abigail Adams

Philadelphia July 29. 1776

How are you all this Morning? Sick, weak, faint, in Pain; or pretty well recovered? By this Time, you are well acquainted with the Small Pox. Pray how do you like it?

We have no News. It is very hard that half a dozen or half a Score Armies cant supply Us, with News. We have a Famine, a perfect Dearth of this necessary Article.

I am at this present Writing perplexed and plagued with two knotty Problems in Politicks. You love to pick a political Bone, so I will even throw it to you.

If a Confederation should take Place, one great Question is how We shall vote. Whether each Colony shall count one? or whether each shall have a Weight in Proportion to its Numbers, or Wealth, or Exports and Imports, or a compound Ratio of all?

Another is whether Congress shall have Authority to limit the Dimensions of each Colony, to prevent those which claim, by Charter, or Proclamation, or Commission to the South Sea, from growing too great and powerfull, so as to be dangerous to the rest.[1]

Shall I write you a Sheet upon each of these Questions. When you are well enough to read, and I can find Leisure enough to write, perhaps I may.

Gerry carried with him a Cannister for you. But he is an old Batchelor, and what is worse a Politician, and what is worse still a kind of Soldier, so that I suppose he will have so much Curiosity to see Armies and Fortifications and Assemblies, that you will loose many a fine Breakfast at a Time when you want them most.[2]

Tell Betcy that this same Gerry is such another, as herself, Sex excepted.—How is my Brother and Friend Cranch. How is his other Self, and their little Selves. And ours. Dont be in the Dumps, above all Things. I am hard put to it, to keep out of them, when I look at home. But I will be gay, if I can.

Adieu.

RC and LbC (Adams Papers).

¹ On 12 July the committee that had been appointed for the purpose just one month earlier reported John Dickinson's draft of the Articles of Confederation, and it was ordered printed for the exclusive use of the members. On the 22d, Congress, in a committee of the whole, began a debate thereon, which continued at intervals until 20 Aug., when a revised text was submitted and ordered printed for later consideration. See JCC, 5:433, 546–556, 600 ff., 674–689. JA entered minutes of some parts of this debate in his Diary, 25 July–2 Aug., particularly on the question of the territorial claims of certain states (Article XV in the Dickinson draft) and the question of the basis of voting by the states in Congress (Article XVII); see

his *Diary and Autobiography*, 2:241–250. JA's notes of debates are supplemented by Jefferson's for 30 July–1 Aug., which include speeches by JA (Jefferson, *Papers*, ed. Boyd, 1:320–327).

² Gerry not only dawdled on the way home but through a misunderstanding delivered the precious canister of tea to the wrong person, namely Mrs. Samuel Adams, who with much satisfaction served some of it to AA during her stay in Boston. To make matters worse, AA did not receive the present letter until some time in September, so that clarification of the mistake was long delayed. See JA to AA, 5 Sept.; AA to JA, 7 and 20 Sept.; all below.

Abigail Adams to John Adams

July 30 1776

I wrote you by the post, but as Capt. Cuznow [Cazneau] goes to morrow perhaps this may reach [you] first. As to myself I am comfortable. Johnny is cleverly. Nabby I hope has gone thro the distemper, the Eruption was so trifling that to be certain I have had innoculation repeated. Charles and Tommy have neither had Symptoms, nor Eruption. Charles was innoculated last Sabbeth evening a second time, Tommy to Day, the 3 time from some fresh matter taken from Becky Peck who has enough for all the House beside.

This Suspence is painfull. I know not what to do with them. It lengthens out the Time which I can but ill afford, and if they can have it, I know not how to quit till I can get them through. Youth youth is the time, they have no pains but bodily, no anxiety of mind, no fears for themselves or others, and then the Disease is much lighter. The poor Doctor is as anxious as we are, but begs us to make it certain if repeated innoculations will do it. There are now several patients who were innoculated last winter and thought they passd through the Distemper, but have now taken it in the natural way.

Mrs. Cranch and two of her children are in this uncertain State, with a great number of others which I could mention. Tis a pestilence that walketh in Darkness. Mrs. Warren with whom I was yesterday, lay the whole day in a State little better than nonexistance. I greatly feard she would not survive it, but to day she is revived and many pocks appear upon her. But tis a poor Buisness at the best, where I entertaind one terror before, I do ten now. The Season of the year is very unfit for the Distemper, the Tone of every persons vessels are relaxed, very little Spring in the Air, and the medicine too powerfull for weak constitutions.

I hope to be properly thankfull that I and mine are so far so comfortable through—I think I have all my difficulties to Grapple with alone and seperete from my Earthly prop and Support.

I begin to long again for the sweet air of Braintree, and the time to come will be much longer than the time past.

Pray Let Mr. Hancock know that I have availd myself of his kind offer so far as to send for some fruit from his Garden. Every thing here bears such a prize as would surprize you to be told. The Gentery were kind enough to cut down a number of my unkles fruit Trees last winter, and to cut up his Current Bushes, but we have had kind Friends. Mrs. Newall has been exceedingly so.—Pray make my Regards to the presidents Lady and tell her since she baulked me of the wedding cake to which I laid claim by promise, I expect she will remember me upon an other occasion which I hear is like to take place.

O my dear Friend do you know how I feel when I look Back upon a long absence. I look forward with the Thought that the year is but half spent. I often recollect those lines "O ye Gods annialate but time and Space, and make two Lovers happy."

July 31

I have the pleasure to tell you this morning that I think Tommys second innoculation has taken as he was very ill last night and the eruptive fever seems comeing on. Tis ten days since the second.

RC (Adams Papers); endorsed: "Portia," to which was later added the date "July 30. 1776" in the hand of William Gordon(?).

John Adams to Abigail Adams

Philadelphia July 30. 1776 Tuesday

This is one of my fortunate days. The Post brought me, a Letter from you and another from my Friend and Brother.[1]

The particular Account you give me of the Condition of each of the Children is very obliging. I hope the next Post will inform me, that you are all, in a fine Way of Recovery. You say I must tell you of my Health and Situation. As to the latter, my Situation is as far removed from Danger, I suppose, as yours. I never had an Idea of Danger here, nor a single Sensation of Fear. Delaware River is so well fortified with Gallies, fixed and floating Batteries, Chevaux de Frizes, Ships of War, Fire Ships, and Fire Rafts, that I have no Suspicions of an Enemy from Sea, although vast Numbers of People have removed out of this City, into the Country, for fear of one.

By Land, an Enemy must march an hundred Miles, to get here, and they must pass through, Woods, Difiles, and Morasses, besides crossing Rivers, which would take them a long time to accomplish, if We had not a single Man to oppose them. But we have a powerfull Army at New York, and New Jersey, watching their Motions, who will give Us a good Account of their Motions, I presume, whenever they shall think fit to stirr.—My Health has lasted longer than I expected, but with Intermissions of Disorder as usual, and at length, I fear, is departing. Increase of Heat in the Weather, and of Perplexity in Business, if that is possible, have become too much for me. These Circumstances, added to my Concern, for those other Parts of myself in Boston, would certainly have carried me there before now, if I could have got there: But I have no servant, nor Horse.—I am now determined to go home: but the precise Time, I cannot fix. I know not how to go. I have been deliberating whether to go by the stage to New York, and trust to the Chapter of Accidents to get from thence to Boston; or whether to hire, or purchase an Horse here, or whether to get along some other Way, with Coll. Whipple, or Mr. S. Adams. But am still undetermined. If I knew that Bass was at Leisure, and if I knew where you could get Horses, I should request you to send him here, to bring me home. But I dont know what to say. If he should come, he must keep a good look out, and make a strict Enquiry all along the Road, for me, least he should miss me, least I should pass by him on my Way home. After all, I cannot reconcile myself to the Thoughts of staying here so long as will be necessary for a servant and Horses to come for me. I must get along as well as I can by the Stage or by procuring a Horse here.

The Conspiracy, at New York, betrayed the Ignorance, Folly, Timidity and Impotence of the Conspirators, at the same Time, that it disclosed the Turpitude of their Hearts. They had no Plan. They corrupted one another, and engaged to Act, when the Plan should be formed. This they left for an After Consideration. The Tory Interest in America, is extreamly feeble.

Your Successes by Sea, give me great Pleasure, and so did the heartfelt Rejoicings at the Proclamation of Freedom. Mr. Bowdoins Sentiment did him Honour.

Adieu.

RC (Adams Papers). LbC (Adams Papers); at foot of text: "Sent. by post. Saturday. Aug. 3d. inclosed to Mr. Cranch. inclosed Newspapers only to my Wife"; see JA to Cranch, 2 Aug.; the enclosed newspapers have not been found.

[1] AA to JA, 21–22 July, and Richard Cranch to JA, 22 July; both above.

Abigail Adams to John Adams

Boston August 1 1776

I wrote you by Capt. Cazneau a wednesday, but as the post will go to day I will not omit telling you how we do, tho I repeat over what I have written before. If I do you must excuse it as I forget one day what I wrote the day before. This small pox is a great confuser of the mind, I am really put to it to spell the commonest words.

I feel well myself, only much weakened and enfeabled, I want the air of the Country, but cannot yet obtain it. We are bounded in our rides to the Lines which were raised last summer, where a smoak House and Guard are fixed. No person who has had the small pox can go beyond them, under a penalty of [. . .]enty[1] pounds Lawfull money, under a time Limitted and a certificate from their Physician. Every person who comes into Town must be smoaked there upon their return with all their money and papers. Tommy is charmingly, he has about a Dozen out, and many more which just make their appearence. He has been very feverish, but is now so well as to go to School. I gave him a small Quantity of meat every day after his second innoculation till the Symptoms came on. Charles second has taken, I think but cannot be certain till next week.

I Received a wednesday by Mr. Gerry your Letter of july 15. I have not yet seen him to speak to him. I knew him at meeting yesterday some how instinctively; tho I never saw him before. He has not call'd upon me yet. I hope he will, or I shall take it very hard, shall hardly be able to allow him all the merrit you say he possesses. It will be no small pleasure to me to see a person who has so lately seen my best Friend. I could find it in my Heart to envy him.

You complain of me. I believe I was to blame in not writing to you, I ought to have done it. I did not suspect you would hear of my intention till I told you myself. I had many cares upon my hands, many things to do for myself and family before I could leave it. The time granted was only ten days. I got here upon the 6th and then [wrot]e you a very long Letter.[2] Since that I have scarcly omitted a Post, you will have more reason to complain of being tired out; I find the Method of treating the small pox here is similar to that sent by Dr. Rush, except that they use Mercury here. The common Practice here to an Adult is 20 Grains after innoculation. I took but 16; I dont admire this Mercury at this Season of the Year. Loyd I find practicess much more upon Dr. Rushs plan, makes use of the same medicines, but has not had greater success than others.

I greatly rejoice at the Spirit prevailing in the middle colonies. There is a fine company formed in this Town, call'd the independant Company consisting of young Gentlemen of the first families. Their Number is 80, they are the School for forming officers, they take great pains to acquire military Skill and will make a fine figure in a little while. Your Pupil Mason is one. He is an ambitious enterprizing creature and will make a figure some how or other, he always applies to his studies with method and diligence. I have lamented it that you have not been able to take him under your perticuliar care, as I know his abilities would have gratified you.

I Received by the Post a few lines from you july 20. It really greaved me to find you so anxious. Your kindness in so often writing shall be returnd in kind. I know not how you find the time amidst such a multitude of cares as surround you, but I feel myself more obliged by the frequent tokens of your remembrance, but you must not forget that tho my Letters have much less merrit, they have many more words, and I fill all the blank paper you send me. Adieu most affectionately your   Portia

RC (Adams Papers); endorsed: "Portia an. 14. Aug."

[1] MS torn by seal. AA probably wrote "twenty," but this does not square with the pertinent acts passed by the General Court in July; see Mass., *Province Laws*, 5:552–553, 554–555. For the selectmen's regulations see Boston Record Commissioners, *25th Report*, p. 3–5.

[2] Here AA made a characteristic mistake in remembering a date. She had arrived in Boston on 12 July, as her "long Letter" to JA of 13–14 July, above, unequivocally states.

John Adams to Richard Cranch

My dear Sir   Aug. 2. 1776

I received your Favour of 22 July, by last Tuesdays post. I thank you for the Trouble you have taken to inform me of the Circumstances of your Family and my own. It gives me great Joy to think your Symptoms were so favourable.—I had a Letter, from my best Friend by the same Conveyance, which gave me more Pleasure than many Times its Weight in Gold would have done.

You mention the Exultation at a Declaration of Independence. Is not the Change We have seen astonishing? Would any Man, two Years ago have believed it possible, to accomplish such an Alteration in the Prejudices, Passions, Sentiments, and Principles of these thirteen little States as to make every one of them completely republican, and to make them own it? Idolatry to Monarchs, and servility to Aristocratical Pride, was never so totally eradicated, from so many Minds in so short a Time.

I thank you for your Account of the Prizes taken, by our little Fleet. We may judge by a little what a great deal Means. I hope We shall have more Power at sea, before long.

I wish it was in my Power to serve the Interest of Mr. N.C.[1] both for his Merit, services and sufferings. But I dont see, how it will be possible for me to do it. The Appointment of all subordinate Officers in the Quarter Masters and Commissaries Departments is left to the Principals. Promotions of Persons from the Staff Offices, into the Line, gives Disgust, and creates Confusion, if Mr. C's Inclination should lead him to military Preferment. In short there is not the least Probability, that I can see, that any Opportunity will turn Up, in which it will be possible for me to serve him, but if it should I will most chearfully embrace it.—I shall inclose to my other self, some News papers.—Barry has taken another Tender. Another Prize is taken and carried into Egg Harbour, and a Vessell has arrived here with a rich Cargo of Arms, Ammunition, Flints and Lead, and dry Goods from Marseilles. She brings no bad News from France.

Remember me, to the whole Hospital, and all other Friends. Adieu.

RC (Adams Papers); docketed: "Letter from Bror. Adams, when we had the Small Pox. Aug 2d. 1776." LbC (Adams Papers); at foot of text: "Sent by Post Aug. 3d. Saturday." Enclosed newspapers not identified. RC was among those acquired by JQA from William Cranch Greenleaf; see JQA's MS Diary, 21 Sept. 1829.

[1] Nathaniel Cranch. JA mentioned his case to Thomas Mifflin, the quartermaster general, in a letter of 15 Aug. (LbC, Adams Papers).

John Adams to Abigail Adams

Aug. 3. 1776

The Post was later than usual to day, so that I had not yours of July 24 till this Evening. You have made me very happy, by the particular and favourable Account you give me of all the Family. But I dont understand how there are so many who have no Eruptions, and no Symptoms. The Inflammation in the Arm might do, but without these,[1] there is no small Pox.

I will lay a Wager, that your whole Hospital have not had so much small Pox, as Mrs. Katy Quincy. Upon my Word she has had an Abundance of it, but is finely recovered, looks as fresh as a Rose, but pitted all over, as thick as ever you saw any one. I this Evening presented your Compliments and Thanks to Mr. Hancock for his polite offer of his House, and likewise your Compliments to his Lady and Mrs. Katy.

Aug. 4

Went this Morning to the Baptist Meeting, in Hopes of hearing Mr. Stillman, but was dissappointed. He was there, but another Gentleman preached. His Action was violent to a degree bordering on fury. His Gestures, unnatural, and distorted. Not the least Idea of Grace in his Motions, or Elegance in his Style. His Voice was vociferous and boisterous, and his Composition almost wholly destitute of Ingenuity. I wonder extreamly at the Fondness of our People for schollars educated at the Southward and for southern Preachers. There is no one Thing, in which We excell them more, than in our University, our schollars, and Preachers. Particular Gentlemen here, who have improved upon their Education by Travel, shine. But in general, old Massachusetts outshines her younger sisters, still. In several Particulars, they have more Wit, than We. They have Societies; the philosophical Society particularly, which excites a scientific Emulation, and propagates their Fame. If ever I get through this Scene of Politicks and War, I will spend the Remainder of my days, in endeavouring to instruct my Countrymen in the Art of making the most of their Abilities and Virtues, an Art, which they have hitherto, too much neglected. A philosophical society shall be established at Boston, if I have Wit and Address enough to accomplish it, sometime or other.— Pray set Brother Cranch's Philosophical Head to plodding upon this Project. Many of his Lucubrations would have been published and preserved, for the Benefit of Mankind, and for his Honour, if such a Clubb had existed.[2]

My Countrymen want Art and Address. They want Knowledge of the World. They want the exteriour and superficial Accomplishments of Gentlemen, upon which the World has foolishly[3] set so high a Value. In solid Abilities and real Virtues, they vastly excell in general, any People upon this Continent. Our N. England People are Aukward and bashfull; yet they are pert, ostentatious and vain, a Mixture which excites Ridicule and gives Disgust. They have not the faculty of shewing themselves to the best Advantage, nor the Art of concealing this faculty. An Art and Faculty which some People possess in the highest degree. Our Deficiencies in these Respects, are owing wholly to the little Intercourse We have had[4] with strangers, and to our Inexperience in the World. These Imperfections must be remedied, for New England must produce the Heroes, the statesmen, the Philosophers, or America will make no great Figure for some Time.

Our Army is rather sickly at N. York, and We live in daily Expectation of hearing of some great Event. May God almighty grant it may be prosperous for America.—Hope is an Anchor and a Cordial. Disappointment however will not disconcert me.

If you will come to Philadelphia in September, I will stay, as long as you please. I should be as proud and happy as a Bridegroom. Yours.

RC (Adams Papers). LbC (Adams Papers); at foot of text: "Sent. by Post Tuesday, Aug. 6th:"

[1] LbC, more correctly, reads: "that" (referring to the inflammation).
[2] These reflections bore fruit in the founding of the American Academy of Arts and Sciences in 1780. For JA's part in this undertaking see his letters to Benjamin Waterhouse, 7 Aug. 1805 (Ford, ed., *Statesman and Friend*, p. 22–29), and to the editor of the *Boston Patriot*, 31 July 1809 (JA, *Corr. in the Boston Patriot*, p. 159–165).
[3] This word supplied from LbC.
[4] This word supplied from LbC.

Mary Palmer to John Adams

Sir   Germantown August. 4th. 1776

I had the honour of your Letter of the 5th July above a fortnight ago, and should much sooner have acknowledged the favor had not an absolute want of Paper prevented, having none but blank Commissions in the House which we used for little Billets, but wou'd not do to send to the Congress. You do me great honor in receiving my Account of the Evacuation of the Harbour so well. I am sensible it was very imperfect, but it was the best I cou'd do at the time from my informations. One thing I think I greatly err'd in, which was that the Ships did not return the Fire upon Long Island, which I am since inform'd they did by those who were Eye Witnesses. I shou'd not have mention'd it now, but that I am loth that any misinformation of mine shou'd lead to a false Account of a Fact which ought to be represented as it really was, and transmitted to future Ages. Your Compliments are sufficient to make one vain, but still I make Allowances for the Privilege the Gentlemen assume of "flattering the other sex a little." And perhaps it may be tho't necessary sometimes in order to ease us of that Bashful Diffidence so natural to most of us—A Plea for Flattery which I think the Gentlemen much oblig'd to me for. You really make me proud by desiring my future Correspondance, and I will not in hopes of being again ask'd, wholly decline the favour. All I shall say is this, that whenever there is any event of a Public Nature happens of which I can give you a proper Account to the best of my Abilities, it will give me pleasure to do it; but at present there seems little Likelihood of any such in these parts but what will be better told by your good Lady, to whom I shall chearfully resign the Pen on her Recovery from the Small Pox. There is nothing gives Papa much more Concern than his not being able to get time to write to You and Mr. Paine, oftener than he does; It is impossible for one Man to do more than he does, his time is wholly bestow'd on the Publick, both by Day and Night; It is but 3 Days in 2 Years that he has been at Home on his private Affairs, and even part of those 3 Days have been employ'd either in writing Expresses or Planning Forts. Few Gentlemen cou'd say the same. He is now the chief Commander at Hull in the Room of Genll. Lincoln who is innoculated, and very busy every Hour he can steal from Business or Sleep in Planning Fortifications and Salt Works. I am sorry the former are still wanted in our Harbour but every Body is not so Active as Papa, if they were they wou'd not be to be *Plannd* now. I most sincerely thank you for your Present of the Declaration of independancy; nothing cou'd have given me more pleasure. It was universally reciev'd with Joy by the friends of their Country. I dont know what the Tories think but I believe they say nothing. As this is a very important so I hope it may be a very happy Revolution and that the latest Posterity may have Reason to look back to the Year 1776, as the happy Era of their Liberties being secur'd by the Wisdom of the Congress. How pleasing is the reflexion of every true Patriot to be assur'd of having done his duty to his God and Country and of having his Memory rever'd by his Descendants and Countrymen to the End of Time.

The first of this Month was kept as a Day of Fasting and Prayer by this Colony. I hope that our repeated Petitions to the Throne of Grace will be Accepted, and that our unnatural Enemies may be turned from us.

I can say little of your family, only that we hear they are Comfortable. Ours is pretty well, except Miss Paine who has an ill turn, occasion'd by overdoing herself at Work Yesterday. I hope it won't last long but at present she is very ill.—As I don't know but my Letter may find the Way to Staten Island You will excuse my [not][1] putting my Name to it any further than that of Your humble Servt., Myra

RC (Adams Papers).

[1] This word editorially supplied.

Abigail Adams to John Adams

Boston August 5 1776

I this Evening Received Your two Letters of july 10 and 11, and last Evening the Post brought me yours of july 23. I am really astonished at looking over the Number I have received during this month, more I believe than for 3 months before. I hope tis your amusement and relaxation from care to be thus imployed. It has been a feast to me during my absence from Home, and cheerd me in my most painfull Moments. At Last I Hear what I have long expected, and have feard for some time. I was certain that your Nerves must bee new Braced, and your Constitution new moulded, to continue well, through such a load of Buisness. Such intense application, in such a climate through the burning Heats of the Summer, tis too much for a constitution of Steel, and ought not to be required.

I intreat you to return, and that speidily. Mr. Gerry has recoverd his Health and Spirits by his journey. He call'd upon me a few moments. I knew Him by the same instinct by which I first discoverd him, and ventured to call him by Name tho his person was never discribed to me. I cannot account for it but so it was. He appeard a modest Man, and has a fine inteligent Eye. I wanted to ask him many questions which I could not do as he was a stranger, and we had company. He has promised to call upon me again before he returns which he proposes to do in about ten Days.

I have been trying all day to get time to write to you. I am now obliged to Rob my Sleep. Mrs. Cranch, Billy and Lucy are very unwell, all of them with the Symptoms I suppose. Lucy I fear has taken the

Distemper in the natural way, as tis more than 3 weeks since she was innoculated, and her Arm being inflamed deceived us. I took the precaution of having all mine who had not the Symptoms the 9th day innoculated a second time, and I hope they have all pass'd through except Charlly, and what to do with him I know not. I cannot get the small pox to opperate upon him, his Arm both times has been very soar, and he lives freely, that is he eats a small Quantity of meat, and I have given him wine but all will not do. Tommy is cleverly, has about a dozen, and is very gay and happy.

I have abundant reason to be thankfull that we are so many of us carried comfortably through a Disease so formidable in its natural opperation, and though our Symptoms have run high, yet they have been the worst, for the Eruption has been a triffel, really should have been glad to have had them in greater plenty. I hope to be able to return to Braintree the Latter end of next week which will compleat me 5 weeks. I have been unlucky in a Maid, who has not one qualification to recommend her but that she has had the small pox. She has been twice sick since she has been with us, and put us to much difficulty. I have attended publick worship constantly, except one day and a half ever since I have been in Town. I rejoice in a preacher who has some warmth, some energy, some feeling. Deliver me from your cold phlegmatick Preachers, Politicians, Friends, Lovers and Husbands. I thank Heaven I am not so constituted my-self and so connected.

How destitute are they of all those Sensations which sweeten as well as embitter our probationary State! And How seldom do we find true Genious residing in such a constitution, but may I ask if the same temperament and the same Sensibility which constitutes a poet and a painter will not be apt to make a Lover and a Debauchee?

When I reflect upon Humane Nature, the various passions and appetites to which it is subject, I am ready to cry out with the Psalmist Lord what is Man?

You ask me How you shall get Home. I know not. Is there any assistance you can think of that I can procure for you. Pray Let me know. Our Court do not set till the 28 of this month, no delegates can be chosen to releave you till then, but if you are so low in Health do not wait for that. Mr. Bowdoin has the Gout in his Stomack, is very ill. I do not think he could by any means bear close application. Mr. Dana and Mr. Lowell are very good Men, I wish they would appoint them. Our Friend ⟨Warren⟩ has some family difficulties. I know not whether he could possibly leave it. A partner dear to him you know beyond description almost Heart broken, by the Situation of one very dear to *her* whose great attention and care you well know has been to Train them up in the way in which they ought to go. Would to Heaven they did not depart from it. Impaired in Health, impaird in mind, impaird in Morrals, is a Situation truly deplorable, but do not mention the Matter—not even to them by the slightest hint. Tis a wound which cannot be touched.

God grant we may never mourn a similiar Situation, but I have some times the Heartake when I look upon the fire, spirit and vivacity, joind to a comely person in the Eldest, soft, tender and pathetick in the second, Manly, firm and intrepid in the third. I fear less for him, but alass we are short sighted mortals.

> O Blindness to the future kindly given
> that each may fill the circle marked by Heaven.

Adieu dearest Best of Friend[s] adieu.

RC (Adams Papers); addressed in an unidentified hand: "To The Honble: John Adams Esqr. to be left at the Post-Office Philadelphia"; endorsed: "Portia. ansd. 14. Aug."

John Adams to Abigail Adams

Philadelphia August 6. 1776

Yours of 29 July came by this days Post, and made me very happy. Nabby, Charles, and Tommy, will have the small Pox, well, I dont doubt. Tell John he is a very lucky young Gentleman, to have it so much better, than his Mamma, his sister, and Brothers.

Mr. S[amuel] A[dams] will set out for Boston, on Monday, the 12. of August. I shall write by him. But I will not neglect Writing a few Lines by the Post.—I have written a Resignation of my Place here, to the General Court, sometime ago,[1] but it seems, they were adjourned, and therefore will not be able to consider the Matter, untill the 28 of this Month, when they will send some other Person here in my Stead. —How I am to get home I dont know. When I see how Mr. A. goes, I will write you more particularly upon the subject. Whether to hire a Horse here, or to have a Man and two Horses come for me, I am not determined, must leave all undetermined at present. I want the Exercise of a Journey so much, that I must return soon. The General Court will appoint some one to relieve me, I hope,[2] the first Thing they do, after they come together. I shall take it for granted, that they will sett off, accordingly. My Health is so infirm that I can stay no longer.

We are in daily Expectation of some decisive Stroke at N. York. Dunmore has fled from Cheasapeak, and Clinton from Charlestown, and both have joined How, at Staten Island.

RC (Adams Papers). LbC (Adams Papers); at foot of text: "Sent. by Post Aug. 10. 1776. with several Newspapers." Enclosed newspapers not found.

[1] On 25 July; see JA to AA, 11 July, above, and note 3 there. The General Court did not relieve JA, and the military crisis around New York caused him to continue his attendance in Congress until mid-October.

[2] Preceding two words supplied from LbC.

Cotton Tufts to John Adams

Dear Sr.   Weymouth Augt. 6th. 1776

Last Week I received Yours of July the 20th. also Dr. Rushs Letter on Inoculation for which You and the learned and benevolent Dr. have my sincere Thanks.[1] He has thrown much Light upon the Subject and the Simplicity of his Method I admire. The whole Art seems to me to lay in reducing the Body to such a State as to prevent any great Degree of Inflammation or Febrile Motions. An Attention to the Subject must I think convince any Person, that an entire Alteration of the Blood and Juices and the removal of inveterate obstructions is not absolutely necessary to a Persons going thro' the Disorder safely: Indeed where any of the noble organs are unsound, I think it unsafe. It can never be suppos'd that Six or Seven Days Dieting, 30 or 40 Grains of Mercury and 2 or 3 Purges or even Purges administred every Day for that Time, will be sufficient for removing old obstructions that in Common Practice would require Months and perhaps Years—from all which it may be inferd (as People of this Class have it safely) That nothing more is necessary than to discharge from the Body all superfluous Juices and Fluids and especially to free the more open Passages from Impurities.

The Small Pox has this Time (I mean received by Inoculation) provd very untoward in its Operations—not that many have died of it, but the Infection has been extremely slow in its Progress, from Inoculation to Eruption. Many have run from 14 to 16 Days, others as the Physicians aver to 21 Days. Of the last am in doubt, but as it is new to me am seeking for evidence thinking it may be of Importance to have it determined. In 1764 scarce any one exceeded 14 Days and upon a Medium broke out the 10 or 11th. Day. The first Incisions now faild in vast Numbers. Many have been inoculated a first, second and even to the Sixth Time and many after all took it in the natural Way. My Son was inoculated for a 5th. Time after the 20th. Day. Afterwards it was found that his fourth Incision had taken effect. He is now in the Eruptive State.

In my last, wrote about 10 or 15 Days past, I gave You an Accountt of the State of your Family. That wrote the 5th. July You mention the receipt of. Mrs. Adams I suppose did not then write to you ⟨as I expected⟩ being unwell but forwarded mine as deliverd. In my last I believe I mentiond the Recovery of your Family. Mrs. Adams, John and Thomas have *indisputably* gone thro the Distemper and are very well, Nabby and Charles there is some doubt off, and have been re-inoculated. Complaints of the variolous Kind they had, and may possibly be sufficiently securd.

Dr. Bulfinch who inoculated in our Families, out of 13 the first Inoculation faild in 4 or 5 and this has been the Case with other Inoculators in the Town. To what Cause to ascribe it am at a Loss—whether to reducing the Patient too low, to the Season of the Year, to the Age of the Matter or Hurry and Carelessness of the Inoculators—perhaps they may all have their Influence. Indeed should we find the last to be the sole Cause We need not wonder. Messrs. Bulfinch and Jos. Gardner according to the best Information I can obtain have inoculated each 1000 Persons. Think You what Attendance must their Patients have. I have been in Pain for my Friends, and have been with them as much as I could. Multitudes Seven or Eight Days after Inoculation have had their Incisions inflamd—a feverish Turn—some Eruptions—these indeed have died away without filling up—seven or Eight Days or ten after, have had the true Eruptions. Others who supposed that they had gone through with it in this Manner had it afterwards in the natural Way. In short there never was in any Place or among any Physicians such Doubts and Uncertainties with respect to the Eruptions or the Operations of Inoculation. Many are now uncertain whether they have had it after 4 or 5 Weeks stay in Town. It is now 11 at Night, must brake off for the present, propose to Visit our Friends at Boston in the Morning and shall then close my Letter with an Accountt of their State.

7th.

Am now at Boston, find Mrs. Adams, John and Thos. safely through the Disorder. Eruptive Symptoms on Nabby. Charles is free from any Complaints. Mrs. Cranch gone through it very Lightly. Mr. Cranch comfortable with Eruptions, also his Daughter Lucy. Betsy Cranch gone through it. Billy Cranch is in the Doubtful State. My Son well with Eruptions on Him. Jona. Sweetser your Fathers Smiths Boy, has attended upon them ever since they have been in Town (suppos'd to have had it in his Infancy) this Day broke out with it.—Am informd that a Jamaica Vessell with 300 Hhds. Sugar yesterday morning got into Providence taken by our Capt. Chase.—Pray what is Hopkins Fleet about.—Would not our Privateers do service at Newfoundland among the Liverpool Men.

Am Sorry to hear You are out of Health. Wishing You perfect Health & Happiness Am Yr. Friend & H. Servt.

RC (Adams Papers).

[1] Rush's letter, addressed to JA and forwarded by the latter to AA, 23 July, has not been found.

John Adams to Abigail Adams

Aug. 10. 76

Yours of 30. and 31 July was brought me, to day, by Captain Cazneau. I am happy to think that you, and my oldest son, are well through the distemper, and have sufficient Receipts. Nabby, I believe is also through. The Inflammation in her Arm, and the single Eruption, are nearly as much Evidence, as I had to shew—and I have seen [1] Small Pox enough since I had it, to have infected 100 [2] Armies. Tommy, I shall hear by next Post, is happily recoverd of it, I think. Charley, my dear Charley! I am sorry, that it is still pretty clear, that you have not taken it. But never fear, you will have it.

This Suspence and Uncertainty must be very irksome to you. But Patience and Perseverance, will overcome this, as well as all other Difficulties. Dont think of Time, nor Expence. 1000 Guineas is not worth so much as security to a Wife, a good one I mean, and four Children, good ones I mean, against the small Pox. It is an important Event in a Mans Life, to go thro that distemper. It is a very great Thing, for a whole Family, to get well over it.

At the same Time that I am in a State of suspence, Uncertainty and Anxiety about my best, dearest, worthyest, wisest Friend, in this World, and all my Children, I am in a State of equal Suspence, Uncertainty, and Anxiety about our Army at N. York and Ticonderoga, and consequently about our Country and Posterity. The Lives of Thousands, and the Liberties of Millions are as much in Suspence, as the Health of my family. But I submit to the Governance of infinite Wisdom.

Had my Advice been followed, in Season, We should now have been in Safety, Liberty and Peace, or at least We should have had a clear and indisputable Superiority of Power. But my Advice was not regarded. It never was, and never will be, in this World. Had N.Y., N.J. and Pensilvania, only been in compleat Possession of the Powers of Government only 3 Months sooner, We should have had an Army, at N.Y. and Amboy, able to cope with double the Number of our Enemies. But now We trust to Chance: to the Chapter of Accidents: a long Chapter it is, as long as the 119 Psalm: and well it is for us that it is so. If We trusted to Providence, I should be easy, but We do not.

I have now come to a Resolution, upon another Subject, which has kept me in suspence for some Time.—I must request of you, to interceed with your Father to procure for me, two Horses, and send them to Philadelphia, with a servant, as soon as possible. I shall wait for their Arrival, let it be sooner or later. The sooner they come, the more agreable to my Wishes, and the better for my Health. I can live no longer, without Riding. If Bass is in the land of the living, and[3] is willing to take one more Ride with his old Friend, let him come, if he declines, send somebody else. I shall wait for Horses. If the Congress should adjourn, I shall attend the Board of War, untill they come. The General Court, I think might do something. Whether they have ever thought of granting me, a farthing, for my Time, I know not. Mr. A. had an Horse and a fine Chaise, furnished him, by the Committee of Supplies. Perhaps they might furnish me with a Pair of Horses too.[4]—Pray mention this to Coll. Warren or Coll. Palmer.—If nothing can be done by them, if I have Credit enough left, to hire two Horses and a servant, let it be employed. The Loss of my fine Mare, has disconcerted me. The General Court will send some Gentleman here to take my Place. But if my Horses come I shall not wait for that.

RC (Adams Papers). LbC (Adams Papers); at foot of text: "Sent. by Mr. S.A." Written in considerable agitation, the two versions of this letter differ in many details of phrasing, but only a few of these are noted here.

[1] LbC adds: "and smelled."
[2] LbC: "500."
[3] Preceding eight words supplied from LbC.
[4] LbC adds here and then deletes: "But I will say nothing."

Nathan Rice to Abigail Adams

Mrs. Adams   Ticonderoga August. 11th. 1776

Inclosd I send you a Copy of General Carltons Orders of the 7th. Instant, which we received by Major Biggelow of Connecticut, who was sent by the Genl. the 28th. ult: with the Resolutions of Congress, concerning the Carteel stipulated by Genl. Arnold, at the Cedars, which was, not to *ratify* it, unless they would deliver up Capt. Foster and those Officers who were present and suffered the Savages to Murder the Prisoners in cool Blood.[1] The Flagg arrived, and after a Stay of a few Days, (in which Time was treated with Politeness) was dispached, with a Party commanded by Capt. Fraizer [Frazier], to escort him over the Lake.

The Capt. delivered him a Letter, subscribed to George Washington Esqr. He not knowing the Resolution of Congress in that Respect, altho he greatly disliked the Superscription, says "I can take it," at the same Time, the Capt. gave him the inclosed with the Letter, saying that is for you. But Major Biggelow very discreetly refused it.—The Captain insisted on the Majors going with him, putting a Sergt. with the Flagg Boat, whom they had furnished with a Number, and who distributed them to the Men. Thus we have it, cut and dried, an End to Truces. Mr. How, however was more [agreea]ble[2] and wished a more free Intercourse with our [army?].

Now for the Assassination mentioned.—One Lieutenant Whitcomb, in our Army an old Indian Hunter, was sent on a Scout, and if possible to get a Prisoner. His Party which was four, by some means all left him, one Deserted to the Enemy. In the Character of a french Peasant he visited them, after the Desertion however he had like to have been taken, before he left the Place, he discovered an Officer riding by, as he lay conceald in the Bushes, and considering him as his enemy and being accustomed to such Things, having also a great fancy for his Watch and Sword as he says, he fired upon him. Not killing him Dead on the Spott, he was obliged to make his Escape. It proved to be no less than Brigadr. Genl. Gordon, who received two Balls in his Shoulder of which Wound he died next Day. This se[ems] rather Murder, but it is treating them on[ly] in their own Way.

The Malitia are comeing in fast, but am a little surprised they receive such Bounty for no longer Time, and the Continental Army to pay it who have never received any and born the whole.

I am with the greatest Respect your humble Sert.,   N Rice

RC (Adams Papers); addressed: "To Mrs. Abigail Adams   Braintree N England." Enclosure (Adams Papers): copy, in Rice's hand, of Gen. Sir Guy Carleton's orders, "Chamblee," 7 Aug. 1776, prohibiting, on account of the recent "Assassination" of Brig. Gen. Patrick Gordon, all emissaries and messages from "Traitors in Arms against their King"; see, further, note 1.

[1] The events alluded to here and below were sequels to the surrender, in May, by an officer Thomas Jefferson called "The scoundrel, Major [Isaac] Butterfield," of a body of New Hampshire troops at The Cedars, some forty miles above Montreal. Gen. Arnold marched to their rescue, but too late, and was obliged to sign an ignominious cartel in order to prevent further butchery among the captives by the Indians serving with Capt. George Forster, the British officer to whom Butterfield had surrendered. Congress investigated the affair, rejected in part the cartel, and sent Maj. John Bigelow to inform Carleton and Burgoyne. The reply, directed to Washington and supposedly from Carleton but bearing the marks of Burgoyne's style, contained the orders of which a copy was enclosed in the present letter. Rice gives details on both this transaction and the waylaying of Gordon by an American scout within the British lines that are not available in other accounts. See JCC, 5:420, 446, 454–458, 468, 475, 533–539 (text of Congress' report and resolutions on the cartel), 601, 695; Jefferson, *Papers*, ed. Boyd, 1:396–404, 459–460; Washington, *Writings*, ed. Fitzpatrick, 5:465–467.

[2] Here and below, MS is torn by seal.

Abigail Adams to John Adams

[Boston, ca. 12 August 1776] [1]

Yours 30 of July reachd me by Saturdays post, and found me with Johnny and Tommy quite Recoverd from the small Pox. When I first came to Town I was made to believe that the small pox was a very light disorder, and one might pass through it with little or no complaints. Some such instances no doubt there are, and Light it is in comparison of the Natural way, or what it formerly was. As I never saw the disease before I have with those much more experienced been deceived in it now.

Nabby was the first person who had complaints of our number, hers came on about the 8th day attended with a voilent pain in a tooth which she had which was defective. She was cold and shivery, then a voilent Heat insued; the doctor supposed it the Symptoms of the disorder, a day or two after she had 3 Eruptions upon one of her Eyes. I thought it did not appear like what I had seen which they calld small pox, however I submitted my judgment to those who knew better. But when I found some who were innoculated at the same time failing, I requested the dr. to innoculate her again. Symptoms she has had very severely and very diffirent from what she had before and small pox in plenty, she can reckon 500 allready. She is cleverly only soar, I am much better satisfied now, and we rejoice when we can reckon a hundred. I believe I mentiond to you my Aunts Little Daughter having recoverd of it, but there again we were deceived, the child has been ill these 3 Days and now is broke out with small pox.— Here I have been a month Last fryday, and for ought I see must be for this fortnight to come. I have broke through my resolution of not having Charles innoculated again. I saw I must tarry for Nabby long enough to make an other trial upon him, and have accordingly done it.—We clear of some this week. Sister Betsy and her Neice, Mr. Tufts, Betsy Cranch and Johnny are going tomorrow. My affairs at home which for 3 weeks I laid asleep, wake up now, and make me anxious to get there. I fear they will go to ruin. My Expences here too for so long atime will be much more than I expectd for I thought to be at home in a month at furthest.—Lucy Cranch who I mentiond having taken the Distemper in the Natural Way is cleverly—pretty full and large.—And now about your returning. I am shut up here, and wholly unable to do that for you, which I might endeavour to if I was at home, and then the fate of your poor horse which I must ever lament makes it necessary to procure two Horses and a very great Scarcity there are. I think I should advice you if you could light of a good Horse, to procure one there, as you will stand in need of one when you return.

A prize was brought in here Last Saturday with 400 Hogsheads of Sugar, 300 of rum and 400 Bags of cotton taken by one White in Capt. Darbys [Derby's] employ and is the 7th taken by him within these ten days.

Mrs. Temple was here to see me a few days past and requested me to make mention of her case to you, and to desire you to render her all the assistance you can. Said she would write to you and state the Situation she was in. She wrote once to the president but had no reply.[2]

I close to send by the Post rejoiceing in the Prospect I have of soon seeing you. Ever yours.

RC (Adams Papers); endorsed: "Portia."

[1] JA in his reply of 20 Aug., below, supposed this letter was written "about the Twelfth." He was undoubtedly right because AA says herein that she has been in Boston "a month Last fryday" —meaning Friday, 9 Aug., which was four weeks after she had arrived there, Friday, 12 July.

[2] Mrs. Temple's "case" recurs in both the family and the general correspondence of the Adamses. She was Harriet, daughter of the late Gov. William Shirley and wife of Robert Temple (d. 1784), of Ten Hills Farm, the original estate of the Winthrops on the Mystic River in Charlestown (Thomas B. Wyman, *The Genealogies and Estates of Charlestown*, Boston, 1879, 2:938; Mayo, *Winthrop Family*, p. 144). Her husband's politics were ambiguous; he had left Boston for England in 1775, but was at this moment in New York

endeavoring to return home, which with the permission of Gen. Howe, Gen. Washington, and the Continental Congress, he soon did. (See JA to AA, 20 Aug., below; Washington, *Writings*, ed. Fitzpatrick, 5:447; Sabine, *Loyalists*, 2:349; Rowe, *Letters and Diary*, p. 319.) In a letter to JA dated at Ten Hills, 10 Aug. 1776, Mrs. Temple described her "distrest Situation," pointed out that "many Persons in this Province have been paid for thier Trees [cut down for the use of the Continental forces] as Cord Wood," and requested a like indulgence to her (Adams Papers). JA promptly presented her case to Congress, 23 Aug. (JCC, 5:699), and on the 28th Congress "*Resolved*, That, upon the said Harriot's producing to the quarter master general, an account of the trees which were cut down upon the farm of Robert Temple, Esqr. for the purpose of supplying the continental army with wood for firing, or for the purposes of fortification, so far as from the nature of the circumstances such destruction can be ascertained by her, that the quarter master general of the continental army, shall make her a just compensation for the same, in such manner as other persons have been paid, who have supplied the army with wood for these purposes; and that the quarter master general, in his accounts, shall be allowed for the same by this Congress" (same, p. 713).

But long delays followed. On 23 April 1778 James Bowdoin (whose daughter Elizabeth was the wife of Robert Temple's brother John) addressed to his friend Washington a strong plea for action on this claim because Ten Hills was "in so ruined a state, that it will require a great length of time, and great expence upon it to put it in a condition to answer the purpose of supporting [Temple's] family" (MHS, *Colls.*, 6th ser., 9 [1897]:415). On 27 Feb. 1779 Temple himself submitted a memorial to Congress saying that the conditions in Congress' resolve of 1776 had been met on his part but the claim had not been paid (PCC, No. 41, X). Action now followed speedily. The memorial was committed on the same day, and on 6 March, in a most interestingly itemized report, which Congress adopted, Temple was allowed, and the quartermaster general ordered to pay him, £6702 for the destruction of his fruit and timber trees, fences, and farm and wharf buildings, less £2500 already paid him by Massachusetts, or £4202, equal to \$14,006⅔ (JCC, 13:260, 288–289). This was, however, in inflated currency, and Temple in the following year gave up the struggle, sold Ten Hills, and sailed with his family to England. "The Day before yesterday Mr. Robert Temple with all his family, even to the *Cat*, arrived here in 32 Days from Boston; he had disposed of all his property, real and personal, in that Country, and is come, as he says, to lay his bones in England or Ireland" (Jonathan Sewall to Isaac Smith Jr., Bristol, 25 Aug. 1780, MHi:Smith-Carter Papers). He died in Dublin, leaving his wife and three daughters (Robert C. Winthrop Jr., "Account of the Family of Robert Temple," MHi:Fenton Papers, under date of 8 Jan. 1894).

John Adams to Abigail Adams

Aug. 12. 76

Mr. A. setts off, to day, if the Rain should not prevent him, with Coll. Whipple of Portsmouth: a Brother of the celebrated Miss Hannah Whipple, a sensible and worthy Man. By him I have sent you two Bundles of Letters, which I hope you will be carefull of. I thought I should not be likely to find a safer opportunity. By them, you will see that my private Correspondence alone, is Business enough for a lazy Man. I think I have answered all but a few of those large Bundles.

A french Vessell, a pretty large Brigantine, deeply loaden, arrived here yesterday from Martinique. She had 50 Barrells of Limes, which are all sold already, at such Prices, that the Amount of them will be sufficient to load the Brig with Flour. A Trade We see, even now, in the midst of summer is not totally interrupted, by all the Efforts of our Enemies. Prizes are taken in no small Numbers. A Gentleman told me a few days ago that he had summed up the sugar, which has been taken, and it amounted to 3000 Hdds. since which two other ships have been taken and carried into Maryland.

Thousands of schemes for Privateering are afloat in American Imaginations. Some are for taking the Hull ships, with Woolens for Amsterdam and Rotterdam—some are for the Tin ships—some for the Irish Linnen ships—some for outward Bound and others for Inward Bound India Men—some for the Hudsons Bay ships—and many for West India sugar ships. Out of these Speculations many fruitless and some profitable Projects will grow.

We have no News from New York. All is quiet there as yet. Our Expectations are raised—the Eyes of the World are upon Washington and How, and their Armies. The Wishes and Prayers of the virtuous Part of it, I hope, will be answerd. If not, yet Virtues grow out of Affliction.

I repeat my request, that you would ask some of the Members of the G[eneral] Court if they can send me Horses, and if they cannot that you would send them. I can live no longer without a servant, and a Horse.

RC (Adams Papers). LbC (Adams Papers); at foot of text: "Sent. by Coll Whipple."

John Adams to Abigail Adams

Aug. 12 76

Mr. A. and Coll. Whipple, are at length gone. Coll. Tudor went off with them. They went away, about Three o Clock this afternoon. I wrote by A and Coll. Whipple too. By the latter I sent two large Bundles, which he promised to deliver to you.

These middle States begin to taste the Sweets of War. Ten Thousand Difficulties and wants occur, which they had no Conception of before. Their Militia are as clamorous, and impatient of Discipline, and mutinous as ours, and more so. There has been seldom less than four Thousand Men in this City at a Time, for a fortnight past on their March to New Jersey. Here they wait untill We grow very angry, about them, for Canteens, Camp Kettles, Blanketts, Tents, Shoes, Hose, Arms, Flints, and other Dittoes, while We are under a very critical Solicitude for our Army at New York, on Account of the Insufficiency of Men.

I want to be informed of the State of Things with you. Whether there is a Scarcity of Provisions of any Kind, of West India Articles, of Cloathing. Whether any Trade is carried on, any Fishery. Whether any Vessells arrive from abroad, or whether any go to sea, upon foreign Voyages.

I wish to know likewise, what Posture of Defence you are in. What Fortifications are at Nantaskett, at Long Island, Petticks Island &c. and what Men and Officers there are to garrison them. We hear nothing from the Massachusetts, lately, in Comparason of what We did, when the Army was before Boston.

I must not conclude without repeating my Request, that you would ask some of the Members of the General Court to send me Horses— and if they cannot, to send them yourself.

RC (Adams Papers). LbC (Adams Papers); at foot of text: "Sent. by Post Tuesday. Aug. 13."

John Adams to Abigail Adams

Philadelphia Aug 13. 1776

Geography is a Branch of Knowledge, not only very usefull, but absolutely necessary, to every Person of public Character whether in civil or military Life. Nay it is equally necessary for Merchants.

America is our Country, and therefore a minute Knowledge of its Geography, is most important to Us and our Children.

The Board of War are making a Collection of all the Maps of America, and of every Part of it, which are extant, to be hung up in the War Office. As soon as the Collection is compleated, I will send you a List of it. In the mean Time take an Account of a few already collected and framed and hung up in the Room.

A Chart of North and South America, including the Atlantic and Pacific Oceans, with the nearest Coasts of Europe, Africa, and Asia.[1]

A Map of the British and French Dominions in North America with the Roads, Distances, Limits and Extent of the Settlements, humbly inscribed to the right Honourable the Earl of Hallifax and the other Right Honourable the Lords Commissioners for Trade and

Plantations, by their Lordships most obliged and very humble servant John Mitchell.[2]

A Map of the most inhabited Part of New England, containing the Provinces of Massachusetts Bay, and New Hampshire, with the Colonies of Konektikut and Rhode Island, divided into Counties and Townships: The whole composed from actual Surveys and its Situation adjusted by Astronomical Observations.[3]

A new and accurate Map of North America, drawn from the famous Mr. D'Anville, with Improvements from the best English Maps, and engraved by R. W. Seale: Also the new Divisions according to the late Treaty of Peace, by Peter Bell Geo[graphe]r—printed for Carington Bowles, Map and Printseller No. 69 in St. Pauls Church Yard, London, published 1. Jany. 1771.[4]

To the Honourable Thomas Penn and Richard Penn Esquires, true and absolute Proprietaries and Governors of the Province of Pensilvania, and the Territories thereunto belonging, and to the Honourable John Penn Esqr., Lieutenant Governor of the same, This Map of the Province of Pensilvania, is humbly dedicated by their most obedient humble servant W. Scull.[5]

A General Map of the Middle British Colonies, in America, vizt. Virginia, Maryland, Delaware, Pensilvania, New Jersey, New York, Connecticutt and Rhode Island, of Aquanishuonigy the Country of the Confederate Indians, comprehending Aquanishuonigy proper, their Place of Residence: Ohio and Tïiuxsoxruntie their Deer Hunting Countries, Couxsaxrage and Skaniadarade their Beaver Hunting Countries: of the Lakes Erie, Ontario, and Champlain, and of Part of New France, wherein is also shewn the ancient and present Seats of the Indian Nations. By Lewis Evans 1755. Dedicated to T. Pownal Esqr. whom Evans calls the best Judge of it in America.[6]

To the Honourable Thomas Penn and Richard Penn Esqrs. true and absolute Proprietaries and Governors of the Province of Pensilvania and Counties of New Castle, Kent and Sussex on Delaware. This Map of the improved Part of the Province of Pensilvania is humbly dedicated by Nicholas Scull.[7]

You will ask me why I trouble you with all these dry Titles, and Dedications of Maps.—I answer, that I may turn the Attention of the Family to the subject of American Geography.—Really, there ought not to be a State, a City, a Promontory, a River, an Harbour, an Inlett, or a Mountain in all America, but what should be intimately known to every Youth, who has any Pretensions to liberal Education. I am.

N.B. Popples Map is not mentioned here, which was dedicated to

Queen Ann, and is recommended by Dr. Hawley.[8]—It is the largest I ever saw, and the most distinct. Not very accurate. It is Eight foot square.—There is one in the Pensilvania State House.[9]

RC and LbC (Adams Papers). LbC contains two paragraphs (the final two) not in RC, but their omission was almost certainly unintentional, and they have accordingly been printed here as part of the text even though they were not received by AA.

[1] A map in six sheets by Thomas Jefferys, London, 1753; entered in P. Lee Phillips, *A List of Maps of America in the Library of Congress*, Washington, 1901, p. 109.

[2] First published by Jefferys & Faden, London, 1755; in Phillips, *List of Maps*, p. 573.

[3] By John Green, but published without his name by Carington Bowles, London, 1771; in Phillips, *List of Maps*, p. 470.

[4] In Phillips, *List of Maps*, p. 583.

[5] First published in Philadelphia for the author, 1770; in Phillips, *List of Maps*, p. 674.

[6] Published in Philadelphia and London; in Phillips, *List of Maps*, p. 575.

[7] First published in Philadelphia, 1759; in Phillips, *List of Maps*, p. 673. Text of RC ends with this paragraph; remainder taken from LbC.

[8] Unidentified; perhaps this is a misspelling or slip of the pen.

[9] Henry Popple's *Map of the British Empire in America with the French and Spanish Settlements Adjacent Thereto*, London [1732?], with subsequent issues, in twenty folio sheets with an index map as the 21st sheet; see Phillips, *List of Maps*, p. 108; Sabin 64140.

Abigail Adams to John Adams

Boston August 14 1776[1]

Mr. Smith call'd upon me to day and told me he should set out tomorrow for Philadelphia, desired I would write by him.[2] I have shewn him all the civility in my power since he has been here, tho not all I have wished too. Our Situation and numerous family as well as sick family prevented our asking him to dine. He drank tea with us once and Breakfasted once with us. I was much pleasd with the account he gave us of the universal joy of his province upon the Establishment of their New Government, and of the Harmony subsisting between every branch of it. This State seems to be behind hand of their Neighbours. We want some Master workmen here. Those who are capable seem backward in this work and some who are so tenacious of their own perticuliar plan as to be loth to give it up. Some who are for abolishing both House and Counsel, affirming Buisness was never so well done as in provincial Congress, and they perhaps never so important.

Last Sunday after Service the Declaration of Independence was read from the pulpit by order of Counsel. The Dr.[3] concluded with asking a Blessing upon the united States of America even untill the final restitution of all things. Dr. Chancys [Chauncy's] address pleasd me. The Good Man after having read it, lifted his Eyes and hands to Heaven—God Bless the united States of America, and Let all the People say Amen. One of His Audiance told me it universally struck them.

I have no News to write you, I am sure it will be none to tell you that I am ever yours, Portia

RC (Adams Papers); addressed in an unidentified hand: "To The Honble. John Adams Esqr. Philadelphia favr. Mr. Smith"; endorsed: "Portia. ans. Aug. 28."

[1] This date is suspect; probably it should be 15 August. See note 1 on the following letter.

[2] This was Benjamin Smith of South Carolina; see JA to AA, 17 May, above, and 21, 28 Aug., below.

[3] Samuel Cooper.

Abigail Adams to John Adams

August 14 1776[1]

I wrote you to day by Mr. Smith but as I suppose this will reach you sooner, I omitted mentioning any thing of my family in it.

Nabby has enough of the small Pox for all the family beside. She is pretty well coverd, not a spot but what is so soar that she can neither walk sit stand or lay with any comfort. She is as patient as one can expect, but they are a very soar sort. If it was a disorder to which we could be subject more than once I would go as far as it was possible to avoid it. She is sweld a good deal. You will receive a perticuliar account before this reaches you of the uncommon manner in which the small Pox acts, it bafels the skill of the most Experience'd here. Billy Cranch is now out with about 40, and so well as not to be detaind at Home an hour for it. Charlly remains in the same state he did.

Your Letter of August 3 came by this days Post. I find it very conveniant to be so handy. I can receive a Letter at Night, sit down and reply to it, and send it of in the morning.

You remark upon the deficiency of Education in your Countrymen. It never I believe was in a worse state, at least for many years. The Colledge is not in the state one could wish, the Schollars complain that their professer in Philosophy is taken of by publick Buisness to their great detriment.[2] In this Town I never saw so great a neglect of Education. The poorer sort of children are wholly neglected, and left to range the Streets without Schools, without Buisness, given up to all Evil. The Town is not as formerly divided into Wards. There is either too much Buisness left upon the hands of a few, or too little care to do it. We daily see the Necessity of a regular Goverment.— You speak of our Worthy Brother.[3] I often lament it that a Man so peculiarly formed for the Education of youth, and so well qualified as he is in many Branches of Litrature, excelling in Philosiphy and the Mathematicks, should not be imployd in some publick Station. I know not the person who would make half so good a Successor to Dr. Winthrope. He has a peculiar easy manner of communicating his Ideas to Youth, and the Goodness of his Heart, and the purity of his morrals without an affected austerity must have a happy Effect upon the minds of Pupils.

If you complain of neglect of Education in sons, What shall I say with regard to daughters, who every day experience the want of it. With regard to the Education of my own children, I find myself soon out of my debth, and destitute and deficient in every part of Education.

I most sincerely wish that some more liberal plan might be laid and executed for the Benefit of the rising Generation, and that our new constitution may be distinguished for Learning and Virtue. If we mean to have Heroes, Statesmen and Philosophers, we should have learned women. The world perhaps would laugh at me, and accuse me of vanity, But you I know have a mind too enlarged and liberal to disregard the Sentiment. If much depends as is allowed upon the early Education of youth and the first principals which are instilld take the deepest root, great benifit must arise from litirary accomplishments in women.

Excuse me my pen has run away with me. I have no thoughts of comeing to P[hiladelphi]a. The length of time I have [and][4] shall be detaind here would have prevented me, even if you had no thoughts of returning till December, but I live in daily Expectation of seeing you here. Your Health I think requires your immediate return. I expected Mr. Gerry would have set off before now, but he finds it perhaps very hard to leave his Mistress—I wont say harder than some do to leave their wives. Mr. Gerry stood very high in my Esteem— what is meat for one is not for an other—no accounting for fancy. She is a queer dame and leads people wild dances.[5]

But hush—Post, dont betray your trust and loose my Letter.

Nabby is poorly this morning. The pock are near the turn, 6 or 7 hundred boils are no agreable feeling. You and I know not what a feeling it is. Miss Katy can tell. I had but 3 they were very clever and fill'd nicely. The Town instead of being clear of this distemper are now in the height of it, hundreds having it in the natural way through the deceitfulness of innoculation.

Adieu ever yours. Breakfast waits. Portia

RC (Adams Papers); endorsed: "Portia ans. Aug. 25."

[1] This letter was written on more than one day, since there is an earlier letter of the same day, preceding, and yet at the end AA says that "Breakfast waits." Moreover, AA says in her letter of the 17th, below, that she "wrote" (i.e. sent?) JA "two Letters yesterday," and so probably the present letter was actually written on 15–16 Aug. and sent by post on Friday the 16th.

[2] John Winthrop was Hollis professor of mathematics and natural philosophy at Harvard, but he was also a member of the Massachusetts Council and had other public duties.

[3] Richard Cranch.

[4] MS: "I."

[5] Gerry's "Mistress" of the moment was Catherine, daughter of Squire John Hunt, Harvard 1734, a Watertown storekeeper, distiller, excise collector, and sometime representative in the General Court, on whom see Sibley-Shipton, *Harvard Graduates*, 9:414–418. According to the gossipy recollections of Mrs. Royall Tyler (the former Mary Hunt Palmer), her grandfather John Hunt believed that "girls knew quite enough if they could make a shirt and a pudding," and so Catherine and her sisters were never taught to read or write. This proved a handicap to Catherine in her affair with Elbridge Gerry, who was a notable man with a pen and addressed long letters to her from Congress which she could neither read nor answer. Gerry eventually married a New York girl, and Catherine Hunt "lived and died at Watertown an old maid," a victim of "Grandpa's system of female education." See *Grandmother Tyler's Book*, p. 7, 9, 13–14.

John Adams to Abigail Adams

Philadelphia 14. August 1776

This is the Anniversary of a memorable day, in the History of America: a day when the Principle of American Resistance and Independence, was first asserted, and carried into Action.[1] The Stamp Office fell before the rising Spirit of our Countrymen.—It is not impossible that the two *gratefull* Brothers may make their grand Attack this very day: if they should, it is possible it may be more glorious for this Country, than ever: it is certain it will become more memorable.

Your Favours of August 1. and 5. came by Yesterdays Post. I congratulate you all upon your agreable Prospects. Even my pathetic little Hero Charles, I hope will have the Distemper finely. It is very odd that the Dr. cant put Infection enough into his Veigns, nay it is unaccountable to me that he has not taken it, in the natural Way before now. I am under little Apprehension, prepared as he is, if he should. I am concerned about you, much more. So many Persons about you, sick. The Children troublesome—your Mind perplexed— yourself weak and relaxed. The Situation must be disagreable. The Country Air, and Exercise however, will refresh you.

I am put upon a Committee to prepare a Device for a Golden Medal to commemorate the Surrender of Boston to the American Arms, and upon another to prepare Devices for a Great Seal for the confederated States. There is a Gentleman here of French Extraction, whose Name is Du simitiere, a Painter by Profession whose Designs are very ingenious, and his Drawings well executed. He has been applied to for his Advice. I waited on him yesterday, and saw his Sketches. For the Medal he proposes Liberty with her Spear and Pileus, leaning on General Washington. The British Fleet in Boston Harbour, with all their Sterns towards the Town, the American Troops, marching in.[2] For the Seal he proposes. The Arms of the several Nations from whence America has been peopled, as English, Scotch, Irish, Dutch, German &c. each in a Shield. On one side of them Liberty, with her Pileus, on the other a Rifler, in his Uniform, with his Rifled Gun in one Hand, and his Tomahauk, in the other. This Dress and these Troops with this Kind of Armour, being peculiar to America—unless the Dress was known to the Romans. Dr. F[ranklin] shewed me, yesterday, a Book, containing an Account of the Dresses of all the Roman Soldiers, one of which, appeared exactly like it.

This Mr. Du simitiere is a very curious Man. He has begun a Collection of Materials for an History of this Revolution. He begins with the first Advices of the Tea Ships. He cutts out of the News-papers, every Scrap of Intelligence, and every Piece of Speculation, and pastes it upon clean Paper, arranging them under the Head of the State to which they belong and intends to bind them up in Volumes. He has a List of every Speculation and Pamphlet concerning Independence, and another of those concerning Forms of Government.[3]

Dr. F. proposes a Device for a Seal. Moses lifting up his Wand, and dividing the Red Sea, and Pharaoh, in his Chariot overwhelmed with the Waters.—This Motto. Rebellion to Tyrants is Obedience to God.

Mr. Jefferson proposed. The Children of Israel in the Wilderness, led by a Cloud by day, and a Pillar of Fire by night, and on the other Side Hengist and Horsa, the Saxon Chiefs, from whom We claim the Honour of being descended and whose Political Principles and Form of Government We have assumed.

I proposed the Choice of Hercules, as engraved by Gribeline in some

Editions of Lord Shaftsburys Works. The Hero resting on his Clubb. Virtue pointing to her rugged Mountain, on one Hand, and perswading him to ascend. Sloth, glancing at her flowery Paths of Pleasure, wantonly reclining on the Ground, displaying the Charms both of her Eloquence and Person, to seduce him into Vice. But this is too complicated a Group for a Seal or Medal, and it is not original.[4]

I shall conclude by repeating my Request for Horses and a servant. Let the Horses be good ones. I cant ride a bad Horse, so many hundred Miles. If our Affairs had not been in so critical a state at N. York, I should have run away before now. But I am determined now to stay, untill some Gentleman is sent here in my Room, and untill my Horses come. But the Time will be very tedious.

The whole Force is arrived at Staten Island.

RC and LbC (Adams Papers).

[1] For the events in Boston on 14 Aug. 1765, which put an end to any possibility of carrying out the Stamp Act in Massachusetts, see JA, *Diary and Autobiography*, 1:259–261.

[2] It was JA who, on 25 March, had proposed that a medal be presented to Washington for his victory at Boston (JCC, 4:234). For Congress' action, Du Simitière's sketches, and the long-delayed result, see JA, *Diary and Autobiography*, 3:xii, 375–376, and the illustrations facing p. 257; also Jefferson, *Papers*, ed. Boyd, 16:xxxvi, 69–70, and No. I among the illustrations of medals following p. 52.

[3] These materials gathered and compiled by the Swiss-born artist and antiquary Pierre Eugène Du Simitière survive at least in part among the portion of his papers now in the Library of Congress. Other papers and miscellanies of his are calendared in Historical Records Survey, *Descriptive Catalogue of the Du Simitière Papers in the Library Company of Philadelphia*, Phila., 1940. See also Hans Huth, "Pierre Eugène Du Simitière and the Beginnings of the American Historical Museum," *PMHB*, 69:315–325 (Oct. 1945).

[4] On 4 July Congress had voted that Franklin, JA, and Jefferson "be a committee, to bring in a device for a seal for the United States of America" (JCC, 5:517–518). Somewhat variant versions of Franklin's, Jefferson's, and Du Simitière's proposals, together with the committee's report of 20 Aug., prepared by Jefferson, are printed in Jefferson, *Papers*, ed. Boyd, 1:494–497. It is there pointed out that, the report being at once tabled, it was not revived until 1780, when another committee tried but failed to satisfy Congress, and that not until June 1782 was the Seal of the United States, essentially in the form we know it, adopted. Du Simitière's pencil sketch for the obverse, with the motto *E Pluribus Unum* (which JA does not mention but which is almost all that survived in 1782 from the various proposals of 1776), is illustrated in same, facing p. 550. See also Gaillard Hunt, *The History of the Seal of the United States*, Washington, 1909.

JA's proposal for the design of the seal, though it was put forward diffidently and came to nothing, was a revealing and interesting one. The Greek fable of the Choice (or Judgment) of Hercules between Virtue and Vice (or Pleasure) was a popular theme for painters in the 18th century, in part, certainly, because the Earl of Shaftesbury had devoted to it a short but influential treatise on esthetics in the third volume of his *Characteristicks* as collected in 1714. Simon Gribelin's engraving of the allegory is reproduced as an illustration in the present volume from the fifth edition of the *Characteristicks*, printed by Baskerville, Birmingham,

1773. JA's own copy of this edition re- Public Library. See Descriptive List of
mains among his books in the Boston Illustrations.

Abigail Adams to John Adams

Boston, August 17 1776

Tho I wrote you two Letters yesterday [1] one by the Post and one by Mr. Smith, yet I will not omit this by your Worthy Friend Mr. Gerry who has promised to drink tea with me this afternoon; I admire his modesty and his annimatd countanance.

I hope this will meet you upon your return to New england, where I assure you I think you are wanted. If you get back before the last of this month you will be soon enough to attend the Superiour Court if you chuse it which is to sit in your own Town.

As to news we go on Briskly taking prizes. We have a plenty of Sugars. Within these ten days Sugars have fallen from 4 pounds to 3 and 2.8 by the hundred. A Brigg was carried into Newburry this Week, from Antigue laiden with Indigo and hides, and a Jamaca Man carried into Marble Head. Our Men the new Leavies have marched for Canada. Isaac [Copeland] who lived with us is gone as one. I this day Received a Letter from Mr. Rice dated july 27 from Ticondoroga, he give much the same account that you did in a former Letter to me. Their Sufferings have been great indeed. The True Source of these Evils ought to be searched out, and the foul streams cleansed.

As to our Hospital to day, Nabby has not been out of her chamber these 3 Days, neither can she stand or sit her foot to the floor. She has above a thousand pussels as larg as a great Green Pea. She is the Dr. says in a good way tho tis hard to make her think so. Charles complains some to day. I hope tis the Symptoms. I have had a Seige of it, I long for the compaign to be over.

I have really wrote you so much this week that I have little or nothing worth saying or telling you. I have not time to enter upon any subject which requires attention, and can only add that I am ever yours, Portia

RC (Adams Papers); addressed in an unidentified hand: "To the Honble. John Adams Esqr. at Philadelphia. (Pr. Favr. of Mr. Geary)"; endorsed: "Portia Aug. 17. 1776."

[1] That is, *sent* two letters yesterday—those dated 14 Aug., above, but probably written on the 15th and 16th.

John Adams to Abigail Adams

Philadelphia August 18. 1776

My Letters to you are an odd Mixture. They would appear to a Stranger, like the Dish which is sometimes called Omnium Gatherum. This is the first Time, I believe that these two Words were ever put together in Writing. The litteral Interpretation of them, I take to be "A Collection of all Things."[1] But as I said before, the Words having never before been written, it is not possible to be very learned in telling you what the Arabic, Syriac, Chaldaic, Greek and Roman Commentators say upon the Subject.

Amidst all the Rubbish that constitutes the Heap, you will see a Proportion of Affection, for my Friends, my Family and Country, that gives a Complexion to the whole. I have a very tender feeling Heart. This Country knows not, and never can know the Torments, I have endured for its sake. I am glad they never can know, for it would give more Pain to the benevolent and humane, than I could wish, even the wicked and malicious to feel.

I have seen in this World, but a little of that pure flame of Patriotism, which certainly burns in some Breasts.[2] There is much of the Ostentation and Affectation of it.[3] I have known a few who could not bear to entertain a selfish design, nor to be suspected by others of such a Meanness. But these are not the most respected by the World. A Man must be selfish, even to acquire great Popularity. He must grasp for himself, under specious Pretences, for the public Good, and he must attach himself to his Relations, Connections and Friends, by becoming a Champion for their Interests, in order to form a Phalanx, about him for his own defence; to make them Trumpeters of his Praise, and sticklers for his Fame, Fortune, and Honour.

My Friend Warren, the late Governor Ward, and Mr. Gadsden, are three Characters in which I have seen the most generous disdain of every Spice and Species of such Meanness. The two last had not great abilities, but they had pure Hearts. Yet they had less Influence, than many others who had neither so considerable Parts, nor any share at all of their Purity of Intention. Warren has both Talents and Virtues beyond most Men in this World, yet his Character has never been in Proportion. Thus it always is, has been, and will be.

Nothing has ever given me, more Mortification, than a suspicion, that has been propagated of me, that I was actuated by private Views, and have been aiming at high Places. The Office of C[hief] J[ustice] has occasioned this Jealousy, and it never will be allayed, untill I resign it. Let me have my Farm, Family and Goose Quil, and all the Honours and Offices this World has to bestow, may go to those who deserve them better, and desire them more. I covet them not.[4]

There are very few People in this World, with whom I can bear to converse. I can treat all with Decency and Civility, and converse with them, when it is necessary, on Points of Business. But I am never happy in their Company. This has made me a Recluse, and will one day, make me an Hermit.

I had rather build stone Wall upon Penns Hill, than be the first Prince in Europe, the first General, or first senator in America.

Our Expectations are very high of some great Affair at N. York.

RC (Adams Papers). LbC (Adams Papers); at foot of text: "Sent. by Post Aug. 20th." LbC contains several revealing revisions and cancellations that are indicated in the notes below.

[1] *OED* cites this passage (from JA-AA, *Familiar Letters*) for the "Dish" JA alludes to, whatever it may have been; but the expression had been used in other senses in England since at least early in the 16th century.

[2] In LbC JA first wrote "which I feel burning in my own Breast," and then revised his phrasing to read as in RC.

[3] LbC here adds a sentence which JA did not cancel but which, intentionally or unintentionally, he did not copy into RC: "There is a great Deal of Selfishness under the Masque and Disguise of it."

[4] LbC here adds the following passage which is there scratched out and was not copied into RC:
"I have been wounded, more deeply than I have been willing to acknowledge, more deeply than the World suspects, by the Conduct of those Persons, who have been joined with me, here. The sordid Meanness of their Souls, is beneath my Contempt. One of them covers as much of it, as ever disgraced a mortal, under the most splendid Affectation of Generosity, Liberality, and Patriotism.—I have acted in Conjunction with such Characters, while it was

necessary to do so, but when that Necessity ceases, I will renounce them forever.—I had rather shut myself up in the Cell of an Hermit, and bid adieu to the human Face, than to live in Society, with such People."

There can be no doubt that in writing this passage which he immediately and very prudently decided not to entrust to the post, JA had John Hancock primarily in mind and, to a lesser extent, Robert Treat Paine. At this date these two men were his only fellow delegates in attendance at Congress, and they had differed with him on one if not both of the two current "Bones of Contention" in Congress, namely whether Gen. David Wooster and Commodore Esek Hopkins should be censured for their conduct. These questions had been decided on the days just preceding the writing of this letter, but only after bitter debates in which JA had defended both officers. See JA to Samuel Adams, 18 Aug. (NN:Bancroft Coll., printed in Burnett, ed., *Letters of Members*, 2: 53–54, but perhaps not accurately); JCC, 5:658–659, 661–662, 664–665; JA, *Diary and Autobiography*, 3:382, 406, 408–409.

Abigail Adams to John Adams

Monday August 18 [*i.e.* 19], 1776[1]

I set down to write you a few lines by the post, because I would not omit one opportunity. I received yours of August 6 but cannot tell what to do for you confined as I am here. I shall know what you would have me do by Mr. A when he returns. At present all my attention is taken up with the care of our Little Charles who has been very bad. The Symptoms rose to a burning fever, a stupifaction and delirium ensued for 48 hours. The Doctor attended him as tho he had been his own child. He has the Distemper in the natural way. A most plentifull Eruption has taken place. Tho every thing has been done to lessen it that could, his face will be quite coverd, many if not all will run together. He is yet a very ill child, tho his Symptoms are lessend.

I would not have allarmed you. I hope he is not dangerous, but we cannot tell the Event. Heaven grant it may be favorable. I will write you by wedensday Post. I shall see then how he is like to be, and can form a better judgment of Him.—Nabby is Cleverly. They are turning fast upon her; and she can walk to day with borrowing my Shooes and Stockings. Adieu the Post will leave me. Dont forget my Herbs for your own sake as well as mine.—Ever yours.

RC (Adams Papers); addressed in an unidentified hand: "To the Honble. John Adams Esqr. at Philadelphia"; postmarked: "FREE N*York, Aug. 26"; endorsed: "Portia. ans. 27."

[1] This Monday fell on the 19th.

Abigail Adams to John Thaxter

Dear Sir   Boston August 20 1776

My Little Charles has been so ill that I have not had leisure to day to thank you for your obliging favour[1] nor for the present which accompanied it, all of which were very acceptable to us.

After 3 innoculations he has to be sure taken the distemper in the natural way. He has been exceeding ill, stupid and delirious for 48 hours. An exceeding high fever and most plentifull Eruption has succeeded. He will be as full as Miss Becky. You may easily think what a trial it will be both to him and me.

You may think yourself exceeding well of to have had the distemper so lightly. I have had many anxietys about you, and could not help blameing myself for consenting to your going so soon least you should be favour with a second crop, or give the distemper to some of your family, but I hope their is no danger now of either.

All the rest of our Hospital are recoverd, or in a good way. I wish it may be so with Charles, but the poor fellow has several very troublesome Days to pass through if he does well at last. Indeed this Small Pox is no triffel, and we cannot be sufficiently thankfull to our Great Preserver that we are carried so well through so malignant a disease.

You inquire after Mr. Adams. I need not say to you that I rejoice at his return, tho I am sorry for the occasion, but I have long expected it. Inclosed to you is a Letter which will give you a more perticuliar account. You may keep it (till we see each other), to yourself, as the contents will not be agreable to others.

Pray present my Duty to your Worthy Parents and Love to your flock of Sisters not forgeting your Brother. Mr. Cranch and family go out a fryday. I shall be left alone. I long for the day to come when my imprisonment will be over and we can rejoice together at Braintree. Believe me dear sir at all times your affectionate Friend,

Abigail Adams

RC (MB); addressed: "To: Mr. John Thaxter junr Hingham." Enclosure not found, but very likely it was one of JA's recent letters telling of his poor health and his determination to return home.

[1] Not found.

John Adams to Abigail Adams

Philadelphia August 20. 1776

Yours without a Date, but written, as I suppose about the Twelfth of August came by the Post this Morning. I wish Mrs. Nabby Joy that she has at last a Receipt in full. This is much better than to be in doubt. Charles! never fear, Charles! you will have it yet, and as good a Receipt as any of them.

The Drs. cannot account for the numerous Failures of Inoculation. I can. No Phisician has either Head or Hands enough to attend a Thousand Patients. He can neither see that the Matter is good, nor that the Thread is properly covered with it, nor that the Incision is properly made, nor any Thing else. I wish you had taken Dr. Tufts for your Phisician and no other. I never liked your Man, and I like him now less than ever. I wish you had all come to Philadelphia, and had the Distemper here. Then I should not be uneasy about getting

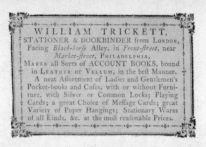

1. TRADE CARD OF JOHN ADAMS' PHILADELPHIA STATIONER
See page vii

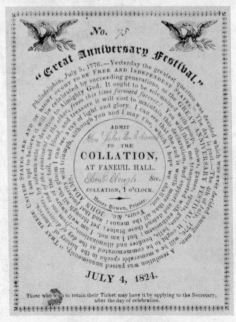

2. "YESTERDAY THE GREATEST QUESTION WAS DECIDED"
See page vii

4. THE HOWES' RECONCILIATION BROADSIDE
See page viii

3. THE BILLOPP HOUSE, STATEN ISLAND
See page viii

In Congress, September 16, 1776.

RESOLVED, That eighty-eight Battalions be inlisted as soon as possible, to serve during the present War, and that each State furnish their respective Quotas in the following Proportions, viz.

New-Hampshire	3 Battalions.
Massachusetts-Bay	15 Ditto.
Rhode-Island	2 Ditto.
Connecticut	8 Ditto.
New-York	4 Ditto.
New-Jersey	4 Ditto.
Pennsylvania	12 Ditto.
Delaware	1 Ditto.
Maryland	8 Ditto.
Virginia	15 Ditto.
North-Carolina	9 Ditto.
South-Carolina	6 Ditto.
Georgia	1 Ditto.

That Twenty Dollars be given as a Bounty to each non-commissioned Officer and private Soldier, who shall inlist to serve during the present War, unless sooner discharged by Congress.

That Congress make Provision for granting Lands in the following Proportions to the Officers and Soldiers who shall so engage in the Service, and continue therein to the Close of the War, or until discharged by Congress; and to the Representatives of such Officers and Soldiers as shall be slain by the Enemy; Such Lands to be provided by the United States, and whatever Expence shall be necessary to procure such Land, the said Expence shall be paid and borne by the States in the same Proportion as the other Expences of the War, viz.

To a	
Colonel,	500 Acres.
a Lieutenant-Colonel	450 Ditto.
a Major	400 Ditto.
a Captain	300 Ditto.
a Lieutenant	200 Ditto.
an Ensign	150 Ditto.

Each non-commissioned Officer and Soldier 100 Acres.

That the Appointment of all Officers and filling up Vacancies (except general Officers) be left to the Governments of the several States, and that every State provide Arms, Cloathing, and every Necessary for its Quota of Troops, according to the foregoing Estimate; the Expence of the Cloathing to be deducted from the pay of the Soldiers as usual.

That all Officers be commissioned by Congress.

That it is recommended to the several States that they take the most speedy and effectual Measures for raising their several Quotas. That the Mustry to be given for Bounties be paid by the Paymaster in the Department where the Soldier shall inlist.

That each Soldier receive Pay and Subsistence from the Time of their Enlistment.

September 18, 1776.

RESOLVED, That if Rations be not issued to the Officers or Privates in the Continental Army in Money, they be paid in Money at the Rate of Ninety-ninth Parts of a Dollar per Ration.

That the Bounty and Grants of Land, offered by Congress by a Resolution of the 16th instant as an Encouragement to the Officers and Soldiers to engage to serve in the Army of the United States during the War, shall extend to all who are or shall be enlisted for that Term; the Money which such Officers and Soldiers have received from Congress, on account of a former Enlistment, to be reckoned in part Payment of the Twenty Dollars offered by said Resolution.

That no Officer in the Continental Army is allowed to hold more than one Commission, or to receive Pay but in one Capacity.

That the Adjutant of Regiments in the Continental Army be allowed the Pay and Rations of a Captain, and that the other Officers, &c.

RESOLVED, That this Congress will not grant Lands to any Person or Persons claiming under the Allegiance of an Officer or Soldier.

By Order of the Congress,

JOHN HANCOCK, President.

6. JOHN ADAMS' PLAN FOR A MILITARY ESTABLISHMENT IN 1776

See page x

TREATISE VII.

VIZ.

A NOTION of the Historical Draught or Tablature

OF THE

JUDGMENT of HERCULES,

According to PRODICUS, Lib. II. Xen. de Mem. Soc.

Potiorà

HERCULIS ærumnas credit, sævosque Labores,
Et Venerej, & cœnis, & pluma SARDANAPALI.
Juv. Sat. 10.

Paulo de Matthæis Pinx.   Sim Gribelin Sculpsit.

Printed first in the Year M.DCC.XIII.

5. THE "CHOICE OF HERCULES," PROPOSED BY JOHN ADAMS FOR THE GREAT SEAL

See page ix

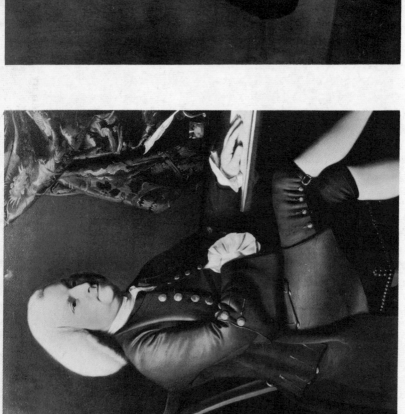

7 · ISAAC SMITH SR. IN 1769, BY JOHN SINGLETON COPLEY
See page x

8 · DR. COTTON TUFTS IN 1804, BY BENJAMIN GREENLEAF
See page xi

home.—I beg Pardon for this Flight about your Dr. I may have done him Wrong. But am afraid you have suffered from his being of rather too much Importance, in the present Scarcity of Phisicians.

With Regard to my Health, as the extream Heat of the Weather has abated, I am better than I was, but not well. I am so comfortable however, as to be determined to wait for a servant and Horses. Horses are so intollerably dear, at this Place, that it will not do for me to purchase one, here. And our Representation is so thin, that it will not do for me to leave this Place, untill another comes in my Room.

I have received a very polite Letter from Mrs. Temple, which I shall answer by the next Post.[1] I wish that something may be done for her Relief, but it will be attended with such Difficulties, that I can promise nothing. I have the Pleasure of congratulating her upon Mr. Temples Arrival. Congress was informed of it, two days ago by the General, and I suppose by this Time, he is on his Way to Ten Hills.

Lord Howe seems afraid to attack and has got to the old Work of Amusement and Chicanery. But he cannot catch old Birds. They are aware of the snare.

RC (Adams Papers). LbC (Adams Papers); at foot of text: "Sent. by Post. Aug. 23d."

[1] Harriet (Shirley) Temple to JA, 10 Aug. 1776 (Adams Papers). See AA to JA, ca. 12 Aug., above, and note 2 there; also JA to Mrs. Temple, 21 Aug. (LbC, Adams Papers).

John Adams to Abigail Adams

Philadelphia August 21. 1776

Yesterday Morning I took a Walk, into Arch Street, to see Mr. Peele's Painters Room. Peele is from Maryland, a tender, soft, affectionate Creature....[1] He shewed me a large Picture containing a Group of Figures, which upon Inquiry I found were his Family. His Mother, and his Wifes Mother, himself and his Wife, his Brothers and sisters, and his Children, Sons and Daughters all young. There was a pleasant, a happy Chearfulness in their Countenances, and a Familiarity in their Airs towards each other.[2]

He shewed me one moving Picture. His Wife, all bathed in Tears, with a Child about six months old, laid out, upon her Lap. This Picture struck me prodigiously.

He has a Variety of Portraits—very well done. But not so well as Copeleys Portraits. Copeley is the greatest Master, that ever was in America. His Portraits far exceed Wests.

Peele has taken General Washington, Dr. Franklin, Mrs. Washington, Mrs. Rush, Mrs. Hopkinson. Mr. Blair McClenachan and his little Daughter in one Picture. His Lady and her little son, in another.

Peele shewed me some Books upon the Art of Painting, among the rest one by Sir Joshua Reynolds, the President of the English Accademy of Painters, by whom the Pictures of General Conway and Coll. Barry [Barré] in Fanuil Hall were taken.

He shewed me too a great Number of Miniature Pictures, among the rest Mr. Hancock and his Lady—Mr. Smith, of S.C. whom you saw the other day in Boston—Mr. Custis, and many others.

He shewed me, likewise, Draughts, or rather Sketches of Gentlemen's Seats in Virginia, where he had been—Mr. Corbins, Mr. Pages, General Washingtons &c.

Also a Variety of rough Drawings, made by great Masters in Italy, which he keeps as Modells.

He shewed me, several Imitations of Heads, which he had made in Clay, as large as the Life, with his Hands only. Among the Rest one of his own Head and Face, which was a great Likeness.

He is ingenious. He has Vanity—loves Finery—Wears a sword—gold Lace—speaks French—is capable of Friendship, and strong Family Attachments and natural Affections.

At this shop I met Mr. Francis Hopkinson, late a Mandamus Councillor of New Jersey, now a Member of the Continental Congress, who it seems is a Native of Philadelphia, a son of a Prothonotary of this County who was a Person much respected. The son was liberally educated, and is a Painter and a Poet.

I have a Curiosity to penetrate a little deeper into the Bosom of this curious Gentleman, and may possibly give you some more particulars concerning him.... He is one of your pretty little, curious, ingenious Men. His Head is not bigger, than a large Apple—less than our Friend Pemberton or Dr. Simon Tufts.[3] I have not met with any Thing in natural History much more amusing and entertaining, than his personal Appearance. Yet he is genteel and well bred, and is very social.

I wish I had Leisure, and Tranquility of Mind to amuse myself with these Elegant, and ingenious Arts of Painting, Sculpture, Statuary, Architecture, and Musick. But I have not. A Taste in all of them, is an agreable Accomplishment.

Mr. Hopkinson has taken in Crayons, with his own Hand, a Picture of Miss Keys, a famous New Jersey Beauty. He talks of bringing it to Town, and in that Case I shall see it, I hope.

RC (Adams Papers). LbC (Adams Papers); at foot of text: "Sent. by Post Aug. 23."

¹ Here and below, suspension points are in MS.

² The thirteen portraits by Peale mentioned by JA in this letter correspond to the following entries in Charles Coleman Sellers, *Portraits and Miniatures by Charles Willson Peale*, Phila., 1952, and six of them are illustrated therein: No. 617, Peale Family (see Illustration 66); No. 645, "Rachel Weeping" (see illustration 49); No. 896, George Washington (see Illustration 354); No. 278, Benjamin Franklin; No. 953, Martha Washington (see Illustration 374); No. 760, Mrs. Benjamin Rush (see Illustrations 89, 90);

No. 387, Mrs. Francis Hopkinson (see Illustration 86); No. 509, Blair McClenachan and Daughter; No. 510, Mrs. Blair McClenachan and Son; No. 351, John Hancock; No. 353, Mrs. John Hancock; No. 804, Benjamin Smith of South Carolina (said by Sellers to be Robert Smith, but see note 3 on JA to AA, 17 May, above, and also JA to AA, 28 Aug., below); No. 170, John Parke Custis.

³ Simon Tufts (1727–1786), Harvard 1744, AA's cousin and an elder brother of Cotton Tufts; he was a physician in Medford. See Adams Genealogy.

Abigail Adams to John Adams

Boston August 22 1776

Yours of August 12 came to hand by last Nights post.¹ Mr. A[dams] and Coll. W[hipple] are not yet returnd so that I know not what you have wrote by them, but by your Letter of this date I suppose tis something relative to your Return. I shall this morning in consequence of your Letter write to Mr. Bass who I make no doubt will be very ready to come for you. I shall write to my Father to request of him that he would endeavour to procure for you a couple of Horses. I shall try some other Friends and will fix of ² Bass as soon as tis possible to procure Horses for you.

As to the other matters you desired to be informed of, at present I am not capable of acquainting [you] any further than that I do not believe we have a 100 men as soldier[s] in this Town. I now and then see a scattering one, but the Militia are not yet come in. Fort Hill is a Beautiful peice of work, I am told not Eaquel to Dorchester. There are about 15 or 20 fine large peices of cannon mounted with Ball &c. by the side of them. We have spaird 700 Barrels of powder to N.Y. We have 600 left as publick Stores. What force we have else where I know not. I have inquired but find every person I have asked as Ignorant as I am. I can learn more in one hour from General Palmer relative to the state of things than I can from all the rest of the persons I converse with and yet I have inquired of those who I think ought to know.

I hear General L[incol]n is appointed in the room of W[ar]d. Has he Spirit enough, has he activity, has he ambition enough for the place?—I will endeavour to be informd of all you inquire about and write you the best account I can. As to applying to ———³ for

Horses, I remember the old proverb, he who waits for dead mens shooes may go barefoot. It would only lengthen out the time, and we should be no better of, than before I askd. I will have them if they are to be had at any price, and they may pay for them. I think you have done your part. I am told that they will appoint somebody to releave you but will not release you.

As to one article you ask about I can tell you we have no scarcity of provisions. In Town upon account of the small pox they are very dear. Ever since june there has been no want of rain and as great a vegatition as was ever known. I have been in Town six weeks yesterday.[4] Charlly is better. He is exceeding full, but the little creature is as patient as a Lamb. We carry him out into the air all we can, in the Height of dog days a very bad time for small pox; but we think he will do well. I hope to be able to get Home by the Last of Next Week.

I shall rejoice exceedingly.

Nabbys are most all turnd and going of. She looks speckled.

I am in great Haste, Mr. Cranch and family leave me tomorrow. I will write by mondays post. Adieu ever Yours,   Portia

RC (Adams Papers); addressed in an unidentified hand: "To The Honble: John Adams Esqr; in Philadelphia"; endorsed: Portia   ans. Aug. 30."

[1] His second letter of that date, above.
[2] Thus in MS, meaning prep..re and send off, dispatch.
[3] JA had suggested that AA might apply to "some of the Members of the General Court."

[4] A mistake. The date of the present letter appears to be correct, but AA's sixth week in Boston (since Friday, 12 July) was not completed until Friday, 23 August.

Abigail Adams to John Adams

Boston August 25 1776

I sent Johnny last Evening to the Post office for Letters. He soon returnd and pulling one from under his Gown gave it me, the young Rogue smiling and watching Mammas countanance draws out an other, and then an other, highly gratified to think he had so many presents to bestow.

Our Friends are very kind. My Father sends his Horse and Dr. Tufts has offerd me an other one he had of unkle Q[uinc]y about 5 year old. He has never been journeys, but is able enough. Mr. Bass is just come, and says he cannot sit out till tomorrow week without great damage to his Buisness. He has been a long time out of Stock, and about a week ago obtain a Quantity and has engaged 20 pair of shooes which will be eaquel to 20 Dollors to him, which he must losse if I will not consent to his tarrying till then. Tho I urged him to sit of tomorrow, yet the Horses will be in a better State as they will not be used and more able to perform the journey. I am obliged to consent to his tarrying till then when you may certainly expect him.

Bass is affraid that the Drs. Horse will not be able to travel so fast as he must go. He will go and see him, and in case he is not your Brother has promised to let one of his go. I only have to regret that I did not sooner make trial of my Friends, and have sent for you 3 weeks ago. I fear you will think me neglegent, and inatentive. If I had been at Home, I should have been sooner in a capacity to have assisted you. I was talking of sending for you and trying to procure horses for you when little Charles who lay upon the couch coverd over with small Pox, and nobody knew that he heard or regarded any thing which was said, lifted up his head and says Mamma, take my Dollor and get a Horse for Pappa. Poor fellow has had a tedious time of it as well as I, but tis now upon the turn, and he is much easier, and better. I hope I shall be able to get out of Town a Saturday next.

Mr. and Mrs. Cranch with their children went out a fryday. I feel rather lonely. Such a change from 1 or 2 and twenty to only 5 or 6 is a great alteration. I took the Liberty of sending my complements to General Lincoln and asking him some questions which you proposed to me, but which I was really unable to answer, and he has promised me a perticuliar reply to them.[1]

As to provisions there is no Scarcity. Tis true they are high, but that is more oweing to the advanced price of Labour than the Scarcity. English Goods of every kind are not purchasable, at least by me. They are extravagantly high, West india articles are very high all except Sugars, which have fallen half since I came into Town. Our New England Rum is 4 Shillings pr. Gallon, Molasses the same price. Loaf Sugar 2s. 4d. pr. pound, cotton wool 4 Shillings pr. pound, sheeps wool 2 Shillings, flax 1 & 6. In short one hundred pound two year ago would purchase more than two will now.

House Rent in this Town is very low. Some of the best and Genteelest houses in Town rent for 20 pounds pr. year. Ben Hollowell [Hallowell's] has been offerd for 10. and Mr. Shurdens [Chardon's] for 13 6 & 8 pence.

The privateer Independance which saild from Plymouth about 3 weeks ago has taken a jamaca man laiden with Sugars and sent her into Marblehead last Saturday. I hear the Defence has taken an other.

I think we make a fine hand at prizes.

Coll. Q[uinc]y desires me to ask you whether you have received a Letter from him, he wrote you some time ago.[2]

I like Dr. F[ranklin's] device for a Seal. It is such a one as will please most—at least it will be most agreable to the Spirit of New england.

We have not any news here—anxiously waiting the Event, and in daily Expectation of hearing tidings from New york. Heaven Grant they may be Glorious for our Country and Country men, then will I glory in being an American. Ever ever Yours,   Portia

PS We are in such want of Lead as to be obliged to take down the Leads from the windows in this Town.

RC (Adams Papers); endorsed: "Portia Aug. 25, 1776."

[1] AA's letter of inquiry to Benjamin Lincoln has not been found, but Lincoln responded directly to JA in a long letter from Boston, 24 Aug. (Adams Papers), concerning the fortifications and the state of supplies and troops in and around Boston.

[2] There is a long, unsigned letter from Col. Josiah Quincy to JA, Braintree, 13–25 June, in Adams Papers, to which no answer has been found.

John Adams to Abigail Adams

Philadelphia August 25. 1776

The day before Yesterday and Yesterday, We expected Letters and Papers by the Post, but by some Accident, or Mismanagement of the Riders, no Post is arrived yet, which has been a great Disappointment to me. I watch, with longing Eyes for the Post, because you have been very good of late in writing by every one. I long to hear, that Charles is in as fair a Way, thro the Distemper as the rest of you.

Poor Barrell is violently ill, in the next Chamber to mine, of an inflammatory Fever. I hear every Cough, Sigh, and Groan. His Fate hangs in a critical Suspence, the least Thing may turn the Scale against him. Miss [Katharine] Quincy is here, very humanely employed in nursing him. This Goodness does her Honour.

Mr. Paine has recovered of his illness, and by present Appearances, is in better Health than before. I hope it will not be my Fate to be sick here. Indeed I am not much afraid of these acute Disorders, mine are more chronical, nervous, and slow.—I must have a Ride. I cannot make it do without it.

We are now approaching rapidly to the autumnal Æquinox, and no great Blow has yet been struck, in the martial Way, by our Enemies nor by Us. If We should be blessed this Year, with a few Storms as happy as those which fell out last Year, in the Beginning of September, they will do much for Us. The British Fleet, where they now lie, have not an Harbour, so convenient, or safe, as they had last Year. Another Winter will do much for Us too. We shall have more and better Soldiers. We shall be better armed. We shall have a greater Force at Sea. We shall have more Trade. Our Artillery will be greatly increased, our Officers will have more Experience, and our Soldiers more Discipline—our Politicians more Courage and Confidence, and our Enemies less Hopes. Our American Commonwealths will be all compleatly form'd and organized, and every Thing, I hope, will go on, with greater Vigour.

After I had written thus far the Post came in and brought me, your Favour of the 14 of August.[1] Nabby, by this Time, I conclude is well, and Charles I hope is broke out. Dont you recollect upon this occasion, Dr. Biles's Benediction to me, when I was innoculated? As you will see the Picquancy of it, now more than ever you could before, I will tell the Story.

After having been 10 or 11 days innoculated, I lay lolling on my Bed, in Major Cunninghams Chamber, under the Tree of Liberty, with half a Dozen young Fellows as lazy as my self, all waiting and wishing for Symptoms and Eruptions. All of a sudden, appeared at the Chamber Door, the reverend Doctor, with his rosy Face, many curled Wigg, and pontifical Air and Gate. I have been thinking, says he, that the Clergy of this Town, ought upon this Occasion, to adopt the Benediction of the Romish Clergy, and, when we enter the Apartments of the sick, to cry, in the foreign Pronunciation *"Pax tecum."* These Words are spoken by foreigners as the Dr. pronounced them *Pox take 'em.* One would think that Sir Isaac Newton's Discovery of the system of Gravitation did not require a deeper reach of Thought, than this frivolous Pun.[2]

Your Plan of making our worthy Brother, Professor, would be very agreable to me.

Your Sentiments of the Importance of Education in Women, are exactly agreable to my own. Yet the Femmes Scavans, are contemptible Characters. So is that of a Pedant, universally, how much soever of a male he may be. In reading History you will generally observe, when you light upon a great Character, whether a General, a Statesman, or Philosopher, some female about him either in the Character of a Mother, Wife, or Sister, who has Knowledge and Ambition above the ordinary Level of Women, and that much of his Emminence is owing to her Precepts, Example, or Instigation, in some shape or other.

Let me mention an Example or two. Sempronius Gracchus, and Caius Gracchus, two great tho unfortunate Men, are said to have been instigated to their great Actions, by their Mother, who, in order to stimulate their Ambition, told them, that she was known in Rome by the Title of the Mother in Law of Scipio, not the Mother of the Gracchi. Thus she excited their Emulation, and put them upon reviving the old Project of an equal Division of the conquered Lands, (a genuine republican Measure, tho it had been too long neglected to be then practicable,) in order to make their Names as illustrious as Scipios.

The great Duke, who first excited the Portuguese to revolt from the Spanish Monarchy, was spurred on, to his great Enterprize by a most artfull, and ambitious Wife. And thus indeed you will find it very generally.

What Tale have you heard of Gerry? What Mistress is he courting?

RC (Adams Papers). LbC (Adams Papers); at foot of text: "Sent. by Post. Tuesday. Aug. 27. with News Papers inclosed." Enclosed newspapers not found.

[1] Her second letter so dated, above, but perhaps written on the 15th and 16th.

[2] Rev. Mather Byles (1707–1778), Harvard 1725, S.T.D., Aberdeen 1765, a nephew of Cotton Mather and minister of the Hollis Street Church; renowned as a wit and punster (*DAB*; Sibley-Shipton, *Harvard Graduates*, 7: 464–493).

John Adams to Abigail Adams

Philadelphia August 27. 1776

Within this half Hour, I received yours of the 18 by the Post. I have only Time before the Post goes out again to thank you for it, and to express my Resignation to the Will of Heaven whatever it may be respecting my dear Charles. I think his Fate is very uncertain. I will hope the best, but Symptoms so terrible indicate the Utmost danger. Besides he will be more troublesome than the rest, if he recovers, because his exquisite Feelings make him more impatient.

You desire me not to forget your "Herbs." I am totally at a Loss for your Meaning.[1] Pray explain—or perhaps your Letter by Mr. Smith,[2] which I have not received, Mr. Smith not being as yet come to Town, will explain it.

RC (Adams Papers); addressed: "Mrs. Adams at Mr. Isaac Smiths Queen Street Boston"; franked: "Free   John Adams"; postmarked: "PHILA. AUG 27." LbC (Adams Papers).

[1] See note 2 on JA's letter to AA of 29 July, above.
[2] Her first letter dated 14 Aug., above.

John Adams to Abigail Adams

Philadelphia August 28. 1776

Mr. Benjamin Smith of S. Carolina, was kind enough to send forward from New York,[1] your Favour of August 14 and it came safely to Hand to day. There is nothing in it, about "your Herbs," which in your Letter of the Eighteenth instant, you wish me to remember. I am yet at a loss for your Meaning. Mr. Gerry carried a Cannister of India Herb for you, which I hope you received. Pray let me know whether you have or not.

Yours of the Eighteenth has fixed an Arrow in my Heart, which will not be drawn out, untill the next Post arrives, and then, perhaps, instead of being withdrawn, it will be driven deeper. My sweet Babe, Charles, is never out of my Thoughts.—Gracious Heaven preserve him!—The Symptoms you describe, are so formidable, that I am afraid almost to flatter myself with Hope.—Why should I repine? Why should I grieve? He is not mine, but conditionally, and subject to the Will of a Superiour, whose Will be done.

I shall inclose with this a Pamphlet, intituled "The present Method of innoculating for the Small Pox, to which are added, some Experiments instituted with a View to discover the Effects of a similar Treatment, in the natural Small Pox, by Thomas Dinsdale M.D."[2] This Pamphlet is recommended to me, by Dr. Khun,[3] an eminent Phisician of this City, as containing the best Method, and that which is practised by the greatest Masters in this City. I send this as a Present to you, but you must lend it to Dr. Tufts. I have not Time to read it.

Every Moment grows more and more critical at New York. We expect every Hour, News of serious Joy, or Sorrow. The two Armies are very near each other, at Long Island.

RC (Adams Papers). LbC (Adams Papers); at foot of text: "Sent with Dr. Dinsdales Pamphlet [see note 2], and several News Papers." Enclosed newspapers not found.

[1] Preceding three words supplied from LbC.

[2] That is, Thomas Dimsdale, a British physician; his tract, first published in 1767, went through numerous editions (*DNB*). Presumably JA sent the Philadelphia edition, 1771 (Evans 12028).

[3] Adam Kuhn (1741–1817), M.D., Edinburgh 1767, professor of materia medica and botany at the College of Philadelphia (*DAB*).

Abigail Adams to John Adams

Dearest Friend   Boston August 29 1776

I have spent the 3 days past almost intirely with you. The weather has been stormy, I have had little company, and I have amused my self in my closet reading over the Letters I have received from you since I have been here.

I have possession of my Aunts chamber in which you know is a very conveniant pretty closet with a window which looks into her flower Garden. In this closet are a number of Book Shelves, which are but poorly furnished, however I have a pretty little desk or cabinet here where I write all my Letters and keep my papers unmollested by any one. I do not covet my Neighbours Goods, but I should like to be the owner of such conveniances. I always had a fancy for a closet with a window which I could more peculiarly call my own.

Here I say I have amused myself in reading and thinking of my absent Friend, sometimes with a mixture of paine, sometimes with pleasure, sometimes anticipating a joyfull and happy meeting, whilst my Heart would bound and palpitate with the pleasing Idea, and with the purest affection I have held you to my Bosom till my whole Soul has dissolved in Tenderness and my pen fallen from my Hand.

How often do I reflect with pleasure that I hold in possession a Heart Eaqually warm with my own, and full as Susceptable of the Tenderest impressions, and Who even now whilst he is reading here, feels all I discribe.

Forgive this Revere, this Delusion, and since I am debared real, suffer me, to enjoy, and indulge In Ideal pleasures—and tell me they are not inconsistant with the stern virtue of a senator and a Patriot.

I must leave my pen to recover myself and write in an other

strain.[1] I feel anxious for a post day, and am full as solicitious for two Letters a week and as uneasy if I do not get them, as I used to be when I got but one in a month or 5 weeks. Thus do I presume upon indulgance, and this is Humane Nature, and brings to my mind a sentiment of one of your correspondents viz. "That Man is the only animal who is hungery with His Belly full."

Last Evening Dr. Cooper came in and brought me your favour from the post office of August 18 and Coll. Whipple arrived yesterday morning and deliverd me the two Bundles you sent, and a Letter of the 12 of August. They have already afforded me much amusement, and I expect much more from them.

I am sorry to find from your last as well as from some others of your Letters that you feel so dissatisfied with the office to which you are chosen. Tho in your acceptance of it, I know you was actuated by the purest motives, and I know of no person here so well qualified to discharge the important Duties of it, Yet I will not urge you to it. In accepting of it you must be excluded from all other employments. There never will be a Salery addequate to the importance of the office or to support you and your family from penury. If you possess a fortune I would urge you to it, in spight of all the flears and gibes of minds who themselves are incapable of acting a disintrested part, and have no conception that others can.

I have never heard any Speaches about it, nor did I know that such insinuations had been Thrown out.

Pure and disintrested Virtue must ever be its own reward. Mankind are too selfish and too depraved to discover the pure Gold from the baser mettle.

I wish for peace and tranquility. All my desires and all my ambition is to be Esteemed and Loved by my Partner, to join with him in the Education and instruction of our Little ones, to set under our own vines in Peace, Liberty and Safety.

Adieu my Dearest Friend, soon, soon return to your most affectionate
Portia

PS Charlly is cleverly. A very odd report has been propagated in Braintree viz. that you were poisond upon your return at N.Y. Bass sets of on monday.

RC (Adams Papers); addressed: "To The Honbl. John Adams Esqr. Philadelphia"; endorsed: "Portia. Ansd. Septr. 8."

[1] This sentence and the three preceding entire paragraphs were omitted by CFA in printing this letter.

Abigail Adams to John Adams

Thursday August 29 1776

I have this moment sent of a Letter to the post office when Mr. Bass came in to let me know that he has got ready sooner than he expected and will now sit of. I cannot let him go without a line to tell you I feel a new flow of spirits, hope to be home and well to receive you. Write me by every Post, and let me know when you expect to sit out. My Best wishes attend you ever yours,   Portia

RC (Adams Papers); addressed: "To The Honbl. John Adams Philadelphia"; on cover: "The Barer has Leve to Go to Philidelphia by order of the Comitey John Johnson Cpt. Sept. 3. 1776"; endorsed: "Portia ans. Sept. 5. 1776."

John Adams to Abigail Adams

Phil. Aug. 30. 1776

The two Armies, on Long Island have been shooting at each other, for this whole Week past, but We have no particular Account of the Advantages gained or Losses suffered, on either side. The General and Officers have been so taken up, with their military Operations, that they have not been able to spare Time to give Us any very particular Information, and the Post which ought to come punctually every day, has been very irregular. I fear We have suffered a good deal.

Amidst all my Concern for the Army, my dear Charles is continually present to my Mind. I dont know what to think. A Load of variolous Matter, sufficient to stupify him for forty Eight Hours, and then to break out so thick, as to threaten a Confluence, I fear will be more than his delicate frame can support. Children of his Age, however, are often seen to bear a great deal. If I had foreseen, that he would have been seized so violently, I should have had no Heart to tell you the vain story of Mather Biles, as I did in my Letter of the 25th.

I have been obliged to hire a servant here, to attend me, untill another shall come for me, with my Horses. My Horses I want beyond Measure. I have never been once on Horse back, since I came here, and I suffer, in my Health, for Want of Exercise. Mr. Barrell is thought to be past recovery.

After I had written the above, my Servant came in from the Post Office, which he watches very diligently, and brought me yours of the 22d. and if you knew how much Joy it gave me, your Benevolence would be satisfied. It has given me fine Spirits. I feel quite light. I did not know what fast Hold that little Pratler Charles had upon me before. Give my Love to my little Speckeled Beauty, Nabby. Tell her I am glad she is like to have a few Pitts. She will not look the worse for them. If she does, she will learn to prize looks less, and Ingenuity more. The best Way to prevent the Pitts from being lasting and conspicuous, is to keep her out of the sun for some time to prevent her from tanning.

John and Tom, hardy fellows! I have hardly had occasion to feel at all anxious about them.

L[incol]n is not appointed. Ward is requested to continue. I hope he will.

I am much pleased with your Spirit, in resolving to procure me Horses your self and not to wait for a Method, which would be more round about and uncertain.—I think I have a Right and that it is my duty, to take a little Respit and Relaxation. If my Life and Health is of any Use to the Public, it is necessary for the Public as well as for me, that I should take a little rest, in order to preserve them. If they are of none, it is no matter how much rest, I take.

RC and LbC (Adams Papers).

Abigail Adams to John Adams

My Dearest Friend   August 31 1776

You know not How dissapointed I was to Night when the Post came in and I received no Letter from You. Tis the first Saturdays post which has come in since I have been in Town without a Letter from you. It has given me more pain to Night than it would any other time, because of some Falce and foolish reports I hope.

I will not, more than I can help, give way to rumours which I have no reason to believe true. Yet at such a time as this when all the Malice of Satan has possessd our foes, when they have recourse to secret poison, assassanation and every wicked art that Hell can Musture, I own my self allarmd and my fears sometimes overpower me.

But I commit you to the great Gaurdian and protecter of the just, and trust in him that we shall meet and rejoice together, in spight of all the Malice of Earth and Hell.

I hope before this time that Bass has arrived with your Horses, and that you are prepairing to return to your own State. How anxiously do I expect you. On Monday I return to my own habitation with our Little Charles who is weak and feeble, and who wants the air and excercise of the Country to restore him. The Little flock have all left me but Him. Mrs. Cranch came into Town yesterday and carried out Nabby and Tommy, the Dr. would not consent to Charles going till Monday. His are but just cleverly turnd. Your Worthy Parent mett them, Mrs. Cranch writes me, upon their return and weept for joy to see them again. I have often pittied her anxiety which I know has been great upon this occasion. My own dear Mother is saved all she would have felt. My Unkle Q[uinc]y has been a parent to us, with us every week, anxious to the greatest Degree about you, solisitious about your return, declared he would sit of for you himself if Bass would not come immediately.

Mr. A did not get here till the 27 of the month, not till I had engaged your Horses and they were ready to come away.

In the Letter by Him[1] you say you wonder whether the G[enera]l C[our]t have thought of doing any thing for you, at which I was a Little surprizd.

When I was at P[lymout]h Coll. W[arre]n mentiond some accounts which were left with Him upon which a committe was orderd but he never got them to do any thing. Said C[ushin]g had got all His setled and he reminded them of that, but nothing had been done. He further said that a Member from Road Island wrote to Him to know what was given to the Delegates here and he asked C——g who told him that they were allowd 12s. pr. day and their expences. 18 was allowd at Road Island to theirs. I replied that it must be something which had been lately done for I knew nothing of it. He said no he understood C——g that it had been allowed from the first, that is from last April twelve month. I however believed that you had never Received any thing more than your expences tho I could not absolutely say.[2]

This I know they will be very willing you should Labour for them as long as your Health and Strength will last, and when they are intirely exausted you may provide for yourself and family as you can.

September 2. 1776

This is a Beautifull Morning. I see it with joy, and I hope thankfullness. I came here with all my treasure of children, have passd thro one of the most terible Diseases to which humane Nature is subject, and not one of us is wanting. I should go home with a much lighter Heart if I had heard from you. I wish you would not miss a Post whilst you tarry tho you write no more than that you are well.

In the Course of the week past we have had many reports of Battles at New York, none of which gain credit. An other peice of Trechery is come to light and as it is in the Military way I hope an Example will be made of the Wretch. What Blindness, what infatuation to suffer the Mayor of the city after having proved himself such a rascel and villan to go at large. To err upon the Leniant Hand is best no doubt, but to suffer such crimes to go unpunished is offensive in the sight of Heaven I doubt not.[3]

Little Charles stands by and sends Duty to Pappa, says Mamma did you get any Letters a Saturday? No. Then why do you write Mamma.

Adieu. Ever ever Yours.

RC (Adams Papers); addressed in an unidentified hand: "To The Honble. John Adams Philadelphia"; endorsed: "Portia ans. Sept. 14."

[1] Of 10 Aug., above.
[2] The information available on JA's payment by the State for service in 1776 does not make clear what his salary was; see his *Diary and Autobiography*, 2:251. But for his 322 days of service in 1777 he was paid at the rate of 24s. a day besides expenses (same, p. 257, citing Mass., *Province Laws*, 20:261).
[3] These allusions remain obscure. The mayor of New York was David Mathews, but he had been jailed after the "Hickey plot"; see Stokes, *Iconography of Manhattan Island*, 4:933–935.

John Adams to Abigail Adams

Wednesday Septr. 4. 1776

Mr. G[erry] arrived Yesterday, and brought me yours of August 17. and soon afterwards the Post came in, with yours of the 25. of Aug. Am happy to find you, in so good a Way, and am glad to learn that Horses and a Man are coming. I want them much. But our Affairs having taken a Turn at Long Island and New York, so much to our Disadvantage, I cannot see my Way clear, to return home so soon as I intended. I shall wait here, untill I see some more decisive Event, in our Favour or against Us. The General Court however will appoint some other Gentleman to relieve me, and my Man and Horses will come, and then I can ride a little in a Morning for my Health, and come home as soon as Circumstances will admit. I am obliged to General Lincoln for his Information, concerning the Fortifications, which I hope will be effectually attended to, as I am not clear, that Boston is yet secure from Invasion.

I hope, the Disasters at Long Island, and New York will not dispirit our People. The Ways of Providence are inscrutable. I have strong suspicions that these Disasters have saved Boston from another Invasion, which I think would have been attempted by the two gratefull Brothers, with their whole Fleet and Army, if they had not obtained Long Island.

RC and LbC (Adams Papers).

Mercy Otis Warren to Abigail Adams

Plimouth Sept. 4th. 1776

Is my Dear Mrs. Adams too Much Engagd with Company, is her Family sick, or is she inattentive to What Gives pleasure to her Friend, that I have not heard a Word from her since I Left the Capital.

How dos my Dear Charles do. I Long to hear if that sweet boy is perfectly Recovered. I felt Great pain in Leaving him so Ill, but as I hear nothing since Conclude he must be better. Has Naby her Health since she Recovered from her Late sprinkling, has she Recoverd her serene and placid Countenence. Tell her she Looked a Little sower upon me when I saw her Last, but I dare say she Never will again for she will have the small pox no more. A sad Enemy this to soft Features, and fine Faces, though I hope Miss Naby will be so Formed both by Example And Education, as to stand in Little Need of any External Accomplishments to Recommend her to the Esteem of the Worthy and Good.

I hope when you Return to Braintree, you will Enjoy the stiller scenes, and take as much Delight in the Cares which Family Oeconomy Require, as one of your Acquaintance at Plimouth dos in her Domestic Circle.

I believe Nothing Gives a Higher Relish to the Calm of Retirement than such a Round of Visits, Visiting, and Visitation as we have Both Lately Experienced.

The Rustling of the Gentle Brezes in my own Little Garden is Music to my Ears, and the Return of my Little Flock from school Marks my Visiting Hour as they are almost the only Guests I have Received. Nor have I Entered any Habitation but my own since my Arrival from the Noisey town. But the frequent Absence of the best of friends prevents to you and to me the full injoyment of the Many Blessings providence has kindly showered Down upon us. I sigh for peace yet it Cannot take place. But while the sword and the pestilence pervade the Land, and Misery is the portion of Millions, why should we Expect to feel No interruption of Happiness.

When Mr. Warren Calls on you again you will not forget to send a Number of Useless Copies, in the full Confidence of Friendship Left in your Hands.

Make my Regards to your sisters And their Families. And do Let me know when you Expect Mr. Adams, and whither he Enjoys better health.

With Every wish for his and your Happiness subscribes your Affectionate Friend,   Marcia Warren

RC (Adams Papers); addressed: "To Mrs. Abigail Adams Braintree pr. Capt. Nicolson."

John Adams to Abigail Adams

Philadelphia Septr. 5. 1776

Mr. Bass arrived this Day, with the joyfull News, that you were all well. By this Opportunity, I shall send you a Cannister of Green Tea, by Mr. Hare.[1]

Before Mr. G[erry] went away from hence, I asked Mrs. Yard to send a Pound of Green Tea to you. She readily agreed. When I came home at Night I was told Mr. G. was gone. I asked Mrs. Y. if she had sent the Cannister? She said Yes and that Mr. G. undertook to deliver it, with a great deal of Pleasure. From that Time I flattered my self, you would have the poor Relief of a dish of good Tea under all your Fatigues with the Children, and under all the disagreabble Circumstances attending the small Pox, and I never conceived a single doubt, that you had received it untill Mr. Gerrys Return. I asked him, accidentally, whether he delivered it, and he said Yes to Mr. S.A.'s Lady.—I was astonished. He misunderstood Mrs. Y. intirely, for upon Inquiry she affirms she told him, it was for Mrs. J.A.

I was so vexed at this, that I have ordered another Cannister, and Mr. Hare has been kind enough to undertake to deliver it. How the Dispute will be settled I dont know. You must send a Card to Mrs. S.A., and let her know that the Cannister was intended for You, and she may send it you if she chooses, as it was charged to me. It is amazingly dear, nothing less than 40s. lawfull Money, a Pound.

I am rejoiced that my Horses are come. I shall now be able to take a ride. But it is uncertain, when I shall set off, for home. I will not go, at present. Affairs are too delicate and critical.—The Panic may seize whom it will, it shall not seize me. I will stay here, untill the public Countenance is better, or much worse. It must and will be better. I think it is not now bad. Lyes by the Million will be told you. Dont believe any of them. There is no danger of the Communication being cutt off, between the northern and southern Colonies. I can go home, when I please, in spight of all the Fleet and Army of Great Britain.

RC and LbC (Adams Papers).

[1] "The Bearer, Mr. Hare, is a Brother of the Gentleman of the same Name in this City, who has made himself so famous by introducing the Brewery of Porter into America. He wants to see our Country, Harvard Colledge, the Town of Boston, etc." (JA to James Warren, 4 Sept. 1776, *Warren-Adams Letters*, 1:273).

John Adams to Abigail Adams

Fryday Septr. 6. 1776

This day, I think, has been the most remarkable of all. Sullivan came here from Lord Howe, five days ago with a Message that his Lordship desired a half an Hours Conversation with some of the Members of Congress, in their private Capacities. We have spent three or four days in debating whether We should take any Notice of it. I have, to the Utmost of my Abilities during the whole Time, opposed our taking any Notice of it. But at last it was determined by a Majority "that the Congress being the Representatives of the free and independent states of America, it was improper to appoint any of their Members to confer, in their private Characters with his Lordship. But they would appoint a Committee of their Body, to wait on him, to know whether he had Power, to treat with Congress upon Terms of Peace and to hear any Propositions, that his Lordship may think proper to make."

When the Committee came to be ballotted for, Dr. Franklin and your humble servant, were unanimously chosen. Coll. R. H. Lee and Mr. [Edward] Rutledge, had an equal Number: but upon a second Vote Mr. R. was chosen. I requested to be excused, but was desired to consider of it untill tomorrow. My Friends here Advise me to go. All the stanch and intrepid, are very earnest with me to go, and the timid and wavering, if any such there are,[1] agree in the request. So I believe I shall undertake the Journey. I doubt whether his Lordship will see Us, but the same Committee will be directed to inquire into the State of the Army, at New York,[2] so that there will be Business enough, if his Lordship makes none.—It would fill this Letter Book, to give you all the Arguments, for and against this Measure, if I had Liberty to attempt it.—His Lordship seems to have been playing off a Number of Machiavillian Maneuvres, in order to throw upon Us the Odium of continuing this War. Those who have been Advocates for the Appointment of this Committee, are for opposing Maneuvre to Maneuvre, and are confident that the Consequence will be, that the Odium will fall upon him. However this may be, my Lesson is plain, to ask a few Questions, and take his Answers.

I can think of but one Reason for their putting me upon this Embassy, and that is this. An Idea has crept into many Minds here that his Lordship is such another as Mr. Hutchinson, and they may possibly think that a Man who has been accustomed to penetrate into the mazy Windings of Hutchinsons Heart, and the serpentine Wiles of his Head, may be tolerably qualified to converse with his Lordship.[3]

Sunday Septr. 8.

Yesterdays Post brought me yours of Aug. 29. The Report you mention "that I was poisoned upon my Return at New York" I suppose will be thought to be a Prophecy, delivered by the Oracle in mystic Language, and meant that I should be politically or morally poisoned by Lord Howe. But the Prophecy shall be false.

RC and LbC (Adams Papers).

[1] Preceding five words not in LbC, added in RC.
[2] As things turned out, the committee was not so instructed.
[3] Maj. Gen. John Sullivan had been captured in the action on Long Island, 27 Aug. (and was afterward exchanged for the British general, Richard Prescott). Sullivan presented Lord Howe's request to Congress on 2 and 3 Sept.; the debate and votes that JA reports here took place on the three following days (*JCC*, 5:723, 730–731, 735, 737–738). See also JA, *Diary and Autobiography*, 3:425; Josiah Bartlett to William Whipple, 3 Sept. 1776 (Burnett, ed., *Letters of Members*, 2:66–67).

Abigail Adams to John Adams

Braintree Sepbr. 7 1776[1]

Last monday I left the Town of Boston, underwent the operation of a smoaking at the lines and arrived at my Brother Cranchs where we go for purification; there I tarried till wedensday, and then came Home, which seem'd greatly endeard to me by my long absence. I think I never felt greater pleasure at comeing Home after an absence in my Life. Yet I felt a vacuum in my Breast and sent a Sigh to P[hiladelphi]a. I long'd for a dear Friend to rejoice with me. Charlly is Banished yet, I keep him at his Aunt Cranch's out of the way of those who have not had the Distemper, his Arm has many Scabs upon it which are yet very soar. He is very weak and sweats a nights prodigiously. I am now giving him the Bark. He recoverd very fast considering how ill he was. I pitty your anxiety and feel sorry that I wrote you when he was so Bad, but I knew not how it might turn with Him, had it been otherways than well, it might have proved a greater Shock than to have known that he was ill.

This Night our good unkle came from Town and brought me yours of August 20, 21, 25, 27 and 28th for all of which I most sincerely thank you. I have felt uneasy to Hear from you. The Report of your being dead, has no doubt reach'd you by Bass who heard enough of it before he came away. It took its rise among the Tories who as Swift said of himself "By their fears betray their Hopes" but How they should ever take it into their Heads that you was poisond at New York a fortnight before that we heard any thing of that villans Zedwitz plan of poisoning the waters of the City, I cannot tell.[2] I am sometimes ready to suspect that there is a communication between the Tories of every State, for they seem to know all news that is passing before tis known by the Whigs.

We Have had many Stories concerning engagements upon Long Island this week, of our Lines being forced and of our Troops retreating to New York. Perticuliars we have not yet obtaind. All we can learn is that we have been unsuccessfull there; having Lost Many Men as prisoners among whom is Lord Sterling and General Sullivan.

But if we should be defeated I think we shall not be conquered. A people fired like the Romans with Love of their Country and of Liberty, a zeal for the publick Good, and a Noble Emulation of Glory, will not be disheartned or dispirited by a Succession of unfortunate Events. But like them may we learn by Defeat the power of becomeing invincible.

I hope to Hear from you by every Post till you return. The Herbs you mention I never Received. I was upon a visit to Mrs. S. Adams about a week after Mr. Gerry returnd, when She entertaind me with a very fine Dish of Green Tea. The Scarcity of the article made me ask her Where she got it. She replied her *Sweet Heart* sent it to her by Mr. Gerry. I said nothing, but thought my Sweet Heart might have been eaquelly kind considering the disease I was visited with, and that [tea] was recommended as a Bracer. A Little after you mention'd a couple of Bundles sent. I supposed one of them might contain the article but found they were Letters. How Mr. Gerry should make such a mistake I know not. I shall take the Liberty of sending for what is left of it tho I suppose it is half gone as it was very freely used. If you had mentiond a single Word of it in your Letter I should have immediately found out the mistake.

Tis said that the Efforts of our Enemies will be to stop the communication between the colonies by taking possession of Hudsons Bay.[3] Can it be effected? The Milford frigate rides triumphant in our Bay, taking vessels every day, and no Colony nor Continental vessel has yet attempted to hinder her. She mounts but 28 Guns but is one of the finest sailors in the British Navy. They complain we have not weighty mettle enough and I suppose truly. The Rage for privateering is as great here as any where and I believe the success has been as great.

It will not be in my power to write you so regularly as when I was in Town. I shall not faill doing it once a week. If you come home the Post Road you must inquire for Letters where ever the Post sit out from.

Tis Here a very General time of Health. I think tis near a twelve month since the pestilance raged here. I fear your being seazd with a fever, tis very prevalant I hear where you are. I pray God preserve you and return you in Health. The Court will not accept your Resignation, they will appoint Mr. Dalton and Dana to releave you.

I am most affectionately Yours.

RC (Adams Papers); endorsed: "Portia ansd. Sep. [21]."

[1] In his reply of 21 Sept., below, JA read this date as 9 Sept., and CFA also printed this letter in *Familiar Letters* with that date. Although AA's 4's, 7's, and 9's are often scarcely distinguishable from each other, the editors believe she intended "7" here.

[2] Lt. Col. Herman Zedtwitz of the New York Line was court-martialed, convicted, and cashiered on 25–26 Aug. for attempting to give intelligence to the enemy, specifically for writing a long letter to Gov. William Tryon (dated 24 Aug. and promptly turned in by an agent Zedtwitz had bribed) which contained a hodgepodge of truth and fancy. One of his fancies was that he had seen "4 Fellows at the Generals [Washington's] Hous wich proposed to Spoil the Watering place [on Staten Island where the British were encamped], they brought along 14 Botles of Stof as Black as an Ink it was Tried and Found good as they [. . . .] The gen: promised Every

one £1000 if it Stands 6 weeks." The proceedings of the court martial are printed and a facsimile of Zedtwitz's letter is reproduced in Force, *Archives*, 5th ser., 1:1159–1162.

[3] Thus in MS, but meaning, surely, the Hudson River.

John Adams to Abigail Adams

Philadelphia Saturday Septr. 14. 1776

Yesterday Morning I returned with Dr. F. and Mr. R. from Staten Island where We met L[ord] H[owe] and had about three Hours Conversation with him. The Result of this Interview, will do no disservice to Us. It is now plain that his L[ordshi]p has no Power, but what is given him in the Act of P[arliament]. His Commission authorises him to grant Pardons upon Submission, and to converse, confer, consult and advise with such Persons as he may think proper, upon American Grievances, upon the Instructions to Governors and the Acts of Parliament, and if any Errors should be found to have crept in, his Majesty and the Ministry were willing they should be rectified.

I found yours of 31. of Aug. and 2d. of September.[1] I now congratulate you on your Return home with the Children. Am sorry to find you anxious on Account of idle Reports.—Dont regard them. I think our Friends are to blame to mention such silly Stories to you. What good do they expect to do by it?

My Ride has been of Service to me. We were absent but four days. It was an agreable Excursion. His L[ordshi]p is about fifty Years of Age. He is a well bred Man, but his Address is not so irresistable, as it has been represented. I could name you many Americans, in your own Neighbourhood, whose Art, Address, and Abilities are greatly superiour. His head is rather confused, I think.[2]

When I shall return I cant say. I expect now, every day, fresh Hands from Watertown.

RC (Adams Papers); addressed: "Mrs. Adams at Mr. John Adams's Braintree Massachusetts Bay"; franked: "free John Adams"; postmarked: "PHILA. SEP 14." LbC (Adams Papers).

[1] A single letter, printed above under its first date.

[2] JA's "Ride" to and from Staten Island, with Benjamin Franklin and Edward Rutledge, began on the 9th and ended on the 13th. The interview with Lord Howe occurred on the 11th at the Christopher Billopp house in Tottenville. JA's retrospective account of the journey and interview is justly famous, and is accompanied by pertinent passages from the Journal of Congress and from his own contemporaneous letters (*Diary and Autobiography*, 3:414–430). Congress published the relevant papers, including the report of the committee, under date of 17 Sept. (broadside in NN; Evans 15168). The best British

account is by Henry Strachey, secretary to the Howe brothers' commission, whom JA was to encounter again during the negotiations for a preliminary peace with Great Britain in the fall of 1782; Strachey's narrative was first printed accurately (from a MS in NN) by Paul L. Ford in an article entitled "Lord Howe's Commission to Pacify the Colonies," *Atlantic Monthly*, 77:758–762 (June 1896); see also Ambrose Serle,

American Journal, ed. Edward H. Tatum Jr., San Marino, Calif., 1940, p. 100–101, and various sources cited in Stokes, *Iconography of Manhattan Island*, 5: 1010. On 19 Sept. the Howes issued in broadside form a further "Declaration," in which they gave up on Congress but appealed again to all persons disposed to reconciliation with Great Britain; an example in MHi is reproduced as an illustration in this volume.

Abigail Adams to John Adams

Sepbr. 15 1776

I have been so much engaged this week with company that, tho I never cease to think of you I have not had leisure to write to you. It has been High Court week with us, judge C[ushin]g and Lady kept here, the judges all dined with me one day and the Bar an other day. The Court sit till Saturday Night, and then were obliged to continue many causes. The people seem to be pleased and gratified at seeing justice returning into its old regular channel again.[1]

I this week received two Letters, one dated july 27 and [another] july 29th. Where they have been these two months I cannot conceive, I hear of an other by the Express but have not yet been able to find it. I write now not knowing where to direct to you, whether you are in the American Senate or on Board the British fleet is a matter of uncertainty. I hear to day that you are one of a committee sent by Congress to hold a conference with Lord How. Some say to negotiate an exchange of General Sulivan, others say you are charged with other matters.

May you be wise as Serpents. I wish to hear from you, the 28 of August was the last date. I may have Letters at the Post office. The Town is not yet clear of the small Pox which makes it dificult for me to get a conveyance from there, unless I send on purpose.

I only write now to let you know that we are all well, anxiously longing for your return.

As this is a child of chance I do not chuse to say any thing more than that I am Sincerely Yours.

RC (Adams Papers); addressed in an unidentified hand: "To The Honble: John Adams Esqr. at New York or Philadelphia"; franked: "Free"; endorsed (twice): "Portia."

[1] This was the first session of the Superior Court in Suffolk co. since its closing in Sept. 1774. In Feb. 1776 the General Court had named Dedham and

Braintree, alternately, as the places of sitting in Suffolk because the British still occupied Boston; and now, although the British had left months ago, the smallpox epidemic in Boston made another meeting place highly advisable. The act of Feb. 1776 was repealed in November, and beginning in Feb. 1777 the sessions returned to Boston. See Mass., *Province Laws*, 5:455–456, 593–594; Quincy, *Reports*, p. 341–342.

For more details on this session of the Superior Court in Braintree, see James Sullivan to JA, 22 Sept. (Adams Papers).

John Adams to Abigail Adams

Monday Septr. 16. 1776

The Postmaster at N. York, in a Panick, about a fortnight ago fled to Dobbs's Ferry, about 30 Miles above N.Y. upon Hudsons River, which has thrown the Office into disorder, and interrupted the Communication so much that I have not received a Line of yours, since that dated the Second of September.[1] Nor have I received a News Paper, or any other Letter from Boston since that date. The same Cause, it is probable has disturbed the Conveyance, to the Eastward, and prevented you from receiving Letters regularly, from me.

One of the Horses, which has been sent me, is very low in flesh. I must wait, some time, I fear for him to recruit.

No new Delegates come yet. I hope to see some in a few days.

We have good News from France and the French West Indies....[2] There is great Reason to think they will not always remain inactive.

You commanded me to write every Post, and I obey altho I have nothing in Particular to say, only that I am as usual, not worse in Health, nor yet well, but ever Yours.

RC (Adams Papers); addressed: "Mrs. Adams at Mr. John Adams's Braintree Massachusetts Bay"; franked: "Free John Adams"; postmarked: "PHILA. SEP 16." LbC (Adams Papers).

[1] Her letter dated 31 Aug. – 2 Sept., above.
[2] Suspension points in MS.

Jonathan Mason to Abigail Adams

Madam   B[oston][1] Sep: 18. 1776

I was extremely sorry I could not pay that attention to your son Johnny, as I should wish to have done, had not I been very diligently employed in other business. Should esteem it as a favour that whenever You trust any of them to town, you would direct them to my father's house, and I am repeatedly desired by my sister to request your consent to Miss Nabby's coming into town and tarrying with us as long as inclination and improvement can make it agreeable. My mite, I doubt not you are assured will be chearfully contributed to her emolument. I forwarded your last letters by the post the first Opportunity, and have only to beg that whenever occasion calls, you would not hesitate to command me to any task. It would afford me great pleasure to have it in my power to compensate in some measure, for many unexpected, unmerited civilities, I mett with at your house. Inclosed you have a letter just handed me, but I am ignorant by whom.—Had not a liberal mind induced you to mention it in your letter,[2] I had notwithstanding determined in my own mind, to have wrote, when Politicks or some other general topic had occurred, and if proper, should be extreemly happy in perusing a return.

I am with great respect Your hum. Servt.,   J Mason Jr.[3]

One Mr. Payne in Boston is a fine tutor for the young ladies.

RC (Adams Papers); addressed: "For Mrs. Adams In Braintree Pr. favour." Enclosure: probably a recent letter from JA to AA, not now identifiable.

[1] MS torn by seal.
[2] Not found.
[3] Mason, who was nominally still apprenticed to JA as law clerk, had written JA on 12 Aug. (Adams Papers), saying that he had "resolved . . . closely to pursue the science of the Law," outlining his progress and plans, and asking whether he should accept an invitation to enter Perez Morton's law office. In his reply of 21 Aug. (LbC, Adams Papers), JA suggested further studies and advised Mason to accept Morton's "kind Offer, provided you dont find the Practice of his Office interferes too much with your studies, which I dont think it will."

Abigail Adams to John Adams

Braintree Sepbr. 20 1777 [*i.e.* 1776]

I sit down this Evening to write you, but I hardly know what to think about your going to N.Y.—The Story has been told so many times, and with circumstances so perticuliar that I with others have given some heed [to] it tho my not hearing any thing of it from you leaves me at a loss.

Yours of Sepbr. 4 came to hand last Night, our Worthy unkle is a constant attendant upon the Post office for me and brought it me.

Yours of Sepbr. 5 came to Night to B[raintre]e and was left as directed with the Cannister. Am sorry you gave yourself so much trouble about them. I got about half you sent me by Mr. Gerry. Am much obliged to you, and hope to have the pleasure of making the greater part of it for you. Your Letter damp't my Spirits; when I had no expectation of your return till December, I endeavourd to bring my mind to acquiess in the too painfull Situation, but I have now been in a state of Hopefull expectation. I have recond the days since Bass went away a hundred times over, and every Letter expected to find the day set for your return.

But now I fear it is far distant. I have frequently been told that the communication would be cut of and that you would not be ever able to return. Sometimes I have been told so by those who really wish'd it might be so, with Malicious pleasure. Sometimes your timid folks have apprehended that it would be so. I wish any thing would bring you nearer. If there is really any danger I should think you would remove. Tis a plan your Enemies would rejoice to see accomplished, and will Effect if it lies in their power.

I am not apt to be intimidated you know. I have given as little heed to that and a thousand other Bug Bear reports as posible. I have slept as soundly since my return not withstanding all the Ghosts and hobgoblings, as ever I did in my life. Tis true I never close my Eyes at night till I have been to P[hiladelphi]a, and my first visit in the morning is there.

How unfealing are the world! They tell me they Heard you was dead with as little sensibility as a stock or a stone, and I have now got to be provoked at it, and can hardly help snubing the person who tells me so.

The Story of your being upon this conference at New york came in a Letter as I am told from R. T. P[aine] to his Brother in Law G[reenlea]fe. Many very many have been the conjectures of the Multitude upon it. Some have supposed the War concluded, the Nation setled, others an exchange of prisoners, others a reconsiliation with Brittain &c. &c.

I cannot consent to your tarrying much longer. I know your Health must greatly suffer from so constant application to Buisness and so little excercise. Besides I shall send you word by and by as Regulus'es steward did, that whilst you are engaged in the Senate your own domestick affairs require your presence at Home, and that your wife and children are in Danger of wanting Bread. If the Senate of America will take care of us, as the Senate of Rome did of the family of Regulus, you may serve them again, but unless you return what little property you possess will be lost. In the first place the House at Boston is going to ruin. When I was there I hired a Girl to clean it, it had a cart load of Dirt in it. I speak within Bounds. One of the chambers was used to keep poultry in, an other sea coal, and an other salt. You may conceive How it look'd. The House is so exceeding damp being shut up, that the floors are mildewd, the sealing falling down, and the paper mouldy and falling from the walls. I took care to have it often opened and aird whilst I tarried in Town. I put it into the best state I could.

In the next place, the Lighter of which you are or should be part owner is lying rotting at the wharf. One year more without any care and she is worth nothing. You have no Bill of Sale, no right to convey any part of her should any person appear to purchase her. The Pew I let, after having paid a tax for the repairs of the meeting House.

As to what is here under my more immediate inspection I do the best I can with it, but it will not at the high price Labour is, pay its way.

I know the weight of publick cares lye so heavey upon you that I have been loth to mention your own private ones.

The Best accounts we can collect from New York assure us that our Men fought valiantly. We are no ways dispiritted here, we possess a Spirit that will not be conquerd. If our Men are all drawn of and we should be attacked, you would find a Race of Amazons in America.

But I trust we shall yet tread down our Enemies.

I must intreat you to remember me often. I never think your Letters half long enough. I do not complain. I have no reason to, no one can boast of more Letters than Your   Portia

RC (Adams Papers); docketed in an unidentified hand: "1777."

Abigail Adams to John Adams

My dear Sir   Sepbr. 21 1774 [*i.e.* 1776]

I wrote you last Night till my Eyes were almost out by the post, but Mr. Eliot has taken pains to send me word that he would carry a Letter for me, and I cannot omit writing a few lines tho tis only to say that I am well, and to inquire how you do? I have a thousand fears for your Health. How is poor Mr. Barrel, is he gone, or does he yet live?

This Month twelve month was attended with so many melancholy Scenes, that my Heart Bleeds afresh at the recollection. The Image of my Dear Mother seems ever before me, and fresh to my memory. I felt more than common depression of spirits the other day when I enterd the House, nor could I enjoy myself whilst I stay'd, a Train of melancholly Ideas forced themselves upon me and made me very unhappy.

My Father enjoys better Health than he has for many year, he possesses a vigirous old age. He call'd here the other day comeing of a journey to dine with me having ride forty miles before dinner. I askd him if he was not fatigued. No says he with his useuel sprightlyness thats a triffell for one so young as I am.

Tis a much healther Season than Last year. Our Neighbour Feild is just gone in a consumption, he has been upon the decline ever since the Spring.

Our Worthy Brother and Sister C[ranc]h are well in Health but a good deal embaressed what course to take. Ever since the Removal of the army and the opening of Boston he has not had half Buisness enough to employ him. I am very loth he should remove, but I know not what he will do. He wants much to purchase a little farm in the Country, but he would I think do better in Town. He had considerable Buisness there, when he had the small Pox.

I had something to say [to] you about the state of Harvard Colledge, but I omit it at present.—The Portsmouth Ship has been waiting for Guns these six weeks. Had an unkle of ours and several other merchants I could mention had the care of her I dare say she would have long ago had Guns. Private adventurours can get Guns even for large Briggs.—The Boston formerly the Zechary Baily which was taken as a prize and bought by private persons has been fitted out, her Guns made and purchased long since the other ought to have saild.

So it is we dream away opportunities by misplaceing Buisness. Adieu, Yours.

RC (Adams Papers); endorsed: "Portia ans. Octr. 5th"; docketed in an unidentified hand: "1777."

John Adams to Abigail Adams

Septr. 21. 1776

Yours of Septr. 9.[1] I have received. Septr. 5. I sent you another Cannister by Mr. Hare. I have only Time to tell you I am not worse in Health than I have been. Where are your new Delegates? None arrived here yet. Our People are as lazy and slothfull, as Congress.[2]

LbC (Adams Papers).

[1] 7 Sept., above; see note 1 on that letter.

[2] The General Court during its session of Sept.–Oct. 1776 took no action on JA's repeated pleas to enlarge the Massachusetts delegation and to send replacements promptly. On 19 Sept. Speaker James Warren wrote JA from

Watertown: "We have not yet made an addition to our Delegates, no Body seems to be against it, many are Indifferent about it, and those who wish to have it done, are at a loss where to find the men; so it is procrastinated and left to the next setting" (Adams Papers). JA drafted a reply, 5 Oct., in so angry and bitter a vein that, cooling off almost immediately after he had written it, he appended this note below the text in his letterbook: "not sent, nor fit to be sent." During its next session the Gen-

eral Court at length, 15 Nov. – 10 Dec., reelected JA and his four colleagues and added two more delegates, James Lovell and Francis Dana; and on 4 Feb. 1777 it went a little further by resolving that "any two or more of the said Delegates, Representing this State in Congress, being the major part present, be, and hereby are, vested with all the powers with which any three ... were vested" previously (Mass., *House Jour.*, 1776–1777, p. 157; JCC, 7:25–26, 169–170).

John Adams to Abigail Adams

22 Sept. 1776

We have at last agreed upon a Plan, for forming a regular Army. We have offered 20 dollars, and 100 Acres of Land to every Man, who will inlist, during the War.[1] And a new sett of Articles of War are agreed on.[2] I will send you, if I can a Copy of these Resolutions and Regulations.

I am at a Loss what to write. News We have not. Congress seems to be forgotten by the Armies. We are most unfaithfully served in the Post Office, as well as many other Offices, civil and military.

Unfaithfullness in public Stations, is deeply criminal. But there is no Encouragement to be faithfull. Neither Profit, nor Honour, nor Applause is acquired by faithfullness. But I know by what. There is too much Corruption, even in this infant Age of our Republic. Virtue is not in Fashion. Vice is not infamous.

October 1. 1776

Since I wrote the foregoing Lines, I have not been able to find Time to write you a Line. Altho I cannot write you, so often as I wish, you are never out of my Thoughts. I am repining at my hard Lot, in being torn from you, much oftener than I ought.

I have often mentioned to you, the Multiplicity of my Engagements, and have been once exposed to the Ridicule and Censure of the World for mentioning the great Importance of the Business which lay upon me, and if this Letter should ever see the Light, it would be again imputed to Vanity, that I mention to you, how busy I am. But I must repeat it by Way of Apology for not writing you oftener. From four O Clock in the Morning untill ten at Night, I have not a single Moment, which I can call my own. I will not say that I expect to run distracted, to grow melancholly, to drop in an Apoplexy, or fall into a Consumption. But I do say, it is little less than a Miracle, that one or other of these Misfortunes has not befallen me before now.

Your Favours of September 15, 20, and 23d. are now before me. Every Line from you gives me inexpressible Pleasure. But it is a great Grief to me, that I can write no oftener to you.

There is one Thing which excites my utmost Indignation and Contempt, I mean the Brutality, with which People talk to you, of my Death. I beg you would openly affront every Man, Woman or Child, for the future who mentions any such Thing to you, except your Relations, and Friends whose Affections you cannot doubt. I expect it of all my Friends, that they resent, as Affronts to me, every Repetition of such Reports.

I shall inclose to you, Governor Livingstons Speech, the most elegant and masterly, ever made in America.[3]

Depend upon it, the Enemy cannot cutt off the Communication. I can come home when I will. They have N. York—and this is their Ne Plus Ultra.[4]

RC and LbC (Adams Papers). Enclosure missing; see note 3 below.

[1] This "Plan," which had occupied JA's thoughts for some time, had been introduced, apparently on 9 Sept., as a report of the Board of War, and was debated on the four following days, principally in committee of the whole. With some amendments it was in large part adopted and spread on the Journal on the 16th. Additional resolutions were proposed and debated next day and again on the 19th. On the 20th Congress ordered that "the resolutions for raising the new army be forthwith published, and copies thereof sent to the commanding officers in the several departments, and to the assemblies and conventions of the respective states." See JCC, 5:747, 749, 751, 754, 756–757, 762–763, 768, 787, 807. They were printed in the *Pennsylvania Gazette* on 25 Sept., and also separately as a broadside (JCC, 6:1125, No. 126; Evans, 15167; an example in MHi is reproduced as an illustration in this volume). No MS version has been found in the Adams Papers or in the Reports of the Board of War and Ordnance (PCC, No. 47), but JA later claimed this important plan for a military establishment as his own

and a sufficient answer to Alexander Hamilton's charge in 1800 that JA had been "an Ennemy to a regular Army" (*Diary and Autobiography*, 3:434–435).

[2] On 5 June JA, Jefferson, and three others had been named a committee "on Spies" to make recommendations concerning persons furnishing intelligence or provisions to the enemy. To this committee, on 14 June, was assigned the further task of revising the Articles of War. They submitted a report on 7 Aug. which was debated on the 19th and again on 19 and 20 Sept., when the old Articles were repealed and the new ones spread on the Journal. See JCC, 5:417, 442, 636, 670, 787, 788–807; for contemporary printings of the revised Articles see the "Bibliographical Notes" in same, vol. 6:1125–1126, Nos. 127–130; Evans 15187–15190. JA's recollections of this affair, while perhaps not entirely accurate, furnish details not elsewhere to be found; see his *Diary and Autobiography*, 3:392, 409–410, 433–434. The MS of the Articles in PCC, No. 27, is a copy in Timothy Pickering's hand and offers no clue to their authorship. JA himself believed

that the new Articles "laid the foundation of a discipline, which in time brought our Troops to a Capacity of contending with British Veterans, and a rivalry with the best Troops of France." His account of his role in their production and adoption was another part of his answer to Hamilton's charges in 1800.

[3] William Livingston (1723–1790) had at the end of August been elected governor of New Jersey under the new state constitution. His first address to the legislature, dated 11 Sept. and greatly admired by JA, was printed in the *Pennsylvania Gazette,* 1 Oct., and is reprinted in *New Jersey Archives,* 2d ser., 1 (1901):200–203.

[4] This is the last entry in Lb/JA/2, which JA had begun in June and devoted mainly to letters addressed to AA. The greater part of the book is blank.

Abigail Adams to John Adams

Sepbr. 23 1776

There are perticuliar times when I feel such an uneasiness, such a restlessness, as neither company, Books, family Cares or any other thing will remove, my Pen is my only pleasure, and writing to you the composure of my mind.

I feel that agitation this Evening, a degree of Melancholy has seazd my mind, owing to the anxiety I feel for the fate of our Arms at New York, and the apprehensions I have for your Health and Safety.

We Have so many rumours and reports that tis imposible to know what to Credit. We are this Evening assurd that there has been a field Battle between a detachment of our Army commanded by General Miflin and a Detachment of British Troops in which the Latter were defeated. An other report says that we have been obliged to Evacuate the city and leave our cannon, Baggage &c. &c. This we cannot credit, we will not Believe it.

Tis a most critical day with us. Heaven Crown our arms with Success.

Did you ever expect that we should hold Long Island? And if that could not be held, the city of New York must lie at their mercy. If they command New York can they cut of the communication between the Colonies?

Tho I sufferd much last winter yet I had rather be in a situation where I can collect the Truth, than at a distance where I am distressd by a thousand vague reports—

> War is our Buisness, but to whom is Give'n
> To die, or triumph, that determine Heav'n!

I write you an abundance, do you read it all? Your last Letters have been very short. Have you buried, stifled or exausted all the—I wont ask the question you must find out my meaning if you can.

I cannot help smileing at your caution in never subscribeing a Letter, yet frank it upon the outside where you are obliged to write your name.

I hope I have a Letter by Saturdays Post. You say you are sometimes dissapointed, you can tell then How I feel. I endeavour to write once a week.

Poor Barrel I see by the paper is dead. So is our Neighbour Feild.

RC (Adams Papers); addressed in John Thaxter's hand: "To The Honble: John Adams Esqr. at Philadelphia"; franked: "Free"; docketed in an unidentified hand: "Portia 1776."

John Adams to Abigail Adams

Septr. 25. 1776

I have only Time to say, by Mr. Taylor, that I am not worse than I have been—that however, I think, the G[eneral] C[our]t might have sent somebody here, before now—and that it will not be many days before I shall sett off. I shall wait for the Completion of a few Things and then go—perhaps in a Week or ten days.

RC (Adams Papers).

Abigail Adams to John Adams

⟨*Braintree*⟩ Sepbr. 29 1776

Not since the 5th of Sepbr. have I had one line from you which makes me very uneasy. Are you all this time confering with his Lordship, is there no communication? or are the post Riders all dismissd.

Let the cause be which it will, not hearing from you has given me much uneasiness.

We seem to be kept in a total Ignorance of affairs at York. I hope you at Congress are more inlightned. Who fell, who wounded, who prisoner or their numbers is as undetermined as it was the day after the Battle. If our Army is in ever so critical a state I wish to know it, and the worst of it—if all America are to be ruind and undone by a pack of Cowards and knaves, I wish to know it. Pitiable is the Lot of their commander. Caesars tenth Leigion never was forgiven. We are told for Truth that a Regiment of Yorkers refused to quit the city and that an other Regiment behaved like a pack of Cowardly villans by quitting their posts. If they are unjustly censured it is for want of proper inteligance.

I am sorry to see a Spirit so venal prevailing every where. When our Men were drawn out for Canady a very large Bounty was given them, and now an other call [is made] [1] upon us no one will go without a large Bounty tho only for two months, and each Town seem to think their Honour engaged in outbiding one an other. The province pay is forty shilings. In addition to that this Town voted to make it up six pounds.[2] They then drew out the persons most unlikely to go and they are obliged to give 3 pounds to Hire a Man. Some pay the whole fine ten pounds; forty men are now draughted from this Town, more than one half from 50 to 16teen are now in the Service. This method of conducting will create a General uneasiness in the Continental Army; I hardly think you can be sensible how much we are thind in this province.

The rage for privateering is as great here as any where. Vast Numbers are employd in that way. If it is necessary to make any more draughts upon us the women must Reap the Harvests. I am willing to do my part. I believe I could gather Corn and Husk it, but I should make a poor figure at diging Potatoes.

There has been a report that a fleet was seen in our Bay yesterday. I cannot conceive from whence, nor do I believe the story.

Tis said you have been upon Staten Island to hold your conference, tis a little odd that I have never Received the least intimation of it from you. Did you think I should be allarmd? Dont you know me better than to think me a Coward? I hope you will write me every thing concerning this affair. I have a great curiosity to know the result.

As to Goverment nothing is yet done about it.[3] The Church is opened here every Sunday, and the king prayed for as usual in open defiance to Congress.[4] Parker of Boston is more discreet and so is Sargant.[5]

You have wrote me once or twice to know whether your Brother inclined to go into the Service. I think he wholy declines it. As to mine I have not heard any thing from him since his application to Court. Natll. Belcher goes Capt. and Tertias Bass Lieut. from this Town. They March tomorrow.

Poor Soper we have lost him with a nerveous fever, he died a fryday.[6] A great loss to this Town a man of so interprizing a temper, more Especially when we are so destitute of them.

I should be obliged to you if you would direct Bass to Buy me a Barcelona Hankerchief and 2 oz. of Thread No. 18. Mr. Gerry said Goods were 5 pr. cent dearer here than with you, and by the way I hope you are not charged Eaquelly dear for the last Canister as for the first, the first is the Best of Hyson the other very Good Suchong.

If the next post does not bring me a Letter I think I will leave of writing, for I shall not believe you get mine.

Adieu yours.

PS Master John has become post rider from Boston to B[raintree].

RC (Adams Papers); endorsed: "Portia   ans. Oct. 8."

[1] Two words editorially supplied.

[2] On 23 Sept. the subject of "Encouragement to the Soldiers" was taken up in Braintree town meeting, and it was "Voted, That each soldier that shall engage to go to New York, in Complyance with the Requesition of the Continentiel Congress, shall have six pounds per month including what is allow'd by the Congress during the time of his being in the service"; it was further voted that each soldier so engaging would receive £2 of his pay "previous to his marching" (*Braintree Town Records*, p. 469–470).

[3] Meaning a plan for a state constitution.

[4] It was Rev. Edward Winslow who continued to pray for the King at Christ Church in Braintree, but under pressure from Attorney General Benjamin Kent in the following spring Winslow preached a farewell sermon and took refuge with British forces at Newport and, later, New York City (Sibley-Shipton, *Harvard Graduates*, 11:104–105; see also AA to JA, 2 April 1777, below).

[5] Rev. Samuel Parker, Harvard 1764, pastor of Trinity Church in Boston; and Rev. Winwood Serjeant, pastor of Christ Church in Cambridge (Weis, *Colonial Clergy of N.E.*).

[6] Edmund Soper, first major in Joseph Palmer's regiment of Suffolk militia, was serving as a Braintree selectman at the time of his death (*Mass. Soldiers and Sailors*; *Braintree Town Records*, p. 464–465).

Samuel Adams to Abigail Adams

Boston Octob. 3. 76

Mr. Samuel Adams sends his affectionate Regards to Mrs. Adams (in which his own Mrs. Adams heartily joyns) and acquaints her that he shall sett off next Week or Monday see'night at the farthest for Philadelphia and is desirous of rendering his best Services to Mrs. A. He wishes to know the State of her Family with Respect to their Health; is very sorry that he has not had the Opportunity of making her a Visit at Braintree, a Pleasure which he has missed of by Reason of constant Avocations, which he begs may excuse him.

He had the pleasure of receiving a Letter from his Friend and Colleague Mr. JA of the 14th of September,[1] and supposes he has written to his Lady since that Date. He only adds that the Conduct of his Friend at Staten Island affords an additional Reason why his Country should still covet and even *demand* his further publick Services.

RC (Adams Papers); addressed: "Mrs. John Adams   Braintree."

[1] LbC (Adams Papers); printed under the wrong date of 17 Sept. in JA's *Works*, 9:443–446.

John Adams to Abigail Adams

Octr. 4. 76

I send you, all the News. When I do not write I suffer more Pain than you do, when you dont receive a Line. I have no greater Pleasure than in Writing to you, but I have not Time.

When I shall come home I dont know. But this you may depend on, I can come when I will. The Communication is open and will remain so. It cannot be cutt off.

The General Court have not appointed any one in my stead. I expected they would—but whether they do or not I shall come home, before long.

RC (Adams Papers).

John Adams to Abigail Adams

Philadelphia Octr: 4th: 1776

I am seated, in a large Library Room, with Eight Gentlemen round about me, all engaged in Conversation. Amidst these Interruptions, how shall I make it out to write a Letter?

The first day of October, the day appointed by the Charter of Pensilvania for the annual Election of Representatives, has passed away, and two Counties only have chosen Members, Bucks and Chester.

The Assembly is therefore dead, and the Convention is dissolved. A new Convention is to be chosen, the Beginning of November.

The Proceedings of the late Convention are not well liked, by the best of the Whiggs.—Their Constitution is reprobated and the Oath with which they have endeavoured to prop it, by obliging every Man to swear that he will not add to, or diminish from or any Way alter that Constitution, before he can vote, is execrated.

We live in the Age of political Experiments. Among many that will fail some, I hope will succeed.—But Pensilvania will be divided and weakend, and rendered much less vigorous in the Cause, by the wretched Ideas of Government, which prevail, in the Minds of many People in it.[1]

RC (Adams Papers); addressed: "Mrs. Adams Braintree Massachusetts Bay"; franked: "free John Adams"; postmarked: "PHILA. OCT. 4."

[1] This proved a true prophecy. The Pennsylvania constitution of 1776, the work of a convention dominated by political radicals, was adopted on 28 Sept. after only a token submission of its articles to the citizens and with a substantial minority of "moderates" in the convention opposed to it. Worse, the Convention adopted a provision for an oath exacting from every elector a promise that he would, in effect, neither oppose nor criticize anything whatever in the form of government now established. One result was that it took six months to organize a new government in Pennsylvania, and another was that for fourteen years, until a new constitution was adopted in 1790, the state was torn and distracted by political factionalism probably bitterer than that in any other state. See J. Paul Selsam, *The Pennsylvania Constitution of 1776*, Phila., 1936, chs. 4-6; Robert L. Brunhouse, *The Counter-Revolution in Pennsylvania, 1776-1790*, Harrisburg, 1942, *passim*.

Among the most vocal critics of the constitution of 1776, both at home and abroad, in public and in private, for many years, was JA, who considered it an epitome of all that was bad in constitution-making and an unadulterated specimen of democratic tyranny. It is not too much to say that his close observation of what happened in Pennsylvania politics in 1776-1777 was one of the principal influences on his mature political thought.

John Adams to Abigail Adams

Oct. 5. 1776

Mr. Eliot brought me yours of Septr. 21, this day. My Health is rather better than worse. The cool Weather, in conjunction with my Ride to Staten Island, has braced me up, a little, but I shall soon relax again and must have another ride.

I sympathize with you, in the Recollection of the melancholly scænes of the last Year; and I rejoice with you, in the vigorous Health of your excellent Father. I hope his Vigour and Vivacity will be long preserved, for the Benefit of all about him. I long to spend one of our social Evenings with him and the Dr., you Girls sitting by and listening to our profound discourse, as you used to do.

I feel a real Sorrow and Affliction at the Loss of my worthy Neighbour Field. His deserving Family have sustained a great Loss. Remember me to them, and tell them that I am an hearty Mourner with them.

I feel as much for my worthy Brother and sister, as I do for my self, and for their family as for mine. Both are going to Wreck, but we shall leave them free tho we leave them poor—And the meanest, poorest American scorns the richest slave, at least I would have it so.

I cannot think his scheme of purchasing a Farm will do.—As to H[arvard] Colledge I know nothing of it.

That Business is misplaced is true. I know more of it, than I have yet thought it prudent to tell the World. I was restrained by dangers of various Kinds, but I will not be always restrained. I will renounce the office of ⟨*Chief Justice*⟩[1] and then I shall be upon equal Ground with other People, and then I will speak and write as freely as my natural Disposition inclines me to do.

I have suffered Indignities to my self, and I have observed without clamouring about Abuses to the Public, when I thought that indulging either public or private Resentment would endanger our Cause—but I will bear it no longer than the public Cause requires this Patience of me.

RC (Adams Papers).

[1] These two words heavily inked out, probably just before the letter was folded and sealed, since there is an inkstain on the facing page.

John Adams to Abigail Adams

Octr: 7th: 1776

I have been here, untill I am stupified. If I set down to write even to you, I am at a Loss what to write.

We expect General Lee, in Town every Hour, He dined at Wilmington Yesterday. His Appearance at Head Quarters on the Heights of Ha'arlem, would give a flow of Spirits to our Army, there. Some Officer of his Spirit and Experience, seems to be wanted.

The Quarter Master Generals Department, the Adjutant Generals Department, and the Surgion Generals Department, have for sometime past, been in great Confusion. The Army have suffered, in their Baggage, Discipline and Health, from those Causes.

RC (Adams Papers); addressed: "Mrs. Adams   Braintree Mass. Bay"; franked: "free   John Adams."

John Adams to Abigail Adams

Oct. 8. 76

I ought to acknowledge with Gratitude, your constant Kindness in Writing to me, by every Post. Your favour of Septr. 29. came by the last. I wish it had been in my Power, to have returned your Civilities with the same Punctuality, but it has not.

Long before this you have received Letters from me, and Newspapers containing a full Account of the Negociation. The Communication is still open and the Post Riders now do their Duty and will continue to do so.

I assure you, We are as much at a Loss, about Affairs at New York, as you are. In general, our Generals were out generalled on Long Island, and Sullivan and Stirling with 1000 Men were made Prisoners, in Consequence of which, and several other unfortunate Circumstances, a Council of War thought it prudent to retreat from that Island, and Governors Island and then from New York. They are now posted at Haarlem about 10 or 11 Miles from the City. They left behind them some Provisions, some Cannon and some Baggage.

Wherever the Men of War have approached, our Militia have most manfully turned their backs and run away, Officers and Men, like sturdy fellows—and their panicks have sometimes seized the regular Regiments.

One little skirmish on Montresors Island, ended with the Loss of the brave Major Henley, and the disgrace of the rest of the Party. Another Skirmish, which might indeed be called an Action, ended in the defeat and shamefull flight of the Enemy, with the Loss of the brave Coll. Knowlton on our Part. The Enemy have Possession of Paulus Hook and Bergen Point, Places on the Jersy side of the North River.

By this Time their Force is so divided between Staten Island, Long Island, New York, Paulus Hook and Bergen Point, that, I think they will do no great Matter more this fall, unless the Expiration of the Term of Inlistment of our Army, should disband it. If our new Inlistments fill up, for Soldiers during the War, We shall do well enough.—Every Body must encourage this.

You are told that a Regiment of Yorkers behaved ill, and it may be true, but I can tell you that several Regiments of Massachusetts Men have behaved ill, too.

The Spirit of Venality, you mention, is the most dreadfull and alarming Enemy, that America has to oppose. It is as rapacious and insatiable as the Grave. We are in the Fæce Romuli, non Republica Platonis. This predominant Avarice will ruin America, if she is ever ruined. If God almighty does not interpose by his Grace to controul this universal Idolatry to the Mammon of Unrighteousness, We shall be given up to the Chastisements of his Judgments. I am ashamed of the Age I live in.

You surprise me with your Account of the Prayers in publick for an Abdicated King, a Pretender to the Crown. Nothing of that Kind is heard in this Place, or any other Part of the Continent, but New York and the Place you mention. This Practice is Treason against the State and cannot be long tolerated.

I lament the Loss of Soper, as an honest, and usefull Member of Society.

Dont leave off writing to me—I write as often as I can.

I am glad Master John has an office so usefull to his Mamma and Pappa, as that of Post rider.

RC (Adams Papers).

John Adams to Abigail Adams

Philadelphia Octr. 11. 1776

I suppose your Ladyship has been in the Twitters, for some Time past, because you have not received a Letter by every Post, as you used to do.—But I am coming to make my Apology in Person. I, Yesterday asked and obtained Leave of Absence. It will take me till next Monday, to get ready, to finish off a few Remnants of public Business, and to put my private Affairs in proper Order. On the 14th. day of October, I shall get away, perhaps. But I dont expect to reach Home, in less than a fortnight, perhaps not in three Weeks, as I shall be obliged to make stops by the Way.[1]

RC (Adams Papers).

[1] No vote on JA's application for leave, 10 Oct., is recorded in the Journal of Congress. He set off from Philadelphia on Sunday the 13th; see the entry of that date in his *Diary and Autobiography*, 2:251. But since his itemized accounts have not been found, we do not know his route beyond Trenton; and since his correspondence broke off abruptly upon his departure from Congress, we do not know when he reached Braintree. He had arrived by 5 Nov., however, for on that date he drafted a letter, probably intended for a colleague in Congress, on the problem of currency inflation; this is in Lb/JA/1 (Adams Papers, Microfilms, Reel No. 89), but appears to be incomplete and may not have been sent.

Mercy Otis Warren to Abigail Adams

October 15 1776

Nothing but the Greatest affection for my dear Mrs. Adams Would Induce me to Break over the Avocations of this busey Morning, and to quit the Conversation of my Friends who Leave me tomorrow, to scrable over a Hasty Line in Token that I have not Forgot you. Mr. Warren promised to Make all the Apoligies Necessary for my Long silence. Mine is the Loss and the Mortifycation and on that Consideration I Could Wish you would not be quite so Ceremonious, But would oftener Favour Your Friend with the News from Abroad and the political Speculations at home, as well as the sentiments of Friendship which Glow in the Bosom of the sociable Portia.

When do You Expect to see Mr. Adams. I Really think it A Great tryal of patience and philosophy to be so Long seperated from the Companion of Your Heart and from the Father of your Little Flock. But the High Enthusiasm of a truly patriotic Lady will Cary Her through Every Difficulty, and Lead Her to Every Exertion. Patience, Fortitude, Public Spirit, Magnanimity and self Denial are the Virtues she Boasts. I wish I Could put in my Claim to those sublime qualities. But oh! the Dread of Loosing all that this World Can Bestow by one Costly sacrifice keeps my Mind in Continual Alarm. I own my weakness and stand Corrected yet Cannot Rise superior to Those Attachments which sweeten Life and Without which the Dregs of this Terestial Existence Would not be Worth preserving.

I have it in Contemplation to Call on you again before the seting in of Winter but if I do not you will be kind Enough to Return some papers I have Frequently Mentiond by Mr. Warren. I Rely With Confidence you will [not] [1] take nor suffer to be taken any Copies.

Our Friends will tell you all you wish to know about Plimouth. They have made me an agreable Visit, and as this is the Last Day I shall have their Company it will not be quite Civil to Leave them Longer than to subscribe the Name of your Ever Affectionate Friend,

M Warren

RC (Adams Papers).

[1] This word has been editorially supplied.

Mercy Otis Warren to Abigail Adams

Plimouth Dec. 1st. 1776

It is A Long time since I had the Happiness of hearing from my Braintree Friends. Dos my dear Mrs. Adams think I am Indebted a Letter. If she dos Let her Recollect A Moment and she will find she is mistaken. Or is she so wholly Engrossed with the Ideas of her own Happiness as to think Little of the absent. Why should I Interrupt for a moment if this is the Case, the Vivacity and Cheerfulness of Portia Encircled by her Children in full health (her kind Companion sharing this felicity,) to Look in upon her Friend in this hour of solitude, my Husband at Boston, my Eldest son absent, my other four at an Hospital Ill with the small pox, my Father on a bed of pain Verging fast towards the Closing scene, no sisters at hand nor Even a Friend to step in and shorten the tedious hour. I feel with the poet, 'poor is the Friendless Master of a World.' But before I quit talking of myself I must tell you that the Lovely Image of Hope still spreads her silken Wing, and Resting on her pinion I sooth myself into tranquility and peace amidst this Group of painful Circumstances. A few days will make a very material Change in the feelings of my Heart. It may be filled with the Highest sentiments of Gratitude for the preservation and Recovery of my Children, with their Father siting by my side partaking the Delight. Or! I May—My pen trembles. I have not the Courage to Reverse the scene. I Leave the Theme, When you in unison with my soul shall Have Breathed a sigh that your Friend may be prepared for Every designation of providence.

I was Greatly Disappointed that you and Mr. Adams did not Come to Plimouth. Can Neither the General, the Marine nor the Superiour Court, Draw him from his own fire side. Well, Let him Indulge there a Little Longer and the Court of Conscience will do more than all, for I know he Reverences Her awful Tribunal. How is his Health, how are his spirits. What dos he think of the surrender of Fort Washington. Twenty other things I want to ask. If you were both to write me a Good Long Letter it would not more than satisfy my Curiosity and my Wishes. But if the acknowlegements of Gratful Esteem will make any Returns you may be assured of them with the most Cordial sincerity from Your unfeigned Friend,   Mercy Warren

PS I hope Mr. Warren will Return on Wensday by whom you will not Fail to send a Certain Copey of A Letter of no Consequence to any body but your Friend.

Mrs. Lothrop has just steped in and desires her Regards to you. Most of her Connexions in town are at the Hospital. Neer a hundred persons are now under Innoculation.

RC (Adams Papers).

John Adams to Abigail Adams

My dear   Dedham January 9. 1777

The irresistable Hospitality of Dr. Sprague and his Lady has prevailed upon me, and my worthy Fellow Traveller, to put up at his happy Seat.—We had an agreable Ride to this Place, and tomorrow Morning We sett off, for Providence, or some other Rout.[1]

Present my affection, in the tenderest Manner to my little deserving Daughter and my amiable sons.

It was cruel Parting this Morning. My Heart was most deeply affected, altho, I had the Presence of Mind, to appear composed.

May God almightys Providence protect you, my dear, and all our little ones. My good Genius, my Guardian Angell whispers me, that We shall see happier Days, and that I shall live to enjoy the Felicities of domestic Life, with her whom my Heart esteems above all earthly Blessings.

RC (Adams Papers); addressed: "Mrs. John Adams Braintree"; docketed in pencil by AA: "Jan 9." (These penciled docketings continue on JA's letters through February and were probably made late in March when AA inventoried the letters she had so far received from him; see AA to JA, 26 March, below.)

[1] JA's host was Dr. John Sprague, a well-to-do physician and warm patriot who has been mentioned earlier in these letters; on Sprague's house in Dedham see Sibley-Shipton, *Harvard Graduates*, 10:241. Accompanying JA were his servant (John Turner) and one of the two recently elected additional Massachusetts delegates, James Lovell. JA's somewhat imperfect account with Massachusetts for his expenses on this journey is printed from the Adams Papers in his *Diary and Autobiography*, 2:252–253, and his experiences on the way are rather fully described in his letters to AA that follow here. Under the threat of Howe's army in the Jerseys, Congress had adjourned from Philadelphia on 12 Dec. 1776 and reassembled at Baltimore on the 20th (JCC, 6:1027–1028). The travelers took a wide arc around the opposing armies, and their precise itinerary is given in a paper docketed by JA "Mr. Lovells Account," which is receipted by Lovell to JA and is in the Adams Papers under the assigned date 1776–1777 (but should be Jan. 1777). The itinerary and payments for food, lodgings, &c. (for the whole party of men and horses), are given by Lovell as follows:

Dedham	6:	
Medfield	4:	6
Medway	7:	
Mendon	1: 1:	
Duglass	2:	
Killingly	4:	
Thompson	9:	4
Pomfrett	4:	
Kenneday	5:	
Windham	15:	6
Coventry	6:	8
East Hartford	10:	6
Hartford	1: 6:	6
Farmington	6:	
Southington	15:	6
Waterbury	5:	
Woodbury	15:	2
New Milford	7:	
New Fairfield	14:	
Beekman's Precinct	6:	
Fish Kills	16:	
Hackinsac	11:	3
Pokeepsie	1: 2:	
River N[or]th	3:	7
New Marlbro'	1:	6
New Windsor	9:	
Bethlehem	13:10	
Goshen	5:	8
Warwick	7:	4
Hardystown	14:	
Sussex Court House	10:	6
Log Jail	1:	4
Oxford Township	9:	4
Oxford	8:	
Greenwich	4:	
Delaware River	1:10	
East Town	1:18:	8
Bethlehem	2:16:11	
Ferry	1:	3
Chester	1:	3

Wilmington	8:	Godsgraces	18: 7
Newark	14: 6		27:12: 1
Notingham	19: 9		
Susquehannah	12:10	JA's two-thirds share is indicated as
Hartford	1: 2: 6	£18 8s.

John Adams to Abigail Adams

Hartford Jan. 13. 1777

The Riding has been so hard and rough, and the Weather so cold that We have not been able to push farther than this Place. My little Colt has performed very well hitherto, and I think will carry me through the Journey, very pleasantly.

Our Spirits have been cheered, by two or three Pieces of good News, which Commissary Trumble[1] who is now with me, tells us, he saw Yesterday in a Letter from G[eneral] Washington, who has gained another considerable Advantage of the Enemy at Stonny Brook in the Jersies, as G[eneral] Putnam has gained another at Burlington, and the Jersy Militia a third.[2] The Particulars, you will have before this reaches you in the public Prints.

The Communication of Intelligence begins to be more open, and We have no Apprehensions of Danger in the Rout We shall take.

How [Howe] has Reason to repent of his Rashness, and will have more.

My Love to my dear little ones. They are all very good Children and I have no doubt will continue so. I will drop a Line as often as I can. Adieu.

RC (Adams Papers); addressed: "Mrs. John Adams Braintree"; franked: "Free John Adams"; docketed in pencil by AA.

[1] Joseph Trumbull (1737–1778), Harvard 1756 (*DAB*).

[2] These were actions in Washington's daring and highly successful winter campaign to drive in the British and Hessian advanced posts in New Jersey, resulting in American victories at Trenton and Princeton. See his letters to Pres. Hancock, 27 Dec. 1776 and 5 Jan. 1777 (Washington, *Writings*, ed. Fitzpatrick, 6:441–444, 467–471).

John Adams to Abigail Adams

Hartford Jany. 14. 1777

It is now generally believed here that G. Washington has killed and taken at least two Thousands of Mr. Howes Army since Christmas. Indeed the Evidence of it is from the Generals own Letters. You know I ever thought Mr. Hows march through the Jerseys a rash Step. It has proved so—but how much more so would it have been thought if the Americans could all have viewed it in that light and exerted themselves as they might and ought. The whole Flock would infallibly have been taken in the Net.

The little Nest of Hornets in Rhode Island—is it to remain unmolested this Winter? The Honour of N[ew] E[ngland] is concerned —if they are not crushed I will never again glory in being a N.E. man. There are now N.E. Generals, Officers and soldiers and if something is not done, any Man may after that call New England men Poltroons with all my Heart.

RC (Adams Papers); addressed: "Mrs. John Adams Braintree"; docketed in pencil by AA.

John Adams to Abigail Adams

Fish Kill [*17 or 18 January*] 1777

After a March like that of Hannibal over the Alps We arrived last Night at this Place, Where We found the Utmost Difficulty to get Forage for our Horses, and Lodgings for ourselves, and at last were indebted to the Hospitality of a private Gentleman Coll. Brinkhoff [Brinckerhoff], who very kindly cared for Us.

We came from Hartford through Farmington, Southington, Waterbury, Woodbury, New Milford, New Fairfield, the Oblong, &c. to Fish Kill. Of all the Mountains I ever passed these are the worst.—We found one Advantage however in the Cheapness of Travelling.

I dont find one half of the Discontent, nor of the Terror here that I left in the Massachusetts. People seem sanguine that they shall do something grand this Winter.

I am well, and in good Spirits.—My Horse performs extreemly well. He clambers over Mountains that my old Mare would have stumbled on. The Weather has been dreadfully severe.

RC (Adams Papers); addressed: "Mrs. John Adams Braintree To be left at Isaac Smith Esqrs. in Queen Street Boston"; docketed in pencil by AA: "Jan 16" (though JA had left only a blank space in the dateline for the month and day).

John Adams to Abigail Adams

Poughkeepsie Jan. 19. 1777

There is too much Ice in Hudsons River to cross it in Ferry Boats and too little to cross it, without, in most Places, which has given Us the Trouble of riding up the Albany Road as far as this Place, where We expect to go over on the Ice, but if We should be dissappointed here, We must go up as far as Esopus about fifteen miles farther.

This, as well as Fish-kill is a pretty Village. We are almost wholly among the Dutch—Zealous against the Tories, who have not half the Tranquillity here that they have in the Town of Boston, after all the Noise that has been made about N. York Tories.

We are treated with the Utmost Respect, wherever We go, and have met with nothing like an Insult, from any Person whatever. I heard ten Reflections, and twenty Sighs and Groans, among my Constituents to one here.

I shall never have done hoping that my Countrymen will contrive some Coup de main, for the Wretches at Newport. The Winter is the Time. Our Enemies have divided their Force. Let Us take Advantage of it.

RC (Adams Papers); addressed: "Mrs. John Adams Braintree"; added on the cover in the hand of Isaac Smith Sr.: "Yrs. IS"; docketed in pencil by AA.

John Adams to Abigail Adams

Bethlehem Orange County, State of N. York
January 20. 1777

This Morning We crossed the North River at Poughkeepsie, on the Ice, after having ridden many Miles on the East side of it to find a proper Place. We landed at New Marlborough, and passed through that and Newborough [Newburgh] to New Windsor, where We dined. This Place is nearly opposite to Fish kill, and but little above the Highlands, where Fort Constitution and Fort Montgomery stand. The Highlands are a grand Sight, a range of vast Mountains, which seem to be rolling like a tumbling Sea.—From New Windser, We came to this Place, Where We put up, and now We have a free and uninterrupted Passage in a good Road to Pensilvania.

General Washington with his little Army is at Morris town. Cornwallis with his larger one at Brunswick. Oh that the Continental Army was full. Now is the Time.

My little Horse holds out, finely, altho We have lost much Time and travelled a great deal of unnecessary Way, to get over the North River.

We have Reports of our Peoples taking Fort Washington again, and taking 400 more Prisoners and six more Pieces of Cannon—but as I know not the Persons who bring these Accounts I pay no Attention to them.

RC (Adams Papers); addressed: "Mrs. John Adams Braintree"; added on the cover in the hand of Isaac Smith Sr.: "Ys. [*i.e.* Yours] IS"; docketed in pencil by AA.

John Adams to Abigail Adams

Easton at the Forks of Delaware River
in the State of Pensilvania, Jan. 24. 1777

We have at last crossed the Delaware, and are agreably lodged in Easton, a little Town, situated on a Point of Land formed by the Delaware on one Side and the River Lehi, on the other. There is an elegant Stone Church here built by the Dutch People,[1] by whom the Town is chiefly inhabited, and what is remarkable because uncommon, the Lutherans and Calvinists united to build this Church, and the Lutheran and Calvinist Minister, alternately officiate in it. There is also an handsome Court House. The Buildings public and private are all of Lime stone.—Here are some Dutch Jews.

Yesterday We had the Pleasure of seeing the Moravian Mills in New Jersey. These Mills belong to the Society of Moravians in Bethlehem in Pensilvania. They are a great Curiosity. The Building is of Limestone four Stories high. It is not in my Power to give a particular Description of this Piece of Mechanism. A vast Quantity of Grain of all sorts is collected here.[2]

We have passed through the famous County of Sussex in New Jersey, where the Sussex Court House stands and where We have so often been told the Tories are so numerous and so dangerous. We met with no Molestation, nor Insult. We stopped at some of the most noted Tory Houses, and were treated every where with the Utmost Respect. Upon the strictest Inquiry I could make, I was assured that a great Majority of the Inhabitants are stanch Whiggs. Sussex they say can take Care of Sussex, and yet all agree that there are more Tories in that County [than in a]ny[3] other. If the British Army should get into that County in sufficient Numbers to protect the Tories there is no doubt to be made they would be insolent enough and malicious and revengefull. But there is no danger at present and will be none untill that Event takes Place.

The Weather has been sometimes bitterly cold, sometimes warm, sometimes rainy and sometimes snowy, and the Roads, abominably hard and rough, so that this Journey has been the most tedious I ever attempted. Our Accommodations have been often, very bad, but much better and cheaper than they would have been if We had taken the Road from Peeks Kill to Morriston where the Army lies.

RC (Adams Papers); addressed: "Mrs. John Adams Braintree To be left at Isaac Smith Esqrs. Queen Street. Boston"; docketed in pencil by AA.

¹ That is, "Pennsylvania Dutch," or Germans.
² These famous mills were at Hope, near Oxford, in Sussex co., N.J. According to Bishop Kenneth G. Hamilton of the Archives of the Moravian Church, Bethlehem, Penna., "the old stone buildings are still standing, and the grist mill is still a showpiece" (communication to the editors, 6 Aug. 1962).
³ MS torn by seal.

Abigail Adams to John Adams

Janry. 26 1777

Tis a Great Grief to me that I know not how to write nor where to send to you. I know not of any conveyance. I risk this by Major R[ic]e who promisses to take what care he can to get it to you.

I have Received 3 Letters from you since you left me, 2 from H[artfor]d and one from D[edha]m. Tis a satisfaction to hear tho only by a line.

We are told the most dissagreable things by use become less so. I cannot say that I find the truth of the observation verified. I am sure no seperation was ever so painfull to me as the last. Many circumstances concur to make it so—the distance and the difficulty of communication, the Hazards which if not real, my immagination represents so, all conspire [to] ¹ make me anxious, as well as what I need not [. . .] mention.²

I wish to Hear often from you and when a conveniant opportunity offers let me know how you like your waiter. Many reports have been circulated since you went away concerning him none of which I regard as I find no proof to support them. One is that he is a deserted Regular, a Spy &c. I find tis all Suspicion or else told with a design to make me uneasy, but it has not that Effect.

The family are all well, and desire Pappa would write to them.— I rejoice in our late Successes. Heaven grant us a continuation of them.

Your M[othe]r desires to be rememberd to you.

I long to hear of your arrival and to get one Letter from B[altimor]e. The Situation will be new and afford me entertainment by an account of it. At all times remember in the tenderest manner her whose happiness depends upon your Welfare,   Portia

RC (Adams Papers); addressed in John Thaxter's hand: "To The Honble: John Adams Esqr. at Baltimore in Maryland"; endorsed: "Portia. Jany. 26."

[1] Here and below, MS is torn by seal.

[2] AA was pregnant. On the following 11 July she was delivered of a stillborn daughter. See various letters in June and July, below, especially John Thaxter to JA, 13 July, and AA to JA, 16 July.

CFA omitted the present letter from his editions of his grandparents' correspondence and, consistently and silently, all allusions to AA's "Circumstances" in such of the following letters as he did include.

Abigail Adams to Mercy Otis Warren

Dear Marcia   [*January?* 1777][1]

Tis so long since I took a pen up to write a line that I fear you have thought me unmindfull of you; I should not have neglected writing to you immediately upon the receipt of your obliging favour especially as you was then under great anxiety. My Eyes ever since the small pox have been great Sufferers. Writing puts them to great pain.—I now congratulate my Friend upon the Recovery of her amiable family from so Malignant a disease and Mr. Winslow in perticuliar who I heard was under some concern and apprehension from it.[2]

You my Friend then experienced in some measure what I passd through in the Summer past only with this difference that your Friend was within a days ride of you mine hundreds of miles Distant.—O Marcia how many hundred miles this moment seperate us—my heart Bleads at the recollection. Many circumstances conspire to make this Seperation more greivious to me than any which has before taken place. The distance, the difficulty of communication, and the many hazards which my immagination represents as real (if they are not so) from Brittains, Hessians and Tories, render me at times very unhappy. I had it in my Heart to disswade him from going and I know I could have prevaild, but our publick affairs at that time wore so gloomy an aspect that I thought if ever his assistance was wanted, it must be at such a time. I therefore resignd my self to suffer much anxiety and many Melancholy hours for this year to come. I know you have a sympathetick feeling Heart or I should not dare indulge myself in relateing my Griefs.

Many unfortunate as well as prosperious Events have taken place in our publick affairs since I had the pleasure of seeing or writing to you. Lee poor Lee—the loss at fort[s] Washington and Lee together did not affect me eaquelly with the loss of that Brave and Experienced General. He has an unconq[uerable] Spirit, imprisonment must be greivious indeed to him.

I am apt to think that our late misfortunes have called out the hidden Excellencies of our Commander in chief—"affliction is the good mans shining time." The critical state of our affairs has shown him to great advantage. Heaven grant that his Successes may be continued to him, tis Natural to estimate the military abilities of a man according to his Successes.

Can you, do you? credit the report that is circulating with regard to the Farmer.[3] We may well adopt the words of the Psalmist—

Lord what is Man?

I was mortified the other day when I heard the Colonel passd this House without calling. I hope he will not forget me when he returns. My Regards to Mrs. Lothrope and all the little folks. Pray write to me soon, I will endeavour to be better for the future. Yours,   Portia

Dft (Adams Papers); dated conjecturally by JQA at head of text: "1776. Novr.," but see note 1.

[1] This undated draft is evidently a reply to Mrs. Warren's "obliging favour" of 1 Dec. 1776, above, but it was not written until some time after JA's departure from Braintree for Baltimore on 9 Jan. 1777. Since it contains one passage nearly identical in phrasing with one in AA to JA, 26 Jan., preceding, it was probably written at about the same time.

[2] Winslow Warren (1759–1791) was the 2d son of James and Mercy (Otis) Warren; he traveled in Europe during the 1780's and crossed the Adamses'

path several times; he was killed in St. Clair's defeat on the Wabash. See Mrs. Washington A. Roebling, *Richard Warren of the Mayflower* . . . , Boston, 1901, p. 28; JA, *Diary and Autobiography*, 2: 402–403; *Warren-Adams Letters, passim*; Charles Warren, "A Young American's Adventures in England and France during the Revolutionary War," MHS, *Procs.*, 65 (1932–1936):234–267, an article based on Winslow Warren's correspondence with his parents in MHi.

[3] John Dickinson. What the current "report" about him was does not appear.

John Adams to Abigail Adams

Baltimore Feby. 2. 1777

Last Evening We arrived safe in this Town after the longest Journey, and through the worst Roads and the worst Weather, that I have ever experienced. My Horses performed extreamly well.

Baltimore is a very pretty Town, situated on Petapsco River, which empties itself into the great Bay of Cheasapeak. The Inhabitants are all good Whiggs, having sometime ago banished all the Tories from among them. The Streets are very dirty and miry, but every Thing else is agreable except the monstrous Prices of Things. We cannot get an Horse kept under a Guinea a Week. Our Friends are well.

The continental Army is filling up fast, here and in Virginia. I pray that the Massachusetts may not fail of its Quota, in Season.

In this Journey, We have crossed four mighty Rivers, Connecticutt, Hudson, Delaware, and Susquehannah. The two first We crossed upon the Ice, the two last in Boats—the last We crossed, a little above the Place where it empties into Cheasapeak Bay.

I think I have never been better pleased with any of our American States than with Maryland. We saw most excellent Farms all along the Road, and what was very striking to me, I saw more sheep and more flax in Maryland than I ever saw in riding a like Distance in any other State. We scarce passed a Farm without seeing a fine flock of sheep, and scarce an House without seeing Men or Women, dressing Flax. Several Times We saw Women, breaking and swingling this necessary Article.

I have been to Meeting, and heard my old Acquaintance Mr. Allison, a worthy Clergyman of this Town whom I have often seen in Philadelphia.

RC (Adams Papers); addressed: "For Mrs. John Adams Braintree To be left at Mr. Isaac Smiths in Queen Street Boston"; docketed in pencil by AA.

John Adams to Abigail Adams

Baltimore Feby. 3. 1777

This Day has been observed in this Place, with exemplary Decency and Solemnity, in Consequence of an Appointment of the Government, in Observance of a Recommendation of Congress, as a Day of Fasting. I went to the Presbyterian Meeting and heard Mr. Allison deliver a most pathetic and animating, as well as pious, patriotic and elegant Discourse. I have seldom been better pleased or more affected with a sermon.

The Presbyterian Meeting House in Baltimore stands upon an Hill just at the Back of the Town, from whence We have a very fair Prospect of the Town, and of the Water upon which it stands, and of the Country round it. Behind this Eminence, which is the Bacon [Beacon] Hill of Baltimore, lies a beautifull Meadow, which is entirely incircled by a Stream of Water. This most beautifull Scæne must be partly natural and partly artificial. Beyond the Meadow and Canall, you have a charming View of the Country. Besides the Meeting House there is upon this Height, a large and elegant Court House, as yet unfinished within, and a small Church of England in which an old Clergyman officiates, Mr. Chase, Father of Mr. Chace[1] one of the Delegates of Maryland, who they say is not so zealous a Whigg as the Son.

I shall take Opportunities to describe this Town and State more particularly to you hereafter. I shall inquire into their Religion, their Laws, their Customs, their Manners, their Descent and Education, their Learning, their Schools and Colledges and their Morals.—It was said of Ulysses I think that he saw the Manners of many Men and many Cities, which is like to be my Case, as far as American Men and Cities extend, provided Congress should continue in the rolling Humour, which I hope they will not. I wish however, that my Mind was more at rest than it is, that I might be able to make more exact Observations of Men and Things as far as I go.

When I reflect upon the Prospect before me of so long an Absence from all that I hold dear in this World, I mean all that contributes to my private personal Happiness, it makes me melancholly. When I think on your *Circumstances* I am more so, and yet I rejoice at them in spight of all this Melancholly.—God almightys Providence protect and bless you and yours and mine.

RC and LbC (Adams Papers). This day JA resumed his practice of keeping copies of his outgoing letters; the present letter is the third in a new folio letter-book (Lb/JA/3) containing entries for both family and other letters. But he wrote numerous letters from Congress during 1777, to both AA and others, of which he did not keep copies; see descriptive notes on JA to AA, 27 April, 25–27 May, both below.

[1] JA long persisted in spelling the name of his friend and fellow delegate Samuel Chase in this way. Samuel's father, an immigrant from England, was Thomas Chase, rector of St. Paul's, Baltimore (*DAB*, under Samuel Chase).

John Adams to Abigail Adams

Baltimore Feby: 7. 1777

I am at last after a great deal of Difficulty, settled in comfortable Quarters, but at an infinite Expence....[1] The Price I pay for my Board is more moderate than any other Gentlemen give, excepting my Colleagues, who are all in the same Quarters,[2] and at the same Rates except Mr. H[ancock] who keeps an House by himself.

The Prices of Things here, are much more intollerable than at Boston.

The Attempt of New England to regulate Prices, is extreamly popular in Congress, who will recommend an Imitation of it to the other States: for my own Part I expect only a partial and a temporary Relief from it. And I fear that after a Time the Evils will break out with greater Violence. The Water will flow with greater Rapidity for having been dammed up for a Time. The only radical Cure will be to stop the Emission of more Paper, and to draw in some that is already out, and devise Means effectually to support the Credit of the Rest.[3]

To this End We must begin forthwith to tax the People, as largely as the distressed Circumstances of the Country will bear. We must raise the Interest from four to six Per Cent. We must if possible borrow Silver and Gold from abroad. We must, above all Things, endeavour this Winter, to gain farther Advantages of the Enemy, that our Power may be in somewhat higher Reputation than it is, or rather than it has been.

RC (Adams Papers); addressed: "Mrs. John Adams Braintree favoured by Mr. Hall"; docketed in pencil by AA. LbC (Adams Papers).

[1] Suspension points in MS.

[2] "at Mrs. Ross'es in Markett Street, Baltimore a few Doors below the fountain Inn" (JA, *Diary and Autobiography*, 2:257).

[3] See JA's speeches in Congress on this subject, 10 and 14 Feb., as recorded in Benjamin Rush's minutes of debates (Burnett, ed., *Letters of Members*, 2: 245, 252). On the Massachusetts price-fixing act of Jan. 1777, see AA to JA, 8 Feb., below, and note there.

John Adams to Abigail Adams

Baltimore Feb. 7. 1777

I think, in some Letter I sent you, since I left Bethlehem, I promised you a more particular Account of that curious and remarkable Town.

When We first came in sight of the Town, We found a Country better cultivated and more agreably diversified with Prospects of orchards and Fields, Groves and Meadows, Hills and Valleys, than any We had seen.

When We came into the Town We were directed to a public House kept by a Mr. Johnson, which I think was the best Inn, I ever saw. It belongs it seems to the Society, is furnished, at their Expence, and is kept for their Profit, or at their Loss. Here you might find every Accommodation that you could wish for yourself, your servants and Horses, and at no extravagant Rates neither.[1]

The Town is regularly laid out, the Streets straight and at right Angles like those in Philadelphia. It stands upon an Eminence and has a fine large Brook flowing on one End of it, and the Lehigh a Branch of the Delaware on the other. Between the Town and the Lehigh are beautifull public Gardens.

They have carried the mechanical Arts to greater Perfection here than in any Place which I have seen. They have a sett of Pumps which go by Water, which force the Water up through leaden Pipes, from the River to the Top of the Hill, near an hundred feet, and to the Top of a little Building, in the shape of a Pyramid, or Obelisk, which stands upon the Top of the Hill and is twenty or thirty feet high. From this Fountain Water is conveyed in Pipes to every Part of the Town.

Upon the River they have a fine Sett of Mills. The best Grist Mills and bolting Mills, that are any where to be found. The best fulling Mills, an oil Mill, a Mill to grind Bark for the Tanyard, a Dying House where all Colours are died, Machines for shearing Cloth &c.

There are three public Institutions here of a very remarkable Nature. One, a Society of the young Men, another of the young Women, and a Third of the Widows. There is a large Building, divided into many Appartments, where the young Men reside, by themselves, and carry on their several Trades. They pay a Rent to the Society for their Rooms, and they pay for their Board, and what they earn is their own.

There is another large Building, appropriated in the same Manner to the young Women. There is a Governess, a little like the Lady Abbess, in some other Institutions, who has the Superintendence of the whole, and they have elders. Each Apartment has a Number of young Women, who are vastly industrious, some Spinning, some Weaving, others employed in all the most curious Works in Linnen, Wool, Cotton, Silver and Gold, Silk and Velvet. This Institution displeased me much. Their Dress was uniform and clean, but very inelegant. Their Rooms were kept extreamly warm with Dutch Stoves: and the Heat, the Want of fresh Air and Exercise, relaxed the poor Girls in such a manner, as must I think destroy their Health. Their Countenances were languid and pale.

The Society of Widows is very similar. Industry and Æconomy are remarkable in all these Institutions.

They shewed Us their Church which is hung round with Pictures of our Saviour from his Birth to his Death, Resurrection and Ascention. It is done with very strong Colours, and very violent Passions, but not in a very elegant Taste. The Painter who is still living in Bethelehem, but very old—he has formerly been in Italy, the school of Paints.[2] They have a very good organ in their Church of their own make. They have a public Building, on Purpose for the Reception of the dead, to which the Corps is carried as soon as it expires, where it lies untill the Time of Sepulture.

Christian Love is their professed Object, but it is said they love

Money and make their public Institutions subservient to the Gratification of that Passion.

They suffer no Law suits with one another, and as few as possible with other Men. It is said that they now profess to be against War.

They have a Custom, peculiar, respecting Courtship and Marriage. The Elders pick out Pairs to be coupled together, who have no Opportunity of Conversing together, more than once or twice, before the Knot is tied. The Youth of the two sexes have very little Conversation with one another, before Marriage.

Mr. Hassey,[3] a very agreable, sensible Gentleman, who shewed Us the Curiosities of the Place, told me, upon Inquiry that they profess the Augsburg Confession of Faith, are Lutherans rather than Calvinists, distinguish between Bishops and Presbyters, but have no Idea of the Necessity of the uninterrupted Succession, are very liberal and candid in their Notions in opposition to Bigottry, and live in Charity with all Denominations.[4]

RC (Adams Papers); docketed in pencil by AA. LbC (Adams Papers).

[1] This was the Sun Inn, kept by Just Jansen (1719–1790), a native of Jutland and former mariner who had come to Bethlehem in the 1750's (William C. Reichel, *The Old Sun Inn at Bethlehem* ..., Doylestown, Penna., 1873, p. 23 and note).

[2] Thus in both RC and LbC.

[3] Brother Johann Christian Hasse (1740–1797), born and educated in Germany, served from 1771 as bookkeeper or secretary for the Moravian Church administration (communication from Bishop Kenneth G. Hamilton, Archives of the Moravian Church, Bethlehem, to the editors, 6 Aug. 1962).

[4] A Moravian diary kept at Bethlehem briefly mentions JA's visit there on 25–26 Jan.; see *PMHB*, 12:397 (Jan. 1889). In September JA visited this Moravian community again and made further observations on it (*Diary and Autobiography*, 2:266–267; see also an illustration in same, facing p. 163).

Abigail Adams to John Adams

Febry 8 1777

Before this time I fancy you at your journeys end; I have pittied you the Season has been a continued cold.

I have heard oftner from you than I ever did in any of your former journeys, it has greatly releaved my mind under its anxiety. I have received six Letters from you, and have the double pleasure of hearing you are well, and that your Thoughts are often turnd this way.

I have wrote once by Major Rice. Two Gentlemen set of for B[altimor]e monday or twesday and have engaged to take this Letter. I feel under so many restraints when I sit down to write that I scarcly know what to say to you. The conveyance of Letters is so precarious that I shall not trust any thing of consequence to them untill we have more regular passes.

Indeed very little of any consequence has taken place since you left us. We seem to be in a state of Tranquility; rather too much so. I wish there was a little more Zeal shewn to join the Army.

Nothing now but the regulating Bill engrosses their attention. The merchant scolds, the farmer growls, and every one seems wroth that he cannot grind his neighbour.[1]

We have a report here said to come in two private Letters that a Considerable Battle has taken place in Brunswick in which we have taken 15000 prisoners. I cannot credit so Good News. The Letters are said to be without date.

I rejoice so much when I only receive a few lines from you, just to hear you are well, that I think I shall give eaquel pleasure by writing to you, tho I cannot say I have enjoyed so much Health since you left me as I did in the begining of winter. Johnny has had an ill turn, but is better.

I beg you would write by every opportunity, and if you cannot send so often as you used write and Let them lay by till you make a pacquet. —What is become of the Farmer, many reports are abroad to his disadvantage.

I feel as if you were gone to a foreign Country. Philadelphia seem'd close by but now I hardly know how to reconcile my self to the Thought that you are 500 miles distant. But tho distant you are always near to

Portia

RC (Adams Papers); addressed in John Thaxter's hand: "To The Honble: John Adams Esqr. at Baltimore in Maryland"; endorsed: "Portia ans. March 7."

[1] The "regulating Bill" was An Act to prevent Monopoly and Oppression, passed 25 Jan. 1777 (Mass., *Province Laws*, 5:583–589). This long and detailed act hopefully fixed wages for labor and the prices of every sort of commodity, both domestic and imported, very precisely. A supplementary act was passed on 10 May (same, p. 642–647), but the ineffectualness of the legislation is attested by complaints from both buyers and sellers in numerous letters that follow.

John Adams to Abigail Adams

Baltimore Feby. 10. 1777

Yesterday, I took a long Walk with our Secretary Mr. Thompson to a Place called Fells Point, a remarkable Piece of Ground about a mile from the Town of Baltimore. It is a Kind of Peninsula which runs out into the Harbour, and forms a Bason before the Town. This Bason, within thirty Years, was deep enough for large Tobacco ships to ride in, but since that Time has filled up ten Feet, so that none but small light Vessells can now come in. Between the Town and the Point We pass a Bridge over a small run of Water which empties itself into the Bason, and is the only Stream which runs into it and is quite insufficient to float away the Earth which every year runs into the Bason from the dirty streets of the Town and the neighbouring Hills and fields.[1]

There are four Men of War just entered Cheasapeak Bay, which makes it difficult for Vessells to go out, and indeed has occasioned an Embargo to be laid here for the present. Your Uncle[2] has two Vessells here, both detained—one is now employed as a Transport for a little While. These Men of War will disappoint you of your Barrell of flour. Your Uncle's Vessells would sell very well here. Hardens would fetch 800 Pounds of this Money.[3]

RC (Adams Papers); addressed: "To Mrs. John Adams Braintree favoured by [*no name given*]"; added in the hand of Isaac Smith Sr.: "Postage 6/ Yrs. I Smith"; docketed in pencil by AA. LbC (Adams Papers) is an abstract: "10 Feb. wrote a short Letter to Portia, which I had not Time to transcribe, and sent it by a Hand of Captn. Arnold who is here from the Mass. Board of War. — The Letter contains nothing but an observation or two concerning Fells Point and the Bason before the Town, and one or Two things about her Uncles Vessells."

[1] JA continued this description in his second letter of this day, following. Compare the entry of 9 Feb. 1777 in his *Diary and Autobiography*, 2:258–259.

[2] Isaac Smith Sr.

[3] Last two words worn in MS and barely legible. Apparently JA means Pennsylvania currency, the money used in Maryland.

John Adams to Abigail Adams

Baltimore Feby. 10. 1777

Fells Point, which I mentioned in a Letter this Morning, has a considerable Number of Houses upon it. The Shipping all lies now at this Point. You have from it on one side a compleat View of the Harbour, and on the other a fine Prospect of the Town of Baltimore. You see the Hill, in full View and the Court House, the Church and Meeting House, upon it. The Court House makes an haughty Appearance, from this Point. There is a Fortification erected, on this Point with a Number of Embrasures for Cannon facing the Narrows which make the Entrance into the Harbour. At the Narrows they have a Fort, with a Garrison in it.

It is now a Month and a few days, since I left you. I have heard nothing from you, nor received a Letter from the Massachusetts. I hope the Post Office will perform better than it has done.

I am anxious to hear how you do. I have in my Mind a Source of Anxiety, which I never had before, since I became such a Wanderer. You know what it is. Cant you convey to me, in Hieroglyphicks, which no other Person can comprehend, Information which will relieve me. Tell me you are as well as can be expected.

My Duty to your Papa and my Mamma. Love to Brothers, and Sisters. Tell Betcy I hope She is married.—Tho I want to throw the Stocking. My Respects to Mr. S[haw]. Tell him he may be a Calvinist if he will, provided always that he preserves his Candour, Charity and Moderation.[1]

What shall I say of or to my N. J. C. and T.?[2] What will they say to me for leaving them, their Education and Fortune so much to the Disposal of Chance?—May almighty and allgracious Providence protect, and bless them.

I have this Day sent my Resignation of a certain mighty office.[3] It has relieved me from a Burden, which has a long Time oppress'd me. But I am determined, that, while I am ruining my Constitution of Mind and Body, and running dayly Risques of my Life and Fortune in Defence of the Independency of my Country, I will not knowingly resign my own.

RC (Adams Papers); addressed: "For Mrs: Adams at Mr. John Adams's Braintree favd. by Mr. Hall"; docketed in pencil by AA. LbC (Adams Papers) is an abstract: "Wrote another Letter the same day to Portia, about indifferent Things of no Consequence—only informed her of the above Resignation [*see note* 3 *below*] and that I was determind that while I was ruining my Constitution both of Mind and Body, and running daily Risques of Life and Fortune in defence of the Independency of my Country, I would not knowingly resign my own."

[1] On the following 16 Oct. AA's sister Elizabeth was to marry Rev. John Shaw at Weymouth. JA did not "throw the Stocking" because he was still attending Congress. AA held very different views of her sister's engagement; see her letter to JA of 8–10 March, below.

[2] Nabby, Johnny, Charley, and Tommy. CFA's text in *Familiar Letters*, p. 244, reads: "my children."

[3] The chief justiceship of Massachusetts. JA's resignation was in a letter to the Massachusetts Council, enclosed in a letter to Deputy Secretary John Avery, both dated this day and both found as letterbook copies in Adams Papers; enclosure printed in JA, *Works*, 3:25. Besides numerous references to JA's appointment and resignation as chief justice in the present volumes from 31 July 1775 on, see also his *Diary and Autobiography*, 3:359–363; Avery to JA, 7 March (Adams Papers); and JA to Avery, 21 March (LbC, Adams Papers, printed in *Works*, 9:457–458).

Abigail Adams to John Adams

Febry 12. 1777

Mr. Bromfield was so obliging as to write me Word that he designd a journey to the Southern States, and would take perticuliar care of a Letter to you. I rejoice in so good an opportunity of letting you know that I am well as usual, but that I have not yet got reconciled to the great distance between us. I have many melancholy Hours when the best company is urksome to me, and solitude the greatest happiness I can enjoy.

I wait most earnestly for a Letter to bring me the welcome tidings of your safe arrival. I hope you will be very perticuliar and let me know how you are after your fatigueing journey. How you are accommodated. How you like Maryland. What state of mind you find the C[ongre]ss in, and what may be communicated relative to their proceedings. You know how little intelegance we received during your stay here with regard to what was passing there or in the Army. We know no better now, all communication seems to be embaressed. I got more knowledge from a Letter wrote to you from your Namesake which I received since you left me,[1] than I had before obtain since you left P[hiladel-phi]a. I find by that Letter that six Hessian officers together with Col. Campel had been offerd in exchange for General Lee. I fear he receives very ill Treatment, the terms were not complied with as poor Campbel finds. He was much surprized when the officers went to take him, and beg'd to know what he had been guilty of? They told him it was no crime of his own but they were obliged tho reluctantly to commit him to Concord jail in consequence of the ill treatment of General Lee. He then beged to know how long his confinement was to last, they told him that was imposible for them to say, since it lay wholy in the power of General How to determine it.[2]

By a vessel from Bilboa we have accounts of the safe arrival of Dr. F————g in France ten day[s] before She saild;[3] a French Gentleman who came passenger says we may rely upon it that 200 thousand Russians will be here in the Spring.

A Lethargy seems to have seazd our Country Men. I hear no more of molessting or routing those troops at Newport than of attacking Great Britain.

We just begin to talk of raising our Men for the Standing Army. I wish to know whether the reports may be Credited of the Southern Regiments being full?

You will write me by the Bearer of this Letter, to whose care you may venture to commit any thing you have Liberty to Communicate. I have wrote you twice before this, hope you have received them. The Children all desire to be rememberd—so does your   Portia

RC (Adams Papers); addressed in an unidentified hand: "To The Honble: John Adams Esqr. at Philadelphia"; endorsed: "Portia. ans. March 7."

¹ Samuel Adams to JA, Baltimore, 9 Jan. 1777 (Adams Papers), printed in JA, *Works*, 9:448–450.

² Lt. Col. Archibald Campbell of the 71st Regiment of Highlanders, a member of Parliament, had been captured when the transport in which he had come out put into Boston harbor just after the British squadron had left there in June 1776 (DNB; William Bell Clark, *George Washington's Navy*, Baton Rouge, 1960, p. 160 ff.). When placed in a common jail at Concord in retalia-tion for alleged British mistreatment of Gen. Charles Lee, Campbell appealed to Washington, who wrote the Massachusetts Council a severe letter on the subject, 28 Feb. 1777 (*Writings*, ed. Fitzpatrick, 7:207–208).

³ AA commonly spelled Franklin's name "Frankling." He had sailed from the Delaware on 29 Oct. and arrived at Nantes on 8 Dec. or a day or so before (Wharton, ed., *Dipl. Corr. Amer. Rev.*, 2:216–217, 221).

John Adams to Abigail Adams

Baltimore Feb. 15. 1777

Mr. Hall, by whom this Letter will be sent, will carry several Letters to you, which have been written and delivered to him, several Days. He has settled his Business, agreably.

I have not received a Line from the Massachusetts, since I left it.

Whether We shall return to Philadelphia, soon, or not, I cannot say. I rather conjecture it will not be long. You may write to me, in Congress, and the Letter will be brought me, wherever I shall be.

I am settled now agreably enough in my Lodgings, there is nothing in this Respect that lies uneasily upon my Mind, except the most extravagant Price which I am obliged to give for every Thing. My Constituents will think me extravagant, but I am not. I wish I could sell or send home my Horses, but I cannot. I must have Horses and a Servant, for Congress will be likely to remove several Times in the Course of the ensuing Year.

I am impatient to hear from you, and most tenderly anxious for your Health and Happiness. I am also most affectionately solicitous for my dear N. J. C. and T. to whom remember Yours.[1]

We long to hear of the Formation of a new Army. We shall loose the most happy opportunity of destroying the Enemy this Spring, if We do not exert ourselves instantly.

We have from New Hampshire a Coll. Thornton, a Physician by

Profession, a Man of Humour. He has a large Budget of droll Stories, with which he entertains Company perpetually.

I heard about Twenty or five and twenty Years ago, a Story of a Physician in Londonderry, who accidentally met with one of our new England Enthusiasts, call'd Exh[orters].[2] The Fanatic soon began to examine the Dr. concerning the Articles of his Faith, and what he thought of original Sin?

Why, says the Dr., I satisfy myself about it in this manner. Either original Sin is divisible or indivisible. If it was divisible every descendant of Adam and Eve must have a Part, and the share which falls to each Individual at this Day, is so small a Particle, that I think it is not worth considering. If indivisible, then the whole Quantity must have descended in a right Line, and must now be possessed by one Person only, and the Chances are Millions and Millions and Millions to one that that Person is now in Asia or Africa, and that I have nothing to do with it.

I told Thornton the story and that I suspected him to be the Man.[3] He said he was. He belongs to Londonderry.

RC (Adams Papers); addressed: "Mrs. Adams at Mr. John Adams's Braintree"; docketed in pencil by AA.

[1] JA evidently intended to break off here, but then resumed on a second page.
[2] MS torn by seal.
[3] That is, the man who answered the exhorter. Dr. Matthew Thornton (ca. 1714–1803) was a delegate to the Continental Congress from New Hampshire, 1776–1777 (*DAB*).

John Adams to Abigail Adams

Baltimore Feb. 17. 1777

It was this Day determined, to adjourn, tomorrow Week to Philadelphia.[1]

How, as you know my opinion always was, will repent his mad march through the Jersies. The People of that Commonwealth, begin to raise their Spirits exceedingly, and to be firmer than ever. They are actuated by Resentment now, and Resentment coinciding with Principle is a very powerfull Motive.

I have got into the old Routine of War Office and Congress, which takes up my Time in such a manner that I can scarce write a Line. I have not Time to think, nor to speak.

There is an united States Lottery abroad.[2] I believe you had better buy a Tickett and make a Present of it to our four sweet ones, not forgetting the other sweet one. Let us try their Luck. I hope they will be more lucky than their Papa has ever been, or ever will be.

I am as well as can be expected. How it happens I dont know nor how long it will last. My Disposition was naturally gay and chearfull, but the ⟨awful⟩ Prospects I have ever had before me, and these cruel Times will make me melancholly. I who would not hurt the Hair of the Head of any Animal, I who am always made miserable by the Misery of every sensible being, that comes to my Knowledge, am obliged to hear continual Accounts of the Barbarities, the cruel Murders in cold Blood, even by the most tormenting Ways of starving and freezing, committed by our Enemies, and continual Accounts of the Deaths and Diseases contracted by our People by their own Imprudence.

These Accounts harrow me beyond Description.[3]

These incarnate Dæmons say in great Composure, ["that][4] Humanity is a Yankey Virtue.—But that they [are] governed by Policy."—Is there any Policy on this side of Hell, that is inconsistent with Humanity? I have no Idea of it. I know of no Policy, God is my Witness but this—Piety, Humanity and Honesty are the best Policy.

Blasphemy, Cruelty, and Villany have prevailed and may again. But they wont prevail against America, in this Contest, because I find the more of them are employed the less they succeed.

RC (Adams Papers); addressed: "Mrs. Adams at Mr. John Adams's Braintree"; docketed in pencil by AA.

[1] That is, Congress was to adjourn at Baltimore on the 25th, but on that day the adjournment was suspended in consequence of letters received from Gen. Washington and Robert Morris. On the 27th Congress adjourned to "Wednesday next [5 March], to meet at the State House in Philadelphia," but a quorum was not assembled there until 12 March.

See *JCC*, 7:127, 157 and note, 168, 169.

[2] Authorized by Congress in Nov. 1776; see Lucius Wilmerding Jr., "The United States Lottery," N.Y. Hist. Soc., *Quart.*, 47:5–39 (Jan. 1963).

[3] MS: "Destription."

[4] Here and below, MS is torn by seal.

John Adams to Abigail Adams

Baltimore Feb. 18. 1777

I shall inclose with this a Newspaper or two.

I am as yet in tollerable Health. My Eyes are somewhat troublesome. I believe I must assume the Appearance of Wisdom, Age and Gravity and put on Spectacles to walk in, about the Streets.

I hear nothing from you, nor from any Part of New England, but

I am endeavouring to devise some better Regulations of the Post Office, so that I hope that Channell of Communication will be opened.[1]

We are told that the Air of Baltimore is unhealthy, and I confess I should dread it, if I were to stay here long. But We shall soon remove.

You may write now by the Post. I am very anxious to hear from you, and to know the State of public Affairs, in your Part of the World.

I have written by Mr. Hall a Resignation of an Office. I suppose it will make a Noise. But I hope not much. I cant help it. But should be glad to hear from you, how it is received. I hope they will fill it up soon, that the Talk may be soon over.

I could not be, at the same Time in Maryland and Massachusetts Bay, which was Reason enough for the Measure, if I had no other, but I have many more, and much stronger.

I have not Health enough, and never shall have to discharge such a Trust. I can but just keep myself alive, and in tollerable Spirits when I am master of my own Time and Course of Life. But this is not all.

I am not formal and ceremonious enough for such a stiff Situation. —But you know I have many Reasons more.

RC (Adams Papers); docketed in pencil by AA. Enclosed newspapers not found or identified.

[1] On 17 Feb. JA was named one of five members of a committee "to revise the regulations of the post office, and report a plan of carrying it on, so as to render the conveyance of intelligence more expeditious and certain" (JCC, 7:127). The committee brought in a report on the 25th, which was read and tabled; the MS is in the hand of the chairman, Thomas Heyward; text printed in same, p. 153–154. For subsequent efforts toward the same end in April and October, see same, p. 258, and vol. 9:816–817.

John Adams to Abigail Adams

Baltimore Feb. 20th. 1777

This Morning I received yours of the 26th. Ult. It is the first I have received from you, and except one from Gen. Palmer of the 28th.[1] it is the first I have received from our State.

Yours made me very happy. Dont be uneasy about my Waiter. He behaves very well to me, and he has not the least Appearance of a Spy or a Deserter. He has not Curiosity, nor Activity nor sense enough for such a Character. He does his Duty extreamly well however in his station. But if he was a Spy he would learn nothing from me. He knows no more, from me, than the Horse he rides, nor shall he know....[2] I have no Conversation with him upon Politicks, nor shall he come to the Sight of Papers.

I hope our Soldiers for the new Army will be all inoculated at Home before they begin their March. The Small Pox is so thick in the Country that there is no Chance of escaping it in the natural Way. Gen. Washington has been obliged to inoculate his whole Army. We are inocculating soldiers here and at Philadelphia.

RC (Adams Papers); addressed: "Mrs. Adams at Mr. John Adams's Braintree"; docketed in pencil by AA.

[1] In Adams Papers. JA's reply, of the present date, is in NN and is printed in part in Burnett, ed., *Letters of Members*, 2:268.
[2] Suspension points in MS.

John Adams to Abigail Adams

Baltimore Feb. 21. 1777

Yesterday, I had the Pleasure of dining with Mr. Purveyance.

There are two Gentlemen of this Name in Baltimore, Samuel and Robert, eminent Merchants, and in Partnership.[1] We had a brillant Company, the two Mrs. Purveyances, the two Mrs. Lees, the Ladies of the two Colonels R[ichard] H[enry] and F[rancis], Mrs. H[ancock] and Miss Katy [Quincy], and a young Lady that belongs to the Family. If this Letter, like some other wise ones, should be intercepted, I suppose I shall be call'd to Account for not adjusting the Rank of these Ladies a little better.

Mr. H., the two Coll. Lees, Coll. Whipple, Coll. Page, Coll. Ewing, the two Mr. Purveyances, and a young Gentleman. I fancy I have named all the Company.

How happy would this Entertainment have been to me if I could by a single Volition have transported one Lady about five hundred miles. But alass! this a greater Felicity than falls to my share.

We have voted to go to Philadelphia next Week.

We have made General Lincoln a Continental Major General.

We shall make Coll. Glover a Brigadier.

I sincerely wish We could hear more from General Heath. Many Persons are extreamly dissatisfied with Numbers of the general Officers of the highest Rank. I dont mean the Commander in Chief, his Character is justly very high, but Schuyler, Putnam, Spencer, Heath, are thought by very few to be capable of the great Commands they hold. We hear of none of their heroic Deeds of Arms. I wish they would all resign.

For my Part I will vote upon the genuine Principles of a Republic for a new Election of general Officers annually, and every Man shall have my Consent to be left out, who does not give sufficient Proof of his Qualifications.

I wish my Lads were old enough. I would send every one of them into the Army, in some Capacity or other. Military Abilities and Experience, are a great Advantage to any Character.

RC (Adams Papers); addressed: "Mrs. John Adams Braintree Mass. Bay"; docketed in pencil by AA.

[1] On the Purviance brothers see entry of this date in JA's *Diary and Autobiography*, 2:260, and note there.

Mercy Otis Warren to Abigail Adams

Plimouth March 1st 1777

For once I have followed the Example of my Friend, and have Long delayed a Reply to her Letter. And though I Cannot Complain of my Eyes as an Excuse, yet I have other Weaknesses to plead that are more than a Ballence, and to say Nothing of the Intelectual system, the Weakness of my Constitution, the Febleness of my Limbs, and the pains in my [spirits?], for several months past is sufficient to damp the Vigour of thought, And Check the inclination for Literary Employment which has heretofore Excited me to spend my Leasure hours in the use of my pen. And I think that Inclination has brought some of my Friends so far in Arrears that I might Claim a Letter or two Exstraordinary on the score of former accounts if the schedule of the Last Year should not happen to be in my Favour.

I do not wonder at the Regrets you Express at the distance and absence of your Excellent Husband.

But why should not the same Heroic Virtue, the same Fortitude, patience and Resolution, that Crowns the memory of the ancient Matron, Adorn the Character of Each modern Fair who Adopts the signature of *Portia*. Surely Rome had not severer tryals than America, nor was Cesar in the senate with his Flatterers, and his Legions about him, more to be Dreaded than George the 3d with his parasites in parliment, and his murdering Mercenaries in the Field.

But as I have several other Letters to write this day, I must speedily descend from the Altitudes of Heroism, and talk in the simple stile of the Manufacturer and the Humbler Language of the Domestic Dame: who seeketh Wool and Flax and Worketh Willingly with her hands.

I would not have you over anxious about the Dispatch of a peice of Bussiness Entrusted to your Care, for though all my household are not Cloathed in scarlet, yet I have not that Reason to be affraid of the snow, with some shivering Mortals at this severe season whose hands perhaps are oftener Layed to the Distaff, but whose Labours at the spindle will not provide fine Linnen for the Merchant, while the Husbandman, who used to Reap the full Grown Ear, and watch the flaxen Harvest is Wading in the Field of Blood.

I do not Exactly Remember how much Wool I sent Forward. It Lies in my mind it was between 94 and 98 weight: but Mr. Warren and his son are Confident it was made up a Neat 100, before it was sent to your Care.

I suppose when it is done we shall be very proud of Braintree Manufactures, more Especially as it is done under the Inspection of one of the Amphyctionic Ladies, to whom the Females of the united states, must in the Future Look up for the Example of Industery and œconimy, whose manners must Lead the Fashion of the times unless any are so Depraved in Their Taste as to prefer the Modes of Paris, and the Frenchefyed airs of Mademoisel from Varssailles to the Lindsey Woolsey of their own Country, and the simplicity and puritanism of N. England.

I am ashamed to ask my Friend again for a paper of so Little Consequence as one in her hands yet I own if it is not Lost I should be Glad you Would send it Forward by some safe hand And in Return for the trouble I have Given You in a matter so unimportant I will promiss no more to pester you with anything of the like Nature from your sincere & Affectionate Friend,   M Warren

My Love to miss Naby and the Young Gentlemen.

If Mrs. Adams has not otherways disposed of the wool should like a Little [...]¹ Worsted.

RC (Adams Papers).

¹ Possibly "stolen," although what this could mean in the present context is not clear.

John Quincy Adams to John Adams

Sir   Braintree March the 3 1777

I write to Congratulate you upon your arrival in baltimore and hope you will not omit writing to me. I have been very earnest to write to you for some time but could not find a subject we have no news here unless telling you that we have had several severe snow storms since you went away and yesterday we had one that banked over the tops of the fences we have not had so much snow before for five years— it has been very cold and severe weather since you left us but very healthy Mamma hears the Post office is a going to be new regulated and then she will be able to write without fear of interruption—if any-thing a new should arise I shall then be able to write you a longer let-ter. My Brothers send thier Duty please to accept of the same from your dutifull son,   John Quincy Adams

RC (Adams Papers); addressed: "To the Honble John Adams at Baltimore"; docketed in an unidentified hand. JQA's open style of punctuation has been preserved.

John Adams to Abigail Adams

Philadelphia March 7. 1777

I am returned in tolerable Health to this Town—have received but one Letter from you since I left you, that which you sent by Mr. Rice.[1]

If you send Letters to Coll. Warren, or your Unkle Smith, they will be conveyed, with safety. I hope the Post Office will be upon a better footing soon.

An Army is gathering in the Jerseys. They have frequent Skirmishes, and the Enemy generally come off second best.—Whether We shall stay long here is uncertain. If We remove it will not be far.

This will go by Dr. Jackson one of the Managers of the Lottery. I hope it will find you all well.

I conjecture you have cold Weather and snow enough. We had at Baltimore last Saturday and Sunday a deep Snow and very sharp frost, such as froze over the Susquehannah, and obliged Us to ride up 15 miles, to cross the River at Bald fryars.[2] We found a deep snow all the Way to this Place.

Maryland and Pensilvania, have at last compleated their Govern-ments. Mr. Johnson is Governor of the first and Thomas Wharton Jur. of the other.

The Delaware State too have finished theirs. McInlay is Governor.[3] They have also chosen new Delegates to Congress. So have S. Carolina —so has Pensilvania. So has Maryland.

There is indeed every where a more chearfull Face upon Things than there was.

South Carolina is said to have a great Trade and a plenty of Things.

Salt comes in frequently and there is a Prospect of supply, though dear.

Our national Revenue is now the most delicate and important Object We have to regulate. If this could be put upon a proper footing, We should be happy.

Money comes in fast upon Loan, which is one great Step—but We must take others.

I sent you from Baltimore, by Captn. Harden, to the Care of your Unkle a Barrell of Burr flour.[4] I hope it will not be taken, but you know I am not lucky in trade.

RC (Adams Papers); addressed: "Mrs. Adams at Mr. John Adams's Braintree favoured by Dr. Jackson. To be left at Mr. Isaac Smiths Queen street Boston."

[1] Dated 26 Jan. and printed above.

[2] Just south of the Pennsylvania-Maryland boundary, near the present Conowingo. See James Lovell's MS map reproduced as an illustration in this volume. JA's companion was William Whipple, a New Hampshire delegate. They had left Baltimore on 2 March and had arrived in Philadelphia on the 5th; see JA's *Diary and Autobiography*, 2:253, 257.

[3] The first governor of the State of Maryland was Thomas Johnson (whose niece, Louisa Catherine, daughter of Joshua Johnson, was to marry JQA in 1797; see Adams Genealogy). After great difficulty in organizing the government under the new constitution, Thomas Wharton Jr. had on 4 March been elected president of the Supreme Executive Council of Pennsylvania. Delaware's chief executive officer was also called a president, and the first to hold the post was Dr. John McKinly.

[4] Flour ground with burr-stones (see *OED*), which were the best kind of millstones and produced "superfine" flour. The flour and barrel, bought from the Purviances, cost JA £2 13s. 1d. Pennsylvania currency; see his *Diary and Autobiography*, 2:253, 256. Isaac Smith reported its arrival in Boston in a letter to JA of 22 March, below.

John Adams to Abigail Adams

Philadelphia March 7. 1777

The President who is just arrived from Baltimore, came in a few Minutes ago and delivered me, yours of Feb. 8, which he found at Susquehannah River, on its way to Baltimore.

It gives me great Pleasure to find that you have received so many Letters from me, altho I knew they contained nothing of importance. I feel a Restraint in Writing like that which you complain of, and am determined to go on trifling. However, the Post now comes regularly, and I believe you may trust it.

I am anxious and impatient to hear of the March of the Massachusetts Soldiers for the new Army. They are much wanted.

This City is a dull Place, in Comparason of what it was. More than one half the Inhabitants have removed into the Country, as it was their Wisdom to do—the Remainder are chiefly Quakers as dull as Beetles. From these neither good is to be expected nor Evil to be apprehended. They are a kind of neutral Tribe, or the Race of the insipids.

How may possibly attempt this Town, and a Pack of sordid Scoundrels male and female, seem to have prepared their Minds and Bodies, Houses and Cellars for his Reception: but these are few, and more despicable in Character than Number. America will loose nothing, by Hows gaining this Town. No such Panick will be spread by it, now as was spread by the Expectation of it in December.

However, if We can get together Twenty thousand Men by the first of April, Mr. How will scarcly cross Delaware River this Year. New Jersey may yet be his Tomb, where he will have a Monument very different from his Brothers in Westminster Abbey.[1]

I am very uneasy that no Attempt is made at Rhode Island. There is but an handfull left there, who might be made an easy Prey. The few invalids who are left there are scattered over the whole Island, which is Eleven Miles in length and three or four wide. Are New England Men such Sons of Sloth and Fear, as to loose this Opportun[ity?][2]

We may possibly remove again from hence, perhaps to Lancaster or Reading. It is good to change Place—it promotes Health and Spirits. It does good many Ways—it does good to the Place We remove from as well as to that We remove to—and it does good to those who move.

I long to be at Home, at the Opening Spring, but this is not my Felicity.—I am tenderly anxious for your Health and for the Welfare of the whole House.

RC (Adams Papers); addressed: "Mrs. John Adams Braintree Mass. Bay"; franked: "free John Adams"; postmarked; "PHILA. MARCH 12 Free"; added on the cover in the hand of Isaac Smith Sr.: "Yrs. IS."

[1] George Augustus, 3d Viscount Howe, older brother of Richard and William Howe, was killed in an action against the French on Lake George in 1758; the Province of Massachusetts Bay voted to erect a monument to him in Westminster Abbey (*DNB*).
[2] MS torn by seal.

John Adams to Abigail Adams

Philadelphia March 7 1777

Yours of Feb. 12. received this day. I have begged a Bundle of Newspapers, to inclose. They contain some Intelligence.

I am pretty well, after all my fatiguing Journeys. The C[ongre]ss are in as good a Temper as ever I knew them—more spirited and determined than ever.

The Southern Battallions are not full. But are in a good Way. Rejoice to learn that Measures are taking to send along the Eastern Quotas.

We are raising a large Body of light Horse—a large Troop of them are this Moment passing the Window. Fine Horses and good Men. The trampling of these Creatures is grand.

Dr. Shippen, whom I just now saw, assures me that he has bought an excellent Assortment of Medicines and has the best Prospect of putting the Hospitals in good order, so that the sick will not suffer this year as they did last.[1]

We have some french Vessells arrived here with Druggs and salt, and other Things.

Let me be remembered by all that I remember. You know who they are.

RC (Adams Papers). Enclosed newspapers not found or identified.

[1] William Shippen Jr. (1736–1808), College of Jersey 1754, M.D., Edinburgh 1761, professor of surgery and anatomy at the College of Philadelphia, was currently director general of Continental hospitals west of the Hudson; he had recently submitted a plan to Congress, where he had influential connections, for reorganizing the hospital department, and on 11 April he replaced Dr. John Morgan, earlier demoted, as director general of all Continental hospitals— a post in which he served with scarcely more success than his predecessor (*DAB*; *JCC*, 6:989; 7:161, 193, 219, 253).

Abigail Adams to John Adams

Braintree March 8 1777

We have had very severe weather almost ever since you left us. About the middle of Febry. came a snow of a foot and half deep upon a Level which made it fine going for about 10 day's when a snow storm succeeded with a High wind and banks 5 and 6 feet high. I do not remember to have seen the Roads so obstructed since my remembrance; there has been no passing since except for a Horse.

I Have wrote you 3 Letters since your absence but whether you have ever received one of them I know not. The Post office has been in such a Situation that there has been no confiding in it, but I hear Hazard is come to put it upon a better footing.[1]

We know not what is passing with you nor with the Army, any more than if we lived with the Antipodes. I want a Bird of passage. It has given me great pleasure to find by your Letters which I have received that your Spirits are so Good, and that your Health has not sufferd by your tedious journey. Posterity who are to reap the Blessings, will scarcly be able to conceive the Hardships and Sufferings of their Ancesstors.—"But tis a day of suffering says the Author of the Crisis, and we ought to expect it. What we contend for is worthy the affliction we may go through. If we get but Bread to eat and any kind of rayment to put on, we ought not only to be contented, but thankfull. What are the inconveniencies of a few Months or years to the Tributary bondage of ages?" [2] These are Sentiments which do Honour to Humane Nature.

We have the Debates of Parliment by which it appears there are Many who apprehend a War inevitable and foresee the precipice upon which they stand. We have a report Here that Letters are come to Congress from administration, and proposals of a treaty, and some other Stories fit to amuse children, but Experienced Birds are not to be caught with chaff. What is said of the english nation by Hume in the Reign of Harry the 8th may very aptly be applied to them now, that they are so thoroughly subdued that like Eastern Slaves they are inclined to admire even those acts of tyranny and violence which are exercised over themselves at their own expence.

Thus far I wrote when I received a Letter dated Febry. 10, favourd by—— but it was a mistake it was not favour by any body, and not being frank'd cost me a Dollor.[3] The Man who deliverd it to my unkle brought him a Letter[4] at the same time for which he paid the same price. If it had containd half as much as I wanted to know I would not have grumbld, but you do not tell me How you do, nor what accommodations you have, which is of more consequence to me than all the discriptions of cities, states and kingdoms in the world. I wish the Men of War better imployd than in taking flower vessels since it creates a Temporary famine Here, if I would give a Guiney for a pound of flower I dont think I could purchase it. There is such a Cry for Bread in the Town of Boston as I suppose was never before Heard, and the Bakers deal out but a loaf a day to the largest families. There is such a demand for Indian and Rye, that a Scarcity will soon take place in the Country. Tis now next to imposible to purchase a Bushel of Rye. In short since the late act there is very little selling. The meat that is carried to market is miserabley poor, and so little of it that many people say they were as well supplied in the Seige.

I am asshamed of my Country men. The Merchant and farmer are both alike. Some there are who have virtue enough to adhere to it, but more who evade it.

March 9

I have this day Received a most agreable packet favourd by Mr. Hall,[5] for which I return you my most hearty thanks, and which contains much amusement, and gave me much pleasure. Rejoice with you in your agreable situation, tho I cannot help wishing you nearer. Shall I tell you how near? You have not given me any politicks tho, have you so much of them that you are sick of them?

I have some thoughts of opening a political correspondence with your namesake. He is much more communicative than you are, but I must agree with him to consider me as part of one of the Members of Congress. You must know that since your absence a Letter designd for you from him fell into my Hands.[6]

You make some inquiries which tenderly affect me. I think upon the whole I have enjoyed as much Health as I ever did in the like situation—a situation I do not repine at, tis a constant remembrancer of an absent Friend, and excites sensations of tenderness which are better felt than expressd.

Our Little ones are well and often talk and wish for ———. Master T. desires I would write a Letter for him which I have promised to do. Your Mamma tenderly inquires after you. I cannot do your Message to B[ets]y since the mortification I endure at the mention of it is so great that I have never changd a word with her upon the subject, altho preparations are making for house keeping. The ordination is the 12th of this month.[7] I would not make an exchange with her for the mountains of Mexico and Peru. She has forfeited all her character with me and the world for taste &c. All her acquaintance stand amazd. —An Idea of 30 years [8] and unmarried is sufficent to make people do very unacountable things. Thank Heaven my Heart was early fix'd and never deviated. The early impression has for succeeding years been gathering strength, and will out last the Brittle frame that contains it—tis a spark of Celestial fire and will burn with Eternal vigor.

Heaven preserve and return in safety the dearest of Friends to His
Portia

March 10

I have just now heard that one of my unkle's flower vessels arrived safe yesterday, at which there is great joy. You can scarcly conceive the distress there has been for Bread, it is but a mouthfull. Flower is sold at 4.16 per Barrell not withstanding what has been done. Indeed the risk and the high price it bears with you, no person can send for it without sinking half the Cargo.

I see by the news papers you sent me that Spado is lost.[9] I mourn for him. If you know any thing of His Master pray Let me hear, what treatment he meets with, where he is confined &c.

A considerable number of our 3 Months Militia have returnd, deserted, some belonging both to this Town and Weymouth, and they say others from other Towns. The Story they tell is this, that a great number of the standing Army were under inoculation for the small pox, and they were obliged to do duty where they were constantly exposed to it, that they would have been innoculated but as they had so short a time to tarry were not allowd to, that they applied to their Col. for leave to come of but could not obtain it, that those who had it in the natural way 4 out [of] 5 died with it, and that it was death for any of the Militia to be innoculated. This does not seem to be likely but is told by all of them. What will be the consequence I know not. I hear of but a few in this Town who are inlisted for the standing Army. Suppose they will be drawn soon.

RC (Adams Papers); addressed in John Thaxter's hand: "To The Honble: John Adams Esqr. Member in Congress"; endorsed: "Portia ans. Ap. 2. 1777"; docketed in CFA's hand: "March 8th." RC evidently enclosed letters from JA's children; see his reply, 2 April, below.

[1] Ebenezer Hazard (1744–1817), College of New Jersey 1762, a bookseller and antiquarian, was currently surveyor general of the Continental post office and afterward postmaster general (*DAB*; see also JA, *Diary and Autobiography*, 2:108–110).

[2] AA is quoting—a little freely, as was her habit—from Thomas Paine, *The American Crisis, No. II*, dated 13 Jan., addressed to Lord Howe, and published as a pamphlet in Philadelphia, 1777. Initial quotation marks have been editorially supplied.

[3] JA's first letter dated 10 Feb., above; see descriptive note there.

[4] Not found.

[5] JA's second letter dated 10 Feb., above.

[6] See AA to JA, 12 Feb., above, and note 1 there.

[7] The ordination of John Shaw, Betsy Smith's fiancé, took place at Haverhill on 12 March (Weis, *Colonial Clergy of N.E.*).

[8] Betsy was in fact a month short of her 27th birthday.

[9] Gen. Charles Lee's dog Spada; see AA to JA, 10 Dec. 1775, above, and note 5 there.

John Adams to Abigail Adams

Philadelphia March 14. 1777

Congress has been sitting several Days and proceeding upon Business. I have been in Town above a Week and have spent much of my Time, in making Inquiries after the cheapest Places in Town for Board and stabling. I have at last removed my Horses from a stable at six and six Pence a Night, to another at three dollars a Week each.

So that for the future I am to pay only six dollars a Week for Hay and Oats for my Horses. Oats they must have here, for the Hay is such as our Horses cannot live upon, nor indeed their own.

I am this day to remove my Quarters, from three Pounds a Week for myself and thirty shillings for my servant, to another Place where they vouchsafe to keep me for forty seven and six Pence, and my servant for twenty shillings. I shall then live at the cheapest Lay.[1] Cheap indeed!

What will become of you, I know not. How you will be able to live is past my Comprehension, but I hope the Regulation of Prices, will be of Service to you. I dont know whether I have mentioned to you in any former Letter, that I sent you a Barrell of burr flour from Baltimore, by Captn. Harden, in your Uncles Vessell. I hope she is not taken.

I wish to hear often from you. Believe the Post may be now trusted. Believe me to be more yours, and more anxious for your Welfare than any Words can express. The Government of Pensilvania is taking Root downwards, and bearing Fruit upwards, notwithstanding the Squibbs in the News Papers. They are making Treason Laws and Militia Laws, &c.

The Jersy Government is making a Militia Law too. The People of that State will be all soldiers. They are exasperated, to a great degree, at the Treatment they have received, and are panting for Revenge. The Quakers too are inflamed with Resentment. They say, that they were used worse, than any other People.

In a Time of Warr, and especially a War like this, one may see the Necessity and Utility, of the divine Prohibitions of Revenge, and the Injunctions of forgiveness of Injuries and love of Enemies, which We find in the Christian Religion. Unrestrained, in some degree by these benevolent Laws, Men would be Devils, at such a Time as this.

Prattle for me to my little Friends. Give them my best Wishes, Blessings and Prayers.

RC and LbC (Adams Papers).

[1] Rate or terms; see *OED* under Lay, noun, 7 (5).

John Adams to Abigail Adams

Philadelphia March 16. 1777

The Spring advances, very rapidly, and all Nature will soon be cloathed in her gayest Robes. The green Grass, which begins to shew itself, here, and there, revives in my longing Imagination my little Farm, and its dear Inhabitants. What Pleasures has not this vile War deprived me of? I want to wander, in my Meadows, to ramble over my Mountains, and to sit in Solitude, or with her who has all my Heart, by the side of the Brooks. These beautifull Scænes would contribute more to my Happiness, than the sublime ones which surround me.

I begin to suspect that I have not much of the Grand in my Composition. The Pride and Pomp of War, the continual Sound of Drums and Fifes as well played, as any in the World, the Prancings and Tramplings of the Light Horse numbers of whom are paraded in the Streets every day, have no Charms for me. I long for rural and domestic scænes, for the warbling of Birds and the Prattle of my Children.— Dont you think I am somewhat poetical this morning, for one of my Years, and considering the Gravity, and Insipidity of my Employment. —As much as I converse with Sages and Heroes, they have very little of my Love or Admiration. I should prefer the Delights of a Garden to the Dominion of a World. I have nothing of Cæsars Greatness in my soul. Power has not my Wishes in her Train. The Gods, by granting me Health, and Peace and Competence, the Society of my Family and Friends, the Perusal of my Books, and the Enjoyment of my Farm and Garden, would make me as happy as my Nature and State will bear.

Of that Ambition which has Power for its Object, I dont believe I have a Spark in my Heart. . . .[1] There [are] other Kinds of Ambition of which I have a great deal.[2]

I am now situated, in a pleasant Part of the Town, in Walnutt Street, in the south side of it, between second and third Streets, at the House of Mr. Duncan, a Gentleman from Boston, who has a Wife and three Children.[3] It is an agreable Family. General Wolcott of Connecticutt, and Coll. Whipple of Portsmouth, are with me in the same House. Mr. Adams has removed to Mrs. Cheasmans [Cheesman's], in fourth Street near the Corner of Markett Street, where he has a curious Group of Company consisting of Characters as opposite, as North and South. Ingersol, the Stamp man and Judge of Admiralty, Sherman, an old Puritan, as honest as an Angell and as ⟨stanch as a blood Hound⟩ firm ⟨as a Rock⟩ in the Cause of American Independence, as Mount Atlass, and Coll. Thornton, as droll and funny as Tristram Shandy. Between the Fun of Thornton, the Gravity of Sherman, and the formal Toryism of Ingersol, Adams will have a curious Life of it. The Landlady too who has buried four Husbands, one Tailor, two shoemakers and Gilbert Tenant [Tennent], and still is ready for a fifth, and well deserves him too, will add to the Entertainment.—Gerry and Lovell are yet at Miss Leonards, under the Auspices of Mrs. Yard.

Mr. Hancock has taken an House in Chesnutt Street, near the Corner of fourth Street near the State House.

March 17.

We this day received Letters from Dr. Franklin and Mr. Deane.[4] I am not at Liberty to mention particulars. But in general the Intelligence is very agreable. I am now convinced, there will be a general War.

LbC (Adams Papers). Though RC is missing (and was missing when CFA first printed this letter, in JA, *Letters,* Boston, 1841, 1:195–197), its receipt was acknowledged by AA in hers to JA of 17 April, below.

[1] Suspension points in MS.

[2] At this point, in the space between paragraphs in LbC, JA later made the following revealing insertion: "Note. Literary and Professional, I suppose.— But is not the Heart deceitfull above all Things? April 9. 1776." There can be no doubt that JA meant to date the insertion 9 April 1777. The handwriting is precisely the same as in the main text (though the ink varies slightly in color); and since JA did not take this letter-book abroad with him, he could not have had access to it on any later 9th of April for more than a decade.

[3] In JA's Account with Massachusetts as a delegate to Congress in 1777, his Philadelphia landlord is called Capt. Robert Duncan (*Diary and Autobiography,* 2:255, 262).

[4] Franklin's letter was to Pres. Hancock, was dated at Nantes, 8 Dec. 1776, and reported his arrival there; it was read in Congress on 19 March (*JCC,* 7:184), and is printed in Wharton, ed., *Dipl. Corr. Amer. Rev.,* 2:221–222. Silas Deane wrote numerous letters home from Paris in late November and early December; probably the one alluded to here was that of 28 Nov., printed in same, p. 196–200; see *JCC,* 7:186.

John Adams to John Quincy Adams

My dear Son   Philadelphia March 16. 1777

There is an observation, which I wish you to make very early in Life because it may be usefull to you, when you grow up. It is this, that a Taste for Literature and a Turn for Business, united in the same Person, never fails to make a great Man. A Taste for Literature, includes the Love of Science and the fine Arts. A Turn for Business, comprehends Industry and Application as well as a faculty of conversing with Men, and managing Affairs.

I hope you will keep these two Objects in View all your Lifetime. As you will not have Property to enable you to pursue your Learning alone, you must apply yourself to Business to procure you the Means of subsistance. But you will find Learning of the utmost Importance to you in Business, as well as the most ingenious and elegant Entertainment, of your Life.

You must acquire the Art of mixing Study with Business and even with your Pleasures and Diversions.—Omne tulit punctum, qui miscuit utile dulci.—There is a Bone for you to pick. Ask Mr. Thaxter, after giving my Love to him, to help you Parse this latin Line. Take it Word by Word, and be able when I come home to give me the Construction of the Line, and the Parsing of every Word in it.—I am your affectionate Father.

LbC (Adams Papers); at foot of text: "J.Q.A."

John Adams to Thomas Boylston Adams

Tommy   Philadelphia March 16. 1777

I believe I must make a Phisician of you. There seems to be a Propriety in your studying Physick, because your Great Great Grandfather after whom you was named, was of that Profession.[1] Would it not please you to study Nature, in all her wonderfull Operations, and to relieve your Fellow Creatures under the severest Pains, and Distresses to which human Nature is liable. Is not this better than to be destroying Mankind by Thousands. If you are of this Opinion, you will change your Title from General to Doctor. It requires the Character of rugged and tough, to go through the hardships of riding and walking Night and Day to visit the sick, as well as to take Care of an Army.—I am your affectionate Father.

LbC (Adams Papers); at foot of text: "T.B.A." Tr, in the hand of LCA and probably from the now missing RC, is in Lb/JA/26, a collection of transcripts of JA's letters made for JQA in 1829 when he was at work on his father's papers.

[1] Thomas Boylston (1644?–1696?), JA's mother's grandfather, "a Surgeon and Apothecary who came from London in 1656" and settled in what is now Brookline, Mass. (JA, *Diary and Autobiography*, 3:256; see Adams Genealogy).

John Adams to Abigail Adams 2d

My dear Daughter   Philadelphia March 17. 1777

I hope by this Time, you can write an handsome Hand; but I wish you would, now and then, send a Specimen of it, to Philadelphia to your Pappa, that he may have the Pleasure of observing the Proficiency you make, not only in your Hand Writing, but in your turn of Thinking, and in your Faculty of expressing your Thoughts.

You have discovered, in your Childhood, a remarkable Modesty, Discretion, and Reserve; I hope these great and amiable Virtues will rather improve, in your riper Years. You are now I think, far advanced in your twelfth Year—a Time when the Understanding generally opens, and the Youth begin to look abroad into that World among whom they are to live.—To be good, and to do good, is all We have to do.

I have seen, in the Progress of my last Journey, a remarkable Institution for the Education of young Ladies, at the Town of Bethlehem, in the Commonwealth of Pensilvania. About one hundred and twenty of them live together under the same Roof; they sleep all together, in the same Garrett every night. I saw one hundred and Twenty Beds, in two long Rows, in the same Room, with a Ventilator about the Middle of the Ceiling, to make a brisk Circulation of the Air, in order to purify it of those gross Vapours, with which the Perspiration of so many Persons would other wise fill it. The Beds and Bed Cloaths were all of them of excellent Quality, and extreamly neat.—How should you like to live in such a Nunnery? I wish you had an opportunity to see and learn the curious Needle Work, and other manufactures, in Flax, Cotton, Silk, silver and Gold which are carried on there. But I would not wish you to live there. The young Misses keep themselves too warm with dutch Stoves, and they take too little Exercise and fresh Air to be healthy.—Remember me, with the tenderest Affection to your Mamma and your Brothers. I am with inexpressible Affection, your Father.

LbC (Adams Papers); at foot of text: "Miss Nabby." RC not found, but a normalized text of it was printed in AA2, *Jour. and Corr.*, 2:5–6.

John Adams to Charles Adams

Charles   Philadelphia March 17. 1777

How do you do?—I hope you are in fine Health and Spirits. What Subject do your Thoughts run upon these Times. You are a thoughtfull Child you know, always meditating upon some deep Thing or other. Your Sensibility is exquisite too. Pray how are your nice Feelings affected by the Times? Dont you wish for Peace—or do you wish to take a Part in the War?

Have you heard of the ill Nature and Cruelty of the Enemies of your

Country, in New Jersey, both to their Prisoners and to the Inhabitants, their wickedest Friends, as well as their most honest foes?—If you have I believe your Resentment is so high as to wish yourself grown up, that you might draw your Sword, to assist in punishing them.

But before you are grown up, I hope this War will be over, and you will have nothing to study but the Arts of Peace. If this should be our happy Lott, pray what Course of Life do you intend to steer? Will you be a Lawyer, a Divine, a Phisician, a Merchant, or what? Something very good and usefull I think you will be, because you have a good Capacity and a good Disposition. Dont loose a Moment, in improving these to the best Advantage, which will be an inexpressible Satisfaction to your Mamma, as well as to me.

Are you a Mechanick? Charles? If you are not, ask your Brothers John and Thomas whether they are? Do you make your own Boats, and Whirligiggs, and other Toys? If you have a Genius for these noble Arts, you would be pleased to see what I saw at Bethlehem, a Pump, which has been constantly going for near Twenty Years, by Water, which forces up into the Air, to the Hight of an hundred feet through a leaden Pipe, Water enough to supply the whole Town. After rising to its utmost Hight it is carried by leaden Pipes, round the whole Town and into the very Kitchen of every Family in it. The Water is admirably sweet, soft and pure. It serves to wash and for all other Purposes, and saves a vast deal of labour to the Women, Maids and servants. Ask your Unkle Cranch how such a surprizing thing can be done with so much Ease and at so little Expence. Ask him too whether a similar Pump at New Boston,[1] might not be made by means of a Wind Mill to supply that whole Town, which has always hitherto suffered, by bad Water, and very often for Want of Water?—I am your affectionate Father.

LbC (Adams Papers).

[1] That is, on Beacon Hill in Boston; the western part of the town was commonly called New Boston at this time (Shurtleff, *Description of Boston*, p. 125).

John Adams to Isaac Smith Sr.

Philadelphia March 20. 1777

In an Hand Bill printed at Baltimore the 17th instant[1] is as well made a Lye as ever I read. It is in these Words viz. "last night Mr. Charles Cook, arrived here in 12 days from Newbern, in North Carolina, and brings the following important Intelligence, vizt.

"That the day before he sat out, Capt. Charles Stedman, of the North Carolina Forces, a Gentleman of Credit, just returned from Charlestown, South Carolina, informed him and others, that he there saw a large French Fleet, consisting of 15 Men of War, two of them 80 Gun Ships, and 40 Merchant Men.—That two of the armed Vessells lay within the Bar. That these Vessells had on Board 200 Pieces of Brass Cannon, 30,000 stand of small Arms, and a vast Quantity of dry Goods, for the Use of the American States. Their Destination was said to be for Delaware and Chesopeak Bays."

When you have read this and the inclosed News Papers, I should be glad if you would send them to my Family.—You are appointed an Arbitrator to settle a Dispute between the Continental Agent and some others, for Want of a Determination of which, the Public suffers. I hope you will accept this Trust, Sir, from Benevolence to the Public. I wish it was a more pleasant Office, but I think your Regard for the Public is such that you will not decline a dissagreable service by which it may be benefited.[2] I am &c.

LbC (Adams Papers). Enclosed newspapers not found or identified.

[1] The editors have not located a copy.
[2] No record of this appointment (which was by the Marine Committee of Congress) appears in JCC. Smith accepted, and served with two colleagues, Ebenezer Storer and William Phillips. They reported on 28 July; see JCC, 8:628–629; 9:836. For a fuller discussion of efforts to untangle the accounts of John Bradford, the Continental agent at Boston, see William Bell Clark, *George Washington's Navy*, Baton Rouge, 1960, p. 203 ff.

John Adams to Abigail Adams

Philadelphia March 22. 1777

The Post now comes regularly, once a Week, and brings me the Boston News Papers, but no Letters from Penns Hill or its Environs. How do you do? Anxious, faint, melancholly? Chear up—dont be distressed. We shall see many good days yet, I hope. I derive a secret Pleasure from a Circumstance which I suppose at present occasions the most of your Apprehensions. I wish I could know more particularly, concerning your Health, but I will presume it to be, as well as can be expected.

The little Folk are all happy I hope. May they continue so, to a good old Age. May they enjoy many happy, usefull and honourable Days.

RC and LbC (Adams Papers).

Isaac Smith Sr. to John Adams

Mr. Adams   Boston March 22d. 1778 [*i.e.* 1777]

Yours of the 25th Ulto.[1] I received sometime since by my Schooner
and have sent your B[arre]l flour—As likewise a packet of yours by a
schooner a few days since. A schooner that came Out with mine
charged by Our Commite of Warr (Arnold Master) is suppos'd to be
taken. As to my Affairs att Baltemore they fell into the hands of those
people not by choice and wish I had known sooner what sort of people
they were.

As to all kinds of provissions, and more especially bread kind I know
not how the Town will be supplyed, As there will scarce any body
Venture Again, and when itt comes there is no satisfaction to the
Owner in doing the business. I Offered itt to the Town or any body
att 5 PC. profit which in fact is nothing because a factor has that for
doing business without any resque, and have sold itt, att that rate and
itt comes Out so high that I am sick of itt.

A great many of the present House as well as [...][2] thinks a person
concernd in trade, what he has comes is all gains, or att least One
would think so by some conduct. As to trade in this province or rather
in this Town I dont know of six Merchants that carries on any and
indeed, we have nothing to send to Europe or the West Indies but
must be subject to a great loss. In short we have nothing that I can
find to send to France or Spain to the Amount of a thousand pounds
ster[ling] in the province.—We cant even buy lumber without pro-
vission or West India goods which is almost gone in the Country and
Armey. Indeed of all the prises [prizes] taken there has not One quarter eenterd in this Town.

I dont know of any more Methods to be taken but what you have
done to keep up the Credit of the Currency.—I have heard you are
About building some ships of 60. or 70. Guns, which will come to a
very large some of money and when built must lay by the Walls.
Whether such a sum that must be made for that purpose wont be a
further means of lessening the Value of the money. Such a ship can
never be got to see from hence, iff we are to judge by the dispatch
lesser Ones make. However I wish itt may prove the reverse.—With
regard to Our regulation of prises [prices], that Ought to have Origi-
nated with the Congress and setled the prises of each states produce,
for were there is no controleing power Over the whole itts imposible
to put things on an equal footing, and Consequently the Thirteen

states cant regulate foreign or the West India Markets, a thing never Accomplisht by any Nation. So that to put prises on Articles when itts imposible to know what they may cost the Owners, is a means of preventing those Articles which are Absolutely Nessesary. Indeed there is nothing got by trade excepting the Owner runs his Own resques, for there can be no Insurance to be Obtaind, under 50 PC. the Voyage³ round which is 100. on the Capital, besides the hire of the Vessell, Victualing and Manning—all which are very high more especially the Wages. So that itt is Imposible [to estima]te⁴ the Value of any commodity before itt Arrives. I have been surprisd my self, att what some Articles have turned Out att, till a Voyage is finisht. I had lately two parcels of Malasses and the Vessells on much easier terms than I can now send them Out att, and the Cargo sent from 10 to 15 PC. under what itt can now be purchast att and the Vessells did as well and much better than Nine tenths of the Vessells that goes to the West Indies, and upon setling the Voyage's itt turnd Out on an Average att 4/4. and as I let Our state have some on consideration of there makeing an Allowance. Otherwise I shall sink from the real cost five pounds L.M. a hhd., and the present regulation as to West India goods the Consequence there will [be] none or but little to be had. N. England Rum would Answer every end for the Armey att 5/ or even 6/ as they must give double for West India.—We have arrived here a french Gen[eral?]⁵ which you have heard of [nearer?] by this.

I should be glad of a line when att leisure—& are Yr. hum servt.,

Isaac Smith

RC (Adams Papers); addressed: "To The Honble. John Adams Esqr. Philadelphia."

¹ Not found.
² Two interlined words illegible.
³ MS: "VG."—one of the many devices of Smith's mercantile shorthand, most of which have been silently expanded by the editors.
⁴ MS torn by seal.

⁵ Probably Philippe Hubert, Chevalier de Preudhomme de Borre, who held the provisional rank of brigadier in the French army and had recently arrived at Portsmouth (*Boston Gazette*, 24 March 1777; Lasseray, *Les français sous les treize étoiles*).

John Thaxter to John Adams

Sir   Braintree March 22d. 1777

You mention, Sir, in the beginning of your Letter,¹ that you are indebted to me for several Letters. I shall never presume to consider you indebted in that Respect, or myself entitled whilst the public at large, or any Individual of it, has a Title to your Attention in preference to mine.

It was not a Consideration of your being indebted Sir, that has prevented my frequent writing to You, but it was a Restraint which I ever have felt and shall feel in writing to Persons of so distinguished Abilities as Yours.

' Your kind Assurances in your Letter deserve my warmest Thanks. The Advice contained in it I shall immediately follow.

Since your Absence, the Sup[erio]r Court has sat in the Counties of Middlesex and Suffolk. In the County of Middlesex there was one Capital Trial, viz. The Trial of a Young woman for the Murder of her Bastard. She was acquitted. Mr. Dana and Mr. Lowell (her Consel) insisted much on two points in their pleadings: 1st That She was insane, and 2dly That the Crime was committed previous to the Declaration of Independence, and during her Allegiance to the King of Great Britain. I did not hear their pleadings; but was informed by a Gentleman who was present that the two points abovementioned were chiefly insisted on.—They admitted She killed the Child; but th[ought?] [2] the fact was done during her Insanity.[3] —The Week the Court sat in that County was mostly taken up in deciding Appeals from the maritime Court.

In Suffolk County there was two Civil Causes bro't up by Demurrer, and several Appeals from the Maritime Court. There was a Man tried at this Court for altering a Bill from the Denomination of one Dollar to that of Ten, and knowingly uttering the same. The Jury found him guilty of knowingly uttering the Bill so altered, but not of the altering of it.

We have very agreeable News indeed from France—The particulars of which I would mention, did not I apprehend they would come to hand before this reaches you.

I am, Sir, yr. very humble Servant,   J. Thaxter Junr.

RC (Adams Papers); addressed: "To The Honble: John Adams Esqr. at Philadelphia"; endorsed: "Mr. Thaxter. ansd. April 8. 1777."

[1] Not found.
[2] MS torn by seal.
[3] The case was that of the Government *v.* Mary Christopher in the Oct. 1776 term of Middlesex Superior Court. According to witnesses whose testimony survives, the mother, who was from Concord, slit her child's throat. But she was not convicted. See Superior Court of Judicature, Minute Book 96; Records, 1775–1778, fol. 56; Suffolk County Court House, Early Court Files, &c., No. 148226.

Abigail Adams to John Adams

March 23 1777

I have a very good opportunity of writing to you by Major Ward, who sits of tomorrow morning.

I most sincerely rejoice at your return to Philadelphia. I shall now be able to hear from you every week or fortnight. You have had journeying this winter and suffucent exercise for a year.

We have very agreable Intelligence from France which suppose will be communicated to you before this reaches you. Our proportion of Men from this State will be sent along soon, our Continental vessels are not yet ready. I have been told that the person who had the care of Building MacNeals Ship,[1] has since built a 20 Gun Ship which has been at Sea some time. Why should a pigmy Build a World?

I yesterday received yours of the 7 of March, with a Bundle of news papers, for which I am much obliged.[2]

Nor would I omit returning my thanks for the Barrell of flower sent by my unkles vessel. I know not a more acceptable present you could have sent, that whole cargo sold for 2.10 per hundred.

There is not a Bushel of Rye to be had within 60 miles of this Town. The late act will annihilate every article we have, unless they will punish the Breaches of it. This person has nothing and the other has nothing, no Coffe, no Sugar, no flax, no wool. They have been so much accustomed to see acts made and repeald that they are endeavouring by every art to make this share the same fate.

If you have not settled your account with Mr. Barrells Estate the next time I write will inclose one I find in your Book against it. There appears one settlement, but since that there is an account which will amount to near 10 pounds.

You mention a Resignation of an office. I have not heard it mentiond, believe tis not much known as yet.

As to news we have none I think. All our Friends are well and desire to be rememberd. I suffer much from my Eyes—otherways am well as usual—and most affectily. Yours,   Portia

RC (Adams Papers); docketed in an unidentified hand.

[1] The *Boston*, a 24-gun Continental frigate, had been launched in June 1776 at Newburyport but was not yet armed and manned; she undertook her first cruise late in May 1777 under the command of Capt. Hector McNeill, and early in 1778, under the command of Capt. Samuel Tucker, carried JA and JQA from Braintree to Bordeaux (*Dict. Amer. Fighting Ships*; JA, *Diary and Autobiography*, 2:269 ff.).

[2] The newspapers accompanied JA's third letter of 7 March, above.

John Quincy Adams to John Adams

Dear Sir   Braintree March ye 23 1777

I received yours of the 19 of Feb[1] and thank you for your perpetual almanack ⟨for⟩ with the assistance of my Mamma I soon found it out and find it is a very useful thing I have been a reading the history of Bamfylde moore carew[2] he went through the ⟨biggest⟩ greatest[3] part of america twice, and he gives a very pretty Desscription of maryland and philadelphia and new york but though he got a great deal of money yet I do not think he got his living either credibly or honestly for surely it is better to work than to beg and better to beg than to lie, for he addicted himself to so many falsehoods that his charecter is odious to all and a disgrace to human nature my Brothers and Sister all send their duty to you please to accept the same from your dutiful son,

John Quincy Adams

[*In AA's hand:*] P S This is a Letter of Mr. Johns own composition.

RC (Adams Papers); addressed: "To The Honble. John Adams esq Philidelphia"; endorsed: "ansd. Ap. 8."; docketed in one or more unidentified hands. The text of this letter is here given with literal fidelity.

[1] Not found.

[2] Bampfylde Moore Carew (1693–1770?), "king of the beggars," son of a Devonshire clergyman, ran away from home as a boy and led a career devoted to "swindling and imposture, very ingeniously carried out" (*DNB*). At one point he was transported to America, escaped, and made his way from Maryland to Connecticut. The veracity of contemporary accounts of his life is, to say the least, subject to question, and their bibliography is complex; see *The King of the Beggars: Bampfylde-Moore Carew*, ed. C. H. Wilkinson, Oxford, 1931. Since no Adams copy of either Carew's *Life and Adventures*, first published in 1745, or his *Apology*, first published in 1749, has been found, one cannot say what version JQA was reading. Very likely it was one of the later and very popular amalgamated editions of the two books.

[3] This correction is in AA's hand.

Abigail Adams to John Adams

March 26 1777

I this morning Received yours of March 7 favour by Dr. Jackson.[1] I rejoice to hear you are so comfortable. Col. Palmer informd me a Sunday that he is going to morrow as far as the Jersies being one of a Committe sent by our assembly to know of the General what proportion of Continental Troops will be allowed to this State; and does not know but he shall be obligd to proceed as far as Philadelphia. I venture to write by Him as he will take good care of a Letter tho he should not go farther than the Jersies.[2]—I fear you will think me neglegent in not writing oftner, but till lately I dare not trust the post office, have sent wholy by private Hands. This Letter is but the sixth that I have wrote since you left me, tho I have to acknowledg the Rec[ei]pt of 20 from you.

We have no news this way except that Manly saild this Morning.— I believe you will not find it difficult to procure Money since you have offerd 6 per cent. I was mentioning the other day to a certain Gentleman in this Town that Congress had agreed to give that, an unusual pleasure lighted up his Countanance immediately, and he instantly replied, they shall have all mine immediately, I only waited for that. You know the Character so perfectly well, that the Speach needs no comment.[3]

You mention my purchaseing a Ticket. I am determined to do it if I find my self able, after having paid the Rate bill, which tis said will amount to near 30 pounds, so that I must be very parsimonious. I met with the Misfortune of loosing a Cow upon the Ice this winter, Ruggles by name, and [having][4] to make her place good purchased an other which cost me 5 pound's.—You know I have ever made it a Rule not to involve an absent Friend in debt.

I have at last Let the House in Q[uee]n S[tree]t to a Good Tenant at £22 per annum, when he gets in, but a very odd affair happend after it was engaged to him. I advertised the House in G[ill]'s paper,[5] and supposing any person would chuse to see it, before they engaged it, desired him to Let them know where the key was to be found. According[ly] Mr. W[illi]s the printer[6] applied to me for the House and I Let it to [him]. Upon his return to Boston and applying to Mr. G—ll for the key he found the famous Dr. W—ship[7] had taken it and would not deliver it to him, tho He let him know that he had hired the House of me, and this same Genious had the Confidence to remove his family into the House without either writing to me or applying to me in any shape whatever, and then upon the other insisting upon having the House, he wrote to Let me know that he had moved in and would pay his Rent Quarterly, and that he supposed Mr. G—ll had the Letting of the House, which was absolutely falce for Mr. G—ll never gave him any leave, and had no right to. In Reply to him I let him know that I had Let the House to Mr. W——s, that I could do nothing about it, that I had nothing more to do with it than with any other House in Town. He and Mr. W——s must settle the matter between themselves. In this Time Mr. W——s had taken advice upon it and was determind to prosecute him; tis near a Month since they have been disputing the

Matter, and the Dr. finding Mr. W——s determind has promised if he will not put him to farther Trouble to remove in about a week.

If you should have an opportunity pray purchase me a Box of Dr. Ryans Wafers for worms, and send them.[8] T[omm]y is much troubled with them, has lost most all his flesh, you would scarcly know him.

Tis now 26 of March and exceeding cold tho the snow is all gone.

Pray what is become of the F[arme]r—has he sunk into forgetfullness. We can not learn any thing about him. Poor General L[e]e how does he fare?

Adieu—Yours.

RC (Adams Papers); addressed in John Thaxter's hand: "To The Honble: John Adams Esqr. at Philadelphia To be left at Mr. Gills printing Office Queen Street Boston Pr. favor of Genl. Palmer"; franked: "Free"; endorsed: "Portia"; docketed in CFA's hand.

[1] JA's first letter of that date, above.

[2] Palmer's trip fell through, and the present letter was sent by post; see JA's reply, 8 April, below.

[3] Possibly (but by no means certainly) this was Col. Josiah Quincy, who a little later on was in difficulties with the General Court because he refused to accept Massachusetts paper money in payment of debts due him; see Mass., *House Jour.*, 1777–1778, p. 25.

[4] MS: "have."

[5] AA's advertisement appeared in John Gill's Boston *Continental Journal*, 6 and 13 Feb., and read: "To be Let, a House in Queen-Street, *Boston*, next Door to *Powers* and *Willis's* printing-office.—For further Particulars enquire of the printer."

[6] Nathaniel Willis Sr., at this time publisher, with Edward E. Powars, of the Boston *Independent Chronicle*.

[7] Presumably a Dr. Winship, and perhaps the Dr. Amos Winship (or, more correctly, Windship), Harvard 1771, whom JA was to see something of in France and who was later a well-known physician in Boston (JA, *Diary and Autobiography*, 2:353 and *passim*; Thwing Catalogue, MHi). But why so young a man was "famous" (even ironically) does not appear. The letters that AA mentions below have not been found.

[8] JA did so. See the entry for 11 April in his Account with Massachusetts for 1777 (*Diary and Autobiography*, 2:253).

John Adams to Abigail Adams

Philadelphia March 28. 1777

"A Plott! a Plott! an horrid Plott, Mr. A." says my Barber, this Morning.—"It must be a Plott 1. because there is British Gold in it. 2. because there is a Woman in it. 3. because there is a Jew in it. 4. because I dont know what to make of it."

The Barber means, that a Villain was taken up, and examined Yesterday, who appears by his own Confession to have been employd by Lord Howe and Jo. Galloway to procure Pilots to conduct the Fleet up Delaware River and through the Chevaux de Frizes. His Confidant was a Woman, who is said to be kept by a Jew. The Fellow and the Woman will suffer for their Wickedness.[1]

RC (Adams Papers).

[1] "The Fellow" was James Molesworth; he was executed three days later. See JA to AA, 31 March, below; William B. Reed, *Life and Correspondence* of *Joseph Reed*, Phila., 1847, 2:30–33; Burnett, ed., *Letters of Members*, 2:333, and references in note there.

John Adams to Abigail Adams 2d

Philadelphia March 30 1777 Sunday

I have been this Afternoon, to a Place of Worship, which I never attended before. It is the Church of the Scotch Seceeders. They have a tolerable Building, but not yet finished. The Congregation is not large, and the People are not very genteel.

The Clergyman, who officiates here, is a Mr. Marshall, a Native of Scotland, whose Speech is yet thick and broad, altho he has officiated in this Place near Ten Years.[1]

By his Prayer and several Passages in his sermon, he appears to be a warm American from whence I conclude, that the most of his Congregation are so too, because I generally suppose that the Minister will in a short time bring his People to his Way of thinking, or they will bring him, to theirs—or else there will be a Seperation.

The Grounds and Reasons, of the Secession of this Society from the other Presbyterian Churches, I know not, but intend to enquire.

After service, the Minister read a long Paper, which he called an Act of the Presbytery of Pensilvania, appointing a Fast, which is to be kept next Thursday. It is as orthodox in Politicks, as it is pious, and zealous in point of Religion.[2]

LbC (Adams Papers); at foot of text: "Miss N." RC not found, but a normalized text of it was printed in AA2, *Jour. and Corr.*, 2:7.

[1] Rev. William Marshall (ca. 1740–1802), minister of the Associate or Scots' Presbyterian Church in Philadelphia, 1768–1786, and afterward of a seceding portion of that congregation that organized the Associate Reformed Church (Benjamin Rush, *Letters*, 2:806–808, and references there).
[2] Text printed from missing RC adds a leavetaking and signature: "I am your affectionate father, John Adams."

John Adams to Charles Adams

Philadelphia March 30 1777

Yesterday, I took a Walk upon the Wharves, to see the Navigation. The new Frigate called The Delaware, is hawled off, into the stream and is ready to sail. Captain Alexander is to command her. She makes a fine Appearance.—I then went to the House of one Humphreys an ingenious shipwright and found him making a Model of a seventy four Gun Ship. He has nearly compleated it. You see every Part of the Ship, in its just Proportion in Miniature. After this Model the new seventy four Gun Ships are to be built, one at Portsmouth, one at Boston and one here.

I then went to the Foundery of brass Cannon. It is in Front street in Southwark, nearly opposite to the Sweedes Church. This Building was formerly a China Manufactory, but is now converted into a Foundery, under the Direction of Mr. Biers [Byers], late of New York. Here is an Air furnace, in which they melt the Metal. There is a great deep Cavern dugg in the Ground in which they place the Mould into which they pour the melted Metal, and thus they cast the Gun in a perpendicular Position. Several brass six Pounders newly cast, were lying there, and several old ones, to be cast over.

There is another Man, one King, who lives in Front street, at the Corner of Norris's Ally, who casts Patterara's[1] and Howitzers.

Thus you see, that a Foundation is laying, in Arts, and Manufactures, of a rising State. May you enjoy the Fruits of it, in greater Tranquility of Mind, than your Father has enjoyed, while it is laying.

LbC (Adams Papers); at foot of text: "Charles A."

[1] That is, pedreros, a kind of small cannon, spelled in a wild variety of ways (*OED*).

John Adams to John Quincy Adams

Philadelphia March 30 1777

Two ingenious Artificers, a Mr. Wheeler and a Mr. Wiley, under the Direction of a Committee, have been lately employed in making a Field Piece, a three Pounder, of bar iron. They have succeeded beyond Expectation. They have finished off a beautifull Piece of ordnance, which from all the Experiments hitherto made, promises great Things.

The Weight of it, is two hundred and twenty six Pounds only. It is made by cutting off short Pieces of bar iron, bending them round and welding them [1] together into Hoops, and then welding one Hoop upon another, untill the Gun is compleated. After which they bore out the Barrell, with a boring Mill, and grind or file the outside into a smooth Surface, and an handsome Shape.

It has been put to the severest Tryal, and has sustained it, unhurt. It has been discharged Eighteen Times, in a succession which they call, quick firing, and was found to be less heated, than any other three Pounder, whether of Brass, or cast Iron. The only Objection to it, which was discovered, was that it rebounded more: but this it is said may be obviated, by making the Carriages and the Tackling a little stronger.

It turns out a great deal cheaper than Brass, and indeed than cast Iron at present. It is so light, that a few Men may easily draw it, by Hand, which will be an Advantage at Times and in Places, where Horses cannot be had. We are about contracting for a Number of them.[2]

We have also made another Acquisition, which We think of Importance. An old Gentleman, by the Name of Butler, who served an Apprenticeship and spent all the former Part of his Life, in the British Works, and was employed all the last War, by the Generals [3] in America, as their principal Armourer, has been drawn, from the interiour Parts of Pensilvania, where he has a Family and Property, and a Character, and from whence he has sent two sons, as Lt. Collonells into our Army, and has taken upon him the Character of principal Armourer, in the middle Department of the united States. He seems to be a Master in his Art, and very desirous of doing service.[4]

We are establishing a laboratory, and an Armory, at Carlisle about one hundred and twenty Miles from this Place. We have a brass Foundery here. Such Foundations I hope will be laid as will place our Artillery, in a respectable situation. I am your affectionate Father,

John Adams

RC and LbC (Adams Papers).

[1] LbC: "welding the Ends."

[2] See JCC, 7:193, 228, 272. In LbC JA at this point added a paragraph which he perhaps inadvertently omitted in RC: "Pray give me your Opinion of them."

[3] LbC: "the British Generals."

[4] Thomas Butler had been appointed "public armourer" by Congress on 22 Jan. 1777 (JCC, 7:55, 188).

John Adams to Abigail Adams

Philadelphia March 31. 1777

I know not the Time, when I have omitted to write you, so long.[1] I have received but three Letters from you, since We parted, and these were short ones. Do you write by the Post? If you do there must have been some Legerdemain. The Post comes now constantly once a Week, and brings me News Papers, but no Letters. I have ventured to write by the Post, but whether my Letters are received or not, I dont know. If you distrust the Post, the Speaker or your Unkle Smith will find frequent Opportunities of conveying Letters.

I never was more desirous of hearing frequently[2] from Home, and never before heard so seldom. We have Reports here, not very favourable to the Town of Boston. It is said that Dissipation prevails and that Toryism abounds, and is openly avowed at the Coffee Houses. I hope the Reports are false. Apostacies in Boston are more abominable than in any other Place. Toryism finds worse Quarter here. A poor fellow, detected here as a Spy, employed as he confesses by Lord Howe and Mr. Galloway to procure Pilots for Delaware River, and for other Purposes, was this day at Noon, executed on the Gallows in the Presence of an immense Crowd of Spectators. His Name was James Molesworth. He has been Mayors Clerk to three or four Mayors.

I believe you will think my Letters, very trifling. Indeed they are. I write in Trammells. Accidents have thrown so many Letters into the Hands of the Enemy, and they take such a malicious Pleasure, in exposing them, that I choose they should have nothing but Trifles from me to expose. For this Reason I never write any Thing of Consequence from Europe, from Philadelphia, from Camp, or any where else. If I could write freely I would lay open to you, the whole system of Politicks and War, and would delineate all the Characters in Either Drama, as minutely, altho I could not do it, so elegantly, as Tully did in his Letters to Atticus.

We have Letters however from France by a Vessell in at Portsmouth—of her important Cargo you have heard.[3] There is News of very great Importance in the Letters, but I am not at Liberty. The News, however, is very agreable.[4]

RC and LbC (Adams Papers).

[1] JA apparently forgot about his brief letter of 28 March, above, of which he had failed to retain a copy and thus supposed his last to AA was that of the 22d, also above. Note that he speaks in the present letter of the spy James Molesworth as if he had not mentioned him before, though his letter of the 28th

deals exclusively with the Molesworth "Plott."

[2] This word supplied from LbC; probably omitted inadvertently from RC.

[3] This was the *Mercure*, which had brought cannon and other military supplies from Nantes, together with the French officer Preudhomme de Borre; the *Mercure* arrived at Portsmouth on 17 March (JCC, 7:211–212; Lasseray, *Les français sous les treize étoiles*, 2:

368; Burnett, ed., *Letters of Members*, 2:352 and note).

[4] One of the letters containing this "very agreable" news was the dispatch from Commissioners Franklin, Deane, and Lee in Paris to the Committee of Secret Correspondence, 17–22 Jan., summarized in JA's next letter to AA, 2 April, below, and printed in Wharton, ed., *Dipl. Corr. Amer. Rev.*, 2:248–251.

Abigail Adams to John Adams

April 2 1777

I sit down to write tho I feel very Languid; the approach of Spring unstrings my nerves, and the South winds have the same Effect upon me which Brydon says the Siroce winds have upon the inhabitants of Sicily.[1] It gives the vapours, blows away all their gaiety and spirits and gives a degree of Lassitude both to the Body and mind, which renders them absolutely incapable of performing their usual functions.

He adds that it is not surprizing that it should produce these Effects upon a phlegmatic English constitution; but that he had just had an Instance that all the Mercury of France must sink under the weight of this Horrid Leaden Atmosphere. A smart Parisian marquis came here, (to Naples) about ten days ago; he was so full of animal Spirits that the people thought him mad. He never remained a moment in the same place; but at their grave conversations used to skip from room to room with such amazing elasticity that the Italians swore he had got springs in his shoes. I met him this morning walking with the step of a philosopher; a smelling bottle in his hand, and all his vivacity extinguishd. I asked what was the matter? "Ah! mon ami," said he "je m'ennui à la mort; moi, qui n'ai jamais sçu L'ennui. Mais cet execrable vent m'accable; et deux jours de plus, et je me pend."

The natives themselves do not suffer less than strangers. A Neapolitian lover avoids his Mistress with the utmost care in the time of the Siroce, the indolence it inspires, is almost sufficent to extinguish every passion. Thus much for the Siroce or South East wind of Naples, which I am persuaided bear[s] a near resemblance to our Southerly Winds, and thus does the happiness of Man depend upon a blast of wind.

I think the Author of common Sense some where says that no persons make use of quotations but those who are destitute of Ideas of their own. Tho this may not att all times be true, yet I am willing to acknowledg it at present.

Yours of the 7 of March received by the Post.[2] Tis said here that How is meditating an other visit to Philadelphia, if so I would advise to taking down all the doors that the panels may not suffer for the future.

Tis said here that General Washington has but 8 thousand troops with him. Can it be true? that we have but 12 hundred at Ticondorogo. I know not who has the care of raising them here, but this I know we are very dilitory about it. All the troops which were station'd upon Nantasket and at Boston are dismissd this week so that we are now very fit to receive an Enemy; I have heard some talk of routing the Enemy at Newport, but if any thing was designd against them, believe tis wholy laid aside. Nobody seems to consider them as dangerous or indeed to care any thing about them.

Where is General Gates? We hear nothing of him.

The Church doors were shut up last Sunday in consequence of a presentment, a farewell Sermon preached and much weeping and wailing. Persecuted [to][3] be sure but not for righteousness sake. The conscientious parson had Taken an oath upon the Holy Evangelist to pray for His most Gracious majesty as his Sovereign Lord, and having no Father Confesser to absolve him, he could not omit it without breaking his oath.[4]

Who is to have the command at Ticondorogo? Where is General Lee? How is he treated? Is there a scarcity of Grain in Philadelphia. How is flower sold there by the Hundred?

Are there any stocking weavers needles to be had. Hardwick has been with me, to desire me to write to you, to send Turner to procure 500 and to beg of you to enclose to me 50 or a Hundred at a time as he is in great want of them. Says Turner knows what sort he wants, and if you will send word what the price is he will pay it, and make me a present of the best pair of Brants he gets this year. He is full of work, but almost out of needles.

We are just begining farming Buisness. I wish most sincerely you was Here to amuse yourself with it, and to unbend your mind from the cares of State. I hope your associates are more to your mind than they have been in times past. I suppose you will be joind this month by two from this state.[5]

Adieu. Yours.

RC (Adams Papers); addressed in John Thaxter's hand: "To The Honble: John Adams Esqr. at Philadelphia To be left at the Post Office in Boston"; endorsed: "Portia ans. Ap. 27"; docketed in CFA's hand.

[1] Patrick Brydone, *A Tour through Sicily and Malta; in a Series of Letters*

to W. *Beckford, Esq.*, London, 1773, and later editions (BM, *Catalogue*). No Adams copy has been found.

[2] JA's second letter of that date, above.

[3] This word editorially supplied for clarity.

[4] Rev. Edward Winslow held his last service in Christ Church, Braintree, on 30 March. See AA to JA, 29 Sept. 1776, above, and note 4 there.

[5] An enlargement of the Massachusetts delegation in Congress, though evidently talked of, did not happen.

John Adams to Abigail Adams

April 2 1777

Yesterdays Post brought me your kind Favour of March 8. 9. 10, with a Letter inclosed for [from] each of my Sons. But where is my Daughters Letter? That is missing. I regret the Loss of it much.[1]

You think I dont write Politicks enough! Indeed I have a surfeit of them. But I shall give you now and then a Taste, since you have such a Goust for them.

By a Letter of 17. Jany.[2] Dr. Franklin, Mr. Deane and Dr. Lee, met in Paris, and on 28. december had an Audience of the Count de Vergennes, Secretary of State and Minister of foreign Affairs; laid before him their Commission, with the Articles of the proposed Treaty of Commerce; were assured of the Protection of his Court, and that due Consideration should be given to what they offered. Soon after they presented a Memorial on the Situation of our States,[3] drawn up at the Ministers Request, together with the Articles of general Confederation, and the Demand for ships of War, agreable to their Instructions. Copies of all which Papers, they gave to the Count D'Aranda, the Spanish Ambassador, to be communicated to his Court.

They were promised an Answer from the french Court, as soon as they could know the Determination of Spain, with whom they design to Act with perfect Unanimity. In the mean Time they are expediting several Vessels laden with Artillery, Arms, Ammunition and Cloathing.

The Ports of France, Spain and Florence (that is Leghorne in the Mediterranean) are open to the American Cruizers, upon the usual Terms of Neutrality.

They write for Commissions to be given to Privateers, and for more frequent and authentic Intelligence.

Great Efforts are now making by the British Ministry, to procure more Troops from Germany. The Princes in Alliance with France, have refused to lend any, or to enter into any Guarrantee of Hanover, which England has been mean enough to ask, being apprehensive for that Electorate if she should draw from it, any more of its Troops.

Four more Regiments (two of them to be light Horse) are raising in Hesse, where there has been an Insurrection, on Account of drafting the People: and now great sums of Money, are distributed for procuring Men. They talk of Ten thousand Men in all to be sent over this Spring.

The Hearts of the French are universally for Us, and the Cry is strong for immediate War with Britain. Indeed every Thing tends that Way, but the Court has Reasons for postponing it, a little longer. In the mean Time, Preparations are making. They have Twenty six sail of the Line manned and fit for the Sea. Spain has seventeen sail in the same State, and more are fitting with such Diligence, that they reckon to have thirty sail in each Kingdom, by April. This must have an immediate good Effect in our Favour, as it keeps the English Fleet at Bay, coops up their Seamen, of whom they will scarce find sufficient to man their next set of Transports, will probably keep Lord Howes fleet more together for fear of a Visit, and leave Us more Sea room, to prey upon their Commerce and a freer Coast to bring in our Prizes, and supplies from abroad.

The Letter then mentions a Circumstance much to our Advantage but this is a secret.[4]

So strong is the Inclination of the Wealthy, in France to assist Us, that our Ambassadors have been offered a Loan of two Millions of Livres, without Interest, and to be repaid when the united States are settled in Peace and Prosperity. No Conditions or securities are required. They have accepted this noble Benefaction, and one half of it is paid into the Hands of their Banker. On the strength of this supply, they are now in Treaty for some strong ships.

Lee is in N.Y. confined, but otherwise treated well.

RC and LbC (Adams Papers).

[1] AA's letter of 8–10 March, above, evidently enclosed, or was intended to enclose, letters from all the Adams children (except TBA?), of which only that from JQA of 3 March, above, has been found.

[2] In Wharton, ed., *Dipl. Corr. Amer. Rev.*, 2:248–251.

[3] Dated 5 Jan. and in same, p. 245–246.

[4] A contract for American tobacco, under the terms of which the Farmers General were to advance a large sum at once for the purchase of French munitions and other military supplies to be sent to America.

Isaac Smith Sr. to John Adams

Mr. Adams   Boston Aprill. 2d. 1777

Yours by Docto. Jackson I received last week,[1] he had letters to Others likewise. I waited on him with some Others att his lodgings.

Mr. Jonathan Williams Offering his servise, itt was not worth while for more to be concerned.[2]

I recommended him to a person att Salem, and to Our Kindsman Tufts att Newbury, who writes me he has undertaken to dispose of a quantity and whose fidellity may be confided in as any person what ever.[3]

I have just received One from you for Mrs. Adams—As likewise some News papers by Colo. Moulton: Bradford['s] paper I take weekly, the Other do not, but iff ever the post gets regurarlly Again and you have a mind to send the Other weekly, to Mrs. Adams I can send itt to her.—I Observe in One of your News papers a ship being taken in your bay. Itt has been a little Misterious that such Valuable Vessells should not have some Guns when they come home. I have known many Vessells taken this Year past for want of even a single Gun.

I Observe what you say as to my Appointment on some dispute but have not heard any thing About itt, and wish may not.

Betscy Cranch is in Town. Your family is well.

I am sorry to here Genl. Washington has no larger Armey got to gether yet. By what I can learn we have already raised as many as he has got with him from all the Other Goverments, however hope Ere this he may have double or ttrible the Number.

I am Sr. Yr. hume. servant,   Isaac Smith

RC (Adams Papers).

[1] Not found. Since it was sent by Dr. David Jackson, described in JA's first letter to AA of 7 March, above, as "one of the Managers of the Lottery," it no doubt discussed (as Smith does in his reply) local agents for the sale of lottery tickets.

[2] This was Jonathan Williams Sr. (1719–1796), a Boston merchant, a nephew by marriage of Benjamin Franklin and father of Jonathan Williams Jr. (1750–1815), who was with Franklin in France (Franklin, *Papers*, ed. Labaree, 1:lvii–lviii).

[3] Samuel Tufts (1735–1799) was a Newburyport merchant and a younger brother of Dr. Cotton Tufts. See Adams Genealogy.

John Adams to Abigail Adams

Philadelphia April 3. 1777

As you seem so inquisitive about Politicks, I will indulge you so far (indulge, I say, observe that Word indulge! I suppose you will say it ought to have been oblige) as to send you a little more News from abroad. As foreign Affairs are now become more interesting to Us than ever, I dare say your political Curiosity has extended itself e'er this all over Europe.[1]

The Agent of the King of Prussia, has often made Proposals of a commercial Nature, to our Agents in France, and expressed a Desire that some American would go to Berlin, at the Instance of his sovereign, who wishes to have a clear Idea of the Nature of our Commerce. You must know, that this Prince has been several Years, dreaming of making his Port of Embden, an Amsterdam.

We cannot as yet, depend that the Dutch Merchants will venture to trade directly to America, at their own Risque. The States [2] however have declared, in Answer to a fresh Remonstrance of General York,[3] that their Ports are open to all Nations, and that their Trade, to and from their own Colonies, shall be unmolested, their subjects complying with the ordinances issued by their high Mightynesses. Their Prohibition of exporting Warlike stores extends to all British subjects.

Without a very material and apparent success of the British Arms in America, a Loan would be very slowly negotiated for England in Amsterdam. Nothing hinders them now from selling out of the English Funds, but their not knowing what to do with their Money. For that Country may be called the Treasury of Europe, and its Stock of Specie is more or less, according to the Necessities of the different Princes in Europe.

The Credit of France has been very low of late. The Mismanagement of the Finances in the late Kings Reign: The Character of the late Comptroller General, Mr. De Olugny,[4] had reduced it so low, that it was impossible to borrow any Thing considerable, on perpetual Funds. By Life Rents, something might be done. Perhaps a Financier, in whose Probity the World have a Confidence, may restore their Credit. The French Stocks rise on the Appointment of Mr. Taboureau. That it is possible for France to borrow, is certain, for at the Time when Mr. Turgot was removed, he was negotiating a Loan, and was likely to succeed, for Sixty Millions of Guilders. The Credit of Spain is extreamly good: That Kingdom may have what Money it will, and on the best Terms. The Emperors Credit is also good, not as Emperor but from his hereditary Dominions. Sweeden and Denmark have good Credit. The first the best. They have Money at four Per Cent. and it is not long since the King of Sweeden borrowed Three Millions of Guilders, at that Interest, to pay off old debts at five Per Cent.—his Interest is paid punctually. Prussia has no Credit but his Treasury is full, by squeezing the last Farthing from his People, and now and then he draws a little Money from Holland, by reviving obsolete Claims. The Credit of the Empress of Russia, is very good, for she has punctually paid the Interest of Twelve Millions of Guilders, which she borrowed in her War with the Turks, and has lately paid off, one Million and an half of the Principal. These are the strongest Recommendations to a mercantile People. As to America, in the present state of Affairs, it is not probable, that a Loan is practicable, but should it appear evident, that We are likely to support our Independency, or should either France or Spain acknowledge it: in either of these Cases We might have Money. And when it shall be seen that We are punctual in our first Payments of the Interest, We should have as much as We pleased.

RC and LbC (Adams Papers).

[1] The remainder of this letter (though JA nowhere says so) is partly quoted and partly paraphrased from a long letter written by William Carmichael from Amsterdam to the Committee of Secret Correspondence, 2 Nov. 1776, the original of which is in PCC, No. 88, I, and a printed text in Wharton, ed., *Dipl. Corr. Amer. Rev.*, 2:184–190. Carmichael, whose name and somewhat shadowy figure will be frequently encountered in JA's later correspondence, was acting strictly as a volunteer in forwarding his information and speculations to Congress from Europe. Born in Maryland, he had been living the life of a well-to-do expatriate in London when the Revolution broke out; then, according to the letter JA abstracted here, he started for Nantes to find passage home but was detained by illness in Paris and "livd with Mr. Deane since his first arrival at Paris" in 1776; he was currently, with Deane's blessing, on his way to Berlin to explore possibilities of developing commercial relations between Prussia and the United States, but had stopped in Amsterdam to see if an American loan could be obtained there. Carmichael spent the rest of 1777 in a similarly busy manner and played a material part in Lafayette's coming to America. On 28 Nov. he was appointed by Congress "secretary to the commissioners at the Court of France" (*JCC*, 9:975), but before he learned of this appointment he sailed for home, just as JA sailed the other direction to replace Carmichael's patron Deane in Paris. Arthur and William Lee strongly suspected Carmichael's patriotism, and JA was given to believe that Carmichael had "contributed much to the Animosities and Exasperations among the Americans at Paris and Passi" (*Diary and Autobiography*, 2:304; 4: 76–77). Nevertheless, Carmichael was soon elected to the Continental Congress and in 1779 was named secretary of legation to John Jay's mission to Spain, where he served (in later years as chargé d'affaires) until his death in 1795. See *DAB* and references there.

The special interest attaching to the present letter from JA to AA is its indication at so early a date of JA's deep interest in international banking arrangements and the question how the resources of the great Dutch banking houses might possibly be tapped by the United States—an anticipation of his own protracted but successful effort a few years later to do what Carmichael here suggests.

[2] The States General of the United Provinces of the Netherlands.

[3] Sir Joseph Yorke (1724–1792), veteran British ambassador at The Hague (*DNB*).

[4] That is, de Clugny—a copying error by JA; Carmichael's "C" looks like an "O" in the letter he sent to the Secret Committee.

John Adams to Abigail Adams

Philadelphia April 6. 1777

You have had many Rumours, propagated among you, which I suppose you know not how to account for. One was, that Congress, the last Summer, had tied the Hands of General Washington, and would not let him fight, particularly on the White Plains. This Report was totally groundless.—Another was, that at last Congress untied the General, and then he instantly fought and conquered at Trenton. This also was without foundation, for as his Hands were never tied, so they were not untied.—Indeed, within a few days past a Question has been asked Congress, to the Surprize I believe of every Member there, whether the General was bound by the Advice of a Council of War? No Member of Congress, that I know of ever harboured or conceived such a Thought. "Taking the Advice of a Council of War" are the Words of the Generals Instructions, but this meant only that Councils of War, should be called and their Opinions and Reasons demanded, but the General like all other Commanders of Armies, was to pursue his own Judgment after all.[1]

Another Report, which has been industriously circulated, is, that the General has been made by Congress, Dictator. But this is as false as the other Stories. Congress it is true, upon removing to Baltimore, gave the General Power, to raise fifteen Battallions, in Addition to those which were ordered to be raised before, and to appoint the Officers, and also to raise three thousand Horse, and to appoint their Officers, and also to take Necessaries for his Army, at an appraised Value.[2] But no more. Congress never thought of making him Dictator, or giving him a Sovereignty.

I wish I could find a Correspondent, who was idle enough to attend to every Report and write it to me. Such false News, uncontradicted, does more or less Harm. Such a Collection of Lyes, would be a Curiosity for Posterity.

The Report you mentioned in your last,[3] that the British Administration had proposed to Congress, a Treaty and Terms, is false and without a Colour. On the Contrary, it is now more than ever past a doubt, that their fixed Determination is Conquest, and unconditional Subjugation. But there will be many Words and Blows too, before they will accomplish their Wishes.—Poor abandoned, infatuated Nation.

Infatuation is one of the Causes to which, great Historians ascribe many Events: and if it ever produced any Effect, it has produced this War, against America.[4]

Arnold, who carries this, was taken in his Passage from Baltimore. He sailed with Harden, for Boston. They took 15 Vessells, while he was on Board the Man of War. Your Flour was highly favoured with good Luck.

RC and LbC (Adams Papers).

[1] See Congress' resolution of 24 March on this subject (JCC, 7:196-197).

[2] See resolutions of 27 Dec. 1776 (same, 6:1045-1046).

[3] AA to JA, 8-10 March, above.

[4] LbC ends at this point.

John Adams to Abigail Adams

Philadelphia April 6. 1777

This Evening Major Ward deliverd me Yours of 23d. of March.—
It is a great Pleasure to me to learn that your Flour has arrived. I begin
to have some opinion of my good Fortune. If I could have been certain,
of the Vessells escaping the many Snares in her Way, I would have
sent a dozen Barrells.

The Act, my dear, that you were so fond of will do no good.[1] Legis-
latures cannot effect Impossibilities. I detest all Embargoes, and all
other Restraints upon Trade.[2] Let it have its own Way, in such a Time
as this and it will cure its own Diseases. The Paper emitted by the
states jointly and separately is too much, it is more than enough to
purchase every Commodity and every Species of Labour that is wanted,
and this Excess of Quantity is the true Cause of the Artificial Scarcity
of Things, but the Price of this will be in Proportion to the Demand,
in spite of all Regulations.—To save my self the Trouble of thinking I
will transcribe for your Amusement a few observations of Lord Kaims,
on the subject of Money, Scarcity, Plenty, and Demand. Read them,
compare them with the Increase of Money in America, the Decrease
of Goods and Labour, and the Increase of Demand for both, and then
judge whether the Regulations and Embargoes can do any good....[3]

LbC (Adams Papers); note at the foot of the text reads: "Sent. most of it";
but no RC has been found.

[1] The Massachusetts act fixing the
prices of wages and commodities; see AA
to JA, 8 Feb. and note, and 23 March,
both above.

[2] In Dec. 1776 the General Court had
laid an embargo on all private vessels,
forbidding them to trade with any but
American coastal ports and banning the
export of a long list of foodstuffs and
other goods from Massachusetts. Though
modified in one way or another in the
following months, the embargo carried
very heavy penalties for violations, was
extended in February to goods carried
out of the state by land as well as water
transport, and (as shown by frequent

allusions in letters that follow) was
much complained of. See the numerous
resolves relating to the embargo, Dec.
1776 – May 1777, in Mass., *Province
Laws*, 19:713-714, 721-722, 773-774,
808-810, 928.

[3] The remainder of this very long
letter, omitted here, is a transcript of
very nearly the entire fourth section, entitled "The Origin and Progress of Commerce," in Henry Home, Lord Kames'
Six Sketches on the History of Man,
Phila., 1776 (Evans 14801), the
abridged first American edition of his
Sketches of the History of Man, 2 vols.,
Edinburgh, 1774. The passage copied

by JA runs to more than 4,000 words and is taken from *Six Sketches*, p. 78–96, with a few omissions and JA's usual small copying errors. In it Kames explains wage and price fluctuation in terms of the classical law of supply and demand, drawing examples, as was his way, from all over the known world.

Abigail Adams to John Adams

Monday April 7. 1777

I hope to receive some Letters from you this week, the date of the last was the 7 of March and now tis the 7 of April. I cannot suppose according to your usual practice but you must have wrote several times since; I sent a Letter to the post office a Saturday, but yesterday hearing of an express I thought to write a few lines by it, just to tell you that the family are well as usual, that I visit you almost every night, or you me, but wakeing the agreable delusion vanishes—"like the Baseless fabrick of a vision."

I have nothing new to write you. The present Subject of discourse is the unfortunate Daughter of Dr. C[oope]r, who having indiscreetly and foolishly married a Stranger, after finding him a Sot, has the additional[1] misery of finding herself the wife of a married Man and the Father of 5 children who are all living. About 3 weeks after he saild for the West Indias a Letter came to Town directed to him which was deliverd to her, and proved to be from his wife, who after condoling with him upon his misfortune in being taken prisoner, Lets him know that she with her 5 children are well, and to add to mortification tis said her complexion is not so fair as the American Laidies.

I most sincerely pitty her unfortunate Father, who having but two children has found himself unhappy in both. This last Stroke is worse than death.[2]

Let me hear from you by the return of this express, and by every other opportunity.

My Brother is going Captain of Marines on board MacNeal.[3] I hear there has been an inquiry at the Counsel Board why he has not saild before? and that the blame falls upon the continental Agent.[4]

I suppose you are in Bloom in your climate whilst we are yet hovering over a fire and shivering with the cold.

Adieu. Yours with an affection that knows no bounds,

Portia

RC (Adams Papers); endorsed: "Portia"; docketed in an unidentified hand.

[1] MS: "additionally."

[2] Rev. Samuel Cooper had two children, both daughters. The elder, Judith, married Gabriel Johonnot, a Boston mer-

chant, in 1766, and died in 1773; their son Samuel Cooper Johonnot was to accompany JA and JQA on their voyage to Spain in 1779 (*NEHGR*, 44 [1890]: 57; JA, *Diary and Autobiography*, 2: 417–418).

Cooper's younger daughter, Abigail (1755–1826), married in Jan. 1777, at Boston, Joseph Sayer Hixon, a well-to-do and well-connected British merchant and slaveowner of Montserrat in the Leeward Islands, who had been captured while on a voyage to London and brought into Boston on a Continental prize ship in Oct. 1776. In the spring of 1777 Hixon went back to Montserrat, but during an insurrection there was captured again and taken to Copenhagen. In 1782 he returned to Boston, was reunited with Abigail, had several children by her, and died in Boston in 1801. (MS letters of Samuel Cooper introducing Hixon to

influential friends in France and England, March 1777, in CSmH; *NEHGR*, 44 [1890]:57–58; Sibley-Shipton, *Harvard Graduates*, 11:206.)

³ William Smith did not sail with McNeill in the *Boston*, but as a captain of marines in the *American Tartar*, a 24-gun privateer, Capt. John Grimes, and after a successful cruise in the Baltic was captured and carried into Newfoundland (AA to JA, 6–9 May and 16 Nov., both below; MHS, *Colls.*, 77 [1927]:73).

⁴ Capt. John Bradford, Continental prize agent for Massachusetts since April 1776 (*JCC*, 4:301; William Bell Clark, *George Washington's Navy*, Baton Rouge, 1960, p. 151 and *passim*). Without much doubt it is to Bradford's conduct as agent that JA alludes darkly in a passage on official peculation in his *Diary and Autobiography*, 2:402.

John Adams to Abigail Adams

Ap. 8. 1777

Yours of 26 March came by this days Post. Am happy to hear you have received so many Letters from me. You need not fear Writing in your cautious Way by the Post, which is now well regulated. But if your Letters should be intercepted, they would do no Harm.

The F[armer] turns out to be the Man, that I have seen him to be, these two Years. He is in total Neglect and Disgrace here. I am sorry for it, because of the forward Part he took, in the Beginning of the Controversy. But there is certainly such a Thing as falling away, in Politicks, if there is none in Grace.

Lee fares as well as a Man in close Prison, can fare, I suppose, constantly guarded and watched. I fancy, Howe will engage that he shall be treated as a Prisoner of War, and in that Case, We shall all be easy. For my own Part, I dont think the Cause depends upon him. I am sorry to see such wild Panegyricks in your Newspapers. I wish they would consider the Woes ¹ against Idolatry.

Ap. 11

Congress is now full. Every one of the thirteen States has a Representation in it, which has not happened before a long Time.

Maryland has taken a Step which will soon compleat their Quota.

They have made it lawfull for their Officers, to inlist servants and Apprentices.

The fine new Frigate, called the Delaware, Capt. Alexander, has sailed down the River. I stood upon the Wharf to see the fine figure and Show she made. They are fitting away the Washington, Captn. Reed [Read], with all possible dispatch.

We have at last finished the System of Officers for the Hospitals, which will be printed Tomorrow. As soon as it is done, I will inclose it to you. A most ample, generous, liberal Provision it is. The Expence will be great. But Humanity overcame Avarice.[2]

RC and LbC (Adams Papers).

[1] Thus clearly in LbC. In RC this word might possibly be read as "Wars," and CFA so rendered it. Neither word makes perfect sense in this context, but the force of the passage is clear enough: JA means "the warnings uttered against idolatry."

[2] Congress' resolutions reorganizing the Continental medical service were adopted on 7–8 April and printed as a broadside by John Dunlap of Philadelphia. See JCC, 7:231–237, 244–246; 9:1083; Evans 15660.

John Adams to John Quincy Adams

My dear Son   Philadelphia April 8. 1777

I received your Letter of 23d. March, and was very much pleased with it, because it is a pretty Composition and your Mamma Assures me it is your own.

The History, you mention of Bamfylde Moore Carew, is worth your Reading altho he was a very wicked Man, because it serves to shew you, what a Variety there is in the Characters of Men, and what Odd, whimsical and extravagant Effects are produced by great Talents, when misapplied, and what Miseries, Dangers and Distresses Men bring themselves into, when they depart from the Paths of Honour, Truth and Virtue.

You, my Son, whom Heaven has blessed with excellent Parts, will never abuse them to bad Purposes, nor dishonour yourself by any Thing unworthy of you. So wishes your [1]

LbC (Adams Papers); at foot of text: "Mr. J.Q.A." RC recorded as in possession of Philip D. Sang, Chicago, 1960; not seen by the present editors.

[1] LbC breaks off thus at foot of page.

John Adams to John Thaxter

Dear Sir   Philadelphia April 8. 1777

Your kind Favour of March 22. reached me Yesterday. I am much obliged to you for your Account of the Proceedings of the Superiour Court, and wish you to continue to give me a regular Account of their Progress. The Order, and Happiness of the State and even its Safety, depend much upon that Court, and I long to learn that they are fully employed in the Distribution of Justice, both in the civil and criminal Branches.

The Restraint you mention you may wholly lay aside, and write to me with the Utmost Freedom and without Reserve....[1] I should be happy, to answer any of your Letters and Enquiries as well as I can at this Distance, and with all my Avocations.

There is one Subject, which I would wish you to turn your Thoughts to, for your Amusement, as soon as possible. It is likely to be the most momentous political Subject of any. It is the Subject of Money. You will find in Mr. Locks Works a Treatise concerning Coins,[2] and in Postlethwait, another of Sir Isaac Newton under the Terms, Coin, Money, &c.[3]

It is a Subject of very curious and ingenious Speculation, and of the last Importance at all Times to Society, but especially at this Time, when a Quantity of Paper more than is necessary for a Medium of Trade, introduces so many Distresses into the Community, and so much Embarrasses our public Councils and Arms.

In the Writings of those great Men you will see the Principles of Commerce and the Nature of Money. And after understanding it perfectly as a Philosopher and a Statesman, I hope you will soon have many honest Opportunities of handling a great deal of it as a Lawyer. I am, sir, with much Esteem your Friend,   John Adams

LbC (Adams Papers).

[1] Suspension points in MS.

[2] In JA's own set of *The Works of John Locke, Esq.*, 4th edn., 3 vols., London, 1740 (in MB, vol. 1 missing), are three papers on money and coining, at vol. 2:1–59, 60–66, 67–106.

[3] The work to which JA refers was Malachy Postlethwayt's great compendium entitled *The Universal Dictionary of Trade and Commerce*, first published in 2 vols., London, 1751–1755, and reissued repeatedly. One would suppose from the present reference that there was a copy of Postlethwayt in JA's library at this time, but the edition among his books in the Boston Public Library is the fourth, 2 vols., folio, London, 1774, which has on the front flyleaf of the first volume "The United States of America" in JA's hand, strongly suggesting that he acquired it during one of his diplomatic missions and charged it to the United States; see his *Diary and Autobiography*, 2:343. In the *Cata-*

logue of JA's Library the book is somewhat perversely entered under the name
of the original compiler, Jacques Savary,
whose work Postlethwayt translated and
greatly enlarged. Under the term "Coin"
Postlethwayt prints two contributions by
Sir Isaac Newton.

Isaac Smith Sr. to John Adams

Mr. Adams   Boston. Aprill. 10. 1777

Yours by post I have received, and with what Armes is Arrived this
way, hope will be a full supply, and wish there were an equal Number to make Use of them. Although Our Number is not compleated,
yet by what we can learn, we have as many or more than any of the
goverments and are marching forward dayly.

The story of the burning the Arsenal att Plymouth wish was more
Authenticated, As we have a prize ship here which Arrived sometime
since, that left Falmouth the 6 Jany. which knows nothing of itt, tho
itt seems there were some damage tho not as has been reported.[1]

I received a packet directed to me and the Other Gentlemen from
the Honble. board of the Marine department, and wish I had been excused in the Matter, but as itt seems to be A Matter of Importance, and
haveing two Gentlemen which are better Capacitated, than my self,
we shall go on the business immediately, but believe will be a Considerable troublesome Affair.

I wish we were better Able to coape with the enemy att sea, for
they have the Advantage of us greatly for they seem to take almost every
thing. They have got Bermudas as a place of rendezvous, by which
they have all the Advantage possible. I had a Master come by the way
of N.York last week, haveing been taken in a brig of mine with 300
hhd. Molasses, [powder?], small Arms and sundry Other Articles, by
which shall be a large sufferer.

Bro. Smith and Cousin Betscy is here. Mrs. Adams and family are
well—and are in haste Yr. H. S.,   Isaac Smith

PS. The loss of the Cabot is an Unhappy Affair.[2]

RC (Adams Papers).

[1] This report doubtless arose from the
exploits of James Aitken, the mad in-
cendiary better known as John the
Painter, who made repeated but largely
abortive attempts during the winter of
1776–1777 to burn the royal dockyards
and shipping at Portsmouth, Plymouth,
and Bristol, England. See William Bell
Clark's engaging and definitive account,
"John the Painter," *PMHB*, 63:1–23
(Jan. 1939).

[2] The Continental brig *Cabot*, Capt.
Joseph Olney, was pursued, beached, and
captured in Nova Scotia waters, March
1777 (William J. Morgan, *Captains to
the Northward* . . . , Barre, Mass., 1959,
p. 83–85).

John Adams to Abigail Adams

Sunday April 13. 1777

Enclosed with this you have a Correspondence, between the two Generals, concerning the Cartell for the Exchange of Prisoners.

Washington is in the Right, and has maintained his Argument with a Delicacy, and a Dignity, which do him much Honour.[1]

He has hinted, at the flagitious Conduct of the two Howes, towards their Prisoners, in so plain and clear a manner, that he cannot be misunderstood; but yet a decency and a Delicacy is preserved which is the more to be applauded, because the natural Resentment of such Atrocious Cruelties renders it very difficult to avoid a more pointed Language, in describing them. They might indeed, without much Impropriety, have been painted in crimson Colours of a deeper Die.

If Mr. Howes Heart is not callous, what must be his Feelings, when he recollects the Starvings, the Freezings, the pestilential Diseases, with which, he coolly and deliberate[ly] destroyed the Lives of so many, unhappy Men. If his Conscience is not seared, how will he bear its Lashes when he remembers his Breach of Honour, his Breach of Faith, his offence against Humanity, and Divinity, his Neighbour and his God, if he thinks there is any such Supream Being, in impairing Health that he ought to have cherished, and in putting an End to Lives that he ought to have preserved, and in choosing the most slow, lingering and torturing Death, that he could have devised?

I charitably suppose, however, that he would have chosen the shortest Course and would have put every Man, to the Sword or Bayonett, and thereby have put an End to their Sufferings, at once, if he could have done it without Detection. But this would have been easily proved upon him, both by his Friends and Enemies. Whereas, by Hunger, Frost and Disease, he might commit the Murders, with equal Certainty, and yet be able to deny that he had done it. He might lay it to Hurry, to Confusion, to the fault of Commissaries and other Officers. Nay might deny, that they were starved, frozen and infected.

He was determined to put them out of the Way, and yet to deny it, to get rid of his Enemies, and yet save his Reputation.—But his Reputation is ruined forever.

The two Brothers will be ranked by Posterity with Pizarro, with Borgia, with Alva, and with others in the Annals of Infamy, whose Memories are intituled to the Hisses and Execrations of all virtuous Men.

These two unprincipled Men are the more detestable, because they were in the opposition at home, their Connections, Friendships and Interest lay with the opposition, to the opposition they owed their Rise, Promotion and Importance. Yet they have basely deserted their Friends and Party, and have made themselves the servile Tools of the worst of Men in the Worst of Causes.

But what will not desperate Circumstances tempt Men to do, who are without Principle? and who have a strong aspiring Ambition, a towering Pride, and a tormenting Avarice.

These two Howes were very poor, and they have spent the little Fortunes they had in bribery at Elections, and having obtained Seats in Parliament, and having some Reputation as brave Men, they had nothing to do but to carry their Votes and their Valour to Markett, and it is very true, they have sold them at an high Price.

Are Titles of Honour, the Reward of Infamy? Is Gold a Compensation for Vice? Can the one or the other, give that Pleasure to the Heart, that Comfort to the Mind, which it derives from doing Good? from a Consciousness of Acting, upon upright and generous Principles, of promoting the Cause of Right, Freedom and the Happiness of Men.

Can Wealth or Titles, soften the Pains of the Mind upon reflecting that a Man has done Evil, and endeavoured to do Evil to Millions, that he has destroyed free Governments and established Tyrannies!

I would not be an Howe, for all the Empires of the Earth, and all the Riches, and Glories thereof.

Who would not rather be brave, even tho unfortunate, in the Cause of Liberty? Who would not rather be Sydney, than Monk?

However, if I am not deceived, Misfortune as well as Infamy awaits these Men. They are doomed to defeat, and Destruction. It may take Time to effect it, but it will certainly come. America is universally convinced of the Necessity of meeting them in the Field in firm Battallion—and American Fire is terrible.

RC (Adams Papers). Enclosures missing, but see note 1.

[1] The "Correspondence" in question was between Washington and sundry British officers relative to a plan for exchanging prisoners; the letters were transmitted to Congress in Washington's letter of 10 April, read next day, and ordered to be published (Washington, *Writings*, ed. Fitzpatrick, 7:375–380, 387–389; JCC, 7:253). Presumably JA sent AA a newspaper printing of these papers. "Enclosed is an *Evening Post*. General Washington's letter [to Sir William Howe, 9 April] is a masterpiece. It has raised his character higher than ever in the opinion of the Congress and his friends" (Benjamin Rush to Mrs. Rush, 14 April, Rush, *Letters*, 1:138–139).

John Adams to Abigail Adams

April 13. 1777

I have spent an Hour, this Morning, in the Congregation of the dead. I took a Walk into the Potters Field, a burying Ground between the new stone Prison, and the Hospital, and I never in my whole Life was affected with so much Melancholly.[1] The Graves of the soldiers, who have been buryed, in this Ground, from the Hospital and bettering House, during the Course of the last Summer, Fall, and Winter, dead of the small Pox, and Camp Diseases, are enough to make the Heart of stone to melt away.

The Sexton told me, that upwards of two Thousand soldiers had been buried there, and by the Appearance, of the Graves, and Trenches, it is most probable to me, he speaks within Bounds.

To what Causes this Plague is to be attributed I dont know. It seems to me, that the Want of Tents, Cloaths, soap, Vegetables, Vinegar, Vaults &c. cannot account for it all.

Oatmeal and Peas, are a great Preservative of our Enemies. Our Frying Pans and Gridirons, slay more than the Sword.

Discipline, Discipline is the great Thing wanted. There can be no order, nor Cleanliness, in an Army without Discipline.

We have at last, determined on a Plan for the Sick, and have called into the Service the best Abilities in Physick and Chirurgery, that the Continent affords. I pray God it may have its desired Effect, and that the Lives and Health of the Soldiers may be saved by it.

Disease has destroyed Ten Men for Us, where the Sword of the Enemy has killed one.

Upon my Return from my pensive melancholly Walk, I heard a Piece of disagreable News—That the ship Morris, Captain Anderson from Nantz, with Cannon, Arms, Gunlocks, Powder &c. was chased into Delaware Bay by two or three Men of War—that she defended herself manfully against their Boats and Barges, but finding no Possibility of getting clear, she run aground. The Crew, and two French Gentlemen Passengers got on shore, but the Captain, determined to disappoint his Enemy in Part, laid a Train and blew up the ship, and lost his own Life unfortunately in the Explosion.[2] I regret the Loss of so brave a Man much more than that of the ship and Cargo. The People are fishing in order to save what they can, and I hope they will save the Cannon. The French Gentlemen, it is said have brought Dispatches from France to the Congress. I hope this is true. If it is, I will let you know the Substance of it, if I may be permitted to disclose it.

RC (Adams Papers).

[1] Potter's Field in 18th-century Philadelphia was the open ground at Sixth and Walnut Streets later converted to Washington Square (Joseph Jackson, *Encyclopedia of Philadelphia*, Harrisburg, 1931–1933).

[2] The *Morris* was a sloop owned by Robert Morris. One of the "French Gentlemen" who escaped was Armand Charles Tuffin, Marquis de La Rouërie, afterward colonel of a French regiment in Continental service (*PMHB*, 2 [1878]:4–5; Lasseray, *Les français sous les treize étoiles*, 2:454–462).

Cotton Tufts to John Adams

Dear Sr. April 14. 1777

We hear of your being at Philadelphia and wish You a comfortable Session there. The spring is now opening and with this (probably) some grand Important Scenes that will call for the Wisdom of the Politician and the Skill and Bravery of the Warrior. Troops are dayly marching from this State to the several Places of their Destination and were all the Levies compleated from the several States, America would make a respectable Figure and under Providence would be able to give a good Account of her Enemies. What Number of Troops are already raisd in this State I am not able to inform You, but am doubtful whether they exceed much more than half the Number required.

An Act for regulating the Prices of Necessaries hath been made. The Cries of People demanded it. Much Pains was taken in framing it and the Prices were upon the whole judiciously set, and it was hoped that a chearful Compliance would have been paid to it. But to tell You the Truth, We are got into a wretched Hobble.

The Act occasiond a sudden Stagnation of Business. All wholesale Business ceas'd at once, and People stood gaping at one another, waiting for the Operation of the Act—some few provoked, that their Avarice should be bounded, took every Method to defeat it. The Farmer began to complain of the Trader and the Trader of the Farmer and each in his Turn contrived to outwit the other. In the mean Time, no Pains taken to enforce the Act. And in this State We have been for some Time. Upon the whole, from all that appears, it must fall through. I hope no other State will adopt such a Measure, unless they fully acquaint themselves with the operation of this Law and the Difficulties attending such a Regulation any where. All have agreed that [it] is necessary that something should have been done, to prevent Monopoly and oppression. But what that is, is a matter of Dispute. Some suppose the lessening of the Medium, would be the most effectual Remedy, and that no other Measure will ever avail. It is of little consequence that You bind the Merchant—in spite of all Laws He will find Means to evade them, and when the Demand for his Goods are great and especially if they are scarce, he will have his Price where Money is plenty. But if Money is scarce, no one will buy but for Necessity and the Merchant will be oblig'd to submit in this Case to such a Price as he can get, and this I suppose will hold good with Respect to the Produce of Lands and other Things.—I am this Moment calld off and must bid You Adieu for the present having only Time to add that all our Families are well and that with the most Ardent Wishes for Your Health and Happiness, I am Yr. Affectionate Friend & H Sert., C.T.

RC (Adams Papers).

John Adams to Abigail Adams

Philadelphia Ap. 16. 1777

We are waiting with some Impatience to hear of the Arrival of some of the Massachusetts Troops at Head Q[uarte]rs.

The Lassitude and Torpor, that has seized our New Englandmen, is to me, very surprizing.

Something will happen I believe, to arrouse them from their Lethargy. If they dont go and crush that little Nest of Hornetts at Newport, I shall think them dead to all Sense of Honour, Virtue, Shame, and Love to their Country.

The continental Troops must all march to Fishkill and Ti....[1] These are the Places to stop the Progress of the Enemy into New England, which I believe is their Intention, notwithstanding all that they give out about coming to Philadelphia. If they come here, they shall get little but bare Walls. And here they will be starved and drubbed.

RC (Adams Papers).
[1] Suspension points in MS.

Abigail Adams to John Adams

April 17. 1777

Your obliging favours of March 14, 16 and 22, have received, and most sincerely thank you for them. I know not How I should support an absence already tedious, and many times attended with melancholy reflections, if it was not for so frequently hearing from you. That is a consolation to me, tho a cold comfort in a winters Night.

As the Summer advances I have many anxieties, some of which I should not feel or at least should find them greatly alleviated if you could be with me. But as that is a Satisfaction I know I must not look for, (tho I have a good mind to hold You to your promise since some perticuliar circumstances were really upon that condition) I must summon all the Phylosophy I am mistress of since what cannot be help'd must be endured.

Mrs. Howard a Lady for whom I know you had a great respect died yesterday to the inexpressible Grief of her Friends.[1] She was deliverd of a Son or Daughter I know not which yesterday week, a mortification in her Bowels occasiond her death. Every thing of this kind naturally shocks a person in similar circumstances. How great the mind that can overcome the fear of Death! How anxious the Heart of a parent who looks round upon a family of young and helpless children and thinks of leaving them to a World full of snares and temptations which they have neither discretion to foresee, nor prudence to avoid.

But I will quit [the][2] Subject least it should excite painfull Sensations in a Heart that I would not willingly wound.

You give me an account in one of your Letters of the removal of your Lodgings. The extravagance of Board is greater there than here tho here every thing is at such prices as was not ever before known. Many articles are not to be had tho at ever so great a price. Sugar, Molasses, Rum, cotton wool, Coffe, chocolate, cannot all be consumed. Yet there are none, or next to none to be sold, perhaps you may procure a pound at a time, but no more. I have sometimes stoped 15 or 20 Butchers in a day with plenty of meat but not a mouthfull to be had unless I would give 4 pence per pound and 2 pence per pound for bringing. I have never yet indulged them and am determined I will not whilst I have a mouthfull of salt meat, to Eat, but the act is no more regarded now than if it had never been made and has only this Effect I think, that it makes people worse than they would have been without it. As to cloathing of any sort for myself or family I think no more of purchaseing any than if they were to live like Adam and Eve in innocence.

I seek wool and flax and can work willingly with my Hands, and tho my Household are not cloathed with fine linnen nor scarlet, they are cloathed with what is perhaps full as Honorary, the plain and decent manufactory of my own family, and tho I do not abound, I am not in want. I have neither poverty nor Riches but food which is conveniant for me and a Heart to be thankfull and content that in such perilous times so large a share of the comforts of life are allotted to me.

I have a large Share of Health to be thankfull for, not only for myself but for my family.

I have enjoyed as much Health since the small pox, as I have known in any year not with standing a paleness which has very near resembled a whited wall, but which for about 3 weeks past I have got the Better of. Coulour and a clumsy figure make their appearence in so much that Master John says, Mar, I never saw any body grow so fat as you do.

I really think this Letter would make a curious figure if it should fall into the Hands of any person but yourself—and pray if it comes safe to you, burn it.

But ever remember with the tenderest Sentiments her who knows no earthly happiness eaquel to that of being tenderly beloved by her dearest Friend.

RC (Adams Papers); endorsed: "Portia. ans. 29."

[1] Elizabeth (Clarke) Mayhew Howard, widow of Rev. Jonathan Mayhew and wife of Mayhew's successor in the West Church in Boston, Rev. Simeon Howard. She had died on the 13th (*Continental* *Journal and Weekly Advertiser,* 17 April 1777); either AA had been misinformed or else she misdated her letter.

[2] MS: "a."

John Adams to Abigail Adams

Ap. 19. 1777

We have now an ample Representation from N. York. It consists of Six Delegates, and they are to all Appearance, as high, as decisive, and as determined, as any Men ever were, or can be.

There is a new Hand, a Mr. Duer, who is a very fine fellow—a Man of sense, Spirit and Activity, and is exceeded by no Man in Zeal. Mr. Duane and Mr. Phillip Livingston, are apparently, as determined as any Men in Congress.

You will see by the inclosed Newspaper, that Duane and Jay have arrived at the Honour of being ranked, with the Two Adams's. I hope they will be duely sensible, of the illustrious Distinction, and be sure to behave in a manner becoming it.

This is the Anniversary of the ever memorable 19. April 1775.— Two compleat Years We have maintained open War, with Great Britain and her Allies, and after all our Difficulties and Misfortunes, are much abler to cope with them now than We were at the Beginning.

RC (Adams Papers). Enclosed newspaper not found or identified.

Zabdiel Adams to John Adams

Dear Sir   Lunenburg April 19th. 1777

The great Distance that separates us occasions that we can hear of each others welfare but seldom. This therefore ought to induce us, as we were formerly much acquainted, to embrace every opportunity to write in order to perpetuate that friendship and regard that once so eminently subsisted between us. It would to me be highly acceptable could Letters be conveyed backwards and forwards frequently. But as this cannot be, I should be inexcusable to let pass those chances which sometimes present of sending a Letter directly to you. One such, I was favored with about 10 months ago, I embraced it, and had in return a most agreeable Letter from yourself. An Opportunity equally safe and convenient now offers in the person of Nathaniel Gorham Esq: who comes charged with a petition to the Congress from the People of Charlestown, praying for a Compensation for the Damage they sustained in the wanton destruction of their Town.[1] This Gentleman now resides in Lunenburg and is one of my nearest neighbors. From an intimate acquaintance with him I can recommend him to you as a person of virtue, patriotism and superior good sense. By him you may receive information of the state of affairs in this part of the Continent. However I cannot forbear to mention a difficulty that is sensibly felt at present, and threatens very great mischief unless a remedy be speedily administered. The difficulty I mean, is the depretiation of our paper currency. The Legislature took up this matter and passed an act regulating the prices of the most essential commodities among us, as you know very well. I hoped this act would have been attended to by the people, and thereby a value given to our circulating medium. My expectations are disappointed. The Prices of the necessary and convenient articles of Life, instead of being lessened are greatly encreasd since the promulgation of that Law. *Nitimur in Vetitum.* But few persons comply with it. Many things Money will not purchase at all, and those for which it is taken are exorbitantly dear. The extreme plenty of it is doubtless the principal reason of its being so greatly undervalued. Whether this redundancy of cash arises from the too copious emission of it by the Congress and the particular states; or from its being counterfeited by our enemies, I cannot tell; tho many worthy persons with whom I converse are ready to impute it chiefly to the latter cause. But let it arise from what quarter soever, it is an evil that deserves the closest attention of those that are in Power. The remedy to be applied I am not competent to point out; neither indeed is it necessary to prescribe or suggest to so wise and discerning a body as the Congress. Doubtless the calling it *in* plentifully by taxes, and then consuming it so far as redundant, and the making it death to counterfeit it would have a Direct tendency greatly to lessen, if not totally to destroy an evil, which if let alone bids fair to Draw after it more serious and troublesome consequences, than the arms of our enraged foes.

You will excuse my mentioning a thing of this Nature as it appears to me a matter of great importance. Money is the sinews of War; and if our enemies can devise a method by which to destroy the credit of our medium they will as effectually gain their point, as tho they were to conquer the country by dint of Arms. We have much need to be upon our guard not only against their power, but also against their policy and cunning. My Dear Sir, we have enemies both within and without to encounter, and what they want in strength they seem determind to supply by artifice. It is shrewdly suspected by those who are far from being inattentive observers, that many who are called Tories among us are possessed of counterfeit money. I am told that several who were known to be poor before the war began and who have done no business since it took place, now appear in pomp and splendor, ride fine horses, buy gay clothes and purchase farms. If this be so, we have too much reason to think they do not come honestly by their riches. *Obsta Principiis* is a good maxim and much to be regarded at this day. I hope those in Power will have wisdom to direct [...] [2] in this perplexed state of our affairs.

As to news perhaps I can tell you none. It is a time of general health, and the season at present is promising. Our Forces in this state are recruited but slowly, altho large bounties have by the several towns been given in addition to the Continental and Provincial ones. I hope however we shall be able in tolerable good season to take the field with a Large and well appointed army who shall have it in their power to counteract and disappoint the designs of our unreasonable enemies. America is now in Labor and attended with hard and severe throws but I trust she will sooner or later be delivered, and then remember no more the anguish, on account of having brought forth the fair Daughter, Liberty, under whose gentle and peaceful reign her sons will enjoy affluence and every blessing.

Permit me Sir, very tenderly to enquire after your health. Your fatigues doub[t]less are great, and situation truly uncomfortable, surrounded as you are by a miscreant host of internal and external foes. But be not discouraged. The time I am firmly persuaded is not very remote when the Congress will be abundantly recompensed for their Noble exertions in their Country's Cause. Go on then with unremitting ardor in the prosecution of the glorious design of extricating your native Land from the worst of all curses, Slavery; and be assured that you are favored with the constant Prayers of by far the greatest part of the people of these united States, that [good?] success may attend you in this important undertaking.

As I Live in a part of the world where we do not receive the earliest intelligence of the movements of the enemy, should take it very kindly if, in answer to this Letter, you would give me the best information of this matter; and let me know what reinforcements the enemy expects this season; where will probably be the seat of the war; how General Washington is supported, and what kind of assistance we are likely to receive from foreign Powers; and whether the honest Quakers are as unfriendly as ever. I have lately been transiently informed that a conspiracy, in which a number of that Denomination were concerned, has been detected. Should be glad to know the certainty of the affair. If you have it in your power to give me information in these particulars it will be pleasing to receive it, but if not, a Letter on any topick from you will be highly acceptable to him who subscribes himself your serious friend & very humble Servant,   Zabdiel Adams

My Best regards to the Honble. Samll. Adams Esq. and the other Gentlemen the Delegates from this state.

RC (Adams Papers); endorsed: "Zabdiel Adams. ansd. May 18"; docketed in CFA's hand. JA's answer of 18 May has not been found.

[1] The Charlestown petition, dated 28 Nov. 1776 and brought to Philadelphia by Nathaniel Gorham and Thomas Russell, prayed for compensation by the United States in the amount of £163,405 3s. 8d. lawful money for losses in real and personal property suffered from the burning of the town and the British occupation which followed (PCC, No. 42, II). On 14 May it was referred to a committee of three members, none of whom was from Massachusetts (JCC, 7:354). Two days later the committee regretfully reported, and Congress agreed, that the payment by the United States of such claims, however justified, would require sums "which, in the present exigency of their affairs, cannot be spared from the support of the present just and necessary war" (same, p. 365–366). See also JA to AA, 17 May, below, and the long and illuminating letter of explanation sent by the Massachusetts delegates to Speaker Warren on 21 May (Burnett, ed., *Letters of Members*, 2:366–368).

[2] A word is here interlined in so fine a hand as to be illegible.

Abigail Adams to John Adams

The post is very Regular and faithfully brings me all your Letters I believe. If I do not write so often as you do be assurd that tis because I have nothing worth your acceptance to write. Whilst the Army lay this way I had constantly something by way of inteligance to write, of late there has been as general a state of Tranquility as if we had no contending Armies.

There seems to be something prepairing against Newport at last. If we are not wise too late it will be well. 2000 Militia are orderd to be Draughted for that place, and last week the independant Company Marchd very generally—expect to tarry six weeks, till the Militia are collected.

Your obliging favours of various dates came safe to Hand last week, and contain a fine parcel of agreable inteligance for which I am much obliged and feel very important to have such a Bugget to communicate.

As to the Town of Boston I cannot give you any very agreable account of it. It seems to be really destitute of the Choice Spirits which once inhabited it. Tho I have not heard any perticuliar charges of Toryism against it, no doubt you had your inteligance from Better authority than I can name. I Have not been into Town since your absence nor do I desire to go till a better Spirit prevails. If tis not Toryism, tis a Spirit of avarice, a Contempt of Authority, an inordinate Love of Gain, that prevails not only in Town, but every where I look or hear from. As to Dissapation, there was always enough of it, in the Town, but I believe not more now than when you left us.

There is a general cry against the Merchants, against monopilizers &c. who tis said have created a partial Scarcity. That a Scarcity prevails of every article not only of Luxery, but even the necessaries of life is a certain fact. Every thing bears an exorbitant price. The act which for a while was in some measure regarded and stemed the torrent of oppression is now no more Heeded than if it had never been made; Indian Corn at 5 shillings, Rye 11 and 12 shilling[s], but none scarcly to be had even at that price, Beaf 8 pence, veal 6 pence and 8 pence, Butter 1 & 6 pence; Mutton none, Lamb none, pork none, Sugar mean Sugar £4 per hundred, Molasses none, cotton wool none, Rum N.E. 8 shilling[s] per Gallon, Coffe 2 & 6 per pound, Chocolate 3 shillings.

What can be done? Will Gold and Silver remedy this Evil? By your accounts of Board, Horse keeping &c. I fancy you are not better of than we are Here. I live in hopes that we see the most difficult time we have to experience. Why is Carolina so much better furnishd than any other State? and at so reasonable prices.

I Hate to tell a Story unless I am fully informd of every perticuliar. As it happned ⟨last Night⟩ yesterday, and to day is Sunday have not been so fully informd as I could wish. About 11 o clock yesterday William Jackson, Dick Green, Harry Perkins, and Sergant of Cape Ann and a Carry of Charlstown were carted out of Boston under the direction of Joice junr. who was mounted on Horse back with a Red coat, a white Wig and a drawn Sword, with Drum and fife following; a Concourse of people to the amount of 500 followed. They proceeded as far as Roxbury when he orderd the cart to be timpd[1] up, then told them if they were ever catchd in Town again it should be at the expence of their lives. He then orderd his Gang to return which they did immediately without any disturbance. Whether they had been guilty of any new offence I cannot learn. Tis said that a week or two ago there was a publick auction at Salem when these 5 Tories went down and bid up the articles to an enormous price, in consequence of which they were complain'd of by the Salem Committee. Two of them I hear took refuge in this Town last Night.[2]

I believe we shall be the last State to assume Goverment. Whilst we Harbour such a number of designing Tories amongst us, we shall find goverment disregarded and every measure brought into contempt, by secretly undermineing and openly contemning them. We abound with designing Tories and Ignorant avaricious Whigs.

Monday. 21

Have now learnt the crime of the carted Tories. It seems they have refused to take paper money and offerd their goods Lower for Silver than for paper—Bought up articles at a dear rate, and then would not part with them for paper.

Yesterday arrived 2 French vessels, one a 20 some say 36 Gun frigate—dry goods and 400 Stands of Arms tis said they contain. I believe I wrote you that Manly had saild, but it was only as far as Cape Ann. He and Mack Neal [McNeill] both lye at Anchor in the Harbour.

Adieu ever yours.

RC (Adams Papers); endorsed: "Portia"; docketed in an unidentified hand.

[1] Thus in MS.

[2] "Joyce Junior," as Albert Matthews has explained in two exemplary pieces of antiquarian research, "was the name by which, for a year or two before the outbreak of the Revolutionary War, the chairman of the committee on tarring and feathering was known, and it was

he who during the war warned and escorted out of town those of Tory proclivities." The name itself rose from the fact that a certain George Joyce, a cornet of horse in Cromwell's army, was the officer who captured the fugitive Charles I in 1647 and was his reputed executioner. See Col. Soc. Mass., *Pubns.*, 8 (1906):90–104; 11 (1910):280–294.

AA's information on the names of the offending merchants was slightly but not seriously defective. They were the notorious William Jackson, who has been identified earlier; Richard Green, a hardware dealer of Boston and an addresser of Gage in Oct. 1775; James (not "Harry") Perkins, another Bostonian and an addresser of Hutchinson and Gage; Epes Sargent, a Gloucester shipowner; and Nathaniel Cary, of Boston or Charlestown, also an addresser of Hutchinson and Gage. See Joyce Junior's "Notification" in the *Boston Gazette* of 21 April 1777, with Matthews' commentary thereon in the first of his articles cited above. On the treatment of Perkins in particular, see Isaac Smith Sr. to JA, 25 April, below.

John Adams to Abigail Adams

Philadelphia Ap. 22. 1777

The Post brought me two Letters from you, this Morning, one of the 7th. instant, and one before.

You seem to be in fine Spirits—I rejoice at it.

General Gates has commanded in Philadelphia, untill about a Fortnight ago, he went to Ticonderoga, where he is to command all Summer.

Schuyler is here, where he now commands. We are crouding along Soldiers to the General, as fast as they get well of Inocculation.

I think our N. Englandmen have been rather tardy, but I hope soon to hear of the Arrival of their Men at Morristown. The Army there, and at Ticonderoga too, is too weak.

But Howes Army is weak too. Let the Tories, and Cowardly Whiggs, exagerate, as much as they will, How has not in all America, Ten Thousand Men fit for Duty, nor in my Opinion Seven.

RC (Adams Papers).

John Adams to Abigail Adams

Ap. 23. 77

My Barber has just left the Chamber. The following curious Dialogue was the Amusement, during the gay Moments of Shaving.

Well, Burn, what is the Lye of the day?—Sir, Mr.   [1] just told me, that a Privateer from Baltimore, has taken two valuable Prizes, with Sixteen Guns each. I can scarcely believe it.—Have you heard of the Success of the Rattlesnake of Philadelphia, and the Sturdy Beggar of Maryland, Mr. Burn? These two Privateers have taken Eleven Prizes, and sent them into the West India Islands, Nine Transports and two Guinea Men.—Confound the ill Luck, sir, I was going to sea myself on board the Rattlesnake and my Wife fell a yelping. These Wives are queer Things. I told her I wondered she had no more Ambition. Now, says I, when you walk the Street, and any Body asks who that is? The Answer is *"Burn the Barbers Wife."* Should you not be better pleased to hear it said "That is *Captain Burns Lady,* the Captain of Marines on board the Rattlesnake"?

Oh! says she, I had rather be called Burn the Barbers Wife, than Captain Burns Widow. I dont desire to live better, than you maintain me, my dear.

So it is, Sir, by this sweet, honey Language I am choused[2] out of my Prizes, and must go on, with my Soap and Razors and Pinchers and Combs. I wish she had more Ambition.—

If this Letter should be intercepted by the Tories, they will get a Booty.—Let them enjoy it. If some of their Wives had been as tender and discreet, as the Barbers, their Husbands Ambition would not have led them into so many Salt Ponds. . . .[3] What an Ignis fatuus this Ambition is! How few of either Sex, have arrived at Mrs. Burns pitch of Moderation, and are able to say, I dont desire to live better: and had rather be the Barbers Wife than the Captains Widow.—Quite smart I think as well as Philosophical.

RC (Adams Papers).

[1] Blank in MS.
[2] Tricked or cheated (*Webster,* 2d edn.).
[3] Suspension points in MS.

Cotton Tufts to John Adams

Dear Sr.　　　　　　　　　　　　　　　　　　April 24. 1777

I wrote to you last Week by Mr. Thos. Russell who was to set out for Philadelphia on Monday last. In it I gave you some Account of the Bill for regulating Prices &c. (entituled an Act to prevent Monopoly and Oppression) and the curious State we have been in since its Publication; it will not be long before I shall be able to give You a more particular Account of its Effects—something decisive must shortly take Place. Many of the necessaries of Life are not to be purchasd such as Corn, Flax and Wool. *Yet no Body* starves—nor *freezes.* Foreign Articles are bought and sold only by those who are daring enough to buy and sell at any Rate or by those whose Necessities compel them to it.

It is reported that the Committee of Salem have thrown open the Mercantile Stores and obliged the owners to an Observance of the Acts. If this Measure is adopted in all the trading Towns, it is likely the Act will be observed, otherwise I think it will fail.

Some have thought, that a general Regulation of the Articles commonly bought and sold in America, made by Congress and binding on all the States would have been more extensively useful and have met with a more chearful Obedience.

Ought not all matters of Trade that affect the whole be directed by that Body that represents the whole and in whom the supreme Power is lodged? If particular States undertake to meddle with matters of Trade and thereby prejudice other States, what must follow, but Disaffection and Disunion.—I do not indeed wish that the Congress would undertake a Matter of this Kind at present like unto what has been done by the New England States, But wish that all Affairs of Commerce may be under the Guidance of that Body and that all Duties, Customs &c. in Trade might be the same throughout America (and its Money the same) unless some local Circumstances forbid.

We hear that a Number of capital Ships are to be built by order of Congress. With respect to the Expediency of it, May not the following Queries have some Weight.—Suppose a Vessell of 60 Guns to be built in so short a Time as the present Exigencies of our affairs require to render it of Use in the present Contest, what Number of Men are to be employd in building and what will be the expence of the same? Suppose it to be built, what Number of Men are required to man her and where are they to be procurd.—Three Frigates built 12 Months past are not yet equipt for sea. What would be the Condition of a 60 Gun Ship. How long must she lay and how is she to be manned.

It has been our Misfortune to be plungd into more Business than we could possibly conduct with any Degree of Clearness and to enter upon *new* Business before we had finishd *old*. Necessity has often compelled us to this. Wisdom points out what is profitable and necessary to be done, but Means are not always at hand. In this Case We must pass on to what is practicable and content ourselves with a Lesser Good where we cant obtain a greater.

Must not a Land Army (under Providence) be our main Security and Dependance? If so Every Measure that materially prevents the raising of Men for that Purpose must necessarily injure us. The greater the Number of Men employ'd at Wages above the Soldiers, the Less Number of Soldiers will be obtaind. Few Men will enter the Service at 2s. per Day when they can get at Home 4s. or 6s. In short must not every Thing bend to that one Point Viz. Raising and maintaining an Army sufficient for our Defence. Should we overcome our Enemies, and enjoy Peace, there will at that Time be multitudes thrown out of Business. Perhaps building Capital Ships would answer a good Purpose and prevent a Stagnation frequently attending Peace.

Our Army is not filled up with that Alacrity and Dispatch that might be wishd for. If We enquire into the true Causes, among others We shall find, that the Demand of Men for Shipping of one kind and another, and the high Wages given to Tradesmen, Labourers &c. may be reckond among the capital Causes. I dont mention the plenty of Money as a cause operating on those mentiond for that may rather be considerd as short livd and limited or rather I would feign consider it so and am strongly in the Faith, that it will eer long be scarce and valuable.

My Dear Sir, I have given You a strange Mess of Politics, and will no longer transgress upon your Patience. Leaving you to your better Thoughts I am with much Esteem, Your Affectionate Friend & H Sert.

[*In the margin*:] Yours and the other Families connected are well.

RC (Adams Papers); addressed: "To Honle. John Adams Esq Philadelphia"; endorsed: "Dr. Tufts"; docketed in CFA's hand.

Isaac Smith Sr. to John Adams

[Mr. Adam]s   Boston, Aprill the 25th. 1777

The bearer is Thomas Russell Esq., who is going to The Congress in order to make Application in behalf of the Town of Charlestown for some temperal releif for the many sufferers amongst which are many widows, more so than in general, and iff any thing could be done for them, under there present dificulties, consistant with the general good I should be glad and hope some method might be found Out for that purpose.

We have two Ships in the bay, and will rain Triumpant As there seems no probabillity of Opozeing them.[1]—By the Ticonderoga post Yesterday itt seems there were but about Two thousand people and the lake Open for the enemy to come Over. I Am A little affraid they will come Over too soon for us.—We have wrote the Marine board how far we have proceeded in the business Appointed us, but we find itt to be a confused business, some part of itt, att least. However hope to get itt Accomplishd as spedily as we can.

There is a ship built att Piscataque, belonging to Mercer & Co. of

Phila. which has taken Out of a fleet Three Vessells and was in persute of more, which ship's keyl was not laid, when [...]² round here.—We have had some very bad carryings on here lately which cant be justifyed by any person that has any regard to the present cause or either to humanity or justice. One of which of the persons referred to is [Mr.?] Perkins that had a son who had run him in debt and borrowed money unbeknown to his father and behaved badly, run of to NY. some time Ago, and on no Other crime Alledged Against the father who knew nothing of his going. To be seized when seting down to breakfast and ludgd.³ into a Cart with his wife and Children hanging round him, not knowing but he was a going to the Gallows, must be shocking to any One that has the sparks of humanity in them. Nothing more inhumane could have been in Spain or Portugal, to be banesht without even the shadow of an Accuation.⁴ I dont know but you think I am pleading the cause of the Torey party, but I abhor a real One and such management has a tendancy to make more of that kind of people. Were any person as the case here, have given bonds With good security for there good behavior, and have never offended, the goverment they are under (for there Own honor) Ought to protect them, or else goverment had as good be att an end.

The Counsel sent a Messuage to the house and people were in hopes some good would have come of itt, but beleive itt will all come to nothing.—Yr. &c.

RC (Adams Papers).

¹ These were British frigates. See James Warren to JA, 27 April, for more details (*Warren-Adams Letters*, 1:318–319).
² MS torn by seal; two or three words missing.
³ Thus in MS, for "lugged"?
⁴ Thus in MS. This must have been James Perkins; see AA to JA, 20 April, above.

John Adams to Abigail Adams

Saturday Evening 26 April 1777

I have been lately more remiss, than usual in Writing to you. There has been a great Dearth of News. Nothing from England, nothing from France, Spain, or any other Part of Europe, nothing from the West Indies. Nothing from Howe, and his Banditti, nothing from General Washington.

There are various Conjectures that Lord How is dead, sick, or gone to England, as the Proclamations run in the Name of Will. Howe only, and nobody from New York can tell any Thing of his Lordship.

I am wearied out, with Expectations that the Massachusetts Troops would have arrived, e'er now, at Head Quarters.—Do our People intend to leave the Continent in the Lurch? Do they mean to submit? or what Fatality attends them? With the noblest Prize in View, that ever Mortals contended for, and with the fairest Prospect of obtaining it upon easy Terms, The People of the Massachusetts Bay, are dead.

Does our State intend to send only half, or a third of their Quota? Do they wish to see another, crippled, disastrous and disgracefull Campaign for Want of an Army?—I am more sick and more ashamed of my own Countrymen, than ever I was before. The Spleen, the Vapours, the Dismals, the Horrors, seem to have seized our whole State.

More Wrath than Terror, has seized me. I am very mad. The gloomy Cowardice of the Times, is intollerable in N. England.

Indeed I feel not a little out of Humour, from Indisposition of Body. You know, I cannot pass a Spring, or fall, without an ill Turn—and I have had one these four or five Weeks—a Cold, as usual. Warm Weather, and a little Exercise, with a little Medicine, I suppose will cure me as usual. I am not confined, but moap about and drudge as usual, like a Gally Slave. I am a Fool if ever there was one to be such a Slave. I wont be much longer. I will be more free, in some World or other.

Is it not intollerable, that the opening Spring, which I should enjoy with my Wife and Children upon my little Farm, should pass away, and laugh at me, for labouring, Day after Day, and Month after Month, in a Conclave, Where neither Taste, nor Fancy, nor Reason, nor Passion, nor Appetite can be gratified?

Posterity! You will never know, how much it cost the present Generation, to preserve your Freedom! I hope you will make a good Use of it. If you do not, I shall repent in Heaven, that I ever took half the Pains to preserve it.

RC (Adams Papers).

John Adams to Abigail Adams

Ap. 27. 1777

Your Favours of Ap. 2 and Ap. 7. I have received.

The inclosed Evening Post, will give you, some Idea, of the Humanity of the present Race of Brittons.[1]—My Barber, whom I quote as often as ever I did any Authority, says "he has read Histories of

Cruelty; and he has read Romances of Cruelty: But the Cruelty of the British exceeds all that he ever read."

For my own Part, I think We cannot dwell too much, on this Part of their Character, and Conduct. It is full of important Lessons. If the Facts only were known, in the Utmost Simplicity of Narration, they would strike every pious, and humane Bosom, in Great Britain with Horror....[2] Every Conscience in that Country is not callous nor every Heart hardened.

The plainest Relation of Facts, would interest the Sympathy, and Compassion of all Europe in our Favour. And it would convince every American that a Nation, so great a Part of which is thus deeply depraved, can never be again trusted with Power over Us.

I think that not only History should perform her Office, but Painting, Sculpture, Statuary, ⟨*Medalling?*⟩ and Poetry ought to assist in publishing to the World, and perpetuating to Posterity, the horrid deeds of our Enemies. It will shew the Persecution, We suffer, in defence of our Rights—it will shew the Fortitude, Patience, Perseverance and Magnanimity of Americans, in as strong a Light, as the Barbarity and Impiety of Britons, in this persecuting War. Surely, Impiety consists, in destroying with such hellish Barbarity, the rational Works of the Deity, as much as in blaspheming and defying his Majesty.

If there is a moral Law: if there is a divine Law—and that there is every intelligent Creature is conscious—to trample on these Laws, to hold them in Contempt and Defyance; is the highest Exertion of Wickedness, and Impiety, that Mortals can be guilty of. The Author of human Nature, who gave it its Rights, will not see it ruined, and suffer its destroyers to escape with Impunity. Divine Vengeance will sometime or other, overtake the Alberts, the Phillips, and Georges—the Alvas, the Grislers[3] and Howes, and vindicate the Wrongs of oppressed human Nature.

I think that Medals in Gold, Silver and Copper ought to be struck in Commemoration of the shocking Cruelties, the brutal Barbarities and the diabolical Impieties of this War, and these should be contrasted with the Kindness, Tenderness, Humanity and Philanthropy, which have marked the Conduct of Americans towards their Prisoners.

It is remarkable, that the Officers and Soldiers of our Enemies, are so totally depraved, so compleatly destitute of the Sentiments of Philanthropy in their own Hearts, that they cannot believe that such delicate Feelings can exist in any other, and therefore have constantly ascribed that Milk and Honey with which We have treated them to Fear, Cowardice, and conscious Weakness.—But in this they are mistaken, and will discover their Mistake too late to answer any good Purpose for them.

RC (Adams Papers). Enclosure not found, but see note 1. An important but perhaps not completely accurate memorandum in JA's letterbook (Lb/JA/3) states that on 27 April he "wrote ten Letters," including "two to Portia. These will go by Captn. Thompson or by next Wednesdays Post.—They are as well worth copying as any others, but I am weary of the Employment." Only four or five of the letters listed by recipients' names in this memorandum are apparently present or recorded *under this date* in the Adams Papers Editorial Files, but others in the list may actually exist and be recorded under slightly later dates. There is, however, no indication that a second letter from JA dated 27 April was ever received by AA; see her acknowledgment of the present letter, 18 May, below.

¹ On 16 Jan. Congress had appointed a committee of seven members, Samuel Chase chairman, "to enquire into the conduct of the British and Hessian generals and officers towards the officers, soldiers and mariners in the service of the United States, and any other persons, inhabitants of these States, in their possession, as prisoners of war, or otherwise, and also into the conduct of the said generals and officers, and the troops under their command, towards the subjects of these States and their property, more especially of the States of New York and New Jersey" (JCC, 7:42–43). The committee acted energetically in collecting evidence and began its report, which was read in Congress on 18 April, as follows:

"That, in every place where the enemy has been, there are heavy complaints of oppression, injury, and insult, suffered by the inhabitants.... The committee found these complaints so greatly diversified, that, as it was impossible to enumerate them, so it appeared exceedingly difficult to give a distinct and comprehensive view of them, or such an account, as would not, if published, appear extremely defective, when read by the unhappy sufferers, or the country in general.

"In order, however, in some degree, to answer the design of their appointment, they determined to divide the object of their enquiry into four parts: First, The wanton and oppressive devas-tation of the country, and destruction of property: Second, The inhuman treatment of those who were so unhappy as to become prisoners: Third, The savage butchery of many who had submitted or were incapable of resistance: Fourth, The lust and brutality of the soldiers in abusing of women.

"They will, therefore, now briefly state, what they found to be the truth upon each of these heads separately, and subjoin to the whole, affidavits and other evidence to support their assertions" (same, p. 276–277).

Congress immediately accepted the report and ordered it published, "with the affidavits." The *Pennsylvania Evening Post* of 24 April devoted its entire front page to the report and continued the supporting affidavits in its issues of 26 and 29 April and 3 May. JA probably sent AA a copy of the issue of 26 April with the present letter, and a copy of that of 3 May with his letter of 4 May, below. On the following 19 July Congress ordered the committee to publish the report and affidavits as a pamphlet, "and that 4,000 copies in English, and 2,000 in German, be struck off and distributed through the several States" (same, 8:565). It is very doubtful if this was done since no copy of a pamphlet printing has been found.

² Suspension points in MS.

³ Hermann Gessler, the more or less legendary persecutor of the Swiss patriot William Tell.

John Adams to Abigail Adams

Ap. 28. 1777

There is a Clock Calm, at this Time, in the political and military Hemispheres. The Surface is smooth and the Air serene. Not a Breath, nor a Wave. No News, nor Noise.

Nothing would promote our Cause more, than Howes March to this Town. Nothing quickens and determines People so much, as a little Smart.—The Germans, who are numerous and wealthy in this state and who have very imperfect Ideas of Freedom, have a violent Attachment to Property. They are passionate and vindictive, in a Degree that is scarce credible to Persons who are unacquainted with them, and the least Injury to their Property, excites a Resentment and a Rage [1] beyond Description. A few Houses and Plantations plundered, as many would be, if Howe should come here, would set them all on Fire. Nothing would unite and determine Pensilvania so effectually.

The Passions of Men must cooperate with their Reason in the Prosecution of a War. The public may be clearly convinced that a War is just, and yet, untill their Passions are excited, will carry it languidly on. The Prejudices, the Anger, the Hatred of the English, against the French, contributes greatly to their Valour and Success. The British Court and their Officers, have studied to excite the same Passions in the Breasts of their Soldiers against the Americans, well knowing their powerfull Effect.

We, on the Contrary, have treated their Characters with too much Tenderness. The Howes, their Officers and Soldiers too, ought to be held up to the Contempt, Derision, Hatred and Abhorrence of the Populace in every State, and of the common Soldiers in every Army. It would give me no Pain, to see them burn'd or hang'd in Effigy in every Town and Village.

RC and LbC (Adams Papers).

[1] Preceding three words, probably inadvertently omitted in RC, supplied from LbC.

John Adams to Abigail Adams

Ap. 29. 1777

This days Post brought me yours of 17th. inst. and Miss Nabbys obliging Favour of the 16.[1] This young Lady writes a very pretty Hand, and expresses her Thoughts with great Propriety.

I shall hardly excuse Miss from writing to me, so long as I have done, now I find she can write so well. I shall carefully preserve her Letter and if she neglects to write me frequently I shall consider this Letter as Proof that it is not Want of Abilities, but Want of Inclination.

The Death of Mrs. Howard I greatly and sincerely lament. She was one of the choice of the Earth.

The Account you give me of the Evasions of your Regulations surprizes me not. I detest the Regulations as well as the Embargo. I find it is necessary for me to resign, for I never, of late, think like my Constituents. I am bound by their Sense in Honour and Principle—But mine differs from them every day. I always knew the Regulations would do more Hurt than good.

The inclosed Speculations upon the Health of the Army, were written I suppose by Dr. Rush,[2] as the former ones I know were done by him.

There is a letter of 20 Feb. from Dr. Lee, which says that Boston was to be attacked by Ten thousand Germans and three thousand British under Burgoin.[3] But Circumstances since may have altered Cases.

RC (Adams Papers). Enclosure missing, but see note 2.

[1] AA's letter is printed above; AA2's has not been found.

[2] This was a remarkable article entitled "Directions for Preserving the Health of Soldiers" which was first printed in the *Pennsylvania Packet*, 22 April 1777, signed "R." It was reprinted as a pamphlet, with a long subtitle and textual changes and additions, by order of the Board of War early in 1778 (Lancaster: John Dunlap; Evans 16064). This brief but pioneering essay in military hygiene was reprinted again and again until as late as 1908 and proved one of the most influential among all of Benjamin Rush's voluminous writings. An annotated text will be found in Rush's *Letters*, 1:140–147.

[3] This was clearly some version of Arthur Lee's letter from Bordeaux, 18 Feb., of which a text is printed in Wharton, ed., *Dipl. Corr. Amer. Rev.*, 2:272–273.

John Adams to Abigail Adams

April 30. 1777

We have a fine Piece of News this Morning of the March of 2000 of the Enemy, and destroying a fine Magazine there—and the stupid sordid cowardly torified Country People let them pass without Opposition.[1]

All New England is petrified, with Astonishment, Horror, and Despair, I believe in my Conscience. They behave worse than any Part of the Continent.[2] Even in N. Jersy 2000 Men could not have marched so far.

RC (Adams Papers).

[1] The reference is to the destructive raid on the Continental stores at Danbury, Conn., from Long Island Sound, 25–27 April, by a British force under Maj. Gen. William Tryon and Brig. Gen. Sir William Erskine; see Washington's letter to Congress, 28 April, read on the 30th (Washington, *Writings*, ed. Fitzpatrick, 7:490–491; JCC, 7: 314); also AA to JA, 6–9 May, below.

[2] The punctuation and capitalization of the MS have been retained in this passage, but in all likelihood JA actually intended a full stop after "Despair" and a comma after "Conscience."

Abigail Adams to John Adams

[*April* 1777][1]

The young folks desire Mamma to return thanks for their Letters which they will properly notice soon. It would have grieved you if you had seen your youngest Son stand by his Mamma and when she deliverd out to the others their Letters, he inquired for one, but none appearing he stood in silent grief with the Tears running down his face, nor could he be pacified till I gave him one of mine.—Pappa does not Love him he says so well as he does Brothers, and many comparisons were made to see whose Letters were the longest.[2]

RC (Adams Papers); addressed in John Thaxter's hand: "To The Honble: John Adams Esqr. Philadelphia"; endorsed: "Portia."

[1] Possibly AA dated this letter, but the seal has torn away part of the top edge of the sheet. On the editors' conjectural date see the following note.

[2] The letters to the "young folks" must have been those JA wrote them on 30 March. Presumably he had received the present letter by 6 May, for on that day he sent TBA an apology for omitting him earlier. On 6 May AA wrote JA, saying, "Tis ten days I believe since I wrote you a Line." Very likely the present short letter is the "Line" she meant, for there is no other from her to JA late in April 1777. All the letters mentioned in this footnote are printed under their respective dates above or below.

John Adams to Abigail Adams

May 1. 1777

This is King Tammany's Day. Tammany was an Indian King, of this Part of the Continent, when Mr. Penn first came here. His Court was in this Town. He was friendly to Mr. Penn and very serviceable to him. He lived here[1] among the first settlers for some Time and untill old Age and at last was burnt.

Some say he lived here with Mr. Penn when he first came here, and upon Mr. Pens Return he heard of it, and called upon his Grandchildren to lead him down to this Place to see his old Friend. But they went off and left him blind and very old. Upon this the old Man finding himself forsaken, he made him up a large Fire and threw himself into it. The People here have sainted him and keep his day.[2]

RC (Adams Papers). There is nothing to prove beyond question that this letter was addressed to AA, and from its tone one might plausibly suppose it was addressed to one of the Adams children, perhaps AA2. But lacking evidence to the contrary, the editors believe, with only the slightest shadow of doubt, that AA was the intended recipient.

[1] MS: "he."
[2] On the history of the St. Tammany Society in Philadelphia, founded in the early 1770's and similar in its politics to the Sons of Liberty in New York and Boston, see a rambling serial article by Francis von A. Cabeen, "The Society of the Sons of Saint Tammany of Philadelphia," *PMHB*, 25 (1901):433–451; 26 (1902):7–24, 207–223, 335–347, 443–463; 27 (1903):29–48. The Society was named for a chief of the Delaware tribe who had died many years before but was endowed with all possible virtues by his admiring followers, particularly the virtue of being indisputably all-American, unlike the legendary patrons of such societies as those of St. George, St. Andrew, and St. Patrick. See *DAB* under Tammany.

John Adams to Abigail Adams

May 2. 1777

We have promoted Arnold, one Step this day, for his Vigilance, Activity, and Bravery, in the late Affair at Connecticutt.[1]—We shall make Huntingdon a Brigadier, I hope.[2]

We shall sleep in a whole Skin for some Time I think in Philadelphia, at least untill a strong Reinforcement arrives.

I want to learn, where Sir William Erskine with his Two Thousand Men, went after his Exploit at Danbury.—Perhaps to Newport.

RC (Adams Papers).

[1] See *JCC*, 7:323.
[2] Jedediah Huntington; see same, p. 347 (12 May).

John Adams to Abigail Adams

May 4. 1777

Inclosed with this you have an Evening Post, containing some of the tender Mercies of the Barbarians to their Prisoners.

If there is a Man, Woman or Child in America, who can read these Depositions, without Resentment, and Horror, that Person has no soul or a very wicked one.

Their Treatment of Prisoners, last Year added to an Act of Parliament, which they have made to enable them to send Prisoners to England, to be there murthered, with still more relentless Cruelty, in Prisons, will bring our Officers and Soldiers to the universal Resolution to *conquer* or *die*.

This Maxim, *conquer or die*, never failed to raise a People who adopted it, to the Head of Man kind.

An Express from Portsmouth last night brought Us News of the Arrival of Arms and ordnance enough to enable Us to take Vengeance of these Foes of Human Nature.

RC (Adams Papers). Enclosure (missing): presumably a copy of the *Pennsylvania Evening Post* for 3 May 1777; see JA to AA, 27 April, above, and note 1 there.

Abigail Adams to John Adams, with a List of American Losses at Danbury

May 6 1777

Tis ten days I believe since I wrote you a Line,[1] yet not ten minuts passes without thinking of you. Tis four Months wanting 3 days since we parted, every day of the time I have mournd the absence of my Friend, and felt a vacancy in my Heart which nothing, nothing can supply. In vain the Spring Blooms or the Birds sing, their Musick has not its formour melody, nor the Spring its usual pleasures. I look round with a melancholy delight and sigh for my absent partner. I fancy I see you worn down with Cares, fatigued with Buisness, and solitary amidst a multitude.

And I think it probabal before this reaches you that you may be driven from the city by our Barbarous and Hostile foes, and the City shareing the fate of Charlestown and Falmouth, Norfolk and Daunbury. So vague and uncertain are the accounts with regard to the Latter that I shall not pretend to mention them. Tis more than a week since the Event, yet we have no accounts which can be depended upon. I wish it may serve the valuable purpose of arousing our degenerated Country Men from that state of security and torpitude into which they seem to be sunk.

May 9

I have been prevented writing for several days by company from Town. Since I wrote you I have received several Letters, 2 of the 13 of April, one of the 19 and one of the 22. Tho some of them were very short, I will not complain. I rejoice to hear from you tho you write but a line. Since the above we have some accounts of the affair at Daunbury and of the loss of General Wocester.[2] That they had no more assistance tis said was owing to six expresses being stoped by the Tories. We shall never prosper till we fall upon some method to extirpate that Blood thirsty set of men. Too much Lenity will prove our ruin. We have rumours too of an action at Brunswick much to our advantage but little credit is yet given to the report. I wish we may be able to meet them in the Feald, to encounter and Conquer so vile an Enemy.

The two Continental frigates lie wind bound with 3 brigs of 20 Guns and some others who are all going out in company. We have had a very long season of cold rainy weather, and the trees are not yet out in Blossome, the wind has been a long time at East, and prevented the vessels from going out.—I was mistaken in my Brothers going with MacNeal. He is going in the Tarter a vessel which mounts 24 Guns, is private property but sails with the Fleat.

I cannot write you half so much as I would. I have left company because I would not loose an opportunity of sending this.

The children are well. I cannot say that I am so well as I have been. The disorder I had in my Eyes has in some measure left them but communicated itself all over me and turnd to the salt rhume which worries me exceedingly, and is very hurtfull in my present situation.[3] However I am doing what I dare to to carry it of.—Believe me at all times most affectionately yours.

I must add a little more. A most Horrid plot has been discoverd of a Band of villans counterfeiting the Hampshire currency to a Great amount, no person scarcly but what has more or less of these Bills. I am unlucky enough to have about 5 pounds LM of it, but this is not the worst of it. One Col. Farington who has been concernd in the plot, was taken sick, and has confessd not only the Counterfeiting, but says they had engaged and inlisted near 2 thousand Men who upon the Troops comeing to Boston were to fall upon the people and make a General Havock. How much more mercifull God than man, in thus providentially bringing to light these Horrid plots and Schemes. I doubt not Heaven will still continue to favour us, unless our iniquities prevent. The Hampshire people have been stupid enough to let one of the principal plotters Col. Holland out upon Baill and he has made his excape.[4]

ENCLOSURE

1700 Barrells Pork
  50 Do: Beef
 700 Basketts Wheat
   7 Hhds. Rum
   6 Do: Bread
  11 Tierces Claret
   3 Quarter Cask Wine
  12 or 1700 Wheat—Rye & Corn
  12 Coile Rope
  10 Waggons
1600 Tents mostly old

The above is a true State of our Loss, in the affair at Danbury. 20 Men killed. 5 Missing. 17 Houses burnt. A Party that went out to bury the Dead have returned, and Report, that they have buried 62 Regulars.

RC (Adams Papers); addressed in John Thaxter's hand: "To The Honble: John Adams Esqr. at Philadelphia"; endorsed: "Portia ans. May 27"; docketed in CFA's hand. Enclosure, in an unidentified hand, printed herewith.

[1] Probably her letter printed under the assigned date of April 1777, above.

[2] Maj. Gen. David Wooster died on 2 May from a wound received in action against the British when they were retreating from Danbury.

[3] "Salt rheum" in U.S. usage, according to *OED*, citing Webster's *Dictionary*, 1854, was "A popular name for 'almost all the non-febrile cutaneous eruptions which are common among adults, except perhaps ringworm and itch.'"

[4] For an account of the career of Col. Stephen Holland of Londonderry, N.H., see Kenneth Scott, *Counterfeiting in Colonial America*, N.Y., 1957, p. 256–260. He was later caught and jailed in Boston (AA to JA, 8 June, below). Lt. Col. Thomas Farrington of the 5th Massachusetts was cashiered from the army this month for counterfeiting (Washington, *Writings*, ed. Fitzpatrick, 8:112 and note).

John Adams to Abigail Adams

May 6. 1777

We have no News here but what comes from you—except that all is well and quiet at Ticonderoga, that We have four Thousand Troops there, and that they were not afraid of Carlton.

The Connecticutt People have given Sir Wm. Erskine a Concord and Lexington Drubbing. But I am very angry at our People for making a Magazine, so near the Water and among such a Gang of high Church Tories. The Loss however, will not be much felt, as We have many Magazines and a plentifull Supply.

Send our Men along and We shall drubb them yet effectually. Ample Vengeance will be yet taken, of these Disturbers of human Nature....[1] There is a chosen Curse, red with uncommon Wrath, yet reserved in the stores of Heaven for these, most mean and most wicked of Men.

RC (Adams Papers).

[1] Suspension points in MS.

John Adams to Thomas Boylston Adams

My dear Son Thomas   Philadelphia May 6. 1777

The only Reason why I omitted to write you when I wrote to your Brothers,[1] was because I thought you was as yet too young to be able to read Writing, not because I had less Affection for you than for them: for you may rely upon it, you have as great a share in your Fathers Esteem and Affection as any of his Children.

I hope you will be good and learn to read and write well, and then I shall take a Pride and Pleasure in your constant Correspondence. Give my Love to your Mamma, your worthy Sister, and Brothers, and to all the rest of the Family.

Pray, when you write me a Letter, let me know how many Calves are raising, how many Ducks and Geese, and how the Garden looks. I long to take a Walk with you to see them, and the green Meadows and Pastures. I am your Father,   John Adams

RC (PPRF); addressed: "Mr. Thomas Adams Braintree."

[1] See AA's letter to JA printed under the assigned date of April 1777, above, and note 2 there.

John Adams to Abigail Adams

Philadelphia May 7. 1777

We have no News here, except what We get from your Country. The Privateers act with great Spirit, and are blessed with remarkable Success. Some Merchant ships are arrived this Week from Maryland. They were first chased by Men of War, in attempting to get into Cheasapeak Bay—they run from them and attempted Delaware Bay—

there they were chased again. Whereupon they again shifted their Course for Cheasapeak and got in safe in spight of all the Men of War could do.

Thus you see We can and will have Trade, in spight of them....[1] And this Trade will probably increase fast. It requires Time for The Stream of Commerce to alter its Channell. Time is necessary, for our Merchants and foreign Merchants to think, plan, and correspond with each other. Time is also necessary for our Masters of Vessells and Mariners to become familiar with the Coasts, Ports and Harbours of foreign Countries—and a longer Time still is needfull for French, Spanish, and Dutch Masters and Mariners to learn our Coasts, and Harbours.

Yours, ever, ever yours.

RC (Adams Papers).

[1] Suspension points in MS.

John Adams to Abigail Adams

Philadelphia May 10. 1777

The Day before Yesterday, I took a Walk, with my Friend Whipple to Mrs. Wells's, the Sister of the famous Mrs. Wright, to see her Waxwork.[1] She has two Chambers filled with it. In one, the Parable of the Prodigal Son, is represented. The Prodigal is prostrate on his Knees, before his Father, whose Joy, and Grief, and Compassion all appear in his Eyes and Face, struggling with each other. A servant Maid, at the Fathers command, is pulling down from a Closet Shelf, the choicest Robes, to cloath the Prodigal, who is all in Rags. At an outward Door, in a Corner of the Room stands the elder Brother, chagrined at this Festivity, a Servant coaxing him to come in. A large Number of Guests, are placed round the Room. In another Chamber, are the Figures of Chatham, Franklin, Sawbridge, Mrs. Maccaulay, and several others. At a Corner is a Miser, sitting at his Table, weighing his Gold, his Bag upon one Side of the Table, and a Thief behind him, endeavouring to pilfer the Bag.

There is Genius, as well as Taste and Art, discovered in this Exhibition: But I must confess, the whole Scæne was disagreable to me. The Imitation of Life was too faint, and I seemed to be walking among a Group of Corps's, standing, sitting, and walking, laughing, singing, crying, and weeping. This Art I think will make but little Progress in the World.

Another Historical Piece I forgot, which is Elisha, restoring to Life the Shunamite's Son. The Joy of the Mother, upon Discerning the first Symptoms of Life in the Child, is pretty strongly expressed.

Dr. Chevots Waxwork, in which all the various Parts of the human Body are represented, for the Benefit of young Students in Anatomy and of which I gave you a particular Description, a Year or two ago, were much more pleasing to me. Wax is much fitter to represent dead Bodies, than living ones.[2]

Upon a Hint, from one of our Commissioners abroad, We are looking about for American Curiosities, to send across the Atlantic as presents to the Ladies.[3] Mr. Rittenhouse's Planetarium, Mr. Arnolds Collection of Rareties in the Virtuoso Way, which I once saw at Norwalk in Connecticutt,[4] Narragansett Pacing Mares, Mooses, Wood ducks, Flying Squirrells, Redwinged Black birds, Cramberries, and Rattlesnakes have all been thought of.[5]

Is not this a pretty Employment for great Statesmen, as We think ourselves to be? Frivolous as it seems, it may be of some Consequence. Little Attentions have great Influence. I think, however, We ought to consult the Ladies upon this Point. Pray what is your Opinion?[6]

RC and LbC (Adams Papers). LbC is entered in Lb/JA/3 as two separate letters, the first ending with JA's remarks on Dr. Chovet's anatomical waxworks, and the second containing only the two final paragraphs as found in RC, on "American Curiosities." Datelines in RC and both LbC entries originally read "April 10.," but the month was corrected to May by overwriting in all three.

[1] Patience (Lovell) Wright (1725–1786), by origin a New Jersey Quaker, gained celebrity as a modeler in wax and has been called the first American sculptor. The Adams ladies were to encounter her in London in the 1780's and to write about her with less than complete admiration. See *DAB*; Groce and Wallace, *Dict. Amer. Artists*; JA, *Diary and Autobiography*, 3:165, with references there. Mrs. Wright's sister, Rachel (Lovell) Wells, was also a modeler in wax, but none of her work is known to survive (Ethel Stanwood Bolton, *American Wax Portraits*, Boston and N.Y., 1929, p. 22, 61). It seems likely that the collection JA viewed included pieces executed by both sisters.

[2] The anatomical waxworks executed by Dr. Abraham Chovet (1704–1790) were among the principal scientific attractions of Philadelphia at this period.

JA was apparently mistaken in supposing that he had described them in an earlier letter to AA, but he had given some account of them in his diary entry for 14 Oct. 1774 (*Diary and Autobiography*, 2:152).

[3] See Silas Deane's letters to the Committee of Secret Correspondence, 28 Nov. 1776, and to John Jay, 3 Dec. 1776, respectively, in Wharton, ed., *Dipl. Corr. Amer. Rev.*, 2:200, 214. Deane's own list of suggestions in the latter is engaging:

"I must mention some trifles. The queen is fond of parade, and I believe wishes a war, and is our friend. She loves riding on horseback. Could you send me a narrowhegansett horse or two; the present might be money exceedingly well laid out. Rittenhouse's orrery, or Arnold's collection of insects, a phaeton of American make and a pair of bay horses, a few barrels of apples, of walnuts, of butternuts, etc., would be great curiosities here, where everything American is gazed at, and where the American contest engages the attention of all ages, ranks, and sexes."

⁴ JA saw this natural history collection in the summer of 1774 when on his way to the first Continental Congress, and he afterward found it incorporated in Sir Ashton Lever's private museum in Leicester House, London; see *Diary and Autobiography*, 3:151.

⁵ In LbC JA did not at first list two of the items as here given but then immediately added: "And why should not Moose's and Rattlesnakes!"

⁶ JA began an additional paragraph in RC, but then rubbed it out: "We have at last accom. . . ." See the beginning of the following letter.

John Adams to Abigail Adams

Philadelphia May 10 [1777]

We have at last accomplished a troublesome Piece of Business. We have chosen a Number of additional Ambassadors. Mr. Ralph Izzard of S. Carolina, a Gentleman of large Fortune, for the Court of the Grand Duke of Tuscany, and Mr. William Lee, formerly Alderman of London, for the Courts of Vienna and Berlin.¹

LbC (Adams Papers). There is no indication that this letter was sent or received. JA perhaps meant to add to it, but did not, and then did not copy and send it. Or perhaps he thought he had included this paragraph in the letter he did send this day, preceding.

¹ Izard was appointed on 7 May, and Lee on 9 May (JCC, 7:334, 343).

Isaac Smith Sr. to John Adams

Mr. Adams   Boston May. 12th. 1777

I duly received your several packets for Mrs. Adams which have been forwarded.—I have thoughts of sending a Vessell to Georgia to load with Rice, and as I should have Occasion to send money for the purchase, I should be glad iff you would enquire of the Gentlemen from Georgia, whether the Continental Loan bills would Answer as some Value in them might be easier conseald in case I should send them by the Vessell, but should rather send them by post iff I could do itt with safety which suppose may be done. I should therefore be glad iff you would enquire of the Gentlemen from Georgia, to whom I might with safety send the bills by land to be lodged in some Gentleman's hands Against the Vessell might Arrive and in case the Vessell should Miscarry, they may remain safe till further orders.

I should be glad to know how long the post is going from Phila. to Georgia.—There are two ships On the Carolina Coast, which takes many Vessells About a fortnight Ago bound here Amongst which I have One.

We have nothing Arrived lately from Europe. There are several may be lookt for from Bilboa about 3 weeks hence and I expect One from France likewise.

I am Yr. hum servt,   Isaac Smith

RC (Adams Papers).

John Adams to Abigail Adams

May 14. 77

Prices with you are much more moderate than here. Yesterday I was obliged to give Forty shillings Pen. Cur.[1] Thirty two L.M. for one Gallon of Rum.

In my station here, I have Business with many Gentlemen who have occasion to visit me, and I am reduced to the Necessity of treating them with plain Toddy and Rum and Water—a Glass of Wine, once in a while to a great stranger, of uncommon Consideration.

The Prices of Beef, Pork, Veal, Mutton, Poultry, Butter, Cheese, Milk is Three Times higher, here than with you.

I live like a Miser, and an Hermit, to save Charges, yet my Constituents will think my Expences beyond all Bounds.—My Love to Dr. Tufts. I have received two agreable Letters from him, which I will answer as soon as I can.

RC (Adams Papers).

[1] Pennsylvania currency, which, as indicated here, had a ratio to New England "lawful money" of 5 to 4.

John Adams to Abigail Adams

May 15. 1777

Gen. Warren writes me, that my Farm never looked better, than when he last saw it, and that Mrs. —— was like to outshine all the Farmers.[1]—I wish I could see it.—But I can make Allowances. He knows the Weakness of his Friends Heart and that nothing flatters it more than praises bestowed upon a certain Lady.

I am suffering every day for Want of my farm to ramble in.—I have been now for near Ten Weeks in a drooping disagreable Way, loaded constantly with a Cold. In the Midst of infinite Noise, Hurry, and Bustle, I lead a lonely melancholly Life, mourning the Loss of all the Charms of Life, which are my family, and all the Amusement that I ever had in Life which is my farm.

If the warm Weather, which is now coming on, should not cure my Cold, and make me better I must come home. If it should and I should get tolerably comfortable, I shall stay, and reconcile my self to the Misery I here suffer as well as I can.

I expect, that I shall be chained to this Oar, untill my Constitution both of Mind and Body are totally destroyed, and rendered wholly useless to my self, and Family for the Remainder of my Days.

However, now We have got over the dreary, dismall, torpid Winter, when We had no Army, not even Three Thousand Men to protect Us against all our Enemies foreign and domestic; and now We have got together a pretty respectable Army, which renders Us tolerably secure against both, I doubt not, We shall be able to perswade some Gentleman or other, in the Massachusetts, to vouch safe, to undertake the dangerous Office of Delegate to Congress.

However, I will neither whine, nor croak. The Moment our Affairs are in a prosperous Way and a little more out of Doubt—that Moment I become a private Gentleman, the respectfull Husband of the amiable Mrs. A. of B. and the affectionate Father of her Children, two Characters, which I have scarcely supported for these three Years past, having done the Duties of neither.

RC (Adams Papers).

[1] "I hope the Court will rise this week and give me a little respite, and time to Study Tull [Jethro Tull, author of *Horse-Hoeing Husbandry*, first published London, 1731] but after all our Study, I don't know but Mrs. Adams Native Genius will Excel us all in Husbandry. She was much Engaged when I came along, and the Farm at Braintree Appeared to be Under Excellent Management. I tryed to persuade her to make A Visit to her Friend Mrs. Warren but she cant leave Home this *Busy Season*" (James Warren to JA, 27 April, Adams Papers).

John Adams to Abigail Adams

Philadelphia May 17. 1777

I never fail to inclose to you the News papers, which contain the most of the Intelligence that comes to my Knowledge.

I am obliged to slacken my Attention to Business a little, and ride and walk for the Sake of my Health, which is but infirm.—Oh that I could wander, upon Penns Hill, and in the Meadows and Mountains in its Neighbourhood free from Care! But this is a Felicity too great for me.

Mr. Gorham and Mr. Russell are here with a Petition from Charlstown. It grieves me that they are to return without success. I feel, most exquisitely, for the unhappy People of that Town. Their Agents have done every Thing in their Power, or in the Power of Men to do, and the Mass. Delegates have seconded their Efforts to the Utmost of their Power, but all in vain.[1]

The Distress of the States, arising from the Quantity of Money abroad, and the monstrous Demands that would be made from Virginia, N. Jersy, N. York and elsewhere, if a Precedent should be once set, has determined the Congress, almost with Tears in their Eyes, to withstand this Application at present.

Every Man expressed the Utmost Tenderness and Humanity, upon the Occasion: But at the same Time every Man except the Mass. Delegates expressed his full Conviction of the ill Policy of granting any Thing at present.

RC (Adams Papers).

[1] See Zabdiel Adams to JA, 19 April, above, and note 1 there.

Abigail Adams to John Adams

Sunday. May 18 1777

I think myself very happy that not a week passes but what I receive a Letter or two, some times more from you; and tho they are longer in comeing than formerly oweing I suppose to the posts being obliged to travel farther round, yet I believe they all faithfully reach me, even the curious conversation between Mr. Burn and your Honour arrived safe and made me laugh very Heartily.

Your Last which I believe came by a private Hand and was dated the 30 of April came to hand in about 12 days which is sooner than any other has reachd me since you came to Philadelphia. Two others accompanied it one of April 26 and 27. In one of them you mention your having been unwell, I hope nothing more than a cold. I feel more anxious than ever for your Health, and must intreat of you if you find it fail in any great measure that you would return during the summer Months; should I hear you were sick the imposibility of my comeing to you would render me misirable indeed.

I think before this time Many of our Troops must have arrived at Head Quarters, for tho we have been dilatory in this and the Neighbouring Towns, others I hear have done their duty better. Not an Hour in the day but what we see soldiers marching. The sure way to prevent their distressing us Here would be to have a strong Army with the General. Their are a number not more than half I believe tho, of this Towns proportion inlisted. The rest were to be drawn at our May meeting, but nothing was done in that way, they concluded to try a little longer to inlist them.[1] The Town send but one Rep. this year and that is Mr. N[ile]s of the middle parish. Give him His pipe and Let him laugh, He will not trouble any body.[2] Philalutheris I suppose will be chosen into the Counsel since He finds that His plan for making them Lackies and Tools to the House was not so acceptable as he expected.[3]

> "Then let me Have the Highest post,
> Suppose it but an inch at most."

I should feel more unhappy and anxious than ever if I realizd our being again invaded by the wickedest and cruelest of Enemies. I should not dare to tarry here in my present situation, nor yet know where to flee for safety; the recital of the inhumane and Brutal Treatment of those poor creatures who have fallen into their Hands, Freazes me with Horrour. My apprehensions are greatly increasd; should they come this way again I know [not][4] what course I should take.

Tis an observation of Bishop Butlers[5] that they who have lost all tenderness and Fellow-feeling for others, have withall contracted a certain Callousness of Heart, which renders them insensible to all other satisfactions, but those of the grossest kind.

Our Enemies have proved the Truth of the observation in every instance of their conduct. Is it not astonishing what Men may at last bring themselves to, by suppressing passions and affections of the best kind, and suffering the worst to rule over them in their full strength.

Infidelity has been a growing part of the British character for many years. It is not so much to be wonderd at that those who pay no regard to a Supreeme Being should throw of all regard to their fellow creatures and to those precepts and doctrines which require peace and good will to Men; and in a perticuliar manner distinguish the followers of him who hath said by this shall all Men know that ye are my deciples if ye have love one towards an other.

Let them reproach us ever so much for our kindness and tenderness to those who have fallen into our Hands, I hope it will never provoke us to retaliate their cruelties; let us put it as much as posible out of their power to injure us, but let us keep in mind the precepts of him who hath commanded us to Love our Enemies; and to excercise towards them acts of Humanity, Benevolence and Kindness, even when they despitefully use us.

And here suffer me to quote an Authority which you greatly Esteem, Dr. Tillotson.[6] It is commonly said that revenge is sweet, but to a calm and considerate mind, patience and forgiveness are sweeter, and do afford a much more rational, and solid and durable pleasure than revenge. The monuments of our Mercy and goodness are a far more pleasing and delightfull Spectacle than of our rage and cruelty, and no sort of thought does usually haunt men with more Terror, than the reflexion upon what they have done in the way of Revenge.

If our cause is just, it will be best supported by justice and righteousness. Tho we have many other crimes to answer for, that of cruelty to our Enemies is not chargable upon Americans, and I hope never will be—if we have err'd it is upon the side of Mercy and have excercised so much lenity to our Enemies as to endanger our Friends—but their Malice and wicked designs against us, has and will oblige every State to proceed against them with more Rigor. Justice and self preservation are duties as much incumbant upon christians, as forgiveness and Love of Enemies.

Adieu. I have devoted an Hour this Day to you. I dare say you are not in debt.

Ever remember with the tenderest affection one whose greatest felicity consists in the firm belief of an unabated Love either by years or absence.   Portia

RC (Adams Papers); addressed in John Thaxter's hand: "To The Honble: John Adams Esqr. at Philadelphia To be left at the Post Office"; endorsed: "Portia ans. 2. June"; docketed in CFA's hand.

[1] From the late fall of 1776 through the following winter and spring, the town had met frequently "To consider and do what the Town may think proper for the Encouragement of Inlisting men for the Continental Army now Required." Committees were appointed to hire recruits, and various other measures were taken. On 15 May, "There being a prospect of a number of men being hired by the said Committee the Town thought proper not to make any Draft, notwithstanding the orders of the [General] Court." But at two special meetings in June the committee reported to the town that only ten men had been hired in a month, and further meetings were held in the following months in an effort to fill up the town's quota without resorting to a draft. (*Braintree Town Records*, p. 473–484.)

[2] Samuel Niles (1711–1804), Harvard 1731, deacon, justice and later chief justice of the Suffolk Inferior Court of Common Pleas, moderator of Braintree town meeting, and from time to time representative in the General Court and member of the Council, had occasionally collaborated with JA at the beginning of the latter's career in politics (Sibley-Shipton, *Harvard Graduates*, 9:71–74; JA, *Diary and Autobiography*,

1:118, 130, 160, 216–217; 3:280, 282).

³ AA is alluding to a five-column communication signed "Phileleutherus" (i.e. a lover of freedom) in the Boston *Independent Chronicle* for 7 March 1777, which embodied a draft constitution for Massachusetts, a subject which was in the forefront of legislative deliberation and popular discussion at this time. Phileleutherus' draft contained a number of features ultimately incorporated in the Massachusetts Constitution of 1780, but it was chiefly remarkable for proposing wholly to subordinate the executive to the legislative branch of government. The "General Assembly" was to elect a "Council of Safety" from its own membership; this council was to serve as a plural executive after the pattern of the Pennsylvania Constitution of 1776. All legislation was to "originate, and be compleated by" the unicameral assembly, the council acting therein only in an advisory capacity. In three signed letters in later issues of the *Chronicle* (20, 27 March, 3 April), Rev. William Gordon severely criticized Phileleutherus' plan; in the second of these he

quoted (without naming) JA on the dangers of unicameralism as set forth in *Thoughts on Government.* Gordon tantalizingly says that he knows who Phileleutherus is but will protect his anonymity. AA speaks as if perhaps she also knew, but unfortunately the present editors do not. (The most detailed account available, though hardly a satisfactory one, of the efforts and maneuvers from Sept. 1776 through May 1777 relating to a new constitution is in Harry A. Cushing, *History of the Transition from Provincial to Commonwealth Government in Massachusetts*, N.Y. 1896, p. 199–207.)

⁴ This word editorially supplied.

⁵ Joseph Butler (1692–1752), Bishop of Durham, author of *The Analogy of Religion . . .* (*DNB*). For works by Butler owned by JA, see *Catalogue of JA's Library*.

⁶ John Tillotson (1630–1694), sometime Archbishop of Canterbury, whose *Works* (10 vols., Edinburgh, 1759–1760) JA owned and had laboriously studied as a young schoolmaster in Worcester (*DNB*; JA, *Diary and Autobiography*, 1:9–10; *Catalogue of JA's Library*).

John Adams to Abigail Adams

May 21. 1777

Dont be two much alarmed at the Report of an Attack of Boston. The British Court are pursuing a system which in the End I think they will find impolitick. They are alarming the Fears of the People, every where. Wentworths Letter was contrived to terrify Portsmouth.[1] Other Threats are given out against Boston. Others against the Eastern shore of Virginia and Maryland. Now Philadelphia is to be invaded—then Albany. Sometimes New London, at others N. Haven.

After all they will make but a poor Figure this Summer. There is some Reason to think, they have sent to Canada, for the Troops there by Water. Their Reinforcement from Europe, I think will not be great. Our Army is grown pretty strong. Pray let my dear Countrymen turn out, and not let a Man be wanting of their Quota.

The Enemy will find it impollitick to awaken the Apprehensions of so many People. Because when the Peoples Fears subside which most of them will, they will be succeeded by Contempt.

My Eyes are weak again, and I am in bad Health but I keep about.

243

I ride every fair Morning and walk every pleasant Evening, so that I cannot write so often as I wish.—Have received no Letter from you by the two last Posts.

The Country here looks most deliciously and the Singing Birds of which Species there is here a great Variety are inspired. The Spring is backward but promised great Fertility, Plenty and Abundance.

I wish I could see your Garden and little Farm.

RC (Adams Papers).

[1] An intercepted letter from former Gov. John Wentworth of New Hampshire, an extract of which was forwarded by Gov. Trumbull of Connecticut, 10 March, read in Congress on the 20th, and referred to "the Committee of Intelligence" (*JCC*, 7:187).

Mercy Otis Warren to Abigail Adams

Plimouth May 21 [1777]

I this day Received a few lines [1] from my Friend, whose Long silence I have not been able to Account for but suppose her Letters are Directed southward. Have you any Late private Inteligence from that quarter, and do our Friends their Really think we shall be Invaded on all sides, or do they mean only to advise us to be Ready. My heart at times almost dies within me only with the Apprehension that we and our Neighbours May in a few months suffer all the distress the Inhabitants of the Jerseys and its Environs have already felt. I then Rally up my Fortitude, but find Nothing but Confidence in Him by whom kings Reign, Who Can Easily turn the Counsels of the Wiked into Foolishness, Can support my spirits, and give me the Courage Necessary for such a day as this.

I purpose to see you soon if Nothing Exstrordinary Intervenes. Mr. Warren proposes to spend Election week at home, and to look Northward the Monday following when I shall accompany him, and promiss myself the pleasure of spending a few days with my Braintree Friends.

Is Betsey agoing to be Maried. Why has she done writing. Do New acquaintance and New prospects Engross all her Attention. Give her my Love and best Wishes.

How do they do down at the Farms.[2] Is Mrs. Lincoln Blind again. Is she Lame or is she Lazy that she Neglects her Friend at Plimouth.

With unfeigned Regards to Yourself and Family Concludes Your Friend,   Marcia Warren

Mrs. Lothrops Compliments &c. to Mrs. Adams.

The papers for which I thank You I send now Least I forget it another time.

RC (Adams Papers). Enclosed "papers" (presumably newspapers) not found or identified.

[1] Not found.

[2] "The Farms" was an early name for the region later known as North Quincy. From the reference to "Mrs. Lincoln" that follows, Mrs. Warren probably is inquiring about Col. Josiah Quincy's family and specifically his daughter Hannah, widow of Dr. Bela Lincoln.

John Adams to Abigail Adams

May 22 [1777]. 4 O Clock in the Morning

After a Series of the souerest,[1] and harshest Weather that ever I felt in this Climate, We are at last, blessed with a bright Sun and a soft Air. The Weather here has been like our old Easterly Winds to me, and southerly Winds to you.

The Charms of the Morning at this Hour, are irresistable. The Streakes of Glory dawning in the East: the freshness and Purity in the Air, the bright blue of the sky, the sweet Warblings of a great Variety of Birds intermingling with the martial Clarions of an hundred Cocks now within my Hearing, all conspire to chear the Spirits.

This kind of puerile Description is a very pretty Employment for an old Fellow whose Brow is furrowed with the Cares of Politicks and War.

I shall be on Horseback in a few Minutes, and then I shall enjoy the Morning, in more Perfection.

I spent last Evening at the War-Office, with General Arnold. . . .[2] He has been basely slandered and libelled. The Regulars say, "he fought like Julius Cæsar."

I am wearied to Death with the Wrangles between military officers, high and low. They Quarrell like Cats and Dogs. They worry one another like Mastiffs. Scrambling for Rank and Pay like Apes for Nutts.

I believe there is no one Principle, which predominates in human Nature so much in every stage of Life, from the Cradle to the Grave, in Males and females, old and young, black and white, rich and poor, high and low, as this Passion for Superiority. . . . Every human Being compares itself in its own Imagination, with every other round about it, and will find some Superiority over every other real or imaginary, or it will die of Grief and Vexation. I have seen it among Boys and Girls at school, among Lads at Colledge, among Practicers at the Bar, among the Clergy in their Associations, among Clubbs of Friends, among the People in Town Meetings, among the Members of an House of Rep[resentative]s, among the Grave Councillors, on the more solemn Bench of Justice, and in that awfully August Body the Congress, and on many of its Committees—and among Ladies every Where—But I never saw it operate with such Keenness, Ferocity and Fury, as among military Officers. They will go terrible Lengths, in their Emulations, their Envy and Revenge, in Consequence of it.

So much for Philosophy.—I hope my five or six Babes are all well. My Duty to my Mother and your Father and Love to sisters and Brothers, Aunts and Uncles.

Pray how does your Asparagus perform? &c.

I would give Three Guineas for a Barrell of your Cyder—not one drop is to be had here for Gold. And wine is not to be had under Six or Eight Dollars a Gallon and that very bad. I would give a Guinea for a Barrell of your Beer. The small beer here is wretchedly bad. In short I can get nothing that I can drink, and I believe I shall be sick from this Cause alone. Rum at forty shillings a Gallon and bad Water, will never do, in this hot Climate in summer where Acid Liquors are necessary against Putrefaction.

RC (Adams Papers).
[1] Thus clearly in MS.
[2] Here and below, suspension points are in MS.

John Adams to Abigail Adams

Philadelphia May 24. 1777

We have an Army in the Jersies, so respectable that We seem to be under no Apprehensions at present, of an Invasion of Philadelphia— at least untill a powerfull Reinforcement shall arrive from Europe. When that will be and how powerfull, it is impossible to say: But I think, it will not be very soon, nor very strong.

Perhaps, the Troops from Canada may come round by Water. If they do, the whole Force they can make, with all the Reinforcements from Europe will do no great Things this Year. I think, our Cause will never again be in so low a state as it was last December—then was the Crisis.

There are four Men of War and four Tenders in Delaware Bay. The Roebuck, and a Fifty Gun ship, and two other Frigates, are the Men of War. They come up the River a little Way to get Water sometimes with Fear and Trembling, and dare not come up far enough to get fresh Water, but content themselves with brackish Water.

They go on shore sometimes to steal some lean Cattle, if any happen to wander into lonely Places, where they dare venture.

My Love to all.

RC (Adams Papers).

John Adams to Abigail Adams

May 25. 1777

At half past four this Morning, I mounted my Horse, and took a ride, in a Road that was new to me. I went to Kensington, and then to Point No Point, by Land, the Place where I went, once before, with a large Company in the Rowe Gallies, by Water. That Frolic was almost two Years ago. I gave you a Relation of it, in the Time, I suppose.[1] The Road to Point No Point lies along the River Delaware, in fair Sight of it, and its opposite shore. For near four Miles the Road is as strait as the Streets of Philadelphia. On each Side, are beautifull Rowes of Trees, Buttonwoods, Oaks, Walnutts, Cherries and Willows, especially down towards the Banks of the River. The Meadows, Pastures, and Grass Plotts, are as Green as Leeks. There are many Fruit Trees and fine orchards, set with the nicest Regularity. But the Fields of Grain, the Rye, and Wheat, exceed all Description. These Fields are all sown in Ridges; and the Furrough between each Couple of Ridges, is as plainly to be seen, as if a swarth[2] had been mown along. Yet it is no wider than a Plough share, and it is as strait as an Arrow. It looks as if the Sower had gone along the Furrough with his Spectacles to pick up every grain that should accidentally fall into it.

The Corn is just coming out of the Ground. The Furroughs struck out for the Hills to be planted in, are each Way, as straight as mathematical right Lines; and the Squares between every four Hills, as exact as they could be done by Plumb and Line, or Scale and Compass.

I am ashamed of our Farmers. They are a lazy, ignorant sett, in Husbandry, I mean—For they know infinitely more of every Thing else, than these. But after all the Native Face of our Country, diversified as it is, with Hill and Dale, Sea and Land, is to me more agreable than this enchanting artificial scæne.

May 27.

The Post brought me yours of May 6th. and 9th.

You express Apprehensions that We may be driven from this City. We have No such Apprehensions here. Howe is unable to do any

Thing but by Stealth. Washington is strong enough to keep Howe, where he is.

How could it happen that you should have £5 of counterfeit New Hampshire Money? Cant you recollect who you had it of? Let me intreat you not to take a shilling of any but continental Money, or Massachusetts—and be very carefull of that. There is a Counterfeit Continental Bill abroad sent out of New York but it will deceive none but Fools, for it is Copper Plate—easily detected, miserably done.

RC and LbC (Adams Papers). LbC does not include the continuation of 27 May. (The present letter is the last to AA entered by JA in Lb/JA/3, which contains only four more entries and breaks off entirely with a copy of a letter written to Nathanael Greene dated 7 July 1777. Thus of the scores of letters he wrote to AA, and the lesser number he wrote to others, during the following summer and fall while still in Congress, JA retained no copies.)

[1] JA's account of his "Excursion" to Point-no-Point, "upon Delaware River in the new Row Gallies built by the Committee of Safety," is in his diary entry of 28 Sept. 1775, not in a letter to AA (*Diary and Autobiography*, 2:187–188).

[2] Obsolete spelling of "swath," which is the spelling found in LbC.

Abigail Adams to John Adams

May 28 1777

This is Election Day, but the news of the day I am not able to inform you of as I have Heard nothing from Town. The House is not so unwealdy a Body this year as the last. Very few Towns have sent more than one, and those are many of them new Members. Whether they have changd for the better time will discover.

I recollect a remark of a writer upon Goverment,[1] who says that a single assembly is subject to all the starts of passion and to the caprices of an individual.

We have lately experienced the Truth of the observation. A French vessel·came into Boston laiden with a large Quantity of dry goods. The War office had the offer of any thing they chose to take, after which some things were offerd for sale by the captain at a higher rate than the Regulated price, whilst some were offerd for less. Upon this a certain B[osto]n Member who comes under the Denomination of a furious Whigg[2] Blusterd about and insisted upon it if he would not comply he ought to be orderd out of the Harbour, and procured a very unanimous vote for it in the House, but upon its being sent up to the Counsel there was but one vote in favour of it.

[*May*] 29.

I have been interrupted by company from writing farther. I have been happy in receiving a number of Letters from you of various dates, since I wrote last. I have not time to notice them now, I will write by the next post, and be more perticular. We Have no News here of any kind. There has been no stir at Newport yet.

Every method is taking to fill up the continental Army which I hope will be effected soon. Many of the soldiers who have inlisted for this Town, are in the Hospital under innoculation. We have two Hospitals in the upper parish, one just opend. Dr. W[ale]s has had great Success. Since March 200 have had the distemper under his care, and not one died. He has now more than a hundred in it from this and the neighbouring Towns.³ 6 or 7 of my neighbours went in yesterday, and one from my own family, Jonathan.⁴

The Spring in general has been very cold, a few extreem Hot days, the rest of the time you might sit by the fire which I now do.

Our Fleet saild Last week and had several days of fine wind and weather.

I hear your president is upon the road Home with his family—I hope He brings me Letters. Adieu most sincerely yours.

RC (Adams Papers); addressed in John Thaxter's hand: "To The Honble: John Adams Esqr. at Philadelphia"; endorsed: "Portia"; docketed in two different hands, one of which is CFA's.

¹ JA, in his *Thoughts on Government* (1776); see his *Works*, 4:206.

² A political type that had recently received rough treatment at the hands of a Philadelphia newspaper essayist whose article was reprinted in Boston: "The Furious Whigs injure the cause of liberty as much by their violence as the timid Whigs do by their fears. They think the destruction of Howe's army of less consequence than the detection and punishment of the most insignificant Tory. They think the common forms of justice should be suspended towards a Tory criminal, and that a man who only *speaks* against our common defence, should be tomahawked, scalped, and roasted alive. Lastly, they are all cowards, and skulk under the cover of an office, or a sickly family, when they are called to oppose the enemy in the field. Woe to that State or Community that is governed by this class of men!" (*Conti-*

nental Journal, 10 April 1777). The particular Boston member and "furious Whigg" to whom AA alludes has not, however, been certainly identified.

³ Dr. Ephraim Wales, Harvard 1768, had settled in the South Precinct of Braintree (now Randolph) about 1770 and was long prominent in town affairs. In March 1777 the town appointed "a Committee to Treat with Doctr. Wales with respect to his Inoculation for the Small pox, contrary to the vote of Town," and "Restrictions" were accordingly laid upon him. The issue was "the distance from the Hospital to the Road," which the committee had found to be "one Hundred and fifteen roods," evidently not enough. However, at its May meeting the town voted, 121 against 70, to permit smallpox inoculation and authorized Dr. Moses Baker and Dr. Ephraim Wales to conduct "Hospitals" for the purpose, "under the Limitation & Regulation of

the Law & the Selectmen of the Town."
(Ebenezer Alden, *The Early History of
the Medical Profession in the County
of Norfolk, Mass.*, Boston, 1853, p. 12;

Braintree Town Records, p. 478–480,
and *passim*.)

⁴ A young servant or farm laborer.

John Adams to Abigail Adams

Philadelphia May 28. 1777

An horrid cold Day for Election—warm work however, in the Afternoon, I suppose.[1]

You will see by the inclosed Papers, among the Advertisements, how the Spirit of Manufacturing grows. There never was a Time when there was such full Employment, for every Man, Woman and Child, in this City. Spinning, Knitting, Weaving, every Tradesman is as full as possible. Wool and Flax in great Demand.

Industry will supply our Necessities, if it is not cramped by injudicious Laws—such as Regulations of Prices &c., Embargoes &c. These discourage Industry and turn that Ingenuity which ought to be employed for the general Good, into Knavery.

RC (Adams Papers). Enclosed newspapers not found or identified.

[1] That is, in the election, by the new House of Representatives, voting jointly with the members of the old Council, of a new council. "Yesterday was our Election of Councellors: a large Number of the Representatives, perhaps 20 or 30 from Hampshire, Berkshire &c. would not vote, being for a single Assembly. I hope this Sentiment will not prevail. They could chuse no more than thirteen by nine o'Clock; and then adjourn'd to this Morning" (Samuel Cooper to JA, 29 May, Adams Papers).

Abigail Adams to John Adams

My dearest Friend   June 1. 1777

I designd to have wrote you by the last Post, but have been so unwell for the week past that I have not been able. We have had very Hot weather which you know never agrees well with me, and greatly distresses me under my present circumstances. I loose my rest a nights, which makes me more unable to bear the Heat of the day. I look forward to the middle of july with more anxiety than I can describe, and the Thoughts of 3 hundreds miles distance are as Greivious as the perils I have to pass through. I am cut of from the privilidge which some of the Brute creation enjoy, that of having their mate sit by them with anxious care during all their Solitary confinement.

You live at an expence however frugal it may be deemed there,

which will astonish your constituents I suppose and be the occasion
of many more gratefull acknowledgments, and speaches. If either of us
were in the least avaricious or even parsimonious we should poorly
Brook the sacrifice we make of property. One Gentleman of the Bar
acknowledged that he had made a thousand pounds sterling since the
opening of Buisness by admiralty causes and others, and there are
some others who have made more than he; and with how much less
fatigue than you have sufferd, you are the best judge. I hope this year
will if we are any way successfull put an end to your fatigues and your
journeys. If you could be at Home and only earnd a Bare subsistance I
should be happeier.

Every thing Here is extravangantly high, but more tolerable than
with you. A Dollor now is not eaquel to what one Quarter was two
years ago, and their is no sort of property which is not held in higher
estimation than money. I have long seen the true causes of this Evil,
and have been out of favour, with the regulating act, as I have seen I
think that it rather served to raise than lower prices.

I endeavour to live with as great frugality as posible. I am obliged to
pay higher wages this year than last; Prince was offerd 8 dollors a
month and left me. I found upon trial that I must give 12, and put to
great difficulty to hire a Hand even at that price, so I sent for Him
again, and he got himself releasd, and is with me for 6 months upon
those terms.

I have paid him his 5 pounds for the winter, have paid the Rates
which amount to 24 pounds 2 & 3 pence, have also paid your Brother
5 hundred & 50 dollors which with what you paid when at Home and
the small sums that were paid before, amount to the whole of the
principal and part of the interest.[1] I would have taken up the bond,
but he chose it should lay as there were Notes of Hand which you have
against him and an account to settle which he has against you—and this
week I propose to send in to the continental Loan office a hundred
pound LM. If I do not explain the matter I fear you will suspect me of
being concerned with the Hampshire money makers. You must know
then that your sister A[dam]s took up a Note to the amount of a
hundred & 27 pounds out of which was oweing to her as you may
remember upon the Settlement 45 pounds and about the same time
my unkle T[haxte]r[2] took up a Note principal and interest amounted
to 56 pounds which enabled me to pay your Brother, and a few day[s]
ago one Stetson took up a Bond of 20 pounds and Clark one of 30
which with a treasurers Note which is due of 20 pounds more and
24 *pounds* which I received for the Sale of a Lighter! will come near

to compleat the Hundred pounds which I propose to send to the office. Every fellow has his pockets full of money and chuses no doubt to pay his debts if he is a good Husband. I have done the best in my power with what I received and hope for your approbation which is always a full compensation to yours—ever yours.

RC (Adams Papers); addressed in John Thaxter's hand: "To The Honble: John Adams Esqr. Philadelphia To be left at the Post Office"; endorsed: "Portia"; docketed in two different hands, one of which is CFA's.

[1] Presumably the final payment to Peter Boylston Adams for what is now called the John Adams Birthplace, the farm that went with it, and a large pasture, all of which JA acquired in 1774 at a price agreed on as £440; see his *Diary and Autobiography*, 2:87–88.

[2] John Thaxter Sr. (1721–1802), Harvard 1741, of Hingham; husband of AA's aunt Anna (Quincy) Thaxter and father of JA's law clerk and (later) private secretary John Thaxter Jr.; see Adams Genealogy.

John Adams to Abigail Adams

June 2 1777

Yesterday, I took a ride to a beautifull Hill eleven Miles out of Town. It is called Rush Hill. An old Lady Mrs. Morris and her Daughter Mrs. Stamper, live here with a Couple of servants, and one little Boy, who is left with the Family for Education.[1]

It is the most airy, and at the same Time the most rural Place in Pensilvania. The good Lady has about sixty Acres of Land, two fine orchards, an excellent Garden, a charming Brook, beautifull Meadows and Clover in Abundance.

This excellent Lady is the Mother of Dr. Rush and Mr. Jacob Rush the Lawyer.[2] I went out with the Lawyer, and I relished the Excursion the more because I know the Pleasure of visiting a Mother.—This ride has refreshed me much. I ride every day. A fine growing Season here—plentifull Crops—and at present perfect Peace.

My Love to N. J. C. and Th. Pray how does the other one, or two?

RC (Adams Papers).

[1] The precise location of Rush Hill is not known to the editors. Presiding over it was Benjamin and Jacob Rush's mother, Susanna (Hall) Harvey Rush Morris, whose younger daughter was Mrs. Thomas Stamper, the former Rebecca Rush. See Benjamin Rush, *Letters*, 1:55, 98, 139–140, 237, and *passim*.

[2] Jacob Rush (1747–1820), College of New Jersey 1765, sometime student at the Middle Temple, and from 1784 to 1806 a prominent judge in the Pennsylvania courts (same, 1:44 and *passim*).

John Adams to Abigail Adams

Monday June 2. 1777

Artillery Election!—I wish I was at it, or near it.

Yours of the 18th. reached me this Morning. The Cause that Letters are so long in travelling, is that there is but one Post in a Week who goes from hence to Peeks Kill, altho there are two that go from thence to Boston.

Riding every day, has made me better than I was, altho I am not yet quite well. I am determined to continue this Practice, which is very necessary for me.

I rejoice to find, that the Town have had the Wisdom to send but one Rep[resentative]. The House last Year was too numerous and unwieldy. The Expence was too great. I suppose you will have a Constitution formed this Year. Who will be the Moses, the Lycurgus, the Solon? Or have you a score or two of such? Whoever they may be and whatever Form may be adopted, I am perswaded there is among the Mass of our People a Fund of Wisdom, Integrity and Humanity, which will preserve their Happiness, in a tolerable Measure.

If the Enemy come to Boston again, fly with your little ones all of them to Philadelphia. But they will scarcely get to Boston, this Campaign.

I admire your Sentiments concerning Revenge.

Revenge, in ancient Days, you will see it through the whole Roman History, was esteemed a generous, and an heroic Passion. Nothing was too good for a Friend or too bad for an Enemy. Hatred and Malice, without Limits, against an Enemy, was indulged, was justified, and no Cruelty was thought unwarrantable.

Our Saviour taught the Immorality of Revenge, and the moral Duty of forgiving Injuries, and even the Duty of loving Enemies. Nothing can shew the amiable, the moral, and divine Excellency of these Christian Doctrines in a stronger Point of Light, than the Characters and Conduct of Marius and Sylla, Cæsar, Pompey, Anthony and Augustus, among innumerable others.

Retaliation, we must practice, in some Instances, in order to make our barbarous Foes respect in some degree the Rights of Humanity. But this will never be done without the most palpable Necessity.

The Apprehension of Retaliation alone, will restrain them from Cruelties which would disgrace Savages.

To omit it then would be cruelty to ourselves, our Officers and Men. We are amused here with Reports of Troops removing from R.

Island, N. York, Staten Island &c.—Waggons, Boats, Bridges &c. pre-pared—two old Indiamen cutt down into floating Batteries mounting 32 Guns sent round into Delaware R[iver] &c. &c.[1] But I heed it no more, than the whistling of the Zephyrs. In short I had rather they should come to Philadelphia than not. It would purify this City of its Dross. Either the Furnace of Affliction would refine it of its Impurities, or it would be purged yet so as by fire.[2]

This Town has been a dead Weight, upon Us—it would be a dead Weight also upon the Enemy. The Mules here would plague them more than all their Money.[3]

RC (Adams Papers).

[1] For Gen. Howe's plans and the move-ments and countermovements of British and American forces in New Jersey dur-ing June, see the succinct and excellent narrative in Leonard Lundin, *Cockpit of the Revolution: The War for Independ-ence in New Jersey*, Princeton, 1940, p. 313–326, and the map in same, fac-ing p. 6.

[2] Thus in MS, though the sense is apparently defective.

[3] Thus in MS. Possibly JA's meaning is: "The Mules here [i.e. the Quakers, who continued willing to accept British money, but not inflated American money, for provisions] would plague them more than all their [the British army's] Money [would help them]." But this may be too ingenious an explanation.

John Quincy Adams to John Adams

Dear Sir   Braintree June the 2d 1777

I Love to recieve Letters very well much better than I love to write them, I make but a poor figure at Composition my head is much too fickle, my Thoughts are running after birds eggs play and trifles, till I get vexd with my Self, Mamma has a troublesome task to keep me Steady, and I own I am ashamed of myself. I Have but Just entered the 3d volume of Smollet[1] tho I had designed to have got it Half through by this time. I have determined this week to be more diligent as Mr. Thaxter will be absent at Court, and I cannot persue my other Studies I have Set myself a Stent, and determine to read the 3d volume Half out, If I can but keep my resolution I will write again at the end of the week, and give a better account of myself. I wish sir you would give me Some instructions with regard to my time and advise me how to proportion my Studies and my Play, in writing and I will keep them by me and endeavour to follow them I am dear Sir with a present determination of growing better yours,   John Quincy Adams

PS Sir if you will be So good as to favour me with a Blank book I will transcribe the most remarkable occurances I mett with in my reading which will Serve to fix them upon my mind.

RC (Adams Papers); addressed: "To The Honble. John Adams esq Philadelphia"; endorsed: "Mr. J. Q. Adams." The writer's punctuation has been left unaltered.

[1] JA's copy of Tobias Smollett's *A Complete History of England . . .*, 16 vols., London, 1758–1765, is in the Boston Public Library and is described in *Catalogue of JA's Library*. See, further, JQA's letter to his father of 8 June, below, and the Descriptive List of Illustrations in the present volume.

John Adams to Abigail Adams

June 4. 1777

I wish I could know, whether your season is cold or warm, wet or dry, fruitfull or barren. Whether you had late Frosts. Whether those Frosts have hurt the Fruit, the Flax, the Corn or Vines, &c. We have a fine season here and a bright Prospect of Abundance.

You will see by the inclosed Papers, in a Letter from my Friend Parsons, a very handsome Narration of one of the prettiest Exploits of this War—a fine Retaliation for the Danbury Mischief. Meigs who was before esteemed a good Officer has acquired by this Expedition a splendid Reputation.[1]

You will see by the same Papers too, that the Writers here in Opposition to the Constitution of Pensilvania, are making a factious Use of my Name and Lucubrations. Much against my Will, I assure you, for altho I am no Admirer of the Form of this Government, yet I think it is agreable to the Body of the People, and if they please themselves they will please me. And I would not choose to be impressed into the service of one Party, or the other—and I am determined I will not inlist.

Besides it is not very genteel in these Writers, to put my Name to a Letter, from which I cautiously withheld it myself.

However, let them take their own Way. I shant trouble myself about it.[2]

I am growing better, by Exercise and Air.

I must write a Letter, in Behalf of Mr. Thaxter, to the Bar and Bench in Boston, in order to get him sworn, at July Court.

Will my Brother, when the Time comes, officiate for his Brother at a Christening?

If it is a young Gentleman call him William after your Father—if a young Lady, call her Elizabeth after your Mother, and sister.

RC (Adams Papers). Enclosures not found, but see the notes below.

[1] Both the *Pennsylvania Gazette* and the *Pennsylvania Journal* of 4 June printed Gen. Samuel Holden Parsons' letter to Washington, New Haven, 25 May, recounting Lt. Col. Return Jonathan Meigs' destruction of an amphibious British foraging party at Sag Harbor, Long Island. Washington forwarded Parsons' letter to Congress in a letter of 31 May, received on 2 June (*Writings*, ed. Fitzpatrick, 8:151; *JCC*, 8:409).

[2] In the *Pennsylvania Journal* of 28 May (of which a copy must have been enclosed in the present letter), "Ludlow," in the second of a series of communications bitterly critical of the new constitution of Pennsylvania, publicly disclosed for the first time the authorship of JA's *Thoughts on Government* (1776). "Ludlow" wrote:

"In order to shew the extreme danger of trusting all the legislative power of a State to a single representation, I shall beg leave to transcribe a few sentences from a letter, written by Mr. JOHN ADAMS, to one of his friends in North Carolina, who requested him to favour him with a plan of a government for that State above a twelve month ago. This illustrious Citizen, who is second to no man in America, in an inflexible attachment to the liberties of America, and to republican forms of government, writes as follows."

Here were added four of the objections JA had urged in his *Thoughts* against unicameralism.

"Ludlow" was actually Dr. Benjamin Rush, who was only one of numerous contributors to the lively newspaper debate then going on over the merits and defects of the new state constitution. See Robert L. Brunhouse, *The Counter-Revolution in Pennsylvania, 1776–1790*, Harrisburg, 1942, p. 28 ff., 240. Rush's letters were promptly gathered in an anonymous pamphlet entitled *Observations upon the Present Government of Pennsylvania. In Four Letters to the People of Pennsylvania*, Phila., 1777; Evans 15589. The purpose of the pamphlet was to sound a call for a new

constitutional convention, and its title-page bore two quotations from "ADAMS on Government."

In an answer to "Ludlow" in the *Pennsylvania Gazette* of 4 June, "Whitlocke" (whose real name is not known) declared JA's objections irrelevant:

"In this view of the subject, the opinions of your Adams's, your Montesquieu's, your Harrington's, Milton's, Addison's, Price's and Bolingbroke's are not only *trifling* but *impertinent*. . . .

"The worthy American patriot's four reasons against a single assembly are not in point, and therefore you can deduce no solid inference from them. As they form a kind of data, on which you found your observations, pointing out their inapplicability to the case before us destroys the whole force of your reasoning. . . . Every one of this gentleman's reasons derive their force from this supposition, that the whole legislative, executive, judicial and military powers of this State are vested in one body of men. . . . How you could introduce them in the present dispute, I cannot conceive, unless to satisfy the public that you did not understand them."

This argument led to the reprinting of JA's essay of 1776 in the *Pennsylvania Gazette* of 11 June, preceded by this note to the printers:

"As two writers in the News-papers have lately quoted Mr. Adams's excellent pamphlet upon a republican form of government, the one to prove that all legislative power should not be lodged in *one* Assembly, the other to prove that the author meant only that the whole power legislative, executive and judicial, should not be lodged in *one* Assembly; your publishing the whole of the pamphlet in your paper, will enable the public to judge for themselves. Your's, &c. A.B."

Interestingly enough, the reprint in the *Gazette* suppressed the last paragraph of JA's tract as printed in 1776, in which JA had requested George Wythe, the original recipient, to keep the author's name "out of sight."

John Thaxter to John Adams

Sir   Boston June 4th. 1777

Last Monday Dr. Mather Byles was tried by Virtue of a late Act of this State, and found by the Jury so inimical, as to render his residence in the State dangerous to the Liberties thereof. He is to be sent to some quarter, where his local Situation will deprive him of the power to injure the State.[1]

Tomorrow some others are to have their Trial—they have engaged Attornies.

The Inferior Court (now sitting) has no great Business to do; most of the Actions are continued, some were called out.

The next Inf[erior] Court sets July the 8th.[2] If you think it advise-able for me to take the Oath at the time proposed, I should be much obliged to You, Sir, to write to the Bar respecting it.[3]

Tho' Sir, unhappy in being deprived of the Advantages of your Company and Instruction, by your absence, yet I should blush to say I lamented the Cause of it. I shall think myself materially benefited in being made a Subject of a firmly establish'd Independence, and shall revere the man to whose Exertions the production of so great an Event was so principally owing as to yours, Sir.

I am Sir, your very hum[...][4]   J. Thaxter Junr.

RC (Adams Papers); addressed: "To The Honble: John Adams Esqr. Philadelphia"; endorsed: "Mr. Thaxter"; docketed in an unidentified hand.

[1] By an Act passed on 10 May 1777, persons complained of and convicted in the Court of General Sessions of the Peace as "internal enemies" of the United States, were to be transported out of the country (Mass., *Province Laws*, 5:648–650). For an account of the trial and conviction of Dr. Mather Byles, see *Boston Gazette*, 9 June, p. 3, col. 1. His sentence was not, however, carried out; he was merely placed under house arrest for two years (Sibley-Shipton, *Harvard Graduates*, 7:482–486).

[2] This sentence was added in the margin.

[3] JA soon afterward wrote letters of recommendation for Thaxter to "the Court and Bar," and Thaxter received them and was duly admitted attorney in Suffolk Inferior Court (JA to AA, 4 Aug.; AA to JA, 27 Aug.; both below); but the letters have not been found.

[4] MS torn by seal.

Abigail Adams to John Adams

June 8. 1777

I generally endeavour to write you once a week, if my Letters do not reach you, tis oweing to the neglect of the post. I generally get Letters from you once a week, but seldom in a fortnight after they are wrote. I am sorry to find that your Health fails. I should greatly rejoice to see you, I know of no earthly blessing which would make me happier, but I cannot wish it upon the terms of ill Health. No seperation was ever more painfull to me than the last, may the joy of meeting again be eaquel to the pain of seperation; I regret that I am in a Situation to wish away one of the most precious Blessings of life, yet as the months pass of[f], I count them up with pleasure and reckon upon tomorrow as the 5th which has passd since your absence. I have some times melancholly reflections, and immagine these seperations as preparatory to a still more painfull one in which even hope the anchor of the Soul is lost, but whilst that remains no Temperary absence can ever wean or abate the ardor of my affection. Bound together by many tender ties, there scarcly wanted an addition, yet I feel that there soon will be an additionall one. Many many are the tender sentiments I have felt for the parent on this occasion. I doubt not they are reciprocal, but I often feel the want of his presence and the soothing tenderness of his affection. Is this weakness or is it not?

I am happy in a daughter who is both a companion and an assistant in my Family affairs and who I think has a prudence and steadiness beyond her years.

You express a longing after the enjoyments of your little Farm. I do not wonder at it, that also wants the care and attention of its master—all that the mistress can do is to see that it does not go to ruin. She would take pleasure in improvements, and study them with assiduity if she was possessd with a sufficency to accomplish them. The season promises plenty at present and the english grass never lookd better.

You inquire after the Asparagrass. It performs very well this year and produces us a great plenty. I long to send you a Barrell of cider, but find it impracticable, as no vessels can pass from this State to yours. I rejoice at the good way our affairs seem to be in and Hope your Herculian Labours will be crownd with more success this year than the last. Every thing wears a better aspect, we have already taken two Transports of theirs with Hessians on board, and this week a prize was carried into Salem taken by the Tyranicide with 4000 Blankets and other valuable articles on board.[1]

I do not feel very apprehensive of an attack upon Boston. I hope we shall be quiet. I should make a misirable hand of running now. Boston is not what it once was. It has no Head, no Men of distinguishd abilities, they behave like children.

Col. Holland the infamous Hampshire counterfeiter was taken last week in Boston and is committed to Jail in Irons. I hope they will now keep a strong guard upon him.[2]

We are not like to get our *now* unpopular act repeald I fear. I own I was in favour of it, but I have seen it fail and the ill consequences arising from it have made me wish it had never been made. Yet the House are nearly divided about it. Genell. W[arre]n will write you I suppose. He and his Lady have spent part of the week with me.

I wish you would be so good as to mention the dates of the Letters you receive from me. The last date of yours was May 22. 5 dated in May since this day week.[3] I wonder how you get time to write so much. I feel very thankfull to you for every line. You will I know remember me often when I cannot write to you.

Good Night tis so dark that I cannot see to add more than that I am with the utmost tenderness Yours ever Yours.

RC (Adams Papers); addressed in John Thaxter's hand: "To The Honble: John Adams Esqr. Philadelphia To be left at the Post Office"; endorsed: "Portia"; docketed in two hands, one of which is CFA's.

[1] The captain of the brig *Tyrannicide* was Jonathan Haraden of Salem. For his capture of a transport carrying Hessians from Ireland to New York, and of the snow *Sally* with blankets and other European goods, see *Boston Gazette,* 9 June, p. 3, col. 1. If, as is probable, AA took these items of news from the *Gazette,* then she either misdated the present letter or wrote it on more than one day.

[2] Col. Stephen Holland, the Londonderry counterfeiter, had escaped from jail in New Hampshire in May and was returned there some days after AA wrote this letter. See *Boston Gazette,* 9, 16 June.

[3] AA means that during the past week she has received five letters from JA dated in May.

John Adams to Abigail Adams

June 8. 1777

Upon an Invitation from the Board of War of Pensilvania, a Committee was appointed a few days ago to go down Delaware River and take a View of the Works there, erected with a View to prevent the Enemy from coming up to Philadelphia by Water. Mr. Duer, your humble servant and Mr. Middleton made the Committee.[1]

Yesterday we went, in three Boats, with Eight Oars each. Mr. Rittenhouse, Coll. Bull and Coll. Deane, went from the Pensilvania Board of War. General Arnold, General De Coudrai, an experienced french officer of Artillery, Monsr. Le Brune, an Engineer, and Mr. Rogers an Aid de Camp of Gen. De Coudray were in Company.[2]

We had a Band of Musick in Company which is very agreable upon the Water.

We went first to Billingsport, about 10 Miles down the River on the Jersey side, where the River is obstructed with Vesseaux de Frizes, and where a large Fort is laid out with a great deal of Work done upon it.

We then came back to Fort Island, or Province Island, where the River is obstructed again, and the only Passage for shipps is commanded by a Fort of 18. 18. Pounders. Here lay the Fire ships, Fire Rafts, floating Batteries, Gallies and the Andrew Doria, and the fine new Frigate Delaware.

We then crossed the River and went to Red Point[3] on the Jersey side, where Coll. Bull has thrown up the strongest Works that I have ever seen. Here We dined, and after Dinner Coll. Bull ordered out his Regiment upon the Parade, where they went through their Exercises and Maneuvres, very well.

We had a long Passage home and made it 9 o Clock before We reached the Wharf. We suffered much with the Heat, yet upon the whole it was an agreable day.

Upon our Return to Town We expected to hear some News but not a Word had been received. All is quiet still. How long will this Calm continue?

I begin to suspect We shall have an unactive Campaign—that How will shut himself up, in some impregnable Post, and lie still. We shall see, however, and I think We shall trouble him whether he moves or lies still.

RC (Adams Papers).

[1] They were appointed on 3 June "to view the works and defences erected at, and near Billingsport, and report their opinion, whether those works ought to be completed or demolished" (*JCC*, 8: 414). There is an excellent map showing the terrain below Philadelphia and the river and shore defenses in 1777, printed by William Faden, 2d edn., London, 1783, and reproduced in Leonard Lundin, *Cockpit of the Revolution*, Princeton, 1940, facing p. 336.

[2] Philippe Tronson du Coudray, a learned and egotistical French artillery officer who had recently arrived with ex-travagant promises from Silas Deane, was to prove much the most controversial among all his countrymen who served in America; see JA, *Diary and Autobiography*, 2:263–264, and references there. His recommendations for improving the Delaware fortifications are printed in *Penna. Archives*, 1st ser., 5: 360–363. Among the numerous officers who accompanied him to America were two Le Brun brothers and Nicolas Roger (Lasseray, *Les français sous les treize étoiles*, 1:278–279; 2:391–394).

[3] Red Bank, Gloucester co., N.J., site of Fort Mercer.

John Quincy Adams to John Adams

Dear Sir   Braintree June the 8 1777

I promised to write In a week again provided I could give a better account of my conduct. I have according to my resolution been more diligent and frugal of my time and when Mr. Thaxter was absent which was 4 days I applied myself for several hours every day to the reading of Smollet and have got almost half through the 3 vol.[1] I find much entertainment in the perusal of history and I must own I am more Satisfied with myself when I have applied part of my time to Some useful employment than when I have Idled it away about Trifles and play.

I have some errants to do for mamma in consequence of Jonathans absence he is broke out and like to have the Distemper lightly—there is nothing remarkable In the news way only that one Davis a printer was catched last week in Boston with a Set of Types to counterfeit our money commonly called The Tobbacco paper or Major Fullers money and was committed to joal[2] I am dear Sir with Sincere affection your Son,
                                                                        J Q A

RC (Adams Papers); endorsed: "Mr. J. Q. Adams"; at head of text in CFA's hand: "J Q A to his father J.A." The punctuation of the original has been retained without correction.

[1] That is, the third volume.

[2] "Saturday last was committed to Goal in this Town, Nathaniel Davis, for counterfeiting the Five Shilling Bills of this State, issued in June 1776" (*Continental Journal*, 12 June 1777).

John Adams to Abigail Adams

Phyladelphia June 14. 1777

This Week has produced an happy Reconciliation between the two Parties in this City and Commonwealth, the Friends of the new Constitution and those who wish for Amendments in it....[1] Mifflin invited the People to assemble in the State House Yard, at the Desire of General Washington, who sent them an Account that the Motions of the Enemy indicated an intention to begin an Expedition, and that every Appearance intimated this City to be their Object.

Mifflin made an Harrangue, in which he applauded the Exertions of the Citizens last December, ascribed the successes of Trenton and Princeton to their Behaviour and exhorted them to the same Spirit, Unanimity and Firmness, upon this occasion. Advised them to choose their Officers, under the new Militia Law and meet him in the common on Fryday.

The Citizens by loud shouts and Huzzas, promised him to turn out, and accordingly, they met him in great Numbers Yesterday.

Mean Time, Generals Armstrong, Mifflin and Reed, waited on the Assembly, to interceed with them, to gratify those who wished Amendments in the Constitution with an Appeal to the People.

The Pensilvania Board of War too, applied, for the same Purpose as you will see by one of the inclosed Papers.

The House agreed to it. Thus the Dispute is in a Way to be determined, and a Coalition formed.[2]

June 15

Yesterday We had an Alarm, and News that the Enemy were on their March, towards Philadelphia in two Divisions—one at Shanks Mills 8 miles from Brunswick, the other at Ten Mile Run, about Ten Miles from Brunswick on another Road, a Road that goes to Corells [Coryell's] Ferry.

We feel pretty bold, here.—If they get Philadelphia, they will hang a Mill stone about their Necks. They must evacuate N. Jersey. The Jersey Militia have turned out, with great Spirit. Magistrates and Subjects, Clergy and Laity, have all marched, like so many Yankees.

If How should get over the Delaware River, and We should not have an Army to stop him, Congress I suppose will remove, fifty or sixty Miles into the Country. But they will not move hastily.

Riding and walking, have given me tolerable Health, and I must confess my Spirits, notwithstanding the Difficulties We have to encounter, are very good.

RC (Adams Papers). Enclosed newspapers not found or precisely identifiable.

[1] Suspension points in MS.

[2] An account of these events is in *Pennsylvania Gazette,* 18 June. See also Kenneth R. Rossman, *Thomas Mifflin and the Politics of the American Revolution,* Chapel Hill, 1952, p. 87–88.

Isaac Smith Sr. to John Adams

Dear Sr.   Boston June the 14th. 1777

I wrote you some time Ago requesting your Asking some of the Gentlemen of the Congress, belonging to Georgia, whether the Continental Certifycates would Answer to purchase a Cargo of Rice.[1]

9. JAMES LOVELL'S MAP OF THE "SEAT OF WAR" IN THE FALL OF 1777

See page xi

Next Month completes Three Years, that I have been devoted to the Servitude of Liberty. — A Slavery it has been to me, whatever the World may think of it. ———

To a Man, whose attachments to his Family, are as Strong as mine, Absence alone from such a Wife and such Children, would be a great Sacrifice. — but in Addition to this Separation, what have I not done? what have I not Suffered? what have I not hazarded? — These are Questions that I may ask you, but I will ask such Questions of none else. — Let the ~~vacant~~ Cymballs of Popularity tinckle still. — Let the Butter flies of Fame glitter with their Wings. — I shall envy neither their Musick nor their Colours. —

The Loss of Property affects me little. — all other hard things I despise, but the Loss of your Company and that of my dear Babes for so long a Time, I consider as a Loss of so much Solid Happiness.

The tender Social Feelings of my Heart, which have distressed me beyond all Utterance, in my most busy, active Scenes, as well as in the numerous Hours of melancholy Solitude, are known only to God and my own Soul.

10. "THE LOSS OF YOUR COMPANY . . . I CONSIDER AS A LOSS
OF SO MUCH SOLID HAPPINESS"
See page xii

July 9 1777.

I sit down to write you this post, and from my present feelings tis the last I shall be able to write for some time if I should do well, I have been very unwell for this week past, with some complaints that have been new to me tho I hope not dangerous. I was last night taken with a shaking fit, and am very apprehensive that a life was lost, as I have no reason to day to think otherways, what may be the consequences to me, Heaven only knows. I know not of any injury to myself, nor any thing which could occasion what I fear. Allarmd, I keep up some spirits yet, tho I would have you prepaird for any Event that may happen. I can add no more than that I am in every Situation unfeignedly Yours, Yours

11. "I KEEP UP SOME SPIRITS YET, THO I WOULD HAVE YOU
PREPAIRD FOR ANY EVENT THAT MAY HAPPEN"
See page xii

ESSAIS
SUR
L'ÉQUITATION,
OU
PRINCIPES RAISONNÉS SUR L'ART
DE MONTER ET DE DRESSER
LES CHEVAUX.

Par M. MOTTIN DE LA BALME,
Capitaine de Cavalerie, & Officier
Major de la Gendarmerie de France.

Hinc bellator equus campo sese arduus infert.
Virg. Georg. L. 3.

A AMSTERDAM,
& se trouve à *PARIS*,
Chez { JOMBERT, Fils aîné, Lib. rue Dauphine.
{ RUAULT, Libraire, rue de la Harpe.

· M. DCC. LXXIII.

A COMPLETE
HISTORY
OF
ENGLAND,
FROM THE
DESCENT of JULIUS CÆSAR,
TO THE
TREATY of AIX LA CHAPELLE, 1748.

Containing the Transactions of
One Thousand Eight Hundred and Three Years.

By T. SMOLLETT, M.D.

THE SECOND EDITION.

VOLUME THE THIRD.

LONDON:
Printed for JAMES RIVINGTON and JAMES FLETCHER, at the
Oxford-Theatre; and R. BALDWIN, at the Rose, in Paternoster-row.
MDCCLVIII.

THE
METHOD
OF
TEACHING and STUDYING
THE
BELLES LETTRES,
OR,
An INTRODUCTION to LANGUAGES, POETRY,
RHETORIC, HISTORY, MORAL PHILOSO-
PHY, PHYSICS, &c.
WITH
REFLECTIONS on TASTE, and INSTRUCTIONS
with regard to the ELOQUENCE of the PULPIT,
the BAR, and the STAGE.

The whole illustrated with PASSAGES from the most famous POETS and ORATORS, ancient and modern,
with CRITICAL REMARKS on them.

Designed more particularly for STUDENTS in the
UNIVERSITIES.

By Mr. ROLLIN,
Late Principal of the University of Paris, Professor of Elo-
quence in the Royal College, and Member of the Royal
Academy of Inscriptions and Belles Lettres.

Translated from the FRENCH.

VOL. I.

The SIXTH EDITION, with ALTERATIONS.

LONDON:
Printed for W. STRAHAN, J. and F. RIVINGTON, R. BALDWIN,
L. HAWES and W. CLARKE and R. COLLINS, R. HORSFIELD,
W. JOHNSTON, W. OWEN, T. CASLON, S. CROWDER, B. LAW,
Z. STUART, ROBINSON and ROBERTS, and NEWBERY and
CARNAN.

M.DCC.LXIX.

THE
PRECEPTOR:
CONTAINING
A General Course of EDUCATION,
WHEREIN
THE FIRST PRINCIPLES
OF
POLITE LEARNING
ARE LAID DOWN
In a Way most suitable for trying the GENIUS,
and advancing the
Instruction of YOUTH.

IN TWELVE PARTS.
Illustrated with MAPS and useful CUTS.

VIZ.

I. On READING, SPEAK-ING, and WRITING LETTERS.	VI. On DRAWING.
II. On ARITHMETIC, GEOMETRY, and AR-CHITECTURE.	VII. On LOGIC.
III. On GEOGRAPHY and ASTRONOMY.	VIII. On NATURAL HIS-TORY.
IV. On CHRONOLOGY and HISTORY.	IX. On ETHICS, or MO-RALITY.
V. On RHETORIC and POETRY.	X. On TRADE and COM-MERCE.
	XI. On LAWS and GO-VERNMENT.
	XII. On HUMAN LIFE and MANNERS.

The FIFTH EDITION, with Additions and Improvements.

THE SECOND VOLUME.

LONDON:
Printed for J. DODSLEY, in Pall-mall.
MDCCLXIX.

---

12. SOME BOOKS THE ADAMSES READ DURING THE REVOLUTION
See page xii

My friends in Europe often you'st to say when nothing Material turnd up worth Adviseing me, they had nothing worth troubling me with so I may say as to my self for sometime past.—But to day we have a prize (a small brig on private Account) loaded with some Cordage, Duck, Cole &c. sent in by Comodore Manley, who with Capt. McNeil only, the Other part of the fleet being seperated, were left indeavouring to take 2 or 3 more which were under Convoy of the Somerset M[an of] W[ar] of 60 Guns from England and as they could Out sail the Somerset, they kept in there persuit.—We have Advise of the Hessian brig and Capt. Skeema with two prizes, being blockt in att a harbour att Townsend, &c. but think iff they Act prudently or those who have the Management of those Affairs they may be all securd.[2] Itt seems on the News of Our fleets sailing A Number of Frigates were immediately ordered Out, from R. Island. Two frigates and a two decker have been in Our bay and are those who have blockt up the Above mentiond Vessells.

I have this day received letters from my Bilboa friends of the 17th. Aprill but dont mention any kind of News. Itt came by two Brigs on the Continent Account which went with fish to purchase salt, but have brought no great quantity, but by order of Mr. Lee who was in Spain have brought a quantity of Cables, Cordage &c. upon the Continant Account which the proper persons for that department will Advise of I suppose. The Capt. tells of a storey which he heard att Bilboa that Capt. Johnson in a brig suppose Capt. Harrey Johnson from Baltimore being in some port of France were lay three ships loaded for England with Wine &c. who gave Out they designd [to] carry him to England iff he went Out with them—he got Out before they and waited there coming, and Accordingly came and he engaged them and took two and was in persute of the third. I wish it may prove true.[3]— I have an Answer by a schooner fited Out here, formerly One of the privateers, Adams now Master which saild the begining of March for France as I understood as an express by order of Congress, which iff they have not heard of her Arrival, probable may be Agreeable.—We are doing all in Our power to facilitate the settlement of the several [...] sales of the Cargos of the several prizes ordered by Our Commissions, two of the most Material are compleated, and A third and fourth near being done. Capt. Bartlet of Beverley who is One of the Agents I called on a day or two ago but is confind with the small pox, but as soon as he gets Out itt may be compleated—but by what Appears there will be large ballances due to the Agents as the Continent took much more than there proportion. You may just let the Gentlemen of the Marine board know we are not Idle in the trust commited to us as we want very much to get itt compleated as soon as may be.—There was a ship to sail from Bilboa and which I let to the Agents in a short time after those Arrived. Iff any News shall Advise you. I had a Vessell come Out with those Arrived which you may remember I told you I had sent to Virginia to load with Tobacco from France and toucht att Bilboa in her way home. She has something considerable of Value On board which iff taken shall suffer greatly.

I am Sr. Yr. hum servt, Isaac Smith

16th.

A Prize with some Irish recruits is arrived into Dartmouth. A Nother from Liverpool in att the Eastward with salt, Linnen and Crockery Ware—am affraid my schooner is gone.

RC (Adams Papers); docketed in JA's later hand.

[1] Smith to JA, 12 May, above.

[2] "Capt. Skeema" was probably John Skimmer, former Boston merchant captain, commanding the Continental schooner *Lee*. Townshend was a settlement on the Maine coast.

[3] Capt. Henry Johnson, commissioned commander of the Continental brig *Lex-ington* in Feb. 1777, was in European waters and ports until the *Lexington* was captured off Ushant in September (*JCC*, 7:90; Ruth Y. Johnston, "American Privateers in French Ports, 1776–1778," *PMHB*, 53 [Oct. 1929]:359–365).

Mercy Otis Warren to Abigail Adams

June 14 1777

Could I write you any agreable Inteligence I would with pleasure Grasp the pen And Call of my Friends Attention a Moment from her Domestic avocations, but so much Avarice and Venallity, so much Annemosity and Contention, so much pride and Weakness predominate both in the Capital and the Cottage that I fear it will be Long: very Long before good tidings are Wafted on Every Wind and the Halcyon days of peace Return to our Land.

I write for the sake of my promise more than anything Else this Morning, for I am very unable to perform as I have been deprived the use of one Eye Ever since I have been in town. Am now Growing better and shall Endeavour to improve them in Future in some useful way.

Mr. Warren has yet no Letter from Mr. Adams. I am with true affection Your Friend, Marcia

Alas! No Repeal of the Regulati[ng] act, nor of Course the Land Embargo.[1]

RC (Adams Papers).

[1] On the Massachusetts "Land Embargo" of Feb. 1777, see note 2 on JA's second letter to AA of 6 April, above, and also Mass., *Province Laws*, 19:808–810.

Abigail Adams to John Adams

[*Braintree, 15 June 1777*]

This is the 15 of June. Tomorrow our new Edition of the Regulating act takes place, and will I fear add wrath to Bitterness. No arguments which were urgd could prevail upon the court to repeal it. A committee in this Town is chosen to see it inforced, and I suppose in other Towns.[1] I am surprizd that when the ill Effects of it are so visible, and the spirit of opposition to it so general and voilent that there should be a determination to enforce it.

There is a very evil spirit opperating and an encreasing Bitterness between the Town and Country. The Town of Boston has lost its leaders, and the respectable figure it once made is exchanged for party squables, for Avarice, venality, Animosity, contention, pride, weakness and dissapation. I wish I could say this spirit was confined to the Capital, but indeed too much of it prevails in the cottage.[2]

Really we are a most ungratefull people, favourd as we have been with peculiar Blessings and favours to make so poor returns. With the best opportunities for becomeing a happy people, and all the materials in our power, yet we have neither skill nor wisdom to put them together.

The House and Counsel have come to a determination to form a Goverment, and to send it out to the people for their inspection. I expect there will be great difficulty as ninety two Towns I am told have sent no representitives, and the Countys of Worcester and Berkshire make up more than a third of the House. Some have instructed their rep's to form a Goverment, others have directly forbid them.[3]

There has been a list of Tories belonging to this Town made out, and Deliverd in to the Town 13 in number. I will enclose the list.[4] Some of them I believe had as goods have been omitted. It will put them to some expence but the practice is to employ one or two gentlemen of the Bar, who generally make out to get them acquitted. Then I expect they will be returnd to us, more Rancorous than before.

There is a movement of Hows, whether he designs for Boston or Road Island or where is as yet unknown—I hope for neither. I think

I could not tarry here with safety should he make an attack upon either, and the thought of being driven from my own Habitation at this time is more distressing than ever. If I had only myself to look after it would be less anxiety to me; if you hear of our being invaded this way, I think you must return. I used to have courage, but you cannot wonder at my apprehensions when you consider my circumstances. I can but poorly walk about House; However I am not of an over anxious make; I will trust in providence that I shall be provided for. I think we shall know in a week whether he designs this way, and you I suppose will know as soon as we. I wish you would advise me what I had best do if we should be attacked this way.—We have not a Man either upon the Castle or at Nantasket. I believe our Enimies know it.

Two continental vessels have arrived with Salt from Bilbo in the last week, and four prizes sent in by the Fleet. As they came in a Saturday have not learnt with what they are loaded.

Have received two letters since I wrote last, one of May 24 and one of May 27.[5] As to your injuntions with regard to my taking any money but this States and continental, I have strictly adhered to them. I know of whom I received the Hampshire money, and returnd it again. I took it of Sister A[dams] as part of the pay for the Lighter, and she of Vose of Milton. She returnd it the same week to Him, which she took it but He refused to receive it, and tho she has twice sent it to Him, and he does not pretend to say He did not pay it to her, Yet he will not take it again. What can be done? I had several other Bills, but knowing of whom I received them, I found no difficulty in returning them again.—There will no money pass in this State after next month but continental and this States.

How is your cold? Are you better than you was? I feel anxious for your Health. Let me know every time you write How you do. A certain Gentleman was ask'd when he expected to go to Philadelphia. O he did not know. That depended upon some of the others returning. He supposed they would be running Home again in a month or two, as they always were. For his part he had tarried so many months.—A great merrit to tarry from Home when a man loves any place better than home. I am for having them all stay now, to keep him at home as a punishment. Tis of no great importance where he is.[6]

Adieu most sincerely yours.

RC (Adams Papers); endorsed: "Portia"; docketed in two different hands, one of which is CFA's. Enclosure not found, but see note 4.

[1] On 9 June the town chose a committee of seven members, "to see that the Act to prevent Monopoly and oppression be not violated in this Town" (*Braintree Town Records*, p. 482). This was in accordance with the Act as amended on 10 May (Mass., *Province Laws*, 5:642–647).

[2] It may be noted that here, as she did on some other occasions, AA borrowed some of her language from Mrs. Warren. See the preceding letter.

[3] On the steps taken by the new General Court to form a new constitution (the abortive Constitution of 1778), see the very informative passages in James Warren's letters to JA of 22 June and 10 July (*Warren-Adams Letters*, 1:334–335, 341).

[4] The enclosed list is missing, but on 9 June, according to the *Braintree Town Records* (p. 481–482), "the Selectmen presented a list to the Town of those

persons they esteemed Inimical to the United States which is a[s] follows, viz. Revd. Edward Winslow, Majr. Ebenezer Miller, John Cheesman, Mr. Joseph Cleverly, James Apthorp, William Veazie, Benj Cleverly, Oliver Gay, & Nedabiah Bent, all which was Voted by the Town to be persons esteemed Inimical.... Then the following Persons was Nominated & voted to be added to the aforesaid List ... viz. Joseph Cleverly second, William Veazie junr. Henry Cleverly & Thomas Brackett."

[5] That is, JA's letters of 24 and 25–27 May, both above.

[6] Robert Treat Paine had been reelected a Massachusetts delegate on 10 Dec. 1776 (as he was to be again in Dec. 1777), but he never resumed his seat in Congress. On 12 June 1777 he was elected attorney general of Massachusetts (Mass., *House Jour.*, 1777–1778, p. 23).

John Adams to Abigail Adams

Philadelphia June 16 1777

I had a most charming Packett from you and my young Correspondents, to day.

I am very happy, to learn that you have done such great Things in the Way of paying Debts. I know not what would become of me, and mine, if I had not such a Friend to take Care of my Interests in my Absence.

You will have Patience with me this Time, I hope, for this Time will be the last.

I shall stay out this Year, if I can preserve my Health, and then come home, and bid farewell to great Affairs. I have a Right to spend the Remainder of my days in small ones.

RC (Adams Papers).

John Adams to Abigail Adams

Philadelphia June 18. 1777

We shall have all the Sages and Heroes of France here before long.

Mr. Du Coudray is here, who is esteemed the most learned Officer in France. He is an Artillery Officer.

267

Mr. De la Balme is here too, a great Writer upon Horsemanship and Cavalry. He has presented me with two Volumes written by himself upon these subjects, elegantly printed, bound and gilt.[1]

Mr. De Vallenais is with him, who speaks very good English.[2]

The inclosed Papers will give you all the News. You get Intelligence sooner and better than We.

We are under no more Apprehensions here than if the British Army was in the Crimea. Our Fabius will be slow, but sure.

Arnold, You see will have at them, if he can.

RC (Adams Papers). Enclosed newspapers not found or identified.

[1] Augustin Mottin de La Balme (1736–1780), a French cavalry officer and writer on cavalry tactics, had left France against orders from Vergennes by disguising himself as a physician. He bore letters of introduction from Franklin to Hancock and from Deane to Washington. In Philadelphia he presented to JA copies of his *Essais sur l'équitation*, Amsterdam and Paris, 1773, and *Elémens de tactique pour la cavalerie*, Paris, 1776, which are still among JA's books in the Boston Public Library; the title-page of the *Essais* is reproduced among the illustrations in the present volume. On 8 July 1777 Congress commissioned La Balme colonel and inspector of cavalry (JCC, 8:539), but he did not gain Washington's support in this post and retired from it early in 1778. The next year he campaigned as a volunteer on the Penobscot and elsewhere, and thereafter among the old French settlements in the West; in Nov. 1780 he and his men were massacred near Miami, Ohio, by a party of Little Turtle's Indians. Most of the information above is drawn from Lasseray's excellent sketch of La Balme in *Les français sous les treize étoiles*, 2:329–336.

[2] Of this officer, whose name was spelled in a great variety of ways, little is definitely known beyond an entry in JCC for 8 July 1777 (8:539): "Resolved . . . That Mons. Vallenais be appointed an aid to Mons. de la Balme, with the rank and pay of captain of cavalry." See also Lasseray, 2:462–463.

John Adams to Abigail Adams

My dearest Friend   Philadelphia June 21. 1777

It would give Pleasure to every Body your Way but the few, unfeeling Tories, to see what a Spirit prevails here.

The Allarm which How was foolish enough to spread by his March out of Brunswick, raised the Militia of [the] Jersies universally, and in this City it united the Whiggs, to exert themselves under their new Militia Law, in such a Degree that nobody here was under any Apprehensions of danger from Hows March. It seemed to be the general Wish that he might persevere in his March that he might meet with certain Destruction.

But the poor Wretches have skulked back to Brunswick.—This is a great Disgrace. It will be considered so in Europe. It is certainly thought so by our People, and it will be felt to be so by their own People—the poor Tories especially.

It will dispirit that Army in such a manner, that Desertions will become very numerous.

The Tories in this Town seem to be in absolute Despair. Chopfallen, in a most remarkable Manner. The Quakers begin to say they are not Tories—that their Principle of passive Obedience will not allow them to be Whiggs, but that they are as far from being Tories as the Presbyterians.

The true Secret of all this is, We have now got together a fine Army, and more are coming in every day. An Officer arrived from Virginia, this day, says he passed by Three Thousand continental Troops between Williamsbourg and this Town.—I am with an Affection, that neither Time nor Place can abate, Yours, ever Yours.

RC (Adams Papers).

Abigail Adams to John Adams

June 23 1777

I have just retird to my Chamber, but an impulce seazes me to write you a few lines before I close my Eye's. Here I often come and sit myself down alone to think of my absent Friend, to ruminate over past scenes, to read over Letters, journals &c.

Tis a melancholy kind of pleasure I find in this amusement, whilst the weighty cares of state scarcly leave room for a tender recollection or sentiment to steal into the Bosome of my Friend.

In my last I expressd some fears least the Enemy should soon invade us here. My apprehensions are in a great measure abated by late accounts received from the General.

We have a very fine Season here, rather cold for a fortnight, but nothing like a drought. You would smile to see what a Farmer our Brother C[ranc]h makes, his whole attention is as much engaged in it, as it ever was in Spermacity Works, Watch Work, or Prophesies. You must know he has purchased, (in spight of the C[olone]ls Threats) that Farm he talkd of.[1] He gave a large price for it tis True, but tis a neat, profitable place, 300 sterling, but money is lookd upon of very little value, and you can scarcly purchase any article now but by Barter. You shall have wool for flax or flax for wool, you shall have veal, Beaf or pork for salt, for sugar, for Rum, &c. but mony we will not take, is the daily language. I will work for you for Corn, for flax or wool, but if I work for money you must give a cart load of it be sure.

What can be done, and which way shall we help ourselves? Every article and necessary of life is rising daily. Gold dear Gold would soon lessen the Evils. I was offerd an article the other day for two dollors in silver for which they askd me six in paper.

I have no more to purchase with than if every dollor was a silver one.[2] Every paper dollor cost a silver one, why then cannot it be eaquelly valuable? You will refer me to Lord Kames I know, who solves the matter. I hope in favour you will not Emit any more paper, till what we have at least becomes more valuable.

Nothing remarkable has occurd since I wrote you last. You do not in your last Letters mention how you do—I will hope better. I want a companion a Nights, many of them are wakefull and Lonesome, and "tierd Natures sweet restorer, Balmy Sleep,"[3] flies me. How hard it is to reconcile myself to six months longer absence! Do you feel it urksome? Do you sigh for Home? And would you willingly share with me what I have to pass through? Perhaps before this reaches you and meets with a Return, ——— I wish the day passt, yet dread its arrival.—Adieu most sincerely most affectionately Yours.

RC (Adams Papers); endorsed: "Portia ansd. July 8."

[1] On 5 May 1777 (though the deed was not recorded until 7 Feb. 1781), Richard Cranch bought of Ebenezer Thayer, Ebenezer Miller, Jonathan Bass, Nathaniel Wales, and Norton Quincy, for £400 lawful money (or £300 sterling), a 32-acre tract of farm land, with the buildings thereon, "being part of the Stoney field so Called"—that is, lying on what is now called Presidents Hill, across the Old Coast Road (now Adams Street) from the Adams National Historic Site in Quincy (Suffolk Registry of Deeds, Boston, vol. 132: fols. 101–102). The name "Cranch Pasture" persisted in this area well into the 19th century, but the farm itself, which abutted on the homestead farm JA purchased in 1787, was bought from Cranch by JA himself in Feb. 1798 (Norfolk Registry of Deeds, Dedham, vol. 8: fol. 77).

As for "the C[olone]ls Threats," the editors can only conjecture who and what they were. Among the Adamses the epithet "the Colonel" ordinarily meant Col. Josiah Quincy of Mount Wollaston, who may have been one of Richard Cranch's creditors.

[2] Thus in MS, though the sense is dubious.

[3] Closing quotation mark editorially supplied.

John Adams to Abigail Adams

My dearest Friend   Philadelphia June 29 1777

The enclosed Newspapers will communicate to you, all the News I know.

The Weather here begins to be very hot. Poor Mortals pant and sweat, under the burning Skies. Faint and feeble as children, We seem as if We were dissolving away. Yet We live along.

The two Armies are now playing off their Arts. Each acts with great Caution. Howe is as much afraid of putting any Thing to Hazard as Washington. What would Britain do, surrounded with formidable Powers in Europe just ready to strike her if Howes Army should meet a Disaster? Where would she find another Army?

How are you?—I hope very well.—Let Mr. Thaxter write, let the Children write, when you cannot. I am very anxious, but Anxiety at 400 Miles distance can do you no more good, than me. I long to hear a certain Piece of News from Home, which will give me great Joy. Thank Mr. John for his kind Letter. I will answer him and all my little Correspondents as soon as I can.

Tell Mr. John, that I am under no Apprehensions about his Proficiency in Learning. With his Capacity, and Opportunities, he can not fail to acquire Knowledge. But let him know, that the moral Sentiments of his Heart, are more important than the Furniture of his Head. Let him be sure that he possesses the great Virtues of Temperance, Justice, Magnanimity, Honour and Generosity, and with these added to his Parts he cannot fail to become a wise and great Man.

Does he read the Newspapers? The Events of this War, should not pass unobserved by him at his Years.

As he reads History you should ask him, what Events strike him most? What Characters he esteems and admires? which he hates and abhors? which he despises?

No doubt he makes some Observations, young as he is.

Treachery, Perfidy, Cruelty, Hypocrisy, Avarice, &c. &c. should be pointed out to him for his Contempt as well as Detestation.

My dear Daughters Education is near my Heart. She will suffer by this War as well as her Brothers. But she is a modest, and discreet Child. Has an excellent Disposition, as well as Understanding. Yet I wish it was in my Power, to give her the Advantages of several Accomplishments, which it is not.

RC (Adams Papers). Enclosed newspapers not found or identified.

John Adams to Abigail Adams

Philadelphia July 1. 1777

We have no News: a long, cold, raw, northeast Storm has chilled our Blood, for two days past. It is unusual, to have a storm from that

Point, in June and July. It is an Omen no doubt. Pray what can it mean?

I have so little Ingenuity, at interpreting the Auspices, that I am unable to say whether it bodes Evil to Howe, or to Us.

I rather think it augurs a fine Crop of Wheat, Rye, Barley, Corn, Spelts, Buckwheat, and Grass. It is a Presage of Plenty. Therefore let the Land rejoice. Flax and Cotton will grow, the better for this Weather.

July 2d.

The News Papers, inclosed, with this, will tell you all, that I know concerning the military operations in N. Jersey.

We have a Letter from Arthur Lee, from Spain, giving Us comfortable Assurances of Friendship and Commerce. We may trade to the Havannah and to New Orleans, as well as to Old Spain.[1]

RC (Adams Papers). Enclosed newspapers not found or identified.

[1] Arthur Lee to the Committee of Secret Correspondence, Vitoria, 18 March, read in Congress on 1 July (*JCC*, 8:514), and printed in Wharton, ed., *Dipl. Corr. Amer. Rev.*, 2:292–296.

Abigail Adams to John Adams

July 2 1777

I sit down to write you a few lines this morning as I am loth the post should go, without telling you that I am well, as usual. Suppose you will be more anxious for me this month than common. I shall write as often and as long as I am able, tho I do not expect that it will be more than two or 3 weeks more at furthest. You will not fail writing me by every opportunity, receiving Letters once a week from you serves to keep up my Spirits and cheer my Heart, which of late does not feel the gayest. I rejoice to find by your last that your Health is better. I should have known it from the stile of your Letter if you had not told me so. The dates run june the 2d, 4th and 8th. Since I wrote last we have had frequent reports of How's sitting out for Philadelphia. I have not been very uneasy about it. I confess I had rather He should make a visit to you than to me, at this time, more especially since you seem so desirous of it. Our last accounts are of a Skirmish in Brunswick and the burning of that Town and of the Troops retreat to Amboy. I think they make no valient appearence this season.—We have an other account from Halifax, that the Gov-

ener there has orderd every House to be cleard and Barrack for that
he expects them there immediately.

Yesterday our Tories so calld appeard in Boston to be tried before
the worshipfull justices Q[uinc]y and Hill; they had engaged counsel
Mr. T——r, who soon let the Court know that Mr. Q——y was not
qualified to try them as he had never taken the oath since the declaration of independance, and that the recognisances were not signed—
so they all marchd back again.[1]

They are pretty much netled and fear being sent on board the guard
ship. Seven are condemnd at Bridgwater.

As to Goverment I can not tell you more than G[e]n. W[arre]n has
wrote you. I hope in time we shall be able to sit down quietly—am sorry
to see so much bickering about it in Pensilvana.

You inquire how our season is here. We have had a very fine one
rather the coldest. There is a prospect of good crops of Grass and
Grain. The fruit will suffer much by the frosts. Not much cider I fear.

Pray write to Dr. T[uft]s by the first opportunity. Our young ones
are all well. We have enjoyd great Health since the small pox, for
which we cannot be sufficently thankfull. Tis very Healthy every
where. We have had a vast deal of thunder and lightning this Summer.—Adieu most Sincerely Yours.

RC (Adams Papers); endorsed: "Portia. Ans. July 16."

[1] The justices were Edmund Quincy,
identified earlier, and John Hill, Harvard
1756. The counsel who defended the
Braintree loyalists was almost certainly
JA's former student William Tudor, who
had recently left the army to resume his
law practice in Boston. There is, however, a little mystification concerning
Tudor's resignation, or resignations, from
military service. On 10 April Tudor had
written to JA from camp in New Jersey:
"I am just going to mount my Horse for
Boston. The offer made me by Genl.
Knox of a Post in the Artillery I have
declined, and shall return to my Books
once more with Pleasure" (Adams Papers). On the same day Washington's
general orders at Morristown stated:
"John Laurence [i.e. Laurance] Esqr. is
appointed Judge Advocate, in the room
of William Tudor Esqr. who has resigned" (Washington, *Writings*, ed.
Fitzpatrick, 7:382). No letter of resignation has been found, but that Tudor was
in Boston thereafter, and practicing law

there, is clear from, among other things,
his appointment by the town on 17
May as its agent "to procure Evidence
that may be had of the inimical Dis-
positions, towards this, or any of the
United States, of any Inhabitants of this
Town" (Boston Record Commissioners,
18th Report, p. 280). Yet all the biographical sketches of Tudor that touch
on the matter, and all the compilations
on Continental officers' service, record
the termination of Tudor's military service as in 1778. Heitman's *Register of
Officers*, for example, gives his resignation as 9 April 1778, just a year after
he had left camp—a coincidence so
striking as to suggest a mistake. To
complicate matters, Tudor was appointed
judge advocate in Jan. 1778 specifically
for the trial by court martial of Col.
David Henley, in Boston, on charges by
Gen. Burgoyne; see Tudor's letter to
AA, 26 June 1778 (Adams Papers). The
explanation appears to be that Tudor's
commission as a lieutenant colonel in

one of the additional Continental regiments, beginning Jan. 1777, ran a year
after he originally gave up his post as

advocate general in April 1777; see
Washington to Heath, 25 March 1778,
Writings, ed. Fitzpatrick, 11:144–145.

John Adams to Abigail Adams 2d

My dear Daughter   Philadelphia, July 5th, 1777

Yesterday, being the anniversary of American Independence, was celebrated here with a festivity and ceremony becoming the occasion.

I am too old to delight in pretty descriptions, if I had a talent for them, otherwise a picture might be drawn, which would please the fancy of a Whig, at least.

The thought of taking any notice of this day, was not conceived, until the second of this month, and it was not mentioned until the third. It was too late to have a sermon, as every one wished, so this must be deferred another year.

Congress determined to adjourn over that day, and to dine together. The general officers and others in town were invited, after the President and Council, and Board of War of this State.

In the morning the Delaware frigate, several large gallies, and other continental armed vessels, the Pennsylvania ship[1] and row gallies and guard boats, were all hawled off in the river, and several of them beautifully dressed in the colours of all nations, displayed about upon the masts, yards, and rigging.

At one o'clock the ships were all manned, that is, the men were all ordered aloft, and arranged upon the tops, yards, and shrouds, making a striking appearance—of companies of men drawn up in order, in the air.

Then I went on board the Delaware, with the President and several gentlemen of the Marine Committee, soon after which we were saluted with a discharge of thirteen guns, which was followed by thirteen others, from each other armed vessel in the river; then the gallies followed the fire, and after them the guard boats. Then the President and company returned in the barge to the shore, and were saluted with three cheers, from every ship, galley, and boat in the river. The wharves and shores, were lined with a vast concourse of people, all shouting and huzzaing, in a manner which gave great joy to every friend to this country, and the utmost terror and dismay to every lurking tory.

At three we went to dinner, and were very agreeably entertained with excellent company, good cheer, fine music from the band of Hessians taken at Trenton, and continual vollies between every toast, from a company of soldiers drawn up in Second-street before the city tavern, where we dined. The toasts were in honour of our country, and the heroes who have fallen in their pious efforts to defend her. After this, two troops of light-horse, raised in Maryland, accidentally here in their way to camp, were paraded through Second-street, after them a train of artillery, and then about a thousand infantry, now in this city on their march to camp, from North Carolina. All these marched into the common, where they went through their firings and manœuvres; but I did not follow them. In the evening, I was walking about the streets for a little fresh air and exercise, and was surprised to find the whole city lighting up their candles at the windows. I walked most of the evening, and I think it was the most splendid illumination I ever saw; a few surly houses were dark; but the lights were very universal. Considering the lateness of the design and the suddenness of the execution, I was amazed at the universal joy and alacrity that was discovered, and at the brilliancy and splendour of every part of this joyful exhibition. I had forgot the ringing of bells all day and evening, and the bonfires in the streets, and the fireworks played off.[2]

Had General Howe been here in disguise, or his master, this show would have given them the heart-ache. I am your affectionate father,

John Adams

MS not found. Printed from *Journal and Correspondence of Miss Adams, ... Edited by Her Daughter,* New York, 1841–1842, 2:8–10.

[1] Probably should read "ships," meaning the ships of the Pennsylvania navy. There was no fighting vessel that bore the name Pennsylvania at this time.

[2] More detailed accounts of this first and very hurriedly gotten-up anniversary celebration of the Fourth of July appeared in the Philadelphia papers (*Penna. Gazette,* 9 July; *Penna. Journal,* same date), but JA's is the fullest account by a participant that is known to the editors. At least one delegate took a much less enthusiastic view of it. William Williams of Connecticut, who had recently resumed his seat, wrote to Gov. Jonathan Trumbull on 5 July:

"Yesterday was in my opinion poorly spent in celebrating the anniversary of the Declaration of Independence, but to avoid singularity and Reflection upon my dear Colony, I thot it my Duty to attend the public Entertainment; a great Expenditure of Liquor, Powder etc. took up the Day, and of Candles thro the City good part of the night. I suppose and I conclude much Tory unilluminated Glass will want replacing etc." (Burnett, ed., *Letters of Members,* 2:401).

Mercy Otis Warren to Abigail Adams

Plimouth July 7th [1777]

Being Necessiated to use a Certain peace of Linnen so Nearly up that I Cannot spare my Friend the bit she Requested I Let her know if I Come across any that I think will suit her I shall not forget her.

I Could spare a Yard of very Good Irish Linnen but the price is more than Adequate to the Goodness so do not send it.

If you are able to write yourself do Let me hear from you soon. If you are not Let some other hand transmit me the agreable Inteligence of the Birth of a young patriot.

What think you of the Runaways at the Jerseys. Will they Come here to try the prowess of the New England Boys. I hope not though I dare say my Country men would be Vallient upon the Occassion. Yet I Wish These Brutal Ravagers May Ever be kept at a Distance from Boston, from New England, from America, from You, and from your unfeigned Friend, Marcia Warren

My Love to My dear Naby and the Young Gentlemen.

Husbandry Must smile after the Late fine showers. If I was to Cultivate the spirit of Farming it should Certainly be in a Driping season.

RC (Adams Papers).

John Adams to Abigail Adams

Philadelphia July 8. 1777 Tuesday

Yours of June 23d. have received. I believe there is no Danger of an Invasion your Way, but the Designs of the Enemy are uncertain and their Motions a little misterious. Before this Letter is sealed, which will not be till Sunday next, I hope I shall be able to inform you better.

I rejoice at your fine Season, and ⟨*still more*⟩ at my Brother Cranches Attention to Husbandry. Am very glad he bought the Farm, and that he likes it so well.

I pant for domestic Life, and rural Felicity like his.

I am better than I have been. But I dread the Heats, which are coming on.

This Day compleats Six Months since I left you. I am wasted and exhausted in Mind and Body, with incessant Application to Business, but if I can possibly endure it, will hold out the Year. It is nonsense to dance backwards and forwards. After this Year I shall take my Leave.

Our Affairs are in a fine prosperous Train, and if they continue so, I can leave this Station with Honour.

Next Month compleats Three Years, that I have been devoted to the Servitude of Liberty. A slavery it has been to me, whatever the World may think of it.

To a Man, whose Attachments to his Family, áre as strong as mine, Absence alone from such a Wife and such Children, would be a great sacrifice. But in Addition to this Seperation, what have I not done? What have I not suffered? What have I not hazarded?—These are Questions that I may ask you, but I will ask such Questions of none else. Let the Cymballs of Popularity tinckle still. Let the Butterflies of Fame glitter with their Wings. I shall envy neither their Musick nor their Colours.

The Loss of Property affects me little. All other hard Things I despize, but the Loss of your Company and that of my dear Babes for so long a Time, I consider as a Loss of so much solid Happiness.

The tender social Feelings of my Heart, which have distressed me beyond all Utterance, in my most busy, active scænes, as well as in the numerous Hours of melancholly solitude, are known only to God and my own soul.

How often have I seen my dearest Friend a Widow and her Charming Prattlers Orphans, exposed to all the Insolence of unfeeling impious Tyrants! Yet, I can appeal to my final Judge, the horrid Vision has never for one Moment shaken the Resolution of my Heart.

RC (Adams Papers). Part of the text of this letter is reproduced from the manuscript as an illustration in the present volume.

Abigail Adams to John Adams

July 9 1777

I sit down to write you this post, and from my present feelings tis the last I shall be able to write for some time if I should do well. I have been very unwell for this week past, with some complaints that have been new to me, tho I hope not dangerous.

I was last night taken with a shaking fit, and am very apprehensive that a life was lost. As I have no reason to day to think otherways; what may be the consequences to me, Heaven only knows. I know not of any injury to myself, nor any thing which could occasion what I fear.

I would not Have you too much allarmd. I keep up some Spirits yet, tho I would have you prepaird for any Event that may happen.

I can add no more than that I am in every Situatìon unfeignedly Yours, Yours.

RC (Adams Papers); addressed in John Thaxter's hand: "To The Honble: John Adams Esqr. Philadelphia"; endorsed: "Portia." This letter is reproduced from the manuscript as an illustration in the present volume.

John Adams to Abigail Adams

Philadelphia July 10. 1777. Thursday

My Mind is again Anxious, and my Heart in Pain for my dearest Friend. . . .[1]

Three Times have I felt the most distressing Sympathy with my Partner, without being able to afford her any Kind of Solace, or Assistance.

When the Family was sick of the Dissentery, and so many of our Friends died of it.

When you all had the small Pox.

And now I think I feel as anxious as ever.—Oh that I could be near, to say a few kind Words, or shew a few Kind Looks, or do a few kind Actions. Oh that I could take from my dearest, a share of her Distress, or relieve her of the whole.

Before this shall rea[c]h you I hope you will be happy in the Embraces of a Daughter, as fair, and good, and wise, and virtuous as the Mother, or if it is a son I hope it will still resemble the Mother in Person, Mind and Heart.[2]

RC (Adams Papers).

[1] Suspension points in MS.

[2] The last sentence as it appears in the MS shows the writer's intensity of feeling in a manner that type cannot show. JA evidently wrote: ". . . or if it is a son I hope it will still resemble the Mother in ⟨Mind, in Face and in [illegible]⟩ Person, Mind and Heart." The words rejected are partly rubbed out by hand and partly scratched out by pen.

Abigail Adams to John Adams

July 10 [1777] 9 o clock Evening

About an Hour ago I received a Letter from my Friend dated June 21: begining in this manner "my dearest Friend." It gave me a most agreable Sensation, it was a cordial to my Heart. That one single expression dwelt upon my mind and playd about my Heart, and was more valuable to me than any part of the Letter, except the close of it. It was because my Heart was softned and my mind enervated by my sufferings, and I wanted the personal and tender soothings of my dearest Friend, that [ren]derd[1] it so valuable to me at this time. I have

[no] doubt of the tenderest affection or sincerest regard of my absent Friend, yet an expression of that kind will sooth my Heart to rest amidst a thousand anxietyes.

Tis now 48 Hours since I can say I really enjoyed any Ease, nor am I ill enough to summons any attendance unless my sisters. Slow, lingering and troublesome is the present situation. The Dr. encourages me to Hope that my apprehensions are groundless respecting what I wrote you yesterday, tho I cannot say I have had any reason to allter my mind. My spirits However are better than they were yesterday, and I almost wish I had not let that Letter go. If there should be agreable News to tell you, you shall know it as soon as the post can convey it. I pray Heaven that it may be soon or it seems to me I shall be worn out. I must lay my pen down this moment, to bear what I cannot fly from—and now I have endured it I reassume my pen and will lay by all my own feelings and thank you for your obligeing Letters.—A prize arrived this week at Marble Head with 400 Hogsheads of rum a board sent in by Manly.—Every article and necessary of life rises here daily. Sugar has got to [8 pounds?] per hundred, Lamb to 1 shilling per pound and all ot[her] things in proportion.—We have the finest Season here that I have known for many years. The fruit was injured by the cold East winds and falls of, the Corn looks well, Hay will be plenty, but your Farm wants manure. I shall endeavour to have Sea weed carted every Leasure moment that can be had. That will not be many. Help is so scarce and so expensive I can not Hire a days mowing under 6 shillings.

How has done himself no honour by his late retreat. We fear most now for Tycon[deroga.] [2] Tis reported to day that tis taken. We have a vast many men who look like officers continually riding about. I wonder what they can be after, why they do not repair to the army.

We wonder too what Congress are a doing? We have not heard of late.

How do you do? Are you glad you are out of the way of sour faces. I could look pleasent upon you in the midst of sufferings—allmighty God carry me safely through them. There I would hope I have a Friend ever nigh and ready to assist me, unto whom I commit myself.

This is Thursday Evening. It [3] cannot go till monday, and then I hope will be accompanied with more agreable inteligance.

Most sincerely Yours.

July 11

I got more rest last night than I expected, this morning am rather

279

more ill than I was yesterday. This day ten years ago master John came into this world. May I have reason again to recollect it with peculiar gratitude. Adieu.

RC (Adams Papers); addressed in John Thaxter's hand: "To The Honble: John Adams Esqr. Philadelphia"; docketed in an unidentified hand.

[1] Here and below, MS is torn by seal.
[2] AA intended to divide this word between two lines but failed to continue it on the second.
[3] This letter.

John Adams to Abigail Adams

Philadelphia July 11. 1777

This Letter will go by the Hand of the Honourable Samuel Hewes Esqr., one of the Delegates in Congress from North Carolina, from the Month of September 1774, untill 1777.[1]

I had the Honour to serve with him upon the naval Committee, who laid the first Foundations, the Corner Stone of an American navy, by fitting to Sea the Alfred, Columbus, Cabott, Andrew Doria, Providence, and several others. An Honour, that I make it a Rule to boast of, upon all Occasions, and I hope my Posterity will have Reason to boast....[2] Hewes has a sharp Eye and keen, penetrating Sense, but what is of much more Value is a Man of Honour and Integrity. If he should call upon you, and you should be about, I hope you will treat him with all the Complaisance that is due to his Character. I almost envy him his Journey, altho he travells for his Health, which at present is infirm. I am yours, yours, yours,   John Adams

My dearest Friend

We have had no News from Camp for 3 or 4 days. Mr. How, by the last Advices, was maneuvring his Fleet and Army in such a Manner, as [to] give Us Expectations of an Expedition, some where. But whether to Rhode Island, Hallifax, up the North River or the Delaware, is left to Conjecture. I am much in doubt whether he knows his own Intentions.

A Faculty of penetrating into the Designs of an Enemy is said to be the first Quality of a General. But it is impossible to discover the Designs of an Enemy who has no Design at all. An Intention that has no Existence, a Plan that is not laid, cannot be divined. Be his Intentions what they may, you have nothing to fear from him—He has not force to penetrate the Country any where.

ATHENEUM

PUBLISHERS

162 EAST 38 STREET   NEW YORK CITY 10016

THE ADAMS PAPERS: ADAMS FAMILY CORRESPONDENCE
                (December 1761–March 1778)

   pub date: September 21, 1965

These are the two new volumes in Atheneum's
paperback publication of THE ADAMS PAPERS
series.

THIS BOOK is sent to you with our com-

pliments. Should you publish any men-

tion of it, we would be grateful for two

clippings of your article. Please do

not review the book before its

publication date.

RC (Adams Papers).

¹ JA of course meant Joseph Hewes (1730–1779), a North Carolina delegate from 1774 through 1776 and a signer of the Declaration of Independence (*DAB*). In a vivid letter written in old age JA credited Hewes with a decisive switch in Congress on the question of independence; see JA to William Plumer, 28 March 1813 (LbC, Adams Papers; printed in JA, *Works*, 10:35–36).

² Suspension points in MS. On the work of the committee in question see JA, *Diary and Autobiography*, 2:198 ff.; 3:345 ff.

John Adams to Abigail Adams

My dearest Friend   Philadelphia July 13. 1777

We have a confused Account, from the Northward, of Something Unlucky, at Ticonderoga, but cannot certainly tell what it is.¹

I am much afraid, We shall loose that Post, as We did Forts Washington and Lee, and indeed, I believe We shall if the Enemy surround it. But it will prove no Benefit to them. I begin to Wish there was not a Fort upon the Continent. Discipline and Disposition, are our Resources.

It is our Policy to draw the Enemy into the Country, where We can avail ourselves of Hills, Woods, Walls, Rivers, Defiles &c. untill our Soldiers are more inured to War.

How and Burgoine will not be able to meet, this Year, and if they were met, it would only be better for Us, for We should draw all our Forces to a Point too.

If they were met, they could not cutt off the Communication, between the Northern and Southern States. But if the Communication was cutt off for a Time, it would be no Misfortune, for New England would defend itself, and the Southern States would defend themselves.

Coll. Miles is come out of N. York on his Parol. His account is, as I am informed, that Mr. Howes Projects are all deranged. His Army has gone round the Circle and is now encamped on the very Spot where he was a Year ago. The Spirits of the Tories are sunk to a great Degree, and those of the Army too. The Tories have been elated with Prospects of coming to this City, and tryumphing, but are miserably disappointed. The Hessians are disgusted, and their General De Heister gone home, in a Miff.²

RC (Adams Papers).

¹ Maj. Gen. Arthur St. Clair on 6 July evacuated Fort Ticonderoga in the face of Burgoyne's army advancing from Canada.

² Lt. Gen. Leopold Philipp, Freiherr von Heister, commander of the Hessian troops in America, had been out of favor with Sir William Howe and with

his own sovereign since the American victory at Trenton. He was replaced by Lt. Gen. Wilhelm von Knyphausen and left the army in June 1777. See Edward J. Lowell, *The Hessians ... in the Revolutionary War*, N.Y., 1884, p. 113–115.

John Thaxter to John Adams

Sir   Braintree July 13th. 1777

The day before Yesterday Mrs. Adams was delivered of a daughter; ⟨but⟩ it grieves me to add, Sir, that it was still born. It was an exceeding fine looking Child.

Mrs. Adams is as comfortable, as She has Just inform'd me, as can be expected; and has desired me to write a few lines to acquaint you that She is in a good Way, which I am very happy in doing.

Every thing in my power that respects her Comfort, or that respects the Children, shall be attended to by Sir, Your most obedient Servt.,

J. Thaxter Junr.

RC (Adams Papers).

Abigail Adams to John Adams

July 16 1777

Join with me my dearest Friend in Gratitude to Heaven, that a life I know you value, has been spaired and carried thro Distress and danger altho the dear Infant is numberd with its ancestors.

My apprehensions with regard to it were well founded. Tho my Friends would have fain perswaded me that the Spleen[1] [or][2] the Vapours had taken hold of me I was as perfectly sensible of its discease as I ever before was of its existance. I was also aware of the danger which awaited me; and which tho my suffering[s] were great thanks be to Heaven I have been supported through, and would silently submit to its dispensations in the loss of a sweet daughter; it appeard to be a very fine Babe, and as it never opened its Eyes in this world it lookd as tho they were only closed for sleep. The circumstance which put an end to its existance, was evident upon its birth, but at this distance and in a Letter which may possibly fall into the Hands of some unfealing Ruffian I must omit particuliars. Suffice it to say that it was not oweing to any injury which I had sustaind, nor could any care of mine have prevented it.

My Heart was much set upon a Daughter. I had had a strong perswasion that my desire would be granted me. It was—but to shew me the uncertanty of all sublinary enjoyments cut of e'er I could call it mine.

No one was so much affected with the loss of it as its Sister who mournd in tears for Hours. I have so much cause for thankfullness amidst my sorrow, that I would not entertain a repineing thought. So short sighted and so little a way can we look into futurity that we ought patiently to submit to the dispensation of Heaven.

I am so comfortable that I am amaizd at myself, after what I have sufferd I did not expect to rise from my Bed for many days. This is but the 5th day and I have set up some Hours.

I However feel myself weakend by this exertion, yet I could not refrain [from] the temptation of writing with my own Hand to you.

Adieu dearest of Friends adieu—Yours most affectionately.

RC (Adams Papers); addressed in Richard Cranch's hand: "To the Honble: John Adams Esqr. at Philadelphia To be left at the Post Office"; endorsed: "Portia."

¹ MS apparently reads: "Splln."
² This word and one other (in the paragraph preceding AA's leavetaking) have been editorially supplied.

John Adams to Abigail Adams

My dearest Friend   Wednesday July 16. 1777

Your Favour of the 2d. instant reached me on the 14th.

The last Letters from me which you had received, were of the 2d. 4th. and 8th. June. Here were 24 days between the 8th. of June and the 2d. July the date of yours. How this could happen I know not. I have inclosed you the Newspapers and written you a Line, every Week, for several Months past. If there is one Week passes without bringing you a Letter from me, it is because the Post does not its Duty.

After another Week, you will probably write me no more Letters for some Days. But I hope you will make Mr. Thaxter, or somebody write. Miss Nabby or Mr. John may write.

We have another Fort Washington and Fort Lee affair at Ticonderoga. I hope at last We shall learn Wisdom. I wished that Post evacuated Three Months ago. We are Fools if We attempt at present to maintain Posts, near navigable Water.

As to the Tories, I think our General Court would do well to imitate the Policy of Pensilvania, who have enjoyned an Oath to be taken by all the People, which has had an amazing Effect.

The Tories have been tolerated, even to long Suffering. Beings so unfeeling, unnatural, ungratefull, as to join an Enemy of their Country so unprincipled, unmerciless[1] and blood thirsty, deserve a Punishment much severer than Banishment.

But you should establish an Oath, and outlaw all who will not take it—that is suffer them to hold no Office, to vote no where for any Thing, to bring no Action, to take out no Execution.

I am grieved to hear that our Fruit is injured by the Frost because as Wine and Rum will wholly fail, from the stoppages of Trade, Cyder will be our only Resource.

However We must drink Water, and Milk, and We should live better, be healthier, and fight bolder[2] than We do with our poisonous Luxuries.

RC (Adams Papers).

[1] Thus in MS. JA first wrote "merciless," but then, looking back and carelessly supposing he had written "merciful," prefixed "un" above the line.
[2] Thus apparently in MS.

John Adams to Abigail Adams

Fryday July 18, 1777

The Papers inclosed will inform you, of the Loss of Ticonderoga, with all its Circumstances of Incapacity and Pusillanimity.—Dont you pitty me to be wasting away my Life, in laborious Exertions, to procure Cannon, Ammunition, Stores, Baggage, Cloathing &c. &c. &c. &c., for Armies, who give them all away to the Enemy, without firing a Gun.

Notwithstanding the Mortification arising from such Considerations, yet I can truly say that this Event is a Relief to my Mind, for I have a long Time expected this Catastrophe, and that it would be aggravated by the Loss of the Garrison, which it seems has been happily saved. My only Hope of holding that Post, has been a long Time founded in a Doubt whether the Enemy had Force enough in Canada, to attempt it.

The Design of the Enemy, is now no doubt to attack poor New England on all sides, from Rhode Island, New York and Ticonderoga.

But I believe their Progress will be stopped, for our Army is pretty numerous, and Discipline, upon which alone We must finally depend, under Providence, for Success, is advancing.

Howes Army is in a miserable Condition, by the best Accounts We can obtain.

My Mind runs upon my Family, as much as upon our public Concerns. I long to hear of the Safety and the Health of my dearest Friend. —May Heaven grant her every Blessing she desires.

Tell my Brother Farmer, I long to study Agriculture with him, and to see the Progress of his Corn and Grass.—Sister too, does she make as good a dairy Woman as your Ladyship?

RC (Adams Papers). Enclosed newspapers not found or precisely identifiable.

John Adams to Abigail Adams

Phila. July 20th. 1777

The little masterly Expedition to Rhode Island has given Us, some Spirits, amidst our Mournings for the Loss of Ti. Barton conducted his Expedition with infinite Address and Gallantry, as Sir Wm. has it.[1] Meigs and Barton must be rewarded.[2]

Although so much Time has elapsed since our Misfortune at Ti, We have no particular Account from General Schuyler or Sinclair [St. Clair]. People here are open mouthed, about the Disgrace and Disaster in that Quarter, and are much disposed to Censure.—For my Part I suspend my Judgment, untill I know the Facts. I hope the People with you will not be too much dejected at the Loss. Burgoine is a wild Man, and will rush into some inconsiderate Measures, which will put him in our Power, but if not, his Career will be stopped.

The Loss of so many Stores is more provoking than that of the Post.

Before this reaches you, I hope you will be happy in the Embraces of a little female Beauty. God bless her. Pray let me continue to hear from you, every Week. When you cant write, make some other Pen do the Duty.

We have had here a few hot days, when Fahrenheits Mercury was at 88, but the Weather has in general been very cool. Such a July was scarcely ever known, which is a fortunate Circumstance for the Health of our Army.

We have The four Months of August, September, October and November, before Us, for the Armies to Act in. There is Time enough to do a great deal of Business. I hope, that the Enemy will not do so much Mischief as last Year, altho their Exploits then have not done them much Good, nor the united States as a Community, much harm.

The Examples of Meigs, and Barton, will be followed I hope, by Numbers. The Sub[t]lety, the Ingenuity, the Activity, the Bravery, the Prudence, with which those Excursions were conducted, are greatly and justly admired.

Connecticutt has the Honour of one, Rhode Island of the other.— Will Mass. be outdone?

RC (Adams Papers).

[1] On 10 July Lt. Col. William Barton with a party of forty Rhode Island militia made a night raid on Maj. Gen. Richard Prescott's headquarters near Newport, captured Prescott and his aide, and almost reached the mainland before an alarm was raised. See Washington to Hancock, 16 July (*Writings*, ed. Fitzpatrick, 8:415–416), and a minutely detailed account, with a map of the terrain, in Frederick Mackenzie, *Diary*, Cambridge, 1930, 1:148–151.

[2] On 25 July Congress voted that both officers be presented with swords—Meigs for his conduct in the raid on Sag Harbor at the end of May (JCC, 8:579–580).

John Adams to Abigail Adams

My best Friend   Philadelphia July 21. 1777

I have long sought for a compleat History of the Revolution in the low Countries, when the Seven united Provinces seperated from the Kingdom of Spain, but without the Success that I wished, untill a few days ago.

Sir William Temples Account is elegant and entertaining, but very brief and general.[1]

Puffendorfs, I have not yet seen.[2] Grotius's I have seen, and read in Part, but it is in Latin, and I had it not in my Possession long enough, to make myself master of the whole.[3]

A few days ago, I heard for the first Time, of an History of the Wars in Flanders, written in Italian by Cardinal Bentivoglio, and translated into English by the Earl of Monmouth. The Cardinal was a Spaniard and a Tory, and his History has about as much Candor towards the Flemish and their Leaders as Clarendon has towards Pym and Hampden, and Cromwell. The Book is in Folio, and is embellished with a Map of the Country and with the Portraits of about Thirty of the Principal Characters.[4]

Mr. Ingersol, who lent me the Book, told me, that in the Year 1765 or 6, being in England, he was invited together with Dr. Franklin to spend a Week in the Country with a Mr. Steel a Gentleman of Fortune, at present an eloquent Speaker in the Society of Arts, descended from Sir Richard Steel.[5] Upon that Visit Mr. Steel told them that the Quarrell which was now begun by the Stamp Act would never be reconciled, but would terminate in a Separation between the two Countries.—Ingersol was surprized at the Prædiction and asked why and how?—I cant tell you how says he, but if you want to know why, when you return to London, enquire at the Booksellers for Bentivoglios History of the Wars in Flanders, read it through, and you will be convinced that such Quarrells cannot be made up.

He bought the Book accordingly and has now lent it to me. It is very similar to the American Quarrell in the Rise and Progress, and will be so in the Conclusion.

RC (Adams Papers).

[1] *Observations upon the United Provinces of the Netherlands*, London, 1672, a brief work but long the principal authority for most English readers on the history and government of the Netherlands. It went through numerous editions and was translated into several languages. JA could have read it in the first volume of his own copy of Temple's *Works*, 2 vols., London, 1731, which is among his books in the Boston Public Library.

[2] The German jurist Pufendorf (1632–1694) wrote *An Introduction to the History of the Principal Kingdoms and States of Europe* . . . , which is not among the works by that writer listed in the *Catalogue of JA's Library*.

[3] Hugo Grotius (1583–1645), *Annales et historiæ de rebus belgicis*, Amsterdam, 1657, likewise not entered in the *Catalogue of JA's Library*.

[4] Guido, Cardinal Bentivoglio's *History of the Warrs in Flanders* was first published in English in this translation by the Earl of Monmouth, London, 1654. Despite his enthusiasm for this book, which led him to copy the entire list of 24 portraits into his letter to JQA of 27 July, below, JA does not seem to have acquired a copy of it, though the *Catalogue of JA's Library* enters two other works by Bentivoglio.

[5] Jared Ingersoll of Connecticut, though a loyalist, was living quietly in Philadelphia at this time; see JA to AA, 16 March, above, and Lawrence H. Gipson, *Jared Ingersoll*, New Haven and London, 1920, p. 355 ff. Joshua Steele (1700–1791) was an Irishman who lived many years in London, was a friend and correspondent of Franklin, wrote treatises on prosody and music, and spent his last years attempting to ameliorate the condition of the slaves on his estates in Barbados (*DNB; Cal. Franklin Papers, A.P.S.*, 2:100; 3:349).

Abigail Adams to John Adams

My dearest Friend   July 23 1777

Notwithstanding my confinement I think I have not omitted writing you by every post. I have recoverd Health and strength beyond expectation; and never was so well in so short a time before. Could I see my Friend in reality as I often do in immagination I think I should feel a happiness beyond expression; I had pleasd myself with the Idea of presenting him a fine son or daughter upon his return, and had figurd to myself the smiles of joy and pleasure with which he would receive it, but [those?][1] dreams are buried in the Grave, transitory as the morning Cloud, short lived as the Dew Drops.

Heaven continue to us those we already have and make them blessings. I think I feel more solicitious for their welfare than ever, and more anxious if posible for the life and Health of their parent. I fear the extreem Heat of the season, and the different temperament of the climate and the continual application to Buisness will finish a constitution naturally feeble.

I know not in what manner you will be affected at the loss, Evacuation, sale, giving up—which of the terms befits the late conduct at Tycondoroga. You may know more of the reasons for this conduct (as I hear the commanding officer went immediately to Congress) than we can devine this way; but this I can truly say no Event since the commencement of the War has appeard so allarming to me, or given me eaquel uneasiness. Had the Enemy fought and conquerd the fort, I could have borne it, but to leave it with all the stores before it was even attackd, has exited a thousand Suspicions, and gives room for more wrath than despondency.

We every day look for an attack upon us this way. The reports of this week are that a number of Transports with Troops have a[rriv]ed at Newport. Some expresses went through this Town yesterday.

Yours of June 30[2] reach'd me last week. I am not a little surprizd that you have not received Letters from me later than the 9 of June.[3] I have never faild for this two months writing you once a week. Tho they contain matters of no great importance I should be glad to know when you receive them.

We have had a remarkable fine Season here, no drought this summer. The Corn looks well, and english Grain promiseing. We cannot be sufficently thankfull to a Bountifull providence that the Horrours of famine are not added to those of war, and that so much more Health prevails in our Camps than in the year past.

Many of your Friends desire to be rememberd to you. Some complain that you do not write them. Adieu. Master Tom stands by and sends duty—he often recollects How *par* used to put him to Jail as he calls it. They are all very Healthy this summer, and are in expectation of a Letter every packet that arrives. Yours, ever yours,   Portia

PS Price Current!! This day I gave 4 dollors a peice for Sythes and a Guiney a Gallon for New england Rum. We come on here finely. What do you think will become of us. If you will come Home and turn Farmer, I will be dairy woman. You will make more than is allowd you, and we shall grow wealthy. Our Boys shall go into the Feild and work with you, and my Girl shall stay in the House and assist me.

RC (Adams Papers); addressed in John Thaxter's hand: "To The Honble: John Adams Esqr. Philadelphia To be left at the Post Office"; franked: *"Free"*; docketed in an unidentified hand.

[1] Here and below, MS is torn by seal.
[2] Not found.
[3] Not found, unless (as is very likely) this is a slip of the pen for 8 June.

John Adams to Abigail Adams

My dearest Friend   Philadelphia July 26. 1777 Saturday

At this Moment, I hope you are abed and happy. I am anxious to hear, and the more so because I had no Letter, from you, nor concerning you by the last Post. I wait with Impatience for Monday Morning, when the Post is to arrive.

I am more Anxious, now, than ever, on another Account. The Enemy's Fleet has sailed—But to what Place, they are destined, is unknown. Some conjecture Philadelphia, some Rhode Island, and some, that they mean only a Feint and intend soon to return to the North River. If they go to Rhode Island, I suppose they will not remain inactive there, which will throw you and your Neighbourhood into Distress.[1]

Poor, unhappy I! who have never an opportunity to share with my Family, their Distresses, nor to contribute in the least degree to relieve them! I suffer more in solitary silence, than I should if I were with them.

RC (Adams Papers).

[1] On 23 July, after long and elaborate preparations that had gone on in plain sight of the Jersey shore, Howe's army sailed out of New York harbor in a fleet of "above 260 Sail" bound for Delaware Bay. Upon its arrival there on 29 July, however, the fleet put out to sea again and reappeared at the entrance to Chesa-peake Bay on 14 August. For a British record of this trying voyage see Ambrose Serle, *American Journal*, ed. Edward H. Tatum Jr., San Marino, 1940, p. 240–242; for the mystification of Americans concerning Howe's intentions see JA's letters to AA of 30 July–21 Aug., below.

John Adams to John Quincy Adams

My dear Son   Philadelphia July 27. 1777

If it should be the Design of Providence that you should live to grow up, you will naturally feel a Curiosity to learn the History of the Causes which have produced the late Revolution of our Government. No Study in which you can engage will be more worthy of you.

It will become you to make yourself Master of all the considerable

Characters, which have figured upon the Stage of civil, political or military Life. This you ought to do with the Utmost Candour, Benevolence and Impartiality, and if you should now and then meet with an Incident, which shall throw some Light upon your Fathers Character, I charge you to consider it with an Attention only to Truth.

It will also be an entertaining and instructive Amusement, to compare our American Revolution with others that Resemble it. The whole Period of English History, from the Accession of James the first, to the Accession of William the third, will deserve your most critical Attention.

The History of the Revolutions in Portugal, Sweeden and Rome by the Abbot de Vertot, is well worth your Reading.[1]

The Seperation of the Helvetic Confederacy from the Dominion of the House of Austria, is also an illustrious Event, that particularly resembles our American Struggle with Great Britain.

But above all others, I would recommend to your study, the History of the Flemish Confederacy, by which the seven united Provinces of the Netherlands, emancipated themselves from the Domination of Spain.

There are several good Histories of this great Revolution. Sir William Temples is short but elegant, and entertaining. Another Account of this Period was written by Puffendorf, and another by Grotius.[2]

But the most full and compleat History, that I have seen, is one that I am now engaged in Reading. It is intituled "The History of the Wars of Flanders, written in Italian by that learned and famous Cardinal Bentivoglio, englished by the Right Honourable Henry Earl of Monmouth, the whole Work illustrated, with a Map of the seventeen Provinces and above twenty Figures of the chief Personages mentioned in the History."

Bentivoglio, like Clarendon, was a Courtier, and on the side of Monarchy and the Hierarchy. But Allowances must be made for that.

The first Cut is of Guido, S.R.E. Cardinalis Bentivolus.

2. The Emperor Charles the 5th. Prince of the low Countries.

3. Phillip the 2d. King of Spain, Prince of the low Countries.

4. William of Nassau, Prince of Orange.

5. Margarett Dutchesse of Parma and Piacenza, Daughter to Charles the 5th. Governesse of the low Countries.

6. Elizabeth Queen of England, France and Ireland.

7. Anthony Perenott Cardinal Granvel, Councillor of state to Margarett of Parma.

8. Peter Ernest Count Mansfeldt Governor of Luxemburg.
9. William Lodowic Count Nassau, Governor of Frisland.
10. John Lignius, Count Aremberg, Governor of Frisland, General at the Battle of Hilligal.
11. Ferdinand of Toledo Duke of Alva, Governor of the Low Countries.
12. Sancho Avila Governor of the Fort, at Antwerp, General at the Battle of Mooch.
13. Chiapino Vitelli Marquiss of Cetona, Camp Master General.
14. Robert Lord Dudley Earl of Leicester, Governor of the united Provinces.
15. Maximillian Hennin Count Bossu, Governor of Holland and Utrecht.
16. Lodovico Requesenes, Great Commandador of Castile, Governor of the Low Countries.
17. Phillip Croy Duke of Areschot, Knight of the golden Fleece, Governor of Flanders.
18. Don John of Austria, son to Charles 5th. Governor of the Low Countries.
19. Mathias, Archduke of Austria, Duke of Burgundy and Governor of the united Provinces.
20. Alexander Farnese, Prince of Parma, Governor of the low Countries.
21. Francis Hercules De Valois, Duke of Anjou, Alencon, Brabant and Protector of the Netherlands.
22. Phillip Count Holach, Baron of Langenberg, first General of the united Provinces.
23. Maurice of Nassau, Prince of Orange, Count Nassau, Governor of the united Provinces.
24. Adolphus Solm Count de Meurs, Governor of Gelderland and Utrecht.

There are three most memorable Seiges described in this History, those of Haerlem, Leyden, and Antwerp.

You will wonder, my dear son, at my writing to you at your tender Age, such dry Things as these: but if you keep this Letter you will in some future Period, thank your Father for writing it. I am my dear son, with the Utmost Affection to your Sister and Brothers as well as to you, your Father,   John Adams

RC (Adams Papers); docketed in CFA's hand.

¹ Not a single work, as JA seems to imply, but three different works by a prolific French historical writer, the Abbé René Aubert de Vertot d'Aubeuf. A copy of *The Revolutions of Portugal*, London, 1721, is among JA's books in MB (*Catalogue of JA's Library*); and two copies in French, published at The Hague in 1734 and 1755 respectively, are still in the family library at Quincy (MQA). JA's copy of *The History of the Revolution in Sweden*, London, 1716, is also in MB (*Catalogue of JA's Library*), and no fewer than three copies in French

are in MQA: Paris, 1722, 1811; The Hague, 1734. Of Vertot's *Histoire des révolutions arrivées dans le gouvernement de la république romaine* there is a copy, 3 vols., The Hague, 1737, in MQA.

² On these works and also on Bentivoglio's *History*, described at such length immediately below, see JA to AA, 21 July, above, and notes there. The title of Bentivoglio's book as given below by JA is a reasonably accurate copy from the titlepage of the London, 1654, translation; and the titles of the plates are also copied with unusual accuracy.

John Adams to Abigail Adams

My dearest Friend   Philadelphia July 28. 1777

Never in my whole Life, was my Heart affected with such Emotions and Sensations, as were this Day occasioned by your Letters of the 9. 10. 11. and 16 of July. Devoutly do I return Thanks to God, whose kind Providence has preserved to me a Life that is dearer to me than all other Blessings in this World. Most fervently do I pray, for a Continuance of his Goodness in the compleat Restoration of my best Friend to perfect Health.

Is it not unaccountable, that one should feel so strong an Affection for an Infant, that one has never seen, nor shall see? Yet I must confess to you, the Loss of this sweet little Girl, has most tenderly and sensibly affected me. I feel a Grief and Mortification, that is heightened tho it is not wholly occasioned, by my Sympathy with the Mother. My dear little Nabbys Tears are sweetly becoming her generous Tenderness and sensibility of Nature. They are Arguments too of her good sense and Discretion.

RC (Adams Papers).

Isaac Smith Sr. to John Adams

Mr. Adams   Boston July 28th. 1777

Not haveing anything worth troubling you with for sometime have been silent. The late Affair of Ticonderogia, makes us all sick. I have been of Opinion for sometime itt would have been best iff itt had been evacuated last spring and come down lower by which means the laboring Oar would have fell more on the Enemy, but to give itt up with such immence stores and charge we have been att, is beyaund all conseption. I cant Care to dwell on so disagreeable a subject and so say no more.

I have a Vessell that went away a little before the Lexington Affair and things soon after became more dificult. I ordered the Master iff he should here that the dificulties still remain, he might imploy the Vessell in freighting from Spain to any Other places and Accordingly he imployed her in that way as was the case of many Others. I have heard he went from Spain with a freight to London and back to Spain Again, in consequence of which I suppose he took Out a New regester to cover his Vessell. I have wrote to London and sundry times to my friends Gardoquis in Bilbao and inclosed letters to the Master to purchase a load of Salt in Spain or Portugal and to come directly home— but have no Account whether he ever received my letters. I have wrote the Master upon supposition that he had got a british regester to distroy itt and come without any, but since I have thought of Another method, which think may be supported, on principle of justice and patreoticism, and am inform'd has been countenanst by the Honbl. Continental Congress in order to get One's Interest into this part of the world, and that is to have two setts of papers—but what I think will Answer my purpose, is Only to have a Certifycate from the Congress sertifying liberty for the Vessell to return into any of these states with a load of Salt, and that no Arm'd Vessell in any of the United states should stop or hinder her in prosecution of her returning home.

I had thoughts to have Applyed to Our goverment, which might easily be effected but then there Authority extends no further than Our Own state wereas One from Your body would extend through the United states.

The Vessell is a schooner of 100 Tons called the Success, Ignatius Webber Master. I have had often upwards (say upwards of Twenty times) Three thousand bushels salt, which att this time would be a publick benifit. I think there need but a very little wrote upon the Matter, iff any charge Attending itt to the under Clerks iff you will pay itt, will Account with you. You will send two as itt is Nessesary these times to have a duplecate.

I am Sr. Yr. h S, Isaac Smith

31st.

PS I have just returned from Weymouth w[h]ere have been a day or two. I forward you a letter from Mrs. Adams.[1] Mr. Cranch is a[s] busey as a bee and seems to be in his Elliment about his New farm. I find a letter from you by Mr. Hewes.[2] I have not seen the Gentleman yet, but shall take proper Notice of him.—Yesterday there was an Account come that How's fleet had saild. Att present we here nothing more so that we suppose they are gone your way.

I Observe what you say about salt and the Necessity of the Importation. I have not time to say any thing on that subject as the post is near going but will let you know in my next the dificulty we labour under here in the Navigation way, & are Y[ours],   IS

RC (Adams Papers); docketed in an unidentified hand.

[1] The letter immediately following?
[2] Not found.

Abigail Adams to John Adams

July 30 1777

I dare say before this Time you have interpreted the Northern Storm; if the presages chill'd your Blood, how must you be froze and stiffend at the Disgrace brought upon our Arms unless some warmer passion seaze you, and Anger and resentment Fire your Breast.

How are all our vast Magazines of Cannon, powder, Arms, cloathing, provision, Medicine &c. to be restored to us—but what is vastly more, How shall the Disgrace be wiped away? How shall our lost Honour be retreaved? The reports with regard to that fortress are very vague and uncertain. Some write from thence, that there was not force suffcient to defend it, others say it might have stood a long Siege. Some there are who ought to know why and wherefore we have given away a place of such importance.

That the inquiry will be made I make no doubt, and if Cowardice, Guilt, Deceit, are found upon any one How high or exalted soever his station, may shame, reproach, infamy, hatred, and the execrations of the publick be his portion.

I would not be so narrow minded as to suppose that there are not many Men of all Nations possessd of Honour, Virtue and Integrety; yet tis to be lamented that we have not Men among ourselves sufficently qualified for War to take upon them the most important command.

It was customary among the Carthaginians to have a Military School, in which the flower of their Nobility and those whose talants and ambition prompted them to aspire to the first dignities, learnt the art of War. From among these they selected all their general officers, for

tho they employd mercenary Soldiers, they were too jealous and suspicious to employ foreign Generals.

Will a Foreigner whose Interest is not naturally connected with
ours, (any otherways than as the cause of Liberty is the cause of all
mankind), will he act with the same Zeal or expose himself to eaquel
dangers with the same resolution for a Republick of which he is not
a member as He would have done for his own Native Country? And
can the people repose an eaquel confidence in them, even supposing
them Men of integrety and abilities, and that they meet with success
eaquel to their abilities. How much envy and Malice, is employd against
them; and How galling to pride, How mortifying to Humane Nature
to see itself excelld.

July 31

I have nothing new to entertain you with, unless it is an account
of a New Set of Mobility which have lately taken the Lead in B[osto]n.
You must know that there is a great Scarcity of Sugar and Coffe, articles which the Female part of the State are very loth to give up, ex-
pecially whilst they consider the Scarcity occasiond by the merchants
having secreted a large Quantity. There has been much rout and Noise
in the Town for several weeks. Some Stores had been opend by a number of people and the Coffe and Sugar carried into the Market and
dealt out by pounds. It was rumourd that an eminent, wealthy, stingy
Merchant (who is a Batchelor) had a Hogshead of Coffe in his Store
which he refused to sell to the committee under 6 shillings per pound.
A Number of Females some say a hundred, some say more assembled
with a cart and trucks, marchd down to the Ware House and demanded
the keys, which he refused to deliver, upon which one of them seazd
him by his Neck and tossd him into the cart. Upon his finding no
Quarter he deliverd the keys, when they tipd up the cart and dis-
chargd him, then opend the Warehouse, Hoisted out the Coffe themselves, put it into the trucks and drove off.

It was reported that he had a Spanking among them,[1] but this I
believe was not true. A large concourse of Men stood amazd silent
Spectators of the whole transaction.[2]

Your kind favour received dated july 11, favourd by the Hon. Mr.
Hews, left at my unkles in Boston. Tis not like he will make an Excursion this way, if he should shall treat him in the best manner I am
able.—What day does your post arrive, and how long are Letters
travelling from me to you? I receive one from you every week, and
I as regularly write one but you make no mention of receiving any,

or very seldom. In your Hurry do you forget it, or do they not reach you. I am very well for the time, not yet 3 weeks since my confinement and yet I think I have wrote you a very long Letter.

Adieu, your good Mother is just come, desires to be rememberd to you. So does my Father and Sister who have just left me, and so does she whose greatest happiness consists in being tenderly beloved by her absent Friend and subscribes herself ever his   Portia

RC (Adams Papers); addressed in John Thaxter's hand: "To The Honble: John Adams Esqr. Philadelphia To be left at the Post Office"; endorsed: "Portia ans. Aug. 11"; docketed by JA in old age, and later by CFA. Probably enclosed in Isaac Smith's letter, preceding, q.v.

¹ CFA printed this letter at least five times between 1840 and 1876, and in every printing his text of this passage reads: "It was reported that he had personal chastisement among them. . . ."

² Although AA did not say so and although JA in his reply of 11 Aug., below, did not indicate that he knew who was meant, the victim of the ladies' resentful action was Thomas Boylston, a Boston merchant who was rich, miserly, a bachelor, and first cousin to JA's mother; see Adams Genealogy. On 25 July 1777 John Scollay, a Boston selectman, wrote his friend Samuel Phillips Savage:

"Yesterday we had a high Scene in this town. In the Morning a Number of Women waited on Mr. Boyleston. They told him that they kept Little shops to sell Necessarys for Poor People, they understood that he had Coffee to sell and if he would sell it at a reasonable price they would take it of him. He gave them a verry short answer and they Left him, about 3 oClock in the afternoon a Number of Women mostly from the North part of the town Assembled under the direction of one Mrs. Colter. They were not your Maggys but reputable Clean drest Women Some of them with Silk gownes on. They went to Boylestons Warehouse where they found him. They Insisted on having his Coffee at their price. He refused. They without Ceremony put him into a Cart they having one at hand and drove him some way up the Wharf. He found it Impossible to withstand, gave them his Keys, they took one Cask and Carried it off Intending to pay him for it. Poor Boyleston was never so Swetted since he was born. He was verry roughly handled. I am sorry for the Occasion but I cant say I am sorry that he has met with a rebuff.— We had yesterday a Legal town Meeting. The town agreed to raise by Subscription £8000.0 La[wful] Money to put into the hands of a Committee to purchase articles for the Inhabitants to deliver them to the Hucksters at the price they cost, they to sell them to the Inhabitants at a Moderate proffit. I hope this method will be of Service" (MHi: S. P. Savage Papers).

John Adams to Abigail Adams

My dearest Friend   Philadelphia July 30. 1777

I am sorry to find by your late Letter what indeed I expected to hear, that my Farm wants manure. I fear by your Expressions that your Crop of Hay falls short.

But, there has been an Error in our Husbandry in which We have been very inconsiderate and extravagant, that is in pasturing the Mowing Ground. This will ruin any Farm.

The true Maxim of profitable Husbandry is to contrive every Means for the Maintenance of Stock.—Increase your Cattle and inrich your Farm.—We bestow too much manure upon Corn—too little upon Grass. Make Manure, make food for Cattle, increase your stock—this is the Method.

Howes Fleet has been at Sea, these 8 days. We know not where he is gone. We are puzzling ourselves in vain, to conjecture his Intention. Some guess he is gone to Cheasapeak, to land near Susquehanna and cross over Land to Albany to meet Burgoine. But they might as well imagine them gone round Cape horn into the South Seas to land at California, and march across the Continent to attack our back settlements.

Others think them gone to Rhode Island, others think they mean only a Deception and to return to the North River. A few days will reveal their Scheme....[1]

We have now before Us, the Months of August, September, October and November, for the Operations of the Campaign.—Time enough for Mischief.

G[eneral] Washington is so near this City, that if the Enemy come into Delaware Bay, he will meet them before they can come near this City.

RC (Adams Papers).

[1] Suspension points in MS.

John Adams to Abigail Adams

My best Friend   Philadelphia August 1. 1777

The Fleet is in Delaware Bay. 228 of them were seen, in the Offing, from Cape Henlopen, the day before yesterday. They come in but slowly.

G[eneral] Washington, and the light Horse came into Town last Night. His Army will be in, this day—that is the two or three first Divisions of it—Greens, Sterlings and Stevensons [Stephen's].

The rest is following on, as fast as possible. General Nash with about 1500 North Carolina Forces, has taken Post on the Heights of Chester, about 15 miles below this City on the River. The Fire Ships &c. are ready.

I really think that Providence has ordered this Country to be the

Theatre of this Summers Campaign, in Favour to Us, for many Reasons. 1. It will make an entire and final Seperation of the Wheat from the Chaff, the Ore from the Dross, the Whiggs from the Tories. 2. It will give a little Breath to you in N. England. 3. If they should fail in their Attempt upon Philadelphia, it will give Lustre to our Arms and Disgrace to theirs, but if they succeed, it will cutt off this corrupted City, from the Body of the Country, and it will take all their Force to maintain it.

RC (Adams Papers).

John Adams to Abigail Adams

My best Friend   Philadelphia August 2. 1777 Saturday

By an express last night from Cape May, We learn that the Fleet went out of the Bay, the Morning before, i.e. on Thursday Morning and put to Sea, and went out of Sight.

What this Man is after, no Wisdom can discover.

Aug. 3

Last night another Express says the Fleet appeared off the Capes again, i.e. part of it, upwards of one hundred Sail.

After all these Feints and Maneuvres, it is most likely he designs to run up the North River, by and by.

The hot weather grows burthensome. And our Business thickens, and presses. I feel as if I could hardly get along through this Month and the next. But must see it out as well as I can.

We have News from France, from our Embassadors.[1] The French will not declare War, as yet. They tell the English they neither desire War nor fear it. But they will lend Us Money, and they have sold Us Eighty thousand Stands of Arms, and will aid Us in every indirect Way. So will Spain.

I hope by this Time you are in perfect Health. Tomorows Post, I hope will confirm the most agreable Account, in the last I received from you, of your being in a good Way. My Health and Spirits and Life are bound up in yours. May Heaven preserve my dearest Friend, and make her happy.

Never was Wretch, more weary of Misery than I am of the Life I lead, condemned to the dullest servitude and Drudgery, seperated from all that I love, and wedded to all that I hate.

Digging in a Potato Yard upon my own Garden and living in my own Family would be to me Paradise. The next Time I come home, shall be for a long Time.

RC (Adams Papers).

¹ "Congress have this Day recd. a number and very large Letters from Dr Franklin Mr Lee and Dean, with a great variety of Papers, the Letters from 12 Mar. to abt the 26 May" (William Williams to Gov. Jonathan Trumbull of Connecticut, 2 Aug., Burnett, ed., *Letters of Members*, 2:436). Letters from the American Commissioners at Paris, 12 March – 26 May, take up most of the space in Wharton, ed., *Dipl. Corr. Amer. Rev.*, 2:283–327.

John Adams to Abigail Adams

My dearest Friend   Philadelphia August 4. 1777

Your kind Favour of July 23, came by the Post, this Morning. It revives me, to hear of your Health, and Welfare, altho I shall be, and am disappointed of a Blessing, which I hoped to enjoy. But this is the Result of Wisdom superiour to ours and must be submitted to with chearfull Resignation.

The Loss of Ti. has occasioned as loud Complaints and as keen Resentment in Philadelphia as in Boston. And Congress have determined that an Inquiry shall be made, and have ordered the Major Generals Schuyler and St. Clair, to Head Quarters and ordered M.G. Gates to relieve M.G. Schuyler.¹ Lincoln and Arnold are there. These three I believe will restore our Affairs in that Department.

We have Letters from France, Spain and the West Indies, which shew that our Ground in Europe is firm, and that a War is brewing.

We have all the English Papers, till the latter End of May, which shew that Britain is in a wretched Condition indeed—their East India Affairs in Distraction, their Affrican Trade ruined and their West Indian Concerns in the Utmost Distress. Almost all their West India Planters have left in the Kingdom in Despair.²

Their Scavengers of the Streets of Germany have been able to rake together, but a little Filth.

Where How is going No Astrologer can determine. He has left the Capes of Delaware and where he is gone no one can tell.—We expect to hear from him at the North River, or at Rhode Island, but cant tell when.

I, for my Part am very homesick, but I will not leave the Field untill the Campaign is ended—unless I should fall sick. This horrid Hot Weather melts my Marrow within my Bones, and makes me faint away almost. I have no other Way to keep alive, but by Abstinence from Eating and drinking. I should not live a Month if I did not starve myself. When I come home I shall be an Epicure.

Tell Tom, I would give a Guinea to have him climb upon my shoulder, and another to chase him into his Jail.—My Love to all the rest. I will write them as soon as I can. I wrote Mr. Thaxter inclosing Letters to the Court and Bar. Has he received them?[3]

RC (Adams Papers).

[1] These important measures, in which JA was very much concerned, were the nub of the "Business [which] thickens, and presses" alluded to in the preceding letter. On 30 July and 1 Aug. respectively, Congress had ordered St. Clair and Schuyler back to Washington's headquarters, and on the latter day JA and four others were appointed a committee "to digest and report the mode of conducting the enquiry [voted 29 July] into the reasons of the evacuation of Ticonderoga and Fort Independence, and into the conduct of the officers who were in the northern department at the time of the evacuation" (*JCC*, 8:585, 590, 596). The subject was a difficult one, Congress was sharply divided on it, and much of Congress' as well as JA's time in the following weeks was given to it. The only visible progress made was a vote on 27 Aug. to conduct a much more elaborate inquiry, and on the 28th Henry Laurens, R. H. Lee, and JA were named the members of a committee to do so.

See same, p. 653, 659, 668–669, 681–687, 688. The investigation and its sequels lasted until long after JA had left Congress; see Burnett's valuable notes in *Letters of Members*, 2:458, 469.

On 2 Aug. JA had also been appointed, with four others, "to take into consideration the state of the northern department," to "confer with General Washington," and to "report as soon as possible." Losing no time, this committee next day recommended, and Congress resolved, that Washington be requested to appoint Schuyler's successor. But Washington declined, and on the 4th Congress elected Maj. Gen. Horatio Gates to command the northern army. See *JCC*, 8:599, 600, 603–604; also JA to AA, 7 Aug., below.

[2] Thus in MS. Probably JA meant: "have left the Kingdom in Despair."

[3] These letters were received and they accomplished their purpose, but they have not been found; see Thaxter to JA, 4 June, above, and note 3 there.

Abigail Adams to John Adams

August 5. [*1777*]

If allarming half a dozen places at the same time is an act of Generalship *How* may boast of his late conduct. We have never since the Evacuation of Boston been under apprehensions of an invasion from them eaquel to what we sufferd last week. All Boston was in confusion, packing up and carting out of Town, Household furniture, military stores, goods &c. Not less than a thousand Teams were imployd a fryday and saturday—and to their shame be it told, not a small trunk would they carry under 8 dollors and many of them I am told askd a hundred dollors a load, for carting a Hogshead of Molasses 8 miles 30 dollors.—O! Humane Nature, or rather O! inhumane nature what art thou? The report of the Fleets being seen of[f] of Cape Ann a fryday Night, gave me the allarm, and tho pretty weak, I set about packing up my things and a saturday removed a load.

When I looked around me and beheld the bounties of Heaven so liberally bestowed in fine Feilds of corn, grass, flax and english grain, and thought it might soon become a prey to these merciless ravagers, our habitations laid waste, and if our flight preserved our lives, we must return to barren Feilds, empty barns and desolated habitations if any we found, perhaps no[1] where to lay our Heads, my Heart was too full to bear the weight of affliction which I thought just ready to overtake us, and my body too weak almost to bear the shock unsupported by my better Half.

But thanks be to Heaven we are at present releaved from our Fears, respecting ourselves. I now feel anxious for your safety but hope prudence will direct to a proper care and attention to yourselves.

May this second attempt of Hows prove his utter ruin. May destruction overtake him as a whirlwind.

We have a report of an engagement at the Northward in which our troops behaved well, drove the Enemy into their lines, killd and took 300 & 50 prisoners. The account came in last Night. I have not perticuliars.[2]—We are under apprehensions that the Hancock is taken.[3]

Your obligeing Letters of the 8th, 10th and 13th came to hand last week. I hope before this time you are releaved from the anxiety you express for your Bosom Friend. I feel my sufferings amply rewarded in the tenderness you express for me, but in one of your Letters you have drawn a picture which drew a flood of tears from my Eyes, and rung my Heart with anguish inexpressible. I pray Heaven I may not live to realize it.[4]

Tis almost 14[5] years since we were united, but not more than half that time have we had the happiness of living together.

The unfealing world may consider it in what light they please, I consider it as a sacrifice to my Country and one of my greatest misfortunes [for my husband][6] to be seperated from my children at a time of life when the joint instructions and admonition of parents sink deeper than in maturer years.

The Hopes of the smiles and approbation of my Friend sweetens all my toil and Labours—

> Ye pow'rs whom Men, and birds obey,
> Great rulers of your creatures, say
> Why mourning comes, by bliss convey'd

And ev'n the Sweets of Love allay'd?
Where grows enjoyment, tall and fair,
Around it twines entangling care
While fear for what our Souls possess
Enervates ev'ry powe'r to Bless.
Yet Friendship forms the Bliss above
And life! what art thou without love?

RC (Adams Papers); endorsed: "Portia"; docketed in an unidentified hand.

¹ MS: "not."
² It was a groundless account.
³ The *Hancock* frigate, Capt. John Manley, was captured after a stiff fight on 8 July by H.M.S. *Rainbow* and carried into Halifax.
⁴ See the last paragraph of JA's letter to AA of 8 July, above.
⁵ Actually thirteen.
⁶ Three words editorially supplied for sense.

John Adams to Abigail Adams

Philadelphia Aug. 6. 1777 Wednesday

Price current.—Oak Wood £4:15s:od. Pr. Cord. Bad Beer; not so good as your Small Beer, 15d: Pr. Quart. Butter one Dollar Pr. Pound. Beef 2s:6d. Coffee a dollar a Pound. Bohea 8 dollars. Souchong £4: 10s. Hyson £6. Mean brown sugar 6s. 6d. a pound. Loaf sugar 18s. a pound. Rum 45s. a Gallon. Wine 2 dollars a Bottle.¹

The Hounds are all still at a Fault. Where the game is gone, is the Question. The Scent is quite lost.

Sullivan Thinks the Fleet is gone to Portsmouth—Green to Newport—Parsons, up the North River—Mifflin to Philadelphia. Thus each one secures his Reputation among his Townsmen for Penetration and Foresight, in Case the Enemy should go against his Town.

Some Conjecture Charlestown S.C.—others, Georgia—others Cheasapeak Bay.

For my Part, I have formed an Opinion, in which I am as clear and positive as ever I was in my Life. I think I can adduce Arguments enough to convince any impartial, cool Mind, that I am in the Right.

My Opinion is, that four Months Time will discover where the Fleet is gone—perhaps less Time than that.

Some begin to be whimsical, and guess them gone to the West Indies. But this is impossible. Some surmise Hallifax—some old England. But these are too flattering Conjectures.

RC (Adams Papers).

¹ Here, for some reason, JA left a blank space of over half a page and continued his letter on a new page of his folded sheet.

John Adams to Abigail Adams

My dearest   Philadelphia Aug. 7. 1777 Thursday
We have not yet the least Intimation of Howes Design. He is wasting away the Time. Let him aim at what Object he will, he will have scarcely Time to secure that, and will have none left to pursue his Advantage, if he gains any.

Burgoine I hope will be checked, and driven back. I hope the New Englandmen will now exert themselves, for it has cost Us, severe Conflicts, to get Affairs in that Department, in the Order they are. Gates cost Us a great deal of Pains.

RC (Adams Papers).

John Adams to Abigail Adams

Philadelphia August 8. 1777

I have concluded to run the Risque of sending Turner Home. It will save me the Expence of his Board and Horse.

The Moment he arrives, I hope you will send his Horse to Boston to be sold at Vendue. If he rides the Horse let him be sold immediately. If he rides the Mare, you may keep her if you chuse to do so and sell the old Horse, provided the Mare will go in a Carriage which must be tried, because I dont know that she ever was in one.

We have heard nothing from the Enemys Fleet, since they left the Capes of Delaware. They may intend for Philadelphia yet, which makes me a little irresolute about sending away my Man and Horse without which I should be puzzled to get away from this Place, if it should be invaded. I believe I shall delay his Journey for a few days. Perhaps We shall hear more within that Time.

This day compleats Seven Months, since I left all that I delight in. When shall I return? Not untill the Year is out, provided I can keep myself tolerably well.

Our Accounts from the Northward are still gloomy. Gates is gone, and I hope will restore some degree of Spirits and Confidence there. Burgoigne is laying himself open to destruction, in that Quarter, every day. It is strange that no Check is given him.

These vile Panicks, that seize People and Soldiers too, are very difficult to get over.—But at last they turn to Vigour, Fury and Desperation, as they did in the Jerseys. I suppose a few Tories in New York, in the Grants [1] and in Berkshire and Hampshire will join Burgoigne, but they will soon repent their rash Folly, and be sick of their Masters. For indeed they will find that neither Burgoigne nor Howe, nor their Master are kind Masters.

The longer We live, the more clearly We see, that nothing will serve our Purpose, but discipline and Experience. Discipline—Discipline, is wanting and must be introduced. The Affair of Ti. will introduce it. The Public calls for Justice, and will have it. This Demand does Honour to the People and is a sure Omen of future Success and Prosperity.

RC (Adams Papers).

[1] The New Hampshire Grants, territory which was long disputed between New Hampshire and New York and which subsequently became Vermont (*DAH*).

John Adams to Abigail Adams

P[hiladelphia] Aug. 11. 1777 [1]

I have paid Turner, his Wages up to this day, and settled all Accounts with him. Besides which I have given him £3:2s:od. L.M. towards his Expences home.[2] When he arrives he is to produce his Account to you, of the Expences of his Journey. See that he produces Receipts from the Tavern Keepers. Dont pay a Farthing, but what he produces a Receipt for.

I am glad he is going, for between you and me he is a very stupid, and a very intemperate Fellow, very fit for a Companion of the Man who recommended him. Yet He is honest. I never saw any Thing knavish in him. He has had a fine Opportunity weaving Stockings to the Tune of 2 dollars a Day—besides, receiving Wages and Board from me. If he has drank it all, it is his own fault.[3]

At the End of the Year, when you send Horses for me again, send some other Man. I will not have him. A low lived Fellow, playing Cards with Negroes, and behaving like a Rival with them for Wenches.

I intend to write you, to perswade your Father or my Brother to purchase me, too [4] other Horses. These I will sell.

I am &c.

RC (Adams Papers); addressed: "Mrs. Adams Braintree Mass: Bay favd. by Mr. John Turner."

[1] JA wrote three letters to AA this day; since there is nothing to indicate the order in which he wrote them, they are printed in merely plausible order.

² See entries in JA's Accounts with Massachusetts, Jan.–Sept. 1777 (*Diary and Autobiography*, 2:255).

³ It is not known who recommended Turner to JA. But evidently Turner per-sisted in one of his bad habits, for in 1796 JA compared his drunken farm hand Billings with "Turner the Stocking Weaver" (same, 3:230).

⁴ Thus in MS.

John Adams to Abigail Adams

Aug. 11. 1777

Your kind Favour of July 30. and 31. was handed me, just now from the Post office.

I have regularly received a Letter from you every Week excepting one, for a long Time past, and as regularly send a Line to you inclosing Papers.—My Letters are scarcely worth sending. Indeed I dont choose to indulge much Speculation, lest a Letter should miscarry, and free Sentiments upon public Affairs intercepted, from me, might do much hurt.

Where the Scourge of God, and the Plague of Mankind is gone, no one can guess. An Express from Sinnepuxent, a Place between the Capes of Delaware and the Capes of Cheasapeak, informs that a fleet of 100 sail was seen off that Place last Thursday.[1] But whether this is Fishermens News like that from Cape Ann, I know not.

The Time spends and the Campaign wears away and Howe makes no great Figure yet.—How many Men and Horses will he cripple by this strange Coasting Vo[y]age of 5 Weeks.

We have given N. Englandmen what they will think a compleat Tryumph in the Removal of Generals from the Northward and sending Gates there. I hope every Part of New England will now exert itself, to its Utmost Efforts. Never was a more glorious Opportunity than Burgoine has given Us of destroying him, by marching down so far towards Albany. Let New England turn out and cutt off his Retreat.

Pray continue to write me every Week. You have made me merry with the female Frolic, with the Miser. But I hope the Females will leave off their Attachment to Coffee. I assure you, the best Families in this Place have left off in a great Measure the Use of West India Goods. We must bring ourselves to live upon the Produce of our own Country. What would I give for some of your Cyder?

Milk has become the Breakfast of many of the wealthiest and genteelest Families here.

Fenno² put me into a Kind of Frenzy to go home, by the Description he gave me last night of the Fertility of the Season, the Plenty of

Fish, &c. &c. &c. in Boston and about it.—I am condemned to this Place a miserable Exile from every Thing that is agreable to me. God will my Banishment shall not last long.

RC (Adams Papers).

[1] That is, on the 7th. Sinepuxent, an Indian name spelled in many ways, was formerly applied to a bay and inlet on the Atlantic coast of Maryland in the present Ocean City area.

[2] Perhaps John Fenno (1751–1798), the Boston writing master who in 1789 founded the *Gazette of the United States* in New York City (*DAB*); but this is a very tentative identification.

John Adams to Abigail Adams

My dearest Friend   Phila. Aug. 11. 1777

I think I have sometimes observed to you in Conversation, that upon examining the Biography of illustrious Men, you will generally find some Female about them in the Relation of Mother or Wife or Sister, to whose Instigation, a great Part of their Merit is to be ascribed.

You will find a curious Example of this, in the Case of Aspasia, the Wife of Pericles. She was a Woman of the greatest Beauty and the first Genius. She taught him, it is said, his refined Maxims of Policy, his lofty imperial Eloquence; nay, even composed the Speeches, on which so great a Share of his Reputation was founded. The best Men in Athens frequented her House, and brought their Wives to receive Lessons from her of Œconomy and right Deportment. Socrates himself was her Pupil in Eloquence and gives her the Honour of that funeral oration which he delivers in the Menexenus of Plato. Aristophanes indeed abuses this famous Lady but Socrates does her Honour.

I wish some of our great Men had such Wives. By the Account in your last Letter, it seems the Women in Boston begin to think themselves able to serve their Country. What a Pity it is that our Generals in the Northern District had not Aspasias to their Wives!

I believe, the two Howes have not very great Women for Wives. If they had We should suffer more from their Exertions than We do. This is our good Fortune. A Woman of good Sense would not let her Husband spend five Weeks at Sea, in such a season of the Year. A smart Wife would have put Howe in Possession of Philadelphia, a long Time ago.

RC (Adams Papers).

John Adams to John Quincy Adams

My dear Son   Philadelphia August 11. 1777

As the War in which your Country is engaged will probably hereafter attract your Attention, more than it does at this Time, and as
the future Circumstances of your Country, may require other Wars,
as well as Councils and Negotiations, similar to those which are now
in Agitation, I wish to turn your Thoughts early to such Studies, as
will afford you the most solid Instruction and Improvement for the
Part which may be allotted you to act on the Stage of Life.

There is no History, perhaps, better adapted to this usefull Purpose
than that of Thucidides, an Author, of whom I hope you will make
yourself perfect Master, in original Language, which is Greek, the
most perfect of all human Languages. In order to understand him
fully in his own Tongue, you must however take Advantage, of every
Help you can procure and particularly of Translations of him into
your own Mother Tongue.

You will find in your Fathers Library, the Works of Mr. Hobbes,
in which among a great deal of mischievous Philosophy, you will find
a learned and exact Translation of Thucidides, which will be usefull
to you.

But there is another Translation of him, much more elegant, intituled "The History of the Peloponnesian War, translated from the
Greek of Thucidides in two Volumes Quarto, by William Smith A.M.
Rector of the Parish of the holy Trinity in Chester, and Chaplain to
the Right Honourable the Earl of Derby."

If you preserve this Letter, it may hereafter remind you, to procure
the Book.

You will find it full of Instruction to the Orator, the Statesman,
the General, as well as to the Historian and the Philosopher.[1] You may
find Something of the Peloponnesian War, in Rollin.

I am with much Affection your Father,   John Adams

RC (Adams Papers); docketed twice in JQA's mature hand: "J. Adams. 11.
Augt: 1777," and "Mr: Adams. Augt: 11. 1777."

[1] Among JA's books in MB are two
editions of Thucydides' *History of the
Peloponnesian War*, with Greek and
Latin texts in parallel columns, one of
them published at Frankfort, 1594,
bearing JQA's signature, and the other
at Amsterdam, 1731 (*Catalogue of
JA's Library*). At the Stone Library in
Quincy (MQA) there are no fewer than
six other editions in various languages,
including William Smith's translation, 2
vols., London, 1781, and Thomas
Hobbes' translation, 2 vols., London,
1812. JA's edition of *The Moral and*

Political Works of Thomas Hobbes of
Malmesbury, London, 1750 (also in
MB), contains Hobbes' discourse preliminary to his translation of Thucydides, but not the translation itself.

Abigail Adams to John Adams

August 12. [1777]

A few lines by way of remembrance every week tho I have nothing
new to write you if I may judge you by myself are very acceptable.
I long for a wedensday which to me is the happiest day of the week.
I never fail of a pacquet, tis soon read, and then the next wedensday
is thought of with the same Solisitude—

"Man never is but always to be blest."

The last post brought me yours of july 16, 18 and 20th.

You have often of late mentiond a daughter with much tenderness
and affection, but before this time you must know of our Bereavement.
I felt it last Sunday with all its poignancy. It was the first time of my
going out. Your Brother held up a daughter and call'd it by the Name
of Susana.[1] I wishd to have call'd ours had it lived after my own dear
Mother, and was much gratified by your mentioning it and requesting
it. But tis now of no importance either the Name or the Relation.
Do you feel in your own Breast any Sentiments of tenderness for one
you never knew, for one who could scarcly be said ever to have had an
existance? The loss occasions very different Sensation[s] from those
I once before experienced, but still I found I had a tenderness and an
affection greater than I immagined could have possess'd my Heart for
one who was not endeard to me by its smiles and its graces. But the
Parent is dear to me, dear to me beyond the power of words to discribe.
I always feel a perticuliar regard for the young fellow who has attended
upon him in the capacity of a servant. Nay even the sight of a Garment
⟨worn⟩ belonging to him will raise a mixture both of pleasure and
pain in my Bosome.

Can it then be strange that I should feel a fondness and a tender
affection for a pledg of unabated Love, a Love pure as the Gold without alloy—

"I Glory in the sacred ties
Which Modern Wits and fools dispise
Of Husband and of Wife."

August 13

I have seen an advertisement in your papers of some Select Essays upon Husbandry containing the manner of whitening and Bleaching cloth, raising flax and hemp &c. If you think the Book worth purchaseing should be obliged to you for it.[2] We must study to make the most of our Husbandery or we must starve. 3 dollors will not purchase what one would (of any article that can be mentiond) two months ago.

I believe we are no way behind hand in prices with any of the other States.

You wish yourself at Home to study agriculture with your Brother Farmer. Tis a wish I most heartily join in, but he is a great practisser I assure you. He has cut the chief of his Hay this summer and made the whole of it with his own hands, and he has several tons too. He has New Built his barn which he has done much of himself. His whole Heart is engaged in Farming. You never took more pleasure in your meddows and Feilds in their greatest perfection.

Hardwick begs me to apply to you to purchase him some needles as he is now obliged to stand still for want of them, will send the money for them if you think it may be conveyd with safety. If you would send along only one hundred in a Letter to me he would be greatly obliged, he has wrote to Turner the Numbers.

We wish to know where the Enemy are and what they are about, but it seems to me your inteligance is very uncertain and in general bad. General ⟨Skliler Skiler⟩ Schuyler has calld upon us for 2000 militia. We seem to be already striped of so many Hands as scarcly to leave enough to perform our Farming. They make strange work in this Town in procuring their Men as usual, it always was a croocked place.

I hear nothing new—nothing worth writing you.

Enclosed is a Letter your Brother desires you would take care of.

Adieu most sincerely yours,   Portia

RC (Adams Papers); endorsed: "Ans. Aug. 25"; docketed in an unidentified hand. Enclosed letter from Peter Boylston Adams, or concerning his affairs, not found.

[1] This was Peter Boylston and Mary (Crosby) Adams' second daughter named Susanna, born on or just before 10 Aug., their first Susanna having lived less than a year (1775–1776). The second Susanna became Mrs. Darius Boardman in 1803 and died in 1816. See Adams Genealogy.

[2] This work, a compilation from a number of sources, was advertised in the Philadelphia papers during June and July as just published and for sale by Robert Hill. For its full title see Evans 15597.

John Adams to Abigail Adams

My dearest Friend   Phila. Aug. 13. 1777

We have been sweltering here, for a great Number of days together, under the scalding Wrath of the Dog Star. So severe a Spell
of Heat has scarcely been known these twenty Years. The Air of the
City has been like the fierce Breath of an hot oven. Every Body has
been running to the Pumps all day long. There has been no finding
a Place of Comfort—the shade, and the very Entrys of Houses where
they have the best Draughts of Air, have been scarcely tolerable. This
season always affects me, deeply. It exhausts my Spirits, and takes
away all my Strength of Mind and Body. I have never lived here in
Dog days, without becoming so enfeebled, and irritated, as to be unable to sleep soundly and regularly and to be still more reduced by
Night Sweats. If I can avoid these Inconveniences, this year, I shall
be happy. But I have experienced something of it, already, altho not
in any great Degree.

When the Weather is so extream, the Fatigue of even holding a
Pen to write a Letter, is distressing.

We have no News from the Fleet since last Thursday when about
200 of them were seen off of Synepuxent.

What will our People do with Burgoigne? He has put himself in
the Power of the People in that Quarter, and if they do not make him
repent his Folly, they will be to blame. It is a Shame that such an
handfull should ravage in a Country so populous.

You will see by the Papers that Manly is taken.—What a Disappointment to Us!—Yet We might have expected it. What rational
Creatures could order two thirty Gun Frigates to cruise on the American Coast, for the Protection of Trade. They should have been ordered
to some other Seas—to France, to Spaign, to the Baltic, the Mediterranean—any where but where they were.

The Ship and Men are a Loss, but We must build more.

RC (Adams Papers).

Isaac Smith Sr. to John Adams

Mr. Adams   Boston August the 13th. 77

I wrote you the post before last to which refer you.[1] In your last[2]
you mention the prize [price] of Salt, which am very sorry to see was
so high. I had a little parcel lately which I retaild Out att 12/ a single

bushel, and sold a Gentleman from the Jerseys who are deprived from geting that Article and to compasionate there case let him have itt att 10/ tho was offerd 20/ for itt, but as he wanted a considerable quantity more his southward friends who had salt here in a prize sold him theres att 30/ which was sorry itt should get to.—You Ask why the Merchants cant get in those Articles now as when the Elicet trade was carried On and M[en of] W[ar] &c. were here. The case is very differant for more than half the Vessells that have been fited Out this Winter have been taken and we have had Three ships for Near Two Months past Cruseing in the bay and come up so near the Lighthouse as that the Flagg att the Castle has been hoisted for them, and the many Captures in the West Indies has risen Insurance near double. Inded there is hardly geting any done att any rate, and itts very dificult to get hands to go, to give 50 P[er] C[ent] Insurance you must pay as much as your Vessell and Cargo is worth to cover your Interest but to give 75 PC still Inhances the Value which is to be laid with all Other Charges On the bare Cargo, and there is Nothing of any Value of the produce of this Province that can be bought to send but that itt must sink 100 PC and we have no Other way to get any Cargo that will any ways Answer than by sending to the southward which makes the Insurance the Vo[yage] round very great.—I have several Vessells tho small I purpose sending that way when itt comes a little later in the season but am put to dificulty of geting money to the southward, without being att the Charge of sending on purpose. I want to get about 8. or 10.000 Dls. lodged that way. I have talkt with Mr. Hewes and find itt very dificult to have any Exchange of money that way.—Mr. Hewes is gone to Piscataque. I have Askt him Once or twice to dine with me, but has been engaged. When he returns I expect he will.

A Commite of Ours and the Other States have met to Consider of what method to take in order to Establish the Currency or rather to prevent itts further deprecasion.[3] I wish some method could be found Out but itt Appears to be a thing that is very dificult.—I was Agoing to give you my sentiments sometime Ago when I heard you had Orderd several large ships to be built, but, as you was the best judges of the Motives of your doing itt, Omited itt as itt could not have any Other merit than a private sentiment. The money to be made to carry on and Compleat these Ships must be immence. I reckon itt will require a Wagon load to be sent Once a Month and such a sum to be made which is the Means of the depresasion, and not to have any benifit Ariseing from itt Appears to me they had never been thought off for I will Venture to say they wont get to see [sea] unless we can make Men this six Years, and to have the Frigates that are building got to see likewise. Frigates I Apprehend would be more servisable, Altho we have lost One, not to exceed 36 or 40 Gun ships, under proper regulations.

I am Sr. Your hum. servant,   Isaac Smith

PS I dont mean by any thing I have said to be Only my private sentiments to you.[4]

RC (Adams Papers); endorsed: "Mr. Smith."

[1] Smith to JA, 28–31 July, above.
[2] Not found.
[3] This convention of delegates from four New England states and New York was held at Springfield, Mass., on 30 July – 6 Aug.; its proceedings are printed in *The Public Records of the State of*

Connecticut, Hartford, 1894–1953, 1: 599–606.
[4] Smith probably meant just the opposite of what he wrote: he wished his views as here expressed to be considered as *no other than* "private sentiments."

Mercy Otis Warren to Abigail Adams

[Plymouth, ante 14 August 1777][1]

Most sincerely do I Congratulate My Friend on her Restoration to Health after pain, peril and Disappointment. May she Long be spared [to] her Family and Friends, And be happy in Domestic Life, Though the political sky Looks Dark and Lowry and the Convulsions of War! shake the Lower Creation.

You ask My opinion with Regard to affairs in the North. All I Can say is I am Mortifyed and Chagrind at the surrender of Ti, but suspend my Resentment till Those who have a better Right than myself have scrutinized, judged and Condemned.

I have not Yet been able to purchase any Coffe. Shall Remember you when I do. My son has had no Returns from France. I begin to fear the Vessels on which he Ventured have fallen into the hands of the Enemy.

I think you desired me to Let you know if I met with any thing suitable for Childrens wear. I have 2 peaces of Blue and White striped French Cottons the one 5 quarters the other, 6 in Width. Very Good and very pretty for boys or Girls, but the price is somewhat Modernized, though not to the Extent of the Fashion, only 20/ £[2] per yard. If you Incline to have any of it Let me know and I will keep it till I have an opportunity to send it. What is become of the sagathe[3]

&c. I only inquire Least you may have sent it forward by some hand that has Neglected to Deliver it to your Friend unfeignedly,

M Warren

I wish you would let your Neghbour the stoken Weaver know I Could not send him the Cotton but intend to send him some Worsted Work as soon as I can Get it spun.

Do Give me the Inteligence from Mr. Lees Letter.[4] Mr. Lothrop has forgot Every Word.

If you are in want of a Little Nice Black Russel[5] for shew, Let your Friend know it.

RC (Adams Papers); addressed: "Mrs. Adams Braintree"; at head of text in CFA's hand: "July 1777."

[1] It is clear from several allusions in this letter that it is a reply to one from AA that has not been found; and it is equally clear that AA's letter to Mrs. Warren, dated 14–16 Aug., following, is a reply in turn to the present letter—in all likelihood a prompt reply.

[2] Thus in MS.

[3] Sagathy, variously spelled, was a woolen fabric somewhat like serge (*OED*).

[4] A copy of a letter from Arthur Lee sent on earlier by JA to AA; perhaps Lee's letter of 18 March, mentioned by JA in his letter of 1–2 July, q.v. above.

[5] Russel, variously spelled, was also a woolen fabric, "formerly used for articles of attire, esp. in the 16th century" (*OED*). But Mrs. Warren may mean the apparently more elegant "Russell cord . . . a ribbed or corded fabric, usually made with a cotton warp and woollen weft" (same). See AA's answer, following.

Abigail Adams to Mercy Otis Warren

August 14. 1777. Braintree

This is the memorable fourteenth of August. This day 12 years the Stamp office was distroyd.[1] Since that time what have we endured? What have we suffer'd? Many very many memorable Events which ought to be handed down to posterity will be buried in oblivion merely for want of a proper Hand to record them, whilst upon the opposite side many venal pens will be imployd to misrepresent facts and to render all our actions odious in the Eyes of future Generations. I have always been sorry that a certain person who once put their Hand to the pen, should be discouraged, and give up so important a service. Many things would have been recorded by the penetrateing Genious of that person which thro the multiplicity of Events and the avocations of the times will wholly escape the notice of any future Historian.

The History and the Events of the present day must fill every Humane Breast with Horrour. Every week produces some Horrid Scene perpetrated by our Barbarous foes, not content with a uniform Series of cruelties practised by their own Hands, but they must let loose the infernal Savages "those dogs of War" and cry Havock to them. Cruelty, impiety and an utter oblivion of the natural Sentiments of probity and Honour with the voilation of all Laws Humane and Divine rise at one veiw and characterise a George, a How and a Burgoine.

O my dear Friend when I bring Home to my own Dwelling these tragical Scenes which are every week presented in the publick papers to us, and only in Idea realize them, my whole Soul is distress'd. Were I a man I must be in the Feild. I could not live to endure the Thought of my Habitation desolated, my children Butcherd, and I an inactive Spectator.

August 15

I enclose to you a Coppy of Mr. Lees Letter. It came to me with some restrictions to be shewn only to those whom I could confide in. I think by that our affairs abroad look'd as favorable as we could expect, but we have a great many hardships to endure yet I fear e'er we shall receive any assistance from others.

Letters from my Friend to the 20 of july mention the loss of Ticondoroga with much regreat, but says tis an Event which he has feard would take place for some time. People that way were much disposed to censure, but that they had not received any perticuliar accounts by which a true judgment could be formd.

August 16

We are bless'd my Friend with a fine Season. I hope the charming rains this afternoon have reachd Plimouth and refreshd the Feilds of Eal [Eel] river.

You mention some French cotton. I am much obliged to you but I have since I saw you been accommodated in that way. The Russel I should be very glad of either one or two yards just as you can spair it, and Shooe binding, if it is to be had. Garlick thread I am in great want of, if you should know of any be so good as to let me know.[2]

I am really asshamed to tell my Friend that I have not yet been able to get Home the cloth. All that was in my power to do to it, has been done 3 months ago and I have been sending and going almost every week since. I saw the Man yesterday and he has promised me that I shall have it next week, but if his word prove no better than it has done I cannot say you may depend upon it. All I can say is that my endeavours have not been wanting. As soon as I can get it it shall be forwarded by your affectionate Friend,   Portia

RC (MHi:Warren-Adams Coll.); docketed in two later unidentified hands: "Mrs. Adams Augt. 1777 No. 9." Enclosed copy of a letter from Arthur Lee not found, but see note 4 on preceding letter.

¹ See JA's entry of 15 Aug. 1765 in his *Diary and Autobiography*, 1:259–261.
² The editors have not found a definition of "Garlick thread."

John Adams to Abigail Adams

Philadelphia August 14. 1777
My dearest Friend   Thursday

We are still parching under the fierce Heats of Dog days. It is agreed, by most People, that so long and so intense a Heat has scarcely been known. The Day before Yesterday, Dr. Ewing an eminent Philosopher as well as Mathematician, and Divine told me, the Spirit in his Glass, was at 91 in his cool Room, and from thence he concludes that it was above an hundred abroad in the Shade, because he says it is generally ten degrees lower, in his cool Room, than it is in the Shade out of Doors. Yesterday, it was at 94, abroad in the Shade. He placed his Thermometer, against a Post which had been heated by the Sun, and the Spirit arose to an 100, but removing it to another Place, and suspending it at a distance from any warm Object and the Spirit subsided and settled at 94.—How we shall live through these Heats I dont know.

If Howes Army is at Sea, his Men between Decks will suffer, beyond Expression. Persons, here, who have been at Sea, upon this Coast, at this Season of the Year, say, the Heat is more intollerable, on Shipboard than on Land. There is no Comfort to be had any where, and the Reflection of the Sun Rays from the Deck, are insufferable.

I wish this Wiseacre may continue to coast about untill an equinoctial Storm shall overtake him. Such a Thing would make fine Sport for his Fleet.

The Summer is consuming, and there is not Time enough left, for accomplishing many Things. If he should land tomorrow, it would take him three Weeks to reach Philadelphia. On the Jersey Side of the Delaware, is an ugly Road for him—many Rivers, Bridges, Causeys, Morasses, by breaking up of which, a Measure which is intended, and for which Preparations are made, his Army might be obstructed, puzzled and confounded in their March. His Army cannot proceed without many Horses, Waggons, and Cannon with their Carriages, for the Passage of which he must make new Bridges and Causeys, which would consume much Time, besides that he would be exposed, to the Militia and to the regular Army. On the other side the River there are several Streams and one large River to cross—the Schuylkill. And We have many fine Fire ships to annoy his Fleet. It would be happy for Us if he should aim at this Place, Because it would give Us an Opportunity of exerting the whole Force of the Continent against him. The Militia of the Jerseys, Pensilvania, Delaware and Maryland, would cooperate with Washington here—those of N.Y. and N. England with Gates.

Writing this Letter, at Six o Clock in the Morning in my cool Chamber has thrown me into a profuse and universal sweat.

RC (Adams Papers).

John Adams to Abigail Adams

My dearest Friend   Philadelphia Aug. 15. 1777

The Weather continues, as hot as ever. Upon my Word I dont know how to sustain it. Oh for a Bowl of your Punch, a Bottle of your Cyder, or something or other that is acid. I am obliged to have recourse to the Liquor of the Roman soldiers and put about a Wine Glass of Vinegar into a Pint of Water. You would laugh to see me pouring down a Pint of this Vinegar and Water at a Time, and admiring it as a great Refreshment.[1]

Nothing yet of Howes Army. It begins to be suspected that they are out at Pasture on Long Island. No further Account of the Fleet as yet. No further Account from the northern Army. If the Militia dont turn out now, and drive Burgoigne to his own Place, they deserve to suffer.

Half after 9 at Night.—The Wind blows, the Clowds gather, the lightnings Play and the Thunder rolls. You can have no adequate Idea of the Joy occasioned here by such a Scæne. They call it a Gust. Dr. Franklin in his Letters on Electricity has explained the Philosophy of it.[2] After a Continuance of Heat it seldom fails to occasion a Change of Weather. It is followed by a cooler and purer Air.

The hot Weather has now continued in an extreme for two Weeks together. The People here generally agree that an Heat so intense in Degree and of so long Continuance, has scarcely ever been known. Cold Water has kill'd Numbers.

But now it rains a Torrent and thunders and lightens most delightfully. It will clean our streets, it will purge our Air. It will be cool, and comfortable after this Gust.

Half after 10.—It is now a constant, plentifull Rain and the World is all of a Blaze with Lightning, and the grand Rolls of Thunder shake the very Chamber where I am. The Windows jarr, the shutters Clatter, and the floor trembles.

RC (Adams Papers).

[1] JA was following the advice of his friend Dr. Rush on the subject of drinks in hot weather. See Benjamin Rush, *Directions for Preserving the Health of Soldiers*, Lancaster, 1778, first published in a newspaper in April 1777 and reprinted in Rush's *Letters*, 1:140–147.
[2] See Franklin's letter to Dr. John Mitchell, 29 April 1749, published in Franklin's *Experiments and Observations on Electricity*, London, 1751, and subsequent editions, as "Observations and Suppositions towards forming a new Hypothesis for explaining the several Phaenomena of Thunder Gusts" (Franklin, *Papers*, ed. Labaree, 3:365–376).

John Adams to Abigail Adams

Philadelphia August 17. 1777
My dearest Friend   Sunday

Yesterday We had a cool Day, the Wind Easterly and cloudy, this Morning there is a brisk northeast Wind and cool Rain, which restores Us, to some Comfort. A Number of People died here with excessive Heat, besides others, who fell Sacrifices to their own Imprudence in drinking cold Water.

This Wind will oblige the Knight Errant and his Fleet, to go somewhere or other. We have had no Intelligence of it, since last Thursday week.

We have a Letter from G[eneral] Schuyler, in which he "is not insensible of the Indignity of being call'd away, when an Action must soon take Place." But I hope, the People will not resent this Indignity, so as not to turn out. G[eneral] Gates I hope, will be able to find Men, who will stand by him. Never was there a fairer opportunity, than now presents of ruining Burgoigne. By the same Letter, We have confused Hints, that an Attack has been made upon Fort Schuyler, and the Enemy repulsed.[1] The Letter seems to suppose, that he had written a fuller Account of it before.—But no such Account has reached Us.

The Enemy at Niagara and Detroit, are endeavouring to seduce the Indians, to take up the Hatchet, but as yet, with little success. They seem determined to maintain their Neutrality.

I read a Letter[2] last Evening directed to Mr. Serjeant, and in his Absence to me from Mr. Clark a Delegate from N. Jersey who is gone Home to Elizabeth Town for his Health, giving a particular Account of Howes Army, in their late precipitate Retreat from Westfield. They were seized with the Utmost Terror, and thrown into the Utmost Confusion. They were so weak and sickly, and had gorged themselves so with fresh Meat, that they fell down in the Roads, many died, and were half buried, &c. &c. &c.

We have many new Members of Congress, among whom are Mr. Vandyke of Delaware, Mr. Jones of Virginia, and Mr. Lawrence [Laurens] of S. Carolina. This last Gentleman is a great acquisition— of the first Rank in his State, Lt. Governor, of ample Fortune, of great Experience, having been 20 Years in their assembly, of a clear Head and a firm Temper, of extensive Knowledge, and much Travel. He has hitherto appeared as good a Member, as any We ever had in Congress. I wish that all the States would imitate this Example and send their best Men. Vandyke is a Lawyer, and a very worthy Man, his Abilities very good and his Intensions very sincere. Mr. Jones also is a Lawyer, but has so lately come in that We have seen as yet no Exhibitions of him.

RC (Adams Papers).

[1] Schuyler to Congress, Albany, 10 Aug., read in Congress on the 16th (*JCC,* 8:647). The original is in PCC, No. 153, III, and reported the action of 6 Aug. now known as the battle of Oriskany, in which the New York militia under Brig. Gen. Nicholas Herkimer inflicted heavy losses on a body of British, tories, and Indians under Sir John Johnson, near Fort Schuyler (formerly Fort Stanwix, on the site of present Rome, N.Y.).

[2] Not found.

John Adams to Abigail Adams

My best Friend   Aug. 19. 1777 Tuesday

Your obliging Favour of the 5th. came by Yesterdays Post, and I intended to have answered it by this Mornings Post, but was delayed by many Matters, untill he gave me the slip.

I am sorry that you and the People of Boston were put to so much Trouble, but glad to hear that such Numbers determined to fly. The Prices for Carting which were demanded, were detestable. I wish your Fatigue and Anxiety may not have injured your Health.

Dont be anxious, for my Safety. If Howe comes here I shall run away, I suppose with the rest. We are too brittle ware you know to stand the Dashing of Balls and Bombs. I wonder upon what Principle the Roman Senators refused to fly from the Gauls and determined to sit, with their Ivory Staves and hoary Beards in the Porticoes of their Houses untill the Enemy entered the City, and altho they confessed they resembled the Gods, put them to the Sword.

I should not choose to indulge this sort of Dignity, but I confess I feel myself so much injured by these barbarean Britains, that I have a strong Inclination to meet them in the Field. This is not Revenge I believe, but there is something sweet and delicious in the Contemplation of it. There is in our Hearts, an Indignation against Wrong, that is righteous and benevolent, and he who is destitute of it, is defective in the Ballance of his Affections and in his moral Character.

As long as there is a Conscience in our Breasts, a moral Sense which distinguishes between Right and Wrong, approving, esteeming, loving the former, and condemning and detesting the other, We must feel a Pleasure in the Punishment, of so eminent a Contemner of all that is Right and good and just, as Howe is. They are virtuous and pious Passions that prompt Us to desire his Destruction, and to lament and deplore his success and Prosperity.

The Desire of assisting towards his Disgrace, is an honest Wish.

It is too late in Life, my Constitution is too much debilitated by Speculation, and indeed it is too late a Period in the War, for me to think of girding on a sword: But if I had the last four Years to run over again, I certainly would.

RC (Adams Papers).

John Adams to Abigail Adams

Philadelphia August 19. 1777
My best Friend   Tuesday

The Weather still continues cloudy and cool and the Wind Easterly.

Howe's Fleet and Army is still incognito. The Gentlemen from South Carolina, begin to tremble for Charlestown.

If Howe is under a judicial Blindness, he may be gone there. But what will be the Fate of a scorbutic Army cooped up in a Fleet for Six, Seven or Eight Weeks in such intemperate Weather, as We have had.

What will be their Condition landing, on a burning shore abounding with Agues and Musquetos, in the most unwholesome Season of the whole Year?

If he should get Charlestown, or indeed the whole State, what Progress will this make towards the Conquest of America? He will stop the Trade of Rice and Indigo, but what then?—Besides he will get some ugly Knocks. They are honest, sincere and brave and will make his Life uncomfortable.

I feel a strong Affection for S. Carolina, for several Reasons. 1. I think them as stanch Patriots as any in America. 2. I think them as brave. 3. They are the only People in America, who have maintained a Post and defended a Fort. 4. They have sent Us a new Delegate, whom I greatly admire, Mr. Lawrence, their Lt. Governor, a Gentleman of great Fortune, great Abilities, Modesty and Integrity—and great Experience too. If all the States would send Us such Men, it would be a Pleasure to be here.

In the Northern Department they begin to fight. The Family of Johnson, the black part of it as well as the white, are pretty well thinned.[1] Rascals! they deserve Extermination. I presume Gates will be so supported that Burgoingne will be obliged to retreat. He will stop at Ticonderoga I suppose for they can maintain Posts, altho We cannot.

I think We shall never defend a Post, untill We shoot a General. After that We shall defend Posts, and this Event in my Opinion is not far off. No other Fort will ever be evacuated without an Enquiry, nor any Officer come off without a Court Martial. We must trifle no more. We have suffered too many Disgraces to pass unexpiated. Every Disgrace must be wiped off.

We have been several Days, hammering upon Money. We are contriving every Way We can, to redress the Evils We feel and fear, from too great a Quantity of Paper. Taxation, as deep as possible, is the only radical Cure. I hope you will pay every Tax that is brought you, if you sell my Books, or Cloaths, or oxen or your Cows to pay it.

RC (Adams Papers).

[1] William Johnson, halfbreed son of the late famous Sir William Johnson (1715–1774) of Johnson Hall on the Mohawk, had been reported killed in the battle of Oriskany (Arthur Pound, *Johnson of the Mohawks*, N.Y., 1930, p. 422).

John Adams to Abigail Adams

Philadelphia August 20th. 1777
My best Friend   Wednesday

This Day compleats three Years since I stepped into the Coach, at Mr. Cushings Door, in Boston, to go to Philadelphia in Quest of Adventures.—And Adventures I have found.

I feel an Inclination sometimes, to write the History of the last Three Years, in Imitation of Thucidides. There is a striking Resemblance, in several Particulars, between the Peloponnesian and the

American War. The real Motive to the former was a Jealousy of the growing Power of Athens, by Sea and Land. . . .[1] The genuine Motive to the latter, was a similar Jealousy of the growing Power of America. The true Causes which incite to War, are seldom professed, or Acknowledged.

We are now afloat upon a full Sea: When We shall arrive at a safe Harbour, no Mariner has Skill and experience enough to foretell. But, by the Favour of Heaven, We shall make a prosperous Voyage, after all the Storms, and Shoals are passed.

5. o Clock afternoon

It is now fair sunshine again and very warm. Not a Word, yet, from Hows Fleet. The most general Suspicion, now, is that it is gone to Charlestown S.C.—But it is a wild Supposition. It may be right however: for Howe is a wild General.

We have been hammering to day, upon a Mode of Tryal for the General Officers at Ti. Whether an Enquiry will preceed the Court Martial, and whether the Enquiry shall be made by a Committee of Congress or by a Council of General Officers, is not determined, but Enquiry and Tryal both I conjecture there will be.[2]

If How is gone to Charlestown, you will have a little Quiet, and enjoy your Corn and Rye and Flax and Hay, and other good Things, untill another Summer.

But What shall We do for Sugar, and Wine and Rum?—Why truly I believe We must leave them off. Loaf Sugar is only four Dollars a Pound here, and Brown only a Dollar, for the meanest sort, and Ten shillings for that a little better. Every Body here is leaving off loaf Sugar, and most are laying aside brown. As to Rum and Wine—give me Cyder and I would compound. N.E. Rum is but 40s. a Gallon. But, if Wine was Ten Dollars a Bottle, I would have one Glass a Day, in Water, while the hot weather continues, unless I could get Cyder.

RC (Adams Papers).

[1] Suspension points in MS.
[2] See JA to AA, 4 Aug., above, and note 1 there.

John Adams to Abigail Adams

Philadelphia August 21. 1777.

My best Friend   Thursday

This Morning, We have heard again from the Fleet. At 9 o Clock at Night, on the 14. Inst. upwards of an hundred Sail were seen, standing in between the Capes of Cheasapeak Bay. They had been seen from the Eastern shore of Virginia, standing off, and on, for two days before.—This Method of coasting along the shore, and standing off, and on, is very curious. First seen off Egg Harbour, then several Times off the Capes of Delaware, standing in and out, then off Sinepuxent, then off the Eastern shore of Virginia, then standing in to Cheasapeak Bay. How many Men, and Horses, will he loose in this Sea Ramble, in the Heat of Dog days. Whether he is going to Virginia to steal Tobacco, to N. Carolina to pilfer Pitch and Tar, or to South to plunder Rice and Indigo, who can tell? He will seduce a few Negroes from their Masters let him go to which he will. But is this conquering America?

From the Northward We learn that Arnold has marched with about 2000 Men to the Relief of Fort Schuyler.

Our People have given Sir John Johnson and his Regulars, Tories and Indians, a very fine Drubbing. The Indians scarcely ever had such a Mauling. The Devils are so frightened that they are all run away to howl and mourn.

The Papers, inclosed with this, will give you, more particular Information.—Can nothing be done at Rhode Island at this critical Time. —Opprobrium Novangliæ!

What is become of all the Massachusetts continental Troops. Every Regiment and every Man of them is at the Northward, under Gates— and yet We are told they have not 4000 Men fit for Duty Officers included. And there are 3 Regiments there from N. Hampshire too.

10 0 Clock at Night

Just come in from Congress. We have within this Hour, received Letters of G[enerals] Schuyler and Lincoln, giving an Account of the Battle of Bennington, wherein Gen. Starks has acquired great Glory, and so has his Militia. The Particulars are to be out in an Hand Bill, tomorrow Morning. I will inclose you one.[1]

RC (Adams Papers). Enclosed newspapers not found or identified; as to the "Hand Bill" JA said he would enclose, see note 1.

[1] The news of Brig. Gen. John Stark's defeat of Lt. Col. Friedrich Baum at Bennington, Vt., 16 Aug., reached Congress in a letter from Schuyler of the 18th enclosing one from Gen. Lincoln of the same date (JCC, 8:663). Though its Journal does not mention it, Congress ordered the pertinent documents published in a handbill and widely distributed: *Philadelphia, August 22, 1777. By an Express arrived last Evening from General Schuyler to Congress, we have the following important Intelligence* ... [Philadelphia:] John Dunlap (JCC, 9:1086; Evans 15686; see Committee of Intelligence to Washington, 2 Sept., Burnett, ed., *Letters of Members,* 2: 473). A copy of the broadside is in MHi, but none has been found in the Adams Papers.

Abigail Adams to John Adams

My dearest Friend   Boston August 22 1777

I came yesterday to this Town for a ride after my confinement, and to see my Friends. I have not been into it since I had the happiness of spending a week here with you. I am feeble and faint with the Heat of the weather, but otherways very well. I feel very anxious for your Health and almost fear to hear from you least I should hear you were sick; but hope your temperance and caution will preserve your Health. I hope, if you can get any way through these Hot months you will recruit. Tis very Healthy throughout Town and Country for the Season, the chin cough[1] prevails in Town among children but has not yet reachd the Country.

Your Letters of August 1, 3 and 4th came by last nights post, and I have to acknowledge the recept of yours of july 27, 28 and 30th[2] by last wedensdays post. I acknowledge my self greatly indebted to you for so frequently writing amidst all your other cares and attentions. I would fain believe that tis a releafe to you after the cares of the day, to converse with your Friend. I most sincerely wish your situation was such that the amusements your family could afford you, might have been intermixed with the weighty cares that oppress you.—

> "My Bosome is thy dearest home;
> I'd lull you there to rest."

As to *How* I wish we could know what he means that we might be able to gaurd against him. I hope however that he will not come this way, and I believe the Season is so far advanced, that he will not venture.

At the Northward our affairs look more favorable. We have been successfull in several of our late engagements. Heaven preserve our dear Countrymen who behave worthy of us and reward them both here and hereafter. Our Militia are chiefly raisd, and will I hope be marchd of immediately. There has been a most shamefull neglect some where. This continent has paid thousands to officers and Men who have been loitering about playing foot-Ball and nine pins, and doing their own private buisness whilst they ought to have been defending our forts and we are now suffering for the neglect.

The late call of Men from us will distress us in our Husbandry. I am a great sufferer as the High Bounty one hundred dollors, has tempted of my Negro Head,[3] and left me just in the midst of our Hay. The english and fresh indeed we have finishd, but the salt is just comeing on, and How to turn my self, or what to do I know not. His going away would not worry me so much if it was not for the rapid depretiation of our money. We can scarcly get a days work done for money and if money is paid tis at such a rate that tis almost imposible to live. I live as I never did before, but I am not agoing to complain. Heaven has blessd us with fine crops. I hope to have 200 hundred Bushels of corn and a hundred & 50 weight of flax. English Hay we have more than we had last year, notwithstanding your ground wants manure. We are like to have a plenty of sause.[4] I shall fat Beaf and pork enough, make butter and cheesse enough. If I have neither Sugar, molasses, coffe nor Tea I have no right to complain. I can live without any of them and if what I enjoy I can share with my partner and with Liberty, I can sing o be joyfull and sit down content—

> "Man wants but little here below
> Nor wants that little long."

As to cloathing I have heithertoo procured materials sufficent to cloath my children and servants which I have done wholy in Home Spun. I have contracted no debts that I have not discharg'd, and one of our Labourers Prince I have paid seven months wages to since you left me. Besides that I have paid Bracket near all we owed him which was to the amount of 15 pounds lawfull money, set up a cider press &c., besides procuring and repairing many other articles in the Husbandery way, which you know are constantly wanted. I should do exceeding well if we could but keep the money good, but at the rate we go on I know not what will become of us.

But I must bid you adieu or the post will go of without my Letter.— Dearest Friend, adieu. Words cannot convey to you the tenderness of my affection.   Portia

RC (Adams Papers); docketed in an unidentified hand: "Portia. Aug. 22."

[1] Whooping cough. See *Webster* under *chincough* and *kinkhost.* For other variants and a different etymology, apparently overlooked by lexicographers, see Robley Dunglison, *A Dictionary of Medical Science,* Phila., 1844, under *pertussis*: "*Chin-cough, Kin-cough, Kind-cough* (Germ. Kind, 'a child')."

[2] All of these letters except that of 27 July are above, but AA probably meant JA's to her of 26 July or just possibly his to JQA of the 27th, also above.

[3] Thus clearly in MS; perhaps a mistake for "Hand," possibly a personal name, or, more likely, her "head" laborer.

[4] That is, "garden sauce," meaning vegetables eaten with meat; see *Webster* under *sauce,* noun, 4.

John Adams to Abigail Adams

My best Friend   Philadelphia August 23 1777

It is now no longer a Secret, where Mr. Hows Fleet is. We have authentic Intelligence that it is arrived, at the Head of Cheasopeak Bay, above the River Petapsco upon which the Town of Baltimore stands.[1]

I wish I could describe to you the Geography of this Country, so as to give you an Adequate Idea of the Situation of the two great Bays of Cheasopeak and Delaware, because it would enable you to form a Conjecture, concerning the Object, he aims at.—The Distance across Land from the Heads of these Bays is but small, and forms an Istmus, below which is a large Peninsula comprehending the Counties of Accomack and Northampton in Virginia, the Counties of Somersett and Worcester in Maryland, and the Counties of Kent and Sussex on Delaware. His March by Land to Philadelphia, may be about sixty or seventy Miles.[2] I think there can be no doubt that he aims at this Place, and he has taken this Voyage of six Weeks, long enough to have gone to London, merely to avoid an Army in his Rear. He found he could not march this Way from Somersett Court House, without leaving G. Washington in his Rear.

We have called out the Militia of Virginia, Maryland, Delaware, and Pensilvania, to oppose him,[3] and G. Washington is handy enough, to meet him, and as G. Washington saved Philadelphia last Winter, by crossing the Delaware and marching to Morristown, and so getting in the Rear of Howe, so I conjecture he will still find Means to get in his Rear between him and Cheasapeak Bay.

You may now sit under your own Vine, and have none to make you afraid.—I sent off my Man and Horse at an unlucky Time, but, if We should be obliged to remove from hence, We shall not go far.

If Congress had deliberated and debated a Month they could not have concerted a Plan for Mr. Howe more to our Advantage than that which he has adopted. He gives Us an Opportunity of exerting the Strength of all the middle States against him, while N.Y. and N.E. are destroying Burgoine. Now is the Time, never was so good an Opportunity, for my Countrymen to turn out and crush that vapouring, blustering Bully to Attoms.

RC (Adams Papers).

[1] See an entry under 22 Aug. in JCC, 8:665, and note there.

[2] For geographical details in this and following letters, see James Lovell's MS

map, enclosed in his letter to AA of 29 Aug. (below), which is reproduced as an illustration in the present volume.

[3] See resolutions of 22 Aug. in *JCC*, 8:666–667.

John Adams to Abigail Adams

Philadelphia August 23d. [1777]

My best Friend   Saturday 4 O Clock

We have an Express, today from Governor Johnson, Captn. Nicholson and several other Gentlemen with an Account that the Fleet, to the Number of Two hundred and Sixty Three Sail, have gone up towards the Head of Cheasapeak Bay.[1] They lie over against the Shore between the River Sassafras and the River Elke.

We have also a Letter from General Washington acquainting Us that Tommorrow Morning at seven O Clock, he shall march his Army through the City of Philadelphia, along Front Street, and then turn up Chesnutt Street, in his Way to cross over the Bridge at Schuylkill River, so that General How will have a grand Continental Army, to oppose him, in very good Season, aided by a formidable Collection of Militia.

I like this Movement of the General, through the City, because, such a show of Artillery, Waggons, Light Horse and Infantry, which takes up a Line of 9 or 10 Miles upon their March and will not be less than 5 or 6 Hours passing through the Town, will make a good Impression upon the Minds of the timourous Whiggs for their Confirmation, upon the cunning Quakers for their Restraint and upon the rascally Tories for their Confusion.

I think there is a reasonable Ground for Confidence with the Favour of Heaven that How will not be able to reach this City.—Yet I really doubt whether it would not be more for our Interest that he should come here and get Possession of the Town.

1. Because there are Impurities here which will never be so soon or so fully purged away, as by that Fire of Affliction which How inkindles wherever he goes.
2. Because it would employ nearly the whole of his Force to keep Possession of this Town, and the rest of the Continent would be more at Liberty.
3. We could counteract him here better than in many other Places.
4. He would leave N. England and N.Y. at Leisure to kill or catch Burgoine.

In all Events I think you may rejoice and sing, for the season is so far gone, that he cannot remove to you.

RC (Adams Papers).

[1] See JCC, 8:668, and note.

John Adams to Abigail Adams

My dearest Friend   Philadelphia August 24. 1777

We had last Evening a Thunder Gust, very sharp and violent, attended with plentifull Rain. The Lightning struck in several Places. It struck the Quaker Alms House in Walnut Street, between third and fourth Streets, not far from Captn. Duncans, where I lodge. They had been wise enough to place an Iron Rod upon the Top of the Steeple, for a Vane to turn on, and had provided no Conductor to the Ground. It also struck in fourth Street, near Mrs. Cheesmans. No Person was hurt.

This Morning was fair, but now it is overcast and rains very hard which will spoil our Show, and wett the Army.

12. O Clock. The Rain ceased and the Army marched through the Town, between Seven and Ten O Clock. The Waggons went another Road. Four Regiments of Light Horse—Blands, Bailers [Baylor's], Sheldons, and Moylands [Moylan's]. Four Grand Divisions of the Army—and the Artillery with the Matrosses. They marched Twelve deep, and yet took up above two Hours in passing by.

General Washington and the other General Officers, with their Aids on Horse back. The Colonels and other Field Officers on Horse back.

We have now an Army, well appointed between Us and Mr. Howe, and this Army will be immediately joined, by ten Thousand Militia. So that I feel as secure here, as if I was at Braintree, but not so happy. My Happiness is no where to be found, but there.

After viewing this fine Spectacle and firm Defence I went to Mr. Duffields Meeting, to hear him pray, as he did most fervently, and I believe he was very sincerely joined by all present, for its success.

The Army, upon an accurate Inspection of it, I find to be extreamly well armed, pretty well cloathed, and tolerably disciplined. ⟨*Edes*⟩ Gill and Town by the Mottoes to their Newspapers, will bring Discipline into Vogue, in Time.[1]—There is such a Mixture of the Sublime, and the Beautifull, together with the Usefull, in military Discipline, that I wonder, every Officer We have is not charmed with it.—Much remains yet to be done. Our soldiers have not yet, quite the Air of Soldiers. They dont step exactly in Time. They dont hold up their Heads, quite erect, nor turn out their Toes, so exactly as they ought. They dont all of them cock their Hats—and such as do, dont all wear them the same Way.

A Disciplinarian has affixed to him commonly the Ideas of Cruelty, severity, Tyranny &c. But if I were an Officer I am convinced I should be the most decisive Disciplinarian in the Army. I am convinced their is no other effectual Way of indulging Benevolence, Humanity, and the tender Social Passions, in an Army. There is no other Way of preserving the Health and Spirits of the Men. There is no other Way of making them active, and skillfull, in War—no other Method of guarding an Army against Destruction by surprizes, and no other Method of giving them Confidence in one another, or making them stand by one another, in the Hour of Battle.

Discipline in an Army, is like the Laws, in civil Society.

There can be no Liberty, in a Commonwealth, where the Laws are not revered, and most sacredly observed, nor can there be Happiness or Safety in an Army, for a single Hour, where the Discipline is not observed.

Obedience is the only Thing wanting now for our Salvation—Obedience to the Laws, in the States, and Obedience to Officers, in the Army.

12 O Clock. No Express, nor accidental News from Maryland to day, as yet.

RC (Adams Papers).

[1] In a letter from New York, 20 July 1776, Brig. Gen. William Heath congratulated JA on Congress' declaring independence and went on to discuss military prospects, saying, among other things, that "The Prussian monarch tells us that the Entire Prosperity of every State rests upon the Discipline of its Army" (Adams Papers). JA was struck by this and, probably while on leave from Congress later that year, suggested to John Gill, printer of the Boston *Continental Journal*, that it be given wider circulation. Beginning on 2 Jan. 1777 the *Continental Journal* quoted it at the head of each issue, altering "Army" to "armies" and correctly attributing the maxim to Frederick of Prussia. See, further, JA's not altogether accurate recollections in a letter to Heath of 11 May 1807 (LbC, Adams Papers; JA, *Works*, 9:594–595).

Benjamin Towne, the printer of the *Pennsylvania Evening Post* in Philadelphia, carried on the masthead of his paper from 21 Aug. through 21 Oct. 1777 the following sentiment: "The finest spectacle, and the firmest defence, is the uniform observation of discipline by a numerous army. Archidamus." Very likely JA had suggested to Towne that he do so.

John Adams to Abigail Adams

Phila. Aug. 25. 1777

Yours of Aug. 12 and 13,[1] came by this Mornings Post.

A letter from Cheasopeak Bay, dated Yesterday Morning, informs that the Enemy had not then landed.[2]

This Morning General Nash, with his Brigade of North Carolina Forces, marched thro the Town with their Band of Musick, their Train of Artillery, and their Bagage Waggons, their Bread Waggons, travelling Forges &c.

General Washingtons Army encamped last Night at Derby. Sullivans Division is expected along in two days.

Our Intelligence of the Fleet has been as good as could be expected —they have been 6 Weeks at sea.

If our People do not now turn out and destroy Burgoines Gang root and branch, they may justly be reproached as lost to Honour and to Virtue. He is compleatly in our Power. Gates writes to congress, that Burgoine is lessened 1200 Men by the Bennington Action.

I inclosed Needles from Turner to Hardwick lately. But Turner is gone home and reached it eer now.

RC (Adams Papers).

[1] A single letter, above.
[2] For the letters mentioned here and below as received by Congress this day, see JCC, 8:670, and note.

John Adams to Abigail Adams

Philadelphia August 26th. 1777

My best Friend　　　　　　　　　　　　　　　Tuesday

Howes Army, at least about 5000 of them besides his Light Horse, are landed, upon the Banks of the Elke River, and the Disposition he has made of his Forces, indicate a Design to rest and refresh both Men and Horses.[1]

General Washington was at Wilmington last Night, and his Army is there to day. The Militia are turning out with great Alacrity both in Maryland and Pensilvania. They are distressed for Want of Arms. Many have none—others have only little fowling Pieces. However, We shall rake and scrape enough to do Howes Business, by the favour of Heaven.

Howe must have intended that Washington should have sent his Army up to fight Burgoine. But He is disappointed.

The Kindness of Heaven, towards Us, has in nothing appeared more conspicuous, than in this Motion of Howe. If the Infatuation is not so universal as to seize Americans, as well as him, it will prove the certain Destruction of Burgoines Army.

The New England Troops and N. York Troops are every Man of them at Peeks Kill and with Gates. The Massachusetts Regiments are all with Gates.

Gen. Washington has none but Southern Troops with him, and he has much the largest Army to encounter.

If My Countrymen do not now turn out and do something, I shall be disappointed indeed. One fifth Part of Burgoines Force has been totally destroyed by Starks and Herkermer. The Remainder must be shocked and terrified at the Stroke. Now is the Time to strike.—New Englandmen! strike home.

RC (Adams Papers). A large sheet which served as a wrapper for this letter (and possibly for one or more of the immediately preceding letters from JA to AA) is in Adams Papers and was subsequently used by AA for her draft letter to James Lovell, 24 June 1778. On this wrapper appear the following address, frank, and postmark: "Mrs. Adams Braintree Mass. Bay free John Adams [PHI]LA. AUGUST 26."

[1] Howe's army landed on the 25th at Head of Elk (modern Elkton, Md.), as far up as ships could go on the Elk River, a tributary of Chesapeake Bay pointing toward Wilmington, Chester, and Philadelphia.

Abigail Adams to John Adams

August 27 1777

Your Man and Horse arrived the 22 day of this Month. The Horse and Man look pretty low in flesh. You advise me to sell the Horse, but I think upon the whole after consulting my Friends it will not be prudent. It will be but a little more than 3 months before I hope to send for you. If I should sell him, I should be put to great difficulty to procure an other as good Horses are very scarce. This you have, we know will perform a journey. An other reason is that tho I might to day sell this Horse well, tomorrow or in a months time I must give double the price for an other, according as other things rise. I have therefore determined to have him Bled and turn him away to get into good Heart till I send for you. Bracket who has had the Small Pox since you left us, desires he may come for you. If you approve him let me know. I believe he will do very well.

We have had a turn of extreem Hot weather when we could neither work or sleep. If I sufferd so much here, what I often think must you, in that climate. The Hot weather here you know is of short Duration and generally succeeded by a cold storm or an Easterly Breaze which soon revives our Languid Spirits. The fruit this Season is very poor and very little of it. Our Good unkle says he never tastes a drop of cider but he thinks of you, and wishes you could partake with him. The Season is fine for grain and grass. We have had nothing like a drought this Summer. How much pleasure would you have taken in rambling over your meddows and Feilds. I endure with more patience this long and tedious absence, hoping that you will have served long enough to ensure you a release.

I Most sincerely congratulate you upon our late successes at the Northward, which is attended with the most agreable circumstances which have taken place since the commencment of the War. Attacking the Enemy in their entrenchments and with the Militia too, is plucking a feather from the plume of the continentall Troops. I wish it may inspire all with an Emulation to conquer and subdue these Bloodthirsty wretches. It has given a spring to our Troops, and vigor to all our countanances.

Tis really strange that no certain inteligance can be obtaind where How is gone, or what his intention is, nor is it certain that he has his Troops aboard, but let it be what it will this late affair will be a damper. I believe we may rest pretty secure in this Quarter this Season.

We have no News but what will reach you before this Letter will, a Ship came in a Sunday where from I have not learnt, but hear she brought cannon and stores for the 74 Gun Ship which is a Building.

Master Tom sends his duty and longs to see Pappa. The poor fellow met with a bad accident a week ago. He saw some Hens robing the pea vines and went into the garden to order them out. Our people had very carelessly set a Scythe there which he did not see, he run against it, and cut him across one of his legs so bad that the Doctor was obliged to sew it up, which he bore like a Soldier as he has the wound ever since. The confinement was the most grevious part of it, the wound is in a good way and he begin[s] to run again.

All the children are well. Mr. Thaxter received the Letters you mention and was sworn in accordingly.[1]

Adieu *yours* Ever *yours*.

RC (Adams Papers); addressed in Richard Cranch's hand: "To The Honble: John Adams Esqr. at Philadelphia"; postmarked: "BOSTON 28 AV"; docketed in two hands, one of which is CFA's.

[1] See Thaxter to JA, 4 June, above, and note 3 there.

John Adams to Abigail Adams

Philadelphia August 29. 1777
Fryday

My dearest Friend

The Newspapers enclosed, will give you, all the Intelligence, of any Consequence.

General Washington with a very numerous Army, is between Wilmington and the Head of Elke. How will make but a pitifull Figure. The Militia of four States, are turning out, with much Alacrity, and chearfull Spirits. The Continental Army, under Washington, Sullivan and Nash, besides is in my Opinion more numerous, by several Thousands, than Howes whole Force. I am afraid that He will be frightened and run on board his ships and go away, plundering, to some other Place.

I almost wish he had Philadelphia, for then he could not get away. I really think it would be the best Policy to retreat before him, and let him into this Snare, where his Army must be ruined.—However this Policy will not be adopted.

In a Letter from good Authority, Mr. Paca,[1] we are informed that many dead Horses have been driven on the Eastern shore of Maryland. —Horses thrown overboard, from the Fleet, no doubt.

Price current. £4 a Week for Board, besides finding your own Washing, shaving, Candles, Liquors, Pipes, Tobacco, Wood &c. Thirty shillings a Week for a servant. It ought to be 30s. for the Gentleman and £4 for the servant, because he generally eats twice as much and makes twice as much trouble.

Shoes five Dollars a Pair. Salt, 27 dollars a Bushell. Butter 10s. a Pound. Punch twenty shillings a Bowl.

All the old Women and young Children are gone down to the Jersey shore to make Salt. Salt Water is boiling all round the Coast, and I hope it will increase. For it is nothing but heedlessness, and shiftlessness that prevents Us from making Salt enough for a Supply. But Necessity will bring Us to it.

As to sugar, Molasses, Rum &c. We must leave them off. Whisky is used here instead of Rum, and I dont see but it is just as good. Of this, the Wheat and Rye Countries[2] can easily distill enough, for the Use of the Country.

If I could get Cyder, I would be content.

The Business of the Continent has been in so critical and dangerous a situation for the last 12 Months, that it was necessary the Massachusetts should have a full Representation, but the Expences of living are grown so enormous, that I believe it will be necessary to reduce the Number of Delegates to three after this Campaign is over.

RC (Adams Papers). Enclosed newspapers not found or identified.

[1] Paca's letter has not been located.
[2] Thus in MS, but JA may have meant to write "Counties."

James Lovell to Abigail Adams

Dear Madam   Philada: Augst. 29th. 1777

It is probable that Genl. Howe will waste the fall of this year between Chesapeak Bay and Delaware River. I send you a copied sketch of part of the country to which the Gazettes will frequently refer; as I know You give singular attention to the interesting concerns of America in the present struggle.

This knowledge is only part of the foundation of my affectionate esteem of you. Nor will I mention the whole.

I shall rather apologize for what there is already of Gallantry in my manner of conveying this little Present to your hand.

I could, it is true, have delivered it to your Husband. But, I could not with delicacy have told him, *to his face,* that your having given your heart to *such* a man is what, most of all, makes me yours, in the manner I have above sincerely professed myself to be.

                                                                    James Lovell

RC (Adams Papers); addressed: "Mrs. John Adams at Braintree near Boston Mr. Clymer To the Care of Isaac Smyth Esqr. in Boston"; franked: "free Jas. Lovell." Enclosure: MS map, in ink, in James Lovell's hand, one folio sheet, 12⅝" x 8", representing the region lying between Philadelphia on the northeast, Delaware Bay and New Jersey on the east, the upper part of Chesapeake Bay and Baltimore on the south and southwest, York on the northwest, and Lancaster on the north. This map is reproduced as an illustration in the present volume; see Descriptive List of Illustrations.

John Adams to Abigail Adams

                                             Philadelphia August 30th: 1777
My Friend   Saturday

A Letter from General Washington, was received last Night by the President, which I read. It is dated the 29th. Yesterday.[1]

The Enemy are in Possession of the Head of Elke, a little Town, at the Head of the River Elke, in which they found a Quantity of

Corn and Oats, belonging to the States. Waggons were so universally taken up, in conveying away the valuable Effects of the Inhabitants, that none could be procured to transport this Grain. Part of their Army, is advanced to Grays Hill about two Miles from the Head of Elke, but whether to take Post there, or only to cover while they remove their Plunder, from the Head of Elke is uncertain.

Our Army is at Wilmington. We have many Officers out reconnoitring the Country and the Enemy. Our Scouting Parties have taken between Thirty and Forty Prisoners, and Twelve Deserters are come in from the Fleet and Eight from the Army.

They say the Men are generally healthy, but their Horses have suffered much by the Voyage.

These Prisoners and Deserters are unable to give any other Intelligence. The Enemy give out, that they are Eighteen Thousand strong. But these are like Burgoines "Make Believes" and "Insinuations." We know better; and that they have not Ten Thousands.

The Militia from four States are joining General Washington, in large Numbers.

The Plan of their military Operations, this Campaign, is well calculated for our Advantage. I hope We shall have heads and Hearts to improve it.

For my own Part, I feel a secret Wish, that they might get into this City, because I think it more for our Interest that they should be cooped up here than that they should run away again to N. York. But according to present Appearances they will not be able to get here. By going into Cheasapeak Bay, they have betrayed a Dread of the Fire Works in the River Delaware, which indeed are formidable.— They must make the most of their Time, for, They cannot rationally depend upon so fine a Season, late in the fall, and Early in Winter, as they had the last Year. September, October, and November are all that remain.

We expect Hourly, Advices from Gates and Arnold. We have Rumours of an Expedition to Long Island under Parsons, and another to Staten Island, under Sullivan, but no regular Accounts. I suppose it certain that such Expeditions have been made, but know not the success.

RC (Adams Papers).

[1] From Headquarters at Wilmington; read on the 30th in Congress (*JCC,* 8:697); printed in Washington's *Writings,* ed. Fitzpatrick, 9:145–146. The following three paragraphs in JA's letter paraphrase Washington's letter.

John Adams to Abigail Adams

My dear   Philadelphia September 1. 1777. Monday

We have now run through the Summer, and altho the Weather is still warm, the fiercest of the Heats is over. And altho the extream Intemperance of the late Season has weakened and exhausted me, much, yet I think upon the whole I have got thro it, as well as upon any former Occasion.

A Letter from General Washington, dated Saturday, informs that our light Parties have brought in four and twenty Prisoners, more.[1] So that the Prisoners and Deserters, since Mr. Howe landed is near an hundred.

The Question now is, whether there will be a general Engagement? In the first Place I think, after all that has past it is not good Policy for Us to attack them unless We can get a favourable Advantage of them, in the Situation of the Ground, or an Opportunity to attack a Detachment of their Army, with superiour Numbers. It would be imprudent, perhaps for Us, with our whole Force to attack them with all theirs.

But another Question arises, whether Mr. Howe will not be able to compell Us to a General Engagement?—Perhaps he may: but I make a Question of it: Washington will maneuvre it with him, a good deal to avoid it. A General Engagement, in which Howe should be defeated, would be ruin to him. If We should be defeated, his Army would be crippled, and perhaps, We might suddenly reinforce our Army which he could not. However all that he could gain by a Victory would be the Possession of this Town which would be the worst Situation he could be in, because it would employ his whole Force by Sea and Land to keep it, and the Command of the River.

Their principal Dependence is not upon their Arms, I believe so much, as upon the Failure of our Revenue. They think, they have taken such Measures, by circulating Counterfeit Bills, to depreciate the Currency, that it cannot hold its Credit longer than this Campaign. But they are mistaken.

We however must disappoint them, by renouncing all Luxuries, and by a severe Œconomy. General Washington setts a fine Example. He has banished Wine from his Table and entertains his Friends with Rum and Water. This is much to the Honour of his Wisdom, his Policy, and his Patriotism, and the Example must be followed, by banishing sugar, and all imported Articles, from all our Families. If Necessity should reduce Us to a Simplicity of Dress, and Diet, be-

335

coming Republicans, it would be an happy and a glorious Necessity. Yours—Yours—Yours.

RC (Adams Papers).

[1] Washington's letter was dated at Wilmington, 30 Aug., was read in Congress on 1 Sept. (JCC, 8:699), and is printed in his *Writings*, ed. Fitzpatrick, 9:148.

John Adams to Abigail Adams

My dear Friend   Philadelphia Tuesday September 2. 1777

I had Yesterday the Pleasure of yours of   [1] from Boston, and am happy to find that you have been able to do so well, amidst all your Difficulties.—There is but one Course for Us to take and that is to renounce the Use of all foreign Commodities. For my own Part I never lived in my whole Life, so meanly and poorly as I do now, and yet my Constituents will growl at my Extravagance. Happy should I be indeed if I could share with you, in the Produce of your little Farm. Milk and Apples and Pork and Beef, and the Fruits of the Garden would be Luxury to me.

We had nothing Yesterday from the General.—Howes Army are in a very unwholesome Situation. Their Water is very bad and brackish, there are frequent Morning and Evening Fogs, which produce Intermittent Fevers in Abundance.—Washington has a great Body of Militia assembled and assembling, in Addition to a grand Continental Army. Whether he will strike or not, I cant say. He is very prudent, you know, and will not unnecessarily hazard his Army. By my own inward Feelings, I judge, I should put more to risque if I were in his shoes. But perhaps he is right.

Gansevoort has proved, that it is possible to hold a Post.[2] Harkermer [Herkimer] has shewn that it is possible to fight Indians, and Stark has proved that it is practicable, even to attack Lines and Posts, with Militia.—I wish the Continental Army would prove, that any Thing can be done. But this is sedition at least. I am weary however, I own, with so much Insipidity.

St. Ledger [St. Leger] and his Party have run away. So will Burgoine. I wish Stark had the Supream Command in the Northern Department. I am sick of Fabian[3] Systems in all Quarters. The Officers drink a long and moderate War. My Toast is a short and violent War. They would call me mad and rash &c. but I know better. I am as cool as any of them and cooler too, for my Mind is not inflamed with Fear nor Anger, whereas I believe theirs are with both.—If this Letter should be intercepted and published, it would do as much good, as another did two Years ago.

Adieu.

RC (Adams Papers).

¹ Blank in MS, but JA is answering AA's letter of 22 Aug., above.

² Col. Peter Gansevoort, commanding Fort Schuyler at the head of navigation on the Mohawk (Heitman, *Register Continental Army*).

³ On the application of this adjective to Washington's strategy, see an interesting article by Albert Matthews, "Some Sobriquets Applied to Washington," Col. Soc. Mass., *Pubns.*, 8 (1906):275–287.

John Adams to Abigail Adams

My dear   Philadelphia Monday Septr. 8. 1777

There has been a very general Apprehension, during the last Week that a general Action would happen, as on Yesterday. But We hear of none.

Our Army is incamped between Newport and White-Clay Creek on advantageous Ground. The General has harrangued his Army and published in General orders, in order to prepare their Minds for something great, and has held up the Example of Starks, Harkemer, Gansevoort and their Troops, to animate his Officers and Men with Emulation.—Whether he expects to be attacked, or whether he designs to offend, I cant say.

A General Action which should terminate in a Defeat of How would be compleat and final Ruin to him, if it should terminate only in a drawn Battle, it would be the same Thing. If He should gain a Victory, and maintain Possession of the Field, he would loose so many Men killed and wounded, that he would scarcely have enough left to march to Philadelphia, surrounded as he would be with Militia, and the broken remains of the Continental Army.

But if there should be no general Battle, and the two Armies should lounge away the Remainder of the Campain, in silent Inactivity gazing at each other, Howes Reputation would be ruined in his own Country and in all Europe, and the Dread of him would cease in all America. The American mind, which I think has more Firmness now than it ever had before since this War begun, would acquire a Confidence and Strength, that all the Efforts of Great Britain afterwards would not be able to relax.

You will see by the Papers inclosed, that We have been obliged to attempt to humble the Pride of some Jesuits who call themselves

Quakers, but who love Money and Land better than Liberty or Religion. The Hypocrites are endeavouring to raise the Cry of Persecution, and to give this Matter a religious Turn, but they cant succeed. The World knows them and their Communications. Actuated by a land jobbing Spirit, like that of William Penn, they have been soliciting Grants of immense Regions of Land on the Ohio. American Independence has disappointed them, which makes them hate it. Yet the Dastards dare not avow their Hatred to it, it seems.[1]

The Moments are critical here. We know not, but the next, will bring Us an Account of a general Engagement begun—and when once begun We know not how it will end, for the Battle is not always to the strong. The Events of War are uncertain. All that We can do is to pray, as I do most devoutly, that We may be victorious—at least that We may not be vanquished. But if it should be the Will of Heaven that our Army should be defeated, our Artillery lost, our best Generals kill'd, and Philadelphia fall into Mr. Howes Hands, still America is not conquered. America would yet be possessed of great Resources, and capable of great Exertions. As Mankind would see.—It may for what I know be the Design of Providence that this should be the Case. Because it would only lay the Foundations of American Independence deeper, and cement them stronger. It would cure Americans of their vicious and luxurious and effeminate Appetites, Passions and Habits, a more dangerous Army to American Liberty than Mr. Howes.

However, without the Loss of Philadelphia, We must be brought to an entire Renunciation of foreign Commodities, at least of West India produce. People are coming to this Resolution, very fast here. Loaf sugar at four dollars a Pound, Wine at Three Dollars a Bottle, &c. will soon introduce Œconomy in the Use of these Articles.

This Spirit of Œconomy would be more terrible to Great Britain, than any Thing else—and it would make Us more respectable in the Eyes of all Europe.

Instead of acrimonious Altercations between Town and Country and between Farmer and Merchant, I wish, that my dear Countrymen would agree in this Virtuous Resolution, of depending on themselves alone. Let them make salt, and live without sugar—and Rum.

I am grieved to hear of the Angry Contentions among you. That improvident Act, for limiting Prices, has done great Injury, and in my sincere Opinion if not repealed, will ruin the state, and introduce a civil War.—I know not how unpopular, this sentiment may be: but it is sincerely mine.—There are Rascally Upstarts in Trade I doubt not, who have made great Fortunes in a small Period, who are Monopolizing, and oppressing. But how this can be avoided entirely I know not, but by disusing their Goods and letting them perish in their Hands.

RC (Adams Papers). Enclosures missing, but they were presumably the *Pennsylvania Packet* of 9 Sept. and the *Pennsylvania Gazette* of 10 Sept.; see note 1.

[1] On 28 Aug. Congress received a letter of the 25th from Maj. Gen. Sullivan at Hanover, near Newark, N.J., with sundry enclosures; these were read and referred to a committee of three, of which JA was chairman. The enclosures were papers found among baggage recently captured in a raid on Staten Island and, if genuine, indicated that New Jersey Quakers were systematically furnishing intelligence to the British concerning the numbers and movements of the American forces. The committee brought in its report on the day it was appointed, recommending, among other things, that the Supreme Executive Council of Pennsylvania "apprehend and secure the persons" of a number of prominent Quakers in Philadelphia, "together with all such papers in their possession as may be of a political nature." Congress so resolved (and also ordered the papers published, though this order does not appear in the Journal, and publication was delayed for a time). Some twenty Philadelphia Quaker leaders were promptly arrested by the Pennsylvania authorities, who on 3 Sept. sent Congress the papers seized when the arrests were made and recommended that the prisoners be sent to Virginia to prevent their cooperating with the British. The papers were turned over to the committee on Sullivan's letter, which reported on the 5th, and next day Congress ordered these (or some of these) papers published as well as those sent by Sullivan. They were printed in the *Packet* and the *Gazette* on 9 and 10 Sept. respectively. Meanwhile there were sharp debates in Congress on whether remonstrances from the prisoners themselves should be heard, but the military crisis superseded all other considerations, and on the 11th all the prisoners who refused to swear or affirm allegiance were started on their exile at Winchester, Va., which lasted until the following spring.

Sullivan's letter of 25 Aug. is in PCC, No. 160, and is printed, without the enclosures, in his *Letters and Papers*, ed. Otis G. Hammond, Concord, N.H., 1930–1939, 1:443–444. The Quaker documents he sent are in PCC, No. 53. See also JCC, 8:688–689, 694–695, 708, 713–714, 718–719, 722–723; Burnett, ed., *Letters of Members*, 2:471 (with references in note there), 476–477, 486–487. For the Quaker side of these events, see [Thomas Gilpin,] *Exiles in Virginia: with Observations on the Conduct of the Society of Friends during the Revolutionary War, ... 1777–1778*, Phila., 1848. Gilpin prints the papers that incriminated the Quakers in the eyes of Congress and others, but argues persuasively from discrepancies of dates and other evidence that the paper which most offended, the so-called Memorial of the Spanktown Yearly Meeting, was a fabrication; see p. 36–37, 61–63.

Abigail Adams to John Adams

My dearest Friend   Septr. 10 1777

The accounts you give of the Heat of the weather, gives me great uneasiness upon account of your Health. I fear it will through [throw] you into a fever, or relax you so as to ruin your Health. We have had some extreem Hot weather here when the glasses have been at 92. I have slept many Nights this Summer with all my windows open which I do not remember ever to have done before. Our Hot weather you know never lasts more than 3 days at a time, and since Sepbr. came in I have been glad to sit at a fire morning and Evening; we had a small frost a night or two ago, but I believe it did not hurt any thing.

Yesterday compleated Eight months since you left me. When shall I see you. I often dream of you, but the other Night I was very unhappy. Methought you was returnd but met me so Coldly that my Heart ackd half an hour after I waked. It would ake in earnest if I once realizd such a reception, and yet if I had a Friend whom I cared little or nothing about, I should be saved many an anxious hour. Yet I would not be destitute of that tender Solisitude notwithstanding all the pain it costs me.

I have setled with Turner and paid him his account which amounted to £10 16s. 8d. including what you paid him. He is not in so good Bread as he was at Philadelphia, he cannot procure any Materials to work up.[1] Sheeps wool is 8 shillings a pound, Cotton 12, other articles in proportion. What can be done? Our money will soon be as useless as blank paper. Tis True I have not much to be anxious about, but it will soon take all I have to pay my day labourers, mowing 12 shillings a day, and much obliged to them to come at that. Butter is 3 shillings, cheeses 2, Mutton 18 pence, Beaf 18 pence, Lamb 1 & 4 pence. Corn at no price, none to be had. Barly 8 shillings a Bushel, Rye none, sold only by way of Barter. Sugar 15 pounds per hundred, Coffe 10 shillings per pound, Molasses 24 per Gallon, Rum 28 ditto. What is to become of sallery people? With Hard money not one article of the produce of this Country but what I could purchase cheeper than ever it was sold, nor do they value offering 8 dollors for one.

Necessity is the Mother of invention. There is a Manufactory of Molasses set up in several Towns. Green corn Storks ground and boild down to Molasses, tis said an acre will produce a Barrel. I have seen some of it, it both tastes and looks like Sugar Bakers molasses.

Tis confidently reported that How has landed his Troops between Philadel[phia] and Baltimore. We are anxious to hear. We have not had any late News from our Army at the Northward. The papers will inform you of several valuable prizes which have been sent in, and with their contents.

Tis almost a fortnight since I wrote you before. I have had but one baulk from you. I mean a News paper without a Letter. Our good unkle to whom you wrote as he thought, was very eager to get his

Letter. He heard of it and rode up in Town on purpose, but behold when he opend it a News paper presented itself. He wanted to know if you had not a House call'd a bettering House proper for persons who were out of their Senses.[2]

Adieu. I have nothing worth writing I think, and my Eyes are very weak which unfits me for writing much in the Evening.

Believe me at all times yours ever yours, Portia

RC (Adams Papers); addressed in John Thaxter's hand: "To the Honble: John Adams Esqr. Philadelphia To be left at the Post Office"; endorsed: "Portia"; docketed in an unidentified hand.

[1] "JOHN TURNER, HEREBY informs the Public, That he is just arrived from *Philadelphia*, and is now going to carry on the Stocking Manufactory, in the best and neatest Manner. All Persons who please to favour him with their Custom, may depend on having their Business done on the shortest Notice. Also, Weaves Men's Gloves, Women's Gloves and Mitts, Men's Caps, and Patterns for Jacket and Breeches.—He will Work for the Produce of this Country or Cash. He desires his Employers, that Spins their own Yarn, to Spin it Fine and not Twist it hard, and to leave it at Mr. *Bracket*'s Tavern in Braintree" (*Boston Gazette*, 8 Sept. 1777).

[2] There is no good clue as to which "unkle" this was, but the editors are inclined to think the incident a little more in character for Norton Quincy than Cotton Tufts.

Peter Cunningham to John Adams

Honner'd Sir   Boston September the 10. 1777

I have been So missfortinate as to be out of my native Country when those unhappy wars began, and have not got home before now. Deturmind to Serve in the United States Service (by Sea) and not Presumeing to Sirlissett any Considerable station on board a Frigate for want of experence in the art of war, I have tacking a masters Berth on board an arm'd Vessell belonging to this State, Cald the Hazard, Commanded by Simmion Sampson, and entended for a Six weeks Cruise. At the time I return, I hope sir, to be Reckermended to you by Some respecttable Jentlemen hear that Shall best now my Capaserty. In the time I am goon I hope Sir you will bare me in mind, and use your great Influance in my be half, to get me appinted to Some office wharein I shall be able to do Service and honner to my Country. I have been and am now, in Perfick't helth, and am Sir your most Obedant and very humble Servant,

Peter Cunningham[1]

Their is a thirty six guns frigat now bilding at Newbery—will be redy to Lanch very soon—should be glad And think my Self happy in being Appinted a Liutenant on board her.

Expect to Sail [in all?] next month. Should be highly honerd to have a line from you as soon as wold be Convenant.

RC (Adams Papers). Originally enclosed in Caleb Davis to JA, Boston, same date, which pronounced Cunningham "a Seaman I belive ... Inferiour to Very few on the Continent," and recommended him for a lieutenantcy "on Board one of the Continental Frigates" (Adams Papers).

[1] The writer was a first cousin to JA, being the son of JA's uncle James and aunt Elizabeth (Boylston) Cunningham of Boston and Dedham. See Adams Genealogy. Cunningham's service on the state armed vessel *Hazard* during the next two years is set forth in *Mass. Soldiers and Sailors.*

John Adams to Abigail Adams

My dearest Friend   Philadelphia Septr. 14. 1777

You will learn from the Newspapers before this reaches you, the situation of Things here. Mr. Howes Army is at Chester, about fifteen Miles from this Town. Gen. Washingtons is over the Schuylkill, awaiting the Flank of Mr. Howes Army.—How much longer Congress will stay here is uncertain. I hope We shall not move untill the last Necessity, that is untill it shall be rendered certain, that Mr. How will get the City. If We should move it will be to Reading, Lancaster, York, Easton or Bethlehem, some Town in this state. It is the Determination not to leave this state. Dont be anxious about me—nor about our great and sacred Cause—it is the Cause of Truth and will prevail. If How gets the City, it will cost him all his Force to keep it, and so he can get nothing else.—My Love to all Friends. Yours,

John Adams[1]

RC (Adams Papers).

[1] On 11 Sept. in a general engagement at Chadd's Ford on Brandywine Creek, Washington had, in his own words, "been obliged to leave the enemy masters of the field" and to retreat first to Chester and then to the eastern bank of the Schuylkill at Germantown. On the 12th JA had moved from Capt. Duncan's in Walnut Street to Rev. Mr. Sproat's in Third Street, for what was to prove a short stay and a precipitant departure. On the day he wrote the present letter Congress resolved that if it should prove necessary to leave Philadelphia, "Lancaster shall be the place at which they shall meet." A warning received early on the morning of the 19th that Howe was in possession of a ford over the Schuylkill caused the members to depart that day. They sat at Lancaster, however, only on the 27th and adjourned to meet at York on the 30th. See JA to AA, 30 Sept., below; to Speaker of Massachusetts House of Representatives, 15 Jan. 1778, NN:Emmet Coll.; *Diary and Autobiography*, 2:262–267; Washington, *Writings*, ed. Fitzpatrick, 9:207; JCC, 8:742, 754-756.

Abigail Adams to John Adams

Best of Friends   Sep 17. [*1777*]

I have to acknowlidge a feast of Letters from you since I wrote last, their dates from August 19 to Sepbr. 1. It is a very great satisfaction to me to know from day to day the Movements of How, and his Bantitti. We live in hourly expectation of important inteligance from both armies. Heaven Grant us victory and peace, two Blessing[s] I fear we are very undeserving of.

Enclosed you will find a Letter to Mr. L[ovel]l who was so obliging as to send me a plan of that part of the Country which is like to be the present seat of war.[1] He accompanied it with a very polite Letter, and I esteem myself much obliged to him, but there is no reward this side the grave that would be a temptation to me to undergo the agitation and distress I was thrown into by receiving a Letter in his Handwriting franked by him. It seems almost imposible that the Humane mind could take in, in so small a space of time, so many Ideas as rushd upon mine in the space of a moment, I cannot describe to you what I felt.

The sickness or death of the dearest of Friends with ten thousand horrours seazd my immagination. I took up the Letter, then laid it down, then gave it out of my Hand unable to open it, then collected resolution enough to unseal it, but dared not read it, begun at the bottom, read a line, then attempted to begin it, but could not. A paper was enclosed, I venturd upon that, and finding it a plan, recoverd enough to read the Letter——but I pray Heaven I may never realize such a nother moment of distress.

I designd to have wrote you a long Letter for really I owe you one, but have been prevented by our worthy P[lymout]h Friends who are Here upon a visit in their way Home and tis now so late at Night just struck 12 that I will defer any thing further till the next post. Good Night Friend of my Heart, companion of my youth—Husband and Lover—Angles watch thy Repose.

RC (Adams Papers); addressed in John Thaxter's hand: "To The Honble: John Adams Esqr. Philadelphia To be left at the Post Office"; postmarked: "BOSTON 22 SE"; docketed in CFA's hand. Enclosed letter from AA to James Lovell is printed (from an undated draft) immediately below.

[1] See Lovell to AA, 29 Aug., above, and descriptive note there.

Abigail Adams to James Lovell

Sir   [*Braintree, 17? September 1777*]

Your very polite favour was handed me this Evening.[1] I esteem myself much obliged for the enclosed plan, but I cannot describe to you the distress and agitation which the reception of your Letter threw me into. It was some time before I could get resolution to open it, and when I had opend it I dared not read it. Ten thousand horrid Ideas rushd upon my Soul. I thought it would announce to me the sickness or death of all my earthly happiness.

As I could not read the Letter I opened the paper enclosed and upon finding it a plan, was releaved from my distress.

Your professions of esteem Sir are very flattering to me. No person possessed with common Humanity can be an inattentive unconcernd Spectator of the present contest. The suffering virtue of individuals if recorded upon the faithfull page of History will astonish future ages, and demands from the present gratitude and veneration. A large share of each will ever be retained for the unfortunate Mr. L[ovell][2] in the Breast of his obliged Humble Servant,

Abigail Adams

Dft (Adams Papers); undated. Missing RC was enclosed in AA to JA, 17 Sept., preceding.

[1] Lovell's letter of 29 Aug., above. This might, of course, have been received (and the present letter might therefore have been drafted) a day or two before the 17th, when AA wrote JA the letter in which she enclosed her reply to Lovell.

[2] An allusion to Lovell's sufferings as a prisoner of the British in Boston and Halifax, 1775–1776; see *DAB*.

Cotton Tufts to John Adams

Dear Sr.   Sept. 18. 1777

Our Spring was cold and Wet, Our Summer fruitful and the Fall forbodes a plentiful Harvest. We had but very little warm Weather untill August. Our Rains were frequent, attended with Thunder and followed by fair Weather which continued for several Days and then Showers again—and such a Succession of Rains and Fair Weather I hardly ever remember which continue to this Instant. Indeed we have this Day a very cold blowing Storm of rain N.N.E. I expect all our Apples will tremble, then fall short of the usual Quantity this Year, so that a Mug of Cyder next Summer will be a Rarity. However We have had good Crops of Barley, and are every where making Molasses from Corn Stalks. We may hope for good Beer. An Acre of Corn Stalks will produce Ten Gallns. of Molasses, according to the best Authority I can get. Believe me, Our People are as diligent as Bees in collecting their Stalks, grinding, and boiling up the Juice. The Mill is formed of Three Rolls perfectly round and smooth, the middle one has a Neck to which the Sweep is fastned and by which the Horse draws, and each Roll has at the Head cogs. In short they are formd upon the Plan of Sugar Mills and are a very simple Construction.— It does not please me very well. I much want a universal Distaste to all sweet Things that will in any wise keep up the vitiated Taste for foreign Articles.—I forgot to tell You that the Crops of Flax exceeded by Three or Four Times at least whatever was raised amongst us before. This Flax [is] in general good and well grown.

Notwithstanding the Plenty which we are favour'd with unhappy it is that there is no freer Distribution or Disposal of the necessaries of Life than what is now found amongst us. Indeed no Body perishes for want of the Necessaries of Life; but they are obtain'd with Difficulty and almost wholly in the Way of Barter. We may truly assent to what indeed many have been loth to believe Viz. That Money is the Root of all Evil. Never was stronger Evidence had of the Truth of it than at this Day. And I have wrote it in my Creed, that no Greater Curse can befall Mankind than a Flood of Money. I have ever been of the Mind that there ought to be but one Currency to this Continent and under the Direction of the Supreme Power for in the Seperate States and in the representative Bodies there will be often Men either of desperate Fortunes or plung'd into Debt, who will never be willing to keep down the Quantity to a State of due Credit. There are many other Reasons some of which in former Letters I have mentioned and every Day more and more convinces me of the Expediency of such a Measure—and I must tell You freely, that if some Measures are not speedily adopted for lessening the Quantity and raising the Credit of the Money, I fear, Destruction will more speedily come upon us than what Our Enemies could accomplish by Success in Arms.— A judicious Taxation may possibly in some Measure remedy the Evil. Vigour and Energy in Government were never more wanted and scarcely ever less seen. Laws without Execution only serve to discourage the virtuous and embolden the vicious. Of this We have had ample Proof. And if We ever hope to see our Affairs wear a better Countenance, We must pursue a different Course. We must regard the Person of no one, but make the Rules of Justice and Righteousness the Standard by which to try the Conduct of every Man.—Without Discipline in the State, Without Discipline in the Army, We must not expect Prosperity. For want of this We suffer dayly, and are incident to innumerable Losses, Disappointments and amazing Expences.— Is not the Appointment of superfluous Generals and other Officers in the Army and State upon the whole a Disadvantage. Would not the general Interest be better servd by fewer General Officers, in this particular have we not outstript Great Britain. Are not Generals and Brigadier Generals often calld to head parties, that in other Nations would be devolved on no higher Officer than a Coll. or Lieut. Col. Are we not in this Way often put under Disadvantages in the Exchange of Prisoners, as our Field Officers are more frequently taken than theirs.

But this is a ramble which You must excuse, and to make up a Variety must tell You that Miss Betsy is shortly to change the Scene and enter upon the Field of Matrimony, soon after which she takes her abode at Haverhill where her Partner is agreably settled. Her Servant Phœbe is about to make the Leap—she takes the [Start?] with Mr. Bristol (a Freeman) of Boston, a Gentleman (to adopt the Language of News Papers in such Cases) *possessed of all the amiable Qualities necessary to render the married State happy.*—The good old Gentleman will be deprived of all his domestic Connections and will be necessitated to seek new ones. But where he will obtain them Time must discover, at present He is undetermind.

Thus the Scene is perpetually varying—every change promising new Felicity. This buoys up the Mind, untill we wear out and drop into Dust.—That Happiness may attend You through all the changing Scenes of this Life and Happiness in the next is the fervent Wish of Yr. Friend & H Servt.

RC (Adams Papers); endorsed: "Dr. Tufts"; docketed in an unidentified hand.

Abigail Adams to John Adams

Sepbr. 21 [*1777*]

I immagine before this reaches you some very important Event must take place betwen the two Armies. Affairs on all Sides seem to be workd up to a crisis, *How* is putting his whole force in action and seems determined to drive or be driven.

I feel in a most painfull situation between hope and fear, there must be fighting and very Bloody Battles too I apprehend. O! how my

Heart recoils at the Idea. Why is Man calld *Humane* when he delights so much in Blood, Slaughter and devastation; even those who are stiled civilizd Nations think this little Spot worth contending for, even to Blood.

Sep 23

We have confused accounts of a Battle at the Northward Last fryday, in which the Enemy were put to flight. God grant it may prove true. Vigorous Exertions now on all sides may prove of the most happy concequence and terminate this cruel War. I long for a decissive Battle—and for peace, an honourable peace. I hope the enemy are as much in our power as you fancy them.

Sepbr. 24

Have just read a hand Bill giving a perticuliar account of the engagement, at the Northward.[1] You will have it long before this reaches you. The loss of Ticondoroga has awakened the sleeping Genious of America and call'd forth all her Martial fire, may it never again be lulld to rest till crownd with victory and peace. Good officers will make good Soldiers. Xanthippus, the Lacedæmonian General who had been educated in the Discipline of Sparta, and learnt the Art of War in that renowned and Excellent School, when he was call'd to assist the Carthaginians, who had been defeated in several Battles against the Romans, declared publickly, and repeated it often in the hearing of their officers, that the misfortune[s] of the Carthaginians were oweing intirely to the incapacity of their Generals, and he proved clearly to the Counsel that by a conduct opposite to the former they would not only secure their dominions but drive the Enemy out of them. Upon his accepting the command of the Carthaginians, the gloomy conste[r]nation (says Rolin) which had before seized the whole Army was succeeded by joy and Alacrity. The Soldiers were urgent to be led against the Enemy, in the firm Assurance of being victorious under their new leader and of obliterating the disgrace of former defeats. Xanthippus did not suffer their ardour to cool but led them on to Battle and entirely routed and deafeated the Romans making Regulas their prisoner. That General who a few days before was insolent with Victory, inexorable to the conquerd, and deaf to all their Remonstrances in a few days experienced by the fate of war a sad reverse of fortune.

This is a case I think very similar to our own, may it prove so in the end. Their are two ways says Rolin of acquiring improvement and instruction, first by ones own experience, and secondly by that of

347

other men. It is much more wise and usefull to improve by other mens miscarriages than by our own.

We have not yet Received any inteligance from the Southern Army since the accounts of the engagement on the 11th, which must have been very severe upon both sides. You now experience what we sufferd when the Army lay this way. I feel very anxious for their Success. The Suspence which the distance occassions is painfull but still I find very different sensations between having the Enemy at such a distance and having them in my own Neighbourhood. I hope you will all look to your own Safety. As you are not calld to action, kidnapping would be rather dissagreable but were you in the Army I should dispise myself for such a Sentiment—as much as I did a certain Gentleman who was in the Horrours a few days ago upon hearing that General Washington had retreated within six miles of Phi[ladelphi]a. If How should get possession of that city it would immediately negotiate a peace. I could not help warmly replying, that I did not believe it even tho that should be the case and the General with his whole Army should be cut of. I hoped then that an Army of women would oppose him. Was it not the Sarassens who turnd their Backs upon the Enemy and were slain by their women who were placed behind them for that purpose?

Your favours of 2d. and 8th. reachd me upon the 20th. Your observation[s] with regard to Luxery are very just, but trade and commerce will always support it. The Necessity of the times will be a temporary restraint upon it, and put us upon seeking Resources among ourselves. An instance of that may be seen in the progress which is made of grinding corn storks and boiling the Liquor into Molasses. Scarcly a Town or parish within 40 miles of us but what have several mills at work, and had the experiment been made a month sooner many thousand Barrels would have been made, no less than 80 have already been made in the small Town of Manchester. It answers very well to distill, and may be boild down to Sugar. There are two mills sitting up in this parish. They have 3 Rollers one with cogs and two smooth, the storks are striped of the leaves and tops so that tis no Robbery upon the cattle, and the juce ground ⟨out⟩. Tis said 4 Barrels of juice will make one of Molasses, but in this people differ widely. They have a method of refining it so that it looks as well as the best imported molasses.

Thus you see we go from Step to Step in our improvements. We can live much better than we deserve within ourselves. Why should we borrow foreign Luxeries. Why should we wish to bring ruin upon ourselves. I feel as content when I have Breakfasted upon milk, as ever I did with Hyson or Suchong.

Coffe and sugar I use only as a rarity. There are none of these things but I could totally renounce. My dear Friend knows that I could always conform to times and circumstances. As yet I know nothing of hardships. My children have never cried for Bread, nor been destitute of cloathing—nor have the poor or the needy gone empty from my Door whenever it was in my power to assist them.

Heaven grant that I may continue to receive its Blessings. One of its greatest is that I can subscribe myself wholy Yours.

RC (Adams Papers); addressed in John Thaxter's hand: "To The Honble: John Adams Esqr. in Congress Philadelphia To be left at the Post Office"; postmarked: "BOSTON 29 SE"; endorsed (perhaps not contemporaneously): "Portia," to which is added in an unidentified hand: "1777."

[1] Burgoyne's repulse in the battle of Freeman's Farm or Stillwater (also known as the first battle of Bemis Heights) occurred on 19 September. No "hand Bill" reporting this action in Boston at so early a date as 24 Sept. has been found.

John Adams to Abigail Adams

York Town Pensylvania,
My best Friend   Septr. 30. 1777 Tuesday

It is now a long Time, since I had an Opportunity of writing to you, and I fear you have suffered unnecessary Anxiety on my Account.—In the Morning of the 19th. Inst., the Congress were allarmed, in their Beds, by a Letter from Mr. Hamilton one of General Washingtons Family, that the Enemy were in Possession of the Ford over the Schuylkill, and the Boats, so that they had it in their Power to be in Philadelphia, before Morning. The Papers of Congress, belonging to the Secretary's Office, the War Office, the Treasury Office, &c. were before sent to Bristol. The President, and all the other Gentlemen were gone that Road, so I followed, with my Friend Mr. Merchant [Marchant] of Rhode Island, to Trenton in the Jersies. We stayed at Trenton, untill the 21. when We set off, to Easton upon the Forks of Delaware. From Easton We went to Bethlehem, from thence to Reading, from thence to Lancaster, and from thence to this Town, which is about a dozen Miles over the Susquehannah River.—Here Congress is to sit.

In order to convey the Papers, with safety, which are of more Importance than all the Members, We were induced to take this Circuit, which is near 180 Miles, whereas this Town by the directest Road is not more than 88 Miles from Philadelphia. This Tour has given me an Opportunity of seeing many Parts of this Country, which I never saw before.[1]

This Morning Major Throop arrived here with a large Packett from General Gates, containing very agreable Intelligence, which I need not repeat, as you have much earlier Intelligence from that Part than We have.[2]

I wish Affairs here wore as pleasing an Aspect.—But alass they do not.

I shall avoid every Thing like History, and make no Reflections.

However, General Washington is in a Condition tolerably respectable, and the Militia are now turning out, from Virginia, Maryland and Pensilvania, in small Numbers. All the Apology that can be made, for this Part of the World is that Mr. Howes march from Elke to Philadelphia, was thro the very Regions of Passive obedience. The whole Country thro which he passed, is inhabited by Quakers. There is not such another Body of Quakers in all America, perhaps not in all the World.

I am still of Opinion that Philadelphia will be no Loss to Us.

I am very comfortably situated, here, in the House of General Roberdeau, whose Hospitality has taken in Mr. S[amuel] A[dams], Mr. G[erry] and me.[3] My Health is as good as common, and I assure you my Spirits not the worse for the Loss of Philadelphia.

Biddle in the Continental Frigate at S. Carolina has made a noble Cruise and taken four very valuable W.I. Prizes.

Continue to write me by the Post, and I shall pay my Debts.

RC (Adams Papers).

[1] For more details on the first part of this "Tour" see JA's *Diary and Autobiography*, 2:264–267; see also JA to AA, 14 Sept., above, and note there.

[2] "Major Throop" (as New Englanders persisted in spelling his name) was Robert Troup of New York, an aide-decamp to Gen. Gates. He brought one or more letters from Gates of 22 Sept. that contained numerous enclosures and reported the action at Freeman's Farm on the 19th and antecedent events. These were read in Congress on 1 Oct., and on the 4th Troup was promoted to a lieutenant colonelcy (*JCC*, 8:756; 9:770; see also Burnett, ed., *Letters of Members*, 2:503–505, 509).

[3] Daniel Roberdeau (1727–1795), of Philadelphia and York, was of Huguenot descent, a brigadier general in the Pennsylvania militia, and a delegate to the Continental Congress, 1777–1779 (*DAB*). For further comments on his career and family see JA to AA, 7 and 9 Oct., below.

Abigail Adams to John Adams

Dearest Friend October 6 [*i.e.* 5]. 1777. Sunday[1]

I know not where to direct to you, but hope you are secure. Tis said in some part of the Jersies, but I know this only from report. I sent to Town yesterday (saturday) but the Post did not get in till the person by whom I sent came out of Town. I could not rest but sent again this morning. The Post came but brought no Letters for me, and but two for any person that I could learn, and no late intelligence.

To the removal of congress I attribute my not hearing, but I never was more anxious to hear. I want to know every movement of the Armies. Mr. Niles by whom I send this sets of tomorrow and promises to find you and deliver this into your Hand. I doubt not you will let me hear from you by the first conveyance. Tell me where you are, how you are situated and how you do? Whether your spirits are good, and what you think of the present state of our Arms. Will Mr. How get possession of the city? Tis a day of doubtfull expectation, Heaven only knows our destiny. I observe often in the account of actions that our Men are sometimes obliged to retreat for want of ammunition, their cartridges are spent. How is this? Is it good Generalship. We never hear of that complaint in the regular Army.—There is a private expedition tis said. The Troops have all marched last monday. I own I have no great faith in it. I wish it may succeed better than I apprehend.[2]

No News of any importance from the Northward; I long for spirited exertions every where. I want some grand important actions to take place. We have both armies from their Shipping. Tis what we have long sought for, now is the important Day; Heaven seems to have granted us our desire, may it also direct us to improve it aright.

We are all well. I write nothing of any importance, till I know where you are, and how to convey to you. Believe me at all times unalterably yours—yours.

RC (Adams Papers); addressed in Richard Cranch's hand: "To The Honble: John Adams Esqr. in Congress (Pr. favr: of ⟨Saml.⟩ Lieut. Niles ⟨Esqr.⟩)"; endorsed (perhaps not contemporaneously): "Portia"; docketed in an unidentified hand.

[1] Sunday fell on the 5th in Oct. 1777.
[2] The attack so long contemplated and at long last mounted against the British forces based at Newport, R.I., was a joint venture of Massachusetts and Connecticut, was intended to be utterly secret, and proved a fiasco. Maj. Gen. Joseph Spencer, a Connecticut officer in the Continental Line, commanded the expedition; the Adamses' friend and neighbor Joseph Palmer, brigadier general of militia, commanded the Massa-

chusetts troops. Palmer established headquarters at Tiverton, R.I., at the beginning of October, but the troops from neither state turned out promptly and in full strength; boats and other essential equipment and supplies were not forwarded as promised; the wind was never right; the officers disagreed on when to strike; morale sagged; and intelligence furnished by American deserters enabled the enemy to put itself in a good posture of defense. By late October Palmer saw that the "surprise" planned for the beginning of that month would certainly fail if now attempted, and recommended withdrawal—a move that permitted Spencer to throw the blame for

failure on his subordinate. A court of inquiry acquitted Palmer, but he never lived down what many considered incompetent and negligent conduct on his part. See AA's remark (quoting Gen. Gates) about "dreaming deacons" as military commanders, in her letter to JA, 16–18 Nov., below, and Cotton Tufts to JA, 21 Nov., also below.

Palmer's letters documenting the planning of the expedition, its delays and failure, and his defense of himself thereafter, Aug. 1777 – March 1778, were printed in the *New Englander*, 3 (1845):13–22, before his papers were dispersed. See also under Palmer in *Mass. Soldiers and Sailors*.

John Adams to Abigail Adams

York Town Octr. 7. 1777

I have no Time, nor Accommodations to write of late—besides I seldom know what to write, and when I do, I dont love to write it.

One Thing is now becoming more and more certain every day. That is that our People will and do fight, and altho they make a clumsy Hand of it, yet they do better and better.

I am lodged in the House of General Roberdeau, an Israelite indeed, I believe, who, with his sisters and Children and servants, do every Thing to make Us happy. We are highly favoured. No other Delegates are so well off.

I am as well as usual. Your Dream will never come to pass. You never can be cooly received by me, while my Heart beats and my senses remain.—I had no Letter from you by the last Post.

Yours, yours, yours,   John Adams

RC (Adams Papers).

John Adams to Abigail Adams

My dearest Friend   York Town Octr. 9. 1777

I told you, in a former Letter, that I lodged at Gen. Roberdeau's.

This Gentleman is of French Extraction, his Father was a rich Planter of the Island of St. Christophers, where my Friend was born, and where he has or had an Estate. He has large Property in England, in Virginia, in Philadelphia, in York Town and in various other Parts of Pensilvania. He has also large Property in our American Funds, have[1] put great Sums into the Loan Office.

He was an intimate Friend, and a passionate Admirer of Mr. Whitfield, who always made his House an Home. He has the Reputation, I believe very justly of a pious Man.

His Wife was a Daughter of Mr. Bostwick of New York, a famous Minister, Sister to Mrs. McDougall, the Lady of General McDougal, two as fine Women as ever America produced, excepting one. Mrs. Roberdeau was a beauty. A fine Figure—good Taste—great sense—much Knowledge—a fine Temper. But she is no more.[2]

The Generals two sisters keep his House—the one a Widow, Mrs. Climer [Clymer], who has a son—the other a Maiden Lady, Miss Elizabeth Roberdeau.

RC (Adams Papers).

[1] Thus in MS.

[2] Mrs. Daniel Roberdeau, the former Mary Bostwick, had died earlier this year while nursing her husband through a serious illness (*DAB*, under her husband's name).

John Adams to Abigail Adams

My dearest Friend   York Town Octr. 15. 1777

I have not been able of late to keep up my Correspondence with you, so constantly, as my Heart inclined me to do. But I hope now to write you oftener—but I dont incline to write, very particularly, least my Letters should be intercepted.

I am in tolerable Health, but oppressed, with a Load of public Cares.

I have long foreseen, that We should be brought down to a great Degree of Depression before the People of America would be convinced of their real Danger, of the true Causes of it, and be stimulated to take the necessary Steps for a Reformation.

Government and Law in the states, large Taxation, and Strict Discipline in our Armies, are the only Things Wanting, as human Means. These with the Blessing of Heaven, will certainly produce Glory, Tryumph, Liberty and Safety and Peace, and nothing but these will do.

I long with the Utmost Impatience to come home—dont send a servant for me. The Expence is so enormous that I cannot bear the Thought of it. I will crawl home, upon my little Pony, and wait upon myself as well as I can. I think you had better sell my Horse. ⟨*I am, yours.*⟩

The People are universally calling for Fighting and for Blood. Washington is getting into the Humour of fighting and How begins to dread it—and well he may. Fighting will certainly answer the End altho We may be beaten every Time for a great While.

We have been heretofore greatly deceived concerning[1] the Numbers of Militia. But there are Numbers enough if they knew how to fight, which as soon as their Generals will let them, they will learn.— I am, with every tender Sentiment, yours forevermore.

RC (Adams Papers).
[1] MS: "concing."

Abigail Adams to John Adams

October 20. 1777

Tis true my dearest Friend that I have spent an anxious 3 weeks, and the sight of a Letter from you gave me joy beyond expression. I had sent every post day, and every post was dissapointed. For 3 week[s] I could not learn one word with certainty—nor can I now determine whether you are 88 miles nearer to me or farther of than you were before.

I was greatly surprizd when I heard that the Enemy were in possession of Philadelphia without any engagement upon our part. If Men will not fight and defend their own perticuliar spot, if they will not drive the Enemy from their Doors, they deserve the slavery and subjection which awaits them.[1]

There is much I think comprised in that short Sentance, "I shall avoid all history and make no reflections." I think I can construe a volum from it, I will follow the example least a miscarrage of this should give triumph to an Enemy.

Our affairs at the Northward wear a more pleasing aspect. The Sunshine from the North gilds the dark Clouds of the South or the Storm would look dismal indeed.

It is a Newengland observation that in some late general orders when many motives and stimulatives were set before the men to excite them to action, they were assured of conquest without once acknowledgeing the Superintendance of divine providence. Our favorite Dr. Tillotson "observes that in all our concernments we ought to have a perticuliar regard to the Supreme disposer of all things and earnestly to seek his favour and blessing upon all our undertakeings, but more especially in the affairs of war, in which the providence of God is pleasd many times in a very peculiar manner to interpose and interest itself, because all war is as it were an appeal to God, and a reference of those causes to the decision of his providence which through the pride, and injustice, and perverse passions of men can receive no other determination."

Tis not more than 3 weeks since I thought our affairs looked in a more prosperious train than they had done since the commencement of the War. Tho they have not taken the turn I hoped for, yet I doubt not they will finally terminate in our favour. Providence for wise purposes has oftentimes since the commencement of this war brought about our deliverence by ways and means which have appeard to us the most improbable and unlikely—has given into our hands those things which we were destitute of, and in the greatest necessity for. So true it is acknowledge him in all thy ways, and he shall direct thy paths.

To you my dear Friend I need not excuse these Moral reflections. I have ever considerd it as a happiness to be united to one whose Sentiments in Religion were not only agreable to my own, but to what I have ever esteemed the Truth.

October 22

I believe I may venture to congratulate my Love upon the completion of his wishes with regard to Burgoin. Tis reported to day from many ways that he has with his whole Army fallen into our hands and tis said the post brings the same inteligance.[2] If true, as I most sincerely hope, let us with gratitude acknowledg the interposition of Heaven in our favour.

We have accounts too of an engagement at the southard. I am glad to hear of fighting even tho we come of second best, not because Heaven is my witness that I delight in the Effusion of humane Blood, but because I believe by delay we should loose more lives than by the sword. It sinks our spirits, disheartens our soldiers, makes them both Idle and wicked. How great would be my joy could I see peace and quietness once more restored to this distressed land.

> "Peace o'er this land her olive Branch extend
> And white Robed Innocence from heaven desend."

It gave me great pleasure to hear of your Health and Spirits. Did you save your cloaths, or have they fallen into the hands of the

Enemy? We are all very well in the family. The hooping cough prevails much and is just comeing into the family. I long for the month of your return to come. I wrote you with regard to B[racket]t[3] but received no answer. You will let me know, and when to send. Dr. T[uft]s desires to know if you have received a Letter from him within these two months, he fears that it did not reach you, as it was about the time of your removal.

The Spirit of Barter and exchange predominates so much here that people dispose of their own Bodies. Matrimony prevails among all orders and Ages; the scarcity of the Commodity enhances the value. Men are a very scarce article to be sure. Among the late mariages which have taken place and are like to, Miss B[ets]y S[mit]h to Mr. S[ha]w last thursday, old Deacon W[eb]b of this Town to a maiden Sister of John Ruggles'es wife, who has lived to the age of 66 unmarried, our Friend Mrs. L[incol]n of this Town to Deacon S[tore]r of Boston, an exceeding good match and much approved of. Numbers of others in the lower class not worth mentioning, but I ask my Cousin P[oll]y S[mit]hs pardon for omitting her. She marries in about 2 months to a Mr. Gray, a Brother of Mr. Eliss Grays of B[osto]n.[4]

Tis very cold for the Season. We had Snow yesterday and Ice in the Streets this morning. When shall I see my Friend? Tis more than Nine long months since we parted. Shall I send the beginning of december? Heaven grant us a joyfull meeting.

Ever yours.

RC (Adams Papers); addressed in John Thaxter's hand: "To The Honble: John Adams Esqr. in Congress at Yorktown in Pensylvania"; franked: "Free."

[1] Howe's army had entered Philadelphia on 27 Sept.; Washington's attack in force on Germantown, 4 Oct., failed because of fog.

[2] Burgoyne was defeated at Bemis Heights on 7 Oct., proposed to capitulate on the 14th, signed the articles of convention on the 16th, and formally surrendered at Saratoga the next day.

[3] See AA to JA, 27 Aug., above.

[4] Elizabeth Smith, AA's younger sister, married Rev. John Shaw on 16 Oct.; see Adams Genealogy. Deacon Jonathan Webb of Braintree married Elizabeth Jones on 7 Oct. (*Braintree Town Records*, p. 867). Hannah (Quincy) Lincoln, a widow since 1773, and Ebenezer Storer, a Boston merchant, newly appointed treasurer of Harvard College, and a widower since 1774, filed marriage intentions in Braintree on 17 Oct. and were married on 6 Nov.; see Adams Genealogy. AA's cousin Polly, i.e. Mary, daughter of Isaac Smith of Boston, was to marry Edward Gray on 11 Dec.; he died two years later, and she subsequently married Samuel Allyne Otis, first and for many years clerk of the U.S. Senate; see Adams Genealogy.

John Adams to Abigail Adams

My dearest Friend　　　　　　　　　York Town Octr. 24. 1777

It is with shame that I recollect that I have not written you more than two or three Letters these 5 Weeks, and those very short.

News I am afraid to write, because I never know untill it is too late what is true. From last Sunday to this Moment Fryday afternoon 4 o Clock, We have been in a state of tormenting Uncertainty concerning our Affairs at the Northward. On Sunday, We had News, from the Committee of Albany, through Governor Clinton and G. Washington, of a Capitulation of Burgoine and his whole Army.[1] To this Moment We have no Express from Gates, nor any Authentic Confirmation.[2]

Howe has drawn his Army into the City and Washington is at Germantown. Supplies will be cutt off, from the British Army, in a great Measure.

I am &c. yours forever,　　　　　　　　　　John Adams

We shall finish a Plan of Confederation in a few days.[3]

RC (Adams Papers).

[1] The earliest news of Burgoyne's capitulation reached York on Sunday the 19th, though this was actually premature, since Burgoyne had only *offered* to surrender on the 14th, the letter of the Albany committee, transmitted through various hands, was dated the 15th, and the Saratoga convention was not signed until the following day. See the very careful and enlightening editorial note on the transmission of the news, with locations of the relevant texts, in Burnett, ed., *Letters of Members*, 2:526–527. The record in JCC is incomplete and otherwise unsatisfactory on this important affair.

[2] The reason was that Lt. Col. James Wilkinson, Gates' adjutant, took twelve days to bring Gates' dispatch of the 18th and a copy of the convention from Saratoga to York. Dawdling sociably on the way, he did not arrive until 31 Oct. (JCC, 9:851), by which time the news he brought had reached Congress from various unofficial sources. In a letter written many years later, Thomas McKean recalled that Samuel Adams had formally proposed that Congress reward Wilkinson by voting him "a pair of spurs" (McKean to JA, 20 Nov. 1815, Adams Papers). JA's recollection was that his own "impatience" had never in his life been "wrought up to an higher pitch, than by the total failure of all Intelligence Official and unofficial from Saratoga, for so long a time after We had heard a confused fugitive rumour of the defeat of Burgoine," and that on the morning after Wilkinson's arrival "a jocular Suggestion [was] thrown out in a private Conversation" among JA, Samuel Adams, and John Hancock, "that it would be proper to present the Courier with a horsewhip and a pair of Spurrs" (to McKean, 26 Nov. 1815, PHi). What in fact happened, however, was that Congress on 6 Nov., acting on Gates' strong recommendation, breveted Wilkinson a brigadier general (JCC, 9:870). Wilkinson's own account of his journey from Saratoga and arrival in York, with the text of Gates' dispatch which he carried and of other pertinent documents, is in James Wilkinson, *Memoirs of My Own Times*, Phila., 1816, 1:323–332.

² This was premature. Debate over the Articles of Confederation had occupied Congress during the present session intermittently since early April, but a final text to be submitted to the states for adoption was not agreed on until 15 Nov., some days after JA had left York for Braintree. See JCC, 9:907–928, and entries under Articles of Confederation in index to JA's *Diary and Autobiography*.

Abigail Adams to John Adams

Boston October 25 1777 Saturday Evening

The joyfull News of the Surrender of General Burgoin and all his Army to our Victorious Troops prompted me to take a ride this afternoon with my daughter to Town to join to morrow with my Friends in thanksgiving and praise to the Supreem Being who hath so remarkably deliverd our Enimies into our Hands.

And hearing that an express is to go of tomorrow morning, I have retired to write you a few line's. I have received no letters from you since you left P[hiladelphi]a by the post, and but one by any private Hand. I have wrote you once before this. Do not fail writing by the return of this express and direct your Letters to the care of my unkle who has been a kind and faithfull hand to me through the whole Season and a constant attendant upon the post office.

Burgoine is expected in by the middle of the week. I have read many Articles of Capitulation, but none which ever containd so generous Terms before. Many people find fault with them but perhaps do not consider sufficently the circumstances of General Gates, who ⟨perhaps⟩ by delaying and exacting more might have lost all. This must be said of him that he has followed the golden rule and done as he would wish himself in like circumstances to be dealt with.—Must not the vapouring Burgoine who tis said possesses great Sensibility, be humbled to the dust. He may now write the Blocade of Saratago.[1] I have heard it proposed that he should take up his quarters in the old South,[2] but believe he will not be permitted to come to this Town.—Heaven grant us success at the Southard. That saying of king Richard often occurs to my mind "God helps those who help themselves" but if Men turn their backs and run from an Enemy they cannot surely expect to conquer them.

This day dearest of Friends compleats 13 years since we were solemly united in wedlock; 3 years of the time we have been cruelly seperated. I have patiently as I could endured it with the Belief that you were serving your Country, and rendering your fellow creatures essential Benefits. May future Generations rise up and call you

Blessed, and the present behave worthy of the blessings you are Labouring to secure to them, and I shall have less reason to regreat the deprivation of my own perticuliar felicity.

Adieu dearest of Friends adieu.

[*Added in the hand of William Smith:*] Please to enquire of Mr. Reese Meredeth if he has received a Letter from my father enclosing a Bill upon Philadelphia.—Yrs., WS[3]

RC (Adams Papers); addressed in the hand of William Smith (see note 3): "To The Honble. John Adams Esqr. Member of Congress at York-Town State of Pensylvania"; endorsed (perhaps not contemporaneously): "Portia"; docketed in an unidentified hand.

[1] An allusion to *The Blockade of Boston*, acted in Boston by British army officers in 1776; see AA to JA, 14 April 1776, note 4.

[2] In allusion to the fact that the Old South Meeting House had been converted to a riding school for officers during the British occupation of Boston. See William Heath, *Memoirs*, new edn., ed. William Abbatt, N.Y., 1901, p. 126.

[3] AA's cousin, William Smith (1755–1816), Harvard 1775, second son of Isaac Smith Sr. of Boston; see Adams Genealogy. AA was staying at her uncle Isaac Smith's home in Queen (later Court) Street, Boston.

John Adams to Abigail Adams

My best Friend   York Town Octr. 25. 1777

This Town is a small one, not larger than Plymouth.—There are in it, two German Churches, the one Lutheran, the other Calvinistical. The Congregations are pretty numerous, and their Attendance upon public Worship is decent. It is remarkable that the Germans, wherever they are found, are carefull to maintain the public Worship, which is more than can be said of the other Denominations of Christians, this Way. There is one Church here erected by the joint Contributions of Episcopalians and Presbyterians, but the Minister, who is a Missionary, is confined for Toryism, so that they have had for a long Time no publick Worship....[1] Congress have appointed two Chaplains, Mr. White and Mr. Duffield, the former of whom an Episcopalian is arrived and opens Congress with Prayers every Day.[2] The latter is expected every Hour. Mr. Duche I am sorry to inform you has turned out an Apostate and a Traytor. Poor Man! I pitty his Weakness, and detest his Wickedness.[3]

As to News, We are yet in a painfull Suspense about Affairs at the Northward, but from Philadelphia, We have Accounts that are very pleasing. Commodore Hazelwood, with his Gallies, and Lt. Coll.

Smith in the Garrison of Fort Mifflin, have behaved in a manner the most gallant and glorious. They have defended the River, and the Fort with a Firmness and Perseverance, which does Honour to human Nature.[4]

If the News from the Northward is true, Mr. Howe will scarcely venture upon Winter Quarters in Philadelphia.

We are waiting, for News, from Rhode Island.

I am wearied with the Life I lead, and long for the Joys of my Family. God grant I may enjoy it, in Peace. Peace is my dear Delight. War has no Charms for me.—If I live much longer in Banishment I shall scarcely know my own Children.

Tell my little ones, that if they will be very good, Pappa will come home.

RC (Adams Papers).

[1] Suspension points in MS.

[2] Rev. (later Bishop) William White and Rev. George Duffield had been appointed chaplains to Congress on 1 Oct. (JCC, 8:756).

[3] On Rev. Jacob Duché, Congress' first chaplain in 1774, see JA to AA, 16 Sept. 1774, above, and note 3 there. His eventually notorious letter to Washington, dated at Philadelphia, 8 Oct., urging him to negotiate for peace at once and asking him "Are the Dregs of a Congress, then, still to influence a mind like yours?" was forwarded by Washington to Congress in a letter of 16 Oct. (Washington, *Writings*, ed. Fitzpatrick, 9:382–383). The original is in PCC, No. 152, V; a copy in John Thaxter's hand was enclosed in Thaxter to AA, 20 Jan. 1778, printed below, and is in Adams Papers. Duché's letter was read in Congress on the 20th, and although it provoked private cries of outrage, the members thought it best treated with official silence (JCC, 9:822; Burnett, ed., *Letters of Members*, 2:523, note, 526–527, 538). All the relevant correspondence was gathered and published, with useful commentary, by Worthington C. Ford in *The Washington-Duché Letters*, Brooklyn, 1890.

[4] In mid-October Commodore John Hazelwood of the Pennsylvania navy and Lt. Col. Samuel Smith of Maryland, commanding at Fort Mifflin on the Delaware, repulsed British attacks designed to open supply lines to Philadelphia. On 4 Nov. these two officers were voted swords by Congress (JCC, 9:862).

John Adams to Abigail Adams

My dearest Friend   York Town Octr. 26. 1777

Mr. Colman goes off for Boston Tomorrow.

I have seized a Moment, to congratulate you on the great and glorious Success of our Arms at the Northward, and in Delaware River. The Forts at Province Island and Red Bank have been defended, with a Magnanimity, which will give our Country a Reputation in Europe.

Coll. Green repulsed the Enemy from Red bank and took Count

Donop and his Aid Prisoners. Coll. Smith repulsed a bold Attack upon
Fort Mifflin, and our Gallies disabled two Men of War a 64 and 20
Gun ship in such a Manner, that the Enemy blew them up. This
comes confirmed this Evening, in Letters from Gen. Washington inclosing Original Letters from Officers in the Forts.[1]

Congress will appoint a Thanksgiving, and one Cause of it ought
to be that the Glory of turning the Tide of Arms, is not immediately
due to the Commander in Chief, nor to southern Troops. If it had
been, Idolatry, and Adulation would have been unbounded, so
excessive as to endanger our Liberties for what I know.

Now We can allow a certain Citizen to be wise, virtuous, and good,
without thinking him a Deity or a saviour.

RC (Adams Papers).

[1] Washington's letter of 24 Oct. informing Congress of the bitter (and, so
far, successful) fighting cn 21–22 Oct.
to keep control of Forts Mifflin and Mercer on the Delaware below Philadelphia,
with large extracts of his enclosures, are
printed in Washington, *Writings*, ed.
Fitzpatrick, 9:422–424. They were read
in Congress on the 27th (*JCC*, 9:841).
Col. Christopher Greene, of the 1st
Rhode Island regiment, was voted a
sword by Congress on 4 Nov. (same, p.
862).

John Adams to Abigail Adams

My dearest Friend   York Town, Octr. 28. 1777

We have been three days, soaking and poaching in the heavyest
Rain, that has been known for several Years, and what adds to the
Gloom is the Uncertainty in which We remain to this Moment,
concerning the Fate of Gates and Burgoigne.—We are out of Patience.
It is impossible to bear this suspense, with any Temper.

I am in comfortable Lodgings, which is a Felicity that has fallen
to the Lott of a very few of our Members. Yet the House where I
am is so thronged, that I cannot enjoy such Accommodations as I
wish. I cannot have a Room as I used, and therefore cannot find
Opportunities to write as I once did.

The People of this Country, are chiefly Germans, who have Schools
in their own Language, as well as Prayers, Psalms and Sermons, so
that Multitudes are born, grow up and die here, without ever learning
the English.—In Politicks they are a Breed of Mongrels or Neutrals,
and benumbed with a general Torpor.

If the People, in Pensylvania, Maryland, Delaware and Jersy had
the Feelings and the Spirit of some People that I know, Howe would

be soon ensnared in a Trap, more fatal than that in which, as it is said, Burgoigne was taken.

Howe is compleatly in our Power, and if he is not totally ruined it will be entirely owing to the Aukwardness and Indolence of this Country.

Fighting however, begins to become fashionable. Coll. Green has exhibited a glorious Example, in the Defence of Red bank. But this must be done by a New Englandman at the Head of two N. England Regiments, Rhode Islanders.

Coll. Smith however, is a Marylander, from Baltimore. He has shewn another Example of Magnanimity, which gives me the most agreable Hopes. Commodore Hazelwood too, has behaved in a manner that exceeds all Praise. This Spirit will be caught by other Officers, for Bravery is epidemical and contagious as the Plague.

This Army suffers much for Want of Blanketts and Shoes.

I celebrated the 25th. of this Month, in my own Mind and Heart, much more than I shall the 30th.—because I think the first a more fortunate day than the last.[1]

My Duty to your Father and my Mother—to Unkles and Aunts. Love to Brothers and sisters—but above all, present all the Affection that Words can express to our dear Babes.

RC (Adams Papers).

[1] The 25th was his wedding anniversary; the 30th was his birthday, according to the New Style calendar.

Abigail Adams to Isaac Smith Jr.

Dear Sir   [October 30, 1777][1]

A favourable opportunity offering by Mr. Austin[2] of writing to you, I embrace it, in compliance to your pappa's request as well as my own inclination.

The uncertainty of a conveyance to you has prevented many of your Friends from writing to you, and when an opportunity has offerd the fear of a miscarrage has obliged them to say little else than what regards the State of their Health and the place of their abode.

But having taken the pen I am determined to write freely regardless of consequences.[3]

When you left your Native land it was in a state little able to defend itself[4] against the force which had invaded it, but providence remarkably smild upon our virtuous exertions in defence of our injured and oppressed land, and has opened resources for us beyond our most sanguine expectations, so that we have been able not only to repel, but conquer, the Regular Troops of Britain, the Mercinaries of Germany, the Savages of the wilderness and the still more cruel paricides of America with one of the most celebrated British Generals at their head.

I have the pleasure Sir to inform you that the British arms have submitted to American fortitude, courage and bravery, and have received terms tho humiliating to them the most generous ever granted to an Enemy[5] cruel and inhumane as these have been.

But true courage is always humane, and we submit the punishment of their crimes to that Being who has stiled himself the Husband of the widow, the Father of the orphan and the avenger of the oppressed. Cruel have been the depredations of these foes of the rights of Humane Nature. Our Commerce has been distroyed, our cities burnt with fire, our Houses plunderd, our women a sacrifice to brutal Lust, our children murderd, and the hoary head of age has oftentimes glutted their savage malice.

These Sir are indisputable facts and will I hope be recorded by the faithfull Historyan to the everlasting infamy and disgrace of Britain, and would almost tempt one to immitate the *parent* of Hannible and swear the rising generation to Eternal Enmity against them. —But as christians tho we abhor the[6] deeds we wish them reformation and repentance.

We most sincerely wish for peace upon honorable terms. Heaven is our witness that we rejoice not in the Effusion of Blood, nor the Carnage of the Humane Speicies but having forced us to draw the Sword we are determined never to sheathe it the Slaves of Britains— and whether it is creditted or not tis a truth for which we have great reason to be thankfull, we are at this day in a much better situation to continue the war for 6 years to come, than we were to contend for 6 months in the commencment of it. We have defended ourselves against a force which would have shaken any kingdom in Europe without becomeing tributary to any power whatever, and I trust we shall continue too, with the blessing of heaven.

Providence has permitted for wise ends that every one of the united States should feel the cruel depredations of the Enemy, that each one should be able to sympathize with the other—and this so far from weakening has served to strengthen our bond of union. Tis a thirteenfold cord which all the Efforts of our Enemies have not been able to break.

The perticuliars of the Capture of General Burgoyne and his whole Army will be transmitted you by other hands. I hope soon to congratulate you upon a similar account from the Southard, but whether I am [can] or not [7] you may rely upon it that the invincible american Spirit is as far from being conquerd as it was the day the cruel mandates were issued against her. She gathers strength by oppression and grows firmer by resistance.[8] Tis the cause of truth and justice and will finally prevail tho the combined force of Earth and hell rise against it.

To this Cause I have sacrificed much of my own personal happiness by giving up to the counsels of America one of my dearest connexions and living for more than 3 years in a State of widowhood.

A return to your native land with a heart and mind truly american would rejoice all your connexions perticuliarly your Friend and former Correspondent,[9]   AA [10]

Dft (Adams Papers); undated; at head of text in JQA's hand: "To Isaac Smith junr. November," to which CFA added "1777." RC not found, but a printed text of it appeared in a British periodical, the *Monthly Repository of Theology and General Literature*, 17:670–671 (Nov. 1822), with this editorial note prefixed: "Copy of a Letter from Mrs. ADAMS, Wife of Mr. Adams, a Member of the American Congress, to the Rev. Mr. SMITH, then of Sidmouth, in Devonshire, but a Native of Boston, in New England, which place he left at the Commencement of the War, and returned to it at the Peace. (*Communicated by the Rev.* Joseph Cornish.)" Dft has been followed in the present text because it better represents AA's usage than RC in its normalized printing; but the more important variations between Dft and RC have been recorded in notes below.

[1] Supplied from RC. AA was evidently writing from Boston. It is hardly necessary to point out how promptly she seized the advantage of the first great American military victory to lecture her (as she believed) errant cousin.

[2] Jonathan Loring Austin (1748–1826), Harvard 1766, sailed the next day from Boston for Nantes in the brigantine *Perch* to carry the news of Burgoyne's surrender to the American Commissioners at Paris; he then served Franklin in various capacities in Europe, and during the summer of 1778 acted as JA's secretary at Passy. See JA, *Diary and Autobiography*, 2:300, and references there; also E. E. Hale and E. E. Hale Jr., *Franklin in France*, Boston, 1887–1888, 1:154–160.

[3] This sentence was revised in RC to read: "But whether this meets with the fate of some others or not, I am determined to congratulate you upon our present situation."

[4] RC here inserts a phrase in commas: "to all human appearance."

[5] RC has a full stop here and continues, without a paragraph break: "Their deserts they never can receive in this world, nor we inflict, but must submit them to that Being who will equally distribute both rewards and punishments, and who hath assured us that he will espouse the cause of the widow, the fatherless and the oppressed."

[6] RC: "their"—probably AA's intended wording in the draft, though she did not write it.

⁷ RC here inserts a phrase in commas: "as the events of war are uncertain."

⁸ This sentence omitted from RC, perhaps unintentionally.

⁹ RC reads, instead: "I hope before long you will be able to return to your native land with a heart truly American;

as such, no one will rejoice more to see you than your affectionate friend and former correspondent."

¹⁰ RC adds a sentence below signature: "If you can write to me with safety, a letter would be very acceptable."

John Adams to Abigail Adams

My dearest Friend   York Town November 3. 1777

This Moment I received your favour of Octr. 6. by Mr. Niles.—I am as well as can be expected.

We have no News, but such as is old to you.

I congratulate you on the great and glorious Events in the northern Department. Congress have ordered a Thanksgiving, and have done great Honour to the Officers.[1]

We shall finish the Confederation in a few days.

RC (Adams Papers); docketed by JA in old age: "J.A. to A.A. Nov. 3. 1777." The letter was written on a blank leaf torn from an earlier letter addressed to JA in an unidentified hand: "The Honble: Jo[. . .] in Congress."

[1] See the Journal for 31 Oct., 1, 4 Nov. (JCC, 9:851, 854–855, 861–862).

James Lovell to Abigail Adams

York Town Novr. 10th. 1777

As the delivery of this Billet cannot be attended with the disagreable allarm which the amiable Mrs. Adams some time ago suffered from a well meant but indiscretely-managed little Compliment of one of her Admirers,[1] I improve this fair opportunity to congratulate her, thus, upon the late happy events at Saratoga, greatly important to the Public and, consequently, interesting to her patriotic mind. At the same time, I wish her many years continuance of that domestic Felicity which will be restored to her at the hour when she receives this written assurance of affectionate Esteem from her very humble Servant,   James Lovell

RC (Adams Papers).

[1] See Lovell to AA, 29 Aug., and AA's reply of 17? Sept., both above. The present letter was obviously brought by JA himself to Braintree; see the following letter and note 1 there.

John Adams to Abigail Adams, with an Extract of a Letter from St. Eustatius

Easton, at the Forks of Delaware in Pensylvania
Novr. 14. 1777

Here I am.—I am bound home.—I suppose it will take me 14 days, perhaps 18 or 20, to reach Home.—Mr. S.A. is with me.—I am tolerably well.[1]

The American Colours are still flying at Fort Mifflin.

The News on the other Side, is from a Merchant to his Partner.[2]

I am in great Haste, most affectionately yours.

ENCLOSURE[3]

17. Sept.

Business still continues dull but am in Hopes of a Speedy Change as it seems by the last Accounts from Amsterdam that a War with France and England is inevitable. Lord Stormont, the English Ambassador has left the Court of France,[4] upon meeting with an unsatisfactory Answer relative to the French's supporting the Americans which they and the Spaniards are determined to do. And you may soon expect to see a Number of Vessells from his Christian and Catholick Majestyes Dominions in America with every necessary Supply for carrying on the War, and the King of Prussia has opened the Port of Mendin[5] for the Americans to carry their Prizes in and to trade. Stocks fell in England 15 Pr. Ct. upon the Ambassadors leaving the french Court. I hope a french War may break out as it will be the Means of our making great Fortunes which I should be happy to acquaint you with.

RC (Adams Papers). Concerning the enclosure, if it can be truly called one, see notes 2 and 3.

[1] On 7 Nov. JA and Samuel Adams were voted a "leave of absence to visit their families" (JCC, 9:880). On the 11th they set off from York and proceeded by way of Lancaster, Reading, and Bethlehem to Easton, meeting Francis Dana, who was on his way to help fill up the depleted Massachusetts delegation, near Reading; their route from Easton home is at least partly indicated in JA's fragmentary diary entries (*Diary and Autobiography*, 2:267–269). According to a letter he wrote James Lovell on 6 Dec.

(LbC, Adams Papers), JA reached Braintree on 27 November.

[2] This appears on the verso of JA's letter, which is written on an irregularly shaped sheet. Paper was scarce, and, although there is no evidence that the letter from "Eustatia" was read in Congress, JA may have copied it before leaving York and then found the blank side of the sheet convenient for writing his note to AA.

[3] The caption in the original reads: "Extract of a Letter from a G[entleman]

at Eustatia 17. Sept." The editors have no certain clue as to who the writer was.
⁴ This was premature. Stormont was
not recalled until March 1778.
⁵ Minden, on the Weser River, in Westphalia.

Abigail Adams to John Adams

My dearest Friend   November 16 1777

In a Letter which came to me to Night you chide yourself for neglecting writing so frequently as you had done. Tis true a very long space of near a fortnight past, without my hearing one word from you. I cannot help feeling anxious when such a space elapses without receiving a line, but I have no reason to complain. You have considering your avocations been more attentive than I had reason to expect.

> "Heaven sure taught Letters for some wretches aid,
> Some banishd Lover or some captive maid."

I have been more fearfull than formerly of writing by the post as I have never received a Letter from you by that conveyance since you left Philadelphia. Mr. Coleman brought me yours of october 25 and 26. You have before this time received from me one of the same date, since which I have not wrote. I have been too much mortified with a late expedition to write you any perticuliars concerning it. Indeed it was from the begining a subject of Burlesque, oweing I believe to the small opinion most people had of the Heroick talents of the commanders. It was call'd a secret Expedition to Newport. A fortnight before the troops marchd, there were by all accounts as fine a set of troops collected, as any spiritted commanders could have wishd for, and tis said for 20 Days the Island might have been succesfully (to all appearence) attacked. The publick are very angry as well they may be, and demand an enquiry.

I know you will be mortified, because it has been a favorite object with you—but if you want your Arms crownd with victory you should not appoint what General Gates calls dreaming deacons to conduct them.[1]

General Burgoine and his troops arrived last week in Cambridge —all seems to be quietness at present. From the southard we get no very authentick accounts. To day How and his whole Army are captives! To morrow they have got possession of our forts and weighd the Cheveaux de Frize.

November 18

No News at all, our Mountabank Story of Captivating How and his Army is come to nothing.

The Southern Troops must have some assistance from the Northern before any thing very Brilliant will take place. Providence over rules all things for the best, and will work out our Salvation for us in the wisest and best manner—provided we perform our Duty.

My Brother has had the misfortune to be taken upon his return from a cruise up the Baltick. They had a valuable prize with them loaded with duck and cordage. He was captain of Marines on board the Tartar Capt. Grimes Master, and was carried into Newfoundland since which we have not heard from him.[2]

Now my dear Friend shall I ask you when you will return, a Question I have not asked you for these ten Months. Knowing your determination when you left me I have summond patience, and endeavourd to submit to my destiny. By the time this reaches you Eleven months will be Elapsed, and you I hope prepairing for your journey. It will be a tedious one I fear in the depth of winter, but let the thought of the cordial reception you will be assured of meeting warm the cold wintry blasts, and make your return joyfull.

You make no mention of receiving any Letters from me for a long time. I hope none have miscarried. I must beg you would write whilst you continue absent. We have had very great rains this fall, and severe cold weather for the Season. A flight of snow yesterday and to day as cold as January.

Adieu yours.

RC (Adams Papers); addressed in an unidentified hand: "To The Honble: John Adams Esqr. at Congress in Pensilvania"; endorsed (probably not contemporaneously): "Portia"; docketed in an unidentified hand.

[1] Concerning the abortive expedition to Rhode Island, in which Deacon and Brig. Gen. Joseph Palmer commanded the Massachusetts militia, see note 2 on AA to JA, [5] Oct., above; also Cotton Tufts to JA, following.

[2] On 12 July Capt. John Grimes' *American Tartar* attempted unsuccessfully to capture the Liverpool vessel *Pole* and was perhaps disabled in the engagement, which lasted several hours. For an account deriving from a Liverpool newspaper, see MHS, *Colls.*, 77 (1927):73.

Cotton Tufts to John Adams

Dear Sr.   Nov. 21. 1777

Sometime in September last I wrote to You,[1] and am not a little anxious to know whether you receivd my Letter, as it was sent about the Time You were removing from Philadelphia; In Your next to me or to Your Bosom Friend dont forget to inform me.

I congratulate You on Our Success to the Northward.—When I saw Burgoines Proclamation I read the Man, when I saw his Orders to Col. Baum I was confident that the Imagination of the Poet would work the Destruction of the Soldier. True it is that Vanity worketh a Lye.

You may be anxious no Doubt to hear of the Event of the Rhode Island Expedition. I wish it were in my Power to give You a satisfactory Accountt of it (that indeed is more than can be expected from those Conductors of it as some are pleased to say). It is said an Enquiry is making or hath already been made, why it prov'd abortive.

From what I can collect, The Failure principally arose from a Want of previous Preparations. When the Troops arrivd, Boats were wanting &c.&c. The Inlistment was but for a Month and by the Time every Thing was in readiness, the Enemy was reinforced and such Works erected by them as might require a regular Siege, which could not be entered upon without an Assurance of the Mens continuing untill the Conquest could be effected in that Way.—A fine set of Men composed the Soldiery, who were Zealous in the Cause and urgent for attempting, untill worried out by Expectations disappointed and by Measures ill conducted.

Adieu.

RC (Adams Papers); addressed: "To The Honble. John Adams Esq Member of the Continental Congress At York Town in the State of Pensylvania"; endorsed: "Dr. Tufts"; docketed in an unidentified hand.

¹ On 18 Sept.; this letter is printed above.

John Adams to Abigail Adams

My dear   Newbury Port Decr. 13. 1777

Yesterday was as fine for Travell as ever occurred at this season of the Year.—I reached Ipswich, and lodged, at the House where I used to put up, old Mrs. Treadwells.¹

This Morning I satt off, in a horrid cold Rain, and after getting wett through all my Coverings, I putt up at our Friend Mr. Tufts's, having no Courage to proceed farther.

Tomorrow Morning, I must proceed. Coll. Doane who was in a stage Coach and his son who was in a close sulky proceeded on, today.²

The fashionable Conversation all along the Journey is that Goods

are fallen and falling in Consequence of calling in the Money.³—
I am—&c.

RC (Adams Papers); addressed: "Mrs. Adams At Mr. John Adams's Braintree To be left at Mr. Isaac Smiths in Queen Street Boston"; postal marking:
"NP——2."

¹ For a lively sketch of her and her
husband, Capt. Nathaniel Treadwell, see
JA, *Diary and Autobiography*, 2:38.
² JA had been engaged by Col. Elisha
Doane, a wealthy Cape Cod shipowner,
and his son-in-law, Shearjashub Bourne,
to defend them in a case about to come
before a maritime court sitting in Portsmouth. The case was that of Penhal-
low and Treadwell *v.* Brig *Lusanna* and
Cargo. Doane was the owner and Bourne
had been supercargo of *Lusanna*, which
had been captured by a New Hampshire
privateer under circumstances strongly
indicating that she had been trading
with the enemy. The case was in the
courts for many years because the question of the authority of the Continental Congress, as opposed to that of individual states, was at issue; it was not
in fact settled until the United States

Supreme Court rendered a final decision
in 1795, which was in favor of JA's
clients. But JA's connection with it was
brief, his argument for the Doanes in
Portsmouth in Dec. 1777 being probably
his last appearance as a practicing lawyer. See his recollections of the trial as
given in his *Diary and Autobiography*,
4:2–3, and the editorial note there. His
MS minutes of the case are in M/JA/6,
Adams Papers, Microfilms, Reel No.
185, and will presumably be printed in
JA, *Legal Papers*.
³ On 13 Oct. the General Court repealed the "regulatory" (or price-fixing)
acts that had proved so objectionable and
unworkable, and passed an act to draw
in the state's badly depreciated bills of
credit (Mass., *Province Laws*, 5:733–
737).

Abigail Adams to James Lovell

Dear Sir   [*Braintree, ca. 15 December 1777*]

Your Letters arrived in the absence of Mr. Adams who is gone
as far as Portsmouth, little thinking of your plot against him.¹

O Sir you who are possessd of Sensibility, and a tender Heart,
how could you contrive to rob me of all my happiness?

I can forgive Mr. Geary because he is a Stranger to domestick
felicity and knows no tenderer attachment than that which he feel[s]
for his Country, tho I think the Stoickism which every Batchelor
discovers ought to be attributed to him as a fault.

He may retort upon me and ask if in such an Instance as this he
is not the happier Man of the two, for tho destitute of the highest
felicity in life he is not exposed to the keen pangs which attend a
Seperation from our dear connexions. This is reasoning like a
Batchelor still.

Desire him from me to make trial of a different Situation and
then tell me his Sentiments.

But you Sir I can hardly be reconciled to you, you who so lately experienced what it was to be restored to your family after a painfull absence from it, and then in a few weeks torn from it by a call from your Country. You disinterestedly obeyed the Summons. But how could you so soon forget your sufferings and place your Friend in a more painfull situation considering the Risk and hazard of a foreign voyage. I pittied the conflict I saw in your mind, and tho a Stranger to your worthy partner sympathized with her and thought it cruel in your Friends to insist upon such a Sacrifice.

I know Sir by this appointment you mean the publick good, or you would not thus call upon me to sacrifice my tranquility and happiness.

The deputing my Friend upon so important an Embassy is a gratefull proof to me of the esteem of his Country. Tho I would not wish him to be less deserving I am sometimes almost selfish enough to wish his abilities confind to private life, and the more so for that wish is according with his own inclinations.

I have often experienced the want of his aid and assistance in the last 3 years of his absence and that Demand increases as our little ones grow up 3 of whom are sons and at this time of life stand most in need of the joint force of his example and precepts.

And can I Sir consent to be seperated from him whom my Heart esteems above all earthly things, and for an unlimited time? My life will be one continued scene of anxiety and apprehension, and must I cheerfully comply with the Demand of my Country?

I know you think I ought, or you [would] [2] not have been accessary to the Call.

I have improved this absence to bring my mind to bear the Event with fortitude and resignation, tho I own it has been at the expence both of food and rest.

I beg your Excuse Sir for writing thus freely, it has been a relief to my mind to drop some of my sorrows through my pen, which had your Friend been present would have been poured only into his bosome.

Accept my sincere wishes for your welfare and happiness and Rank among the Number of your Friend[s], Your Humble Servant,

AA

Dft (Adams Papers); undated; at head of text in JQA's hand: "to James Lovell," to which CFA added: "1778."

[1] "I am charged by all those who are truly anxious here for the best prosperity of our affairs in France to press your acceptance of the Commission which has this day been voted you. The great sacrifices which you have made of private

happiness has encouraged them to hope you will undertake this new business. As one I hope that you will not allow the consideration of your partial defect in the Language to weigh any thing, when you surmount others of a different nature. Doctor Franklin's Age allarms us. We want one man of inflexible Integrity on that Embassy.... You see I am ripe in hope about your acceptance, however your dear amiable Partner may be tempted to condemn my Persuasions of you to distance yourself from her farther than Baltimore or York Town. [¢] Great as Brother Geary's hurry is he threatens to take his Pen in hand because I am not enough urgent with you; he feels all the Callosity of a Bachelor. I am but too ready to pardon his hard heartedness on this occasion where the eminent Interest of my Country is pleaded in excuse for him." (James Lovell to JA, undated, but undoubtedly written on 28 Nov. 1777, Adams Papers.)

On 28 Nov. Henry Laurens, recently elected John Hancock's successor as president of the Continental Congress, wrote JA enclosing "an extract from the Minutes of Congress" in Charles Thomson's hand (letter and enclosure in Adams Papers), as follows:

"In Congress Novr. 28. 1777
"Congress proceeded to the election of a commissioner at the court of France in the room of S. Deane esqr. and the ballots being taken
"John Adams esqr. was elected
Extract from the minutes
Charles Thomson secy"

Though the Journal is, as usual, uninformative, it is known that the nomination of JA was made by Elbridge Gerry, who told Congress that he had sounded out JA on the subject before the latter left York. In a letter to JA of 29 Sept. 1779 (Adams Papers; printed in JA's *Works*, 9:491–496), Gerry told JA some of the story behind the nomination and the vote, which was between JA and Robert R. Livingston, who had been nominated by the New York delegates. By marking a copy of the *Journals* for 1777, called Volume III, just printed by Dunlap in Philadelphia, Gerry signified to JA who had voted for him (and by implication who had not). This marked copy is among JA's books in the Boston Public Library (shelfmark 200.1, vol. 3; see p. 547 therein). CFA recorded Gerry's tabulation of the vote in a note in JA's *Works*, 9:492. See also note 3 on JA to AA, 15 Dec., below.

[2] This word editorially supplied.

Abigail Adams to Daniel Roberdeau

Dear Sir   *[Braintree, ca. 15 December 1777]*

Your obliging favour came to hand yesterday in the absence of my dearest Friend, and as he will not I fear reach home before tis too late to write by the post, or this conveyance, I have venturd to take up the pen least you should accuse him of neglect or inattention.[1]

I have been the more readily induced to write as it gives me an opportunity of acknowledging with gratitude the many civilities which Mr. Adams assures me he received from you and your worthy Sisters whilst he was an inmate in your family.

Be pleased Sir to acquaint them that I shall ever retain a gratefull Sence of their kindness.

The fresh instance of your regard to my worthy partner, and the honour conferd upon him by the important Embassy to which you have deputed him, together with the Sympathy you discover for his domestick happiness demands my warmest acknowledgments, tho I feel that the distinction given him by his Country must be at the expence of my present tranquility and happiness.

Taught both by his precept and example to sacrifice every private view to the publick good, ought I to say that I fear he will not be able to withstand the solicitations of his Friends upon this occassion, tho his partial knowledg of the Language will be an objection with him.

O Sir you who know as my dear Mr. Adams has informd me by melancholy experience, what it is to be seperated from one of the worthyest of women, and the dearest connexion in life, will forgive me when I say this is the hardest conflict I ever endured.

Danger and hazard, fear and anxiety will ever be uppermost in my mind, tho I have made use of his absence to prepare my mind for what I apprehend must take place least I should unnecessaryly embarras him.

I could easily su[r]mount the Dangers of the Sea and every other impediment, provided his tenderness would suffer me to accompany him.

At present he knows nothing of the appointment as the Presidents and all other Letters have come to my hand in his absence.

I shall endeavour as much as posible to leave him free to act ⟨*for himself*⟩ as he thinks best.

My most respectfull regards to Mrs. Climer and Roberdeau whom Mr. Adams always speaks of with the affection of a Brother. Love to Miss Nancy and the other little folks whose Names I have forgot. I must beg your Excuse for troubling you with this Epistle, and ask leave to subscribe myself your obliged Friend,   AA

Dft (Adams Papers); undated; at head of text in CFA's hand: "Jany. 1778."

¹ "Your domestick views of happiness was not consulted on this occasion, but the necessity of your Country for your Talents, which being devoted to her service, I expect a chearful acquiescence with a call so honorable, which I doubt not will prove a lasting honor to you and your Connections as well as a blessing to these States. . . . I wish you had improved the opportunity when here of studying the French language, which our friend Mr. Garry is now doing. I would advise your taking french books with you and a french Companion, and if an Opportunity does not immediately present from Boston a trip to the West Indies and a passage in a french vessel to Paris would be of considerable advantage" (Roberdeau to JA, "York Town," Penna., 28 Nov. 1777, Adams Papers).

John Adams to Abigail Adams

My dear   Portsmouth Decr. 15. 1777

I arrived here, last Evening, in good Health. This Morning, General Whipple made me a Visit, at the Tavern, Tiltons, and insists upon my taking a Bed at his House, in so very affectionate, and urgent a Manner, that I believe I shall go to his House.[1]

The Cause comes on Tomorrow, before my old Friend Dr. Joshua Brackett, as Judge of Admiralty. How it will go I know not. The Captors are a numerous Company, and are said to be very tenacious, and have many Connections; so that We have Prejudice, and Influence to fear: Justice, Policy and Law, are, I am very sure, on our Side.

I have had many Opportunities, in the Course of this Journey, to observe, how deeply rooted, our righteous Cause is in the Minds of the People—and could write you many Anecdotes in Proof of it. But I will reserve them for private Conversation. But on 2d Thoughts why should I?

One Evening, as I satt in one Room, I overheard Company of the Common sort of People in another, conversing upon serious subjects. One of them, whom I afterwards found upon Enquiry to be a reputable, religious Man, was more eloquent than the rest—he was[2] upon the Danger of despizing and neglecting serious Things. Said whatever Person or People made light of them would soon find themselves terribly mistaken. At length I heard these Words—"it appears to me the eternal son of God is opperating Powerfully against the British Nation for their treating lightly serious Things."

One Morning, I asked my Landlady what I had to pay? Nothing she said—"I was welcome, and she hoped I would always make her House my Home, and she should be happy to entertain all those Gentlemen who had been raised up by Providence to be the Saviours of their Country." This was flattering enough to my vain Heart. But it made a greater Impression on me, as a Proof, how deeply this Cause had sunk into the Minds and Hearts of the People.—In short every Thing I see and hear, indicates the same Thing.[3]

RC (Adams Papers); addressed: "Mrs. Adams Braintree To be left at Mr. Isaac Smiths Queen Street Boston."

[1] William Whipple (1730–1785), formerly a New Hampshire delegate to the Continental Congress and a signer of the Declaration of Independence, had left Congress in June of this year to command state troops in the campaign against Burgoyne (*Biog. Dir. Cong.*). Ezra Stiles was in Portsmouth at this time and recorded conversations with JA at Whipple's (and elsewhere), in

which JA spoke very freely of persons and measures; see Stiles' *Literary Diary*, 2:236–238.

² A word may be missing here, perhaps "discoursing" or "speaking."

³ As JA recalled in 1806, it was "while I was speaking" in the *Lusanna* trial at Portsmouth that "Mr. [John?] Langdon came in from Phyladelphia and leaning over the Bar whispered to me, that Mr. Deane was recalled, and I was appointed to go to France. As I could scarcely believe the News to be true, and suspected Langdon [to] be sporting with me, it did not disconcert me. As I had never solicited such an Appointment, nor intimated to any one, the smallest inclination for it, the News was altogether unexpected." To be sure, Gerry had mentioned this possibility just as JA was mounting his horse to leave York for home, but "I entreated him that neither [he] nor any one else would think of me" as Deane's successor, "for I was altogether unqualified" for that post, and thereafter, JA added, he quite dismissed the whole matter from his mind. (JA, *Diary and Autobiography*, 4:2–3.) Stiles in his *Literary Diary* (2:239) records the news of JA's appointment on 20 December. JA must have left Portsmouth that day or the day before, because he arrived in Boston on the 22d and received "Large Packetts from Congress" which AA had sent from Braintree in order for them to reach JA at the earliest possible moment. Getting home later the same day, JA made his decision at once and during the following two days answered—feelingly but affirmatively—all the official notifications and personal pleas he had received from York. See his letters of 23 Dec. to Henry Laurens, PCC, No. 84, I, printed in Wharton, ed., *Dipl. Corr. Amer. Rev.*, 2:458 (LbC, Adams Papers, printed in JA's *Works*, 7:7–8), and to Elbridge Gerry, LbC, Adams Papers. Also his letters of 24 Dec. to R. H. Lee and James Lovell jointly as members of the Committee for Foreign Affairs (who had sent him his commission in a letter of 3 Dec., Adams Papers), PCC, No. 84, I, printed in Wharton, 2:459–460 (LbC, Adams Papers, printed in *Works*, 7:8); to Lovell personally, LbC, Adams Papers, printed in *Works*, 9:471; and to Daniel Roberdeau, LbC, Adams Papers. The letter to Laurens and the letter to Lee and Lovell jointly are formal acceptances. To Gerry, JA said: "You wish for the Concurrence of a certain Lady, in a certain Appointment.—This Concurrence may be had upon one Condition, which is that her Ladyship become a Party in the Voyage, to which she has a great Inclination. She would run the Risque of the Seas and of Enemies, for the Sake of accompanying her humble servant.—But I believe it will not be expedient." To Lovell JA ruefully observed: "I should have wanted no Motives nor Arguments to induce me to accept of this momentous Trust, if I could be sure that the Public would be benefited by it.—But when I see my Brothers at the Bar, here, so easily making Fortunes for themselves and their Families, and when I recollect that for four Years I have abandoned myself and mine, and when I see my own Children growing up, in something very like real Want, because I have taken no Care of them, it requires as much Philosophy as I am Master of, to determine to persevere in public Life, and engage in a new Scæne, for which I fear I am very ill qualified. [¶]However, by the Innuendoes in your Letter, if I cannot do much good in this new Department, I may possibly do less Harm, than some others." And to Roberdeau he communicated his doubts about his acquiring a speaking knowledge of French at so late an age: "I shall try the Experiment, however, and if I find any great Inconvenience by which the Public may be likely to suffer I shall ask Leave to return. [¶]I shall devote my Time henceforward, to the Acquisition of a Language, to which I am not a total Stranger, having had some Knowledge of the Grammer and Construction of it, early in Life, and having practised Reading something in [it] all along, but which however, I never before aimed at learning to speak."

JA's decision to accept his appointment, though difficult, was speedy; indeed there seems never to have been any real question in either his or AA's mind about what that decision would be. Much more difficult to answer were the closely related questions whether AA would accompany him and which, if any, of the children would accompany him or them. When John Thaxter left for York, Penna., two or three days after JA had returned from Portsmouth, he had the impression that JA would take not only AA but the two oldest children, AA2 and JQA, as well (Thaxter to AA, "York Town," 20 Jan. 1778, below). But the very serious possibility of capture by the enemy at sea changed the Adamses' first tentative decision; and in the end only JQA, on his own plea, was permitted to sail with his father.

See AA's letters printed under the present date, above, and others to family and friends in Feb.–March 1778, below; also, JA's *Diary and Autobiography*, 4:4–5, 15–16; and his conversations in old age recorded by Harriet Welsh: "I never would have gone any where without my Wife. Nothing but the *deadly* fear that I might be in the tower and she not permitted to be there with me prevented my taking her" (transcript in CFA's hand, Adams Papers, M/CFA/31, Microfilms, Reel No. 327).

Mercy Otis Warren to Abigail Adams

My Dear Friend   Plimouth Jan 2d. 1778

Great Advantages are often Attended with Great Inconveniencies, And Great Minds Called to severe tryals. If your Dearest Friend had not Abilities to Render such important services to his Country, he would not be Called to the self Denying task of leaving for a time His Beloved Wife and Little pratling Brood. Therefore while I Weep with my Friend the painful abscence, I Congratulate her that she is so Nearly Connected with a Gentleman Whose Learning, patriotism And prudence qualify Him to Negotiate at Foreign Courts the affairs of America at this Very Critical period.

I think I know your public spirit and Fortitude to be such that you will Throw no Impediment in his way. Why should you. You are yet young and May set Down together many Years in peace after He has finished the Work to his own Honour, to the satisfaction of his Constituants and to the Approbation of his Conscience. You Cannot my Dear avoid Anticipating the Advantages that will probably Redound from this Honorable Embassy to Your self, to your Children and your Country.

But while I wish to say somewhat to support your Resolution and spirits Methinks somthing Wispers me within that you will justly say we are very Ready to Give advice when we but Illy practice upon the principles we lay down. True—but we may profit by the advice Though we despise the Weakness of the Adviser. Yet I have not so Ill an opinion of myself as to think were I just in your situation I shoud not strive for the Exertion of a Little Heroism upon such an Occasion.

I was in hopes we should have had the pleasure of seeing Mr. Adams at Plimouth before he left America. I should be very happy to see you together by my fire side if it was but for one day before he Crosses the Atlantic, but if that Cannot be my best Wishes await him. Assure him that my Fervant prayer is that he May Experience the peculier protection of providence through Every stage of his useful Life.

But I think before we part I Must desire him to Look into A Letter from Marcia Dated March 1776 (if he has not Destroyed it) which will Remind him of a Certain Bargin which I Expect he will fulfill.[1] His Excuse was once that he should Never be Called to the Different Courts of Europe. But I have seen Events so precipitated, and the Wheels of Revolution so Rapidly Move on, that I have Expected it for several Years. And if I am Notwithstanding His Vast Avocations Gratifyed with one Letter from the Court of France, however high I May Esteem the Indulgence, I shall not be More pleased with the Honour done me by the Embassadour of America, than obliged by this Mark of Friendship from Mr. Adams.

One thing More I Must beg you to assure him that if it is possible for me or mine to do any thing to Lessen the Inconvenience or pain of absence that His Portia or Her Children May suffer, He May Depend upon the Ready aid of His And Your Very Affectionate Friend,

Marcia Warren

RC (Adams Papers); addressed: "Mrs. Adams."

[1] In a letter to her of 8 Jan. 1776 JA praised certain "Characters" Mrs. Warren had drawn, and added: "I think I will make a Bargain with you, to draw the Character of every new Personage I have an Opportunity of knowing, on Condition you will do the same" (MHi: Warren-Adams Coll.; *Warren-Adams Letters*, 1:201). In replying, 10 March, Mrs. Warren agreed to the bargain but said she would be the gainer by it: "I Expect to be made Acquainted with the Genius, the taste, and Manners, not only of the Most Distinguished Characters in America, but of the Nobility of Britain, And Perhaps before the Conflict is Ended, with some of Those Dignifyed personages who have held the Regalia of Crowns And Scepters, and in the Zenith of power are the Dancing Puppets of other European Courts" (Adams Papers). To the latter part of this prediction JA strongly demurred in a characteristic passage in his reply of 16 April, q.v. in *Warren-Adams Letters*, 1:223.

Samuel Tufts to John Adams, with Enclosure

Hond. Sr.   Newburyport the 6 Jany. 1778

Inclosed you have a letter from Saml. Moody Esqr. dated the 5th. Inst. came to my hands by his Brother, unsealed. You will therein read his proposals respecting your son. If you should send him, I shall be ready to offer him my Service so far as lays in my power, in any respect, to make his life happy in his Absence from his Friends.[1]

The Owners and Agents of the Civel Usage have followed your Advice to me respecting the Unloading the Prize Brigantine Lafortune. As Capt. Bertrand declined giving his Consent to Takeing out the goods, had the goods been taken out upon her Arrival, I Imagine it would have been a means of saving many Thousands of Dollars to the Concerned. The Next Superior Court, Which you with Messrs. Lowell and Parsons will Attend in our behalf, Will (I suppose) decide the Dispute, between the Captain and those Concerned in the Prize.[2]—With my complements to Mrs. Adams and all friends, I am Sr. your Honor's Obedt. Hume. sert., Samll. Tufts

Mrs. Tufts desires her Compliments to be deliverd to Mrs. Adams &c.

RC (Adams Papers). Enclosure: Samuel Moody to Samuel Tufts, 5 Jan. 1778, printed herewith.

[1] Samuel Moody (1726–1795), Harvard 1746, was the first master of Governor Dummer Academy in Byfield, founded in 1763, and during more than a quarter-century in that post acquired great repute for his success in preparing boys for Harvard and other New England colleges. His brother Joseph and wife "ran the academy farm and boarded the boys." See Sibley-Shipton, *Harvard Graduates*, 12:48–54; James Duncan Phillips, "Harvard College and Governor Dummer's School," MHS, *Procs.*, 69 (1947–1950):194–206.

Doubtless JA discussed with Tufts (whose wife was a Moody) arrangements for placing JQA at Dummer Academy when JA stopped at Tufts' home in December. But the family's decision to let JQA accompany his father to Europe made any such plans obsolete.

[2] Tufts had no doubt consulted JA on this case in December. He was acting as agent for the officers of the *Civil Usage*, Capt. Andrew Giddings, a Newburyport privateer, which in September had captured a French vessel, *La Fortune*, Capt. Yves Bertrand K'Enguen, carrying a cargo of British goods. The maritime court in Boston had condemned the cargo (though not the vessel) in Nov. 1777, but the French captain appealed to the Superior Court, which in its Suffolk session of Feb. 1778 upheld the previous decree. John Lowell and Theophilus Parsons represented Capt. Giddings when the appeal came on. See Superior Court of Judicature, Minute Book 103, Records, 1775–1778, fol. 203–205; MHS, *Colls.*, 77 (1927):99.

ENCLOSURE

Samuel Moody to Samuel Tufts

Dear Sir   Newbury 5 Jan. 1778

With a very particular Satisfaction shall I take into our School and Family the Son of your respectable Friend Mr. Adams but as we are now so full and incumbered I believe it must be postponed till the 22 April after our Spring Vacation when he may be Chumm or Chambermate to the Son of the Hon. William Ellery of the State of Rhode Island. Our Pupils find their Bed and Bedding. Board a

Dollar per Week when Silver was our Currency and not more now allowing for the Difference of the Money. My Perquisite a Guinea in hard Money a Year which in Compassion to the present Times I reduced to less than that Sum in Paper Money. My Agreement with Mr. Shimmin is equivalent in Paper Money to a Guinea in Silver a Year. That your worthy Friend may have the full Completion of his Wishes in the present Accomplishment and Future Usefulness and Prosperity of his Son is the sincere Wish of My dear Sir Your assured Friend & hum. sert., Samuel Moody

The present fluctuating State of Things renders it impossible to be more explicit on the Subject. My Brother can be particular.

RC (Adams Papers); addressed: "To Mr. Samuel Tufts In Newbury-Port." Enclosed in Samuel Tufts to JA of 6 Jan. 1778, preceding.

Mercy Otis Warren to Abigail Adams

Jan. 8th. 1778

Did I think it in my power to afford any Consolation to my Friend I Would Readily undertake the tender task and as she Request[s] offer many Arguments for her support. But is it Really Necessary to Muster up arguments to prevail with my dear Mrs. Adams to Consent to what she knows is Right, to what she is sensible will Contribute Much to the welfare of the public. No [surely?] she has Already Consented And I hope from the best Motives.

In your Late hasty scrip[1] You ask 3 questions, Viz. what I think of a Certain appointment, what You ought to do, and what I would do. To the first I answer I think the Appointment most Judicious— and though we want his services hear I think the *Stat Holder* the best qualified of any man on the Continent to Represent the united States of America. By his penetrating Genius he May see through and Defeat the tricks of old statsmen and Courtiers at the same time He Gaurds against the Imbecility and Wickedness of more Modern politicians. To the second I Reply you Must be too sensible of the path that duty points out and the part you ought to act to stand in Need of the premonitions of Friendship. To your 3d question I have too Great a Regard to my own Character to [say][2] Frankly No, Yet am too suspicious of my own Heart positively to say Yes. Therefore must Leave it a Little *problematical* till further Examination and tryal.

I had some secret hopes that a Certain Embarkation would have

379

been made from Plimouth, but if there is a better place Layed you will with my best Regards bid your Friend Adieu in my Name, and suffer me to accompany your Every Good wish for his safty, success And happy Return.

I am sorry I Cannot supply you with the Little Articles you wrote for, but I Lend out of my own store 1/2 oz. of different threads just to keep you At Work till Either You or myself Can Get a Larger supply.

My son has no Cambrick. But there is A Frenchman here with whom I should have traded for you but he Cannot Yet Give me his price, and I dare not purchase at a Venture as he seems fully acquainted with the spirit of the Country, and knows no bounds to his Demands. If you will Limit me I will follow your Directions and purchase whatever You want. He has a Great Variety of those Luxeries we have been Fond off.

This European Commerce is Attended with some Inconveniences, for though we want their Cloathing, Warlike stores &c. &c., They Throw in upon us such an Innundation [of][3] useless Baubles, that the Wealthy may purchase, and the poorer Will, that I fear Their will be Little of that Frugality and Oeconomy so Necessary to support the Increasing public Burdens.

12 Jan

Since the Above was wrote I have been trying to trade with Monsieur, but find it will not do for Either of us. I Cannot Get a bit of Cambrick fit for your use under £4 per yd. Threads he has in plenty at 1/ per scain. I therefore send 10 scains of a sort from my Little stock till You Can do better.

With Great sincerity subscribes your Friend,

Marcia Warren

RC (Adams Papers).

[1] Not found.
[2] This word editorially supplied.
[3] This word editorially supplied.

Elizabeth Smith Shaw to Mary Smith Cranch

My Dear Sister   Haverhill January 10. 1778

I am very sorry I lost the Opportunity of conveying a Letter to Braintree by Mr. Thayer last week. We had company engaged to dine with us, expected Ladies to visit here in the PM and a very cold, short Day, when he called upon us. Otherwise I would have perswaded him to have tarried while I wrote a few Lines and thanked you for your very kind enquiries after *Madam* and her *Spouse*.—I have the Pleasure of assuring you they are in fine Health, are exceedingly pleased with their Situation, have every thing they want, more than a Clergyman just entered into a Family could expect, in such perilous Times. She is as happy as she can, or ought to be, at such a distance from her dear Friends. You my Sister have experienced how much kindness, affection, and tender assiduity contributed to make you easy even in this particular; and Without these Cordials of Life, I should be miserable was I situated even in the midst of my numerous Friends.

You say I must give you an account of every thing a sister ought to know.—In the first place I will begin with our Family matters—Of which I cannot give you a very Economick Discription. In short we spend our Time in Eating, Drinking, sleeping, geting victuals, cleaning house, Dressing, receving, and returning Visits, like other fine Folks.—A dismal kind of life I hear you say. I acknowledge it. But while we are in this World, Society is essential to Man's happiness, and we are induced to conform, and suffer many things dissagreeable, for the sake of the Blessings, and the Comforts that flow from it. Charity, and Benevolence are thus spread from Family to Family, and Friendships are formed that soften the Cares, and mitigate the Ills of Life.

Among other things I suppose I must tell you what oppinion the People have formed of me. In general, they say my Character was very good, and they are no ways dissappointed, (thats clever). One says that I am a little heavenly body. Others are so favourable as to say "that she talks, and is as sociable as one of *Us*," and the Children think that I am a *dear pretty woman*.—The People appear kind and hospitable, and as far as I can discern, no ways disposed to censure each other. If I live, I hope to gain their Affections, and to grow more and more worthy of their regards and Esteem.

Haverhill was once a beautiful and wealthy Town, flourished by Commerce, but now the best Families have quitted Trade, and live upon the Interest of their Money, which has greatly reduced their Estates.—This is now the Case of most populous Places.—I rejoice that you are out of them, and are the happy possessor of a long desired little Farm.

I am really troubled with Brother Adams for not returning from Portsmouth this way, it would have been but a few miles, if any, out of his way, and it would have rejoiced our Hearts to have seen him after so long an abscence. We congratulate Sister Adams however, on his Health, and safe return, and wish that e'er long he may see Peace restored to the Commonwealth, and after toiling for the publick Good, enjoy unmolested, the sweets of domestic Life.

I want to hear from our Friends at Weymouth, how they do, whether Sister Smith has got to bed, and whether it is a son or Daughter.[1] From my Father, from the Doctors Family, from Yours, from Sister Adams, from Miss Lucy, from Cousin Betsy, from Phebe, and all—every thing indeed that you, in exchange of places would wish to know.

January 16

This Day I was invited to a very elegant Entertainment at Mr. Duncan's, where I meet with Mr. Black from Boston who courted the once beautiful and amiable Polly Duncan, who instead of enjoying the fond endearments of a kind husband, lies now folded in the cold arms of Death. This is the dark side—a brighter Scene (from her Character) I trust she is the possesor of, than any earthly prospect could afford her.[2]

By this unhappy Lover, (for he had a tender and ardent affection for her) I propose to send a letter to Uncle Smith's, and from thence I hope it will soon be conveyed to my dear Sister, from Your truly affectionate
Eliza Shaw

PS My Love to Brother Cranch, and my little Cousins. Mr. Shaw desires to be remembered to every branch of my Connections.—When when shall I see them.

RC (DLC:Shaw Family Papers); docketed in Richard Cranch's hand: "Letter from Mrs. E. Shaw Jan. 10th. 1778."

[1] "Sister Smith" was the former Catharine Louisa Salmon (1749–1824), wife of William Smith, the writer's brother. The fourth of the Smiths' six children, Isaac, was born about this time, but neither his birth date nor much else about him is known to the editors. See Adams Genealogy.

[2] Mary, daughter of James Duncan, a prominent Haverhill merchant, died on 31 Oct. 1777, aged 28 (*Vital Records of Haverhill*, Topsfield, Mass., 1910–1911, 2:387; George W. Chase, *The History of Haverhill, Massachusetts*, Haverhill, 1861, p. 452).

John Thaxter to John Adams

Dear Sir   York Town Jany. 10th. 1777 [*i.e.* 1778]

The morning after my arrival to this place, I waited on the President with your letter; upon reading of which, he informed me, that he did not think it in his power to give me the place which you so kindly sollicited for me, but assured me he would use his Endeavours to procure some place for me.[1] I then waited upon General Roberdeau and the Massachusetts Delegates, who gave me the same assurances. Mr. Lovell, who has been particularly friendly, advised me to write in the Secretary's Office for the present, till some other Employment could be found. In pursuance of his Advice, I have enter'd the Office, with an Allowance of fifty five Dollars pr. Month. Ten Dollars and better, I am obliged to give a Week for Board, besides paying a seperate Bill for washing. My board is cheaper than I could have expected from Mr. Lovell's Representation of matters; who says a Man must pay ten dollars for glancing at a Tavern, and ten or twelve Shillings a night for his horse's gnawing the Rack.—I am in great hopes something will turn up for me, in another department, or that my present allowance will be augmented; otherwise I must return home, as the present office will not support me.

Lord Cornwallis, it is said, was kill'd in an Action lately, in which the Marquiss de Fayette was engaged. The Report seems tolerably well founded. Dr. Rush says the following facts are well attested, viz., That an Officer was seen carried off the field, to a certain House —that about a fortnight after, a very elegant Coffin was carried to that House—that a most pompous funeral was made—and that the Officers of the Army wear black Crape on their Arms. The Doctor, however, is not positive. There is an Account also that his Lordship's baggage is on board the Vessel bound to England, but no Certainty of *his* being on board; it is said he is not.

Mr. Duchè is gone to England: very penitent, Dr. Rush says. The illiberal manner in which he has treated Congress and General Washington has excited some Emotions of Grief and penitence. This may be depended on.—Please to give my respects to Mrs. Adams and Love to the Children.

I am, Sir, your most obedient Servt.,   John Thaxter Junr.

RC (Adams Papers); endorsed: "Mr. thaxter"; docketed by CFA: "Jany. 10th. 1777."

[1] Thaxter had arrived at York after "a long, cold and tedious Journey of 16 days" from Hingham (Thaxter to John Thaxter Sr., 10 Jan. 1778, MHi:Thaxter Papers). He was armed with five letters of introduction from JA, all dated 9 Dec. and all found in Adams Papers, Lb/JA/1; they were directed to Pres. Henry Laurens, to three Massachusetts delegates (Dana, Gerry, and Lovell), and to Daniel Roberdeau; and they commended Thaxter's qualifications for a secretarial post in the office of the President or elsewhere. Laurens' reply (which is in his own hand, not that of a clerk) contains a paragraph sufficiently remarkable to be quoted here even though the full text will presumably be included in Series III of *The Adams Papers*: "I desired that Young Gentleman to

call on me the Morning after he arrived intending to have conversed with him and to have aimed at some plan for procuring a suitable employment for him, but I found that by the Interest of his friends he had been introduced into the Secretary's Office. You may depend upon it Sir, if it shall hereafter be in my power, I will not fail to join those friends in order to give him a lift in proportion to his merit. For my own part long experience has convinced me that inaccuracy and confusion attend supernumerary Clerks in any Office. The duties of mine demand the Eye and hand of the principal and afford sufficient, oftentimes heavy employment for every moment between adjournments and Meetings of Congress, borrowing deeply of the Night and stirring very early every Morning but there is not half work enough for a Clerk who would have the whole day for the easy business of Copying which is all he ought to be entrusted with. I have a Young Man who serves me tolerably well in that branch and at intervals he finds other necessary work to do" (to JA, 15 Jan. 1778, Adams Papers).

Daniel Roberdeau to Abigail Adams

Dear Madam   York Town in Pennsilvania Jany. 19th. 1778

So much good sense, prudence, conjugal affection and patriotism blended in your favor to me [1] was a juster portraiture of the dear deceased, the subject of your compassionate sympathy, than I have met with, since the awful Catastrophe from which you borrow a comparison, to illustrate your feelings by anticipating a separation from your worthy partner my friend. Nor be offended at the comparison, which needs no apology, for truely She was "the worthyest of women" the loss of whom would beggar discription. But permit me to say your Subject will not bear a comparison. You may go with or follow Mr. Adams, at a more agreeable season, or suffer only a temporary separation whereas time fixes no limits to my sufferings. I most earnes[t]ly wish Mr. Adams may be long preserved a comfort to you and a blessing to his Country. I rejoice to find he purposes to go, and congratulate you on that fortitude of mind, which I presaged from your Letter, you have shown on the occasion. Please to accept the salutations of my Sisters and my thanks for your remembrance of my poor motherless Children. May yours be long blessed with maternal care, which cannot be supplied. I am with tender regard to your whole Household Dear Madam Yr. most obt. & very hume. Servt.,

Danl. Roberdeau

RC (Adams Papers).

[1] Printed above, from AA's undated draft, under the assigned date ca. 15 Dec. 1777.

John Thaxter to Abigail Adams

Dear Madam   York Town Jany. 20th. 1778

I am happy in having it in my power to furnish you with a Copy of Mr. Duchè's Letter, which is inclosed, as also an Extract from the public Ledger of Sept. 10.

By the Journals it appears that Mr. Adams has accepted the appointment.[1] The Appointment marks the Wisdom of Congress, and the Acceptation evinces his zeal in "the great and sacred Cause." Upon those great and important Exertions which he will make in our favour, depend under heaven the salvation of an insulted Country. It is my sincere belief—I have long thought so, and still maintain it. It may have the Air of Adulation, but it is not. It is the effusion of a heart sincere at least in this. Adulation I offer to those whose breasts contain Altars to recieve its incense. He is possessed of all those qualifications requisite to fill the Station.

I presume your Ladyship accompanies him. It gives me great pain on your account to indulge an Idea to the Contrary.

It would give me great Satisfaction to see my very worthy friends and the two you mentioned that you should take if you accompanied Mr. Adams, before they set out [on] their Journey. I should part with them very reluctantly. I shall hereafter feel lost in Braintree, when ever I go there.

My Duty to your Father, and Uncle Quincy if you please, not forgetting other friends.

My Love to Miss Nabby, Master John, my little friend Charley, and Master Tommy.

I wish you a safe and an agreeable Journey Madam, if you go, as also Miss Nabby and Mast: John. I shall journey far with Mr. Adams and You in Idea.

I am, Madam, your most obdt. Servt.,   J. Thaxter Junr.

RC (Adams Papers); addressed: "To Mrs. Abigail Adams Braintree"; endorsed: "Janry. 20." Enclosures: (1) Jacob Duché to George Washington, 8 Oct. 1777, copy in Thaxter's hand (in Adams Papers, filed under date of original); see JA to AA, 25 Oct. 1777, above, and note 3 there. (2) "Extract from the public Ledger of Sept. 10," not found or identified.

[1] JA's formal acceptance of his appointment as joint commissioner to France, in a letter to Pres. Laurens, 23 Dec. 1777 (RC in PCC, No. 84, I; printed in Wharton, ed., *Dipl. Corr.*, *Amer. Rev.*, 2:458), reached York and was read in Congress on 19 Jan. (JCC, 10:64; Laurens to JA, 22 Jan., Adams Papers). But there was no public announcement.

John Thaxter to John Adams

Dear Sir York Town Jany: 20th. 1778

Mr. Lovell informed me last Evening of your acceptation of the appointment; and also that he should send an express immediately to the Eastward with dispatches, by whom I write.[1]

I feel a mixture of joy and grief on this event. As a Patriot, I ought to congratulate my Countrymen upon it, as having thereby a glorious prospect of seeing the liberties of America supported by so able an advocate; but as an interested individual the event is exceedingly grievous—as thereby an invaluable friend and patron is lost to me for a time.

We are informed by Genl: Gates (who arrived here yesterday) that a general disaffection prevails mong the Canadians; Genl: Carleton, by scourging and bastinading 20 or 30 prisoners under the convention, has obliged them to enlist. By this Conduct, he has evidenced to the world that he is possessed of a Howe's humanity and a Burgoyne's faith. They are fit instruments for executing the wicked projects of the sanguinary Administration of Britain.

It is currently reported here that Genl: Lee is exchanged.[2] A man, who saw him in New York, says, that upon asking the Commissary of Prisoners who the Genl: was exchanged for, was answered that it was none of his business, that he was exchanged and that was sufficient. The same man further adds, that the Genl: told him, that he should come out of New York in a day or two.

If there is any thing respecting your domestic matters that can be left to my Care, I will manage them with the utmost Cheerfulness and fidelity.

Permit me, Sir, after most sincerely wishing you a good——— and that your life, health and Usefulness may be preserved, to subscribe myself, Your very hble. Sevt., J. Thaxter Jr.

RC (Adams Papers); addressed: "Honble. John Adams Esqr. Braintree"; endorsed: "Mr. thaxter"; docketed by JA in old age: "Jan. 20 1778 Yorktown."

[1] Lovell's letter to JA of the present date, which originally enclosed numerous papers—mostly to be forwarded or to be carried by JA to France—is in Adams Papers.

[2] A false rumor, like so much else that Thaxter reported from York at third or fourth hand.

John Thaxter to John Adams

Dear Sir   York Town Jany: 28th. 1778

One day last week a number of british waggoners, who were carrying Cloathing &c. to some of their soldiers in our power, had the honor of being introduced to a goal, for attempting to pass counterfeit money. These waggoners with a number of Serjeants of the enemy, were sent out by Genl: Howe, and permitted to pass by Genl: Washington's leave. When they arrived at Lancaster, they din'd or took lodgings there, and endeavoured to impose a counterfeit bill in payment of their reckoning. This induced some suspicions, that they might be furnished with some considerable quantity of said money; and upon examining their pockets, a pretty large Sum was found to be lodged there. The people, alarmed at this Villany, immediately applied to proper Authority to have these Villains confined. Upon which, they were apprehended and committed to close goal. The one that did actually pass the money, it is said, will hardly return a waggoner, before trial, to the General. If he is not hanged, I shall think Justice is hunted from our Courts.

Congress has adopted Retaliation at last; a copy of the resolution I have the honor to enclose you.[1] I think it a debt of Justice and humanity our poor soldiers, in their power, have a right to think due to them. It would be needless to mention the Cruelty and Inhumanity that have been invariably and uniformly exercised towards them; it is a matter of too much notoriety. The delay of this measure has been construed into timidity. I hope they will now be convinced to the Contrary.

A most valuable prize has been taken by the Jersey Militia. She was bound to Philadelphia from New York. The ice obstructed the navigation up the Delaware in such a manner as to force her so near shore as give the militia an opportunity of firing Cannon balls from Reedy Island. Her Cargo consists of 300 hogsheads of loaf sugar, near 200 of Rum, a quantity of Tea and a number of other articles of English goods. There were 90 Soldiers on board.

Yesterday afternoon and this morning was spent by a Committee of Congress in hearing Doctors Shippen and Rush. Dr. Rush informed me this morning, that he imagined the favorite System of Shippen's would be essentially altered in consequence of it. Dr. Brown says in a letter, that one half of the soldiers that died last year, perished by the present medical Establishment. A shocking black picture indeed Dr. Rush painted. But by all accounts it is a just one. It is a very melancholy reflection, that buildings erected for the relief and comfort of the sick and wounded, should become tombs to them. A bad System and a bad administration have produced great mischiefs in the Hospital. Peculation and embezzlement of Stores prevail as much in this department as in others. I do not alledge these things without authority or proof. They are facts too well authenticated.[2]

Please to give my respects to Mrs. Adams and love to the Children. I am Sir, with great respect your very Hble Servt.,

J. Thaxter Junr.

RC (Adams Papers); docketed by JA in old age: "John Thaxter Jan 28 1778." Enclosure not found; see note 1.

[1] This was presumably the report of the Board of War brought in on 21 Jan. setting forth British mistreatment of American prisoners and recommending retaliatory measures (*JCC*, 10:74–81). It was to have been followed by a published manifesto, which, however, was not adopted until the following 30 Oct. (same, p. 81–82, and 12:1080–1082, 1281; see also Burnett, ed., *Letters of Members*, 3:42–43).

[2] Rush wrote Pres. Laurens on 25 Jan. offering to furnish proof for his charges against Dr. William Shippen's management of the Continental hospitals. On the 27th a committee was appointed to hear both doctors. The committee and Congress sustained Shippen, and on the 30th Rush resigned. See Rush's letters to JA, 22 Jan., 8 Feb., and to Laurens, 25, 30 Jan. (*Letters*, 1:190–194, 199–200); *JCC*, 10:92, 93–94, 101.

John Adams to Abigail Adams

Uncle Quincys half after 11. O Clock

Dearest of Friends
Feby. 13. 1778[1]

I had not been 20 Minutes in this House before I had the Happiness to see Captn. Tucker, and a Midshipman, coming for me.[2] We shall be soon on Board, and may God prosper our Voyage, in every Stage of it, as much as at the Beginning, and send to you, my dear Children and all my Friends, the choisest of Blessings—so Wishes and prays yours, with an Ardour, that neither Absence, nor any other Event can abate,
John Adams

Johnny sends his Duty to his Mamma and his Love to his sister and Brothers. He behaves like a Man.

RC (Adams Papers); addressed: "Mrs. Adams"; docketed in an unidentified hand.

[1] The house of AA's uncle Norton Quincy was on his Mount Wollaston farm, in that part of Quincy Bay still known as Adams Shore, just east of where Black's Creek empties into the Atlantic. (This farm later passed into the possession of the Adamses, and here soon after the Civil War JQA2 built his

home called "Merrymount" from its proximity to the site of Thomas Morton's famous maypole. See CFA2, *Three Episodes*, vol. 1: chs. 10–19. A state highway marker has been placed near the site of the maypole.) Norton Quincy's house is pretty accurately located, by a building called "Quinzey," on "A Plan of the Town and Chart of the Harbour of Boston" in the *Gentleman's Magazine* for Jan. 1775, which is reproduced in the first volume of the present work.

² Capt. Samuel Tucker (1747–1833) commanded the *Boston*, a 24-gun Continental frigate launched at Newburyport in June 1776 (DAB; *Dict. Amer. Fighting Ships*). His instructions from the Navy Board in Boston concerning this voyage are printed in JA's *Works*,

3:94, note. There is implied if not explicit evidence in JA's papers, comparatively scanty as they are at this time, that his appointment as joint minister and particularly his sailing arrangements were kept as secret as possible, no doubt in order to avoid alerting British cruisers in New England waters. This may well be the reason why he embarked at Braintree rather than Boston. It will be noted from subsequent letters (and there are others in the files to the same effect) that JA left for France without taking care of pressing legal business and that some of his close friends and family connections did not know of his appointment until after he had sailed.

John Adams to Abigail Adams

On Board the Frigate Boston
5 O Clock in the Afternoon
Feb. 13. 1778

Dearest of Friends

I am favoured with an unexpected Opportunity, by Mr. Woodward the lame Man who once lived at Mr. Belchers, and who promises in a very kind manner to take great Care of the Letter, to inform you of our Safe Passage from the Moon head, on Board the ship.¹— The seas ran very high, and the Spray of the seas would have wet Us, but Captn. Tucker kindly brought great Coats on Purpose with which he covered Up me and John so that We came very dry.—Tomorrow Morning We sail.—God bless you, and my Nabby, my Charley, my Tommy and all my Friends.

Yours, ever, ever, ever yours,   John Adams

RC (Adams Papers).

¹ JA's term "Moon head" is puzzling, but from various sources it is known that he and JQA walked from Norton Quincy's across Hough's Neck (the peninsula that forms Quincy Bay on the southeast) to a barge which took them to the *Boston* lying in Nantasket Roads. See AA to Thaxter, 15–18 Feb., following; JA, *Diary and Autobiography*,

2:269–271; 4:6–7. The fullest contemporary record of the voyage is JA's own Diary, beginning in vol. 2 as just cited, supplemented by Tucker's log (quoted in editorial notes on the Diary entries) and also by the retrospective account in JA's Autobiography, beginning in vol. 4 as cited.

Abigail Adams to John Thaxter

Dear Sir   Braintree Febry 15 1778[1]

I little thought when you left me, that so much time would have Elapsed before I had taken my pen to write to you, but indeed Sir my Hands and my Heart have both been full. My whole Time has been taken up in prepareing my dearest Friend, and Master John for their Voyage, and yesterday they Embarked from this Town, the place you well know, Hofs Neck.[2] I think the wind has been fair for them to day, but they have not yet saild. I hope before I close this Letter to acquaint you that they are gone, tis a mortification to me to have them one day inactive. Since they are seperated from me I long to know that they are making the best of their Way to their desired Haven.

And now cannot you immagine me seated by my fire side Bereft of my better Half, and added to that a Limb lopt of to heighten the anguish. In vain have I summoned philosiphy, its aid is vain. Come then Religion thy force can alone support the Mind under the severest trials and hardest conflicts humane Nature is subject to.

> "Religion Noble comfort brings
> Disarms our Greifs or Blunts their Stings."

You were not ignorant of the agitation of my mind upon this occasion. The World may talk of Honour, and the ignorant multitude of profit, but sure I am no Consideration weighd with me, but the belief that the abilities and integrity of Your Friend might be more extensively usefull to his Country in this Department at this perticuliar time, than in any other. I resign my own personal felicity and look for my satisfaction in the Consciousness of having discharged my duty to the publick.

My desire was you know to have run all hazards and accompanied him, but I could not prevail upon him to consent. The Dangers from Enemies was so great, and their treatment to prisoners so inhumane and Brutal, that in case of a Capture my sufferings would enhance his misiry, and perhaps I might be subjected to worse treatment on account of my connection with him. These arguments prevaild upon me to give up the favorite wish of my Heart. Master John was very happy in his pappa's consent to accompany him, But young as he is a Mothers Heart will feel a thousand Fears and anxieties upon the occasion. There are many snares and temptations, I hope some of the worst [of] which on account of his age he will be likely to escape. Yet there are many very many which may stain his morals even at this early period of life. But to exclude him from temptation would be to exclude him from the World in which he is to live, and the only method which can be persued with advantage is to fix the padlock upon the mind.

I have to acknowledg the Recept of your very obliging favour of Janry. 10th, and the papers which accompanied it.³ Mr. Duche has acquired immortal fame by his performance if fame consists in being talked of, but tis a fame similar to what I have heard of a Man who murderd his Friend that he might not die unnoticed.

It gives me pleasure to see so distinguished a Genious as Mrs. Macauly Honourd with a Statue, yet she wanted it not to render her Name immortal. The Gentleman who erected it has sullied the glory of his deed by the narrow contracted Spirit which he discovers in the inscription, and if a Quotation from Lord Lyttleton (as I understand it) it is a pitty that what was meant to perpetuate the memory of that Lady should cast a shade upon the character of that Nobleman for whom heretofore I have had a great veneration. Even the most Excellent monody which he wrote upon the Death of his Lady will not atone for a mind contracted enough to wish that but one woman in an age might excell, and she only for the sake of a prodigy. What must be that Genious which cannot do justice to one Lady, but at the expence of the whole Sex?⁴

It is really mortifying Sir, when a woman possessd of a common share of understanding considers the difference of Education between the male and female Sex, even in those families where Education is attended too. Every assistance and advantage which can be procured is afforded to the sons, whilst the daughters are totally neglected in point of Literature. Writing and Arithmetick comprise all their Learning. Why should children of the same parents be thus distinguished? Why should the Females who have a part to act upon the great Theater, and a part not less important to Society, (as the care of a family and the first instruction of Children falls to their share, and if as we are told that first impressions are most durable), is it not of great importance that those who are to instill the first principals should be suiteably qualified for the Trust, Especially when we consider that families compose communities, and individuals make up the sum total. Nay why should your sex wish for such a disparity in those whom they one day intend for companions and associates. Pardon me Sir if I cannot help sometimes suspecting that this Neglect arises in some measure from an ungenerous jealosy of rivals near the Throne—but I quit the Subject or it will run away with my pen.

Present my Regards to Mr. L[ovel]l and tell him I will compound with him for the Robbery he has lately been accessory to, since his motives were such as I cannot condemn, if he will permit you to communicate to me all the News and intelligence from your Quarter of the world which may be communicated to a *Woman*. Tell him I have a large share of Grandmother Eves curiosity and have had a very indulgent partner, but being deprived of him I claim some small right of knowledge from others.—I feel very lonely and miss you more than ever.[5] The Boston saild a Sunday morning 6 o clock with a fair wind.

This Moment a Letter is deliverd me from on Board the Boston.[6] I will note the contents and tell you.

They are these, that they got on Board safe tho the Sea ran very high, and that they saild on Sunday, but a Snow Storm obliged them to put in to Marble Head, from whence they saild a twe.sday since which I know they have had fair weather and a fine wind. I dont know whether you know it, but I am governd by impulces a little, and cruel as the Seperation is I receive some comfort from a secret impulse that they will have a short and favourable passage. God Grant it is my fervent prayer.

You must write me by every opportunity unless discouraged by the length of this Epistle from Your Assured Friend,   Portia

Febry. 18
PS Enclosed you will find a Letter from your old Friend.[7] All the young folks desire to be rememberd.

RC (MHi:Waterston Coll.); addressed: "To Mr. John Thaxter York Town"; endorsed: "Mrs. Adams 15th. Feby. 1778." Dft (Adams Papers); incomplete and dated only "Saturday"; at head of text in JQA's hand: "to John Thaxter Yorktown Pa.," to which CFA added: "Feby. 1778." There are numerous small variations in phrasing between Dft and RC, but they have not been recorded here. Enclosure not found; see note 7.

[1] AA's letter was almost entirely composed, in draft form, on Saturday the 14th, the day after JA and JQA had gone on board the *Boston*. She copied it fair, so far as her draft extended (see note 5) on Sunday the 15th, but in doing so she did not correct her reference to the embarkation "yesterday" (i.e. Friday the 13th). The last three paragraphs of text in RC, together with the postscript, must all have been added on Wednesday the 18th after AA heard from Marblehead that the *Boston* had sailed from there on Tuesday the 17th.

[2] Hough's Neck; see note on preceding letter.

[3] AA means Thaxter's letter to her of 20 Jan., above.

⁴ All this relates to an incident in the life of Catharine (Sawbridge) Macaulay that caused a good deal of talk in England at this time and evidently also in America, where she had many admirers. In 1777 her generous but eccentric patron, Rev. Dr. Thomas Wilson, rector of St. Stephen, Walbrook, London, caused to be erected in his church (where he seldom officiated because he resided mostly at Bath) a white marble statue of her as Clio, leaning on the five stout volumes of her *History*. Whatever the merits of the statue, which was by a well-known sculptor, J. F. Moore, and heroic in its proportions, the vestry of St. Stephen's did not like it where it was and demanded its removal. Wilson eventually acceded, having lost some of his interest in Mrs. Macaulay after she married, in Dec. 1778, a 21-year-old surgeon's mate named William Graham. In 1872 the statue was given to the town of Warrington and placed in its town hall. A photograph of it is reproduced in Lucy M. Donnelly's article, "The Celebrated Mrs. Macaulay," *WMQ*, 3d ser., 6:173–207 (April 1949).

The inscription of which AA speaks here was on a marble table at the base of the statue: "You speak of Mrs. Macaulay; She is a Kind of Prodigy! I revere her Abilities; I cannot bear to hear her Name sarcastically mentioned; I would have her taste the exalted Pleasure of universal Applause; I would have Statues erected to her Memory; and once in every Age I could wish such a Woman to appear, as a proof that Genius is not confined to Sex; but at the same time—you will pardon me— We want no more than One Mrs. Macaulay. 'Late Lord Lyttelton's Letters to Mrs. Peach,' p. 114." There is reason to believe that the quotation from Lord Lyttelton was spurious. On the whole incident see the article on Mrs. Macaulay in *DNB*, and the very detailed and careful communications of Robert Pierpoint in *Notes and Queries*, 11th ser., 1 (1910):101–103, 142–144.

⁵ Dft breaks off here at foot of page with the phrase: "—a Sunday morning Six."

⁶ One can only suppose that this was a letter from JA, written from Marblehead when the *Boston* sailed from there; but it has unaccountably not survived. See AA to JA, 8 March, below.

⁷ Not found. In a letter to AA from York on 13 March (Adams Papers), Thaxter mentions receiving "letters from Mr. Adams and master John," presumably written before they left Braintree.

John Lowell to Abigail Adams

Dear Madam　　　　　　　　　　Boston Feby. 22d. 1778

I am not displeased that the Call of Business obliges me to address you at this Time, and gives me an Opportunity of expressing my sincere good Wishes, that Mr. Adams's Voyage may be agreable, and happy; I am sensible that the Prospect of so long a Seperation must be painfull to you, the tender social Connection which you have so highly enjoyed, must make the Struggle hard, but the Consideration that he is called to so honourable an Employment in the Service of his Country, I doubt not will greatly alleviate your Trouble. If during his Absence I can be of any Service in your Affairs, I hope you will command me freely, and be assured I shall be highly gratified in executing your Commands.—Judge Tyng of Dunstable will be the Bearer of this, there were two Actions of considerable Importance in one of which he was Plaintiff, and in the other Col. Eleazer Tyng, both against Dr. Gardner and others.[1] Mr. Adams was engaged for Dr. Gardner, and by the Clerks Minutes divers Papers filed in these Causes, were delivered to Mr. Adams, if they are at Braintree Judge Tyng will be obliged if you will let him look into them, and see whether some, which he must otherwise seek after, are among them. I do not propose, that Judge Tyng should take them as he was not Mr. Adams's Client, but if you will send them to Mr. Tudor there can be no Inconvenience as he is engaged on the same Side with Mr. Adams.

I am with most Esteem your most obedt. Servt.,   J Lowell

RC (Adams Papers); addressed: "To Mrs. Abigail Adams In Braintree."

[1] The cases were John Tyng *v.* Silvester Gardiner et al. and Eleazar Tyng *v.* Silvester Gardiner et al. (Eleazar was John's uncle; see sketches in Sibley-Shipton, *Harvard Graduates*, at 5:651–653, and 7:595–601, respectively.) They were part of the complex litigation over the Maine lands of the Plymouth or Kennebec Company, in which JA had been involved for some years before the Revolution; see his *Diary and Autobiography*, 1:54; 2:5–6; 3:280–282; and also a collection of printed tracts and MSS in the Robert Treat Paine Papers (MHi), mounted in a volume and labeled "Tyng v Gardiner / Kennebeck Purchase." The particular cases to which Lowell alludes were subject to repeated delays and were in the courts until 1785, when, at length, the record of the Supreme Judicial Court reads: "Neither party appears." See the letter immediately following, and Superior Court of Judicature, Minute Books 99, 105; Supreme Judicial Court, Minute Book 56; Records, June–Nov. 1785, fol. 21. Paine acted for the Kennebec Company in the later stages of this litigation.

——— ——— to Abigail Adams

Madam   Boston Feby. 23d. 1778

Mr. Adams for a long time has been engaged by the Kennebeck Company in a cause in which Colo. Tyng is a Party, which was reduced in one or more points to a special Verdict and was to have been argued this Court, but unfortunately being deprived of Mr. Adams to conduct the cause, by his sudden departure for France, the matter is suspended untill April, to give us time to provide for the debate.

When I had the pleasure to see Mr. Adams in Town he expected to conduct the cause and I gave him a Copy of the special Verdict, which with any other papers he may have left should be glad you will send by Colo. Tyng who will be so good as bring them to Boston.

I am not without expectations that Mr. Adams has left some minutes of importance to the Company as he promised me in consequence of his recommending Mr. Tudor to be joined with him, to confer with Tudor on the subject in dispute, who informs me he has had no opportunity for it, and therefore hopes to be assisted by his advice on paper.[1]

If Mr. Adams has not mentioned any thing on this head to you, probably he did to the Young Gentleman who studied with him; should be much obliged to you to desire him to make sarch and if he finds any thing to seal it up and send it by this opportunity.

I sincerely hope Mr. Adams will have a safe and pleasant Passage; and that the consideration that he may be extensively usefull to his Country will console you who are more entimately connected, and his other Friends, in the absence of so agreable a Companion.

I am with great respect Your most obedint hum. servt.

RC (Adams Papers). Signature omitted inadvertently, but this doubtless indicates that the body of the letter is in a clerk's hand, prepared for another to sign. The intended signer was either a partner or agent of the Kennebec Company and may have been James Bowdoin. The tone and substance of the letter both suggest Bowdoin, but since he did not sign it and the clerk's hand has not been identified, this is only a plausible conjecture.

[1] In R. T. Paine's collection of papers on Tyng *v.* Gardiner (see note on preceding letter), there are a few notes in JA's hand which may or may not be the "minutes" here inquired for.

So secret and "sudden" had been JA's preparations and departure that as late as 11 Feb. his friend and colleague William Tudor had written him from Cambridge: "Col. Henley waits upon You to engage You as Council upon the Prosecution against him by Genl. Burgoyne. Should You appear for him, which I hope You will, I would wish for an Opportunity of talking with You on the Subject. . . . Can You not come to Boston on Thursday or friday?" (Adams Papers).

Hannah Quincy Lincoln Storer to Abigail Adams

Feby. 24 1778

I have often thought of You My good friend, and as often wish'd to See You, and did flatter Myself that I should injoy that happiness before Mr. A—— departure. I am really Sorry that I was so unfortunate as to be absent from home when your first friend call'd to see Me. You Must Surely have call'd up all your Philosophy to Stand the Shock of his Absence a Second time for a Year.—Will My owning a truth lessen Me in your Esteem, if I thought it would, I Shoud be cautious how I confessed it. Indeed My good friend, I am Not so Stanch a friend to My Country as I find You are, for upon Examineing My heart I can't [say][1] that I should be willing to Make Such S[acrifices] as I think you have done. I hope that My patriotism will Never be proved in the way that Yours has, for I am confidant, that I should Make but a poor Figure in the like Situation.

I had wrote thus far a few days back, but interruptions of Various kinds prevented My proceeding, and Now I have only time to Let My Worthy friend know that it would afford great pleasure both to Mr. Storer and Me to See you with your Children at the habitation, where I know that you'd receive a Sincere Welcome. I can [write] [2] No More at present but am   H. Storer

P.S. Mr. Storer presents his Respects. My Love to Miss Nabby, and a[lso] to C——, T——.

RC (Adams Papers); addressed: "To Mrs. Abigail Adams In Braintree."

[1] Here and immediately below, MS is torn by seal.
[2] This word editorially supplied.

Abigail Adams to James Lovell

Dear Sir   Braintree March 1 1778
    I am greatly allarmed and distressd at the intelligence from Bordeaux, with regard to Dr. Franklin, which if true must be attended with very serious consequences. I had just acquired fortitude sufficent to withstand the dangers of the Sea and open and avowed Enemies, but was not prepaird for the assassinateing knife of a Ravellick.[1]— Is there no method that congress can take to chain these infernal Emissarys, and render the persons of their Commissioners safe? Indeed Sir I wanted not this additional terror to heighten my anxiety.[2]
    I want words to express my indignation at this black and infamous deed. Such a barbarous act of cruelty and injustice must fill every mind with horrour and can be eaqueld only by the "Macedonian Madman and the Sweede." Must a Man so Respectable as the Dr., known and revered throughout Europe both as a Philo[so]pher and a Statesman, whose only crime is that of defending the rights and privileges of his Country, be meanly assassinated for fulfilling the first of duties. O Britain can the Lusture of former deeds, or the Splendor of high atchivements blot out such baseness or cover such cruelty. May all Nations detest thee and the indelible Stains of this Haughty Tyrants Reign decend upon his posterity even to the third and fourth Generation.
    I should be very much obliged to you Sir if you would let me know by the first opportunity what foundation you have for this report, tis said that it comes confirmd in a Letter from you. You cannot wonder at my concern when what I hold dearest on Earth is embarked in the same hazardous enterprize.

Your Letters of the 8 and 10th of Febry. have just arrived.[3] Those which accompanied them I deliverd to General Warren to be forwarded by the first opportunity.

Tell Mr. G[err]y that if my heart was more at Ease I would rally him upon his Defence of Batchelors. I am sure he can shine in a good cause, but I will not affront his abilities so much as to take this as a Specimen of them.

When ever any perticulars arrive with regard to this black affair I must beg of you to acquaint me with them. They cannot add too, but may possibly Mitigate the anxiety of your Friend & Humble Servant, Portia

Dft (Adams Papers).

[1] François Ravaillac assassinated Henry IV of France, 1610 (*Century Cyclo. of Names*).

[2] The "intelligence" that so agitated AA was a news story published in the *Boston Gazette*, 23 Feb., p. 3, col. 1: "A Letter from Bourdeaux of December 12, mentions, That the illustrious Patriot Dr. Benjamin Franklin has been assassinated in his Bed-Chamber, at the Instance of Lord Stormont. The Villain left him for dead; but one of the Doctor's Ribs prevented the Stab from being instantly fatal, and he lay in a languishing Condition when the Vessel sail'd that brings this Account." This rumor was not discredited for more than a month; see Thaxter to AA, 31 March, below, and Lovell to AA, 1 April 1778 (Adams Papers).

[3] These were both addressed to JA and are in Adams Papers.

Abigail Adams to Hannah Quincy Lincoln Storer

[Braintree, ca. 1 March 1778]

My dear Mrs. Storers obliging favour was handed me to day. It found me with an additional Weight of anxiety upon my mind. I had been just able by the force of philosophy and I would fain hope by nobler Motives, to acquire a sufficent Stock of fortitude to support me under the most painfull Seperation I have yet been call'd to endure, when last Mondays paper gave me a Shock that I was not armd against.

Against an open and avowed Enemy we may find some guard, but the Secret Murderer and the dark assassin none but that Being without whose Notice not a Sparrow falls to the ground, can protect or secure us. My own solicitude[1] will not avail. When I was call'd to this trial, I asked not my Heart what it could, but what it ought to do, and being convinced that my Friend might be more extensively usefull in this department at this perticuliar time than in any other, hard as the Struggle was I consented to the Seperation. Most willingly would I have hazarded the danger of the Sea to have accompanied him, but the dangers from Enemies was so great that I could not obtain his consent.

You have a sympathetick Heart, and have often I dare say compasioned your Friend who feels as if she was left alone in the world, unsupported and defenceless, with the important weight of Education upon her hands at a time of life when the young charge stand most in need of the joint Efforts and assistance of both parents. I have sacrificed my own personal happiness and must look for my Sati[s]faction in the consciousness of having discharged my duty to the publick. Indulge me my Friend when I say few people have so valuable a treasure to resign, none know the Struggle it has cost me. Tender as Maternal affection is, it was swallowed up in what I found a much stronger, nor had it, its full opperation till after the departure of my Son when I found a larger portion of my Heart gone than I was aware of.

I was in hopes that a few Months would releave me from a Large Share of anxiety by the happy tidings of the safe arrival of my Friend, but a new Source of Distress has opened to my view. I was not aware of the assasinating knife of a Ravelick. Join with me my Friend in Suplications to Heaven for the safety of my Friend, and for the success and faithfull discharge of the important trust committed to him.

I rejoice in the happiness of my Friend, tho my own felicity is over cast. I little thought so much time would have elapsed before I had the pleasure of seeing her in her own habitation. She has left a vacancy here which cannot be supplied, but I will not regret it since she has contributed to the happiness of a worthy Man, and a deserving family—to whom as a peculiar Blessing of Heaven may she long be continued which will contribute much to the happiness of her affectionate   Portia

Dft (Adams Papers); at head of text in CFA's hand: "March 1778."
[1] MS: "solicituted."

Samuel Cooper to Abigail Adams

My dear Madam   Boston 2d. March 1778
Many besides my self partake with you in the Sollicitude you express respecting our dear Friend; for no Man could carry with him more of the ardent good Wishes of his Country than Mr. Adams did.

His Merit is great in denying himself so much for the Service of his Country, and your's not a little in giving up so much domestic Happiness for the Sake of this Service. Heaven, I trust, will protect and reward you both. I deferr'd till this Time answering your Letter,[1] in Hopes of an exact Copy of the Account you refer to, but have not been able to procure it; I remember, however, all the material Circumstances distinctly. Mr. Purveyance, a Gentleman of Character in Maryland, writes to his Friend at Congress, that Capt. Moore had arriv'd there from France, which he left the 12th. Decr.; that on the Day before he sail'd the Governor of the Place where he was receiv'd Dispatches from Paris, among which was an Account that Dr. Franklin had been assassinated by an Emissary, as was suppos'd, of L[ord] Stormont, who got into his Chamber, stabb'd him with a Knife, left him for dead, and made his Escape; but the Knife striking upon a Rib, it was hoped the Wound was not mortal. The Governor's Secretary gave this Account to Capt. Moore. Nothing can be more just than your Reflection on the Horror of this Deed. How many keenly feel the Weapon that pierc'd the Bosom of a Franklin! But this Assassination at once heightens his own Glory, and the Infamy of our Enemies; and the Abhorrence and Indignation it cannot fail to excite, must prove in the End highly advantageous to our Cause, and to the future Safety of our Friends in that Quarter: for it must unavoidably produce such Precautions on all Sides, and particularly in the Court of France, as to render the illustrious Sufferer himself, should he survive, as well as all his Colleagues, more secure than ever from such Attempts. It is in this Way I sooth my own Mind upon so affecting an Occasion, and would alleviate the Anxiety of your's.

The Sentiments and Expressions of your Letter have given me so much Pleasure that I cannot but wish to have it repeated as often as your Leisure will allow; and must beg you to command me in ev'ry Thing in which I can be suppos'd capable of doing you the best Service.

I am, Madam, with particular Regard, Your Friend and humble Servant,   Saml: Cooper

Mrs. Cooper and my Daughter remember you in the most affectionate Manner.

RC (Adams Papers).

[1] Not found. AA had presumably asked Cooper to inquire more closely into the origin of the story of Franklin's supposed assassination. See, further, James Lovell to AA, 1 April 1778 (Adams Papers).

John Thaxter to Abigail Adams

Dear Madam   York Town March 6th. 1778

Your much esteemed favor came to hand this day, in which you inform me of the departure of your "dearest Friend." I sincerely wish for your sake it had been convenient and safe for you to have accompanied him: But the danger you mention must, I think, have made the voyage disagreeable and had the event taken place, doubly aggravating on his part.—I can picture to myself the separation and your present situation; but it is too affecting a picture. My feelings are exceedingly interested. I feel the force of sympathy sensibly on the occasion. But let the consideration of its being a sacrifice to the glorious American Cause draw a shade o'er this affecting Picture, and Religion, which supplies the place of weak failing philosophy, on which you rely not, support you. To this source you have applied to blunt the edge of keen anguish—the sincerity of the application must ensure those consolations which "disarm grief or blunts it's stings." The principle, on which you assented to his departure, was noble, and marks that zeal and attachment to the cause of our country, which has so eminently distinguished you. Honor or profit weighed not with either of you, I am certain. Let the inadvertent and ignora[n]t amuse themselves with the rattle of Honor and profit. Time will convince them that far more noble and disinterested principles actuated the bosom of him who under heaven, is securing and will be securing and establishing that Independance which haughty Britain compelled us to avow.

A sacrifice like this is almost without parallel. But I will no longer dwell on a subject, which must wound that exquisite sensibility which your delicately susceptible mind is possessed of.

You will pardon me Madam for not writing oftener when I tell you that I have been in suspense ever since you had thoughts of going. I did not know till I received your letter, but that you was gone. I will now trouble [you][1] often with my Scrolls.

I cannot pass over that part of your agreeable favor which contain some strictures on the statue of [Mrs.][2] McCaulay, and the difference in point of Education between [male] and female, without an acknowledgment of the justice of the observations. They are so ingenious, and at the same time so just, that if complaisance did not suggest silence, Reason would tell me that the subterfuges of sophistication would be defied in breaking silence and attempting to explain them away. After mentioning that our sex wish a disparity, you subjoin a suspicion that Jealousy of rivalship is the foundation of the neglect of your sex. Madam, I am positive it is too often the case. It is an "ungenerous Jealousy" as you justly term it.

General Burgoyne and his family have leave to embark for England. This was in consequence of a representation of his ill state of health. He is desirous of going to the Baths in England—he thinks the only method of saving his life—he has tried the Bath often he says with success. He gives his parole and the officers of his family to return and redeliver themselves when called upon.

Congress will not recede from their resolutions of the 8th. of Jany. for suspending the embarkation of the troops. There is nothing they say in his last long argumentative letter sufficient to induce them to recede.[3]

⟨. . . .⟩[4] My duty is excessively laborious—eight, ten or twelve hours in the day at the pen. This York Town is a vile quarter. The streets and its Dutch inhabitants are happily assimilated.

Remember me to all friends—your little remaining flock. Poor Johnny is gone you tell me. I think he is now laying the foundations of a great man.

I hope to be honored with your further correspondence, and believe me when I say there was sufficient encouragement in the last for the perusal of many however long, yet to be sent to Your most obedient & very humble Servant,   J T.

RC (Adams Papers); addressed: "To Mrs. Abigail Adams Braintree"; endorsed: "March 16 [*sic*]."

[1] This word editorially supplied.

[2] Here and immediately below, MS is torn by seal.

[3] The report of a committee recommending that the embarkation of Burgoyne and his army be suspended "till a distinct and explicit ratification of the convention of Saratoga shall be properly notified by the court of Great Britain to Congress" was adopted by Congress on 8 Jan. and is printed with the accompanying resolves in *JCC*, 10:29–35. This action had been preceded and was to be followed by a controversy which still continues in historical discussions of the "Convention troops" and their

fate. Burgoyne's remonstrance mentioned by Thaxter was in a letter to Congress of 11 Feb., in PCC, No. 57, printed at p. 73–76 in Charles Deane's still valuable memoir on the Convention of Saratoga, Amer. Antiq. Soc., *Procs.*, Oct. 1877, p. 12–77. On 3 March Congress voted to permit Burgoyne and his immediate military family to sail home on parole (*JCC*, 10:218).

[4] One or two sentences at the beginning of this paragraph were heavily scratched and blotted out, probably but not certainly just after they were written. They cannot now be read.

Abigail Adams to John Adams

March 8 1778

Tis a little more than 3 week[s] since the dearest of Friends and tenderest of Husbands left his solitary partner, and quitted all the fond endearments of domestick felicity for the dangers of the Sea, exposed perhaps to the attack of a Hostile foe, and o good Heaven can I add to the dark assassin, to the secret Murderer and the Bloody Emissary of as cruel a Tyrant as God in his Riteous judgments ever sufferd to Discrace the Throne of Brittain.

I have travelled with you over the wide Atlantick, and could have landed you safe with humble confidence at your desired Haven, and then have set myself down to have enjoyed a negative kind of happiness, in the painfull part which it has pleased Heaven to allot me, but this intelligance with Regard to that great Philosopher, able Statesman and unshaken Friend of his Country, has planted a Dagger in my Breast and I feel with a double Edge the weapon that pierced the Bosom of a Franklin—

> "For Nought avails the Virtues of the Heart
> Nor tow'ring Genious claims its due Reward
> From Britains fury, as from Deaths keen dart
> No worth can save us and no Fame can guard."

The more distinguished the person the greater the inveteracy of these foes of Humane Nature. The Arguments of my Friends to alleviate my anxiety by perswading me that this shocking attempt will put you more upon your Gaurd and render your person more secure than if it had never taken place, is kind in them and has some weight, but my greatest comfort and consolation arrisses from the Belief of a Superintending providence to whom I can with confidence commit you since not a Sparrow falls to the ground without his Notice. Were it not for this I should be misirable and overwhelmed by my fears and apprehensions.

Freedom of sentiment the life and soul of Friendship is in a great measure cut of by the Danger of Miscarrages, and the apprehension of Letters falling into the hands of our Enemies. Should this meet with that fate may they Blush for their connexion with a Nation who have renderd themselves infamous and abhorred by a long list of crimes which not their high atchivements nor the Lusture of former Deeds, nor the tender appellation of parent nor the fond connexion which once subsisted, can ever blot from our remembrance or wipe out those indellible stains ⟨of their⟩ cruelty and baseness.[1] They have engraven them with a pen of Iron and Led in a Rock forever.

To my dear Son Remember me in the most affectionate terms. I would have wrote to him but my notice is so short that I have not time. Injoin it upon him Never to Disgrace his Mother, and to behave worthy of his Father. Tender as Maternal affection is, it was swallowed up in what I found a stronger, or so intermingld that I felt it not in its full force till after he had left me. I console myself with the hopes of his reaping advantages under the carefull Eye of a tender parent which it was not in my power to bestow upon him.

There is nothing material taken place in the politicall world since you left us. This Letter will go by a vessel for Bilboa from whence you may perhaps get better opportunities of conveyance than from any other place. The Letter you deliverd to the pilot came safe to hand.[2] All the little folks are anxious for the Safety of their Pappa and Brother to whom they desire to be rememberd—to which is added the tenderest Sentiments of affection and the fervent prayers for your happiness and Safty of Your   Portia

Dft (Adams Papers). RC, sent by a vessel bound for Bilbao, has not been found, was never acknowledged by JA, and therefore probably never reached him.

[1] Thus in MS. The sentence is defective, but only because it is not clear which words AA would have omitted and which she would have let stand in her fair copy.

[2] His second letter of 13 Feb., above, sent from the *Boston* in Nantasket Roads, or a missing letter sent from Marblehead when the *Boston* sailed from there? See AA to Thaxter, 15–18 Feb., above.

James Lovell to Abigail Adams

York Town
Dear Ma'am   21st. of March 1777 [*i.e.* 1778]

I am to thank you, in my own name, and on the public account, for that exercise of laudable patriotic prudence, which you have modestly termed the "Freedom" of inclosing to me Mr. McCreary's letter to your worthy Husband.[1] I read it in Congress, and I think it will be useful to the commercial Committee. The same Gentleman wrote to Mr. Adams in Sepr. some interesting history,[2] of which he gave me a copy, just before he undertook his late vast Sacrifice to his Country's Wellfare.—I fear I shall have wounded you by carrying your mind back to a day which you ought to strive to forget, by confining your imagination strictly to that of your future reunion: but, your billet under my eye, by developing your character, made my pen mark the expression *"vast* Sacrifice," while my heart acknowledged its individual portion of the debt of gratitude, which *our* Mr. Adams may charge against the Public.

All the intelligence which we received from France, about the period of Mr. McCreary's letter, was of the same tenor; our friends in Martinique wrote in like style on Decr. 3d.; but, on the 28th. of that month and the 26th. of January we have an ecclaircisement of the gallic finesse. The most open protection is afforded to our trade, privateers are fitted out, and their prizes not only sold, but a duty of 1 pr. Ct. regularly paid upon their cargoes towards the governmental revenue. The Governor of Antigua has no resource left but impotent threats to the General at St. Pierres of the Resentment that may arise in the breast of his Britannic Majesty, when the affair is properly represented. I suspect that England will more easily draw France in to open War by talking about Reconciliation than by boasting of subduing us by force. Louis thinks the latter impossible: his only fears are about the former.

I cannot give you any thing agreable from this neighbourhood. I cannot promise you that we shall owe our prosperity to our own spirit and preperations, in any degree comparable to what we shall owe to the Enemy's embarrassments and the unmerited favour of Providence, but, our hope of the latter is hardly supported in a ballance by the Justice of our Cause, counteracted by the *selfish* spirit of the Times: Justly may I be turned to the Parable of the Beam and Mote while I beg you to count me among yr. affectionate humb Servant[s].

RC (Adams Papers).

[1] AA's letter to which Lovell is replying has not been found. In the Adams Papers, however, is a paper in AA's hand containing copies of two letters to JA from William McCreery at Bordeaux, 10 and 25 Oct. 1777, the substance of either or both of which AA may have furnished to Lovell. There is no record in the Journal that they were read in Congress. Concerning McCreery, a Maryland merchant who had some acquaintance with JA and had recently established himself in Bordeaux, see JA's *Diary and Autobiography*, 2:293–294, and *passim*; also AA to JA, 18 May (Adams Papers). JA and McCreery corresponded for some years on commercial matters.

[2] This may refer to McCreery's letter to JA from Nantes, 29 Sept. 1777 (Adams Papers).

John Thaxter to Abigail Adams

Madam   York Town March 31st. 1778

Since I wrote you last,[1] the mystery of blank Dispatches being sent by Capt. Folgier from France has been developed. One Capt. Hinson (who was honored with Dr. Franklin's confidence) was guilty of the treachery and robbery. Hinson it seems was to have brought the Dispatches if Folgier declined. But when he found that Folgier accepted the trust, he, from his knowledge of the position and, I believe, nature of the dispatches, was not put to any difficulty which to select for Stormont. He carried the dispatches from the Dr. to Havre de Grace where Folgier was. There was a circumstance which render'd Hinson's conduct rather suspicious previous to the delivery of the packet containing the dispatches. He went to a certain place after he found that Folgier was determined to take charge of them, where it is conjectured he took such papers as he wanted. Folgier says he was at a loss to conceive what he could have to do at that place with the Dispatches. However the affair is now unfolded, and it is beyond the reach of doubt that he robbed the packet at said place.[2]

How few men, Madam, have virtue enough to withstand the temptation of a glittering bribe. May it not shelter this perfidious wretch when apprehended, from the hand of strict Justice. The secret machinations and subterfuges as well as the open assaults of our enemies are to be guarded against.

Men of inflexible fidelity and uncorrupted virtue should only be employed, and honoured with the confidence of our Commissioners. Such [men][3] will be hereafter engaged.

It gave me great uneasiness to find your apprehensions alarmed respecting the attempt on Dr. Franklin's life; I have now the pleasure to inform you that the report appears to be without foundation. Mr. Lovell will write you particularly about the matter[4] as also the foreign news, which I would have done myself the pleasure of transmitting you, had he not with great cheerfulness undertaken the business himself. I will postpone my congratulations till the agreeable and important news receives an authentic confirmation from proper authority.[5]

It comes, says the gentlemen[6] at Martinico, through so many channels, that the most incredulous cannot doubt. The General of Martinico pays full credit to it, altho, he has not received any particular advices. The proposal of Ld. Chatham for an accomodation, and the relinquishment of that Independence which American virtue first established, and still supports with unabated fortitude, will produce some serious deliberations in the cabinet of Versailles if America inclines to accede to it. The French Court will defeat the possibility of an accomodation says the Gentlemen at Martinico. America will not easily be flattered or frightened into an accession. Lord Chatham is a great and good man I sincerely believe, but I must subjoin with great deference to his Lordship, that he is a stranger to American politicks, if he thinks to mediate an accomodation upon that footing.

I am with great respect Your very humble Servt.,   J T.

RC (Adams Papers); addressed: "To Mrs. Abigail Adams Braintree"; endorsed: "March 31."

[1] Since his letter of 6 March, above, Thaxter had written to AA on the 7th, the 13th, and the 21st. None of these except the last was of much moment, but in that letter he gave a long paraphrase of Burgoyne's "argumentative" letter to Congress of 11 Feb., with critical comments thereon. The letters of the 7th and 13th are in the Adams Papers; that of the 21st is in MHi:Thaxter Papers, is incomplete, and may be a retained copy.
[2] The story of the "blank Dispatches," innocently brought to Congress in January by Capt. John Folger, is told in detail by Lewis Einstein in *Divided Loyalties*, Boston and N.Y., 1933, p. 55–71. The originals, being a large packet of letters from the American Commissioners in France, had been stolen and taken to London by Joseph Hynson, a Marylander who had been very confidentially entrusted with the dispatches by Silas Deane but who was in the pay of the British secret service.

[3] MS torn by seal.
[4] See Lovell to AA, 1 April (Adams Papers).
[5] This may be the first hint of the proposals by the British ministry that developed into the famous but wholly abortive Carlisle conciliatory mission. Contrary to Thaxter's present assurance, Lovell did not think himself at liberty to discuss this highly secret matter outside Congress so soon and so freely as the young clerk in the Secretary's office did. For a connected and authoritative account of the British conciliatory mission of 1778, see Carl Van Doren, *Secret History of the American Revolution*, N.Y., 1941, chs. 3–4.
[6] Thus in MS, here and below.

Abigail Adams to Elizabeth Smith Shaw

[Braintree, March 1778] [1]

I was meditating a Letter to my dear Sister when her agreable favour [2] reachd my Hands. Tho my own felicity is over cast, I can rejoice in that of my Friends and tis with pleasure I hear of your Health and happiness which are very dear to me.

The Scene which I have had to pass through, and in which you so kindly sympathize has put to the full proof all my fortitude and patriotism, and required the aid and assistance of a still nobler motive to bear up and support the pained anxious mind.

> "Religion noble comfort brings
> Disarms our Greifs or blunts their Stings."

Known only to my own Heart, is the Sacrifice I have made, and the conflict it has cost me. Call'd by the unanimous voice of his Country to an Embassy important to America and attended with much greater difficulties than tis prudence to represent—willing to resign all his domestick felicity and to devote fame, fortune and life to the Service of his Country, he bid defiance to ease, affluence and the allurements of ambition on the one hand and pushd forward against the threats of Calamity on the other. Satisfied as I was that his integrity and abilities were calculated to do essential Service at this critical season, I was determined to resign my own personal felicity and happiness and at all Events to bring my mind to acquiese in the cruel Seperation from the dearest conexion on Earth—a connexion formed early in life, matured by age and strengthend by the virtues of a Heart all my own, a Seperation for an unlimitted time, if it should please Heaven to preserve his life—seldom like to hear from him, unable to afford him any assistance in case of sickness, exposed to the Dangers of the Sea, to the open assaults of Enemies, and O Good Heaven, perhaps to the dark assassin and secret Murderer.

In this conflict my Heart has sufferd a distress which words cannot discribe and which nothing could alleviate but a confidence in that Being without whose notice not a sparrow falls to the ground.

The infamous attack upon the life of a Man so respectable as Dr. Franklin is a convincing proof that no regard is paid even to venerable age dignified by virtue, and distinguished by abilities which do honour to humane Nature.

> For Nought avails the virtues of the Heart
> Nor tow'ring Genious claims its due reward
> From Britains Fury as from Deaths keen dart
> No Worth can save us and no fame can guard.

Tis with a double edg I feel the weapon that pirced the Bosome of a Franklin. Nor can I refrain from imprecating the just vengance of Heaven upon the base and diabolical Counsels of a Nation who have not only deprived individuals of happiness, but by their cruelty, Rage and rapine laid waste oppulent cities, populus Towns, fruitfull villigaes and pleasent Feilds, but reduced to misiry and famine the widow, the Fatherless and the orphan. No former atchievements of Glory, illusterious deeds nor high renown can wipe out the indelliable stains dyed with Rivers of American Blood, and shed by the hands which ought only to have been lifted for her protection.

But I quit the subject and return to my own private affairs. I am endeavouring to put the Farm I am in possession of out of my Hands which will releive me from a load of care, and be more Beneficial to my Interest I believe than to struggle along as I have done from year to year. If I effect this I hope to be more at leisure to visit my Friends. One of the first visits will be to Haverhill.

Our Worthy parent was well this day and in good Spirits. The Roads have been so bad that I have not been to Weymouth since I saw you. I have but a few enducements to encounter difficulties to visit a place which has but one link left of a chain which once bound me to it.

Remember me in affectionate Terms to Mr. S[ha]w, who I dare say from the sympathetick Soul he possesses has participated in my anxiety—and to my Little Neice who I compasionate that she has not a Father whom she can Honour.[3] I thank my Sister for her Remembrance of a Nephew who I hope will never disgrace his parents or bring shame upon his relations. He mantaind a manly firmness at parting tho his Sister and Brothers burst into Tears. I need not add that the Mothers Heart is dissolved at the recollection, yet what ever it pleases Heaven to allot me the knowledg of your happiness will always give joy to Your Sister,
A A

Dft (Adams Papers); at head of text in JQA's hand: "to Mrs. Elizabeth Shaw. Haverhill," to which CFA added: "March 1778."

[1] This letter was answered by Mrs. Shaw on 5 April (Adams Papers).

[2] Not found.

[3] The "Little Neice," presumably staying with the Shaws at the time, was one of the daughters of AA's and Mrs. Shaw's brother, William Smith. This is the first indication in the Adams correspondence —there will be many more and quite explicit indications later—that William was delinquent toward his family.

Index

NOTE ON THE INDEX

This Index covers the first two volumes of the *Adams Family Correspondence*; hereafter an index will appear at the end of each published unit of this series, that is, presumably, at the end of every even-numbered volume. The Indexes are designed in some measure to supplement the annotation. The editors have tried to furnish here the correct spellings of proper names, to supply forenames for persons who appear in the text only with surnames, to indicate places of residence and occupations of persons whose forenames are either unknown or not known with certainty, and finally to distinguish by dates persons with identical or nearly identical names. Markedly variant spellings of proper names have been cross-referenced to what are believed to be their most nearly standard forms, and the variant forms found in the MSS are parenthetically recorded following the standard spellings. Because of the casual orthographic habits of the Adamses and their correspondents, and sometimes for other reasons, the editors' efforts to carry out these practices are admittedly imperfect, and they would warmly welcome corrections.

Wives' names, with a few exceptions for special reasons, follow their husbands' names, with *see*-references under their maiden names.

Under major place names (e.g. Boston, Philadelphia) there are appended separate gatherings of "Buildings, landmarks, streets, &c.," the items in which are arranged alphabetically rather than in the order of their appearance (as other subentries are throughout this Index).

References in the form "*See* (or *See also*) Adams Genealogy" are to a compilation described in the Guide to Editorial Apparatus at vol. 1:lvii and also at vol. 2:xv–xvi.

There is no separate register of writers and recipients of letters, but all letters printed in these volumes are listed in separate paragraphs at the end of the entries for the persons concerned, divided between letters written and letters received, each division arranged alphabetically by correspondent, with the letters dated only by year, and with only the first page (not inclusive pages) of the individual letters given.

Index

AA. *See* Adams, Mrs. John (Abigail Smith, 1744–1818)

AA2. *See* Adams, Abigail, 2d (1765–1813)

ABA. *See* Adams, Mrs. Charles Francis (Abigail Brooks, 1808–1889)

Abercromby (Abbercrombie), Col. James, British officer reported killed at Bunker Hill, 1:228

Abington, Mass., Hobart's iron foundry in, 2:25, 61

Accomac co., Va., 2:325

Adams, Abigail. *See* Adams, Mrs. John (1744–1818)

Adams, Abigail, 2d (1765–1813, daughter of JA and AA, later Mrs. William Stephens Smith, designated as AA2 in *The Adams Papers*): identified, 1:52 (*see also* Adams Genealogy); papers, 1:xxix–xxx; *Journal and Correspondence* (1841–1842), 1:xxx, xli; birth, 1:51–52; infancy, 1:54, 55, 57, 59–60, 61, 62, 63; lives briefly with Warren family, 1:87; requests stationery, 1:350; JA on education of, 1:384, 388; 2:271; illness, 1:391; requests books, 1:408; inoculated with smallpox, 2:47, 55, 57, 69, 80, 82–83, 86–87, 93–95, 98, 101–02, 106, 109, 115–16, 118; Mrs. Warren on appearance of, 2:118; invited to visit Mason family in Boston, 2:126–27; JA advises to learn needlework, 2:179; her "remarkable Modesty, Discretion, and Reserve," 2:179; JA on writing hand and style of, 2:227–28; "has a prudence and steadiness beyond her years," 2:258; "mournd in tears for Hours" over stillborn sister Elizabeth, 2:283, 292; mentioned, 1:xxix, 90, 91, 111, 145, 148, 152, 158, 174, 196, 209, 212, 216, 223, 232, 241, 267, 278, 290, 295, 300, 313, 322–23, 332, 343, 413; 2:144, 159, 161, 167, 195–96, 230, 234, 252, 276, 283, 288, 358, 376, 385, 389, 396

Letters: From JA (in 1774), 1:160; (in 1775), 1:304; (in 1776), 1:387; (in 1777), 2:189, 274

Adams, Abigail. *See* Homans, Mrs. Robert

Adams, Boylston (1771–1829, nephew of JA, *see* Adams Genealogy), 1:311

Adams, Mrs. Boylston (Elizabeth Anne Crosby, *see* Adams Genealogy), 1:311

Adams, Brooks (1848–1927, son of CFA, designated as BA in *The Adams Papers*, *see* Adams Genealogy): destroys his papers, 1:xxvii; unpublished biography of JQA, 1:xxxviii; last occupant of Old House, 1:219

Adams, Charles (1770–1800, son of JA and AA, designated as CA in *The Adams Papers*): identified, 1:84 (*see also* Adams Genealogy); papers of, 1:xxx; illnesses, 1:305, 403, 417; JA on education of, 1:384; requests "History of king and Queen," 1:408; anecdotes about, 1:417; 2:107; inoculated with smallpox, 2:55, 57, 65, 69, 72, 79–80, 82–83, 87, 93, 95–96, 98, 101–02, 106–22; JA: "You are a thoughtfull Child," 2:179; JA advises to increase his mechanical ability, 2:180; mentioned, 1:83, 90, 91, 111, 145, 160, 196, 209, 212, 216, 232, 241, 250, 278, 300, 313, 322, 332, 343, 413; 2:12, 144, 159, 161, 167, 195–96, 234, 252, 276, 288, 385, 389, 396

Letters: From JA (in 1777), 2:179, 190

Adams, Charles Francis (1807–1886, son of JQA, designated as CFA in *The Adams Papers*): identified, 1:6 (*see also* Adams Genealogy); *Diary* (in press 1963), 1:xix; as family archivist and editor, 1:xxiv, xxvii–xxviii, xxxii–xxxviii; letterbooks of, 1:xxix; CFA2's projected biography of, 1:xxxviii; correspondence in *A Cycle of Adams Letters* (1920), 1:xxxix; his silent omissions and

Adams Family Correspondence

ADAMS, JOHN (*continued*)

FINANCES AND ACCOUNTS

1:107, 109, 113–14, 117, 119, 123, 286, 383–84, 408; 2:27, 50, 128–29, 144–45, 251, 267, 288, 304–05, 330, 336, 340, 353–54, 375

HEALTH AND ILLNESSES

inoculated with smallpox, 1:12–47; 2:109; rumor of his being poisoned in New York, 2:113, 115, 121–22, 124, 128, 132; "My Eyes are somewhat troublesome," 2:163, 243; "I cannot pass a Spring, or fall, without an ill Turn," 2:224; "loaded constantly with a Cold," 2:238–40, 266; mentioned, 1:75, 107, 134, 158, 173, 195, 207–08, 213–14, 217, 226, 243, 246, 308, 399, 420; 2:12, 44, 56, 71, 78, 81, 83–84, 94, 103, 108–09, 114, 119, 128–32, 138, 172, 216, 253, 258, 262, 272, 276, 298, 310, 323, 335, 339, 350

LAND TRANSACTIONS

buys woodland in Braintree from Mrs. Elihu Adams, 1:415, 418; 2:12

LEGAL STUDIES AND CAREER

court circuit to Worcester (1763), 1:10; cases and experiences at the bar (1764), 1:48–49; cases and experiences at the bar (1766), 1:52, 54, 56; choice of and apprenticeship in the law, 1:62; cases and experiences at the bar (1767), 1:62; cases and experiences at the bar (1769), 1:66–67; Boston Massacre trials, 1:72, 74, 75; cases and experiences at the bar (1772), 1:83–84; cases and experiences at the bar (1774), 1:108–36; office in Queen Street, Boston, 1:109 ff.; on lawyers in the Province who have made greater fortunes than he, 1:113–14; term of Superior Court of Judicature in Falmouth (Portland), Maine, 1:123–36; King v. Stewart (1774) and its sequels, 1:131–34; cases and experiences at the bar (1775), 1:179–81; "1757 . . . I longed more ardently to be a Soldier than I ever did to be a Lawyer," 1:347; rivalry with Robert Treat Paine at bar, 1:351; writes Suffolk co. bar on behalf of John Thaxter, 2:255, 257, 300, 331; *Lusanna* case (1777 *et seq.*), 2:370, 374–75; *La Fortune* case (1777), 2:378; Tyng v. Gardiner cases, 2:393–95; sought as

counsel by Col. David Henley, 2:395. *See also under the names of JA's law clerks and names of particular cases*

PUBLIC LIFE

Local, Provincial, and State Politics: role in impeachment proceedings against Chief Justice Peter Oliver, 1:97; elected member of Mass. Council but negatived, 1:108, 124, 193–94; Braintree delegate to 1st Provincial Congress, 1:181; member of Mass. Council, 1:263–64, 269, 273, 342; appointed chief justice of Superior Court of Judicature, 1:271–72, 314, 327–28, 333, 342, 351, 405; commissioned justice of peace and quorum in Suffolk co., 1:314; rivalry with Robert Treat Paine, 1:351; resigns chief justiceship of Superior Court, 1:406–07, 417–19; 2:16, 27, 99–100, 113, 139, 159, 164, 185; resigns seat in Council after complaints about plural officeholding, 1:421

Continental Congress: 1774: JA's election to, 1:109, 129, 136; "I dread the Thought of the Congress's falling short of the Expectations of the Continent," 1:129; journey to, 1:129, 139–40, 144–46, 159; 2:237; service in and comments on proceedings of, 1:150–51, 155–61, 162–67; return from, 1:171

1775: JA's reelection and journeys to, 1:188–96, 200, 205, 224, 273, 276, 280–81, 329–31; service in and comments on proceedings of, 1:206–69, 280–333, 338; return from, 1:269, 272–73, 333, 337; CFA on JA's committee work, 1:332

1776: JA's reelection and journey to, 1:342–43, 345, 352, 398, 423–24; 2:131; service in and comments on proceedings of, 1:345–424; 2:1–141; rumor of his defection, 1:352, 363; leave and return from, 1:399; 2:71, 79, 84, 134, 137, 141; committee to confer with Lord Howe on Staten Island, 2:viii, 120–21, 124–25, 127–28, 134–35, 137–38; committee to design Great Seal of U.S., 2:ix–x, 96–97; chairman of Board of War and Ordnance, 2:x, 24, 58, 74, 84, 90, 131–32; drafts plan for a military establishment, 2:x, following 102, 131–32; committee to draft Declaration of Independence, 2:23, 31–32, 46, 48–49; drafts "Plan of Treaties," 2:44; proposal to General Court for alteration of "Plan of Delegation" to

alteration of "Plan of Delegation" to

ADAMS, JOHN (*continued*)
120, 122, 124, 126, 128, 130, 134,
144, 150, 155, 156, 157, 158, 161,
162, 163, 164, 166; (in 1775), 1:188,
189, 191, 192, 195, 206, 207, 208,
211, 213, 214, 215, 224, 226, 238,
241, 251, 252, 254, 255, 267, 268,
280, 285, 289, 291, 294, 299, 300,
302, 309, 311, 314, 316, 317, 318,
319, 326, 327, 331; (in 1776), 1:343,
345, 346, 348, 356, 361, 362, 366,
376, 381, 383, 391, 398, 406, 409,
410, 412, 419; 2:3, 5, 12, 23, 27, 29,
37, 39, 42, 43, 49, 50, 52, 53, 59, 63,
68, 70, 75, 80, 83, 88, 89, 90, 95, 99,
102, 103, 108, 110, 111, 114, 117,
119, 120, 124, 126, 130, 131, 134,
137, 138, 139, 141; (in 1777), 2:143,
145, 146, 147, 148, 151, 152, 153,
154, 157, 158, 161, 162, 163, 164,
165, 168, 169, 170, 174, 175, 181,
188, 192, 195, 197, 199, 201, 203,
207, 209, 211, 213, 219, 223, 224,
227, 228, 229, 230, 233, 234, 235,
237, 238, 239, 243, 245, 246, 247,
250, 252, 253, 255, 259, 261, 267,
268, 270, 271, 276, 278, 280, 281,
283, 284, 285, 286, 289, 292, 296,
297, 298, 299, 302, 303, 304, 305,
306, 310, 315, 316, 317, 318, 319,
320, 321, 325, 326, 327, 329, 332,
333, 335, 336, 337, 342, 349, 352,
353, 357, 359, 360, 361, 365, 366,
369, 374; (in 1778), 2:388, 389, 402;
to AA2 (in 1774), 1:160; (in 1775),
1:304; (in 1776), 1:387; (in 1777),
2:189, 274; to CA (in 1777), 2:179,
190; to JQA (in 1776), 1:388; (in
1777), 2:177, 190, 204, 289, 307; to
Peter Boylston Adams (in 1776), 2:8;
to TBA (in 1775), 1:305; (in 1777),
2:178, 234; to Zabdiel Adams (in
1776), 2:20; to Mary Smith Cranch
(in 1761), 1:1; to Richard Cranch
(in 1766), 1:52; (in 1767), 1:63; (in
1774), 1:159; (in 1776), 2:73; to
Mary Palmer (in 1776), 2:34; to Norton Quincy (in 1776), 1:368; to Isaac
Smith Sr. (in 1775), 1:212; (in 1776),
2:1, 52, 180; to Isaac Smith Jr. (in
1770), 1:67; (in 1771), 1:74, 81; to
John Thaxter (in 1777), 2:205; to
Cotton Tufts (in 1764), 1:19; (in
1776), 1:367; 2:21, 24, 54

Letters: From AA (in 1763), 1:6, 8;
(in 1764), 1:15, 19, 25, 31, 32, 36,
41, 43, 46, 50, 51; (in 1767), 1:62;
(in 1773), 1:90; (in 1774), 1:140,
142, 146, 151, 161, 172; (in 1775),
1:192, 194, 204, 217, 222, 225, 230,
239, 243, 245, 260, 269, 272, 276,
278, 284, 287, 288, 296, 305, 309,
312, 320, 324, 328, 335; (in 1776),
1:350, 352, 357, 369, 374, 378, 386,
389, 401, 404, 407, 415; 2:4, 13, 45,
55, 60, 65, 69, 72, 78, 86, 92, 93, 98,
101, 105, 106, 112, 114, 115, 121,
125, 127, 129, 133, 134; (in 1777),
2:149, 156, 160, 171, 185, 186, 193,
202, 211, 217, 229, 231, 240, 248,
250, 257, 265, 269, 272, 277, 278,
282, 287, 294, 300, 308, 323, 330,
339, 343, 346, 351, 354, 358, 367;
(in 1778), 2:402; from JQA (in
1774), 1:167; (in 1777), 2:167, 186,
254, 261; from Peter Boylston Adams
(in 1776), 1:371; from Zabdiel Adams
(in 1776), 2:6; (in 1777), 2:214;
from Richard Cranch (in 1775), 1:
258; (in 1776), 2:57; from Peter Cunningham (in 1777), 2:341; from John
Hancock (in 1776), 2:51; from Mary
Palmer (in 1776), 2:9, 76; from Elizabeth Smith (in 1774), 1:168; from
Isaac Smith Sr. (in 1775), 1:227, 266;
(in 1776), 1:339, 342, 364, 365, 372,
409, 413; 2:41, 182; (in 1777), 2:
196, 206, 222, 237, 262, 292, 310;
from Isaac Smith Jr. (in 1771), 1:71,
78; from John Thaxter (in 1775), 1:
233, 292; (in 1777), 2:183, 257, 282;
(in 1778), 2:382, 386, 387; from
Cotton Tufts (in 1775), 1:235, 264;
(in 1776), 1:393; 2:17, 35, 61, 81;
(in 1777), 2:210, 220, 344, 368; from
Samuel Tufts (in 1778), 2:377

ADAMS, MRS. JOHN (1744–1818,
Abigail Smith, designated as AA in
The Adams Papers, see Adams Gene-
alogy)

BOOKS AND READING
admiration for Mrs. Macaulay and her
writings, 1:xiii; in French language,
1:3–4, 355, 359–60; James Thomson a
favorite poet, but AA adapts text to her
purpose, 1:54, 85, 389–91; Fordyce's
Sermons to Young Women, 1:61; recommends and sends books to family and
friends, 1:61, 85; on the rearing and
education of children, 1:85–86; comments on Molière, 1:89–90, 93; reads

Index

ADAMS, MRS. JOHN (*continued*)

Rollin's *Ancient History*, 1:142–43; 2: 347; William Collins' "Ode" ("How sleep the brave"), 1:223; comments on Paine's *Common Sense*, 1:350, 352, 354, 376, 390; 2:193; requests copy of Trumbull's *M'Fingal*, 1:350, 352; requests copy of Chesterfield's *Letters*, 1:359, 376, 389; acknowledges receipt of newspapers and pamphlets from JA, 1:374, 390; interest in reading and writing poetry, 1:398; during inoculation with smallpox, 2:112; Hume's *History of England*, 2:172; Paine's *American Crisis, No. II*, 2:172, 174; Brydone's *Tour through Sicily and Malta*, 2:193–95; requests copy of *Select Essays upon Husbandry*, 2:308–09. *See also under particular authors' names*

CHARACTER, APPEARANCE, HABITS

early proposals to publish letters of, 1:xxxii–xxxiii; spelling and grammar, 1:xxxvii; carelessness with dates, 1:xlvii; JA's catalogue of faults of, 1:44–46; "I am lean as a rale," 1:56; "I am not Naturally of a gloomy temper," 1:97; "Some folks say I grow very fat," 1:173; mourns death of Joseph Warren, 1:223, 239–40; "I have been distress'd, but not dismayed," 1:239; "I am not naturally ... of that rastless anxious disposition," 1:255; a British visitor's praise of, 1:286; "my pen is always freer than my tongue," 1:310; "uneaquil to the cares which fall upon me," 1:375; use of literary sources, 1:391; JA on her wifely virtues, 1:412–13; "My Heart is as light as a feather and my Spirits are dancing," 1:416; facsimile of her handwriting in 1777, 2:xii, following 262; JA: "your Letters are much better worth preserving than mine," 2:3; keeps a letterbook for brief period, 2:4; JA: her letters give "clearer and fuller Intelligence, than I can get from a whole Committee of Gentlemen," 2:34; "Deliver me from your cold phlegmatick Preachers, Politicians, Friends, Lovers and Husbands," 2:79; "my Pen is my only pleasure, and writing to you the composure of my mind," 2:133; "I am not of an over anxious make," 2:266; on the current popularity of matrimony, 2:356; "I have a large share of Grandmother Eves curiosity," 2:392

CHILDREN

education of, 1:85–86, 94, 117, 141, 153, 377; views battle of Bunker Hill with JQA, 1:224; and JA's letters to them, 1:229, 250; JA outlines methods of teaching epistolary style to, 2:39–41; characterizes her three sons, 2:80. *See also under the names of the children*

DOMESTIC AND SOCIAL LIFE

dines at Col. Quincy's house, 1:xi, 152, 313, 320–21; comments on and relations with servants, 1:47–50, 60–61; 2:45, 59, 79; marriage to JA, 1:51; housekeeping, 1:52; visit from Samuel Adams and wife, 1:54; "I am still left alone," 1:60; "dined Nine Gentlemen to Day," 1:61; boards JA's law clerks, 1: 141, 153, 193; "I have lived a very recluse life since your absence," 1:154; the Warrens visit, 1:174; Quincys take refuge with, 1:193; seeks commission for JA's brother Elihu, 1:196–97; assumes responsibility for answering important communications received by JA, 1:200–05, 211; lodges soldiers and refugees, 1:205, 218; orders household items through JA in Philadelphia, 1: 219, 240, 243, 249, 277, 308, 314, 337, 350, 380, 383; "We live in continual Expectation of Hostilities," 1: 231; sociableness of neighbors in time of crisis, 1:232; trouble with tenant Hayden, 1:243–45, 305–06; attempts to assist family of George Trott, 1:243–45, 249, 370–71; meets Generals Washington and Lee, 1:246–47; on scarcity of West Indies goods, 1:249; "I endeavour to live in the most frugal manner posible," 1:249; on illness and death of JA's brother Elihu, 1:272; nurses family and servants through serious illnesses, 1:276–79, 286–89, 292, 296–97, 305; on illness and death of her mother, 1: 284, 287, 288–89, 293–94, 297–98, 309–10, 313; "I have been like a nun in a cloister," 1:325; "the House ... shakes with the roar of Cannon," 1:353; "We feel a temporary peace," 1:370; makes family clothing, 1:371; comments on JA's clothing, 2:4, 13; Gerry mistakenly delivers her canister of tea to Mrs. Samuel Adams, 2:68–69, 119, 122–23, 127; wants private chamber where she can write "Letters and keep my papers unmollested," 2:112; Supe-

ADAMS, MRS. JOHN (*continued*)
rior Court judges and members of bar
dine with, 2:125; unfavorable view of
her sister Elizabeth's engagement, 2:
159; requests stocking weaver's needles
for Hardwick, 2:194, 309, 329; won't
buy staples at inflated prices, 2:212–13

FARMING AND FARM MANAGEMENT

hiring and managing farm hands, 1:
117, 119, 359, 375, 377, 380, 398–99,
407–08, 416; 2:251, 269–70, 279,
323–24, 340; complains of drought,
1:147, 154; "a fine growing Season,"
1:205; profits and losses, 1:218, 232,
329; takes cow to Boston when family
undergoes inoculation, 2:45; "the loss
of your Grey Horse," 2:47, 60, 84, 87;
"Misfortune of loosing a Cow upon the
Ice," 2:187; comments on crops and
prospects for the year (1777), 2:194,
258, 273, 279, 288, 301, 323–24;
James Warren praises AA's management
of farm, 2:238–39; pays the tax rates,
2:251–52; advised by JA on crops and
livestock, 2:296–97; requests *Select Essays upon Husbandry*, 2:308–09; plans
to "put the Farm ... out of my Hands"
(1778), 2:407–08

HEALTH AND ILLNESSES

treated by Dr. Cotton Tufts, 1:12,
38; inoculated with smallpox, 1:332,
380, 400; 2:15–16, 27, 37, 41, 45–48,
50–122, 150, 213; pregnancy in 1777,
2:xii, 149–50, 157, 159, 161, 173,
181, 212–13, 232, 250, 252, 255, 258,
266, 271–72, 276–80, 285, 289; delivered of a stillborn daughter in 1777,
2:xii, 150, 282–83, 287, 292, 299,
308; "a nervious pain in my Head to
which I am sometimes subject," 2:5, 13;
death in 1818, 2:32; eye complaints,
2:45, 150, 185, 232, 341; "A most
Excruciating pain in my head and every
Limb and joint," 2:57; "the approach of
Spring unstrings my nerves," 2:193;
has "a paleness which has very near
resembled a whited wall," 2:213; has
"salt rheum," 2:232; "feeble and faint
with the Heat," 2:323; mentioned, 1:
51, 88, 90, 91, 97, 107, 108, 151, 173,
219, 255, 270, 276–78, 285–86, 289,
292, 295, 320, 322, 324, 328–29, 358,
422–23

POLITICAL AND RELATED OPINIONS

on women's rights, 1:76–77, 370,
397–98, 402–03; on superiority of
American society, 1:76–77; on resistance to tea tax, 1:88–89; on the "passion
of Ambition," 1:98; disapproves of
slavery, 1:162, 369; "the arm of
treachery ... is lifted over us as a
Scourge ... for our numerous offences,"
1:173; "Liberty or Death," 1:177–79;
on the "Massachusettensis" papers, 1:
180; "the Sword is now our only, yet
dreadful alternative," 1:183; "We know
too well the blessings of freedom, to
tamely resign it," 1:184; informs Edward Dilly of American crisis, 1:200–
02; disapproves "Olive Branch" petition,
1:262–63; "A patriot without religion
... is as great a paradox, as an honest
Man without the fear of God," 1:323;
"Man is a dangerous creature," 1:329;
on a "Code of Laws" for the new nation,
1:329–30; advocates independence, 1:
329–30, 337–38, 350, 352, 357, 370,
402; comments on trade and taxation,
1:336–37; approves Paine's *Common
Sense*, 1:350, 352; on Amer. rights in
Atlantic fisheries, 1:390–91; suggested
for committee "to examine the Torys
Ladies," 1:391, 398, 406; on inflated
prices of labor and goods, 2:5, 212–13,
217–18, 250–52, 323–24; sorry that
"the most Manly Sentiments in the Declaration are Expunged from the printed
coppy," 2:46, 48; on the need and
nature of a new state constitution, 2:92,
94, 218, 248–49; on scarcity of Boston
political leaders, 2:258; for repeal of
the Regulating Act, 2:265; on method
of training general officers for Continental Army, 2:294–95; on repeal of
the Stamp Act, 2:313; "Why should
we borrow foreign Luxeries [?]," 2:348–
49; "We have both [British] armies from
their Shipping. Tis what we have long
sought for" (1777), 2:351; on signifi-
cance of Burgoyne's defeat, 2:362–64;
on neglect of education of women,
2:391–93

RELATIONSHIP WITH AND
INFLUENCE ON JA

courtship, 1:1–12, 15–19, 22–51;
JA: "You shall ... banish all the un-
social and ill natured Particles in my
Composition," 1:49; marriage, 1:51;
"I have but little of his company," 1:56;

ADAMS, MRS. JOHN (*continued*)
loneliness, 1:62; "ardently I long for your return," 1:172; "I want some sentimental Effusions of the Heart," 1:247; joy upon JA's return from Philadelphia, 1:273; "I am obliged to summons all my patriotism to feel willing to part with him again," 1:276; JA desires her presence in Philadelphia, 1:331–32; "in need of the constant assistance of my Better half," 1:377; "a painfull Seperation from the companion of my youth, and the Friend of my Heart," 1:402; on JA's resignation from chief justiceship, 2:16, 113; inquires about JA's salary as delegate, 2:116–17; urges JA to return from Congress to deal with deteriorating family finances, 2:128–29, 251, 288; JA: "you have done such great Things in the Way of paying Debts," 2:267; comments on painful separation for half of their married life, 2:301–02; and JA's acceptance of first diplomatic appointment, 2:370–77, 379–80, 384–85, 390–92, 395–98, 402–07. *See also* Intercepted letters from JA

RESIDENCES

birthplace in Weymouth, 1:ix–x, 9, facing 80; birthplaces of JA and JQA (JA's patrimonial property in Braintree, now Quincy, Mass.), 1:xv, 76, 217, 222, 226, 244–45, 249, 267, 408, 413; 2:266; residences in Boston, 1:65–66, 139–40, 217–18, 223, 369, 380, 382, 388, 408–09; 2:4–5, 13, 128–29, 187–88; Old House, Braintree (now the Adams National Historic Site, Quincy, Mass.), 1:219

TRAVELS

visits American headquarters in Cambridge, 1:xv, 335–36; accompanies JA on trip to Worcester court, 1:10; visits the Cranches in Salem, 1:53–55; visits parents in Weymouth, 1:60, 90, 154, 176; desire to visit England, 1:76; visits Mercy Warren in Plymouth, 1:84; visits brother in Lincoln, 1:161; in Watertown with JA, 1:273; rides to Boston, 2:323; in Boston following Burgoyne's defeat, 2:358–64

WRITINGS

papers of, 1:xxvii, xxviii, xxx; *Letters* (1840, 1841, 1848), 1:xxxiii–xxxiv; *Familiar Letters* (1876), 1:xxxiv, xxxvi; *New Letters* (1947), 1:xli

Letters: To JA (in 1763), 1:6, 8; (in 1764), 1:15, 19, 25, 31, 32, 36, 41, 43, 46, 50, 51; (in 1767), 1:62; (in 1773), 1:90; (in 1774), 1:140, 142, 146, 151, 161, 172; (in 1775), 1:192, 194, 204, 217, 222, 225, 230, 239, 243, 245, 260, 269, 272, 276, 278, 284, 287, 288, 296, 305, 309, 312, 320, 324, 328, 335; (in 1776), 1:350, 352, 357, 369, 374, 378, 386, 389, 401, 404, 407, 415; 2:4, 13, 45, 55, 60, 65, 69, 72, 78, 86, 92, 93, 98, 101, 105, 106, 112, 114, 115, 121, 125, 127, 129, 133, 134; (in 1777), 2:149, 156, 160, 171, 185, 186, 193, 202, 211, 217, 229, 231, 240, 248, 250, 257, 265, 269, 272, 277, 278, 282, 287, 294, 300, 308, 323, 330, 339, 343, 346, 351, 354, 358, 367; (in 1778), 2:402; to James Bowdoin (in 1775), 1:220; to Mary Smith Cranch (in 1766), 1:53, 55, 56; (in 1767), 1:57, 60; (in 1774), 1:176; to Edward Dilly (in 1775), 1:200; to Hannah Storer Green (in 1765), 1:51; to James Lovell (in 1777), 2:344, 370; (in 1778), 2:396; to Catharine Sawbridge Macaulay (in 1774), 1:177; to Eunice Paine (in 1775), 1:209; to Daniel Roberdeau (in 1777), 2:372; to Elizabeth Smith Shaw (in 1778), 2:406; to Isaac Smith Jr. (in 1763), 1:3; (in 1770), 1:67; (in 1771), 1:76; (in 1777), 2:362; to Hannah Quincy Lincoln Storer (in 1778), 2:397; to John Thaxter (in 1776), 2:37, 101; (in 1778), 2:390; to William Tudor (in 1774), 1:170; to Cotton Tufts (in 1764), 1:12, 20; to Joseph Warren (in 1775), 1:196; to Mercy Otis Warren (in 1773), 1:84, 88; (in 1774), 1:97; (in 1775), 1:179, 183, 190, 254, 275, 301, 322; (in 1776), 1:377, 396, 403, 422; (in 1777), 2:150, 313

Letters: From JA (in 1762), 1:2; (in 1762–1763), 1:2; (in 1763), 1:3, 4, 7, 8; (in 1764), 1:16, 22, 23, 24, 28, 29, 32, 36, 39, 43, 44, 46, 47; (in 1769), 1:66, 67; (in 1771), 1:81; (in 1772), 1:83; (in 1774), 1:96, 107, 108, 109, 111, 113, 114, 116, 118, 120, 122, 124, 126, 128, 130, 134, 144, 150, 155, 156, 157, 158, 161, 162, 163, 164, 166; (in 1775), 1:188, 189, 191, 192, 195, 206, 207, 208, 211, 213, 214, 215, 224,

ADAMS, MRS. JOHN (*continued*)
226, 238, 241, 251, 252, 254, 255,
267, 268, 280, 285, 289, 291, 294, 299,
300, 302, 309, 311, 314, 316, 317,
318, 319, 326, 327, 331; (in 1776),
1:343, 345, 346, 348, 356, 361, 362,
366, 376, 381, 383, 391, 398, 406, 409,
410, 412, 419; 2:3, 5, 12, 23, 27, 29,
37, 39, 42, 43, 49, 50, 52, 53, 59, 63,
68, 70, 75, 80, 83, 88, 89, 90, 95, 99,
102, 103, 108, 110, 111, 114, 117,
119, 120, 124, 126, 130, 131, 134,
137, 138, 139, 141; (in 1777), 2:143,
145, 146, 147, 148, 151, 152, 153,
154, 157, 158, 161, 162, 163, 164,
165, 168, 169, 170, 174, 175, 181,
188, 192, 195, 197, 199, 201, 203,
207, 209, 211, 213, 219, 223, 224,
227, 228, 229, 230, 233, 234, 235,
237, 238, 239, 243, 245, 246, 247,
250, 252, 253, 255, 259, 261, 267,
268, 270, 271, 276, 278, 280, 281,
283, 284, 285, 286, 289, 292, 296,
297, 298, 299, 302, 303, 304, 305,
306, 310, 315, 316, 317, 318, 319,
320, 321, 325, 326, 327, 329, 332,
333, 335, 336, 337, 342, 349, 352,
353, 357, 359, 360, 361, 365, 366,
369, 374; (in 1778) 2:388, 389, 402;
from Samuel Adams (in 1776), 2:136;
from Samuel Cooper (in 1778), 2:398;
from Mary Smith Cranch (in 1767),
1:59; (in 1774), 1:143; from Hannah
Storer Green (in 1763-1764), 1:10;
(in 1764), 1:11; (in 1775), 1:273;
from Joseph Hawley (in 1775), 1:283;
from James Lovell (in 1777), 2:333,
365; (in 1778), 2:403; from John
Lowell (in 1778), 2:393; from Jonathan Mason (in 1776), 2:126; from
Mary Nicolson (in 1775), 1:221; from
Eunice Paine (in 1775), 1:197, 210;
from Elizabeth Palmer (in 1774),
1:137; from Nathan Rice (in 1776),
2:64, 85; from Daniel Roberdeau (in
1778), 2:384; from Elizabeth Smith (in
1774), 1:94, 103; from Isaac Smith
Jr. (in 1771), 1:70; from Hannah
Quincy Lincoln Storer (in 1778),
2:395; from John Thaxter (in 1778),
2:385, 400, 405; from William Tudor
(in 1774), 1:149; from Cotton Tufts
(in 1764), 1:38; from James Warren
(in 1775), 1:286; from Mercy Otis
Warren (in 1773), 1:86; (in 1774),
1:91, 99, 108, 138; (in 1775), 1:181,
186, 198, 274, 281, 338; (in 1776),

1:343, 385, 421; 2:33, 118, 141,
142; (in 1777), 2:166, 244, 264, 275,
312; (in 1778), 2:376, 379; from
an unidentified correspondent (in 1778),
2:394

Adams, John, 2d (1803-1834, son of
JQA, designated as JA2 in *The Adams
Papers, see* Adams Genealogy), 1:xxv

ADAMS, JOHN QUINCY (1767-1848,
son of JA and AA, designated as JQA
in *The Adams Papers*), identified,
1:62 (*see also* Adams Genealogy)

BOOKS AND READING

reads Rollin's *Ancient History*, 1:143,
145; reads to his mother, 1:145, 167;
memorizes Collins' "Ode," 1:224; requests books, 1:408; Smollett's *History
of England*, 2:xiii, 254-55, 261; JA
sends "perpetual almanack" to, 2:186;
reads Bampfylde Moore Carew's *Life
and Adventures*, 2:186, 204; JA advises to read newspapers and history,
2:271; JA sends list of portraits in
Bentivoglio's *History* to, 2:287, 290-92;
JA urges to study histories of revolutions,
2:289-92; JA advises to study ancient
history, 2:307-08; Thucydides' *History*,
2:307-08

CHARACTER, APPEARANCE,
HABITS, DOMESTIC LIFE

youthful letter-writing, 1:xxiii; letterbooks of, 1:xxix; works on family papers
during brief retirement from public life,
1:xxxii, 2, 40-41, 63, 203, 257, 424;
2:74, 151, 178; named for Col. John
Quincy, 1:56; rocked to sleep by AA2,
1:62; earliest known surviving letter of,
1:91; post rider between Braintree and
Boston, 2:106, 136, 141; marriage,
2:169; on AA's pregnancy, 2:213

EDUCATION

JA's comments on, 1:63, 117, 145,
252, 285-86, 384; problem of finding
a school for, 1:117, 193; tutored by
John Thaxter, 1:141, 153, 167; 2:178,
254, 261; on battle of Bunker Hill and
death of Warren, 1:223-24; JA on
writing style of, 1:332; JA: "John has
Genius," 1:384; tutored by Jonathan
Mason, 2:126; JA: "You must acquire
the Art of mixing Study with Business,"
2:177-78; wants a blank book in which

to "transcribe the most remarkable occurances," 2:254–55; plan to place him
in Governor Dummer Academy, 2:377–
79

HEALTH AND ILLNESSES

inoculated with smallpox, 1:332;
2:47, 55, 57, 66, 69, 80, 82–83, 86–
87, 115–16, 157; mentioned, 1:224,
322, 403, 423

TRAVELS

accompanies his father to France
(1778), 1:xvi; 2:185, 376, 390, 408;
accompanies Dana to St. Petersburg as
French interpreter, 1:362; voyage to
Spain in 1779, 2:203; JA: "He behaves
like a Man," 2:388

WRITINGS

CFA's plan to publish JQA's correspondence with his family, 1:xxxiii;
Writings (1913–1917), 1:xxxix

MENTIONED

1:xix, xxxi, xlii, 90–91, 111, 160,
174, 196, 209, 212, 216, 232, 241,
255, 263, 278, 300, 313, 332, 343,
359–60, 388, 413; 2:vii, 31–32, 61,
144, 159, 161, 167, 195–96, 234, 252,
276, 280, 283, 288, 385, 403

LETTERS

Letters: To JA (in 1774), 1:167; (in
1777), 2:167, 186, 254, 261; to Elizabeth Cranch (in 1773), 1:91
Letters: From JA (in 1776), 1:388;
(in 1777), 2:177, 190, 204, 289, 307

Adams, Mrs. John Quincy (1775–1852,
Louisa Catherine Johnson, designated
as LCA in *The Adams Papers*):
identified, 2:169 (*see also* Adams
Genealogy); papers of, 1:xxvii; HA's
plan to publish her journals, &c.,
1:xxxviii; mentioned, 1:xxxix; 2:178
Adams, John Quincy, 2d (1833–1894,
son of CFA, designated as JQA2 in
The Adams Papers, see Adams Genealogy): on not keeping letters,
1:xxvi–xxvii; as letter-writer, 1:xxxix;
home on Adams Shore, Mount Wollaston, called "Merrymount," 2:388–89
Adams, Peter Boylston (1738–1823,
brother of JA): identified, 1:18 (*see
also* Adams Genealogy); helps repulse
British raid on Grape Island, 1:xv,

225, 242; inoculated with smallpox,
1:16–18, 20–21, 23, 28–29, 31, 33,
40, 44; lives with widowed mother,
1:18; residence, 1:244; children,
1:245, 371, 391; 2:308–09; in as-
sault on Dorchester Heights, 1:372;
loses election as Braintree representative, 1:416, 418; 2:8–9, 12; JA
urges to join army, 2:38, 43, 135;
offers to send horse to JA in Philadelphia, 2:107; JA buys what is now
John Adams Birthplace from, 2:251–
52; mentioned, 1:xv, 46, 189, 191,
209, 212, 311; 2:50, 255
Letter: To JA (in 1776), 1:371
Letter: From JA (in 1776), 2:8
Adams, Mrs. Peter Boylston (1749–
1780, Mary Crosby, sister-in-law of
JA, see Adams Genealogy): pregnancy, 1:244; children of, 1:245,
254–55; 2:309; mentioned, 1:311
Adams, Samuel (1722–1803, 2d cousin
of JA): identified, 1:43 (*see also*
Adams Genealogy); personality and
character, 1:54; journey to Continental Congress (1774), 1:139–40,
146, 148, 159; Mass. delegate in Continental Congress, 1:156, 331; 2:5,
71, 160–61, 176, 213, 350; journeys
to Continental Congress (1775),
1:188, 224, 281; and Dr. Thomas
Young, 1:208; excepted in Gage's
pardon proclamation, 1:220; on
Thomas Cushing, 1:267; on adjournment of Continental Congress (1775),
1:268; and Dr. Benjamin Church,
1:299; and the Paine-Warren controversy, 1:351; on Provost William
Smith's *Oration*, 1:361; return from
Continental Congress (1776), 2:80,
84, 88–89, 101, 105, 116; reelected
delegate to Continental Congress
(1776), 2:131; journey to Continental Congress (1776), 2:136;
"much more communicative" than
JA, 2:173; Philadelphia residence
of, 2:176–77; and "a pair of spurs"
for Wilkinson, 2:357; return from
Congress with JA (1777), 2:366;
mentioned, 1:260, 262, 271; 2:100,
123, 216
Letter: To AA (in 1776), 2:136
Adams, Mrs. Samuel (Elizabeth Welles,
see Adams Genealogy): personality
and character, 1:54; AA visits and
comments on, 1:263; Gerry mistakenly delivers AA's canister of tea to,

character of, 1:347; and defense of New York, 1:347-48; AA desires more information on, 1:380; captured on Long Island, 2:122, 140; and Philadelphia campaign, 2:297

Alexander the Great, 1:98

Alfred, Continental ship of war, 2:280

Alison, Rev. Francis: sketch of, 1:167; minister of First Presbyterian Church in Philadelphia, 1:166-67

Allen, Ethan: and Dr. Thomas Young, 1:208; *Narrative* of his captivity, 1:341-42; marriage to daughter of Crean Brush, 1:374; mentioned, 1:214

Allen, James, of Philadelphia, "fallen, like Grass before the Scythe," 2:42

Allen, Mr., carries letters between JA and AA, 1:44, 46

Allen(?), Mr., of Braintree, 1:232

Alliance, Continental ship of war, 1:419

Allison, Rev. Patrick, preaches in Baltimore, 2:152

Allyne, Mary. *See* Otis, Mrs. James

Almon, John, *Remembrancer*, 1:327

Alva, Fernando Alvarez de Toledo, Duque de, 2:207, 225, 291

Amboy, N.J. *See* Perth Amboy, N.J.

American Academy of Arts and Sciences, JA's part in founding, 2:75-76

American Antiquarian Society: Cranch-Adams letters in, 1:xxx, xli; Mather family books and MSS in, 1:243

American Commissioners at Paris: Franklin's arrival in France, 2:160-61, 177; send letters to Congress, 2:193, 298-99; meet with Vergennes, 2:195-96; and proposals for commercial treaty with Prussia, 2:197-98; JA's appointment as joint commissioner (1777), 2:372; and blank dispatches sent to Congress, 2:405-06. *See also* JA–Public Life

American Philosophical Society, 2:59, 75

American Prohibitory Act, 1:401

American Tartar, Mass. privateer, 2:203, 232, 368

Ammunition, JA urges domestic manufacture of, 2:25-26. *See also* Gunpowder

Amory, Mr., Mass. loyalist, 1:234

Amsterdam, Netherlands: Carmichael seeks American loan in, 2:199; mentioned, 2:2, 89, 198, 366

Anabaptists. *See* Baptists

Anderson, Capt., of the Amer. sloop *Morris*, 2:209

Andover, Mass.: gunpowder mill in, 2:61; mentioned, 1:371

Andrews, Amos, Richard King's case against, 1:132

Andrews, John, letters to William Barrell, 1:140, 243

Andrews, Jonathan, Jr., Richard King's case against, 1:132-33

Andrews et al. *v.* King, 1:132-33

Angier, Oakes (JA's law clerk): sketch of, 1:84; AA on character and politics of, 1:140-41, 153; elected to Mass. House of Representatives (1776), 2:4, 13; mentioned, 1:83, 141

Andrew Doria, Continental ship of war, 2:260, 280

Anglicans. *See* Episcopal Church

Annabella, British troop transport, 2:16

Annapolis, Md., 1:252

Anne, Queen of England, 2:15, 92

Antigua (island), 2:42, 98, 404

Antimony (medicine), 1:14, 16, 40

Antipaedobaptists. *See* Baptists

Antony, Mark, 2:253

Antwerp, Belgium, 2:291

Anville, Jean Baptiste Bourguignon d' (French cartographer), 2:91

Apthorp, James, Braintree loyalist voted "Inimical," 2:267

Apthorp, Sarah Wentworth. *See* Morton, Mrs. Perez

Aranda, Pedro Pablo Abarca y Bolea, Conde de, and proposals for Franco-American alliance, 2:195

Arcadian Belles Lettres Society, Rome, 1:315

"Ardelio." *See* Green, Joshua

Arenberg, Jean de Ligne van, 2:291

Aristophanes, 2:306

Arms. *See* Firearms

Armstrong, Maj. Gen. John, urges amendments to Penna. Constitution, 2:262

Arnold, Maj. Gen. Benedict: commands troops in march into Canada, 1:287; signs cartel with Capt. Forster at The Cedars, 2:85-86; promotion, 2:230; allegations against, 2:245; and reorganization of northern army, 2:299; marches to relieve Fort Schuyler, 2:322; mentioned, 1:214, 339, 345; 2:64, 259, 268, 334

Arnold, Capt., mariner in service of

Index

to enforce Regulating Act, 2:265, 267; loyalist inhabitants voted "Inimical to the United States," 2:265, 267, 273; AA on inflation of wages and goods in, 2:269–70, 279, 323–24; molasses mills in, 2:348

Buildings, landmarks, streets, &c. (*alphabetically arranged*): Black's Creek, 2:388; Christ Church (now on School Street, Quincy), 1:407; 2:135–36, 194–95; Commons, 1:366, 413; "Cranch Pasture," 2:270; "The Farms" (later North Quincy), 2:244–45; First or North Precinct Church, 1:146; 2:47; Great Hill (or Spears Hill) on Hough's Neck, 1:204, 248, 251, 358; 2:9–10, 14; Hough's (Hoff's) Neck, 1:xv–xvi, 251, 259, 360; 2:11, 389–90, 392; meetinghouse in Middle Precinct, 1:204, 206; Middle Precinct, 2:241; "Moon head," 2:389; Morton's "Merrymount," 2:389; Mount Wollaston, 1:x, 14, 22, 146, 191, 194, 314; 2:270, 388–89; Norton Quincy's house on Adams Shore, 2:388–89; Penn's Hill, 1:111, 224, 343, 353, 358; 2:33, 100, 181, 239; Powder House, 1:152; Col. Josiah Quincy's house in Wollaston section, 1:190–91, 193–94; Stony Field and Stony Field Hill (later Presidents Hill), 2:32, 270. *See also* JA *and* AA—Residences; Germantown (district of Quincy, Mass.); Quincy, Mass.; Randolph, Mass.).

Brand Hollis, Thomas, 1:xxxii
Brandywine Creek, battle of, 2:xii, 342, 348
Brattle, Thomas, sketch of, 1:252
Brattle, Brig. Gen. William: letter to Gage on preparedness of military companies exposed, 1:147–49; "Address to the Public," 1:149; replaced by Col. Gardner after fleeing to Boston, 1:227; mentioned, 1:400
Breck, Mr., carries letters between JA and AA, 1:153
Breeds Hill. *See* Charlestown, Mass.
Breed's Island. *See* Hog Island
Brewer, Rachel. *See* Peale, Mrs. Charles Willson
Bridesburg (called Point-no-Point), Penna., 2:247–48
Bridgewater, Mass., 1:84, 140–41, 204; 2:4, 61, 273
Brigham, Dr. William T., 2:xi

Brinckerhoff (Brinkhoff), Col. John, JA's host in Fishkill, N.Y., 2:146
Bristol, Mr., of Boston, marriage to Rev. William Smith's slave Phœbe, 2:346
Bristol, England, 1:136; 2:88, 206
Bristol, Penna., 2:349
British Army. *See* British troops in America
British Navy: Vice Adm. Graves' fleet in Boston Harbor, 1:149; contractors for, 1:233; committee of Congress appointed to record hostile acts of, 1:303–04; squadron bombards and burns Falmouth (Portland), Maine, 1:308–10; squadron under Banks patrols Nantasket Roads, 1:381; 2:9–11; operations after evacuation of Boston, 1:414; "fleet" appears in Boston Harbor, 2:47; men of war patrol Chesapeake Bay, 2:158, 234–35; captures vessels importing flour into Boston, 2:172; and Aitken's attempts to burn royal dockyards in England, 2:206; men of war patrol Delaware Bay, 2:246–47; floating batteries sent into Delaware River, 2:254. *See also names of particular officers and ships*
British troops in America: and rumored conspiracy of Negroes in Boston, 1:162; officers tried in Mass. courts, 1:179–81; AA on occupation of Boston by, 1:200–04, 247; losses at Bunker Hill, 1:227, 229–31, 235–36, 241; Boston under martial law, 1:228–29, 236, 239, 247–48, 261, 306–07, 314; contractors for, 1:233; rumored court martials over burning of Charlestown, 1:265; evacuation of Boston, 1:271, 294, 356–58, 366–69, 373–74, 379, 381, 393, 402, 414, 417; Howe supersedes Gage as commander, 1:298–99; committee of Congress appointed to record hostile acts of, 1:303–04; and Amer. fortifications on Dorchester Heights, 1:356; transports carrying Highland soldiers captured in Boston Harbor, 2:11, 15, 17–19, 161; and smallpox, 2:24; The Cedars affair, 2:85–86; in New York campaign (1776), 2:89–90, 108, 111, 117–18, 121, 129, 132–35, 140; in New Jersey campaign (1777), 2:144–46, 162, 168, 180, 318; JA on cruelty of, 1:163; plan for exchanging prisoners, 2:207–08; JA on number and strength of

429

Index

Checkley, William, sketch of, 1:43
Cheesman, John, Braintree loyalist voted "Inimical," 2:267
Cheesman (Cheasman), Mrs., of Philadelphia, 2:176–77, 327
Chelsea, Mass.: naval action at, 1:210, 214, 225; mentioned, 1:xvi
Chesapeake Bay: Lord Dunmore flees from, 2:81; British men of war in, 2:158, 234–35; Howe's army sails into, 2:289, 297, 302, 305, 321–22, 325–26, 329–30, 333–34; mentioned, 2:xi–xii, 151–52, 181
Chester, England, 2:307
Chester, Penna., 2:144, 297, 330, 342
Chester co., Penna., 2:137
Chester River, Penna., 2:xii
Chesterfield, Earl of. See Stanhope, Philip Dormer
Chevot. See Chovet
Chincough (whooping cough) in Boston, 2:323–24
"Choice of Hercules" (Shaftesbury's treatise and Gribelin's engraving), 2:ix–x, 96–98
Choiseul, César Gabriel de, Duc de Praslin, French minister of war and foreign affairs, 1:72, 78
Chovet (Chevot), Dr. Abraham: sketch of, 2:236; anatomical waxworks of, 2:236
Christopher, Mary, of Concord, charged with murdering her child, 2:184
Church, Dr. Benjamin: sketch of, 1:35; inoculates patients with smallpox in Boston, 1:33, 40; mission to Philadelphia, 1:208–09, 213; treats infirmity of JA, 1:214, 243; appointed director and chief physician of Continental hospital, 1:298–99, 312; charged with treason for furnishing information to British command in Boston, 1:298–99, 301–02, 306–07, 312, 314–15, 323, 352; AA on conduct of, 1:307, 323; mentioned, 1:229
Church, Edward ("Ned"), 1:243, 354, 386–87, 389, 409; 2:4
Church of England. See Episcopal (Anglican) Church
Churchill, John, 1st Duke of Marlborough, 1:401
Cicero, Marcus Tullius: "Tully's Orations," 1:xxi; JA on epistolary style of, 2:39; letters to Atticus, 2:192
Cider and cider-making, 1:164; 2:246,

258, 273, 284, 305, 316, 321, 324, 331, 332, 344
Civil Usage, Newburyport privateer, captures La Fortune, 2:378
Clams, poisoning by eating, 1:110
Clarendon, Earl of. See Hyde, Edward
Clark, Abraham, N.J. delegate in Continental Congress, 2:318
Clark, Mr., of Braintree, 2:251
Clarke, Elizabeth. See Howard, Mrs. Simeon
Clarke (Clark), Richard(?), loyalist in London, 1:136
Clarke, Mr., of Stoughton, killed on Moon Island, 1:259
Clements Library, Gage Papers, 1:299
Cleverly, Benjamin, Braintree loyalist voted "Inimical," 2:267
Cleverly, Henry, Braintree loyalist voted "Inimical," 2:267
Cleverly, Joseph: sketch of, 1:235; loyalist opinions of, 1:234–35, 359; voted "Inimical," 2:267
Cleverly, Joseph, 2d, Braintree loyalist voted "Inimical," 2:267
Cleverly (Cleavely), Mr., of Braintree, 1:143–44
Cleverly family of Braintree, 1:152, 154
Climer. See Clymer
Clinton, Gov. George, of N.Y., sends news of Burgoyne's defeat, 2:357
Clinton, Lt. Gen. Sir Henry: threatens to land troops in New York, 1:354; and campaign at Charleston, S.C., 2:52, 81; mentioned, 1:262
Clugny, Jean Etienne Bernard de, 2:198–99
Clymer, Mr., carries letter to Boston for James Lovell, 2:333
Clymer (Climer), Mrs., sister of Daniel Roberdeau, 2:353, 372–73
Cockran, Mr., of Boston, 1:236
Codman, Richard: sketch of, 1:135; extends hospitality to JA in Falmouth (Portland), Maine, 1:134–35
Coffin, John (Boston loyalist in Quebec), sketch of, 1:341
Cohasset, Mass., 1:xvi, 376
Cohasset Rocks, Massachusetts Bay, 2:15–16
Coleman. See Colman
College of Philadelphia. See Pennsylvania, University of
Collins, Ezra, of Boston, brother of Stephen, 1:238
Collins, Stephen: sketch of, 1:238; his

433

also Adams Genealogy); portrait of, 1:xii–xiii, facing 81; appearance of, 1:xiii, 56–58; conducts glassworks in Germantown with Palmer, 1:1, 18, 53; JA's affection for, 1:3; personality and character, 1:52–53; in watch-making business, 1:52–53, 55, 62, 63; house and business on Hanover Street, Boston, 1:53, 111, 121, 143, 160–61, 176; ill health of, 1:55–57, 59; in cardmaking business, 1:61–62; JA requests to read letters to AA, 1:160; plans to move from Boston to Braintree, 1:163, 173; secures family retreat against British invasion, 1:226; Braintree residence near Christ Church, 1:407; inoculated with smallpox, 2:37, 41, 45, 55–57, 62, 73–74, 82–83, 102, 106–07, 130; seeks advancement for Nathaniel Cranch, 2:58, 74; JA wants his help in founding a "philosophical society" in Boston, 2:75–76; AA mentions as possible successor to Winthrop at Harvard, 2:94, 109; contemplates moving because of failing business, 2:130, 138–39; mechanical ability of, 2:180, 269; buys and farms land in Braintree, 2:269–70, 276, 285, 293, 309; mentioned, 1:2, 19, 31, 40–41, 46, 63, 69, 90, 189, 206, 214–15, 232, 242, 250, 263, 265, 300, 311, 316, 322, 371; 2:47, 60, 65, 68, 70, 72, 121, 283, 331, 382

Letters: To JA (in 1775), 1:258; (in 1776), 2:57; to Mary Smith Cranch (in 1761), 1:1

Letters: From JA (in 1766), 1:52; (in 1767), 1:63; (in 1774), 1:159; (in 1776), 2:73

Cranch, Mrs. Richard (1741–1811, Mary Smith, sister of AA): identified, 1:1 (see also Adams Genealogy); inherits Smith parsonage in Weymouth, 1:x, 9; AA's letters to, 1:xxx; fanciful name, "Aurelia," 1:2, 26; pregnancy, 1:3; and Mary Nicolson, 1:26; health and illnesses, 1:143–44, 210, 313, 322; concern over toryism of Isaac Smith Jr., 1:171–72, 174–76; inoculated with smallpox, 2:37, 45, 56, 65, 69, 78, 82, 107; mentioned, 1:xii, 19, 45, 46, 53, 63, 69, 160, 189, 210, 214, 221, 232, 242, 263, 288–89, 300, 316, 325–26; 2:47, 68, 116, 119, 122, 130, 138, 285, 296

Letters: To AA (in 1767), 1:59; (in 1774), 1:143; to Isaac Smith Jr. (in 1774), 1:171

Letters: From AA (in 1766), 1:53, 55, 56; (in 1767), 1:57, 60; (in 1774), 1:176; from JA (in 1761), 1:1; from Richard Cranch (in 1761), 1:1; from Hannah Storer Green (in 1775), 1:282; from Elizabeth Smith Shaw (in 1778), 2:380; from Isaac Smith Jr. (in 1774), 1:174

Cranch, William (1769–1855, nephew of AA): identified, 2:67 (see also Adams Genealogy); papers of, 1:xxxi; inoculated with smallpox, 2:66, 69, 78, 83, 93

Cranch family: dispersion of their papers, 1:xxxi; mentioned, 1:xlii

Crane, Hannah, 1:48

Crane, Mr., housewright, AA's agent in Boston, 1:369, 371

Cresswell, Nicholas, *Journal*, 1:257

Crimea, 2:268

Cromwell, Oliver, 2:219, 286

Cromwell Foundation. See William Nelson Cromwell Foundation

Crosby, Elizabeth Anne. See Adams, Mrs. Boylston

Crosby, Joseph: sketch of, 1:142; keeps school in Braintree, 1:141–42

Crosby, Joseph, Jr., sketch of, 1:311

Crosby, Mary. See Adams, Mrs. Peter Boylston

Crown Point, N.Y.: wretched state of Continental troops at, 2:38; JA urges that New England troops march to aid, 2:43; mentioned, 1:214; 2:65

Croy, Philip, Duke of Areschot, 2:291

Cumberland, Richard, *The West Indian*, 1:71, 77

Cumberland co., Maine, 1:67, 135

Cunningham, Ann Boylston. See Trott, Mrs. George

Cunningham, Archibald, carries off property at evacuation of Boston, 1:365

Cunningham, James (1721–1795, uncle of JA): identified, 1:18 (see also Adams Genealogy); JA inoculated at Boston residence of, 1:16–18, 20, 21, 28, 30, 33, 34, 44; 2:109; mentioned, 1:243, 245; 2:342

Cunningham, Mrs. James (1717–1769, Elizabeth Boylston, aunt of JA): identified, 1:18 (see also Adams Genealogy); mentioned, 1:34; 2:342

Cunningham, Peter (1750–1827, son

Field, Patty, 1:160

Field (Feild), Mr., of Braintree, dies, 2:130, 134, 138

Fine arts, JA's comments on, 2:ix–x, 103–05, 177, 225, 235–36. *See also* Medals; Waxworks in Philadelphia

Firearms: JA urges domestic manufacture of, 2:25–26; Cotton Tufts on manufacturing, 2:61

Fisheries: British in Newfoundland, 1: 212; AA's early assertion of Amer. rights to Atlantic, 1:390–91; Isaac Smith Sr. stiffens JA's stand on, 2:x; mentioned, 2:90

Fishkill, N.Y., 2:144, 146–47, 211

Fishkill Landing (now Beacon), N.Y., 1:xxx

Fitzroy, Augustus Henry, 3d Duke of Grafton, 1:334

Fleeming, John, printer of *Boston Chronicle*, 1:128

Fleet, Thomas and John, printers of *Boston Evening Post*, 1:59–60, 128

Fletcher, Deborah. *See* Cushing, Mrs. Thomas

Florence, Italy, 2:195

Flucker, Thomas, of Boston, 1:73

Folger, Capt. John, brings blank dispatches from France to Congress, 2: 405–06

Folwell, John, of Bucks co., Penna., 1:309

Forbes, Allyn B., 1:xxx

Forbes, Brig. John, 1:315

Force, Peter, *American Archives*, 1:xi, 342; 2:43, 124

Ford, Elisha, Marshfield loyalist, 1:396

Ford, Paul L., edits Strachey's narrative of Staten Island conference, 2:125

Ford, Worthington Chauncey: edits writings of various Adamses, 1: xxxviii–xl; edits letters of William Gordon, 1:229; *Washington-Duché Letters*, 2:360

Fordyce, James, *Sermons to Young Women*, 1:61–62

"Forester, The." *See* Paine, Thomas

Forster, Capt. George (British officer), signs cartel with Arnold at The Cedars, 2:85–86

Fort Constitution. *See* Fort Lee

Fort Hill. *See* Boston, Mass.

Fort Independence, N.Y., inquiry by Congress into evacuation of, 2:300

Fort Island (or Province Island) in Delaware River, 2:260

Fort Lee (Fort Constitution), N.Y., 2: 147, 150, 281, 283

Fort Mercer, N.J., 2:260, 360–62

Fort Mifflin, Mud Island, Penna., 2:360, 366

Fort Montgomery, N.Y., 2:147

Fort Schuyler (formerly Fort Stanwix), N.Y., 2:317–18, 322, 336–37

Fort Ticonderoga. *See* Ticonderoga

Fort Washington, N.Y., in campaign of 1776–1777, 2:143, 147, 150, 281, 283

Foster, Jedidiah, associate justice of Mass. Superior Court, 1:389, 391, 421

Foster, William, Boston merchant, 2:61

Foundries: plan to build in Mass., 2:19, 25; Hobart's iron foundry in Abington, 2:25, 61; in Philadelphia for casting brass cannon, 2:190–91

Fourth of July. *See* Independence Day

Fowle, Abigail. *See* Smith, Mrs. William (1679–1760)

Framingham, Mass., 1:140, 362, 364, 374, 376, 398

France: Isaac Smith Jr. on political situation in, 1:78–79; sends munitions and other military supplies to America, 2:74, 171, 184–85, 192–93, 195–96, 231, 298, 404; trade and commerce with, 2:182, 218, 235, 238, 248, 263–64, 312; chaotic state of the French treasury, 2:198–99; JA on anti-British feeling in, 2:227; support of America predicted, 2:366; mentioned, 2:2, 126, 223, 299, 310. *See also* French language; French Navy; French troops in America

Franco-American alliance: proposed by Amer. commissioners to Vergennes, 2:195–96; Amer. commissioners at Paris on progress of, 2:298–99

Frankford, Penna., 2:55

Franklin, Benjamin: portraits, 1:xlviii; and industrial establishment in Germantown district of Braintree, 1:58; arrival in Philadelphia (1775), 1: 197, 204; and founding of Pennsylvania Hospital, 1:252; JA on role of in Continental Congress, 1:252–53; on committee to visit Washington's camp, 1:301–02, 307; AA dines with, 1:313, 320–21, 325–26; on committee to visit Canada, 1:348; and Staten Island conference, 2:viii, 120–21, 124; proposal for Great Seal of U.S., 2:ix, 96–97, 108; on com-

451

Index

recommends Dimsdale's pamphlet on inoculation, 2:111

La Balme. *See* Mottin de La Balme
Lacedemonians, 2:347
Laertes (character in Shakespeare), 1:68
Lafayette, Marie Joseph Paul Yves Roch Gilbert du Motier, Marquis de: and William Carmichael, 2:199; mentioned, 2:383
La Fortune, French merchant ship, litigation over, 2:378
Lakes. *See the names of particular lakes*
Lancaster, Penna., 1:254; 2:xii, 170, 228, 333, 342, 349, 366, 387
"Land Embargo." *See* Embargoes; Massachusetts — General Court
Langborn, William, Virginia walking traveler, 1:319
Langdon, John(?), brings word of JA's appointment as joint commissioner to France, 2:375
Langdon, Woodbury(?), carries letters between JA and AA, 1:66–67
Lathrop (Lothtrope), Rev. John, and fortification of Boston Harbor, 1:405
Latin language, JA's views on learning, 2:178
Laurance (Laurence), John, judge advocate in Continental Army, 2:273
Laurens (Lawrence), Henry: S.C. delegate in Continental Congress, 2:300, 318, 320; JA on personality and character of, 2:318, 320; and JA's appointment as joint commissioner (1777), 2:372–73, 375; on "supernumerary Clerks," 2:382–84; and Rush-Shippen dispute, 2:388
Laurie, Capt. Walter Sloane, on burial of Joseph Warren in Charlestown, 1:271
Lawyers. *See* JA—Legal Studies and Career; Massachusetts—Courts of Law; Suffolk co. bar; *and names of particular lawyers*
Leach (Leech), John, jailed by British in Boston, 1:248, 260
Le Brun, Augustin, French officer in Amer., 2:259–60
Lechmere Point, East Cambridge, Mass., British raid and repulse at, 1:324–26
Lee, Arthur: sketch of, 1:83; "Junius Americanus," pseudonym of, 1:131, 134; French mission, 2:193, 195–96, 198, 298–99; suspects William Carmichael's patriotism, 2:199; warns

Congress that British troops plan to attack Boston (1777), 2:228; Amer. minister in Spain, 2:263, 272, 313–15; mentioned, 1:81, 304
Lee, Maj. Gen. Charles: departure for army before Boston, 1:226; AA's account of visit to, 1:246–47; exchange of letters with Burgoyne, 1:261, 264; AA on personality and character of, 1:335, 338; 2:150; his dog Spada, 1:335, 338; 2:174; and defense of New York, 1:346–47, 354; Canadian command, 1:349; Southern command, 1:349; on Thomas Paine, 1:400; on victory over British at Sullivan's Island, S.C., 2:52–53, 66; "His Appearance ... would give a flow of Spirits to our Army," 2:139; capture of (1776), 2:150, 160–61, 174, 188, 194, 196, 203; alleged mistreatment of and proposals for exchange (1777), 2:160–61, 386; mentioned, 1:225
Lee, Francis Lightfoot, Va. delegate in Continental Congress, 1:281; 2:165
Lee, Mrs. Francis Lightfoot (Rebecca Tayloe), 2:165
Lee, Jeremiah, of Marblehead, 2:x
Lee, Judge Joseph: receives letter from Jonathan Sewall concerning JA, 1:136–37; forced to resign as mandamus councilor, 1:149
Lee, Richard Henry: Va. delegate in Continental Congress, 1:411; 2:120, 165, 300, 375; moves "certain resolutions respecting independency," 2:22–23, 29
Lee, Mrs. Richard Henry (Anne Gaskins), 2:165
Lee, William: suspects William Carmichael's patriotism, 2:199; commissions to courts of Berlin and Vienna, 2:237
Lee family of Va., 1:83
Lee, Continental armed vessel, 1:338; 2:264
Leech. *See* Leach
Leeward Islands, 2:203
Lefavour, John, 1:18
Lefavour (Le Febure), Mrs. Rebecca, 1:17–21
Legge, William, 2d Earl of Dartmouth, 1:257
Leghorn, Italy, 2:195
Le Havre. *See* Havre, Le
Lehigh River, 2:148, 154–55
Leicester, Earl of. *See* Dudley, Robert

Index

2:32; original JA letters lost through negligence of, 1:164

Niles, Judge Samuel: sketch of, 2:242–43; Braintree representative in General Court, 2:241–42; delivers letter from AA to JA, 2:351, 365

Niles' Weekly Register, 2:32

Noah (Biblical character), 2:35

Noddle's Island (now East Boston), Boston Harbor: fort built on, 2:19; mentioned, 1:168, 210, 367, 387, 393, 402, 405

Norfolk, Va.: destroyed by fire (1776), 2:231; mentioned, 1:266

Norfolk co., Mass., 2:270

North, Frederick, Lord (later 2d Earl of Guilford): British opposition to Amer. policy of, 1:159; mentioned, 1:107, 144, 184, 189–90, 198, 211, 232

Northampton, Mass., 2:25–26

Northampton co., Va., 2:325

North Carolina: Provincial Congress, 1:189, 384; choice of delegates to Continental Congress, 1:189, 194; Assembly, 1:189, 194; JA on progress toward independence in, 1:381; JA prepares text of "Thoughts on Government" for, 1:384; forming a new government, 2:1; troops in Philadelphia, 2:275, 297, 329; mentioned, 1:188; 2:181, 256, 280–81, 322

North Carolina State Department of Archives and History, 1:384

North Quincy. *See* Quincy, Mass.

North River. *See* Hudson River

Northumberland, 2d Duke of. *See* Percy, Hugh, Earl

North Yarmouth, Mass., 1:6

Norton, Elizabeth. *See* Quincy, Mrs. John

Norton, Rev. Jacob (1764–1858, husband of AA's niece, *see* Adams Genealogy): buys Smith parsonage in Weymouth, 1:x, 9; marriage, 1:46

Norton, Mrs. Jacob. *See* Cranch, Elizabeth

Norton, Rev. John (1651?–1716, great-grandfather of AA, *see* Adams Genealogy), courtship letter and ministerial career, 1:xix–xxi

Norton, Mrs. John (1659–1739, Mary Mason, great-grandmother of AA, *see* Adams Genealogy): letter from John Norton (1678), 1:xx; letter from Samuel Shepard (1704), 1:xxi

Norton, Mass., 1:7

Norwalk, Conn., 2:236–37

Norway, 1:64–66

Norwich, Conn.(?), 1:233

Nottingham, Md., 2:145

"Novanglus" essays by JA, 1:7, 181, 187, 202, 234

Nova Scotia, 1:110, 251; 2:206

Oaths: "Money Oath" in Mass., 1:112; in Penna. constitution of 1776, 2:137–38, 283; JA urges "oaths of office" for Mass., 2:283–84

Oblong, The (area in Conn. on N.Y. border), 2:146

Ocean City, Md., 2:306

Ohio country: map of, 2:91; mentioned, 2:xiii

Ohio River, 2:338

Old House (Adams National Historic Site, Quincy, Mass.): Adams Papers at, xxxii; history of, 1:218–19; Cotton Tufts negotiates Adamses' purchase of in 1787, 2:xi. *See also* JA—Residences

Old South Church. *See* Boston, Mass.

"Olive Branch" petition. *See* Petition to the King

Oliver, Andrew, 1:xlviii

Oliver, Peter: impeachment proceedings against, 1:97, 114, 141; support in York co., Maine, 1:110; chief justice of Mass. Superior Court, 1:111, 141; encourages taxation of Americans, 1:125; house in Middleborough, 1:218; and JA's intercepted letters, 1:257

Oliver, Thomas, forced to resign as mandamus councilor, 1:149

Olney, Capt. Joseph, of the *Cabot*, 2:206

Ontario, Lake, 2:91

Orange co., N.Y., 2:25–26, 147

Oriskany, battle of, 2:317–18, 320, 330, 336

Orne, Col. Azor, 1:235, 386

Orne, Mrs. Azor, 1:386

Orr, Mr., Mass. gunmaker, 2:25, 61

Orrery, Rittenhouse's, 2:236

Osgood, Samuel: sketch of, 1:357; mentioned, 1:356

Ostend, Belgium, 2:2

Otis, Col. James, Sr. (1702–1778): says of JA "The Zeal-Pot boils over," 1:135; poor health of, 2:143; mentioned, 1:xiv, 138

Otis, Mrs. James (Mary Allyne), 1:xiv

Otis, James, Jr. (1725–1783): opponent of Thomas Hutchinson, 1:52–

Index

Skene (Skeene), "Governor" Philip, 1:
214, 237

Skillman, Rev. Isaac, and fortification of Boston Harbor, 1:405

Skimmer (Skeema), Capt. John, commands Continental armed schooner Lee, 2:263–64

Slavery, slaves, and slave trade: Trowbridge's and JA's comments on, 1:135; AA's comments on, 1:162, 369; Joshua Steele ameliorates condition of slaves in Barbados, 2:287. See also Negroes

Small, Maj. John(?), reported killed at Bunker Hill, 1:236

Small, Lt., and rumored conspiracy of Negroes in Boston, 1:162

Smallpox: Boston epidemic (1764), 1:14–47; Boston epidemic (1776), 1:358, 369, 373, 379–80, 400; 2:15–122, 125–26; "Cruel small Pox! worse than the sword!," 2:13; "ten times more terrible than Britons, Canadians and Indians together," 2:23–24; rages among the Continental troops, 2:30, 38, 46, 62–64, 67, 165, 174, 209; Philadelphia epidemic (1776), 2:209; mentioned, 1:1, 2, 279, 366, 378. See also Inoculation with smallpox

Smedley (Smelden), Samuel, lieutenant on the Defence, 2:14–16

Smith, Abigail. See Adams, Mrs. John (1744–1818)

Smith, Anna. See Kent, Mrs. Ebenezer

Smith, Benjamin (1717–1770, of Charleston, S.C., grandson of Thomas the sea captain, 1665–1690), 1:69

Smith, Benjamin (1757–1826, of South Carolina, later governor of North Carolina, son of Thomas, 1720–1790): sketch of, 1:412; on new South Carolina constitution, 1:411; 2:92; visits AA in Boston and carries letter back to JA, 2:92–93, 98, 111; miniature by Peale, 2:104–05

Smith, Caroline Amelia. See de Windt, Mrs. John Peter

Smith, Elizabeth (1750–1815). See Shaw, Mrs. John

Smith, Elizabeth (b. 1770, cousin of AA, later Mrs. John P. Hale): identified, 2:48 (see also Adams Genealogy); inoculated with smallpox, 2:45, 87; mentioned, 1:213

Smith, Elizabeth Hall (1843–1911), 1:ix

Smith, Isaac, Sr. (1719–1787, Boston merchant, uncle of AA): identified, 1:4 (see also Adams Genealogy); and toryism of son, 1:171–72; 2:362; in Salem during siege of Boston, 1:198, 212–13, 228; on the conflagration of Charlestown, 1:227–28; business ventures, 1:228, 342, 364–65; his trade and credit in S.C., 1:339–41; request to export fish to West Indies granted, 1:342, 364, 372–73, 409; residence in Boston, 1:364; 2:45, 52, 70, 111–12, 146, 359; and inoculation of AA and her children, 1:373, 400; 2:41, 45, 50–52, 112; on fortifications in Boston Harbor, 1:413–14; portrait, 2:x–xi, facing 103; on problems of conducting trade and commerce in New England, 2:x, 182–83, 293–94, 310–12; his ships in Baltimore, 2:158, 169; forwards AA's letters to JA, 2:168, 192; imports flour into Boston, 2:173, 175, 182, 185, 200; appointed by Marine Committee to arbitrate a dispute, 2:181, 197, 206, 222, 263–64; and the Continental lottery, 2:197; his ships taken by British, 2:206; on British frigates in Boston Harbor, 2:222–23, 263, 311; on mob actions against suspected loyalists in Boston, 2:223; wants to establish credit and trade connections in Ga., 2:237–38, 262, 311; views on building ships for Continental Navy, 2:311–12; mentioned, 1:ix, xv, 50, 58, 60–61, 68, 243; 2:48, 147–49, 152, 170, 172, 295–96, 333, 356, 382

Letters: To JA (in 1775), 1:227, 266; (in 1776), 1:339, 342, 364, 365, 372, 409, 413; 2:41, 182; (in 1777), 2:196, 206, 222, 237, 262, 292, 310

Letters: From JA (in 1775), 1:212; (in 1776), 2:1, 52, 180

Smith, Mrs. Isaac (1726–1786, Elizabeth Storer, aunt of AA): identified, 1:50 (see also Adams Genealogy); and toryism of son, 1:172; moves to Salem, 1:198; AA describes "my Aunts chamber," 2:112; mentioned, 1:49, 68, 213; 2:x–xi, 45, 48, 52

Smith, Rev. Isaac, Jr. (1749–1829, cousin of AA): identified, 1:4 (see also Adams Genealogy); studies for the ministry, 1:65–66, 172, 175; visits kinsmen in Charleston, S.C.,

477

1:67–69; travels in England and France, 1:70–83, 172; toryism of, 1:171–72, 174–76, 333–34, 354, 363–64; minister at Enfield, England, 1:333–34, 354–55; comments on JA's intercepted letters, 1:354, 356, 363–64; mentioned, 1:203, 213; 2:xi, 88

Letters: To AA (in 1771), 1:70; to JA (in 1771), 1:71, 78; to Mary Smith Cranch (in 1774), 1:174; to Rev. William Smith (in 1775), 1:333

Letters: From AA (in 1763), 1:3; (in 1770), 1:67; (in 1771), 1:76; (in 1777), 2:362; from JA (in 1770), 1:67; (in 1771), 1:74, 81; from Mary Smith Cranch (in 1774), 1:171; from Elizabeth Smith (in 1768), 1:63

Smith, Isaac (son of William Smith Jr. and nephew of AA, dates unknown), 2:382

Smith, Louisa Catherine (1773?–1857, niece of AA): identified, 2:47–48 (*see also* Adams Genealogy); inoculated with smallpox, 2:45, 87

Smith, Mary or "Polly" (1757–1839, cousin of AA; later, by 1st marriage, Mrs. Edward Gray; by 2d marriage, Mrs. Samuel Allyne Otis): identified, 1:103 (*see also* Adams Genealogy); marriage to Edward Gray, 2:356; mentioned, 1:213

Smith, Mary (aunt of AA). *See* Austin, Mrs. Ebenezer

Smith, Mary (sister of AA). *See* Cranch, Mrs. Richard

Smith, Richard, N.J. delegate in Continental Congress, 1:346

Smith, Robert, supposed portrait by Peale, 2:105

Smith, Lt. Col. Samuel, commands Fort Mifflin, 2:360–62

Smith, Sarah. *See* Edwards, Mrs. Samuel

Smith, Thomas (d. 1690, of Charlestown, Mass., great-grandfather of AA, *see* Adams Genealogy), 1:69

Smith, Thomas (1665–1690, sea captain, son of preceding), marries and founds family in South Carolina, 1:69

Smith, Thomas (1720–1790, of Charleston, S.C., grandson of preceding), 1:69, 411

Smith, Rev. Thomas, of Falmouth (Portland), Maine, 1:124

Smith, Thomas Carter, 2:xi

Smith, Mrs. William (1679–1760, Abigail Fowle, grandmother of AA), identified, 1:314 (*see also* Adams Genealogy)

Smith, Rev. William (1707–1783, father of AA): identified, 1:18 (*see also* Adams Genealogy); MS diaries of, 1:ix–x; Weymouth parsonage of, 1:ix–x, 9, facing 80, 204, 225; portrait of, 1:xii, facing 81; expenses at Harvard, 1:xxi; and Negro servant Tom, 1:15, 16; lends books to JA, 1:24, 27; and education of JQA, 1:117; JA borrows and wrecks sulky of, 1:195–96, 325, 332; and British raid on Grape Island, 1:204, 209, 274; and conflagration of Charlestown, 1:230, 241; and wife's death, 1:289, 293–94, 300, 303, 307–08, 310, 316, 325; accompanies AA to Mifflin's entertainment in Cambridge, 1:335; requests Zubly's *Law of Liberty*, 1:337; JA borrows horse of, 1:408; Jonathan Sweetser servant or farm boy of, 2:83; AA on good health of, 2:130, 138; marriage of his slave Phœbe, 2:346; mentioned, 1:xxi, 17, 29, 57, 59, 61, 62, 72, 106, 107, 108, 145, 154, 156, 161–62, 176, 189, 206, 216, 224, 237–38, 257, 320, 326, 332, 355–56, 359, 407, 417; 2:x, 12, 65, 84, 105–06, 159, 206, 246, 255, 296, 382, 385, 408

Letter: From Isaac Smith Jr. (in 1775), 1:333

Smith, Mrs. William (1721–1775, Elizabeth Quincy, mother of AA): identified, 1:22 (*see also* Adams Genealogy); health and illnesses, 1:148, 154, 160, 169, 284, 286–88, 295; death, 1:288–89, 292–94, 296–97, 300, 304–05, 307–10, 312–13, 316–17, 335; 2:129, 138; obituary tribute to, 1:293–94; JA's estimate of, 1:316–17; mentioned, 1:xxi, 21, 27, 29, 32, 34, 37, 38, 49, 57, 59, 60, 90, 106, 189, 216, 263; 2:116, 255, 308

Smith, Rev. William (1727–1803, provost of College of Philadelphia): controversy over his *Oration* on death of Gen. Montgomery, 1:345–46, 359, 361, 374, 380–81, 400–01; writes reply to *Common Sense*, 1:380, 390, 400; JA on personality and character of, 1:400–01

Smith, William, Jr. (1746–1787, brother of AA): identified, 1:1 (*see also*

Atheneum Paperbacks

HISTORY

HISTORY—AMERICAN

Atheneum Paperbacks

Atheneum Paperbacks

Atheneum Paperbacks